THE VINLAND MAP

AND THE

TARTAR RELATION

THE VINLAND MAP

AND THE

TARTAR RELATION

by R. A. Skelton, Thomas E. Marston, and George D. Painter

for the Yale University Library

with a Foreword by Alexander O. Vietor

NEW HAVEN AND LONDON | YALE UNIVERSITY PRESS

Copyright © 1965 by Yale University.
Fourth printing, April 1966.
Designed by John O. C. McCrillis,
set in Granjon type,
and printed in the United States of America by
Connecticut Printers, Inc., Hartford, Connecticut.
Facsimiles and maps by The Carl Purington Rollins
Printing-Office of the Yale University Press,
New Haven, Connecticut.
Distributed in Canada by McGill University Press.
All rights reserved. This book may not be
reproduced, in whole or in part, in any form
(except by reviewers for the public press),
without written permission from the publishers.

Library of Congress catalog card number: 65–22339

Published with assistance from an anonymous gift, and
The Ellsworth Eliot Fund
of the Yale University Library
established by Ellsworth Eliot, Jr. B.A. 1884
in memory of Ellsworth Eliot, B.A. 1849.

FOREWORD

In the study of history the documentary source materials available to scholars are often incomplete, equivocal, or lacking in continuity. In some great matters of history, therefore, the discovery of a single new document may significantly alter the accepted pattern; and its publication becomes an imperative responsibility.

These remarks apply with particular force to the early movement of Europeans into Asia, Africa, and America and their reactions to the native cultures. The documents published in this volume are concerned with two episodes of medieval history: the Norse voyages from Iceland and Greenland to North America in the tenth to twelfth centuries, and the expedition of Friar John de Plano Carpini across Central Asia on a mission to the Mongols in 1245–47.

The manuscript consists of a map and text copied about 1440 by an unknown scribe, from lost earlier originals, into a manuscript of Vincent of Beauvais' *Speculum Historiale*. The first is a world map drawn on a folded sheet of vellum, of late medieval type but including the western ocean with representations of Iceland, Greenland, and Vinland. This map is unknown and unrecorded. The second, written on vellum and paper, is an account of the Carpini mission by an unidentified friar who calls himself C. de Bridia. No other manuscript of this text is known. The two documents are referred to here as the Vinland Map (VM) and the Tartar Relation (TR). They had become physically separated from the volume containing the Vincent text, in which the map stood at the beginning and the Tartar Relation at the end, and were rebound together in the nineteenth century. In the present publication, Dr. Marston describes the chance circumstances of the discovery of the remainder of the Vincent manuscript in its fifteenth-century binding, establishing the association of the Vinland Map and the Tartar Relation; and Mr. Painter analyzes the relationship of the surviving elements of the original total manuscript and reconstructs its bibliographical history.

The documents here brought to light are of dramatic novelty. As Mr. Painter's commentary shows, the Tartar Relation helps us to understand how the previously known narratives of the Carpini mission came into being and provides information on Mongol history and legend not to be found in any western source. The Vinland Map contains the earliest known and indisputable cartographic representation of any part of the Americas, and includes a delineation of Greenland so strikingly accurate that it may well have been derived from experience. If, as Mr. Skelton supposes, this part of the map originated in the North, and probably in Iceland, it represents the only surviving medieval example of Norse cartography. These conclusions, if accepted, have far-reaching implications for the history of cartography and of the Viking navigations.

The arresting character of the documents naturally calls into question their genuineness. In the absence of an unbroken record of their history, there can be no absolute and unassailable demonstration that they are not counterfeit. Nevertheless, analysis of content and form in the historical framework may create—and in this case, we believe, has created—a presumption of authenticity so strong as to be difficult, if not impossible, to challenge. All tests that would not involve damage or destruction of the manuscript have been applied. The scripts and the physical nature of the materials used (vellum, paper, and ink) have been examined minutely and have been found compatible with the date in the 1440s here ascribed to the writing of the manuscript, along with the other hypothetical conclusions concerning its place of origin and its execution reached by the editors. All the available evidence, both physical and internal, points beyond reasonable doubt to the presence of the Vinland Map and the Tartar Relation in the manuscript from the beginning. Each of these documents contains matter in text or map-legend which is not known from any other source and which stands up to historical criticism. The editors who have worked on the documents, with the present writer, are satisfied that the evidence, while in part circumstantial and not amounting to legal proof, justifies them in affirming without reservation the genuineness of the manuscript.

The present publication of these remarkable documents is designed to be a preliminary work; completeness or finality is not claimed for the commentaries, which are to be considered a springboard for further investigation.

The principal editorial work has been undertaken by Mr. R. A. Skelton, Superintendent of the Map Room, British Museum; Dr. Thomas E. Marston, Curator of Medieval and Renaissance Literature in the Yale University Library; and Mr. George D. Painter, Assistant Keeper in charge of incunabula in the British Museum. These authors have been in regular communication on specific issues. For the most part, however, they have prepared their respective sections independently of one another; and if in some details of interpretation they differ or diverge, this may be taken as a guarantee of intellectual honesty. The whole work has been supervised by the writer of this Foreword under the direction of Mr. James T. Babb, Librarian (now Emeritus) of Yale University.

A word about the arrangement of the book. Since the Vinland Map appears to have been drawn in part from the Tartar Relation and therefore to follow the latter in time, this general order of materials has been observed in the publication. The history and physical characteristics of the manuscript are set forth in Dr. Marston's general introduction to the facsimile. Mr. Painter, in the first chapter of his remarks on the Tartar Relation, develops the bibliographical analysis of the Vincent of Beauvais manuscript as a whole, showing how the Map and Relation came to be incorporated into it. In further chapters he examines the narrative of C. de Bridia against the background of Mongol history and of the Carpini mission and its records. These are followed by the annotated transcript and translation of the Tartar Relation. Mr. Skelton then describes the Vinland Map and its geography in relation to its sources and discusses its historical importance. In conclusion, Mr. Painter gives a personal interpretation of the connection between the Map and the Tartar Relation, supplementing that of Mr. Skelton.

That the project has been long in completion is explained by the laborious and many-sided character of the investigation, by the need for consultation at both short and long range, and by the illness of two of the authors.

Thanks must be extended to the many interested friends and colleagues who have contributed advice, encouragement, or other assistance. To Mr. Laurence Witten, rare-book dealer of New

Haven, is due the credit for bringing together the separate parts of the Vincent manuscript and for his recognition of the significance of the Map and Relation. Dr. Curt F. Bühler of the Pierpont Morgan Library examined the manuscripts and confirmed Dr. Marston's findings. Mr. Allan Stevenson, whose report is by his kind permission quoted verbatim, identified and dated the watermarks of the paper on which part of the Relation and the text of Vincent de Beauvais was written; and he was even able to suggest the mill in which it might have been made. Mr. Painter has been greatly assisted by consultation on Mongol history, language, and lore with Dr. J. A. Boyle, Reader in Persian in the University of Manchester, who must not be held responsible, however, for the use made of information supplied by him. Mr. Skelton's section was kindly read in typescript by Dr. Lawrence C. Wroth and Professor David B. Quinn, who made helpful comments and criticisms; he also wishes to acknowledge his debt to the published writings of Dr. John K. Wright, sometime Director of the American Geographical Society. The sketch maps were prepared by the skillful hand of Dr. Robert Lee Williams, Director of the Map Laboratory, Yale University. To all these the editors offer their cordial thanks.

Lastly, they wish to express to the Yale University Library their warm appreciation of the opportunity and privilege of preparing these remarkable documents for publication.

March 1965

Alexander Orr Vietor
Curator of Maps
Yale University Library

CONTENTS

LIST OF ILLUSTRATIONS

The Vinland Map and the Tartar Relation are reproduced following page 17.

PLATES

FIGURES

List of Illustrations

THE MANUSCRIPT:

HISTORY AND DESCRIPTION

Thomas E. Marston

CONTENTS

I. Binding of the Vincent of Beauvais Manuscript (front cover).

II. Binding of the Vinland Map and Tartar Relation (front cover).

III. A Page from the Vincent of Beauvais Manuscript (sig. E₁₅ rec

uod cum audissent sancti
maximus epc et antipa
tus proconsul qui nuper in
urbem aduenerat manda
uerunt ciuibus ut eu caute
adducerent et argenteos dum
a ministris traheretur ad ec
clesiam putabat uere q du
ceretur ad imperatorem xpm
igitur et proconsul mirati de
argenteos interrogauerunt eu
ubi thesauru inuentum inue
nisset at ille respondit se
michil penitus inuenisse
sed de saculo parentu coru
eosdem denarios huiusce quid
uero ei mali accederit se pe
nitus ignorare Et interroga
tus cuius ciuitatis esset //
Respondit bene scio q huius
ciuitatis sum si tamen hec
ciuitas ephesiorum proconsul
dixit uac venire parentes tuos
ut testentur de te Quos tu
nominasset et nullus eos co
gnosceret dicebant eum se fin
gere ut aliquo modo euaderet
Et ait proconsul quo te cre
demus tibi q hoc argentum
parentum tuorum fuerit cu
scriptura eius plusq̃ ccc
lxxij annos habeat et sit
primoru decij imperatoris
diez et in nullo similes sit
argenteis nostris Et quo pa
rentes tui ante tn tempus
fuerunt tu vero iuuenis
uir de peze sapientes et se
nes ephesi q̃ auro iubeo te
legibus tradi donec constet

ante quid inuenisti dunt pro
cidens maluit ante eos dni
pro deo dni orate michi q uos
interrogo et ego dicam uobis
qd est in corde meo Decius
imperator qui fuit in hac ciui
tate ubi est / et uie dixit fili
non est hodie in terra qui
decius nomietur Impator at
fuit aute longum tempus et
aut in in hoc dne ita stupeo
q nemo michi credit sed se
quimini me et ostendam uobis
socios meos qui sunt in monte
celio et ipis credite Lo cuiu
sio q afacie decij imperatoris
nos fugimus Et ego uero di
di q ingressus est decius in
pater in hanc urbem si tame
hec est ephesus ciuitas dunt
epc cogitans in se xpo dixit
proconsuli q uisto est quam
uult deus ostendere in iuuene
isto procedunt ergo cu eo et
ciuitatis plurima multitudo
et ingressus est prius malch
ad socios suos et post eu epc
introdierut inuenit inter la
pides litteras sigillatas duo
bus sigillis argenteis et con
notato ipso Legit eas audie
tibz et mirantibus cunctis
et uidentes sanctos sedentes
in speluna et facies eorum q̃
roseas florentes procidetes glo
rificauerunt deum et tatin
epc et proconsul miserunt
ad theodosium imperatore
rogantes ut cito ueniet et
mirabilia dei nup ostensa

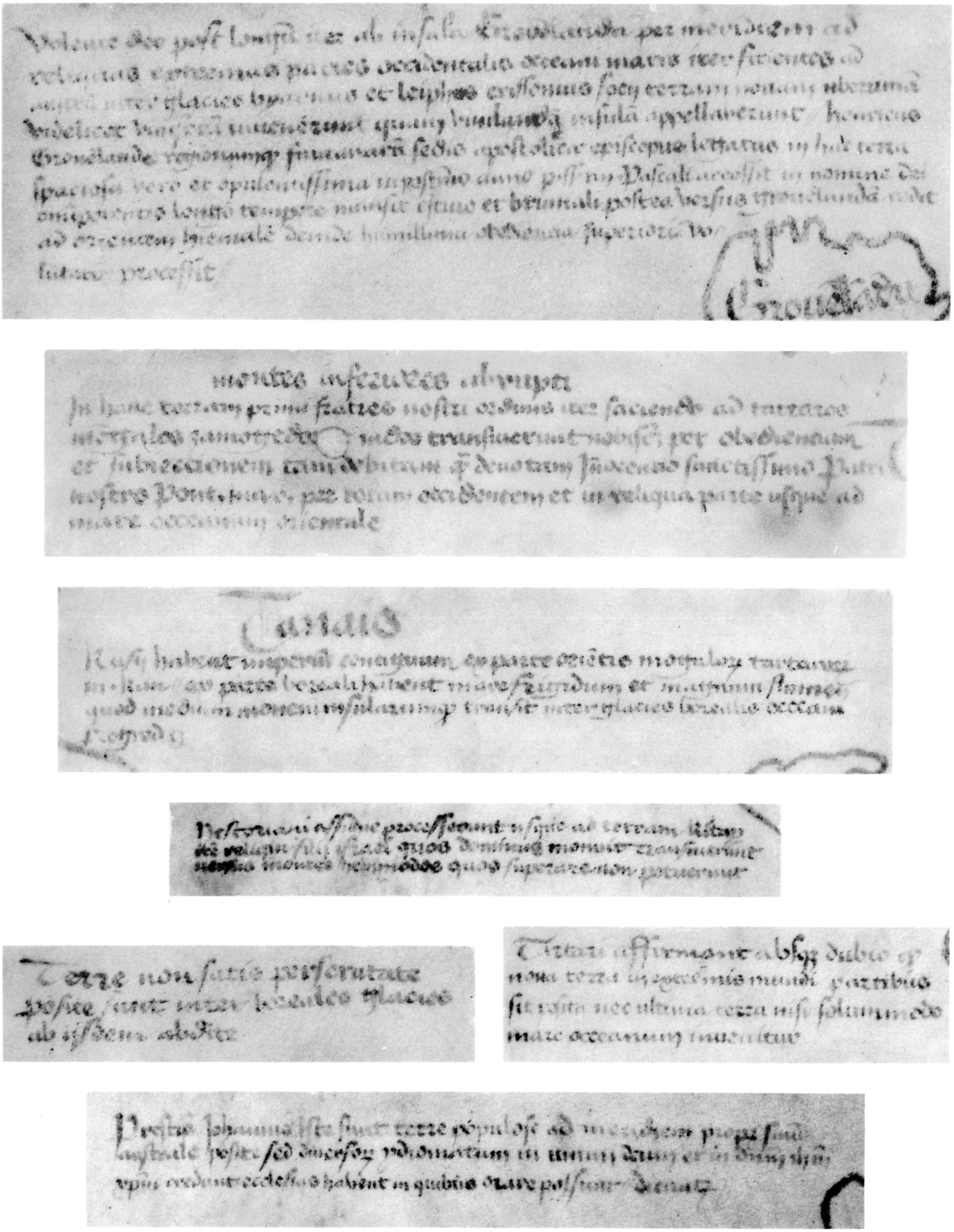

IV. The Longer Legends of the Vinland Map (enlarged). Reading from top to bottom, these are the legends numbered on Pl. VII as: 67, 39, 11/12, 36, 53, 56, 30.

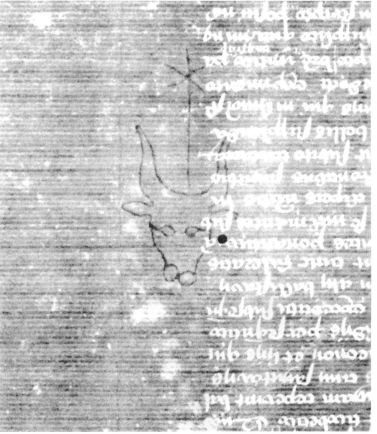

V. Watermarks: *upper,* in the Vincent Manuscript
(sig. e₄ verso); *lower,* in the Tartar Relation
(sig. [TR]₁₀ recto).

1. RECENT HISTORY AND ACQUISITION

As the writer of this section was intimately and personally involved in the recent history of this manuscript, it is impossible for him to write about it except from a personal point of view.

In October 1957 the antiquarian bookseller Laurence Witten, of New Haven, showed to my colleague Alexander O. Vietor and myself a slim volume, bound in recent calf, which contained a map of the world, including Iceland, Greenland, and Vinland, and a hitherto unknown account of the mission of John de Plano Carpini to the Mongols in 1245–47. Mr. Witten told us that he had acquired it from a private collection in Europe.

Mr. Vietor and I examined the volume carefully. Both map and text appeared to us to be genuine and in approximately the same hand, which we judged to be from the Rhineland about the middle of the fifteenth century. A few of the legends on the map, from superficial observation, appeared to come from the manuscript account of the Carpini mission; but two factors made us question whether the manuscript and the map belonged together. The first of these was the incidence of worm holes. Both map and manuscript were slightly wormed, but the worm holes were not in the same positions on the two parts. A more disconcerting feature was a statement on the recto of the first leaf of the map: *Delineatio 1ᵉ ps: 2ᵉ ps. 3ᵉ ps. specl'i,* which can be translated "Delineation of the first part, the second part (and) the third part of the Speculum". Mr. Vietor and I believed that until these two factors could be satisfactorily explained, the map would remain suspect, no matter how convinced we were of its genuineness.

In April 1958 I received an advance copy of a new catalogue of a London bookseller. As often happens in collecting books, one makes a collection within a collection, and I had been fortunate in being able to acquire a group of manuscripts of the writings of Leonardo Bruni Aretino. In the catalogue in question I noted a manuscript of Bruni's translation of Plutarch's lives of Cicero and Demosthenes, a text I did not have; and I went to the firm of C. A. Stonehill, Inc., to ask its owner Mr. Robert J. Barry to cable for it. On my way to Mr. Barry's office I leafed through the catalogue again and noticed a manuscript of a portion of Vincent of Beauvais' *Speculum Historiale* at a very modest price. I had used Vincent's work in historical research and had a great deal of respect for it. While I was aware that a fifteenth-century copy such as this would have no textual value, I thought it would be interesting to add it to my collection, and when I arrived at Mr. Barry's office I asked him to cable for this in addition to the Bruni manuscript.

About three weeks later, Mr. Barry's secretary called me to tell me that the two manuscripts had arrived. Delighted to see that both were in very unusual contemporary bindings, I asked Mr. Witten to examine them. Mr. Witten came to my office late that afternoon, looked at the manuscripts, and asked if he could borrow the Vincent for a few days. I readily acceded. That evening I did not return home until after ten o'clock. I had hardly entered my house when the telephone rang. It was Mr. Witten, very excited. The Vincent manuscript was the key to the puzzle of the map and Tartar Relation. The hand was the same, the watermarks of the paper were the same; and the worm holes showed that the map had been at the front of the volume and the Tartar Relation at the back.

All this placed me in a rather strange position. The Vincent manuscript by itself was of minor intrinsic value. Now it had suddenly become very precious as a piece of scholarly evidence. What its commercial value had become, I had no way of determining. As I tried to figure out the problem, I became more and more convinced that the two pieces had to come under one ownership as soon as possible. Also, as I thought the problem over, it seemed that the cleancut way this could be done was to give the Vincent to Mrs. Witten (who had acquired the map and Tartar Relation). This was not a wholly Quixotic gesture on my part, for I hoped, although I never expressed the hope verbally, that this generosity would give the Yale Library some element of control over the disposition of the map in the event that Mrs. Witten should decide to sell it. I might add that this unexpressed hope was fully realized.

After the finding of the Vincent of Beauvais manuscript, some questions remained. The text ends with the words "*Explicit tertia pars speculi hist(orialis)*" i.e. "Here ends the third part of the *Speculum Historiale*". As the manuscript contains books XX to XXIII (here numbered XXI–XXIV) and the inscription on the map refers to the first, second, and third parts, it seemed that there must have once been two or more other volumes. Mr. Witten returned to the private library whence came the map and the Vincent, but an intensive search was fruitless.

2. DESCRIPTION OF THE MANUSCRIPT

As they exist today the three manuscript works now to be described are found in two separate volumes. We may first describe each volume briefly and then examine the relationship between the two.

The first volume to be found contains, first, a parchment[1] bifolium with a map of the world (VM) drawn on the inner double-opening and otherwise blank except for a brief inscription, mentioned above, on the recto of the first leaf. Second, the volume contains TR, a single quire of sixteen leaves in which the outer and inner sheets (i.e. leaves 1, 8, 9, 16) are of parchment and the remainder of paper, the text being written, two columns to the page, on the first eleven leaves, with the remaining five leaves blank but ruled. No letter-signature has been applied to this gathering, and the first and eighth leaves of it (parchment) show no trace of any signature, which may, however, have been cut away during the original trimming for binding; leaves 2 through 7 are signed in the lower right corner of the recto as follows: ij, iij, iiij, v, vj, vij. VM and TR are bound together in a comparatively recent binding of gilt calf over pasteboard with decorated endpapers. Inscriptions on VM (often in minute writing) and the text of TR are both written in a variety of bastard cursive hand. VM has no rubrication; TR has a few capitals stroked red near the beginning, and its incipit and explicit (one column-line each) are written in red. VM and TR are both slightly wormeaten, but the wormholes through VM, which have been repaired with small squares of parchment, do not match in position or in number those of TR, which are unrepaired. The bifolium of VM has been repaired with parchment at the fold. The leaves of VM and TR measure 285 × 210 mm.

The second volume found contains a portion of the vast *Speculum Historiale* by Vincent of

---

1. *Parchment* is the word used throughout this portion of the text to describe those sheets of the manuscript which are of animal skin rather than of paper. Parchment is the generic term for all such skin-derived writing materials and is employed here in preference to the term, *vellum,* which in fact applies only to the skins of calves and vealers. The tendency of the skins to be yellowish and oily in the present manuscript suggests derivation from sheep or goats, rather than calf or veal hides. The preparation of all parchment from hides, including the finest vellum, is basically the same regardless of derivation.

Beauvais, identified by the scribe as Books XXI–XXIV (lacking a table of chapter headings for Book XXI, which may be presumed to have stood at the beginning on a leaf or leaves now missing). The text is written on 239 leaves of parchment and paper, two columns to each page, consisting of fifteen quires of sixteen leaves each, the quires signed e, f, g, h, i, k, l, m, n, o, p, q, r, s, t, each quire composed of parchment and paper as the TR quire, lacking the first leaf of quire e. The manuscript is fully rubricated, with capitals stroked red, and there are catch-words at quire-endings throughout. Signatures, placed in the lower right corner of the recto and sometimes cut away in the trimming which preceded the original binding of the volume, are applied to the first eight leaves of each quire, the following form being typical: h j, h ij, h iij, h iiij, h v, h vj, h vij, h viij. The lower margins of i_{16} and s_{16}, both parchment leaves, have been cut away causing the loss of the catchwords on these leaves, and have been repaired with blank parchment. The volume is preserved in a worn fifteenth-century binding of brown leather over wooden boards, rebacked with modern leather which is also used to restore some corners, and with new endpapers; the lower cover is cracked vertically. The text is written in a variety of bastard cursive hand, by a single copyist, and even at first glance the handwriting is very similar to that of VM and TR. The manuscript is slightly wormeaten at beginning and end. The leaves measure 285 × 210 mm.

The leaves containing VM, *Speculum,* and TR are all of the same size (285 × 210 mm.), except that the parchment leaves are sometimes of a very slightly differing size because parchment contracts and expands at a different rate and in a degree different from paper. None of the leaf edges of any of the three sections shows any sign whatever of modern cutting; the size of the written space and the number of columns (two) in *Speculum* and TR are identical. The handwriting will be shown to be identical. The composition of the single quire used for TR is identical to that of the fifteen quires employed for *Speculum.* The manner of ruling in *Speculum* and TR is identical. The paper used in TR is identical to that in *Speculum.* But do the three portions fit together and, if they do, how are they to be reconstructed? The answer to these questions is fortunately plain and simple. While the wormholes in VM do not match those of TR in number or position, those of VM do precisely match those at the beginning of *Speculum,* and the worming in TR precisely matches that in the final leaves of *Speculum.* The conclusion is inescapable: VM, *Speculum,* and TR were bound together, in the order indicated, in a single volume before bookworms attacked that volume: Furthermore, since all three parts are the work of one scribe in one identical format, the only reasonable conclusion is that the three were bound together about the time of their writing and remained together until after they had sustained worm damage. They were probably separated only at a comparatively recent date when VM and TR were newly rebound.

It is not difficult to reconstruct what in all probability happened to the original volume. Many years ago the back of the original binding had completely deteriorated. The map at the front of the volume had become detached and had even parted at the fold, and the quire containing TR was also starting to separate or had already separated, with some detached blank leaves now incorrectly rebound. The owner of the volume removed VM and TR and had them rebound separately, while the *Speculum,* which no longer had very much merit of its own, seems to have been left as it was for a considerable period and was only repaired at a much later date, seemingly when both volumes were recently sold. By this time, it appears, the identity of the parts had been completely forgotten or themselves lost sight of; by chance they ultimately followed their separate paths to New Haven and were reunited by the process of mingled accident and deduction described above.

It is possible to argue that VM, *Speculum,* and TR were only bound together some time *after* they were originally written, even long after, since it is impossible to ascertain at what date the worming took place; but there is no very sound reason to suggest this possibility in the absence of any evidence to support it. The evidence of the binding, to be examined later, will tend to support the assumption that the parts were originally bound together.

The volume may now be reconstructed. We know that VM stood first among the preserved portions, and we know that *Speculum* is fragmentary since its quiring begins at the letter *e* and since the first leaf of quire e (a parchment leaf) is missing. It may be assumed that at least sixty-five leaves, consisting of the four quires of sixteen leaves each, signed a, b, c, and d, plus folio e, are now missing entirely. It is probable that they contained an additional book of the *Speculum Historiale* of Vincent of Beauvais, and calculations have shown that these sixty-five missing leaves would conveniently accommodate the book of the *Speculum* which precedes the first one now preserved.[2]

Keeping in mind that VM has no signature, that quires a through d and leaf e_1 are lost, that the *Speculum* fragment has a full set of letter-signatures, and that TR has number-signatures like those of *Speculum,* but no letter assigned to its single quire, the collation of the reconstructed manuscript may be expressed as follows:

VM^2; $a–t^{16}$ (wanting $a_1–e_1$); TR^{16}.

3. THE PALEOGRAPHY

The briefest appraisal of the *Speculum* fragment and TR are sufficient to demonstrate that they are both the work of a single scribe. The writing style is a type of bastard book cursive identified by E. Crouse and J. Kirchner in their pioneering work on Gothic handwritings (*Die gotischen Schriftarten,* Leipzig, 1928, cf. Fig. 32) as "Oberrheinische Bastarda", which may be translated and expanded as "Upper Rhineland bastard (or cursive) book hand." Closely similar varieties of the widespread cursive "Bastarda" were simultaneously in use in Germany, Switzerland, France, Flanders, and Italy in the period *ca.* 1415—*ca.* 1460. Crouse and Kirchner attribute their example to the 1440s. The script of *Speculum* and TR shows the handwriting in fully developed form and is free of accretions from styles which were to develop later. It is in all respects a classical example of the "Oberrheinische Bastarda", and a date in the 1440s seems most appropriate for it.

A slightly later hand has added a running headline for each double-page opening of the Vincent of Beauvais, giving the name of the emperor, the book number, and the subject. A few additional notes have been added in a cursive humanistic script of about 1500. These later notations are so trivial as to be without significance.

To proceed from the general classification of the scribe's style to a more precise dating is a difficult problem. Work extending over years and years on the paleography of the early classical manuscripts in Latin has provided useful guides with facsimile reproductions for their approxi-

2. The calculation is explained in Mr. G. D. Painter's article which follows in the present volume, p. 24.

mate dating. These guides stop, however, about A.D. 1100. After that, except for isolated studies, the paleographer is on his own, dependent largely on observation and experience. This situation is complicated by the fact that relatively few extant manuscripts are precisely dated by the scribe or can be precisely dated by internal evidence. There is also a human element: a scribe could live to a ripe old age and not change his style of writing, unless for professional reasons he had to alter it to meet changing tastes and demands of his customers. The problem of localizing a manuscript is also very difficult, for trained scribes and artists moved around a great deal more than is usually suspected.

It is nevertheless possible to cite several manuscripts, all dated by their scribes or strictly datable on the basis of other evidence, which confirm the attributed date of *Speculum* and TR. Two volumes of the long awaited study by Charles Samaran and Robert Marichal under the auspices of the Comité International de Paléographie, *Catalogue des manuscrits en écriture latine portant des indications de date, de lieu ou de copiste,* Paris, 1959–1962, have now been published, embracing manuscripts from the libraries of Paris and Chantilly. As is to be expected, most of the manuscripts in French libraries are of French origin, but manuscripts of very different origins have been included in this listing because of the close similarity between the various bastard hands, and because of the dating evidence they provide.

The following may be cited:

Mazarine 934, datable 1396–1420. Prepared under the direction of the author Pierre d'Ailly, who died in 1420, and signed by him. I, Plate LXX.

Bibl. nat. lat. 6490, dated 4 November 1406 by the scribe, Ruauldus Silvestre, a cleric of Coutances, France (? or of Constance, Switzerland). II, Plate LXXIX.

Bibl. nat. lat. 6935A, dated by the scribe at the University of Siena, Italy, 6 March 1408, and corrected 22 August 1413 by Nicholaus de Alegro (probably also at Siena). Both the scribe and Nicholaus write cursive bastard hands. II, Plate LXXIX.

Bibl. nat. lat. 4514, dated at Grenoble 13 October 1415 by the scribe. II, Plate LXXXIII. The manuscript is written on parchment and paper mixed, as is VM-*Speculum*-TR.

Bibl. nat. lat. 7831, written in 1416 at the Council of Constance, Switzerland. Other manuscripts written for the same original owner at Constance during the Council, 1415–1417, in very similar hands are preserved at Reims, nos. 381, 1110, 1111, 1112, 1321, 1338. II, Plate LXXXIV.

Mazarine 253, dated 7 August 1417, probably written by a French scribe, Yves (son of?) François. I, Plate LXXXIV.

Arsenal 767, dated 3 May 1424, written by a monk at Emstein near Dordrecht, Holland. I, Plate LXXXV.

Arsenal 731, dated 18 September 1425, and bought for the Abbey of Saint-Victor, Paris, by a prior of the Abbey who died in 1458. I, Plates LXXXVI–LXXXVII. The manuscript is written on parchment and paper mixed, as is VM-*Speculum*-TR.

Mazarine 3524, dated 1427 by the scribe, Brother Alanus Kerfibu of Guingamp, Côtes-du-Nord, France, while he was a student at Poitiers. I, Plate XC.

Bibl. nat. lat. 6658, dated at Florence, Italy, in September 1429, and signed by Gregorius de Interande while he was a student there. II, Plate XCI.

Bibl. nat. lat. 7655, dated 20 March 1432 by the scribe, Cunradus Hoeren of Saint-Gall, Switzerland. II, Plate XCIV.

Bibliothèque Universitaire number 1454. This was written by two scribes, the second of whom dated the manuscript 1456. The hand of the first scribe is similar to the scribe of the Vincent manuscript, that of the second scribe is not.

In addition to these manuscripts cited above, two others in American collections which confirm the attributed date have been examined. One of these, a massive anonymous Chronicle at Yale containing one leaf written in a bastard cursive hand closely comparable to *Speculum* and TR, bears a presentation inscription dated 1446 from a certain Jacobus of Oppenheim to John Capgrave of Oxford. The other, a manuscript written on parchment and paper mixed by several different scribes is dated 1446; the first scribe used a handwriting style very similar to that of *Speculum*-TR, and the manuscript was probably written at Mainz as it has several contemporary ownership notes of the Monastery of St. Jacob in that town.

So much for the handwriting of *Speculum* and TR. VM presents a special problem, since the handwriting of its legends is often so small and so condensed that one does not immediately see that the hand is identical to that of *Speculum* and TR. The latter has comparatively few capital letters, whereas VM has a great many, some of them not represented at all in TR.

The discovery of the Vincent manuscript considerably aided the analysis of the script. While TR appeared to have been written in extreme haste, as though the scribe had it in his possession for a very short time, the *Speculum* is a well-written manuscript, done without the sense of haste which one observes in the Tartar Relation. The Bastarda script is a semi-cursive one with some use of ligatures and frequent inadvertently almost-connected letters (i.e. the letters are not intentionally connected but the pen point hardly leaves the surface). Most distinctive are the letters *x, y, g.* Our scribe starts his *x* from the top left stroke, connecting his first stroke completely with the second coming from top right. At the conclusion of the letter the pen, barely touching the surface, turns sharply to the right, making a light stroke before leaving the surface to form the next letter. In forming the tails of the *g* and *y,* the scribe bears down to the left, then sharply reverses his direction parallel to the down stroke, gradually lifting the pen from the surface. These are the obvious characteristics, apparent in the originals, less so in the reproductions.

The Vincent also provides many capitals for comparison, such as the unusual capital *S,* which always seems to be falling over backward, and the rather ornate capitals *M, B, Q,* and *O.*

Minute examination of every letter form in VM and enlargements made from its inscriptions (Pl. IV) reveal clearly that the hand is identical throughout with *Speculum* and TR. Thus the only special characteristic of VM which sets it slightly apart from the other sections is the tinyness of much of its writing. Since the scribe was forced to write his legends in very small spaces, he had recourse to a fine quill-point and small writing, and he wrote with much more care than in much of *Speculum* and all of TR. The forms of the letters remain identical, as does the ductus of the hand; it is only the scale of the writing which changes. Therefore VM, *Speculum,* and TR are all by a single scribe writing an Oberrheinische Bastarda in the first half of the Fifteenth Century, most probably in the 1440s.

4. THE PAPER, PARCHMENT, AND INK

From the earliest stages of the study of this manuscript the paper and parchment employed in it have assumed signal importance. When Mr. Witten first saw the *Speculum* volume, he was impressed by the make-up of its quiring; before taking it home for comparison with the VM-TR volume, he checked the watermark of its paper in Briquet's *Les Filigranes* and wrote down Briquet's number 15056. When he examined his notes on VM-TR, he found that he had obtained the same number for the paper of TR among the hundreds of bullshead marks in Briquet. It has now been shown that the paper of the manuscript is primary evidence in assigning the date and locale of the writing. In September 1962 the Vincent manuscript together with photographs of the watermarks of the paper leaves in the Tartar Relation were sent for examination to Mr. Allan Stevenson, who was then in England. His letter on the subject is with his permission printed below.

"British Museum
19 October 1962

"Dear Mr. Marston,

"You seem to be in luck regarding the paper in the Tartar Relation and the Vincent de Beauvais. For these manuscripts apparently consist of long runs of a single paper manufactured (except for a sheet or so) on one pair of moulds, in the same state or related states, and thus belonging to one short period in the work of the moulds. As regularly in paper of the Rhine Valley in the fifteenth century, the marks are in the opposite halves of their moulds or sheets. The clear example at the end of the Tartar Relation is mould-side left folio (mLF°), the other mould-side right folio (mRF°). Let us call them L and R. L has spaced eyes and slanted nostrils, R close eyes and nearly level nostrils; and both have the spectacle effect.

"The lucky thing is that L can be identified with Briquet 15056.[3] Ordinarily Briquet's tracings are insufficiently accurate or detailed for absolute identification. Briquet could have made things much easier for scholars by reproducing the pattern of sewing dots by which a mark was attached to its mould, or by including both members of a pair. But here 15056 (traced from the felt side and so reversed) is so nearly congruent with L that we can be 99 per cent sure that they derive from the same mould.

"The main difference is one of *state*. According to my experience, L is in a slightly *earlier* state than the mark in Briquet. Originally the mark was probably centered between the chains; but it has slid along the laid wires (largely through pull of mould on paper at couching) until the 'left' ear just about touches the chain. Here it measures 62.5 × 0[31.5]5.5 mm across the ears in a chainspace of 37 mm. This seems to be the prevailing state in both manuscripts. Briquet's state measures 61 × [1.5:30]7 mm, similarly in a space of 37 mm. The ear has been moved nearly 2 mm farther left, so that it might be sewn twice to the chain. (The same phenomenon occurs in a Bull's-head-tau mark in the *Missale speciale:* cf. Briquet 15161.) In the process the ear has been distorted and the 'left' horn has been squeezed a bit. This is sufficient evidence that the Briquet state is later. Two minor differences are probably due to poor tracing: Briquet cuts the

---

3. See C. M. Briquet, *Les Filigranes,* Tom. 4, 1907, no. 15056, and p. 755, where Briquet records paper with this watermark in the municipal accounts of Colmar, with the date 1441.

'left' horn point short and does not show the 'star' or X beyond its group of sewing dots. Otherwise the X agrees in form and position precisely with that in the last Tartar leaf. It is reassuring that both chainspaces measure 37 mm.

"This statement is 'preliminary', but it may be sufficient. In going through the Vincent I noted a random BHX mark without 'spectacles', and so from a third mould; also a clear instance of *L* in a state with the X-staff tipped left; and there may be other states half-hidden by the script. Though I shall examine these farther, they probably have no real value for your investigation.

"Briquet's date may be close to the right one. As Briquet's note gives only one place and date, he has dated the state he depicts. Another consideration is that the Vincent and the Tartar Relation seem to represent (virtually) one long *run* or supply of paper. Thus one may argue that the manuscript was begun, probably, not long after the paper was manufactured or at least supplied; and that the paper dates from about 1440. One cannot argue so from an individual or random instance of a watermark. The weak point here is that we have only one date and tracing from Briquet and do not know whether his example is random or not—though, as he cites Municipal Accounts, that should mean a consistent supply or run of paper. In any case, I should say that the style of the marks *L* and *R* is indicative of a date not far from 1440.

"The provenance of the Spectacled Bulls is uncertain. At an earlier time BHX papers were made in Piedmont, as Briquet 15046 for example indicates. But it looks as if imitations were made farther north. The main possibilities around 1440 were, I think, Fribourg and Basel. Briquet thought a mill had operated at Marly near Fribourg from 1411 and cites a mention of a mill at Belfaux near Fribourg in 1440. (See Briquet's *Opuscula*, pp. 71–72.) It is worth noting that Br 15057 was used at Fribourg. However, I am more and more persuaded, by the positions of known mills and the areas of use, that a high proportion of early BHX papers was manufactured at Basel. In this case the mill would be the Mühle Zu Allen Winden, established at Klein Basel by Heinrich Halbisen about 1433, apparently to supply paper for the Church Council and a great trade down the Rhine. So far as I know, the only other mill in the region was that at Ravensburg, which made paper marked only with Eyeless Bulls. The fact that Br 15056 (that is, *L*) was found at Colmar in Alsace fits with either Fribourg or Basel. Later, if not already, Fribourg was known for its paper marked rather with Grapes. Of the three sources around 1440, Piedmont, Fribourg, Basel, the chances seem but slightly to favor Basel.

"The investigation that you and Mr. Skelton have been engaged upon is one of the most breathtaking that I have heard of. I am proud to have been let in on a piece of the mystery concerning the Map. And I shall be happy if any notes on the paper should prove of any service in arriving at a date.

Sincerely Yours,
Allan Stevenson"

The parchment acquired by our scribe was definitely of second quality, perhaps the best he could afford. He first had trouble with leaf e_{16}, where he could not get his ink to spread properly. Then on g_{16} recto he ran into a rough hair side of the parchment, which bothered his writing. The same happens with h_1 verso; and to correct this, when he comes to h_{16}, its conjugate leaf, he tries using a finer pen, writing a smaller script and increasing the number of lines in a column from 41 to 48 in the same writing space. One could cite other leaves where the same problems occur. About 20 per cent of the parchment leaves present similar conditions to the scribe.

The map is on an extremely thin piece of parchment, the hair side on the outside. Therefore there should be a conjugate leaf of similar thickness and pliability in the manuscript (unless it had been lost). There is such a leaf, l_1, with its conjugate l_{16}. It is the same in thickness, pliability, and color. To prove that it is part of the same leaf is almost impossible, since the volume has been trimmed by the fifteenth-century binder. Yet here are two sheets of parchment of similar qualities utterly dissimilar from the rest of the parchment in the rest of the volume. Furthermore, as the enlargements of the map legends show (see Pl. IV), the parchment of the map was unevenly cured, for in some places the ink goes into the parchment and in others it does not penetrate the surface.

It would be very convenient if there were some chemical test to indicate either the age or approximately common point of origin of parchment. Such tests of age as exist are at present objectionable for two reasons: they are decidedly not accurate enough for our purposes, and they require the destruction of at least some of the parchment. Possibly examination for trace elements might be a help; again, presumably, this would require the destruction of some of the parchment. But there are other reasons for objecting to it. The manufacture of parchment requires the introduction of two mineral substances, unslaked lime and pumice or a similar material for polishing. Each of these substances could introduce trace elements which would make it difficult to draw conclusions from such tests. The added materials would probably leave varying residual amounts of the foreign minerals that would vary from piece to piece of parchment, particularly because the rougher (or hair) side of each piece would retain varying amounts of the added substances.

The scribe used several different batches of ink in the manuscript, in one case switching to a new batch of ink after writing a column and a half on one of the poorly cured parchment leaves. Since the same ink takes differently on paper and on parchment, the change from one batch to another is sometimes hard to identify.

It has been only recently that ink has ceased being mainly a homemade article and can be bought at stores in bottles. In the medieval period ink was made either of iron salts or of oak galls, or a combination of both. This type of ink does not lend itself to modern spectroscopic tests effective in determining the relationship of one ink to another of chemically known composition. The only kind of test that would yield valid results would require the scraping away of the amount of writing necessary to produce enough material to work on. This would of course be only part of the problem, as the composition of medieval ink was not governed by precise measurements but varied from batch to batch as its maker guessed at its correct composition, and apparently varied within each batch as the constituent of the ink sank to the bottom of its container.

The red in the rubrication of our documents is uniform throughout. As it is a paint— i.e. with a pigment base—rather than an ink, it takes equally well on both paper and parchment.

5. THE BINDING

The reader is referred to the photographic reproductions of the *Speculum* binding (Pl. I) for an understanding of this section. In considering these old binding sides we must first determine if they are original to the *Speculum* and therefore to the whole manuscript.

A cursory examination shows that the volume has been subjected to a complete modern re-backing and a slight restoration of the covers using a leather which does not match the original at all; this work is of very rough and inartistic quality. We may also see that the sewing of the volume has been renewed at head and foot of the spine where it is visible; this is almost certainly true throughout, since the quires of the *Speculum* now present a slight unevenness at the edges (it is virtually impossible to resew an entire volume retaining evenness in the edges; for this reason, most books which have been resewn have also been retrimmed). Since the back and sewing are not intact, it is entirely possible that the sides have nothing to do with the manuscript. However, there are two immediately apparent reasons for thinking that they do belong.

First, it must be recalled that the *Speculum* fragment was offered for sale at a low price in the present binding and there is no reason to suppose that anyone would have troubled to provide it with a pastiche consisting of old sides salvaged from some other fifteenth-century book or manuscript, together with a very crude new back. On the contrary, if the original sides were lacking, it would have been far simpler and cheaper to provide the manuscript with a modest new binding. On the other hand, if the original sides still existed, the obvious thing to do was to put this manuscript back together as inexpensively as possible, retaining the attraction of the remains of the old binding. Second, and much more telling, is the fact that the old sides precisely match the dimensions of VM, the *Speculum* fragment, and TR, none of whose edges have been subjected to a modern trimming. This is important evidence because of the great difficulty involved in finding a pair of fifteenth-century covers which will *exactly* match the original dimensions of any given fifteenth-century manuscript. We cannot, however, rule out the possibility that the unlikely coincidence occurred: that the repairer had on hand, or searched for and located, matching covers for a manuscript of very modest value.

Since the covers do match the manuscripts in size, we must now determine if they are stylistically appropriate. The task is not an easy one, and no final answers will be found in this brief study, partly because of certain truly unusual features of this particular binding and partly because the systematic study of gothic bookbindings from the dozens of locations, chiefly monasteries and larger cities, in which they were made, is still in its infancy. Very little has been published on bindings of the first half or even of the middle of the fifteenth century, except for monographs treating a very small number of master binders whose names and works are known, as will be seen below.

The following data may be recorded in a first view of the exterior of the volume: the binding sides consist of wooden boards covered with brown leather which has been ruled and stamped with binders' tools; one of the tools represents a bird and another a fleur-de-lys, and all impressions of these tools are upside down on the covers with respect to the handwriting of the manuscript inside; there are four wrought brass catches on the upper cover, two on the fore edge, one each at top and bottom; the four leather straps terminating in clasps, now entirely lacking, were fastened on the lower cover by two brass nails each, the heads of which are of asterisk design; the binding is very worn and wormeaten with the bare boards exposed in several places where the leather has worn or been torn away, and impressions of the binder's tools are often visible in the bare boards; one of the boards has cracked vertically with the grain, and the leather covering it has cracked, too; finally, the tooling, identical in each cover, consists of numerous patterned repetitions of a very small number of different tools—in fact, only five different tools are employed, and one of these is always found in conjunction with one other.

Each cover of the binding is divided into concentric rectangular panels by rows of blind fillets; the spaces between these rows of fillets have been filled to a greater or lesser degree by rows of impressions of the five different tools, each row of which occupies the outer perimeter of a rectangle, except for the innermost rectangle on each cover, which is filled by repeated impressions of a single tool arranged in three vertical rows. The tool filling the innermost rectangle is a small square stamp of a bird seen in profile with its wings spread. In the next row outward a small stamp of rosette type is employed. Outside this is found a pattern of circles: a group consisting of six circles surrounds a similar inner one which is gilt, while around the exterior of this group are six tiny circles; separating each group of this type is a single impression of the larger circle which is gilded. The outermost tool employed is a lozenge-shaped stamp containing a fleur-de-lys, except that the pattern of circles, with the center circle gilt, is repeated at the four corners of each cover in the square spaces formed by the pattern of fillets.

The design of the binding may be compared with the series of types described by Hans Loubier, *Der Bucheinband,* Leipzig, 1926 (*Monographien des Kunstgewerbes,* Band XXI/XXII), Illustration 90. This is Loubier's first type, current throughout the fourteenth and the earlier fifteenth century (Loubier, p. 99). The complete absence of large stamps, rolls, or plaques in the present binding is evidence of early date and consistent with the early design of the whole.

What country of origin may be suggested for this binding? In general, its characteristics are decidedly Germanic, and nothing in its overall appearance strongly suggests French, Flemish, English, Italian, or Spanish origin. Its design is of a somewhat standardized and unspecific type, but it is a design perhaps more frequently utilized in Germanic bindings than in those of other countries. Its brown leather, apparently calfskin, is not at all typical of Italian work where this same basic design was also much favored. The bird, fleur-de-lys, and rosette tools are all typically Germanic and not suggestive of any other style.

The binding recalls in some ways the work of two of the most famous early German binders, Conrad Forster and Johannes Fogel. Of these Forster, who was a Dominican monk in Nuremberg, signed and dated bindings from 1433 to 1457; his small stamps included a fleur-de-lys, and perhaps a rosette, very closely comparable to those on the *Speculum* binding (Loubier, Illustration 92). Fogel, who worked at Erfurt, is known from signed bindings dating from 1456 to 1459; after the latter date his tools are in the hands of others. The four catches on the *Speculum* binding are exceedingly like those on one Fogel binding (Loubier, Illustration 95), and his work nearly always includes a bird stamp (Vogel = Bird) and a fleur-de-lys stamp of lozenge shape (Loubier, Illustration 96). Fogel frequently used a design of Loubier's first type, although he elaborated it considerably (compare Loubier, Illustration 95; E. P. Goldschmidt, *Gothic and Renaissance Bookbindings,* London, 1928, vol. 2, Plate I; Léon Gruel, *Manuel Historique et Bibliographique de l'Amateur de Reliures,* vol. II, Paris, 1905, Illustration opposite p. 82). ·

It is not suggested that the *Speculum* binding be attributed to Forster or Fogel, but rather that its general appearance is typical of work not later than about 1450. It is difficult indeed, for example, to cite a single Germanic binding of the later Fifteenth Century which has much similarity to the present example.[4] Unfortunately, no systematic study of specifically Swiss or Upper Rhineland bindings is available for consultation.

Four unusual and puzzling elements in the binding must now be examined: the original position of the covers; the original position of the clasps and catches; the nails which fastened the now missing clasps; and the use of gilt roundels on the binding.

As the covers are now placed, all impressions of the two stamps which have a specific upward-downward character (the bird-stamp and the fleur-de-lys stamp) are upside down. There are only two possible explanations for this fact; either the covers have been reversed accidentally in the rebinding, or the original binder made a very gross blunder. It would have been extremely easy to reverse the covers in rebinding; the modern binder need only have been moderately in-attentive, and with the covers reversed the four brass catches appear on the *upper* cover, which is by far the most common treatment in Germanic and many other fifteenth-century bindings. The mistake is an easy one to make, and the conspicuous catches give it a natural appearance which is betrayed only when one looks closely and finds that the small stamps are upside down. The other possibility, a very gross error on the part of the original binder, seems much less likely, even though it would place the clasps on the lower and the catches on the upper cover where they are most frequently placed in Germanic bindings. Would a monastic library or a rich collector in the fifteenth century have tolerated a binding whose stamps were upside down? It is much more probable that the monastic or layman binder would have been com-pelled to replace his faulty workmanship.

If the covers have been reversed by the modern repairer, we are obliged to accept a positioning of the clasps and catches which is very rare in Germanic workmanship. However, this position-ing is very frequently encountered in Italian bindings of the fifteenth century and may even have been the predominant practice in Italy. This is the first of three specifically Italianate fea-tures which may be observed in the present binding.

Also specifically Italianate are the brass nails with asterisk-like heads serving to attach the leather portion of the clasps to the edges of the (originally upper) cover. Two were used for each of the four clasp-straps; one nail is missing. Such nails may be seen on countless fifteenth-century Italian bindings, whereas other attachment styles predominate outside Italy.

Finally, we must discuss the small gilt circular tool which we may call a roundel, taking note that the literature of bookbinding is almost totally silent on this very interesting topic. Although the gilt is very worn on these roundels (it cannot be readily seen in the photographic repro-ductions), enough traces of it remain to make its original presence a certainty. Tools of pre-cisely this type are commonly seen on North Italian bindings of the period 1440–1500. From the beginning of the period of their usage these roundels were sometimes gilded or silvered and sometimes painted in other colors. Close study shows that all of the coloration was applied as a paint; most importantly, the gilding was not done by means of gold leaf and the hot iron. These little gilt roundels, which always have a coppery tint, doubtless represent the earliest

4. The reader is referred to the long series of illustrations in *Verzierte gotische Einbände im alten deutschen Sprach-gebiet,* by Ernst Kyriss, Stuttgart, 1951–58.

Western European attempt at the decoration of bookbindings with gilding (see T. De Marinis, *La Legatura Artistica in Italia nei Secoli XV e XVI,* Florence, 1960, passim, where many examples are reproduced).

We may summarize the study of the preserved binding sides. They are probably original to the manuscript, the remains of its first binding, and they have very likely been reversed in the recent rebinding. They are readily attributable to the period 1440–1450, like the rest of the manuscript, and they are not likely to be of much later date in any case. They combine Germanic and Italianate features in a way which has not been recorded in any binding so far published. In the absence of data for comparison it is impossible to attribute the binding firmly to any specific place. We may only suggest that such a binding is the product of both Germanic and Italianate techniques mingling at some unknown place about the middle of the fifteenth century.

6. THE TEXT OF THE VINCENT OF BEAUVAIS

No modern critical scholarly text of Vincent of Beauvais' *Speculum Historiale* exists. The attempt made in the Douai edition of 1624 to edit the text is worse than useless, for it incorporates into the text corruptions and misreadings which a better scholar than its editor would have avoided. In making textual comparisons, one is therefore dependent on the early printed editions for the most reliable text.

The first and most obvious problem facing the reader of the Vincent is that the scribe has numbered his books XXI–XXIV, whereas, in the Douai edition of 1624 and in various other texts both printed and manuscript, the same books are numbered XX–XXIII. This variation in the printed editions was noted by Lynn Thorndike (*A History of Magic and Experimental Science,* Vol. 2, 1929, p. 429, n. 3). As Mr. Painter shows (see below, p. 22, n. 5), this difference in numeration arises from an early divergence in the manuscript tradition, through which the books of the *Speculum Historiale* came to be numbered alternatively as 31 or 32, though the text remained in other respects the same. The 32-book numeration turns out to be found not only in the Yale manuscript, but in numerous other fifteenth-century manuscripts and printed texts, and is in no way abnormal.

A rough computation of the space required for Book XX (in the 32-book numeration used by our scribe) shows that it could reasonably be fitted into the missing 65 leaves. On this plausible assumption, the reconstructed manuscript originally contained Books XX–XXIV. The only connection between this portion of the *Speculum* and the map is that it contains the story of St. Brendan's voyage. However, as in the printed editions, Vincent declares his belief that this voyage is a fictitious invention.[5]

As to the text itself, both Mr. Painter and I have checked the contents against the printed editions. While no effort has been made to edit the text, we have both made random spot collations, and neither of us has found any substantive variations between the text of the manuscript and the printed versions.

A close examination of the manuscript reveals the fact that, while our scribe ruled his total writing space, he did not rule in the single lines. Normally he wrote from 38 to 41 lines to a

5. Cf. below, p. 25, n. 8.

column. It has been pointed out in discussing the parchment that, in an effort to cope with the difficulties of the material, he tried a smaller pen and a smaller hand on h_{16}, getting 48 lines into the same space. When he reached signature s, he apparently became worried about getting the remainder of the text into his supply of paper and parchment. Possibly at this point the original of the Tartar Relation had become available to him, and he used one of his precious quires to copy that text. At any rate, the scribe turns to his smaller hand and consistently writes 45 to 49 lines to a column. By the time he reaches t_8, however, he realizes that he has enough writing material to complete the manuscript, and in the last eight leaves he reverts to his earlier practice of 38 to 41 lines to a column.

The *Speculum Historiale* ends with *"Explicit tertia pars speculi hist."*—which must refer to the text in this volume. The inscription on the front of the map refers to the map as illustrating the first, second, and third part of the *Speculum,* presumably meaning the *Speculum Historiale* as a whole. This discrepancy is discussed by Mr. Painter (pp. 22–27 below), with the conclusion that the archetype of the Vinland Map was produced to accompany a three-volume manuscript of the *Speculum,* from which the Yale manuscript, which probably consisted originally of five volumes, descended by way of a four-volume intermediary. Possibly the missing four volumes of the Yale manuscript are still in existence, for nothing would be considered more humble in a collection of medieval manuscripts than an odd volume of a fifteenth-century manuscript of the *Speculum Historiale*. Any cataloguer would glance at it, readily identify it, and forget about it.

7. SUMMARY

What do we know of the early history of the manuscript? By actual tradition, nothing; by internal evidence, a great deal. The structure of the manuscript places it in the first half of the fifteenth century, as does its paleography. The remains of the contemporary binding places it about the middle of the fifteenth century. Its paper, usually secondary evidence, is in this case of primary importance and dates it about 1440, a date that fits in with all the other evidence.

Also, all evidence points to the Upper Rhineland as the source of origin of the manuscript, paper, binding, and paleography. To pinpoint the source of origin is highly speculative, but there seems to be sufficient evidence to point to the Swiss town of Basle. This was the center of an important church council, which lasted from 1431 to 1449. Aside from its importance in the conciliar movement, which is of no interest to us here, this council was important in intellectual history. Attended by church dignitaries and their staffs from all over Europe, the council is noted for introducing to Western European churchmen the Bible in Greek, and in spreading the ideas of the Italian humanists and their works to Northern Europeans. Where else could such a product as this be prepared, combining an East European account of a mission to the Mongols with a medieval historical text and a map (as Mr. Skelton shows) of Northern European origin? Basle certainly seems the most sensible and logical conclusion. As a result, following the custom of booksellers, our description of this manuscript should read "Upper Rhineland (Basle?).*ca.* 1440."

THE VINLAND MAP

AND THE

TARTAR RELATION

Facsimiles of the manuscript originals

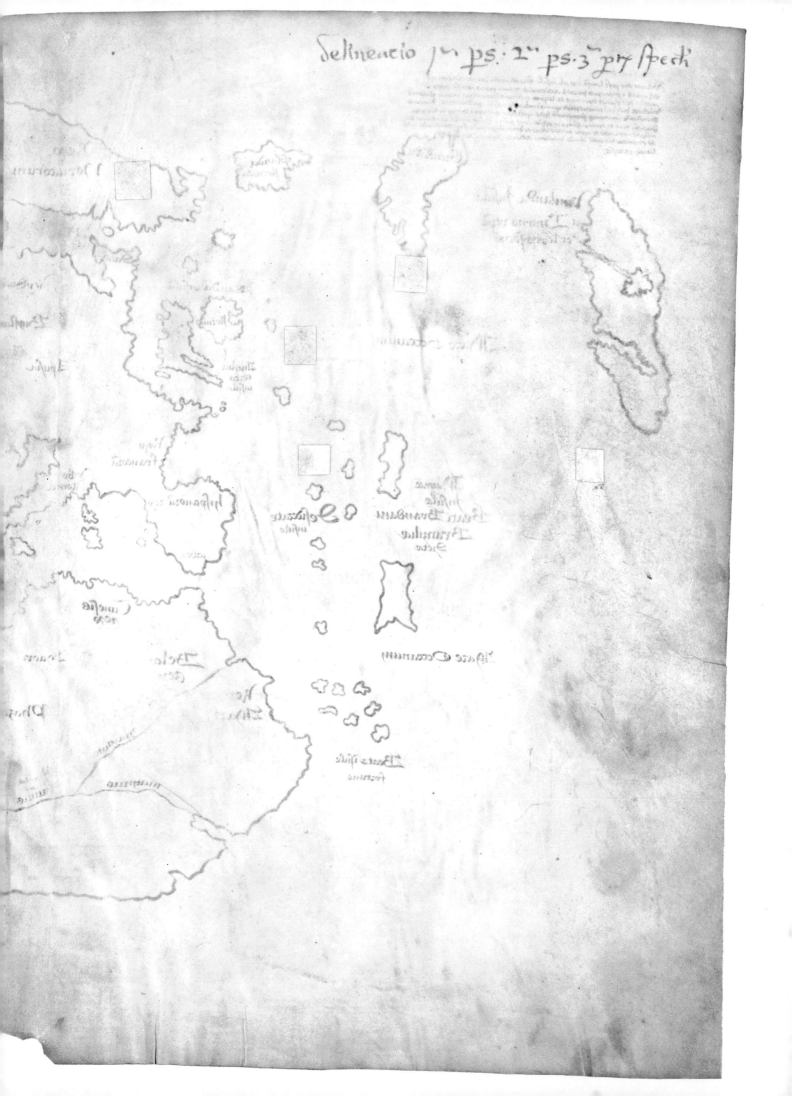

Volente deo post longu[m] iter ab insula Gronelanda per meridiem ad
reliquas extremas partes occidentalis oceani maris iter facientes ad
austru[m] inter glacies hyemales et leiphus crossanus socij terram novam uberrima[m]
videlicet vineti[m] invenerunt qua[m] Vinlanda i[n]sula appellaverunt. heinricus
Gronelande regionumq[ue] finitimar[um] sedis apostolice ep[iscop]us legatus in hac terra
spaciosa vero et opule[n]tissima in postremo an[n]o p[re]sul[is] Pascal[is] accessit in nomine dei
omnipotentis longo tempore mansit estivo et brumali postea versus Gronelanda[m] redijt
ad orientem hiemale[m] deinde humillima obediencia superiori vo-
luntate processit.

Gronelada

Vinlanda Insula
a Byarno repa
et leipho socijs

Isolanda
Ibernica

Rex
Noruicorum

Sacij

Rex Suec[ie]

Bugisla[via]

Isolanda insula

Ibernia

Mare Occeanum

Ipisia

Anglia
terci[a]
insula

Rex
francoru[m]

Urbo
Roma

Magne
Insule
Beati Brandani
Branzilie
dicte

Desiderate
insule

hispanoru[m] rex

aben

Tunesis
rex

Mare Occeanum

Bela
no[...]

Lyaor[a]

Rex
Aliar[um]

Phaza[n]

Beata i[n]sule
fortune

Braziine

magnus

Braz[iine]
u[...]us

septda pars

Thule ultima

Tartarata fluuius

montes inferiores abrupti

Jn hanc terram prius fratres nostri ordinis iter faciendo ad tartaros
mongolos zamorered ? ? ? transiuerunt nobis per orbe? ? ? ?
et subiectionem tam debitam ? deuotam iudicauo ? ? ? ?
nostro Pontifices, per totum occidentem et in reliqua parte usque ad
mare occeanum orientale

Tartatuo Rev

Terre non satis perfcrutate
posite sunt inter boreales glacies
ab iisdem abs? ? ?

mare
Occeanum
Orientale

Jmperiu Tartarorum

kytano

Gotpio

Insule
Sub aquilone
zamorederum

Tartaus

Ruff habeat imperiu? ? ? ? ? ? ex parte orietis mogulos tartaros
? ? ? ? ex parte boreali habent mare frigidum et magnum flumen
quod medium montem insulam? ? transiit interglacies boreales occeani
? ? ? ? ? ?

Matzoti

Jrpun

Morali

Magnum
mare
Tartarorum

magnus Kai

Abad

Jumul

Tartaria magilica

Postreme Insule

Samaca

Tartari affirmant absq dubio ?
noua terra inagcoruenio mundi partibus
sit eam nec ultima terra nisi solumodo
mare occeanum inueniatur

Seseruani affudice pacessserant usque ad terram kitay
ad reliqua filii ? ? ? ? ? ? ? ? ?
uastis montes hermedeos quos superare non potuerunt

kennuod
montes
Superiores
Gozsf siue
? ? ? ?

Terra
Indica

mare
Indicum

Jerusalem

Alexandria

Chaira

Petra

Rev
Soldanus

Sinaius
mons

mare
Indicum

Jmperiu Baseru

Jndicum

Prefto johannis iste sunt terre populose ad meridiem prope ind?
maghalie nostre sed diuerso? ordo? ? ? in iunio? dum orbi ? ? ? ? ?
? ? ordo uo ecclesie habent in quibus oraie possunt demaq?

Ethiopi

Gimbar superior

? ? ? Ethiopicus

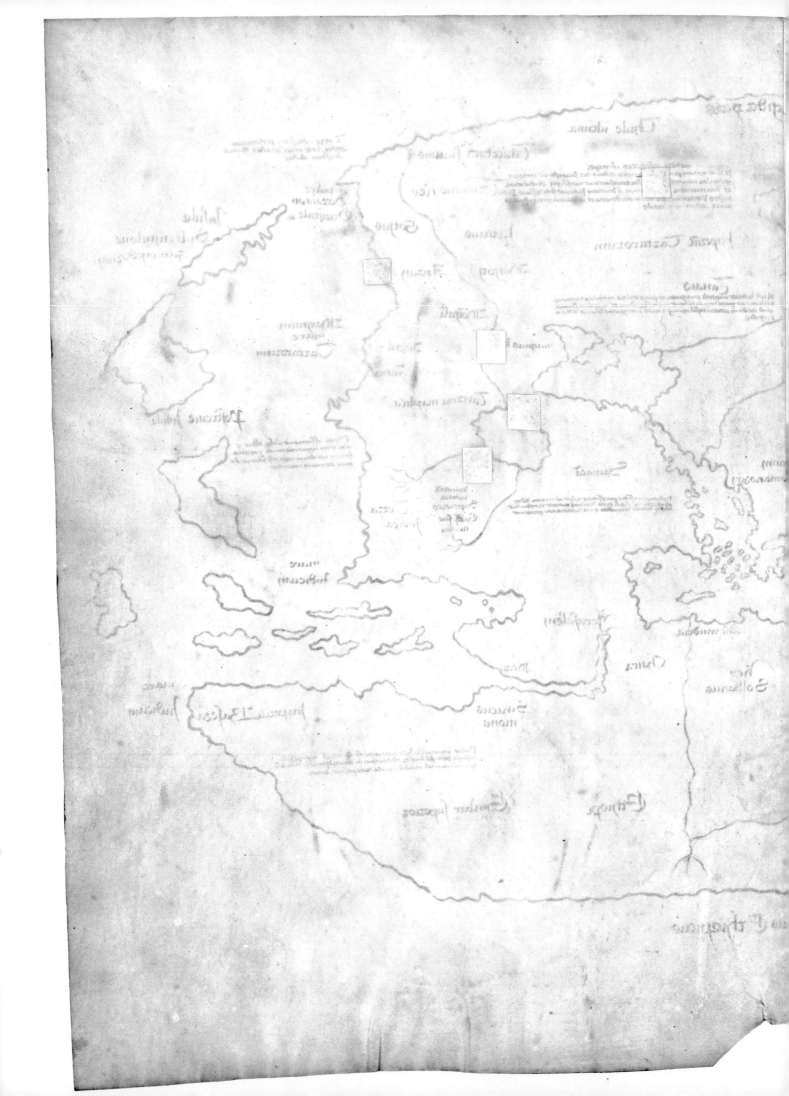

Reverentissimo patri fri
Conrado ministro fratrum
Aymorum in Boemia et polonia
referencium frater C. de brida
inter minores minimus filialis
obediencie subiectionem tam de
bitam quam devotam perfecte obe
diencie hoc exposcit officii ut si
quis meo exercatu desiderat
non solum fieri sed verum eciam
ardua sibi volenti aggredia
tur animo secundum superi
orum voluntatem vestram paterni
tati quamvis supra vires re
mei audiens que vidi de
tartaris intellexi cum venerabi
libus fratribus nostri ordinis
scilicet Johanne sedis aplice
legato ad omnes exteras naciones
precipue et ad tartaros caterot
et fre benedicto polono et fre
ceslao boemo socii eius brevi
ter in scripto posui causes facta
dum legor et ut vera hic audiat
deuoco que de terre incolis novi
utilia elicere et mirabilibus
dei omnipotentis iudicia tam ocu
tis que in fine iam clarescunt
scilicet in quo appropinquat stor
redempto conversat in laudem
eius pariter et amorem. Sciendum
igitur quod secundum tartaros et
quosdam alios habitabilis mun
di humus machina dividitur
in duas principales orientalem
videlicet et occidentalem lat
tyre sumptas secundum quod sol oritur et
occidit estivo tempore et bru
mali iuchoatur autem ab occidente
a terra liuonie et vadit per

sia usque in treciam et deinceps
et continet in se universam et
ecclesiam catholice fidei. Unde et
tartari appellant apostolicum ma
ximum papam per totum occi
dentem. Reliqua vero pars de
orientalis in qua posita est ter
ra tartarorum oriens intersit
aquilonem habens contiguum ma
ze occeanum aquilonem et appel
latur moal. Erat autem in ea
vir quidam nobilis quidem gene
sed moribus crudelis homine
cingis aquo et principium tarta
ri habuerunt hic cum pauces
hominibus suis cepit spolia exter
cere Tandem crudelior effectus
homines furtim capiebat et in sue
inquitatis dominio adiungebat
cumque triginta satellites sibi co
aciasset prorumpens in insaniam
publicam totam terram sue na
tivitatis scilicet moal sue dicacioni
per omnia subiungauit. Quo facto
cepit ut moris est elatorum
appetere ampliora et coniuncta
to exercitu processit versus
terram eis contiguam ex par
te orientis que ab eisdem deno
minatur zumoal id est aquilei mo
gali zu in tartarice aqua dicit
latine id est moal terra mogali in
cole dicitur terre. Ipsi autem
appellabant se tartaros a fluvio
ayayno et impetuoso qui transit
terram eorum et dicitur tarta
tata id est trece the tartar trahens
dicitur in lingua eorum Isti per
brevimet ipsis sic ordinabant. Que
eo autem tempore preficerat
sibi ducem nomine Cauli que

cungis deuincens homines sibiu
gatos suo exercitui adunauit
Consuleuerat enim deuictos se
per sibi atrahere ut maioris
fortitudinis uirtute alias ter
ras superaret sicut patet in
eius posteris manifeste qui ipsi
us malicie sunt sequaces de
inde cum toto exercitu pera
uit ad terram que dicitur mer
bat que etiam tartaris est q
tigua ex parte occidentis est
ualis quam iam ualida sue
Dnacion subiciens apposita for
titudine suo exercitu terram
merkitis co comunitam que
appellatur meerit inuauit et
sibi continuo subiugauit Iste
quatuor s. moal aserbat et
meerit sunt unius labij sz par
differunt inter se sicut boemi et
polom et rutheni uel sicut ro
mani Lumbardi et de foro iulij
aut sicut australes Turingi et
sueui seu saxones feaminji et
vestfali homines terrarum ista
rum assimulantur sibi in facie
competenter Post hec cungis
collecto exercitu processit uersus
terram que dicitur uihur inco
le terre huius vpiam erant de
secta nestarianorum quibus supe
ratis acceptis acceperunt mongja
li eorum literas ad scribendu
no n antea literis vtebantur
et sic reuersi sunt in terram pro
priam deinde cungis mox fortitu
dine grauiori collera adijt tra
orientalem nomine esursakita ho

4 zomoal

mnes vero terre appellant se
kitai quibus mongali et reliq
tres prouincie smigue eorum
quondam fuerant tributarij
hec terra est magna et spaci
osa ualde et opulentissima ha
bens imperatorem strenuum et
potentem qui huiusmodi per
ceptis rumoribus indignatus
uehementer occurrit cungis
et et exercitui eius cum mi
litia de copiosa in quadam
nasta sollitudine et tanta
strages facta est mongalorum
q de viris mongalis tantum
septem remanserunt alia
tamen nacionum plures ho
mines euaserunt Quodcu
nens iam dictus imperator
contempsit etiam spolia collige
occisorum Cumq qum vero
clam in terram fugiens per
temporis modicum sue mali
cie pacem dedit Est autem
autem quedam terra tartaris
contigua a plaga occidenta
li que appellatur namian
montuosa ualde et fortitudinate
modum excedens huius tre
regi tartari et omnes circiad
iacentes prouincie tunc tpris
tributa regalia persoluebat
nt mortuus est eo tempore
quo cungis a plurib quiescebat
Religit tamen sui regni tres
paruulos filios successores Qo
audito cungis cepit aspirare
ad regnum puerorum et col
lecto exercitu cepit inuadere

regnum naymanorum Qui
uidentes fortitudinem eius re
trorsum cesserunt et associatis
sibi karakitaus · l· mgtis kytai/
sz kara · n· tartarice latine in
gyrum dicatur occurrerunt mo
galis in quadam ualle inter duos
montes altissimos et occupantes
uiam qua solus introitus pa
tebat in terram ex parte illius
lateris ducissime restiterunt
hanc uallem et terram fratres
nostri ordinis transiuerunt ad
tartaros iter faciendo Tandem
mongali quidam longe ualde
ab exercitu montes inferiores
transiuerunt Alij uero per ipsa
abrupta moncium q solis ybi
abus sunt peruia per que et
frater benedictus equitare
attemptabat sed a tartaris n
est permissus ne equm perdet
et personam Residuu autem in
ipsa acie exercitus accesserit
et sic commissum est plium in
ipmum ualde nimis ex omni
parte naymanorum in quorz
maior pars eorum interepta
est et residua cum suo dno se
subiecit Tunc interfectis tribz
filijs regis cum ampliori ex
ercitu cum... ad propria est
reuersus / Deinde progrediens
ad bellum inter meridianam
plagam et orientalem cepit
quatuor terras uidelicet uoy
rat Saryphur keranitas et
cosmur Et sic iterum ad ipsia

remeauit uerum quia auiditas
cum dominandi non smebat qes
cere aggregata omi qua poterat
robustorum fortitudine iterato p
cessit aduersus imperatorem ky
taiorum · Tandem post diuturnu
bellum fugato exercitu impera
toris ipsum imperatorem in me
tropoli ciuitate fortissma obsedit
quo aduersz obsidentes p nimia pe
nuria excepto · cumgz decim cum
suis deximu hominem inter se ma
ducarent Obsessi uero cum iam sa
gittaz ac lapidum rectus pate
rentur iacture argenti · ceperut
contra hostes et precipue liquc/
stan Erat · n· hec ciuitas habu'
dans diuicijs huiusmodi Abl
tmum autem obsidentes fecert
uiam subterranea usqz ad mediu
ciuitatis per quam in nocte ir
ruentes in ciuitate imperatorem
cum potentibus interfecto un
iuersa que in ea fuezat possidezet
Cingit ergo parte terre quam
ceperat ordinata cum gaudio
ad propria est reuersus Est · n·
quedam pars ma terre mariti
ma quam etiam usqz ad hodi
ernam diem tartari non pre
ualent obtinere / extunc cumgz
per tempus se precepisse can i.
imperatorem appellari pre/
dicti autem kitai quamuis pa
gani sint habent tamen nouum
et uetus testamentum et li
teras speciales uitas prim mil
tas et heremitas et domos

quasi ecclesias in quibus oramt
statuto tempore dicunt prete
rea se habere sanctos speciales
quosdam hii bonum deum colt
et credunt in dominum ihm xpm
credunt etiam uitam eternam
elemosinas dant largas et re
uerentur xpianos licet mime
baptizentur barbam non hent
nec in facie lati sunt ut mon
goli et habent ydioma speciale
igitur cum emgz iam esse appt
lati et quicuisset per unum
annum siue bellis ordinanit
eo tempore tres exercitus ad
tres mundi partes ut subiu
garent cunctos homines qui hi
tant super terram unum di
rexit cum filio suo cossut qm
etiam can nominabant cotra
comanos qui sti super azad
plagam accidentalem alteru
uero cum alio filio contra ma
iorem indyam ad orientem
hyemalem ipse autem cum
tercio processit contra mon
tes caspeos et cum transset
terram que palancia dicit
tunc temporis eam sibi non
subiaciens assidue ibat tribg
mensibus homicez non inue
mens per dextum cumqz be
misset prope montes caspeos
ubi dicuntur esse inclusi aba
lexandro iudi quos xpi appt
labant gog et magog et
ecce subito omnia ferramenta

sagitte de pharetris autelli et
gladii de uaginis strepede pel
lis habene de freme ferram
ta de equorum pedibus lorite
de corporibus gallee de capiti
bus uersus montem cum
impetu ad maximo strepi
tu processerunt et sicut ip
si fratri mo benedicto com
memorantes hec in quadam
referebant letteria qz grauiora
ferramenta ut pote lority z
gallee super terram ad motes
properanda cum impetu nia
gnum mimis puluerem et stru
pitum excitabant unde ipos
terras et horror mimius in
uadabant creduntur autem
hii montes esse addamantini
tereritus qz cylugis can fugt
cum exercitu dimictens qz
montes ad dextris processit
intes aquilonem et oriente
tamdem cum per tres alios
menses continue in itinere
per desta laborasset precept
desterentibus almoniis ut
decim decimum interse de
norarent hominem post
hos tres menses uenit ad
montes magnos terve q
appellantur navarigen i
homines solis naza emm
tartarice sol dicitur latie
prien homines cumqz in
uemisset itinera cta et nullos

homies/ murari cepit cum suis
uehementer. postmodum inde r
uento vivo vivo cum vroze ce
pit per multos interpretes que
rere de terre homnibus ubi es
sent et percepto qu in domibus
subterraneis sub montibus
habitarent mist iuu qu ceperat
mtie retenta interrogans si
uellent egredi ad bellandum sz
illo redeunte tartari facto ma
ne mortui plus prostrati sut
super terram propter strepi
tum plus ascendentib[us] ad pl
ures ibidem mortui sunt ex e
is/ incole autem terre per
ceptis hostibus irruerunt in
nocte super illos et plures de
tartaris occiderunt quod cer
nens cyngyz can. affugit cu
residuis vrozem captiua ni
chlominus secum deducens.
que postmodum sicut ipi tar
tari referebant sribus cum
vris mansit longo tempore
affirmans absq[ue] dubio qu dra
terra in extremis mundi
partibus sit posita/ nec ultig
terra nisi plummodo mare
occeanum invenitur unde in
ima vicinitate solis ascende
tis in mare extinoc estiuali
tempore tantius ac talis stra
por et sortius ex contrarieta
te solis et firmamenti audi
tur in ea qu millus homine
audet sub divo habitare super
terram quo adusq[ue] sol ad
meridiem per suum zodiacum

protgrediatur quin statim mori
atur tamquam per tonitruu
aut ledatur unde est eaam q[ue]
eo tempore cympana magna
et alia instrumenta percuciu
nt cauertno monau ut sono
tympanorum solis strepitum i
excludant hec terra post tran
situm monau plana est et fer
tilis Sed non est magna du
autem de hac terra cyngyz can.
demutus ad propria cum suis re
dire festinaret et dum in redi
tu montes caspeos conspexi
sset ad eos propter timore
prestmui non accessit videt
tur homies iam de montibz
processe propter strepitum
ante scm qu ad montes pro
parabant serramenta cu eis
ctare cupiebat Cumq[ue] uterq[ue]
sibi appropinquare cepissent
et ecce nubes diuisit eos
stans in medio sicut quonda
cyypcyos et filios israel. unde
satis crude credibile est eos
od iudeos quos dominus mu
niuit et monuit sicut prm et
quandocunq[ue] tartari ad nube
ascendebant cecitate peratie
bantur et quidam eaam plaga
mortis poterant tamen se
videre per nubem ad inuice
quoquo modo postqua vero aut
ad utramq[ue] partem nubis per
duas dietas transire i non
possent quin super nubem
hererent oppositum ceperunt cep
to itinere proficisci/ ituitur ita

l. integra

facientes tartari pedester et fa
me deficientes invenerunt al
uum seu viscera unius animal
animalia satis fortia que ut
ipsi credunt prius eis ibidem
manducantibus fuerant dere
luta et t adamsiz can essent
delata precepit ut trimmodo
grosso fimo manibus expresso
absque ulla rupcione vel lesione
viscerum congererentur quod et
factum est et sic cingiz can au
ceteris iam quasi fame mori
ens manducauit et ex inde sta
tuit cingiz can ut nichil de
pectoribus reiicerentur preter
fimum grossiciem interiorem de
quo plenius dicetur cum de
tradicionibus dicetur tartaro
rum Hiis gestis reuersus est
in terram suam et a contrario
diuino iudicio est percussus
Secundus uero exercitus qui
cum secundo filio cingiz can
missus fuerat contra indeos
deuicit deu minorem ideam i
ethyopiam in qua sunt homines
nigerrimi et paganam au... p
uenisset ad maiorem quam
thomas aplus prespiter iohes
quamuis non bene primum
misit exercitum contra eos 2
fecerunt quandam nouam
inauditam artem contra
tartaros ordinauerunt .n.
specialiter tria milia pug
natorum in quorum sellis in
anteriori parte posuerunt as

.ginlat. stati rex
ereispapllat

dain ferreas siue ereas ymagi
nes ignem uiuum habentes
in sua concauitate et ante
quam pugnite tartarorum ad
ipsos art mittere possent caput
contra ignem emittere suf
flando cum follibus quos ha
bebant ex utraque parte selle
sub utroque femore / post igne
uero sagitas iacere ceperunt
et sic turbatus est exercitus
tartarorum Alii quidem uero
uulnerati fugam inierunt
quos persequentes indi mul
multos strauerunt et reliquos
de suis finibus eiecerunt nec
ultra ad yndos tartari sunt
reuersi Hec eadem ipsi tartari
fratribus nobis referebant di
centes qui ynd... congressum or
dinata acie super equos se d
strepis eleuauerunt et cum ad
mirarentur quid hoc esset re
cederunt subito super sellas
et igne mox prosiliit ad il
sum nos quam etiam sagit
eorum sunt secute et sic
noster exercitus est fugatus
Cumque ynd tartarorum ad
se cederunt infra urbm annos
aut paulo plus nichil uidis
sent miserunt nuper ad eos
nuncios sic dicentes uos in
terram nostram intrauerat
sicut fures et non milites

milites bellicosi sed nunc scitote
quoniam aduentum nostrum coti-
die prestolamur Et si ad nos
uenire nolueritis nostrum ad
uos aduentum cicius expectes
Tartari autem redire non presumentes de propria autem ate
statutum tempus atingit tan-
ne subirent sentenciam capitalem processerunt inter orientalem plagam et meridianam ambulantes plusque mensem per
desertum peruenerunt ad terram
certam que appellatur tataruice nothoy cadzar Nothoy in tartarice canis dicitur latine kadzar
uero tartarice terra dicitur latine inuenerunt tantummodo m-
ulieres preter uiros quibus
captas remanserunt duobus
iuxta flumen quod medium
terre transit Cumque intrassent
de uiris quales et ubi essent
responderunt quod canes naturales et audita fama hostium flu-
me transiuisse Tercia autem
die canes omnes qui in terra
fuerant coadunari apparuerunt
sed tartaris iocum de eis facientibus transito fleumine iud-
uerunt se et ablis quod propter
temporis frigiditatem congelatum est diesque secundo et tercio
fecerunt et quia canes pilosi erant glacies cum pabulo
congelata est ad spissitudinem

unius palme Quo facto super
tartaros iruerunt Qui risu
facientes sagittis eos impetere
ceperunt Sed quia nisi per
os et occlos ledi non poterant
paucissimos peremerunt Canes
uero attauzentes eiaus uno morsu equm detraebant altero ca-
taz strangulabant Tartari
ergo cernentes quod in canibus
nec sagitte nec gladij nocere
poterant fugam inierunt quos
canes persequentes per bi-
duum interfectis plurimis ex
ipsis eos finibus eiecerunt et
sic pacem ab eis de cetero habuerunt Narrauit eciam cuidam
fui B. tartarus patrem suum a
canibus tunc temporis interemptum fratre praetea B. credit
pro certo inter tartaros unam
de canum mulieribus se uidisse
quam eciam dicit pepisse a tartauis ff pueros monstruosos dicti
autem canes sunt matris pilosi intelligentes omnia uerba
mulierum et mulieres intellica-
mim si mulier parit femmaz
humanam formam muris habet
si masculum canis efficiatur sic
patet de hac terra tartari ad
propria reuertentes ceperunt
terram que appellatur Buri-
thebeth Burith dicitur lupi
et bene conuenit medilis terre
qui tamquam lupi seruientes
patrem mortuum parentela

congregata comedere con
sueuerunt Isti pilos in barba
non habent sed si pili nascun
tur extrahunt eos ferreo tena
culo ad hoc facto multum p
terea sunt deformes Tercia
autem exercitus qui ad oc
cidentem iuit cum cosput tan
cum filio emgiz can subiuga
uit primo terram que dicitur
telemen Sm̄ Berezemtas
postea kanoptas ad ultimū
intrauerunt terram cuspras
.i. comonia Comaniautem co
adunati cum zutheins omic
bus pugnauerunt cum tar
tauis iuxta duos riuulos
nomen vnius talc alterig
uero comi comiuyzu .i. oniū
aq̄ cam .n. yrece diaetur
tartauice oues diauntur
latine vzzum vero aqua
et deuicti sunt a tartauis
effusus est sanguis ex utraq̄
parte usq̄ ad frenos equo
zum sic qui bello interfu
erunt referebant nuntis q̄
istas tartari rediue cepert
ad terras proprias et in re
ditu ceperunt ab aquilone
quasdam terras videlicet
Bastarchos .i. maiorem hun
gariam que est contigua
mari occeano ab aquilone .
ab hac terra benerunt ad
parofatas qui longe sunt sta

ture sed graciles sunt et debi
les habentes ventrem paruu
lum et rotundum ad modū ci
phi modici . hij nichil man
ducant pomtaus sed uapore
viuunt . henc enim foramen
puum loco oris et dum car
nes in olla obstctas decoaut
vapore suscepto per apturam
modicam sustentantur car
nes uero non cantes proici
unt ante canes os itaq̄ n
auauerunt quia mult reis
abhominantur monstrosas
post hec uenerunt ad quos
dam qui zamoyedi appellat
Sed neq̄ istos auauerunt
eo q̄ sint homines pauperes
siluestres ox et de uenacione
tantummodo uitam sustenta
tes Postremo uenerunt ad
eos qui uocantur vcolon vco
tartarice latie diaetur boc
colon pedes quasi boues pe
des uel dno diauntur Noto
yterim Nochoy cams tci dr
.q. cams caput latine uero
diauntur camua capita ha
bent caninos pedes a tali de
orsum caput homis ab oca
pite usq̄ ad aupes faciem
autem per omia sicut cams
et ideo a parte denomiant
huiusmodi isti duo uerba lo
cuntur et icui latrant et
idauco eciam canes possunt

nominari Sunt etiam siluestr
es et in cursu agiles compe
tenter et hos similiter cotep
serunt · Reuertentes itaq ade
zam suam cmyrtan percusso a
tonitruo muenerunt Retule
runt preterea tartari fribus
nostris cp fuissent in terra qo
zundam homm qui bini in pede
brent tantu modo et una manu
quibus mchil potuerunt no
cere propter eorum uelocitate
et fortitudmem sagittarum
Nam bnus tenet arcum alt'
nero dirigit sagittam foraus
omni tpente uelocitate etiam
sua ercedere diruntur non
solum hommes terrarum alia
zum uerum etiam cuncta
qua drupedia super terram
Vnde ante aduentum fim
nostrozum ad tartiros duo
cp iam dictis homimbus pat'
et filius ad curiam impeza
tozis tartarozum uementes
sicut dixerunt ob quam cain
nos bellis mquietare attemp
tastis · nonne in sagittarum
iaculis et cursus uelocitate
uos ercedimus Cumqz egi
uelocissimus statutus fuis
set cum eis publice ad pre
dicandum ad currendum api
serunt egm quidem cursu
ucloci procedere Ipi uero
modo mirabili se uelut ro

tam ipe ceperunt uoluere et ·
equin sunt subito infecuti ·
Tandem equo et tartaris terga
uertentes ad terram propriam
cucurrerunt quod cernentes
tartari eos amplius inuadere
noluerunt isti autem vnipedes
uocantur · hiis tpestis octoday
filius eius rnperio ei succes
sit per electionem aliorum re
liquerat · n̄ cmyrtan quatu
or filios s̄ octoday qui et suc
cessit eis · Cosur sthahaday
quarti n̄ nec a fratoibus n̄
ab alijs intellexi filij octoday
sunt tres · s̄ cuiur qui modo
est can · v̄ imperator et bozen
et gyreuen filij secundi · s̄ eoz
sucan filij zbati iste est pote
aor post can orduiste ordu Iste
se moz est inter duces et hono
zabilioz ualde alios duos fili
os habuit de alia uxore · s̄
Syban et chauth terci̇j s̄ stha
day sunt filij can et burimcti
cuius nomen non intellexi
filij sunt autgoz · hic fiut se
moz cuius mater serectam q̄
post m̄rem impatoris est de
tartaros nominata et est pote
cior ptterquam zbati alter be
taht aliorum filiozu nomina
non intellexi hec sunt aute
nomina ducum ordu Iste tn
siut per polomam in hunga
ziam zbati · buz in kadan sy
ban Burtet Isti fuerunt

m hungaria Cyrbodan adhuc co
tra Soldanum damasci pliatur
sz in terra tartarorum remaserat
ajango Coten Cyrenen. et alij
quam plures quos nomiare no
opportet octoday vero cum esset
foras multitudine tres co pa
tris exercitus ordinauit po
prefecit Bati filium suos et
misit ad occidentem contra ec
clesiam dei et omes prouicias
occidentis Qui veniendo sub
mugauit terram alti joldams
terram bisermenorum. Hij sar
racem erant comamcul loqu
tes Cepit ibidem eaam forty
simam ciuitatem nomine Baz/
chin licet cum bello diuturi
no. Alia vero ciuitas pponte
se reddidit nomine sakint/
qua de re ciuitatem no de
saruit sed acceptis spolijs
et interstis ut ut moris eo
rum est nobilioribus alijs
hoibus ciuitatem locans
incolas tiisseuui fecit et pro
cessit aduersus vrnaz ciui
tatem maxmam repleta fra
ms s Gazaris et alams nec
non et alijs sarracems paraui
duersarum Est autem sita
super fluuiu magna habente
partem maris et q transibat
ciuitatem tartari obsentes
in superiori parte fluuium
diuiserunt aquam cu ipeta

et submerserunt ciuitatem
cum oibus que in se ciuitas
contmebat preterea Bat tuc
tempois submirauit terram
terlromen et terram traurta
rum atqz magnam camoniam
necnon et ursiam et capta ky
oma metropoli rusie ciuitate
maxma et nominatissma
per stratzem multam iploru
et bellam plurima que ad
pns transeo quia scriptore
exigunt specialem Cumqz fili
us octoday paruelis Bati
qui modo est cuj. reuersus
est prius occulte intitu intel
lecto in reditu autem cepit
terram Gazarorum terra
et alanorum postea terra
et et AD ultimum terram
tartarorum Iste sunt terre
xpia nou sed diuersorum
ydromatum et posite sunt
ad meridiem iupta mare
hijs actus ad terram propriam
est reuersus Bati vero exim
in rusia contra pilaxoe id est
bulgariam magna et mordu
anos et captis eis suos eos
exercatui submirauit Co
tunt postea processit contra
polomam et hungariam di
inso qz exercatui immeris
terrauum cum frie suo
ordu misit contra poloma
decem milia pugnatorum
eo quibus in terre prmcipio

apolinis ecclesiarum. et sandomeriensis
ducatus perturbati plurimo
rum prelio ceciderunt verum quia
inuidia post fomentum iuicio
virium plurimorum idem ideo
poloni non fouentes vnitate
mutua bonum quod ceperat
ob fastum superbie inuidentes
inuicem a tartaris miserabi
liter sunt percussi Tartari
uero ulterius procedentes in
se in silesiam cum henrico du
ce tunc temporis cristianissimo
eiusdem terre in prelio sunt
congressi et dum iam sicut ipsi
fratri benedicto referebant
fugere uoluissent ex insperato
cristianorum acies ad fugam su
bito sunt conuersi Tunc ducem
henricum capientes et totaliter
spoliantes coram duce mortuo
qui in sandomiriam occisus fuerat
flectere genua preceperunt
Sicque caput eius uelut oui
s morauiam in bulgariam ad
bati detulerunt et inter cetera
capita cadauerum postmodum
proiecerunt Ipso autem bati
intrante hungariam ultra m
dium terre ipsius spacium occu
perunt et iuxta quendam flu
uium cum multitudine copi
osa duo reges fratres beter...
bela uidelicet qui adhuc reg
nat et colomanus felicis me

morie quam morte propria de pote
ipsius fecunus principalem ducem
tartarorum in primo congressu
cum equo et armis mortis pre
cipitauit in abyssum sicque resti
tit eis etiam secundo et tercio
quo adusque in fugam tartaris
conuersi Medio autem tempore
Bathi misit exercitum ultra
flumen in supiori parte ad die
tam unam siue duas qui istis
in ponte pugnantibus caute
super hostes irruerunt Ex adui
so et factum est Nam rei cue
tus se probabit sic sic probauit
experimentibus. n. bulgaris mo
nitia retus colomon pontem tar
tari transfluent et quod etiam
ipsi tartari referebant uidelicet
quod ipsis iam fugientibus ante
bulgarios bati euaginato gladio
redire eos compulit ad bellandu
et dum hungari quasi securi
quiescerent uilipendentes tarta
ros quod polonis inuidia hoc terris
presumptuosa superbia miscuit
Nam tartari irruentes strauue
runt plurimos et usque ad m
re belam et regem hungarie pro
secuti Bathi uero in hungaria
existens percepta morte octoday
can. qui impociatus periit
a sorore et sepultus est cum dice
in inferno statim redyt in coma
mam quam etiam uiderunt
fratres ibidem ad dominum pro a tartaris

redeundo dicunt preterea fratres q̄
iam ad cui[us]uocan̄. cu[m] ip̄ius im
perio reuertat[ur] in[su]p[er] m̄t
bos est discordia magn̄a que p̄
processum habu[er]it ypiam pote
runt per plures an̄os a tataris
respirare. Ednus aut[em] ep̄c̄
acius cū p[re]l[a]t[us] Gyrddan q̄
uicat contra meridiem subin
trauit t[er]ram que appellat[ur]
kiuchz hom̄es t[er]re hui[us] pa
triam st̄ nec hēnt pilos in bar
ba et cu[m] q[uis]q[ue] pat[er] morit[ur] ab
una aure usq[ue] ad aliā p[re]ncti
madit corrigiam de morte pa
tris ostendens gemitum et dolo
rem. Item subiugauit arme
niam. Item georgianā. Ite[m] nu
biam. Item aud[r]iam it[em] bal
dat et saracenoz soldanos.
alios q̄ plures. Iste admic sol
danus damasci dicit[ur] imp[er]
ynaue. Teraus aut[em] excerci
tus pugnat contra quosdam
orientales qui adhuc non sub
iacent per om̄ia d[omi]nio tarta
rorum. a p[ar]cio iṗitur ottoduy cū
tartaris c[on]uen[er]unt c[ur]ib[us] aid
et ideo ad plagam occidentaloz
inc pugnau[er]unt p[ro] p[re]sentj
bus aut[em] f[rat]rib[us] nostris cui̇it
filium eius in cham p[er] b[ur]ng
a[r]bitru̇m eleg[er]u[n]t Cuiu[s]
eo ut electus est eṗ erexit be
xillu[m] triumphale contra
dei ecc[les]iam et ypianoru[m] ṗ
pu[m] et regn̄a om̄ia occide

tis et de om̄i sua fortitudine de
stinauit partem tercia[m] ad bel
landu[m]. ben̄iunt aut[em] vbin
annis contin̄uic pugitauit nec
app[re]ciantur q̄m nec potentem
nec imp[er]atorem neq[ue] reges
et quamuis sciant q̄ debeāt
int[er]sic in medio tempore ypia
nis nec tam[en] diem nez t[er]ram
in qua hoc de[us] disposucrit
fieri ut eo imp[er]ato sangu[in]em
m[u]ltorum ulciscatur de[us] in eo
rum. Nom̄ia aut[em] eov vabium
q[u]as submittauerunt tartari
sint hec kytai Solangi Keyo
pia Voyrath[z] keramte huvite
bet vnhiur kyrgiz. Savi[n]uhir
ayerkyte kezam̄te ayctuig Nay
ma[n]. kyrakytaz Turkia Nu
bia Baldac Urum Soldan. 2Bi
zerunhte Campite Armema.
Georgiam̄a. Alam̄ qui dicunt
se azzos. Ciraasi Gazari Coma
m̄ qui dicunt se kusitar. a[l]ordui
Bastart. i. magn̄a ungaria 2By
lee Corola Cassidi Parozici ca
mina Zamoyedi Nestoriam Nusia
p[er]sarum Soldani om̄s isti sar
racen̄ p[er] se vocant[ur] de scrip
tis igit[ur] sellis tartarorum 2
unde ortu̇m habu[er]int Vbi eā
eorum t[er]ra sit Nunc sciendu̇
est p̄ t[er]ra eadem est in parte
aliqua mont[u]osa m[u]ltum in
aliqua plana valde infertuosa
qua arenosa est in aere nim̄s
distempata et hoc forte ratio[n]e
moncium et plaçi ventis for
tissim[us] lıumdat[i] sint etiam
ubi sublmia tonitrua et tempe

states et extra tempus dicebant
enim scribus quod a paucis annis in
cepissent mutabiliter aput eos
minutari. Nam sepe nubes que
nubes iuxta terram quasi pu
gnare uidentur. Dicebant enim
preterea quod parum ante aduect
fum adeos ignis de celo et co
sumpsit equorum multa mili
a et pecorum cum seruis omnibus
pascentibus preter paucos fra
tribus autem presentibus in
electione eam .i. imperatoris
tanta grando cecidit quod ex sui
resolutione subita plus .c. ho
homines submersit et res cum
habitaculis procul Duo frum
nero habitaculum quod pre
erat penitus non offendit
fratribus insuper uidentibus et
cum aliis hoc idem pacientibus
maximus uentus exurgens
tantum puluerem exalauit
quod nemo equitare poterat nec
stare isti tartari sunt stature
mediocris et satis grossiles
roo lactis iumentum quod sub
tilem facit hominem et laboris
in facie uero sunt lati gonas
prminentes habentes corona
preterea sicut uri tela habent
in capite a qua radere necesse
utramque autem spacium tri
um digitorum in fronte bene
habent aures usque ad supercilia
in modum cumule deprehendentes reliquos autem
comes componunt et mitiut

sicut sarracem. De uestibus eorum
sciendum est quod uniformes uestes
habent uiri cum feminis et ideo non
subito dinoscuntur et quia her
mari curiosa quam utilia uidentur
ideo de uestibus cetera et
ornatu eorum scribere non cura
uit. Domus eorum stationes uoca
tur et sunt rotunde facte de uir
et de sudibus superius rotunda
habent fenestram per quam fumum et luce
tectum et hostium et sunt de fi
differunt tamen in quantitate
et duci possunt. Sed quod fatas
exigunt ad portandum stationes eorum
et prmacrum ordea tartarite
apellantur uillas non habent
sed in diuersis locis per stationes
ordinantur et ciuitatem unam
habent que ciatura dicitur
uiso quam fres nostri fuerunt ad
dietam diundum quando erat
apud syram ordea imperatoris
ciam meliorem. Habent fomenta
itmus non nobiles et simplices
propter suorum paupertate
paucitatem nisi de boum ster
coribus et equorum coadiacob
undam tartarorum cynthican
inuentor extitit sed plurimus
autores fres inter eos longo
existentes tempore minime inue
nerunt. Et credunt tamen unum deum
creatorem uerum uisibilium et in
uisibilium et datorem bonoru
m hoc seculo pariter et maloru
Nec tamen ideo eum uenerant
sicut decet. Habent enim ydola

A[?] ceterar[um]

diuersa quasdam ymagines hoi[um]
de filo[rum] h[ab]ent · quas ponunt ex
utraq[ue] parte hostii stacionis sr
utr[? de] filo[rum] similiter et has
affirmant esse custodes pecor[um]
et eis offerunt lac et carnes
Sed quedam ydola cericea plus
honorant potentes ⁊ super eorum tectum aut hostium stacio[n]is
et si q[ui]s in eo q[uo]d fricatus
fuerit mox necatur a illena
Z[?] autem pellem [?]na repl[et]am
tam feno uel stramine h[ab]ent ⁊
medio stacionis offerunt [?]
ei lac om[n]ib[us] temp[or]ib[us] · ydolo uero
q[uo]d est[?] cu[i]u[?] com[m]ed[er]e siue
bibere incipientes offerunt cor
animalis in scutella q[uo]d mac[?]
auff[er]unt et manducant/fe-
cerunt p[re]terea p[ri]mo [?]
ca[?] · ydolum q[uo]d ante stacionem cuiuslibet ca[?] · ponunt
offerentes ei munera/ S[un]t at
q[ui] ei offeruntur ultim[?] no[n]
equitant[ur] animalia etiam q[ue]
occidunt ad manducandu[m]
ei p[ri]us offerunt / de a[n]i[m]alib[us]
non confri[n]gunt eidem ydo-
lo inclinant ad meridie[m] quasi deo et ad idem multos a[?]
pellunt p[re]cipue nobiles sub
iugatos Unde nup[er] accidit
q[uod] do[?] antiqad de maioribz
[?] duabus dum se eoru[m]
dominio subiaceret et nollet
inito ydolo inclinare dicens
hoc illicitum ee[?] [?] et dum

constans in fide xpi p[er]sisteret
iussus est tac[?] pedib[us] ad p[re]-
cordia p[er]cuti ad [?]sm euor-
tante aute[m] milite suo ad constanciam martyrii inuitus[?]
ei cutello p[re]cisu[m] est et caput amputatum militi Exp-
hortat[us] Libant etiam mi[n]a
soli lune aque terre et hoc
p[re]cipue mane facere consueuerunt h[ab]ent preterea q[uas]-
dam tradiciones acyrnz[?] can
quas observant qui statuit
ut int[er]iora g[r]ossaciei ventris
animalis sicut dictum est superius per apcionem ysterii[?]
non purgetur sed exp[ri]m[?]t
manibus et uenter sic p[re]gat[?]
ad co[m]edend[um] m[?] preparetur ·
Item si q[ui]s ante per suplia
auctoritate p[ro]pria ca[m] de-
uoluerit mox necetur ideo
ante elecionem g[r]yng[?] ca[n]
nepos g[r]yng[?] ca[n] occisus fuit
qua ad imperium aspirauit
Item statuit ut om[n]es terras
mundi subiug[ar]ent et cum
nullis pacem facerent nisi
simpliciter se eis redderent
s[i]ne pacto et cu[n]c[?] p[re]cep[it]
q[uod] om[n]ib[us] nobiliores int[er]fici
ant[ur] iusticiis reseruatis p[ro]-
phetatu[m] est eciam eis q[uod] ad
ultimu[m] debent om[n]es int[er]-
fici in terru[m] p[ro]prio nou[?] pau
ci tamen residui tenebunt
legem terre in qua patres

Rasnicz

corundum diuersis mortibus occide
tur. Item statuit eor temerarios
decanos m exceratum millena
rios et decem millenarios i. dece
millia sub vno quia autem so
lent tumbas appellare. Et vero
re preterita prim suorum pecca
quedam asserunt esse magi
vnum est fingere ignem uel q
quo modo tangere m cultello.
Item carnes de caldario extra
here cum cultello. Item iuxta
ignem ligna findere cum secur
ri. Post hoc n. capit ignis as
serunt amputare. Item appodiare
ad flagella equor quia calca
ribus non utuntur uel flagel
lo quibus tangere uel iuuenes
annulas demodo accipere. Item
cum freno equum percutere. Item
m stacione urinare q si facit uo
luntarie tunc necatur si non
oportet ut det pecuniam ca
tatori qui purificet inter du
os ignes prius staciones cum
rebus suaens per transire et p
us q fiat hoc millus audet
res stacionis attrectare. Item
si quis morsellum siue bollum
quod idem est sibi impositum
de ore eicit deglutire non ualet
suffocatur stacio eius et per illud
foramen extraitur et non cal
catur. Item si quis calcat limen
stacionis duas absq misericor
dia uita caret. Ideo fratres
nostri super limen docti fuerint
non calcare. Item pectum repu

tant in terra sua sponte lac effun
dere iumentum et quando fres
dicebant eis peccatum esse hu
manum fundere. Inebriari alie
na rapere et huius ridebat
et pmtus non curabant. Non m
credunt esse storum uitam eter
nam nec dampnacionem ppetu
am. Sed eommodo q post morte
uiuant iterum et greges multi
plicant et manducent. Ostendunt
etiam ueneficia et incantaciones
Responsa uero demonus/credit
dei q deum appellant ingra. Sed
communem codar. Nec cogunt que
piam fidem fide sua relinquere
dum pt modo per omnia eis obedi
at in preceptis. Alioquum creg
uiolenter aut occidunt vnde
Item iunicorem ducis andree i
Rusia quem flo iudicio interfe
cerunt coegerunt feris relicta
accipere etiam in eos in vno
lecto coram alijs publice com
ponentes. Item in principio lu
nacionis uelim plenilunio so
lent incipere q q opus. Item
dicunt lunam magnam esse im
peratorem et gembus flexis
adorant eam. Solem uero dnt
esse matrem lune eo q ab eo
lumen recipiat et ignee na
ture est quam ipi pre omnibus
reuerencur credunt credunt
n. per ignem omnia purificari
Inde munas qualescunq et
munera que portant inter
duos ignes ad dominas eor

transire opportet ut bene nisi qd
portauerint aut malesitu corri-
gietur qua de re ad ignes tran-
siuerint etiam fres noi cum a-
quus inter eos infirmatur gra-
uiter hasta nouem cubitorum
circumdata filo erigitur circa stacionem eius et extunc nullus
alienus audet intrare termino
illarum stacionum cum aute
agonizare cepit raro aliquis
aput eum remanet qui in mul-
tibus posset qui morti interesse
ordin ducis alicuius aut
imperatoris introire nisi sit
nona luniacio ut probauetur
Quod si diues morit occulte in campo sepellitur cum stacione sua sedendo in ea et cum
alueolo pleno carnibus et ciso
lactis iumenti sepellitur etia
cum eo pumetia cum pullo equi-
tum freno et sella utceg cu pro-
bazetur et fatitie vinum aut
equum comme dunt anima et coreum eius repleto feno eleua-
tium super ligna cremant ut
hijs omnibus mundeat in futuro
iumento .s. ad lactandum equo
ad equitandum et sic de alijs
simili modo ponitur aurum et
argentum Quosdam etiam
maiores sic sepelliuntur vna
occultam foueam in campo faciunt cuius oriniu est quadrum et satis paruum iuxta
autem ad utramque parte illa

tatur et alia faciunt prope staciones publice et aperte ni q
se mortuum simulant sepelire
sepcru uero qui pre ceterie dilexit in uita ponunt subtus
corpus mortui sepulc? aperto remanente qui si tertio
sub eo agonizando surrexerit
liber erit et in tota parentela illa honorabilis atque potes
Post hc sepulc oprientes iumenta seu pectora etia per
noctem desuper locum ut
planato loco non posset ab eo-
neis thesaurus cum eo po-
situs muenui. Quandoque
etiam prius reposita frimia
supponunt duo ipsa cimi-
teria habent in terra propria
vnum simplicium aliud imperatorum ducum et nobilium
et si quomodo fieri potest
de omnibus terris in quibus
occiduntur ad istud mortui
nobiles redducuntur si aut
de hijs fuit sint qui in bu-
ngaria fuerunt interfecti
Si quis ad hoc cimiterium
accesserit exceptis custodibus male multimodis per-
tractatur vnde et fres nostros qui ignoranter intra-
uerant offendissent trauiti-
quum fuissent nunciy mag-
ni ps q forent tartari rul.

boba · ꝓ magnus ꝑꝑ cortuo at
aliquo oportet ꝑuiſitaui oꝵa
que ad eue ꝑtinent ſtacoi
ꝓantur itaqꝫ duo ignes iuxta
huos coniunguntur in directum
due haſte in directum ni ca
triuie colligate zona h̄ēte in
ſe quaſdam ſtiſſuras de buke
zano alligatas ⁊ ſub hac ꝛon
ꝫ haſtas et ignes oꝑtꝫ
transire homines beſtias et
ſtacionem due autem m̄cāta
trices ſtant hīc atꝫ inde
aquam ꝓicentes et carmia
recitantes q̇ ſi currus trāſeund̄
frangitur ſeu tres aliqꝫ ꝯcade
zint moꝛ eas m̄cātatrices ac
cipiunt iꝑo nǒe ⁊ ſimiliter
ſi quis a tom̄tuo ꝑcuſſus
omā que habꝫ ꝯtēpnuntur
ab hoībus quouſqꝫ dictoꝛ
fuerint expurgata Quoꝛⸯqꝫ
poſſunt in expenſis teneꝛe
uxores tot habent emūt aūt
eas generaliter oīb̄ ideo ſunt
quaſi ꝓprie ꝑtꝫ nobilio
res et ducunt indifferenter
excepta nǒe et filia et ſoro
re ex eadem matre Noueꝛcā
moꝛtuo patre ducunt et re
lictam frīs iunioꝛ frater uel
cognatus uxores faciunt oīa
opera · ſ· tal̄ceos pellitea et
huiꝰ cā vero ſagittas triuū
et exercent cum arcubus ſa
gitando Compellunt etiam
pueros triuū aut qⁱatuoꝛ

gracia ihu xpi. Quam sepe
plusqm xxx boemica miliaria
vna die equitabant super eos
subductos tartar non gustan
tes panem neque aquam s
tantummodo in meridie aut in
nocte parumper de temisso
brodio carti milij nec habebant
nec mouum si tantum equi
tabant. deficientibus enim
equis etiam preuisi paupa
re ceptabant alios fortes et
recentes tartari adducebat
ad imperium etiam can omes
manent stationes et moue
tur ipe namque assignat lo
ca ducibus qui millenari
is qui centenariisque de
canis. Omes insuper nobi
les et pauperes auarissimj
sunt et maximj ajunera
extorsores statim etiam si
si munera non recipiunt
multa fame ac cause pro
tellatione nuncios afflixit
ita ut ipi sponte dare neq
loquerunt coffantur offerre
munera postmodum sue
sponte. hinc est qp fres mi
elemosinam bonoru homi
qp pascendo excepto nucio
sedis aplice spali acceperit
pro magna parte in muni
bus expendunt alioqui
multum fuissent in negro
cio vniuersalis ecclesie in

pediti priuiter et contempti
inter homini aliarum nac
ones sunt latissimj contemp
tores. Vnde etiam interpre
tes tartarici licet contemp
tibiles precedunt tamen
nuncios sibi commendati
in ambulando et sedendo
siue sint nuncij uel legati
sedis aplice siue regum inter
ter nulla ueritatem siuat
aliens. Sunt enim multa
bona in principio promitte
tes sed ad ultimum infini
tas crudelitates nihiluat
exercentes eorum namque g
misso est ut scorpio qui li
cet facie blandiri uideat
per cautit tamen subito cau
de aculeo uenenoso inf ine
briantur super omnes nacoes
huius mundi gricule in de
nimia potucde per uentre
se euacuant bibere stati
in code loco incipiunt ite
zato et hoc indie bna sepi
us lacere consueuerunt
Solent ppea lactis bibere
de gremis inter omia inun
da commedunt absqz modo
lupos uulpes canes morticini
na adsimones mures et
in necitate carnes humana
nas comisceret et inter uo
latilia nulla reiciunt sed
commedunt immunda pit er
cum mundis pannis et mic

salibus ad prandia non vtitur
et ideo immunde commedunt
super modum scutellas raro
et pessime lauant simili modo
fiunt cocleariis Sed tamen
inter se pacifici formicatio et
adulterium inter eos perit
valde raro mulieres eorum
castitate excedunt feminas
aliarum nationum excepto
quod in trufa sepe proferunt
verba impudica siuul me
eos esse non consueuit ideo
staciones et des res earum
non seruantur Si qui aut
equi aut boues aut aliqua
huiusmodi iumenta fuerint aut
libere ne permutantur aut
ad proprios dominos reducuntur
habundant enim equis et
iumentis bobus vaccis et
omnibus magis quam aliqui
homines super terram satis
eciam humani sunt inter se
et libenter res suas libenter
communicant ad inuicem co
cedendo paciencia ppea si
multum Sepe namque licet
per diem aut per duos in
cibu addant tamen cantat
et iocantur tamquam per op
timo manducassent libenter
namque eciam vnius alium

promouet ad honorem Karo ad
pda sediciones inter eos excitatur
nec motum si siuant quia vt pcia
dixi superius transgressores in
ter eos absque mia puniuntur
Nunc de preliis eorum et qua
liter eis occurri posset breuit
est notandum quandocumque tar
tari terras aliquas proponunt
impugnare exercitus qui ad
eas dirigitur congregandas
cum omni familia vxoribus
videlicet pueris et ancillis
tentorum et omni superlectili cu
armentis et omnibus in curri
bus et in equis proparat valde
caute duces sciat in maxima mul
titudine armorum arcuum pharetras
et sagittas Cumque tartari pro
pinquare ceperint P mittunt
velocissimos cursores qui ter
reant eo impauto homines et oc
cidant et ne possit contra eos
exercitus subito congregari Ad
si obstaculu non huerunt proce
dunt semper et multitudo sequitur
cum suis omnibus sano plane si aut
viderint turbam insuperabilem
confestim ad suos reuertunt et
exercitus ordinat tali modo ro
bus exercitus disponunt acies
vexillum triumphalem medio
cum multitudine copiosa in ar
mis lateribus suas acies po
nunt vtrumque vnum parium distan
tes et eminentes ante aciem in
paucos autem relinquunt in

custodia mulierum debilium
puerorum et eorum que du
xerunt cum itaq; deben
dum hostibus plures expis
se pluribus muniunt plura
tris et sagittis et antequam
adversarior eos possunt sagit
te attingere acies diviserunt
quandoq; etiam ante tempus
ad plenum iacere non valentes
quando vero sine obstaculo sa
gittis possunt attingere applicue
pocaus dicuntur qua iacere
tum sagittis et hoc propter
sagittarum nimiam densita
tem Et si hostes incautos
repererint circundant eos i
modum corone subito dimit
tentes eis unicam viam ad
fugiendum eos per impetu
facilis valde absq; modo ita
ut si quis in medio express
non fuerit peat fugiendo q
de re melius arbitror pugna
do bene mori quam conspice
malam fugam Notandum p
ea si eis prosperatum fuerit
q semper procedendo ordinat
post s terrium stationes per
millenarios centenarios scdm
q eis expedit cum hominibus
et iumentis ordinat in biam
ores sibi forciores et maiores
stationes et si que civitates
sine castra in terris quas ex
pugnaverint manserunt et

bene possunt subsistere ante
eos ubi sagittabilium impetus
potest divigi et iactius ma
in thearum et ubi expense
cibi et potus defuerint aut
ligna pt came sit loci suple
fortitudo aut audacia aplor
sic in terra antiquor sagit
tim sint scim qui sepint prim
ci expressi de civitate plures
ex tartaris occidebant et mu
lieribus extinguentibus suc
censam civitatem a tartaris
viri inerma deffendebant
necnon exteriores tartaros
in medio civitatis per biam
subterraneam penetravint
et reliquos fugaverunt in
mutis autem silvis abscondi
possunt homines ubi estate
et hyeme ateni pt morat
homines tamquam feras in
mari tamen securitas est
et in locis superius pre
tavitis Qualis autem tur
tavis sit occurrendum sat
intelligendum est intelligi
potest ex successu regni
machabedr hystoriis ubi
et precedentes sanctuary
exercitium et inside hostib
diversimode posito describit
si me tu necessitatem robi
tior patem principum ob hoc
factum ut in vini congregati
ex adverso hostium tres
aut plures exercitus ordi

nent prout pugnancium qualitas
hoc exposcit/ ex late nichilominus
in insidiis in equis optimis
adaptatis ballistariis vero
ad minus tribus ordinibus
ante exceratus disponatur
qui iacere sagitas debent priu
etiam post possint tartaroru
aciem attingere bene bono mo
ut sit tempestiue prosacies a
fugiat aut turbetur Quod
si hostes fugam ceperint bal
listarii eos cum sagitariis
accurrunt necnon et hiis qui
sunt in insidiis persequitur
paulatim exercitatis subsequen
te si autem alii ballistarii
non fuerint tunc faleratis
equis utentes ponantur a
tergus qui se intel mantes sub
fortissimis clipeis nditis in
equozum frontibus sagittas
confundant subito tartaros
cetera de bellis supplenda
relinquo hiis qui in simili st
exercitio edocti experimento
plusg scripto brevitatum pa
ternitati supplico qua minus
edmate in scripto posui non
voluntati sed ignorancie me
pocius imputetis Actum ab
incarnacione dni aptis dei albi
nis kl augusti
Explicit hystoria tartaroru

THE TARTAR RELATION

Edited, with introduction, translation, and commentary

by George D. Painter

CONTENTS

1. FOREWORD

Like the Vinland Map with which it is associated, the Tartar Relation has remained unknown since the late middle ages, and is here published for the first time. This text is of vital significance in its relevance to the Vinland Map, the compiler of which used it as one of the chief source materials for the captions in the Asian portion of his work; though the Relation unfortunately has no direct contribution to make to the Vinland or northwestern sections of the Map, which to the modern reader are by far the most interesting. In any reasonable appraisal of the importance of these two manuscripts the Vinland Map as a document in the history of Western civilization must be admitted as paramount; and it is surely proper in this context to value the Tartar Relation predominantly for the light it can throw on the Vinland Map, and on the intentions, resources, and psychology of the Vinland Map's compiler.

Nevertheless, the Tartar Relation remains highly important and interesting in its own right, as an independent primary source on the Carpini Mission to Central Asia in 1245–47, and the history and folklore of the Mongols at the zenith of their conquests. In the following introduction the editor has endeavored, after first tracing the stages in the transmission of the text, to outline the background information which will make these aspects of the Tartar Relation clear to the general reader. Further sections on the sources of the Relation, with an assessment of its value as a contribution to knowledge and an explanation of the editorial method here employed, are followed by the *editio princeps* of the original Latin text, with English translation and commentary. An "appreciation" by the present editor, on the use of the Tartar Relation by the compiler of the Vinland Map and the hypothetical significance of the map caption concerning Vinland, is given after Mr. Skelton's essay, pp. 241–62 below.*

2. THE TRANSMISSION OF THE TARTAR RELATION

On 30 July 1247 a Franciscan friar named C. de Bridia wrote the last words of an intelligence report on the Tartars or Mongols, which he had compiled during the last few weeks at the request of his superior, Friar Boguslaus, then minister in charge of the Franciscan Order in Bohemia and Poland. The Franciscan mission sent from Lyons in April 1245 by Pope Innocent IV to the Mongols was now on its way home, and its distinguished leader, Friar John de Plano Carpini, with his two companions, Benedict the Pole and Ceslaus of Bohemia, had passed through Poland on the return journey from Karakorum shortly before. C. de Bridia, according to his own statement, obtained his material from contact with all three of these, but mainly, as we shall see reason to believe, through access to a draft already prepared by Friar Benedict, and from Benedict's own spoken comments on matters raised in this document. De Bridia's terms of reference did not include the actual journey and adventures of the friars, exciting as these would have been to tell and read. The primary subjects of his report were the history of the Mongols and their conquests, their character, way of life, social customs, and religious

* Books, articles, and other texts referred to below are cited in abbreviated forms, consisting of the author's surname or any other convenient reference, followed when necessary by the date of publication. Full particulars of each work are given under these abbreviated forms in the Bibliography, pp. 263–69 below. Carpini's *Historia Mongalorum* is cited as *Carpini,* with references to chapter and paragraph in Wyngaert's edition. Friar Benedict's journey-narrative is cited with references to page number in Wyngaert's edition.

beliefs, their methods of making war and their future intentions; and these were then matters not of idle curiosity but of urgent and sinister practical importance to every dweller in Eastern Europe. Only a few years before, in 1241, the Mongols had overrun Poland, Silesia, and Hungary with appalling destruction and bloodshed; and they had now announced their intention of returning to conquer the whole of Europe. De Bridia entitled his report *Historia Tartarorum,* that is, *Description of the Tartars,* or, as it will be more convenient to name it here, the Tartar Relation, TR for short.

Three other reports on the Carpini mission were issued in the same year, 1247, and have been known ever since. First, Carpini produced his own *Historia Mongalorum* [sic] *quos nos Tartaros appellamus* (*Description of the Mongols Whom We Call Tartars*), in two versions. The first version was communicated, as Carpini states, to interested parties in Poland, Bohemia, Germany, Liège, and Champagne on the homeward journey in June–November 1247. It gives in eight chapters a fuller account of the subjects discussed in the Tartar Relation, although the latter contains in its turn much valuable information not given by Carpini. This first version exists in five early manuscripts.[1] Carpini's second version, published after his arrival at Lyons in November 1247, comprises the same text as the first, but with 31 minor additions[2] and with a ninth chapter containing Carpini's detailed account of the journey to Karakorum and back. This second version is known in two manuscripts.[3] Thirdly, Benedict's own much briefer but independent narrative of the journey was taken down in abridged form from dictation at Cologne toward the end of September 1247. This account by Benedict is found only in two manuscripts[4] of Carpini's first version, in which it immediately precedes Carpini's text and has no separate title of its own.

At the time of the Carpini Mission the Dominican Friar Vincent of Beauvais (*ca.* 1190–*ca.* 1264) was already at work on his *Speculum Majus,* a vast encyclopedia of human knowledge which included a chronicle of world history from the creation to his own time, entitled *Speculum Historiale* (*Mirror of History*) and comprising thirty-two sections or "books".[5] Vincent was a familiar in the court at Paris of Louis IX, King of France, later canonized as Saint Louis, who was then preparing his Seventh Crusade (1248–52). Early in 1248, after reporting to Pope Innocent IV at Lyons in November 1247, Carpini was sent by Innocent on a mission to Louis in Paris, to request him, unsuccessfully as it turned out, to postpone his departure on the Crusade. It was no doubt on this occasion that Vincent acquired a manuscript of Carpini's *Historia Mongalorum,* complete with the final chapter IX containing the narrative of his

---

1. Paris, Bibliothèque Nationale, Colbert no. 2477; Vienna, National Library, MSS nos. 362, 512; London, British Museum, Royal MS 13.A.XIV; Oxford, Bodleian Library, Digby 11. See Wyngaert, pp. 11–13; Pullé, pp. 33–40. Turin, Biblioteca Nazionale, MS E.V.8, which Golubovich (vol. 1, pp. 200–14) took to be Carpini's original short version, is in fact a later abridgment of the first version by an ignorant scribe, and has no independent authority (Pullé, pp. 37–40).

2. Listed by Beazley, *Texts,* pp. ix–xiii.

3. Corpus Christi College, Cambridge, MS no. 181; Leyden University Library, MS no. 104.

4. Paris; Vienna no. 512.

5. The 32-book numeration, counting Vincent's preface as Book I, is found in the Yale manuscript and in most others; though Vincent himself left the preface unnumbered, and numbered the succeeding sections as Books I–XXXI. For convenience the 32-book numeration will be used here. The present references can readily be identified in editions using the 31-book numeration (e.g. the Augsburg edition of 1474, printed at the monastery of Saints Ulrich and Afra, and the Douai edition of 1624) by subtracting one from the book numbers here given.

journey. However this may be, in the thirty-second and last book of the *Speculum Historiale* Vincent embodied an abridgment of both sections of Carpini's treatise.[6]

It is to this lucky accident that we owe the survival of the Tartar Relation, the only known exemplar of which is associated in the company of the Vinland Map with the Yale manuscript of part of the *Speculum Historiale*. Clearly any circulation TR may have had in separate form was too limited, in view of the normal wastage of medieval manuscripts, to ensure transmission to the present day. The fate of the *Speculum Historiale* was very different, for Vincent's work became a standard reference book on the shelves of monastic libraries and was constantly multiplied during the next two centuries in manuscript form. It is because the Tartar Relation had the good fortune to become embodied in a manuscript of this popular work—and because, in general, a bulky manuscript like the *Speculum Historiale* had a better chance of physical survival than a slender one like TR—that it has reached us today. And the Vinland Map owes not only its survival, in the same way, to its incorporation in a *Speculum Historiale* manuscript, but even its actual creation, since it was produced as a cartographic illustration to the *Speculum Historiale* in association with TR.

How did this juxtaposition of the *Speculum Historiale* and the Tartar Relation first occur? It seems evident that some scribe of the *Speculum Historiale,* who also happened to be familiar with the Tartar Relation, was impressed by the relevance of the latter to the Carpini and Mongol subject matter of the *Speculum Historiale,* Book XXXII, and brought the two texts together. This event may have occurred at any time from the original publication of the *Speculum Historiale, ca.* 1255, to the compilation of the Vinland Map apparently within a few decades before 1440. The person responsible can hardly have been Vincent of Beauvais himself; first be-

---

6. For the abridgment of Carpini see *Speculum Historiale,* Book XXXII, chs. 3–25, 30–31, 33, 35–39. Vincent also added (Book XXX, chs. 69–89; XXXI, chs. 95–98, 139–47, 150–51; XXXII, chs. 26–29, 32, 34, 40–52), passages from the otherwise unknown narrative by Friar Simon of Saint-Quentin of the Dominican mission of Friar Ascelin (see also Pelliot, 1924, pp. 271–80). Ascelin was sent by Innocent IV, at about the time of Carpini's departure in 1245, to the Mongol Khan Baiju in Armenia, where he arrived in 1247, returning home in 1250. Most modern authorities give 1247 as the date of Ascelin's departure, which is clearly impossible, since the time would be too short for his arrival at Baiju's camp in the early summer of 1247; and Vincent's statement (Book XXXII, ch. 2 and ch. 26) that he left in 1245 is no doubt correct. Pelliot (1924), p. 293, infers that he left in March 1245, a month before Carpini. Although Friar Simon's narrative was available to the compiler of the Vinland Map, since he used a manuscript of De Bridia's Tartar Relation in conjunction with a *Speculum Historiale,* there is no feature in the Map which shows any use of it. Vincent first completed Book XXXII, as he states in ch. 105 thereof, in 1244. The final publication of the *Speculum Historiale,* allowing time for him to acquire and insert Carpini's and Friar Simon's material and the information on the Seventh Crusade up to 1250 (ch. 89–102), with a final entry in ch. 103 relating to 'the tenth year of Innocent IV' (25 June 1252–24 June 1253), may be dated *ca.* 1255 or a little before. Friar Simon's narrative of Ascelin's sojourn with Baiju (*Speculum Historiale,* Book XXXII, loc. cit.) is well known, but the preceding extracts from his work (Books XXX, XXXI, loc. cit.) have been unduly neglected. They include an account of Mongol history and customs which forms a valuable supplement to Carpini and TR, a discussion of the Georgians and Armenians, and the earliest extant history of the recent Mongol invasion of Armenia and Turkey. The passages on Mongol history include notably (1) a story furnished to Friar Simon by the Nestorian priest Rabban-ata (Book XXX, ch. 69) of Chingis Khan's slaying "David, son of Prester John, King of India" in "1202" and marrying his daughter, which seems to allude to Chingis Khan's victory over the Keraits in 1203, when he slew the Wang Khan Toghril and married his niece Ibaka-beki (cf. below, p. 48 and n. 65), and (2) an account (ibid., ch. 88) of Chingis Khan's conquest of the Khorasmian Empire in 1219–21, a historical event of which *Carpini* seems virtually unaware, except insofar as it concerns the campaigns of Chingis Khan's son Jochi (cf. below, p. 46; TR, ¶20, ¶24, ¶25, and notes).

cause it was Vincent's method to embody his sources, suitably abridged, in his own text, never, as far as we know, to add a document verbatim in the form of an appendix; and secondly because, in view of the wide circulation of the *Speculum Historiale,* the Tartar Relation would surely be known in other extant manuscripts of the *Speculum,* if it had been present from the beginning in one of the exemplars issued by the author himself. It is equally unlikely, on grounds which will now be examined, that the juxtaposition of *Speculum Historiale* and TR first occurred in the Yale manuscript of *ca.* 1440. In other words, the Yale manuscript is itself a copy of an earlier manuscript, now unknown, in which the *Speculum Historiale,* Tartar Relation, and Vinland Map were already conjoined.

The Yale Vincent manuscript now consists of 239 leaves in 15 quires of 16 leaves each, the inner and outer sheets of each quire on large quarto vellum (leaves 1, 8, 9, 16), the rest on small folio paper. These quires are signed e–t, and comprise Books XXI–XXIV of the *Speculum Historiale* in the 32-book numeration. The first leaf of quire e and the first four quires (a–d) are wanting. Calculation shows, however, that these 65 leaves would have exactly sufficed for the table and text of Book XX and the missing table of contents to Book XXI; and there can be no reasonable doubt that the volume originally contained Books XX–XXIV.[7] The colophon at the end of Book XXIV reads: *"Explicit tertia pars speculi hist.",* i.e. "Here ends part 3 of the *Speculum Historiale".* We shall return to the real significance of these words a little later.

Although they originally formed part of the Vincent volume, the Vinland Map and the Tartar Relation are now bound together in a separate volume. VM consists of a two-leaf quire of vellum, with the title (contractions resolved) *"Delineatio 1e partis, 2e partis, 3e partis speculi",* i.e. "Delineation of the 1st, 2nd, 3rd part of the *Speculum",* written at the top right of the first page, and the map itself broadside over the inner opening. TR is written on the first 11 leaves (the rest being blank) of an unsigned 16-leaf quire of mixed vellum and paper, in exactly the same make-up as the Vincent quires.

Despite their present separate state, which is due to the late-nineteenth century rebinding, the evidence that the Vincent manuscript, VM, and TR were produced in the same scriptorium at the same time *ca.* 1440 and were then physically joined is remarkably varied, consistent, and conclusive, as Dr. Marston has shown in the first section of this publication. The scribal hand in all three is apparently the same; and the hand of the corrector is certainly identical in the Vincent manuscript and TR. The quality of the vellum is the same in TR and the greater part of the *Speculum,* while the vellum in VM matches that in the half-sheet 1 1/16 of the *Speculum.* The 16-leaf make-up of each quire and the same quite unusual combination of vellum and paper in the quire are common to both the Vincent manuscript and TR. Perhaps most decisive of all, as Mr. Allan Stevenson has shown, is the fact that the paper of the Vincent manuscript was made in the same molds as that of TR; it belongs, that is, to the same batch of paper as received from the paper merchant. Moreover, the paper can be dated with certainty to a few years on either side of 1440, a date that is consistent with all other evidence, both material and internal, relating to all three items. Lastly, the physical presence, and order of VM and TR in the original Vincent volume is determined by the wormholes. Those in VM fit those in the beginning of the *Speculum;* VM was therefore at the front of the volume. The single wormhole at the beginning of TR fits that at the end of the *Speculum;* TR was therefore at the end of the volume.

7. Books XX–XXIV cover the period A.D. 411–801.

This evidence, besides being more than sufficient to establish the joint origin *ca.* 1440 of all three manuscripts, includes certain features that enable us to reconstruct the unknown stages in the transmission of TR and VM to their present form, the only one in which we know them as yet.

At first sight the colophon to the Vincent manuscript, stating that it concludes "the third part of the *Speculum Historiale*", and the title of the Vinland Map, stating that it is the "delineation of the 1st, 2nd, 3rd part of the *Speculum*", seem to give further documentary evidence that VM and the Vincent fragment belong together. On the face of it they should mean that VM was intended to illustrate the very three parts of the *Speculum* which are here concluded. But further thought shows that there are latent contradictions here, which demand to be resolved; and perhaps, as is the way when difficulties occur in a chain of evidence, their resolution may supply the very clues we need.

In fact, four puzzling discrepancies are involved in the original presence of TR and VM in the Yale Vincent volume, in the VM title, and in the Vincent colophon.

First, as we have seen, the Tartar Relation is linked by its subject matter with the final book (XXXII) of the *Speculum Historiale*. It has nothing whatever to do with the subjects covered by Books XX–XXIV, which formed the original contents of the Yale Vincent manuscript. If, as may well be, the manuscript was originally completed by a final volume, now lost, containing the later books of the *Speculum,* then TR ought to have been inserted there, at the end of Book XXXII. It certainly does not belong here, at the end of Book XXIV.

Secondly, the Vinland Map, in its declared function as an illustration to the *Speculum Historiale,* is equally out of place in a volume containing Books XX–XXIV of the *Speculum.* It would be naturally placed either at the very beginning of the *Speculum,* before Book I, or, better still, in the final volume, because this is the proper position for its close companion, the Tartar Relation. It certainly does not make sense in Books XX–XXIV, with which it has no conceivable connection.[8]

Thirdly, it follows that the title of the Vinland Map, "Delineation of the 1st, 2nd, 3rd part of the *Speculum*" conflicts with the colophon of the Vincent manuscript, 'Here ends the third part of the *Speculum Historiale',* if we take the '3rd part' mentioned in the former to be the same as that in the latter; since, as we have just seen, VM belongs not here but in the final volume of the *Speculum.*

Fourthly, and no less strangely, the colophon of the Vincent manuscript is inconsistent with itself, if we take it to mean that this volume consists of the "third part" of a manuscript of the *Speculum.* The volume originally contained (counting the missing quires a–d, the 2-leaf VM quire, and the 16-leaf TR quire) 21 quires totaling 322 leaves, containing the five books, XX–XXIV, from the total 32 books of the *Speculum.* A simple calculation shows that the preceding Books I–XIX would have occupied about 1100 leaves, which on this basis would have formed

8. The remote possibility that the VM compiler noticed the allusion to St. Brendan in Book XXII, ch. 81, and had it in mind when delineating *"Magnae Insulae Beati Brandani Branziliae dictae",* may be mentioned only to be dismissed. As R. A. Skelton shows (p. 138 below), the compiler undoubtedly copied this feature from his cartographic model. Moreover (apart from the compiler's general lack of interest in or knowledge of the *Speculum* text), Vincent names Brendan only to reject the credibility of his reputed voyages. "I have deleted the story of his voyage from this work," he explains, "because of certain apocryphal ravings which seem to be contained in it". Here, as elsewhere, the Yale text is identical with the normal *Speculum* text. Cf. above, p. 15.

two "parts" of about 550 leaves each. Such an incongruity with the size of the "third part" is almost if not quite impossible. It seems that, despite the ostensible meaning of its colophon, the Yale manuscript could hardly have formed, in this sense, the "third part" of a *Speculum Historiale* text.

All these difficulties turn upon the meaning of "part", and especially "third part", in a manuscript of the *Speculum Historiale*. If we investigate this meaning, the solution of the problem becomes evident. The only basic division of the *Speculum* is that into 32 "books", and it does not call, textually speaking, for any division into "parts". But this enormous work of approximately 1,450,000 words was only occasionally, by the use of a large folio format and small script, crowded into the compass of a single volume. More usually, both in manuscript and in printed form, it was apportioned into two, three, or more volumes of manageable size, which were customarily called "parts". At the end of each, by way of information to both binder and reader, the scribe added the colophon: "Here ends the first (second, etc.) part".[9] Here, beyond doubt, is the explanation of the title of the Vinland Map. The Map was originally drawn to illustrate a three-volume manuscript of the *Speculum,* and the title means, simply, that the Map is a "delineation" illustrating the whole work. The original Vinland Map was presumably bound in the third volume, probably at the beginning; and at the end of this volume was a manuscript of the Tartar Relation.

The word "part" was as easy to misunderstand for the medieval scribe as it is for us: he was always liable to mistake it for a genuine textual division, intended by the author himself, and to copy it as such. Apparently this happened at the end of the Yale volume, where, as we have seen, the words "third part" are inappropriate as a volume-numeration, as well as in several of the manuscripts cited in note 9 above. The scribe of the Yale manuscript, or his predecessor, must have copied from a four-volume text in which Book XXIV (as in the Paris manuscripts cited in note 9) was in fact the last of the third volume. Evidently the binder shared his misapprehension, and inserted the Vinland Map and the Tartar Relation not in the last volume (as the words of the Map title, "1st, 2nd, 3rd part of the *Speculum*" were intended to signify), but in the "third part", wrongly so called, of the present manuscript. The Yale manuscript, con-

9. The following relevant examples may be cited. The Augsburg edition of 1474 is in three volumes, numbered parts 1, 2, 3 in the incipits and colophons, and also, in the British Museum copy, on contemporary manuscript labels affixed to the top covers of the binding. See *Catalogue of XVth Century Books now in the British Museum*, Pt. II (1912), p. 339. Bodleian Library (Western) MS 2435 consists of Books I–XVI in one volume, with the colophon *"Explicit prima pars Speculi hystorialis"* (presumably taken from a 4-volume text) at the end of Book IX. (See F. Madan and H. H. E. Craster, *Summary Catalogue of Western Manuscripts in the Bodleian Library*, Vol. 2, Pt. 1 (1922), pp. 362–63). Similarly, British Museum Royal MS 13.D.VIII consists of Books I–XVI in one volume, with the colophons *"Explicit primum (secundum) volumen speculi historialis"* at the end of Books VIII and XVI respectively. See G. F. Warner and J. P. Gilson, *British Museum. Catalogue of Western Manuscripts in the Old Royal and King's Collections,* Vol. 2 (1921), p. 111. Exeter College, Oxford, MS XV has the whole *Speculum Historiale* in one volume of 463 leaves, beginning *"Prima pars Speculi"*. See H. O. Coxe, *Catalogus codicum MSS. in collegiis aulisque Oxoniensibus*, Pt. I (1852). Bibliothèque Nationale, Paris, Fonds latin MSS nos. 4900, 4901 each contain Books XXV–XXXII only, being evidently relics of 4-volume sets corresponding in coverage to the 4-volume model of the Yale manuscript. See *Catalogus codicum manuscriptorum Bibliothecae Regiae*, Pt. III, tom. 4 (1744), pp. 15–16. It may be mentioned that the majority of surviving *Speculum Historiale* manuscripts are, like the Yale manuscript, incomplete; and that according to S. De Ricci, *Census of Medieval and Renaissance MSS. in the United States* (1935–40), and Supplement (1962), there is no other Latin manuscript of this work in the U.S.A. For lists of the known extant manuscripts see A. Pottehast, *Bibliotheca historica medii aevi*, Vol. 2 (1896), p. 1095, and *Histoire littéraire de la France*, vol. 18, pp. 449–519.

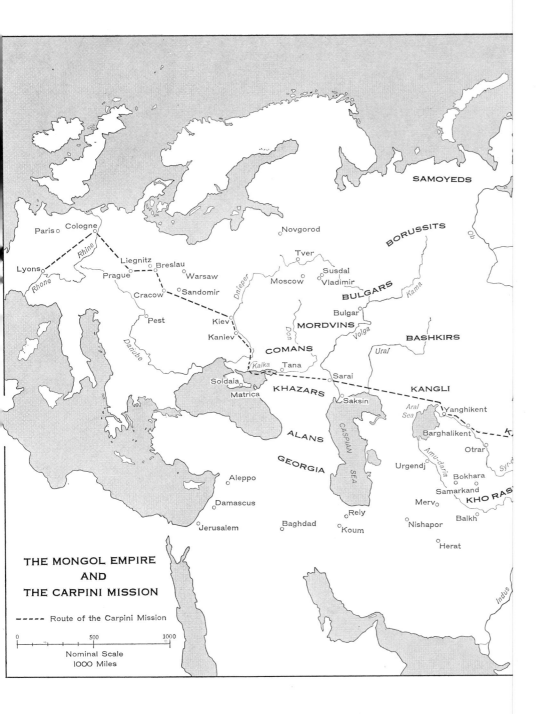

SAMOYEDS

BORUSSITS

Paris Cologne

Rhine

Lyons

Rhone

Liegnitz Breslau

Prague Warsaw

Cracow Sandomir

Pest

Kiev

Kaniev

Novgorod

Tver

Moscow

Susdal
Vladimir

Bulgar

MORDVINS

COMANS

Kalka Tana

Soldaia

Matrica

KHAZARS

Saksin

ALANS

GEORGIA

Aleppo

Damascus

Jerusalem

Baghdad

Reiy

Koum

BULGARS

Kama

Volga

Don

Ural

Sarai

BASHKIRS

KANGLI

Aral
Sea

Yanghikent

Barghalikent

Otrar

Urgendj

Amu-daria

Bokhara

Samarkand

Merv

Nishapor

Balkh

KHO RAS

Herat

Syr-d

CASPIAN SEA

Ob

Dnieper

Danube

Indus

THE MONGOL EMPIRE
AND
THE CARPINI MISSION

- - - - Route of the Carpini Mission

0   500   1000

Nominal Scale
1000 Miles

sisting originally of the five books, XX–XXIV, in all probability represents the fourth volume in a set of five volumes, with the first three containing six or seven books each, and the fifth and last, comprising eight books, a little oversize.[10]

It seems, therefore, that the Yale manuscript, originally of five volumes, was derived, by way of a four-volume intermediary copy, from a three-volume manuscript of the *Speculum Historiale* which contained the Vinland Map and the Tartar Relation in the third and last volume. This strongly confirms the inference, reached on several other grounds by Mr. Skelton, that the Vinland Map as we have it is a copy, perhaps at more removes than one, and not an original. Such a three-volume text may well have had a tall folio format rather than the small folio format of the Yale manuscript; and it follows that the original Vinland Map may have had a larger format to match, which would help to account for the curiously minute script of the longer captions on the existing reduced copy. The remote but exciting possibility remains that the present publication may lead to the discovery of a hitherto unnoticed three-volume *Speculum Historiale* manuscript complete with the original Vinland Map and an earlier Tartar Relation. Perhaps it is too much to hope that such a manuscript might also include as an additional appendix the unknown source for the Vinland area and captions of the Map. But it would at least be likely to provide a more correct version of the Vinland Map and a less corrupt text of the Tartar Relation.

3. THE MONGOL CONQUESTS[1]

Throughout the Middle Ages, along the belt of grassland that stretches between the 40th and 50th parallels from the Pacific coast of Asia to the Ukraine, dwelt nomadic, horse-breeding, hunting, and raiding tribes of evolving Turco-Mongol race and language. In times of climatic and political pressure their hordes of mounted bowmen rode east and west along the highway of the steppes to ravage the sedentary civilizations of China and Europe. The first of these invaders of the West were the proto-Mongol Huns in the fifth century; they were followed by the Turkish Avars in the sixth, the Bulgars in the seventh to eighth, the Magyars (Finno-Ugrians with a Turkish admixture) in the ninth, the Pechenegs in the tenth and eleventh, and the Kipchaks or Comans in the eleventh century. The last and most formidable of all were the true Mongols, also known customarily though incorrectly as Tartars, sent by their rulers Chingis Khan and Ogedei in the thirteenth century.

In the twelfth century the Mongols proper occupied the steppe-country north of the eastern Gobi Desert, between the rivers Onon and Kerulen, headwaters of the Amur, which flows into the Pacific a thousand miles to the east. Their first attempt at unity under a single Khan, *ca.* 1140–61, was overthrown by the Kin rulers of Northern China in alliance with the Mongolized Turkish tribe of the Tatars, the Mongols' neighbors and hereditary enemies to the southeast of the Kerulen. The name of the Tatars (incorrectly known to the West as Tartars) derives from

---

10. Possibly the fourth volume was originally meant to contain six books, which would have evened the numbers, by leaving only seven books for the fifth and last volume; indeed, the absence from the signature-letters of the last four, v, x, y, z, which would exactly suffice for Book XXV, tends to suggest this. The binder was perhaps led by the colophon to suppose that Book XXIV was intended to be the last in the volume.

1. The following account of Mongol history is based mainly upon Grousset (1939 and 1941), with recourse to d'Ohsson and Howorth, and to other sources cited in the footnotes. See the Bibliography, below, pp. 263–69.

the Mongol word for "drag" or "carry", and means simply "nomads";[2] its extension by both Chinese and Europeans to mean the Mongols in general was resented by the Mongols themselves,[3] and remains difficult to explain.

The true Mongols were bordered on the northwest, between the Onon and Lake Baikal, by the forest-dwelling Mongol Merkits, on the west by the Naimans, and on the southwest by the Keraits; these two latter tribes were semi-Mongolized Turkish nomads, of mixed shamanistic and Nestorian-Christian religion. North of the Naimans, between the headstreams of the Yenisei, were the Mongol Uirats, west of whom were the Turkish Kirghiz, while southwest of the Naimans were the comparatively civilized Uighurs, a Turkish tribe that had adopted Nestorian Christianity, together with the use of the Syrian alphabet and a strong element of Buddhism. West of the Uighurs, in Turkestan to the south of Lake Balkhash, lay the empire of the Karakhitai or Black Khitai, founded by Khitayan Mongol exiles dispossessed from North China by the Kin in the 1120s. At the time of the rise of Chingis Khan the Karakhitai were overlords of the Uighurs and of the Moslem Turkish Karakhanids of northern Transoxiana, but were yielding ground in the southwest to the new and short-lived Khorasmian Empire, which between 1180 and 1220 united the vast expanses of Persia, Transoxiana, and Afghanistan between the Caspian and the Persian Gulf, the Aral Sea, and the Indus.

On the northwestern border of China, between the Keraits and the upper Hoang-Ho or Yellow River, were the semi-civilized, sub-Tibetan Tanguts, notorious for banditry on the caravan route from China to the west. China itself was divided into two hostile empires by the Hoang-Ho. In Southern China reigned the Sung dynasty, while Northern China was occupied by the Jurchets or Kin, a Tungusic people, now civilized, whom the southern Chinese, true to their age-old policy of using a worse barbarian to chase away a better, had invited *ca.* 1120 to expel the Mongol Khitai.

In the last quarter of the twelfth century the nomad tribes, over the three thousand miles of steppe-land between the two civilizations of Khorasmia in the west and Northern China in the east, were in an explosive state of instability and fermentation, and the time was ripe for the rise of a new world conqueror.

The future Chingis Khan was the son of Yesugei, chieftain of the Kiyats, a clan of the Borjigin subtribe of the Mongols proper, whose uncle Kutula (*d.* 1161) had been the last holder of the defunct Mongol Khanate. He was born on the banks of the Onon River in 1167,[4] and named Temujin, meaning blacksmith, after a Tatar chief captured by his father. Orphaned at the age of thirteen, when Yesugei was poisoned at a Tatar feast, Temujin was deserted by his father's followers and left alone with his mother and young brothers. The sources for his next twenty years are obscure in chronology and contaminated with magnificent but unreliable legendary material. Toward 1185 he submitted himself as vassal to his father's former overlord, Toghril, the Nestorian Christian king of the Keraits, and soon afterward, with the help of Toghril and of his own blood-brother Jamuka, made a first successful raid on the Merkits, who

---

2. Cf. Rockhill, pp. 112–13; TR, ¶3, n. 3.

3. Rubruck, ed. Rockhill, pp. 107, 115.

4. The previously accepted dates of 1155 or 1162 have been refuted by Pelliot (Grousset, 1941, pp. 51, 53–54; J. A. Boyle, art. Chingis Khan in *Encyclopaedia of Islam,* new edition).

had kidnapped his young bride Borte. It remained ever doubtful whether the child Jochi, with whom Borte returned home after nine months, was the son of Temujin or of her captor.

Both Temujin and Jamuka had ambitions to restore the Khanate, each in his own person, and their friendship was short-lived. About 1193, seeing the possibility of future power under the rising star of Temujin, the Mongol princes elected him as their Khan. Toward 1194, at the request of the Kin and with the aid of Toghril and the Keraits, he made a first campaign against the Tatars, slew their chief Megujin-se'ultu, and massacred his prisoners. The grateful Kin gave Toghril the honorific title of Wang (i.e. prince) Khan, by which he was thereafter known, and to Temujin the lesser title of "commander of hundreds". In 1196 Temujin in turn aided the Wang Khan, whose brother had driven him into exile, defeated his Merkit enemies in 1197 and gave him the booty, and restored him to the Kerait throne in 1198. In the same year the Wang Khan led his own expedition against the Merkit, but unwisely preferred to keep the booty for himself.

The Naiman king Inanch-Bilga had recently died, and his realm descended not to the "three little boys" of the Tartar Relation[5] but to his two stalwart rival sons, Taibuka and Buyuruk. In 1199 Temujin and the Wang Khan defeated Buyuruk, but were driven back by a Naiman counterattack in which the Wang Khan unscrupulously deserted, and was later rescued by Temujin. In 1201 the allies defeated a coalition of dissident Mongol tribes with Tatars, Merkits, Naimans, and Uirats, under the Mongol anti-Khan Jamuka, the former blood-brother of Temujin; and in 1202 Temujin finally exterminated the Tatars, incorporating the few survivors in his own tribes. In 1203 a rupture with the Wang Khan followed this crucial change in the balance of power. Jamuka joined the Keraits, and, after an indecisive battle in which both sides suffered enormous losses, Temujin was forced to retreat northeast to the marshland called Baljuna with only two thousand faithful warriors. In the autumn he surprised the Keraits and defeated them in a three-day battle; the Wang Khan fled to the Naimans, who slew him and carried his head to their king Taibuka. Temujin annexed the country of the Keraits and amalgamated their warriors with his own army. "There are a sun and a moon in the sky, but there cannot be two kings on earth", said Taibuka, and allied himself with the Merkits and Jamuka; but in 1204 he was surrounded and overwhelmed by Temujin on Mount Namogo near Karakorum. In 1205 Temujin killed Buyuruk, destroyed the Merkits and slew their king Toktoa near the Siberian Altai, and executed Jamuka. In 1206, at a grand Kuriltai (i.e. assembly) by the Onon, he proclaimed himself supreme ruler of the Mongol peoples under the title of Chingis Khan, or Universal Emperor. He completed the reorganization of his army in tens, hundreds, and thousands, under ninety-three thousand-commanders, and began the compilation of his legal code, the Yasa. In 1207 the Uighurs, Uirats, and Kirghiz submitted voluntarily.

Chingis was now master of all Central Asia up to the Karakhitai, to whom Taibuka's son Kuchluk had fled. First, however, he determined to secure his rear in China. After making the Tanguts his vassals in two campaigns (1205–07, 1209) in which he failed to take their fortified cities, he "spat to the south", as the Chinese source relates,[6] and in 1211 began a war against the Kin of Northern China, which was to last until 1234. Here for the first time the Mongol

5. Cf. TR, ¶7, n. 1.
6. Grousset, 1941, p. 216.

custom of tribal massacre led, in a civilized country of farmers and town-dwellers, to the tragic slaughter of noncombatant millions. Gradually, with the help of captured Kin engineers, the Mongols learned the art of siege warfare, broke through the fortresses of the Great Wall in 1213, and in 1215 captured Peking. In 1216, leaving a small army under his general Mukali, who slowly forced the Kin south of the Hoang-Ho by 1223, Chingis retired to prepare his attack on the West.

Meanwhile, in 1211, the Naiman heir Kuchluk, with a band of Naiman and Merkit fugitives, had made himself master of the Karakhitayan Empire, where he became hated for his persecution of the Moslems. In 1218 the Karakhitai welcomed Chingis Khan's general Jebe as a deliverer, and Kuchluk was pursued through Kashgar and slain. Chingis Khan now confronted the new and unstable empire of Khorasmia, ruled since 1194 by Shah Mohammed. In the same year a trading caravan from Mongolia was destroyed by Mohammed's governor at the frontier town of Otrar, and in the autumn of 1219 Chingis Khan invaded Khorasmia with an army of 200,000 men. Mohammed's forces were superior in numbers but hired, potentially disloyal, and dispersed along the line of the Syr-daria (Iaxartes) River. Leaving his sons Chaghatai and Ogedei to besiege Otrar and sending his eldest son Jochi down the Syr-daria to capture the cities of Barghalikent and Yanghikent (the Barchin and Iankint of TR), Chingis Khan overwhelmed Mohammed's army and marched south in February 1220 with his youngest son Tolui on Bokhara, where he spared the submissive inhabitants but sacked and burned the city. Samarkand resisted, and the populace were massacred, excepting the craftsmen, who were deported to Mongolia. Mohammed fled, pursued by Subetei and Jebe, via Balkh and Nishapor to an island on the Caspian, where he died in December 1220 of pleurisy and despair. After a long siege under Jochi and Chaghatai, who quarreled and were subordinated to Ogodei, Mohammed's capital city of Urgendj was captured in April 1221, submerged by damming the Amu-daria (Oxus), and pillaged with total massacre. Meanwhile, Chingis Khan advanced south with Tolui, who slaughtered the inhabitants of Merv and Nishapor and the garrison of Herat in the spring of 1221. Balkh surrendered to Chingis, but was nonetheless put to the sword. Mohammed's brave son Jelal-ed-din heavily defeated a Mongol army under Shigi-Kutuku in Afghanistan, but retreated before Chingis Khan to the Indus, where he was beaten on 24 November 1221 and fled to Delhi. According to a legend, which is to some degree supported by the statement of TR and *Carpini* that the Mongols conquered Kashmir,[7] Chingis Khan attempted to return home along the upper Indus but was halted by the insuperable Himalayas. He retired in 1222–23 to rest and hunt north of the Syr-daria, and in 1225 returned home to Mongolia.

In the winter of 1220–21, thwarted south of the Caspian by news of the death of Mohammed, Subetei and Jebe with 25,000 men continued the extraordinary raid that was to lead them over the frontier of Europe. After sacking Reiy, Koum, and other cities south of the Caspian, defeating the Georgians near Tiflis in February, and abandoning the project of marching on Baghdad,[8] they again defeated the Georgians, in November 1221, and reached the Iron Gates of Derbend between the Caucasus and the Caspian, where Alexander the Great was said to have walled in the cannibal lost ten tribes of the Jews known as Gog and Magog. Bypassing

---

7. Cf. TR, ¶8, n. 5, where a different possibility is suggested.
8. Grousset, 1939, p. 307; TR, ¶31, n. 4.

the impregnable citadel of Derbend, they defeated the coalition of the Alans or Ases, the Lesgis, Circassians, and Kipchaks or Comans, and burst through the south Russian steppes to the Dnieper. Here the fleeing Comans turned, reinforced by the Russian princes with an army of 80,000. The Mongols made a feigned retreat for nine days, and on 31 May 1222[9] destroyed the Russians by the river Kalka, now the Kal'chik, which flows into the Sea of Azov near Mariupol. They pillaged the Genoese port of Soldaia in the Crimea, and returned to Chingis Khan on the Syr-daria, after suffering a defeat on the way from the Bulgars on the middle Volga and attacking the Turkish Kanglis between the Caspian and the Aral Sea.

On 18 August 1227, during a successful campaign against the rebellious Tanguts, Chingis Khan died of fever, aged sixty. His son Jochi had died in the previous February, and Jochi's appanage from the Aral to the Volga "and as far as Mongol horsemen have trodden"[10] passed to his son Batu. Chaghatai received the country from Bokhara to the Uighurs, Ogedei the Naiman lands east and north of Lake Balkhash, while to the regent Tolui, now married to the Christian Kerait princess Sorghoktani, fell the Mongol homeland. On 13 September 1229, in accordance with Chingis Khan's wishes, a Kuriltai elected Ogedei, the most intelligent, affable, and drunken of the four sons, as Grand Khan of the Mongol Empire.

Ogedei made his headquarters at the city of Karakorum, once capital of the Uighurs and recently of the Naimans. The era of barbaric pillage was replaced by organization of the conquered territories in the Chinese manner through a literate Uighur, Kerait, and Kin secretariat, using the Syrian-Nestorian-Uighur alphabet, encouraging trade, and with a fixed tithing and taxation of 10 per cent. Post-stations at intervals of a day's ride were established from east to west throughout the vast empire.

The Kin resistance had revived. In 1231–34, aided by Tolui and Subetei, Ogedei annexed the last province of their empire, Ho-nan, south of the Hoang-Ho. In the sieges of fortified towns the Mongols used siege-towers, mine-tunnels, and catapults hurling millstones. At Lo-yang the Kin are said to have made arrowheads from copper money,[11] and at their capital Kai-feng they fired burning rockets on the Mongols. Their emperor Ai-tsung committed suicide in his last city, Ju-nan. In 1236 Ogedei began the long war against the Sung dynasty of Southern China, recently his allies against the Kin, which was to drag on until the final victory under Kubilai in 1279. Korea was conquered in two campaigns in 1231 and 1236.

Jelal-ed-din had returned in 1224 to reoccupy Azerbaijan and northwestern Persia, defeat the Georgians thrice (1225, 1226, 1228), and embroil himself with the Seljuk Turks of Asia Minor. He had just been defeated by the Seljuks in 1230 when he was overwhelmed by a Mongol army sent by Ogedei under Chormaghan (who is said to have been charged by Chingis in 1220, abortively, with the advance on Baghdad).[12] In his flight he was murdered by a Kurdish peasant on 12 August 1231; but the remnants of the Khorasmian warriors fought their way west over the Euphrates and took Jerusalem from the Crusaders in 1244, thus causing the crusade of Saint Louis. Chormaghan reconquered the Georgians in 1236 and attacked Armenia in 1239;

9. Grousset, 1941, pp. 260, 517–20.

10. Juvaini, Vol. 1, p. 42.

11. Cf. TR, ¶9, n. 3.

12. Cf. TR, ¶31, n. 4.

but the Christians in his dominions were protected, at Ogedei's command, by the Syrian priest Simeon, otherwise known as Rabban-ata.[13] Chormaghan died or retired in 1241 and was succeeded by Baiju, who sacked Erzerum in 1242 and made the Seljuk sultan his vassal after defeating him near Erzinjan in 1243. In 1244 King Hetoum I of Armenia submitted voluntarily to Baiju, who was visited in 1247 by the Dominican mission of Friar Ascelin.

Meanwhile, in 1236, Ogedei ordered a great attack on Europe by an army of 150,000 warriors under the nominal command of Jochi's son Batu, now Khan of the steppe-land from the Aral to the Volga, but using primarily the strategic genius of the sixty-year-old Subetei. With these fought Batu's brothers, Ordu, Berke, and Siban; Ogedei's sons, Kuyuk and Kadan; his grandson Kaidu; Tolui's son Mongke; and Chaghatai's son Baidar and grandson Buri. In 1236–37, between the Aral and the Kama, they conquered the Kangli, the Bashkirs or Old Hungarians, and the Old Bulgarians, the two latter being the stay-at-home remnants of the Bulgars and Magyars who had invaded Europe in the seventh to ninth centuries. The Bulgarian capital, the merchant-city of Bulgar, near the confluence of the Volga and Kama, was sacked. In 1237–38 the Kipchaks in the south Russian steppes were attacked; many submitted and joined the Mongol armies, many resisted and were destroyed, and 40,000 families fled under their chief Kutan to Hungary, where they became Christians but proved unwelcome guests.

In the winter of 1237–38 the Mongols advanced over the frozen steppes from Bulgar through the country of the Finnish Mordvins against the north Russian cities. Riazan was taken in December 1237; Moscow, Susdal, and Vladimir in February 1238; Yaroslav and Tver in March —all with massacre, sacking, and burning. Wealthy Novgorod itself was saved from Batu only by the spring thaw. A pause of two years followed, occupied partly by mopping-up operations against the Kipchaks and Mordvins, partly by Mongke's conquest of the Alans or Ases between the Black Sea and the Caspian in 1239–40. In the winter of 1240 the terrible advance was resumed. Kiev was destroyed on 6 December 1240. On 13 February 1241 a detachment under Baidar and Kaidu crossed the frozen Vistula into Poland, where they sacked Sandomir, defeated a Polish army at Chmielnik on 18 March, and burned Cracow, whence the Polish king Boleslaus IV had fled to Moravia. They advanced into Silesia, where at the Battle of Liegnitz on 9 April they routed an army of 40,000 Poles and Teutonic Knights under Duke Henry II of Silesia. Henry was killed, and nine sacks were filled with the right ears of the slain. Turning south they ravaged Moravia, failing to take the fortified city of Olmütz, and joined the main army in Hungary under Batu and Subetei, whose right flank they had thus covered.

Early in April the main Mongol army had concentrated before Pest and retreated strategically for a hundred miles east to the juncture of the Theiss and Sayo rivers, followed by the Hungarian army, 100,000 strong, under King Bela IV and his brother Coloman. The Battle of the Sayo was fought on 11 April 1241. While Batu held the enemy in a fight by the bridge, Subetei crossed the river upstream and surrounded the Hungarians from the rear, opening a path for those who tried to flee. After immense slaughter the survivors fled with Bela and Coloman, who soon died of his wounds, to Croatia. The Mongols returned to sack Pest and devastate

13. See Pelliot, 1924, pp. 238–53; Vincent, *Speculum Historiale,* Book XXX, chs. 69, 70, 87, 88. Simeon befriended Friar Ascelin's mission to Baiju in 1247, and gave them the curious Nestorian version of the rise of the Mongols: that Chingis Khan, immediately before invading Khorasmia, had slain his overlord David, King of India, son of Prester John, and married his daughter. Cf. above, p. 23, n. 6.

western Hungary, reaching their farthest west at Neustadt near Vienna in July. They were joined in their ravaging by the exiled Kipchaks, whom the rash Hungarians, unjustly suspecting them of collusion with the Mongols, had attacked in March. The wretched peasants were spared to bring in the harvest, and then massacred. Early in 1242, true to the Mongol habit by which Toktoa, Kuchluk, Mohammed, and Jelal-ed-din had formerly been hunted down, Kadan rode through Croatia and Dalmatia to the Adriatic coast in pursuit of Bela, who escaped to an offshore island and lived to resurrect his stricken kingdom. Probably Batu would in any case have paused for some years to consolidate before tackling the remainder of Europe; probably, too, the Mongol hordes of light cavalry would eventually have been cut off and destroyed in those lands of walled towns, fortresses, and feudal armies; but when in the spring of 1242 news arrived of the death of Ogedei and Batu slowly retreated to Russia, it seemed that the West had been spared by a miracle.

While Batu was absent in Hungary, his deputy Sinkur made a further campaign on the upper Kama against the Bulgars, and continued north to the Finnish Permiaks or Borassits, whose refugees were given lands in Norway by King Haakon II, perhaps even—as *Carpini* and TR affirm—as far as the harmless Samoyeds of the tundra, beyond whom lay only the fabulous ox-footed and dog-faced Tchouds.[14]

During the Russian campaign Batu's cousins Kuyuk and Buri had quarreled violently with him over a question of precedence in drinking. "He's an old woman with a quiverful of arrows, and I'll have him bastinadoed", Kuyuk declared.[15] The two rebels were recalled by Ogedei, after last appearing at the sack of Kiev in December 1240. Ogedei, however, died on 11 December 1241 of drink, to which he had become increasingly addicted since the death of Tolui from the same cause in 1232: "whenever he was drunk," records a chronicler, "he used to remember Tolui and weep".[16] His vigorous widow Turakina, a Christian Naiman princess, held the regency for four and a half years, supported by Chaghatai, who died in 1242. She ignored Ogedei's dying wish that his grandson Siremun should be made Khan, dismissed her husband's civilized and popular Uighur and Chinese ministers, and prepared the way for her beloved son Kuyuk. A Kuriltai, which Batu refused to attend under the diplomatic plea of rheumatism, was at last summoned for the summer of 1246; and among the humbler spectators at Kuyuk's election on 24 August were the members of the Carpini mission.

Although contemporaries could hardly foresee it, the Mongol menace to Europe was ended. Kuyuk was determined to renew the offensive, but was hampered by his breach with Batu. In the spring of 1248 the two potentates advanced slowly to a rendezvous near Lake Balkhash, where it is vain to speculate whether they would have been reconciled or have fought to the death; for when they were only a few days' journey apart Kuyuk died of drink, like his father and uncle before him. Batu supported Tolui's widow Sorghoktani in carrying the election on 1 July 1251 of her son Mongke, who settled accounts with the Ogedeist opposition by executing Kuyuk's sorceress widow Oghul Ghaimish, Buri, and Siremun. Mongke, like his successor and brother the wise Kubilai, who reigned 1260–94, looked only to the consolidation of Asia and the conquest of Southern China. Mongke's brother Hulagu wiped out the Assassin strong-

14. Cf. TR, ¶20, n. 7; ¶21, nn. 1–3.
15. *Secret History*, ¶275.
16. d'Ohsson, Vol. 2, p. 59; Juvaini, Vol. 2, pp. 549–50.

holds south of the Caspian in 1256, took Baghdad in 1258, but in 1260, after capturing Aleppo and Damascus, was driven from Syria by the Mamelukes of Egypt.

In Russia under the "Tartar Yoke", in Asia under the "Tartar Peace", the Mongols turned from havoc to order, civilization, justice, and religious tolerance. Their early atrocities were the most enormous and unpardonable recorded in history until our own century; the grim habits of petty tribal warfare had been senselessly extended to the mass slaughter of capitulated armies, fallen cities, harmless civilians, and unfortunate peasants. But the modern student of their epic traditions may justifiably feel something of the same reluctant admiration for the savage bravery, generosity, poetry, and nobility of the Mongols, as for the same qualities in Homer's Greeks, or in his own barbaric ancestors who overthrew Rome.

For more than a century, until the rise of the Ottoman Turks severed the caravan routes, Asia remained open to European missionaries and merchants. Of two of these—Saint Louis' envoy the Franciscan Friar William Rubruck in 1253–55 and the Polos in 1256–95—we have accounts that surpass even *Carpini* and TR in vivid detail, though not in knowledge of Mongol history. But the brave friars of the Carpini mission could not know that the Tartar Peace had begun, and that they would return in safety from the pitiless murderers, only four years since, of Poland and Hungary. "We feared we might be slain or imprisoned for life by the Tartars," wrote Carpini, "or afflicted beyond our strength by hunger, thirst, cold, heat, insults and excessive toil; all of which, except death and captivity, came to us far more than we had expected."[17]

4. THE CARPINI MISSION

Western Europe had viewed the approach of the Mongols with a characteristic mingling of undue optimism, terror, and selfish indifference. When Chingis Khan overwhelmed the Khorasmian Empire, it seemed that Islam might providentially be crushed between the Mongols and the Crusaders; and the pagan conqueror was hopefully identified as the mysterious Prester John, the fabulous Christian king of Central Asia. But when Batu's appalling invasion descended, men believed that the Mongols, "pouring forth like devils from Tartarus, so that they are rightly called Tartars," were the tribes of Gog and Magog, broken loose at last from the Caspian Mountains. Herrings, the chronicler Matthew Paris recorded, were in glut at Yarmouth in 1238, because the merchants of Gotland and Frisia dared not leave home to fetch them.[1] But the popes Gregory IX, who died on 21 August 1241, and Innocent IV, elected in 1243, were preoccupied with their war in Northern Italy against the Hohenstaufen Emperor Frederick II. It seemed that the calamities of Eastern Europe would fall first on the Eastern Church, next on Frederick's German homeland, and that the Mongols were fighting the enemies of the Church of Rome. Duke Frederick of Austria was so unfeeling as to attack his stricken foe Bela of Hungary from the rear.[2] The retreat of Batu in 1242 seemed to justify the masterly inactivity of the Church. It was not until 1245, when the urgent danger appeared to have receded, that Innocent decided to send two missions to the Mongols, ostensibly to expostulate on the errors of their ways and to urge the merits of baptism, but primarily to spy upon their

17. *Carpini,* Prologus, ¶2.
1. Matthew Paris, Vol. 3, p. 488. Cf. Rockhill, pp. xiv–xvii.
2. Howorth, Vol. 1, pp. 150–51; d'Ohsson, Vol. 2, pp. 156–57.

resources and intentions. The first, as we have seen, was sent under the Franciscan Friar John of Plano Carpini by the northern route to Karakorum; the second, under the Dominican Friar Ascelin, proceeded via Syria to Baiju in Persia.

Carpini, then aged about sixty, was born at the village of Piano del Carpini, later Piano della Magione, near Lake Trasimene a few miles northwest of Perugia, and became one of the first companions of St. Francis (1182–1226) in the nearby town of Assisi. At the General Chapter of the Franciscan Order in 1221 he was sent to prepare the way for the Franciscans in Germany, where he served mainly in Saxony, with an interval in Spain in 1230–32. In 1232 he was appointed to the important post of Minister of the Franciscan province of Saxony, where he preached, organized, founded convents, and sent Franciscan outposts to Bohemia, Hungary, Poland, Denmark, and Norway. He was removed on 15 May 1239 by the General Chapter of the Order, perhaps in view of the approach of the Mongols, and possibly (for a frequent change of post was customary among the higher Franciscan officials) to take an appointment in the Papal court, where he is found in 1245 as a protonotary. "He cherished and ruled his friars as a hen does her chickens," wrote a fellow-Franciscan, who also recorded that Carpini was so corpulent that he had to ride a donkey; "and the men of that time showed more reverence to his donkey than they now feel for a Minister of the Order!"[3] This experienced and widely traveled administrator, with his devoted energy, keen intelligence, brave heart, and exceptional knowledge of Eastern Europe, was an ideal choice as an envoy to the Mongols and the first Catholic missionary in Central Asia.

Innocent had summoned the Council of Lyons, at which the Mongol menace and the excommunication of the rebel Frederick were the chief items on the agenda, for June 1245. To avoid delay, Carpini was furnished on 5 March with the Papal brief, addressed without name, since the identity of the future Khan was unsettled, "to the King and nation of the Tartars". Here Innocent "warns, begs and earnestly exhorts your Universality" to desist and repent for fear of the wrath of God, and asks pointblank "what urged you to exterminate other nations, and what are your future intentions?" He requests safe conduct for "our beloved son Friar John and his companions", whom he has chosen, he explains, with a view to their knowledge of the Scriptures and their Christian humility; "but if we had thought them more likely to be useful and welcome to you, we would have sent either bishops or other potentates".[4] Among Carpini's companions was a certain Friar Stephen of Bohemia;[5] but at least one more is

---

3. *AF*, Vol. 1, p. 17. For the career of Carpini see Golubovich, Vol. 1, pp. 191–95; Vol. 2, pp. 318–19; Sbaralea, Supplementum, Vol. 2, pp. 117–18; Pullé, pp. 22–31; *AF*, Vol. 1, pp. 8–12, 16–18; Vol. 2, pp. 21, 23, 29, 31, 48–50, 56, 59, 61; Vol. 3, p. 266.

4. Innocent wrote two letters, dated 5 March and 13 March 1245. Carpini's own summary of Innocent's message, as made on 24 February 1246 to the captains of the first Mongol outpost (*Carpini*, ch. IX, ¶8), contains material from both letters, and similarly Kuyuk's reply answers points found in one or the other letter but not in both. It follows that Carpini must either have carried both letters, or, much more probably, a third letter now unknown which embodied the material of both. Cf. Pelliot, 1922–23, pp. 6–9. In the first of these letters the bearer is named as Friar Lawrence of Portugal, of whom nothing more is known (cf. Golubovich, Vol. 1, pp. 215–16, Vol. 2, pp. 350–55, and Pelliot, 1924, p. 270, denying his identity with Laurentius de Orte, legate in the Near East from 7 July 1246, though this identity is assumed by Roncaglia, pp. 92–99). Perhaps he led another and abortive mission to the Mongols; or perhaps he was superseded between 5 and 13 March by Carpini, who is named as the bearer of the second letter. For the texts see Wadding, Vol. 3, pp. 133–36, Sbaralea, Vol. 1, pp. 353–55.

5. Wadding, *Scriptores ordinis minorum*, p. 149. Wadding does not cite his source, which is presumably the

required to justify Innocent's use of the plural, and this third man may possibly have been the Ceslaus of Bohemia named in the Tartar Relation.

The travelers left Lyons on Easter Day, 16 April 1245. They were helped on their way by Carpini's friend King Wenceslaus IV of Bohemia, who advised them to proceed by way of Poland and Russia, by Boleslaus IV Duke of Silesia, also a personal friend of Carpini, in whose territory Carpini acquired at Breslau the services of Friar Benedict the Pole as "comrade of my tribulation and interpreter", by Conrad Duke of Poland at Cracow, who gave them beaver furs as indispensable presents to Mongol officials, and by Vasiliko (Basil), the Russian Duke of Vladimir, who politely evaded (on the pretext of his brother Daniel's absence on a visit to Batu) Innocent's letter urging him to abandon his allegiance to the Eastern Church, and sent them on to Kiev. Here Carpini arrived by sledge over the snow, "sick unto death", and left his horses, being assured that only Mongol mounts were trained to dig for grass beneath the snow.[6]

Leaving Kiev on 3 February 1246, and Kaniev on the Dnieper on 19 February, they reached the first Mongol outpost on 23 February—where "the Tartars rushed in upon us hideously armed, enquiring what manner of men we were".[7] Here they parted at the Mongols' order with the exhausted Friar Stephen and their servants. Continuing their journey by the strenuous but highly efficient system of Mongol post-horses, they followed the Dnieper to the camp of the Mongol frontier general Khurumsi, i.e. the Khorasmian, a son of Batu's elder brother Ordu, whose name Carpini transcribed as "Corenza".[8] In accordance with protocol this general extorted gifts, warned them not to touch his threshold, made them kneel before him, heard the purpose of their mission, and forwarded them to Batu. They continued down the Dnieper on the ice, traversed the territory of Chaghatai's son Mochi to the Sea of Azov, where they occasionally crossed the dangerous sea-ice,[9] passed the Don and the lands of Batu's sister's husband Karton,[10] and reached Batu's winter seat at Sarai on the Volga delta, some 65 miles north of Astra-

---

Chronica generalium ministrorum OFM (*AF*, Vol. 3, p. 266; cf. also Vol. 2, p. 71). Carpini's choice of the two Czechs Stephen and Ceslaus and the Polish Benedict as his companions is significant. They belonged to the jurisdiction of the newly formed Franciscan province of Bohemia and Poland, where he may well have known them when he himself was minister of the previous and overlapping province of Saxony and Bohemia in 1232–39; and their special experience and knowledge of Slavonic languages would be valuable on the journey outward and homeward through Eastern Europe.

6. *Carpini*, ch. IX, ¶3–¶5. The text of Innocent's letter to Daniel and Vasiliko was in all probability identical with that of his letter of 21 March 1245 to King Coloman of Bulgaria (Sbaralea, Vol. 1, p. 359), which uses much of the same phraseology as his letters of 5 and 13 March to Kuyuk (see n. 4, above), and invites Coloman's adhesion to the Roman Church and his support for the mission in terms that would suit any ruler in Eastern Europe. The bearer of the letter to King Coloman is unnamed. He may have been the leader of an otherwise unknown mission, possibly the Friar Lawrence of Portugal named in the letter of 5 March 1245; or, equally well, he may have been Carpini himself, since Carpini's route was left to his own discretion, and he would have passed through Bulgaria via Hungary if he had chosen the Black Sea route.

7. *Carpini,* ch. IX, ¶7.

8. *Carpini,* ch. IX, ¶9. For Khurumsi, see Pelliot, 1938, pp. 151–52; Idem, *Horde d'Or*, p. 9.

9. *Carpini,* ch. IX, ¶13. The context names the Mare Magnum, i.e. the Black Sea, and shows clearly that the friars crossed the ice of the Sea of Azov, not of the Caspian which they never saw, as they passed the Volga at Batu's camp some eighty miles north of the Caspian. D'Avezac and Rockhill incorrectly show them on their route-maps as traveling well to the north of the Sea of Azov and close to the northern shore of the Caspian. This feature is therefore amended in the map included in the present publication (facing p. 26).

10. Karton, who appears in the *Carpini* manuscripts (ch. IX, ¶13, ¶49) under the various readings *Carton* and *Carbon,* and in Vincent, *Speculum Historiale*, Book XXXII, ch. 21, as *Tirbon,* is not otherwise known. He may possibly be the same as the Scatay or Scatatay (i.e. Chaghatai—otherwise unknown, but several persons were named after

khan, on 4 April. Here the additional rites of passing between two fires, "lest you should harbour evil thoughts against our lord, or carry poison", and bowing to a golden image of the deified Chingis Khan, were enforced upon the reluctant envoys; and then, in his fine linen tent, looted from King Bela of Hungary, they confronted the formidable Batu—"kindly enough to his own people, though they fear him greatly, but most cruel in war", says Carpini.[11] A Russian serving in the retinue of the future Saint Alexander Nevsky, who was then visiting Batu, acted as their interpreter and translated Innocent's letter into Russian, Turkish, and Mongol. Batu, after reading the latter text with great attention, sent them on to Karakorum, giving orders to their Mongol guides that they should travel fast in order to be in time for the great Kuriltai.[12]

They left on Easter Monday, 8 April, "with many tears, not knowing whether we went to death or to life", their legs swathed in puttees against the friction of riding, and weak from lack of food, for they had fasted scrupulously throughout Lent, "on boiled millet and salt, with nothing to drink but snow melted in a kettle".[13] On 16 April they crossed the Ural River into the country of the Kangli Turks, reaching the frontiers of northern Khorasmia on 17 May, of the Karakhitai about 16 June, the Naimans on 28 June, and the Mongols' imperial summer station of Sira Ordu (Superior Court), half a day's journey south of Karakorum, which they never actually saw,[14] on 22 July. Riding all day and sometimes far into the night, and changing horses several times a day, the indomitable friars had covered little less than 3,000 miles from Batu's camp in 106 days, an average of nearly 30 miles a day.

Three thousand envoys, of whom they were the least, had gathered from all Asia for the Kuriltai, including Alexander Nevsky's father Yaroslav, Duke of Susdal in Russia, who died soon after and turned "marvellously green", from Mongol poison, as the friars darkly but unjustly suspected.[15] Kuyuk's election was not a foregone conclusion, for his brother Koten had hopes, and an opposition party favored his nephew Siremun, although the boy was still under age. A great hailstorm fell on 15 August, alarming the friars and causing the shamans to postpone the election; but Kuyuk was duly made Khan on 24 August. A week of wild rejoicing followed; "all set the foot of merriment in the arena of amusement", says the Persian chronicler Juvaini, who was present.[16] For a time the friars knew better days, with largesse of roasted meat, and such torrents of wine and beer that, after doing their gallant best, they could only beg

---

the great Chaghatai, son of Chingis Khan—cf. Juvaini, Vol. 2, p. 724, n. 4), also a relative of Batu, encountered by Rubruck in 1253 (Rockhill, p. 84); but this was much further west, in the district between Soldaia and the Don, commanded in Carpini's time by Mochi. One or other of Batu's brother Berke and son Sartak would be no more remote paleographically from *Carton-Carbon*, and it would be easy enough for Carpini to misunderstand their precise relationship to Batu. Berke was in command at Derbend and northward (article Berke in *Encyclopaedia of Islam*, new edition), while Sartak controlled the very region in question, between the Don and the Volga (Hammer-Purgstall, p. 141).

11. *Carpini*, ch. IX, ¶17. Sarai as a town had only recently been founded at the time of Rubruck's return journey in 1255 (see Rockhill, p. 256; art. Batu in *Encyclopaedia of Islam*, new edition); but it is likely enough that Batu's previous winter seat on the Volga was at or near the same site.

12. *Carpini*, ch. IX, ¶16, ¶19, ¶28.

13. *Carpini*, ch. IX, ¶19; Benedict, ed. Wyngaert, p. 137.

14. *Carpini*, ch. I, ¶4; TR, ¶38.

15. *Carpini*, ch. IX, ¶37. Carpini took the opportunity to convert Yaroslav from the Orthodox Church to Rome before his death, as is stated by a letter of Innocent IV dated 23 January 1248 to his son Alexander Nevsky, urging him to follow his father's example (Sbaralea, Vol. 1, p. 506).

16. Juvaini, Vol. 1, p. 256.

to be excused. But when they were admitted at last to the stern Kuyuk, "a clever man who was seldom seen to smile",[17] and their names were read by the Kerait Christian chancellor Chingay, and the other envoys gave silk, samite, and camels, the poor friars had nothing left to give. A lean time followed this breach of etiquette, "the rations for four were scarcely enough for one", and without the providential kindness of the Russian Cosmas, Kuyuk's favorite gold-smith, they would have starved to death.[18]

Kuyuk proceeded to business, setting up his ceremonial standard for total war against the West, Persia, and the Sungs of Southern China. His rival brother Koten had died, rather conveniently, during the Kuriltai, and Turakina's favorite, Fatima, was put to death for murdering him by witchcraft.[19] Kuyuk's own uncle Otegin, Chingis Khan's youngest brother, who had tried to seize the Khanate after Ogedei's death, was also tried for conspiracy and executed.[20] It was not until November that Kuyuk received the long-suffering friars, heard their business as interpreted by Yaroslav's attendant knight Temer, and asked if the Pope had men who understood Russian, Persian, or Mongol writing. The friars proposed that Kuyuk's answer to Innocent should be written in Mongol and interpreted for them to transcribe in Latin, which was done in conference with the Christian procurator of the Mongol Empire Kadak and the chancellors Chingay and Bala on 11 November, with a third version in Persian that survives in the Vatican archives to this day.[21] Kuyuk's message was far from conciliatory. He professed to be unable to comprehend the Pope's request that he should be baptized, still less his presuming to complain of the massacres in Poland and Hungary: it was God Himself that ordained these men to be slain, for otherwise, "what could man do against man?" If the West wanted peace, then Pope, emperors, kings and all leading men must come to him without delay to learn his will. If they did not, "we know not what will come of it, but God knows".[22] On 13 November the friars received Kuyuk's uncompromising letter, sealed with his seal made by the goldsmith Cosmas; their good friend Turakina (who was now in disfavor and died soon after) gave them each a fox-fur cloak;[23] and they set out on the long way home.

For fifteen days they journeyed with the envoys of the Sultan of Egypt, who then turned away to the southern route through Kashgar and Persia. The friars traveled all winter, sleeping on the snow and waking to find themselves covered by the blizzard.[24] After nearly six months, on 9 May 1247, they reached the camp of Batu, who gave them safe conduct to Mochi, with whom they found Stephen and their servants safe and sound. Khurumsi demanded gifts, this time in vain, but gave them an escort to Kiev, where they were received on 25 May with rejoicing, "as if we had come back from the dead". Daniel and Basil feasted them at Vladimir for a week, "detaining us against our will", and sent letters of submission to the Pope and the Roman Church;[25] but when Innocent responded only by naming Daniel King, Daniel replied:

17. *Carpini,* ch. IX, ¶43.
18. *Carpini,* ch. IX, ¶34, ¶38.
19. Juvaini, Vol. 1, pp. 244–46. Cf. *Carpini,* ch. IX, ¶36, and TR, ¶30, n. 2.
20. Juvaini, Vol. 1, pp. 244, 255. Cf. *Carpini,* ch. V, ¶18; TR, ¶41, n. 3.
21. Pelliot, 1922–23, with text and facsimile.
22. *Carpini,* ch. IX, ¶47.
23. *Carpini,* ch. IX, ¶39, ¶45; Pelliot, 1931–32, p. 57.
24. *Carpini,* ch. IX, ¶46; Benedict, ed. Wyngaert, pp. 140–41.
25. *Carpini,* ch. IX, ¶47, ¶48.

"I wanted you to send an army, not a title".[26] They crossed Poland, Bohemia, and Germany to Cologne, presumably making this detour because Bavaria was loyal to the rebel Frederick,[27] and via Liège and Champagne reached Innocent at Lyons on 18 November. After his mission to Louis in the spring of 1248 Carpini was made bishop of Antivari in Dalmatia: "because you have been faithful in little things," said Innocent, to whom a perilous journey of some 8,000 miles seemed a little thing, "I will entrust you with great."[28] Unfortunately, Carpini's jurisdiction was disputed by the Archbishop of Ragusa, the populace sided against him, and he was ejected from his see. The much-enduring friar died in Italy, possibly at Perugia—where he may have gone to plead his cause with Innocent—on 1 August 1252.[29]

5. THE AUTHORITY OF THE TARTAR RELATION

During their return through Europe the friars repeatedly gave lectures on their experiences to eager audiences. Carpini himself states that "people through whom I passed in Poland, Bohemia, Germany, Liège and Champagne were so pleased with the present treatise that they copied it down before it was complete, as I had not yet had leisure enough to finish it fully"[1]—meaning, of course, when it was still in its first version, before he revised this and augmented it with the narrative of his journey. "He wrote a great book about the deeds of the Tartars," says the chronicler Friar Salimbene, who met Carpini nearing Lyons a little after 2 November 1247, "and caused this book to be read aloud, as I myself saw and heard, whenever he found it too laborious to tell the story; and when the readers were astonished or did not understand, he himself expounded or discussed matters of detail."[2] Similarly Friar Benedict, by way of division of labor, had made his own narrative of the journey, which he dictated at Cologne, as a chronicler of that city records,[3] and no doubt in other places—including, as we shall see, Poland or Bohemia.

26. Howorth, Vol. 2, p. 77; Rockhill, p. 2, n. 4.

27. Frederick was excommunicated on 17 July 1245, and was now besieging Parma. The friars' route between Lyons and Prague on the outward journey is unstated and unknown; but a journey through Southern Germany in the summer of 1245, when the Council of Lyons was sitting with the express intention of deposing Frederick, would have been no less dangerous for papal envoys than in 1247, so it is likely that in 1245 also they made the same or a similar detour via northern France and Germany. For the visit to Cologne see below, p. 39, n. 3.

28. As reported by Salimbene, in Golubovich, Vol. 1, p. 194. To do Innocent justice these tactless words are quoted from Matthew 25:23, the Parable of the Talents, where they are addressed by the Master to the good and faithful servant; so they were no doubt intended as a great compliment.

29. Letters of Innocent IV from Perugia dated 20–22 April 1252 last mention Carpini as still alive (Potthast, Vol. 2, p. 1201; Farlati, Vol. 7, pp. 38, 40). His successor to the see of Antivari was appointed on 12 April 1253 (Sbaralea, Vol. 1, pp. 653–54). The *Martyrologium Franciscanum*, p. 321, states that Carpini died in Italy on 1 August (cf. Farlati, Vol. 7, p. 41). If so, it is possible that his life may have come full circle in the Perugia of his youth and of his master St. Francis. It is perhaps significant that Innocent IV, who had left Lyons in March 1251, resided at Perugia and Assisi until he at last returned to Rome in October 1253 (Sbaralea, Vol. 1, pp. 574–684).

1. *Carpini*, ch. IX, ¶52.

2. *MGH*, Vol. 32, p. 207; Pelliot, 1922–23, p. 13, suggesting that this meeting occurred at Villefranche. The readings attended by Salimbene took place at Sens during Carpini's mission to Louis IX in the spring of 1248 (*MGH*, Vol. 32, p. 213). Salimbene says that Carpini was a frequent diner-out on the strength of his story—"and I ate with him not only at Franciscan convents but at abbeys and other important places". The monks of Cluny said: "Would that all papal legates were like Friar John who came back from the Tartars! For other legates loot our churches and take away all they can carry, but he would only accept a piece of cloth to make a tunic for his companion" (ibid.).

3. See *Annales Sancti Pantaleonis Coloniensis*, in *MGH*, Vol. 22, p. 542. The friars arrived in Cologne during the

In this context of a triumphal lecture tour across Europe, in which the story of the friars was attentively heard and copied down, the Tartar Relation finds a natural place. It is, in fact, a transcript of one of these lectures or readings, taken down and edited by a certain C. de Bridia. De Bridia finished his report on 30 July 1247,[4] and allowing a week or two for his task we may suppose that the lecture took place toward the middle of July. This date fits very well between the friars' arrival on 25 May at Kiev (where they no doubt stayed for a week or so as they did shortly afterward at Vladimir) and their entry into Cologne late in September. The whereabouts of the session is not stated, but either Cracow or Breslau, at which the friars had touched on their outward journey, or Prague, through which they probably passed on their way through Bohemia, would be suitable places.

Nothing is known of C. de Bridia from any other source. Owing to a labor-saving but deplorable foible of the scribe, who gives only the initial "C."[5] and similarly twice refers to Benedict himself by his initial as "Friar B.",[6] even De Bridia's first name is lost. He refers to himself modestly as *inter Minores minimus,* "most minor of the Minorites"; but this was a universal polite formula of Franciscans, used by Rubruck among others,[7] and does not necessarily mean that his status was insignificant. He may well have been, for example, a private secretary or deputy to the Friar Boguslaus in "filial obedience" to whom, as he says, he has "set down in writing what I have understood of the Tartars on the authority of the venerable friars of our order, namely Friar Johannes . . . and his companions Friar Benedict the Pole and Friar Ceslaus the Bohemian".[8] Friar Ceslaus, likewise, is otherwise unrecorded. Boguslaus himself, "a man of great mildness and modesty", is well known. He had been appointed in that very year of 1247, by a chapter held at Znoimo in Moravia, as the fifth in succession to the post of Minister of the Franciscan province of Bohemia and Poland, an office he held for four years, being succeeded in 1251 by a certain Friar Aegidius. He died, it is said, on 19 August 1299.[9]

Both from De Bridia's position as a mere reporter to his superior, and from the entire ab-

---

election, at the nearby town of Worringen, of William, Count of Holland, as anti-King of the Empire in opposition to the Emperor Frederick's son Conrad—a pro-papal maneuver occasioned by Innocent's excommunication and deposition of Frederick and Conrad, which these latter of course did not recognize. Cologne had previously been loyal to Frederick, and kept William waiting for several days before allowing his ceremonial entry on 3 October 1247. The friars would therefore have arrived in Cologne toward the end of September. Benedict, says the chronicler, told everything "to a certain bishop and former university professor (*scholastico*) of Cologne as he saw and heard it", including Kuyuk's letter to Innocent and "the whole narrative of the journey; which things were added, as the friar declared them with his own mouth, to a special book on the origin, religion and other circumstances of the Tartars, which the friars brought back with them", i.e. the first version of *Carpini.* In all probability Benedict's journey-narrative as we have it, told in the third person with evident abridgments and comments by the copyist, is the very version taken down at Cologne, since (1) it consists only of the journey-narrative and Kuyuk's letter, (2) in both the known manuscripts it is prefixed to the first version of *Carpini,* and (3) the only detail of the homeward journey here mentioned is that "the friars crossed the Rhine at Cologne and went on their way to our lord the Pope at Lyons" (Benedict, ed. Wyngaert, p. 141).

4. TR, ¶62.

5. TR, ¶1.

6. TR, ¶18. This could have occurred at any stage in the transmission of the text of TR, including its last transcription in the Yale manuscript. But the culprit could equally well have been De Bridia himself.

7. *"In ordine fratrum minorum minimus"* (Wyngaert, p. 164; Rockhill, p. 40).

8. TR, ¶1.

9. Biernacki, pp. 223–24. The date given for Friar Boguslaus' death is surprisingly late, and a misprint may be suspected.

sence in the Tartar Relation or elsewhere of any mention of his presence on the journey or of any statement on Mongol matters made on his own authority, it seems quite certain that he did not accompany the friars. The misleading word "seen" in his preface must be taken either as a textual corruption (as is both paleographically and grammatically feasible), or as an unintentional ambiguity.[10]

Analysis of the Tartar Relation, and of the features in which it resembles or differs from Carpini's *Historia Mongalorum,* throws considerable light on its origins and authority. TR lacks, as we have seen, any narrative of the friars' journey, and deals primarily with the history, sociology, and intentions of the Mongols. Its affinities lie, therefore, with the first version of Carpini's treatise, in which the same subjects are handled and the narrative of the journey does not appear. Rather more than half the material in TR is present also in *Carpini,* as will be seen at a glance from the present edition, in which the matter common to both is printed in roman type, with marginal references to Wyngaert's edition of *Carpini,* and matter peculiar to TR is italicized.

However, it is impossible to believe that TR represents, even in this common material alone, a mere recasting by De Bridia of the existing text of *Carpini.* Comparison shows that, even where the sense of TR closely resembles that of *Carpini,* the actual Latin wording is almost always entirely different. Verbal identity is so rare, indeed, and so strictly limited to an occasional single word or two, that it can reasonably be ascribed to accident. Still more significantly, TR persistently condenses or expands the expression of the common material, in an apparently random manner. Moreover, a single section of TR often contains matter found in a different order in several widely separated sections of *Carpini;* or, similarly, the order in which individual sections occur in *Carpini* is often inverted or dislocated in TR. New material, ranging from single words to whole sections and sometimes trivial but often of great factual importance, is embodied in the midst of the common material. There is a marked tendency for the common material to express only the basic facts, which TR and *Carpini* then proceed to explain or elaborate in a different manner. Often these elaborations are more intelligible or interesting in *Carpini* than in TR; or again, *Carpini* contains, apart from the common material, much important or attractive information which is absent from TR; so that it seems improbable that even so comparatively unintelligent a compiler as C. de Bridia would have chosen his TR source in preference to *Carpini,* if he had access to both. We may conclude with certainty that De Bridia's main informant was not Carpini, and that his text was not based on Carpini's.

Fortunately there can be little doubt as to De Bridia's chief—if not sole—source for the matter peculiar to TR. Except in his preface he never mentions Carpini himself, nor Friar Ceslaus of Bohemia. Possibly some of the information for which he cites "our friars" as authority[11] may have been gathered from Carpini or Ceslaus; but even here the expression may well be a circumlocution, indicating that his informant is speaking both for himself and for his companions. Much of the new material—in particular that on Mongol legends, Mongol etymology, the campaigns in Russia and the West, and statements for which the Mongols themselves are quoted as source—seems to show the personal interests of a single individual. On four occasions, the last three of which are in contexts of this nature, De Bridia names Friar Benedict as his in-

10. See TR, ¶1, n. 3.
11. TR, ¶14, ¶17, ¶22, ¶30, ¶35, ¶38, ¶42, ¶43, ¶47, ¶51, ¶52.

formant.[12] It seems reasonable to infer that, except for the few unidentifiable details which could possibly have been derived from Carpini or Ceslaus, De Bridia's information was supplied by Benedict.

The following hypothesis appears to be the only complete or even tenable explanation of the above facts. Carpini and Benedict evidently kept each his own diary of the journey, since their journey-narratives, although each of course tells the same basic story, differ throughout. Similarly, each must have kept his own notebook on Mongol history, customs, etc., from which Carpini compiled his *Historia Mongalorum* and Benedict the version on which TR is based. To account for the material common to *Carpini* and TR we may postulate a brief preliminary sketch available to both Carpini and Benedict and written, probably during their sojourn near Karakorum or on the return through Central Asia, by one or the other or by both in collaboration. This was expanded by Carpini into the first issue of his *Historia Mongalorum* and by Benedict, in accordance with his own information and special interests, into the version reported by TR. TR, in fact, is to Benedict's narrative of the journey what *Carpini,* chs. I–VIII is to *Carpini,* ch. IX; and we may identify TR as representing the hitherto missing portion of Benedict's own complete account of the mission.

By a curious coincidence, however, Benedict's account, in its surviving form, has been substantially altered in both sections by the respective scribes. His narrative of the journey is found only in the abridged form taken down, apparently, at Cologne; similarly, the remainder survives only as edited by De Bridia in TR.

De Bridia's editing comprises four main features. The first of these may be deduced from the perplexing fact that the Latin wording of the common material in TR differs throughout, though the sense remains the same, from that in *Carpini.* For this discrepancy there seems to be only one natural explanation: that Benedict's text passed at some point through the medium of another language and was then retranslated back into Latin. The two friars, as we have seen, divided the labor of their lecture tour by telling each his own version to their different audiences. It may be conjectured that, at the session in Poland or Bohemia attended by De Bridia, Carpini addressed a gathering of church dignitaries in Latin, a language common to all clerics irrespective of nationality, while Benedict spoke in his native Polish or in Czech to a meeting of noblemen and their retinues, city officials and the like, who did not understand Latin. For some reason De Bridia attended Benedict's meeting and not Carpini's: possibly he arrived too late to hear Carpini, or possibly he may have been a personal friend of Benedict, or possibly the two lectures were held simultaneously, and Boguslaus may have sent another friar to collect Carpini's report. De Bridia then translated Benedict's vernacular into his own Latin. The process would apply, of course, not merely to the common material (though it is only here that its symptoms are directly visible), but to the whole. It is clear from the prefatory and final paragraphs of TR, where De Bridia is writing in his own person, that he was sadly inferior to Carpini and Benedict both in intelligence and in command of Latin. De Bridia's retranslation and editing no doubt account, it must be said with regret, for TR's deficiency in prose style as compared to *Carpini* and to Benedict's journey-narrative, and for its indefinable but pervasive air of having passed through a second-rate mind.

12. TR, ¶7, ¶12, ¶18, ¶28.

A more beneficial result of De Bridia's intervention is seen in his reporting of Benedict's valuable spoken comments and replies to questioning. Perhaps it is more likely that these occurred in the general hurlyburly of the press conference than in a private interview with De Bridia, since the latter never writes: "Friar Benedict told me . . .", but only: "Friar Benedict says . . ." The material which he claims in his preface to have obtained from Carpini and Ceslaus remains unidentified, but was apparently small in quantity. The only explicit trace of this information is a negative one, when De Bridia states that he was unable to learn the name of Chingis Khan's fourth son (i.e. Tolui) "either from the friars or from the rest of the party".[13] Lastly, besides his opening and closing paragraphs addressed to his superior Friar Boguslaus, De Bridia carried out an unknown but perhaps not very extensive amount of editorial abridgment of Benedict's spoken text, of which signs are visible in his refusal to discuss more fully Batu's Russian campaign ("because the subject demands a special writer"), Mongol clothing ("because these matters seem more curious than useful"), and military tactics (a topic he leaves "to those who are instructed in its practice more by experience than by book-learning").[14]

At first sight it is surprising, in view of the formidable language barriers, that the friars could travel many thousands of miles into Mongol- and Turkish-speaking Asia and return with a vast body of detailed and valuable information derived from word of mouth. Both Carpini and Benedict were excellent linguists in European tongues, for Carpini spoke Italian, Latin, and probably German, French, and Spanish,[15] while Benedict, "the companion and interpreter of our tribulation",[16] spoke at least Latin and his native Polish, and probably had a working knowledge of other languages such as German, Czech, and Russian.[17] But their ability to acquire knowledge of Mongol matters is amply explained by Carpini's extensive remarks upon their interpreters and sources. As far as Khurumsi's camp they had an interpreter hired at Kiev, though his command of Mongol turned out to be second-rate.[18] Khurumsi gave them two Mongol sergeants (decani, or leaders of ten), who accompanied them all the way to Karakorum[19] and presumably knew enough of a common language, probably Russian, to supply the many topographical observations on their journey which the friars could not have made from mere eyesight. At Batu's camp they were supplied with interpreters, including a Russian from Susdal, for the translation of Innocent's letter into Russian, Turkish, and Mongol, and also met Alexander Nevsky's attendant knight Sangor, a Coman converted to Christianity, who would have known at least Turkish and Russian.[20] At Kuyuk's court they found not only the vast concourse of envoys from many races to the great kuriltai but many educated and Mongol-speaking captives from Eastern Europe, some of whom had dwelt in Mongolia since Subetei's and Jebe's great raid twenty-four years ago. "We learned many of Kuyuk's secrets",

13. TR, ¶23, and nn. 4, 11.

14. TR, ¶25, ¶37, ¶61, respectively.

15. Italian was his native language; he served for sixteen years in Germany and for two in Spain, and was chosen as envoy to Louis IX of France in 1248. The friars used French in their conversations with the Russians and Hungarians at Kuyuk's court (*Carpini*, ch. IX, ¶39).

16. *Carpini*, Prologus, ¶3.

17. These, at least, would be the languages to be expected of a Polish Franciscan stationed at Breslau and chosen for his ability as an interpreter for a journey through Eastern Europe.

18. *Carpini*, ch. IX, ¶11.

19. Ibid., ¶11, ¶19.

20. Ibid., ¶15, ¶49.

says Carpini, "from persons who came with other princes, numerous Russians and Hungarians who knew French and Latin, and Russian priests, and others who had been with the Mongols, some for thirty [*sic*] years, in their wars and other deeds, and were acquainted with all their affairs, because they knew their language and stayed with them constantly for ten or twenty years, some for longer and some for less, by means of whom we could examine everything. And they told us all voluntarily and sometimes without questioning, because they knew our wishes".[21] As interpreters with Kuyuk they had Duke Yaroslav's knight Temer, his priest Duboslav, and a Russian priest in the service of Kuyuk himself.[22] Another Mongol-speaking friend was Kuyuk's Russian goldsmith Cosmas, "a great favorite of the Emperor", who saved them from starving, showed them in his workshop the throne and seal he had made for his master, and translated for them the inscription on the seal, an impression of which still survives on Kuyuk's letter to Innocent.[23] They also interviewed non-Mongol soldiers in the Mongol army, who declared that "if they saw the chance, and had confidence that we would not kill them, they would fight the Mongols and do them worse harm than their open enemies".[24]

"We either saw everything with our own eyes, or heard it from Christians who are captives among the Mongols and, as we consider, worthy of belief," says Carpini in his prologue.[25] Carpini cites the Russian priests of Karakorum only twice, when he felt their stories were particularly tall: once for the tale of the dog-warriors of Nochoy Kadzar, "told firmly by Russian priests and others who were long among the Mongols", and again for the embassy of the Unipeds, told "by Russian priests at Kuyuk's court who dwell with the aforesaid Emperor".[26] Yet these are among the very subjects for which TR quotes Mongol sources,[27] and we may perhaps envisage the friars interviewing a joint session of Russian priests and Mongol informants. A minority of place names and personal names represent Turkish rather than Mongol forms—such as Zumoal,[28] Burithebet,[29] Tossuc (for Jochi),[30] Mangu (for Mongke),[31] and the Pope's name *yul boba*[32]—and were no doubt derived either from Comans in Batu's territory or from Uighurs or Keraits at Karakorum. Bati (for Batu), on the other hand, is the Russian form.[33]

First-hand contact with the Mongols was not lacking, though it seems to have been entrusted mainly to Benedict (if we agree that he was the primary author of TR), rather than to Carpini himself, who never quotes a direct Mongol source. TR cites interviews with Mongols on ten topics—the magnetic effects of the Caspian Mountains,[34] the woman prisoner from

21. Ibid., ¶39.
22. Ibid., ¶40, ¶49.
23. Ibid., ¶38, ¶39. Cf. Pelliot, 1922–23, p. 24, with text and facsimile of letter and seal; TR, ¶2, n. 5.
24. Ibid., ch. VIII, ¶14.
25. Ibid., Prologus, ¶3.
26. Ibid., ch. V, ¶13, ¶33, respectively.
27. TR, ¶18, ¶22.
28. TR, ¶3, n. 2.
29. TR, ¶19, n. 1.
30. TR, ¶11, n. 2.
31. TR, ¶23, n. 12.
32. TR, ¶47, n. 3.
33. TR, ¶23, n. 6.
34. TR, ¶12.

Narayrgen,[35] Prester John's firearms,[36] the battle with the dogs of Nochoy Kadzar,[37] the blood-shed at the Battle of the Kalka,[38] the Unipeds,[39] the Mongols' incipient panic at Liegnitz,[40] the same at the Battle of the Sayo and Batu's action to halt it,[41] the recent strange weather in Mongolia,[42] and the friars' sermon on the sinfulness of homicide, drink, and looting ("at which they"—the Mongol audience—"laughed and paid no attention whatever").[43] All these, except the last, involve special points on which Benedict felt it necessary to cite his authority, and no doubt reflect only a small proportion of the material obtained from Mongol sources. In particular, it seems highly probable that the many Mongol names and derivations of places and peoples, most of which are peculiar to TR, indicate Mongol sources for the matters to which they relate.[44]

Carpini and TR give by far the most detailed and correct account of Mongol history, genealogy, ethnography, and military methods to be found in any western medieval source, not excluding Rubruck and Marco Polo;[45] on the two latter subjects, indeed, they are superior to medieval oriental sources.[46] On ethnographical and military matters TR is inferior to *Carpini*, omitting much valuable detail found in *Carpini* and supplying only a small, though still notable, amount of new material.[47] It seems that in these sections the friars' original brief draft which formed the basis of both *Carpini* and TR was enriched from their notebooks far more in *Carpini* than in TR, though De Bridia's editorial lack of interest may be partly to blame for the bareness of TR. In the historical section, however, TR not only is more nearly equivalent to *Carpini* in the common material but also supplies further information of the highest importance. Herein lies the chief value of TR as a new primary source.

A detailed survey of the features peculiar to TR will be found in the italicized portions of the Latin text and translation, and in the notes on these. The following, however, may be selected as deserving special mention.

One of the chief gaps in knowledge of early Mongol history has lain in the almost complete silence of contemporary sources, both western and oriental, on the last years of Chingis Khan's eldest son Jochi, between his retirement after the capture of Urgendj in 1221 to the steppes north of the Aral Sea, where he is generally thought to have remained sullen and idle,[48] and his death

35. TR, ¶14.
36. TR, ¶17.
37. TR, ¶18.
38. TR, ¶20.
39. TR, ¶22.
40. TR, ¶28.
41. TR, ¶29.
42. TR, ¶35.
43. TR, ¶42.
44. Cf. TR, ¶3, n. 3 (*Tatar*); ¶13, n. 4 (*Narayrgen*); ¶18, n. 2 (*Nochoy ḳadzar*); ¶20, n. 6 (*Coniuzzu*); ¶21, n. 3 (*Ucorcolon, Nochoyterim*); ¶38, n. 1 (*Sira ordu*).
45. Rubruck, however, is a close rival as an observer of ethnographical matters (cf. Rockhill, pp. 53–83, and passim). For Polo's account see Yule, *Polo,* Vol. 1, pp. 226–69.
46. Cf., e.g., the account in Juvaini, Vol. 1, pp. 19–34. Cf. Wyngaert, pp. 10–11, on the merits of *Carpini*.
47. Including, in particular, an interesting though brief account of Mongol invasion strategy, which *Carpini* omits apparently from mere oversight (see TR, ¶56, ¶59, and ¶56, n. 1).
48. Cf. Grousset, 1939, pp. 300, 308–09; 317–18; idem., 1941, pp. 236–38, 278, 391; d'Ohsson, Vol. 1, pp. 294, 322, 353–54, 447.

in 1227. Yet he was confirmed shortly before his death in the possession of a vast appanage, including not only his own conquests of the cities on the lower Syr-daria and of Urgendj, but the land westward "to the remotest parts of Saksin and Bulgar (on the Volga) and as far in that direction as the hoof of Mongol horse had penetrated";[49] and in 1236 Batu's great invasion of the West set out from "the horde of the sons of Jochi" near the frontier of the Bulgars.[50] Wolff, without citing any authority, represents Jochi as advancing from Urgendj in 1221 between the Aral and the Caspian to the Volga, receiving the submission of the Kangli, Pechenegs, and Saksins on the way and lending to Subetei and Jebe a large part of his army in time for the Kalka battle in 1222.[51] Wolff's account—whether it draws from sources not yet rediscovered or, as is more likely, is merely an unconfessed but intelligent guess—is strikingly confirmed by the narrative in TR, garbled as it is. Jochi, we are told, conquered the Turcomans, the Bisermins (i.e. the Khorasmians), and the Kangits and beat the Comans and Russians on the Kalka.[52] Then, strangely but significantly, part of the same story is retold of Jochi's son Batu, though it manifestly belongs in reality to Jochi. "Batu"—in fact Jochi—conquers the Bisermins, capturing the cities of Barchin, Iankint and Ornas (Barghalikent, Yanghikent and Urgendj, taken by Jochi in 1219–21), and then subdues the Turcomans, the Kangli and the Comans[53]—at which point the tale leaps from the lifetime of Jochi to Batu's actual capture of Kiev in 1240.[54] Jochi, who was rumored to be a bastard and had quarreled with his brothers and father,[55] had a bad press in his homeland, which accounts for the silence of eastern sources. But in his Kipchak appanage, it seems, the truth was known and remembered, though with exaggeration, and was recorded there by the friars. In the light of *Carpini*-TR the expeditions of Jochi and of Subetei and Jebe may be seen as inseparable parts of a huge pincer movement, executed under the orders of Chingis Khan and the supreme command of Jochi and planned to meet at the Volga.[56] In the version current at Batu's camp and reported by TR, the whole operation is carried out by Jochi, and the names of Subetei and Jebe have disappeared even from the Battle of the Kalka in 1222. Similarly, a generation later, Batu is known to have been jealous of Subetei and to have tried to minimize his preponderant part in the strategy of the Hungarian campaign of 1241.[57] The friars seem to have heard the story twice over, recording first the campaign of 1219–22 as told of Jochi alone, and secondly the two campaigns of 1219–22 and 1240–42 as of Batu, without realizing that only the latter belonged to Batu. With all its confusions and exaggerations, if the TR narrative can bear the burden here placed upon it, this new light on Jochi is TR's most important contribution to historical knowledge.

49. Juvaini, Vol. 1, p. 42.

50. d'Ohsson, Vol. 2, pp. 110–12, 619–24; Bretschneider, Vol. 1, p. 309.

51. Wolff, pp. 97–8, 100–01.

52. TR, ¶20, and nn.

53. TR, ¶24, ¶25, and nn.

54. TR, ¶25, n. 2.

55. Grousset, 1941, pp. 67–71, 228–30, 236–38; *Secret History*, ¶99, ¶102, ¶254–55, ¶260.

56. Had this not been so, the mission of Subetei and Jebe would have been impossibly dangerous, and contrary to Mongol strategy, since their left flank would have been exposed to the Bulgars on their return eastward; and in fact, even with Jochi's support, they were severely mauled by the Bulgars during this stage of their journey (TR, ¶20, n. 7). Ibn-el-ethir and Rashid-ed-din indeed state that Chingis Khan ordered Jochi to attack the Comans, but that he disobeyed (d'Ohsson, Vol. 1, p. 447).

57. Bretschneider, Vol. 1, p. 332; Grousset, 1941, pp. 299–300.

In the new context of TR a decisive solution can be given to the long-fought controversy concerning the identity of "Ornas". The arguments for equating that city with Tana at the mouth of the Don can be shown to be ill-founded, and it now seems certain that "Ornas" is Urgendj, with elements drawn probably from Matrica on the straits of Kerch and from Soldaia in the Crimea, rather than from Tana.[58]

The account of Batu's Polish and Hungarian campaigns in 1241, detailed and accurate in TR but somewhat perfunctory in *Carpini,* is unique among western sources in drawing directly from Mongol information, which the friars no doubt acquired in Batu's own territory. The friars learned new details of the Mongols' losses in the early stages of their invasion of Poland, their difficulties in the great battles of Liegnitz and the Sayo river, the slaying of two of their generals, the fate of Duke Henry of Silesia and his severed head, and Batu's harangue, in the true spirit of Mongol epic, at the bridge over the Sayo—though this last is given fully only in *Carpini.*[59] The Polish and Hungarian campaigns would be of special interest to the Polish Benedict; and the TR version, in blaming the Poles for envious disunion and the Hungarians for arrogant negligence, and in giving a preponderant role at the Sayo to the heroic Duke Coloman, seems to reflect Benedict's personal views.

A further highly remarkable feature of TR is the list of nations conquered by the Mongols. A similar catalogue appears in *Carpini* but has never attracted sufficient attention, partly owing to its chaotic order. The TR list, however, shows a significant order and grouping, which appears to follow the Mongol's own geographical division of their empire into left-hand (i.e. east), center (i.e. Mongolia) and right-hand (i.e. west). It seems likely that the two lists derive from two otherwise unknown Mongol documents, perhaps inscriptions, giving variant versions of a comprehensive catalogue of Mongol conquests, in the manner of the briefer, regional lists recorded in the *Secret History.*[60]

Paradoxically, however, although the contributions of *Carpini*-TR to historical evidence are unique and important, the fabulous elements in their account of Mongol history are no less significant and valuable. The still recent events of the reign of Ogedei are told with relative accuracy, more so than in any other western source; but the early stages of Chingis Khan's rise to power are here and there strangely distorted, while the largely unhistorical expeditions of Chingis Khan and Tolui, which occupy the middle place in the narrative, are a wild romance of monsters and the supernatural. This section contrasts not only with the objective and scholarly accounts of the later Persian and Chinese sources, on which our knowledge of Mongol history is mainly founded, but even with the epic but still basically factual *Secret History* of the Mongols themselves.

The failure of the friars to obtain veracious information is neither mysterious nor unusual. Rashid-ed-din, writing in 1303, complained that previous histories of the Mongols were "based on popular stories, capriciously arranged, and the few facts they reported were denied by the princes of the house of Chingis Khan and the chiefs of the Mongol nation".[61] At the time of the Carpini mission the original Mongol documents, such as the *Secret History,* later used in the

---

58. TR, ¶24, and Excursus A, pp. 102–04 below.
59. TR, ¶27–30, and nn.
60. TR, ¶34, and Excursus B, pp. 104–06 below.
61. d'Ohsson, Vol. 1, pp. xxxiv–xxxv.

Chinese *Yuan-shi,* and the lost *Altan Debter* or *Golden Book,* afterward consulted by Rashid-ed-din, were still the private property of the Mongol princes. In the absence of reliable sources all reports of the rise of Chingis Khan available to the West, both before and long after the Carpini mission, were mainly fabulous.

Such reports fall into two main classes, both arising in the Near East from rumors of the Khorasmian War, and deriving one from Nestorian Christian, the other from Mohammedan sources. In the first of these the onslaught of the Mongols was connected in various ways with the Nestorian hero Prester John, the semilegendary Christian priest-king of an indeterminate realm in central or further Asia, who was expected for more than a century to destroy Islam and join arms with the Crusaders in Palestine.[62] The legend of Prester John first reached Europe toward 1145, originating in Nestorian rumors of the foundation of the Karakhitayan Empire, partly Buddhist and partly Nestorian Christian, by the Khitayan exiles expelled from North China in the 1120s by the Kin (Jurchet) invaders, and the defeat by their Gurkhan Yeliu-Tache of the Mohammedan Karakhanids of Kashgar and Transoxiana, the Seljuk Sultan of Iran, and the Shah of Khorasmia in 1128–41.[63] The strength, persistence, and ubiquity of the legend were due not only to credulity and wishful thinking but to the real existence in many parts of Asia of semi-Christian kingdoms hostile to Islam, and of Nestorian communities which conserved and spread in good faith the tales created by their distant co-believers. In the time of the Khorasmian War, Prester John, or his equally legendary son David, was at first briefly identified as Chingis Khan himself, in his capacity as the great destroyer of the Mohammedans.[64] Next, and more lastingly, when it became too clear that Chingis Khan was the enemy no less of Christendom than of Islam, and when further rumors from the Nestorians of the Far East reached their fellows in the Near East and became preponderant in the evolution of the legend, Prester John or King David was equated with yet another historical figure, the Nestorian Wang Khan of the Keraits, whom Chingis Khan had conquered in 1203; though their imaginary realm remained located in India. Chingis Khan, it was now believed, was the rebellious vassal of John or David; his overlord had demanded his help for the invasion of Khorasmia, whereupon Chingis Khan had fought and slain him, married his daughter (actually Chingis Khan married the Wang Khan's niece Ibaka Beki and gave another niece, the Christian Sorghoktani, to his son Tolui), usurped his kingdom, and invaded Khorasmia himself.[65]

62. For general accounts of the Prester John legend see d'Avezac, pp. 547–64; d'Ohsson, Vol. 1, pp. 52–53, 629–32; Oppert, passim; Beazley, *Texts,* pp. 278–80; Yule, *Cathay,* Vol. 1, pp. 173–82; Yule, *Polo,* Vol. 1, pp. 226–45; Rockhill, pp. xxxi–xxxii, 108–15. The relevant texts are collected and edited by Zarncke.

63. Grousset, 1939, pp. 219–22; ibid., 1941, pp. 18–21.

64. The first version involving the Mongols to reach Europe arose early in the Khorasmian War, when Jacques de Vitry, writing at Acre in Palestine in 1221, ascribed the invasion of Khorasmia to "David, King of India, commonly known as Prester John" (Zarncke, pp. 4–59).

65. Cf. Albericus Trium Fontium, *Chronicon,* under the year 1237, in *MGH,* Vol. 23, p. 942; Zarncke, pp. 60–62, and the similar version told in 1247 to Friar Ascelin's mission by the Nestorian priest Simeon, otherwise Rabban-ata, who claimed, perhaps truly, to have been a courtier of Prester John himself (i.e. the Wang Khan, who was slain in 1203) in his youth (Zarncke, pp. 62–67; Vincent, *Speculum Historiale,* Book XXX, chs. 69, 70; Pelliot, 1924, pp. 239, 242–43, 247). The same story was still current when Marco Polo recorded it *ca.* 1275 (Yule, *Polo,* Vol. 1, pp. 226–45). A unique but most significant variant is told by Rubruck, who confuses the first Gurkhan of the Karakhitai, Yeliu-Tache, with Chingis Khan's enemy the Gurkhan Kuchluk of the Naimans nearly a century later, and identifies this composite figure as "King John", saying accordingly that he was a Naiman. Rubruck regards the Wang Khan Toghril as King John's brother, and complains that the Nestorians say of King John "ten times more than was true", because it is their

In the alternative report, based primarily on the Mongol legend that their ancestors had broken from the mountain barrier of Ergene-kun, the Mongols were identified with the tribes of Gog-Magog whom Alexander the Great was said to have enclosed within the Caspian Mountains.[66] Mixed versions followed, in which Chingis Khan was supposed first to have led his people from the Caspian Mountains and then to have slain Prester John before invading Khorasmia.[67]

Modified traces of both these rumors are visible in the *Carpini*-TR narrative, in which Chingis Khan encounters the enclosed tribes of the Caspian Mountains[68] and his son Tolui fights a battle with Prester John.[69] Here, however, both episodes result in an ignominious defeat of the Mongols. The two common elements, preceded as they are by a relatively historical account of the rise of Chingis Khan, are no longer needed to explain that rise; they have lost their aetiological function and become peripheral. They now play only a vestigial part in an elaborate series of folk tales, told of Chingis Khan in no other known source, in which (as is shown below by the detailed analysis in the notes to TR) ingredients from the Alexander Romance, Mongol and Chinese legend, the epic of Oghuz Khan the mythical ancestor of the Turks, the Nestorian concepts of Gog-Magog and Prester John, together with a modicum of historical fact, are all blended to form a Chingis Romance.[70]

At first sight the fact that the story was obtained by the friars at the Mongol court—together with the new evidence of TR, in which Mongol informants are explicitly cited and Mongol names (*Narayrgen* and *Nochoy kadzar*) are given for the People of the Sun and the Land of Dogs[71]—may tempt us to believe that this Chingis Romance is of actual Mongol creation. But it seems impossible to ascribe a truly Mongol origin, however ignorant and popular, to a tale so oblivious of recent historical fact and so counter to national pride, where the Alexander and Nestorian components are preponderant and the Mongol themes are minimal, and the attitude toward Chingis Khan and Tolui, who suffer a series of semicomic and fantastic defeats, is overtly hostile and contemptuous. An origin among Uighur Nestorians in the Mongol court, followed when elaboration was complete by a degree of Mongol acceptance (perhaps only as of an amusing fiction) and Mongol nomenclature, would seem to account for the facts.[72] The pre-

---

way "to make a great story out of nothing", and that when he passed through King John's country, "no one knew anything of him except for a few Nestorians" (Rockhill, pp. 108–15).

66. The earliest version to reach Europe was apparently that brought by the envoys of the Ishmaelite Assassins, seeking aid against Chormaghan, to Louis IX of France and Henry II of England in 1238, where the Mongols are said to have burst from the Caspian Mountains or "from the mountains of the Arctic". The Assassins had no help from the English: "Let these dogs devour one another," said Peter des Roches, Bishop of Winchester. See Matthew Paris, Vol. 3, pp. 488–89; Vol. 4, pp. 76–78; Rockhill, pp. xiv–xvii.

67. E.g. Joinville, the historian of the Seventh Crusade, writing *ca.* 1300, in Zarncke, pp. 81–87, and Ricoldus de Monte Crucis, also writing *ca.* 1300 (Ricoldus, pp. 118–20). Ricoldus significantly says, whether truly or not, that the Mongols themselves say they are descended from Gog-Magog, and adds that their name *Mogoli* is a corruption of *Magogoli!* As a further proof he remarks: "They hate Alexander the Great exceedingly, and cannot bear to hear his name without losing their temper"!

68. TR, ¶12, ¶15, and nn.

69. TR, ¶17, and nn.

70. TR, ¶11–¶18, and nn.

71. TR, ¶13, n. 4; ¶18, n. 2.

72. Chingis Khan's adoption of the Uighur script and of Uighur civil servants, many of whom were Nestorian Christians, led to the acclimatization of Uighur culture and literature in the Mongol court. "They consider the Uighur

ceding narrative, although relatively closer to history, shows the same derogatory view of Chingis Khan, together with a historical bias and ignorance—notably in the strange misunderstanding of the role of the Keraits and the Karakhitayans[73]—appropriate to a foreign source but inconceivable in an indigenous Mongol origin. It appears, therefore, that the whole of the friars' account of Mongol history up to the death of Chingis Khan, with the exception of the information concerning Jochi obtained in Batu's territory, must be ascribed to this Chingis Romance.

Although the Romance, as such, must be admitted as genuine, it remains manifestly unlikely that the Mongols themselves were unaware of their own recent past. It may well be that the friars, who came partly as spies, were deliberately deceived and mocked. Several passages show that their informants were in a jesting mood;[74] and it would be absurd to suppose that no more historically accurate narrative would have been available in the Mongol court if Carpini and Benedict had sought further and been allowed to find the truth. The part played by the captive Russian priests, who acted as their interpreters during the interview and swore stoutly in corroboration of its most amazing features,[75] is open to grave suspicion! The Russian Orthodox clerics may well have enjoyed the opportunity of deluding the friars, whose church was the immemorial enemy of theirs and who converted their own Grand Duke Yaroslav to Rome beneath their very noses.[76] But the Chingis Romance, which bears all the evidence of extended elaboration from varied sources, can hardly have been concocted for the occasion and must be accepted as an authentic folk myth. It is noteworthy that the prevalence of equally fabulous reports is attested in *Carpini*-TR even outside the context of the Chingis Romance, and in relation to the events of still more recent times. The same trends appear in the tales of the steam-fed Parossits and the Dog-heads and Ox-foots obtained in Batu's country,[77] in the story of wild men with jointless legs in the desert south of Ogedei's city of Omyl,[78] and in the *conte drôlatique* of the Unipeds said (in *Carpini* only) to have been encountered by Chormaghan during his Armenian expedition of 1239.[79]

The relevance of the *Carpini*-TR Chingis Romance extends far beyond its immediate associations with the Carpini mission and medieval Asian folklore. We have here a unique labora-

language and script to be the height of knowledge and learning", Juvaini complains (Vol. 1, p. 7; Vol. 2, p. 523). A Turkish Alexander Romance once existed, though now lost, and was presumably available to the Uighurs; indeed, it may be conjectured that the recently discovered Mongol fragment of an Alexander Romance in Uighur script (see TR, ¶13, n. 5; ¶15, n. 2) is perhaps a translation or adaptation of such an Uighur-Turkish version. Similarly the Uighurs might be expected to possess an Oghuz Khan epic (cf. TR, ¶18, n. 3). An Uighur Nestorian source in the Mongol court would account for all the elements in the Chingis Romance here listed, and no alternative hypothesis seems conceivable. A Kerait Nestorian source seems to be ruled out by the curious misunderstanding and ignorance of the Kerait role in Mongol history which is shown in the Chingis Romance as recorded in TR (cf. the following note 73).

73. TR, ¶4, n. 2; ¶5, n. 1; ¶6, n. 1; ¶7, n. 1; ¶8, n. 4.

74. TR, ¶12, and n. 5; ¶17. But a comic note is evident throughout the successive discomfitures of Chingis Khan and Tolui.

75. See above, n. 26.

76. See above, p. 37, n. 15.

77. *Carpini*, ch. V, ¶30, ¶31; TR, ¶21, and nn.

78. *Carpini*, ch. V, ¶6; not in TR. Incidentally, these monsters are noted at lat. 65°–70°, long. 165° in the Strassburg Ptolemy Atlas of 1522 (Nordenskiöld, *Facsimile Atlas*, p. 101, fig. 63), where the source is presumably the abridgment of *Carpini* in Vincent, *Speculum Historiale*, Book XXXII, ch. 8.

79. *Carpini*, ch. V, ¶33; TR, ¶22, and nn.

tory specimen of a popular myth embroidering upon events beginning only fifty years and ending only nineteen years before it was recorded. We are able to compare it not only with the diverse legendary ingredients from which it was compounded but with our abundant knowledge of the objective historical facts from which it so astonishingly departs, and even with a contemporary but entirely different epic and aristocratic treatment of the same happenings, the Mongol *Secret History*. The implications of this situation for the evolution of other epics or romances founded more or less distantly upon real events—the Homeric lays, the Alexander Romance, *Beowulf,* the Arthurian and Charlemagne cycles—are far-reaching and demand further investigation.

The fiction in TR, it may be claimed, is no less valuable than the fact; but our chief gratitude to Friar Benedict and his editor C. de Bridia is due, perhaps, to their unwitting collaboration, nearly two centuries later, in the compilation of the Vinland Map.

6. EDITORIAL METHOD

The following first presentation of the Latin text of the Tartar Relation is intended to supply a serviceable and readable reconstruction of the archetype, together with a schematic collation with the text of *Carpini.*

The manuscript of TR is legible and not unduly corrupt, but heavily contracted, unparagraphed, and capricious in spelling, punctuation, and capitalization. An exact transcription would only transfer to the reader a burden that belongs to the editor, and is fortunately made unnecessary by the photographic facsimile of the original included in the present publication. In the working text here offered contractions are resolved, numbered paragraphing is supplied, and punctuation and capitalization are normalized. The spelling of the TR manuscript has been retained when it falls within the usual range of medieval Latin orthography, but various unimportant vagaries of the scribe (e.g. *excercitus* for *exercitus, habundans* for *abundans, sagita* for *sagitta, y* for *i*) have been silently corrected—although they may conceivably go back to the editor De Bridia himself. All significant departures from the manuscript original are recorded in the textual footnotes.

When a text exists only in a single exemplar, emendation must depend mainly upon the presumable sense and upon paleographical probability or possibility. Except in proper names, the Latin wording of *Carpini* differs almost always from that of TR and therefore gives little aid in verbal emendation; but it occasionally gives a useful correction of the sense. Most of the proper names, however, are fortunately common to both TR and *Carpini;* accordingly, where the TR reading is corrupt the best reading available in *Carpini* manuscripts has been substituted, as giving in all probability the reading of the TR archetype. Much further work upon the text will have to be undertaken by future editors; and if a new manuscript of TR should ever come to light, it will doubtless reveal other unforeseeable corrections. However, the present editor has done all in his power to detect and solve textual difficulties, and trusts that in most cases the emendations he offers may seem certain, probable, or at least acceptable. The chief points of doubt, few of which appear to affect any fundamental issue, are discussed in the commentary.

The new evidence of TR involves many and various reinterpretations of the significance of *Carpini,* which call for an ultimate full-scale edition of both works, preferably by a specialist in

Mongol matters, and including parallel texts of both *Carpini* and TR. The present edition provides the minimal basis for collation through marginal references to Wyngaert's edition of *Carpini,* the only one that is equipped with satisfactory paragraph divisions, and by printing in italics the passages of TR that are not found in *Carpini.*

In the English translation, as well as in the commentary and introduction, the proper names of persons, tribes, and places have generally been conventionalized or modernized, and should be compared with the actual forms in the Latin text. The available forms of Mongol names differ bewilderingly in spelling and phonetics according to the language and personal preferences both of the primary sources and of later authors; while the rigorously accurate system of transliteration adopted by present-day Mongolists is probably too formidable for the general reader, and certainly beyond the competence of this editor. The forms here given represent an eclectic and no doubt unsatisfactory compromise between all these factors. The incorrect but traditional term "Tartar", which is generally found as a synonym for "Mongol" in the Latin text of TR, is retained in the translation; but in the introduction and commentary the Mongols proper are called by their true name.

The commentary is based partly on the editions of *Carpini* by d'Avezac, Rockhill, Beazley, Pullé, Wyngaert, and Risch, partly on the other sources cited in the references and the Bibliography, but with particular heed to the work of Pelliot, Grousset, Professor F. W. Cleaves, Dr. J. A. Boyle, and others who in the past fifty years have transformed the face of Mongol studies. Wherever possible, however, the editor has endeavored to form his own opinion, in the light of all these, from examination of the primary sources as far as these were available to him in European languages.

The editor is deeply grateful to Dr. J. A. Boyle of the Department of Persian Studies in the University of Manchester for much generous help in philological and other matters, but remains responsible for all errors. He hopes that this pioneering effort by a well-meaning layman may meet with more leniency than it deserves from the expert scholars who will assess, for many years to come, the true significance of that amazing document the Tartar Relation.

[1ʳ] *Here begins the History of the Tartars:*

¶1. *To the very reverend father Friar Boguslaus,*[1] *minister of the Minorite friars dwelling in Bohemia and Poland, Friar C. de Bridia,*[2] *most minor of Minorites, duly and devotedly submits his filial obedience, and requests in return for the obedient accomplishment of his task that whosoever desires to study the subject should approach not only easy but even difficult matters with willing heart in accordance with the wish of his superior. In deference to your paternal authority, although the task is beyond the powers of my talent, I have briefly set down in writing what I have understood*[3] *of the Tartars along with the venerable friars of our order, namely Friar John, legate of the Apostolic See to all nations outside Christendom, especially the Tartars,*[4,5] *and his companions Friar Benedict the Pole and Friar Ceslaus the Bohemian;*[6] *and I have tried to avoid boring the reader, so that your devotion, hearing my story, and knowing how to extract useful knowledge on earthly matters from the marvellous and hidden judgments of Almighty God, which now grow clear at the end of the centuries when the redemption of the saints draws near, may rise to His praise and love.*[7]

¶2. *Be it known therefore that according to the Tartars and certain others the habitable fabric of this world*[1] *is divided into two principal parts, namely East and West, extending in breadth between the points of summer and winter sunrise and sunset. The West begins at Livonia and reaches all the way from Prussia*[2] *to Greece and so further, and includes the Universal Church of the Catholic Faith.*[3] *Accordingly even the Tartars recognize the apostolic authority of the Pope throughout the West.*[4] *The remaining part, however, is called* the East, in which the coun-

¶1. 1. See above, p. 40.

2. See above, p. 40. The place name Bridia (not in Graesse, *Orbis Latinus*) is perhaps corrupt; but so many suitable place names can be produced by changing a letter or two—e.g. Brixia = Brescia, Brigia = Brie in Champagne, Frisia, etc.—that emendation seems impracticable. If "De Bridia" was himself a native of Eastern Europe, as his apparent knowledge of Polish or Czech perhaps implies (see above, p. 42), then Brega or Briga, meaning Brieg in Silesia, might be suggested. The editor is indebted to Mr. Laurence Witten for the latter conjecture.

3. The MS text *"que vidi de Tartaris intellexi"* is ungrammatical, and demands either the deletion of *vidi,* or the insertion of *et* or *vel* before *intellexi. Vidi* could be explained either as a dittography of the adjacent letters *ue de,* or as a well-meaning interpolation by a later scribe. If genuine, it could either be a mechanical repetition of Benedict's own apparent words as recorded by the chronicler of *Annales sancti Pantaleonis* at Cologne (*MGH,* Vol. 21, p. 542), *"sicut vidit et audivit",* corresponding to Carpini's *"vidimus . . . vel audivimus"* (*Carpini,* Prologus, ¶3), or De Bridia's own unintentionally ambiguous statement, meaning no more than that he saw the friars, and perhaps the Mongol clothing (cf. *Carpini,* ch. IX, ¶44) and other objects which they brought with them, with his own eyes. However this may be, the word presents no real difficulty, as it is quite certain that De Bridia did not accompany them on their journey (see above, p. 41).

4. Carpini himself gives his title as *"Sedis Apostolice nuntius ad Tartaros et ad nationes alias orientis"* (*Carpini,* Prologus, ¶1). Either version indicates that, besides his main mission to the Mongols, he had powers to transact papal business in every country he might visit which lay outside the jurisdiction of the Church of Rome. In particular, he carried Innocent's letters inviting rulers adhering to the Eastern Church to declare allegiance to Rome (see above, p. 36).

5. The MS reading *"Tartaros cacoros"* suggests that the original reading was *Tataros.* This unusual form occurs several times in TR (e.g. ¶13, ¶30), and was perhaps used by Benedict himself. Carpini likewise told Friar Salimbene "that the Tartars were called Tattars [*sic*], not Tartars" (Golubovich, Vol. 1, p. 192). The correct Mongol

HISTORIA TARTARORUM

[1ʳ] *Incipit historia Tartarorum:*

¶1. *Reverendissimo patri fratri Boguslao*⁽ᵃ⁾ *ministro fratrum minorum in Boemia et Polonia degentium*⁽ᵇ⁾ *frater C. de Bridia inter minores minimus filialis obediencie subiectionem tam debitam quam devotam perfecte obediencie hoc exposcit officium ut si quis in eo exercitari desiderat non solum facilia verum etiam ardua sibi volenti aggrediatur animo secundum sui superioris voluntatem. Vestre paternitati quamvis supra vires ingenii mei obaudiens que de*⁽ᶜ⁾ *Tartaris intellexi cum venerabilibus fratribus nostri ordinis, fratre videlicet Johanne sedis apostolice legato ad omnes externas nationes precipue tamen ad Tartaros*⁽ᵈ⁾ *et fratre Benedicto Polono et fratre Ceslao Boemo sociis eius, breviter in scripto posui cavens fastidium lectorum et ut vestra haec audiens devotio que de terrenicis novit utilia elicere ex mirabilibus*⁽ᵉ⁾ *dei omnipotentis iudiciis tam occultis que in fine iam clarescunt saeculorum in quo appropinquat sanctorum redempcio exurgat in laudem eius pariter et amorem.*

¶2. *Sciendum igitur quod secundum Tartaros et quosdam alios habitabilis mundi huius machina dividitur in duas principales partes*⁽ᵃ⁾ *orientalem videlicet et occidentalem large sumptas secundum quod sol oritur et occidit estivo tempore et brumali. Inchoatur autem occidens a terra Livonie et vadit a Prusia*⁽ᵇ⁾ *usque in Greciam et deinceps et continet in se universam ecclesiam catholice fidei. Unde et Tartari appellant apostolicum magnum papam per totum occidentem.*

¶1. (*a*) MS *Reverentissimo ... Bogirdao.*   (*b*) MS *regentium.*   (*c*) MS *que vidi de.*   (*d*) MS *tartaros cacoros.*
(*e*) MS *mirabililibus.*
¶2. (*a*) MS omits *partes.*   (*b*) MS *vadit apusia*, with *r* above *u* inserted by corrector.

---

form was in fact *Tatar*, which was generally corrupted by Europeans into *Tartari*, from false analogy with the classical *Tartarus*, meaning Hell.

6. See above, pp. 35–36.

7. The obscure syntax of the opening paragraph, though there may be latent corruptions, gives a fair idea of De Bridia's poor Latinity when left to his own devices. The closing words suggest the idea current among the early Franciscans, who were influenced by the heretical writings of Joachim de Flore, that the world was now in its third and last age, that of the Holy Ghost (cf. *SCMH*, Vol. 2, p. 671). Boguslaus and De Bridia probably identified the Mongols, as others did, with the armies of Anti-Christ heralding Judgment Day (cf. Rockhill, p. xvi, n. 3).

¶2. 1. Evidently an echo of the words *"mundialia elementa machinae"* in Innocent's letter to Kuyuk of 13 March 1245, beginning *"Cum non solum ..."* (Wadding, Vol. 3, p. 135), which in turn derive ultimately from Lucretius, 5.96, *"moles et machina mundi"*.

2. Livonia, the district round the Gulf of Riga in the Baltic, was then an outpost of the Roman Church controlled under the Bishop of Riga by the Brethren of the Sword, who in 1237 were amalgamated with the Teutonic Order (*SCMH*, Vol. 2, pp. 745–46). Prussia, roughly corresponding to the modern East Prussia, lay southwest of Livonia, and was occupied by the knights of the Teutonic Order, who fought in alliance with the Poles against the Mongols at the battle of Liegnitz in 1241 (see above, p. 32; below, ¶33, n. 3).

3. This idea of the division between East and West is politicoreligious rather than geographical, since instead of the customary meridian of Jerusalem or the frontier of Asia on the Don (as Rubruck, ed. Rockhill, p. 96), the eastern limit of the Church of Rome is taken as the dividing line. It may be true that the Mongols adopted a similar division, which would correspond roughly to the boundary of their own empire in the 1240s.

4. Carpini himself, as he told Friar Salimbene, was asked by Kuyuk which was the more powerful in the West, the Pope or the Emperor, and dutifully replied: "The Pope" (Golubovich, Vol. 1, p. 192). Cf. below, ¶47, n. 3.

try of the Tartars is situated, at the point where the East adjoins the Arctic, being adjacent to the Arctic Ocean, and is called Moal.[5]

¶3. In this country lived a certain man *of noble birth but cruel character* named Chingis, *from whom the Tartars took their origin. With the aid of a few followers* he commenced a life of plunder and *in due course, becoming crueler than ever,* began to capture other men *by stealth* and add them to the bondage of his iniquity.[1] *When he had amassed thirty henchmen he burst into open frenzy,* and entirely subdued to his command his native country *of Moal. Thereupon, as is the way of haughty men, he began to crave for more, and gathering an army proceeded against the country adjacent to the Tartars on the east,* which is called by them Zumoal, meaning Aquatic Mongols; *for zu in Tartar and aqua in Latin mean "water", moal means "earth", and "Mongols" signifies "natives of the earth".*[2] The inhabitants, however, called themselves Tartars after a *great and rushing* river named Tatar, which flows through their country. *Tata and Tartar correspond in their language to the Latin trahere and trahens, meaning "carry along".*[3] *It was their custom to choose a leader to rule over them, and at that time they had elected one named Cauli,*[4] whom [1ᵛ] Chingis conquered and incorporated his beaten followers in his own army. *For he had acquired the invariable habit of conscripting the soldiers of a conquered army into his own, with the object of subduing other countries by virtue of his increasing strength, as is clearly evident in his successors, who imitate his wicked cunning.*

¶4. Next with his entire army he hastened to the country called Merkit, which is adjacent to the Tartars *on the southwest,*[1] and subdued it by force to his own domination; and *adding its forces to his army* he entered the country bordering on the Merkits, which is called Mecrit,[2] and immediately conquered it. These four countries, namely Moal, Zumoal, Merkit, and Mecrit, have the same language, *but differ slightly one from the other in dialect, like the Bohemians, Poles, and Russians, or the people of Rome, Lombardy, and Friuli, or those of Austria, Thuringia, and Swabia, or those of Saxony, Flanders, and Westfalia.*[3] The natives of these countries resemble one another more or less closely in appearance.

---

5. TR typically prefers the form Moal, which is also used by Rubruck (Rockhill, pp. 112–15), representing the Turkish *Moghal,* the Mongol form being *Mongghol. Carpini* has *Mongal* (ch. V, ¶2). *Carpini* alone (ibid.) calls the tribe of Chingis "Yekamongal, that is Great Mongols", which may be compared with Kuyuk's seal as affixed to his reply to Innocent IV delivered by Carpini, in which he calls himself "Oceanic Khan of the Great Mongols (*yeke Mongghol ulusun dalain Khanu*)". See Pelliot (1922–23), p. 24.

¶3. 1. TR's account of Chingis's early conquests, though much telescoped, is mainly correct in topography and chronological order, and contains true details—his noble birth, small beginnings, and habit of embodying conquered warriors in his own army—which are not in *Carpini.*

2. Zumoal (*Carpini* has *Sumongal,* and gives the meaning but not the derivation) is a Turkish rather than a Mongol form, the Turkish for water being *su,* Mongol *usu* (Lessing, p. 887). Rubruck has *Su-Moal,* but does not explicitly identify these with the Tatars (Rockhill, p. 196). The name is also found in Persian and Chinese sources (d'Avezac, p. 532; Juvaini, Vol. 1, p. 196), and is possibly related to the Shui-Tatar or Water Tatar of the Chinese, though these seem to have been a Tungusic subtribe of the Kin in their homeland in eastern Manchuria (Bretschneider, Vol. 2, p. 275; Juvaini, Vol. 1, p. 296, n. 19). The Tatars dwelt on the lower Kerulen and by the lakes Bur Nor and Khulun Nor, hence perhaps their epithet. *Mongol* is in fact a proper name, without derivation, though Rashid-ed-din and other authors have given meanings such as "simple", "weak", and "brave" (Rockhill, p. 112).

3. The derivation of Tartar from a river Tatar is given independently by Matthew Paris (*Chronica Majora,* Vol. 7, p. 78; Rockhill, p. xvii), but lacks eastern authority; perhaps this, too, comes from confusion with the Su-Mongol,

Reliqua vero pars *dicitur* orientalis, in qua posita est terra Tartarorum ubi oriens iungitur aqui- [I, ¶3]
loni, habens contiguum mare oceanum aquilonis, et appellatur Moal. [V, ¶2]

¶3. Erat autem in ea vir quidam *nobilis quidem genere sed moribus crudelis,* nomine Cingis, *a* [V, ¶3]
quo et principium Tartari habuerunt. Hic *cum paucis hominibus suis* cepit spolia exercere.
Tandem crudelior effectus homines *furtim* capiebat et in sue iniquitatis dominio adiungebat.
Cumque triginta satellites sibi coacervasset prorumpens in vesaniam publicam totam terram sue
nativitatis *scilicet Moal* sue dominacioni per omnia subiugavit. *Quo facto cepit ut moris est*
elatorum appetere ampliora et congregato exercitu processit versus terram eis contiguam ex
parte orientis que ab eisdem denominatur Zumoal id est Aquatici Mongali, *zu enim Tartarice* [V, ¶2]
aqua dicitur latine moal terra, Mongali incole dicuntur terre. Ipsi autem appellabant se Tartaros
a fluvio *magno et impetuoso* qui transit terram eorum et dicitur Tatar. *Tata enim latine tra-*
here[a] *tartar trahens dicitur in lingua eorum. Isti sibimet ipsis superordinabant ducem, eo autem*
tempore prefecerant sibi ducem nomine Cauli quem [1ᵛ] Cingis devincens homines subiugatos [V, ¶3]
suo exercitui adunavit. *Consueverat enim devictos semper sibi aggregare ut maioris fortitudinis*
virtute alias terras superaret sicut patet in eius posteris manifeste qui ipsius malicie sunt sequaces.
¶4. Deinde cum toto exercitu properavit ad terram que dicitur Merkit[a] que etiam Tartaris est
contigua *ex parte occidentis estivalis,* quam manu valida sue dominacioni subiciens *apposita*
fortitudine suo exercitui terram Merkitis coniunctam que appellatur Mecrit[b] intravit et sibi [V, ¶2]
continuo subiugavit. Iste quatuor scilicet Moal, Zumoal, Merkit,[c] et Mecrit sunt unius labii
sed parum differunt inter se sicut Boemi et Poloni et Rutheni vel sicut Romani Lumbardi et
de Foro Iulii aut sicut Australes Turingi et Suevi seu Saxones Flamingi et Westfali. Homines
terrarum istarum assimulantur sibi in facie competenter.

¶3. (*a*) MS *dicitur tatar tata enim grece trahere,* with deletion dots under *grece.*
¶4. (*a*) MS *merbat.*   (*b*) MS *meerit.*   (*c*) MS *Zomoal merkat.*

---

since the Turkish *su* can mean river as well as water. The compiler of VM is alone both in showing this river (but see
below, p. 247, n. 9) and in calling it Tatartata, evidently through erroneously running together the two words *tatar*
and *tata,* which are unpunctuated in the TR MS. The derivation of Tatar from the Mongol for "carry" or "pull"
(Lessing, p. 785) is correct and peculiar to TR. Chingis in fact made two wars against the Tatars, *ca.* 1194 and 1202.
4. Cauli, peculiar to TR, does not resemble the name of any Tatar chieftain named in the Mongol records (cf.
Poucha, p. 57). It may be a confusion with Kao-li, the name of the reigning dynasty in Korea, named Caule by
Rubruck (Rockhill, p. 201).

¶4. 1. The Merkits dwelt northwest of the Mongols, not southwest. *Carpini*-TR conflate Chingis's campaigns of *ca.*
1187, 1197, 1201, 1204–05 against the Merkits into one.
2. The Mecrits, also named by Marco Polo (Yule, *Polo,* Vol. 1, p. 269), and called Crits by Rubruck (Rockhill, p.
111), are the Keraits, presumably, whom Chingis defeated after an initial setback in 1203. The prefix Me- may be
either a contamination with the Merkits, or a "double jumble", to use Yule's picturesque term, like Gog and
Magog, etc. Cf. d'Avezac, pp. 534–36; Beazley, *Texts,* p. 322.
3. The remark on the four nations speaking the same language in different dialects is not quite correct. The Tatars
and Merkits spoke dialects of Mongol, but the Keraits were Turks, though somewhat Mongolized, and spoke
Turkish (see Poucha, pp. 57–62). However, Mongol and Turkish were both offshoots from the ancient Altaic stem,
remained in constant contact, and retained or borrowed many words in common. The comparison with European
language-groups, peculiar to TR, seems typical of Benedict's philological interests. In the district of Friuli, between
the head of the Adriatic and the Carnic and Julian Alps, a dialect of the Rhaeto-Romance group, evolved from
Latin with Celtic elements, is spoken to this day.

¶5. Next[1] Chingis collected an army and marched against the country called Uighur,[2] whose inhabitants were Christians of the Nestorian sect. After conquering them the Mongols adopted their alphabet for writing (for previously they had no alphabet), and so returned to their own country.

¶6. Soon afterward Chingis collected a still more powerful force and entered *the eastern country called Esurscakita, the natives of which call themselves* Kitai, *to whom the Mongols, and the other three provinces speaking their language, had formerly paid tribute. This country is large, very extensive, and was then extremely rich,* having a *powerful and energetic* Emperor who, hearing the news and *violently enraged,* met Chingis and his army with a numerous multitude *in a certain vast desert,* inflicting such slaughter on the Mongols that only seven survived, *though a larger number of other nationalities succeeded in escaping. Seeing this the aforesaid Emperor scorned even to gather spoil from the slain.*[1] Chingis, however, fled *unnoticed* to his own country and for a short time abated his wickedness.

¶7. Next to the Tartars on the west, however, is a certain country called Naiman, *very mountainous and immoderately cold,* to whose king the Tartars and all the neighboring provinces at that time paid royal tribute. The king died *at the period when Chingis was resting from war,* but left *three* little sons as successors to the throne. Hearing of this, Chingis *began to covet the boys' kingdom,* and collecting an army commenced to invade [2^r] the realm of the Naimans. *Seeing his strength, they retreated,* and joining forces with the Karakitai, or Black Kitai (*kara in Tartar means 'black'*) attacked the Mongols in a valley between two lofty mountains; *and occupying the road which afforded the only access into the country from that direction, they resisted for a very long time.* The friars of our Order traveled through this valley and country on their journey to the Tartars. *At last some of the Mongols crossed the mountains at a lower point a long way from the army, while others climbed the precipices where only mountain goats can find a way. Friar Benedict tried to take this route on horseback, but the Tartars would not allow him, lest he should lose both horse and life. The rest advanced upon the front line*

¶5. 1. The events of TR ¶5–9 correspond to *Carpini,* ch. V, ¶4–9. *Carpini* diverges somewhat from the historical facts and from their chronological order, while TR differs still more curiously from *Carpini.* The correct order of events after the defeat of the Keraits in the autumn of 1203 would be as follows (cf. above, pp. 29–30): (1) Defeat of Naimans in 1204; (2) Final defeat of Merkits in 1205; (3) Tangut campaigns of 1205–09; (4) Proclamation of Chingis Khan in 1206; (5) Submission of Uighurs, Uirats, and other tribes in 1207; (6) War against the Kin of Northern China from 1211 onward; (7) Defeat of Kuchluk, Gur-Khan of the Karakhitai, in 1218. This historical order of events becomes the following in *Carpini* and TR:

(1), (7) *Carpini,* ch. V, ¶4, 5 = TR ¶7. Defeat of Naimans and Karakhitai.

——[*Carpini,* ch. V, ¶6, not in TR.

Digression on the foundation of the town of Omyl in the country of the Karakhitai by Ogedei, and on a tribe of wild men to the south of Omyl.]

——*Carpini,* ch. V, ¶7 = TR, ¶6. Defeat of Chingis by the "Kitai", i.e. Keraits.

(5) *Carpini,* ch. V, ¶8 = TR, ¶5, ¶8. Defeat of Uighurs (TR, ¶5), and of Uirats, etc. (TR, ¶8).

(6), (4) *Carpini,* ch. V, ¶9 = TR, ¶9. War against Kitai (i.e. Kin), followed by proclamation of Chingis Khan. Neither *Carpini* nor TR mention (2) and (3). However, (2) is accounted for in the general account of the Merkits in TR ¶4 = *Carpini,* ch. V, ¶3, while for (3) see TR ¶6, n. 1, below. Both *Carpini* and TR combine (1) with (7), for reasons that are suggested below (TR ¶7, n. 1). Lastly, each tells the story of an overwhelming defeat of Chingis by the "Kitai", which seems (see TR ¶6, n. 1) to be a conflation of (3) and (6) with the temporary repulse of Chingis by the Keraits in 1203. The order in which *Carpini* tells of the defeat of the Naimans, the defeat by the "Kitai", and the conquest of the Uighurs, etc. (*Carpini,* ch. V, ¶4–5, ¶7, ¶8 respectively) is exactly reversed in TR

¶5. Post hec Cingis collecto exercitu processit versus terram que dicitur Uihur.[a] Incole terre   [V, ¶8]
huius christiani erant de secta Nestorianorum.[b] Quibus superatis acceperunt Mongali eorum
litteras ad scribendum, non enim antea litteris utebantur, et sic reversi sunt in terram propriam.   [V, ¶9]
¶6. Deinde Cingis mox fortitudine graviori collecta[a] adiit *terram orientalem nomine Esurs-*   [V, ¶7]
cakita. Homines vero terre appellant se Kitai, quibus Mongali et reliquae tres provinciae lingue
eorum quondam fuerant tributarii. Hec terra est magna et spatiosa valde et erat opulentissima
habens imperatorem *strenuum et potentem* qui huiusmodi perceptis rumoribus *indignatus*
vehementer occurrit Cingis et exercitui eius cum multitudine copiosa *in quadam vasta solitudine*
et tanta strages facta est Mongalorum quod de viris Mongalis tantummodo septem remanserunt, *aliarum tamen nacionum plures homines evaserunt. Quod cernens iam dictus imperator*
contempsit etiam spolia colligere occisorum. Cingis[b] vero *clam* in terram fugiens per temporis   [V, ¶8]
modicum sue malicie pacem dedit.
¶7. Est autem quedam terra Tartaris contigua a plaga occidentali que appellatur Nayman[a]   [I, ¶3]
montuosa valde et frigiditate[b] *modum excedens.* Huius terre regi Tartari et omnes circum   [V, ¶4]
adiacentes provincie tunc temporis tributa regalia persolvebant. Hic mortuus est *eo tempore*
quo Cingis a proeliis quiescebat. Reliquit[c] tamen sui regni *tres* parvulos filios successores. Quo
audito Cingis *cepit aspirare ad regnum puerorum* et collecto exercitu cepit invadere [2ʳ] regnum   [V, ¶5]
Naymanorum. *Qui videntes fortitudinem eius retrorsum cesserunt* et associatis sibi Karakitais vel
Nigris Kitais,[d] *kara enim Tartarice Latine nigrum dicitur,* occurrerunt Mongalis in quadam
valle inter duos montes altissimos *et occupantes viam qua solus introitus patebat in terram ex*
parte illius lateris diutissime restiterunt. Hanc vallem et terram fratres nostri ordinis transiverunt
ad Tartaros iter faciendo. *Tandem Mongali quidam longe valde ab excercitu montes inferiores*
transiverunt alii vero per ipsa abrupta moncium quae solis ibycibus[e] *sunt pervia, per que etiam*

¶5. (*a*) MS *Vihur.*   (*b*) MS *nestarianorum.*
¶6. (*a*) MS *collera.*   (*b*) MS *Cingiz,* and so frequently *infra.*
¶7. (*a*) MS *Naiman.*   (*b*) MS *frigiditatem.*   (*c*) MS *Reliqui.*   (*d*) MS *kytai si.*   (*e*) MS *ybicibus.*

(TR, ¶7, ¶6, ¶5 respectively). Insofar as the conquest of the Naimans did in fact precede that of the Uighurs, *Carpini*
is right here, and TR is wrong.

2. TR's account of the Uighurs agrees with *Carpini,* except in order, and is correct, save that their chief Barchuk, far
from being defeated, placed himself voluntarily under the protection of Chingis Khan in 1207 (Grousset, 1941, pp.
197–98). The first founder of Chingis Khan's Uighur secretariat, however, was the Naiman chief Taibuka's Uighur
chancellor, Tata-tonga, taken prisoner in 1204 (Grousset, 1941, pp. 168, 267–68).

¶6. 1. This story of an attack on North China, though the country, the emperor, and the former liability of the
Mongol and Turkish neighboring tribes to pay tribute are correctly described, is unhistorical, for Chingis Khan's
campaigns against the Kin in 1211–16 were overwhelmingly successful, with only a few minor reverses. The first
three syllables of *Esurscakita,* peculiar to TR and perhaps a little corrupt, presumably represent *Jurchet,* the name
of the Tungusic invaders who founded the Kin dynasty in the 1120s, though the Northern Chinese, as *Carpini*-TR
correctly state, continued to be called Khitai. The Tangut campaigns of 1205–09 are perhaps a further element in the
confusion, but in these also, although progress was slow, the Mongols suffered no serious defeat. The rest of the story
is evidently a garbled version of the first indecisive battle in 1203 against Toghril, the Wang Khan of the Keraits,
after which Chingis fled with a few loyal survivors (but 2,000, not 7) to the district of Baljuna. The Mongols regarded this with pride as the great crisis of their early history, and *Carpini* (ch. V, ¶7) adds that they declare, when
warned of the power of an enemy: "Once before we were all slain but seven, and soon increased to a great multitude,
wherefore we are not frightened by such things." TR's statement about spoils apparently alludes (reversing the
roles) to Chingis's waiving the Merkit spoils in favor of the Wang Khan in 1197. See above, p. 29.

of the army, and so an exceedingly great battle ensued in which the Naimans were assailed from every side, and perished for the most part, the survivors submitting to the rule of Chingis, who then *put the king's three sons to death and* returned home *with an augmented army.*[1]

¶8. Next he set out to war *toward the southeast* and took four countries,[1] namely Uirat,[2] Sari-Uighur,[3] the Karanitae,[4] and *Cosmir,*[5] and again made his way home.

¶9. *Since his lust for power would not let him rest,* he gathered all the force of *strong* men he could and *again* marched against the emperor of the Kitai. At last, after a long war, he *put the emperor's army to flight* and beleaguered the emperor himself in his very strong capital city,[1] until the besiegers were compelled by extreme famine to eat one man in each platoon of ten, with the exception of Chingis himself.[2] The besieged, however, as they were now suffering under the fire of arrows and stones, began hurling silver at the enemy, mostly molten, for the city was rich in wealth of this kind.[3] At last the besiegers dug an underground tunnel to the center of the city,[4] burst in at night, killed the emperor[5] and his officials, and took possession of everything that therein was. So Chingis set the part of the country that he had conquered in

¶7. 1. The topography of the Naimans is correctly described, but the remark about tribute is incorrect. TR pathetically represents the deceased Inanch-Bilga's stalwart and rival sons Taibuka and Buyuruk as "three little sons"—*Carpini* does not give the number. The third "son" is presumably Taibuka's son Kuchluk, who fled to the Karakhitai—hence perhaps the erroneous supposition of *Carpini*-TR that the Karakhitai fought beside the Naimans—and was ejected and hunted down by Chingis Khan's general Jebe only in 1218 (see above, p. 30). Chingis fought two mountain battles with the Naimans: the first on Mount Namogo near Karakorum in 1204, when Taibuka was slain, and the second against the fugitives under Kuchluk and Toktoa's surviving Merkits in 1205 some 600 miles to the west in the Siberian Altai, on the upper Irtish. The friars would have had to cross the Altai near this point, whereas they would have reached Karakorum without touching upon Mount Namogo. Probably the story here told is of the Mount Namogo battle, which was by far the more famous in Mongol epic (see Grousset, 1941, pp. 163–68; Martin, pp. 88–91; *Secret History,* ¶193–96), but the friars have confused it with the site of the later battle in the Altai (cf. Grousset, 1941, pp. 171–72; Martin, p. 103). For the Mongol word kara (khara) = black, see Lessing, p. 931.

¶8. 1. In Carpini, ch. V, ¶8, this section follows immediately and correctly on the account of the Uighurs, from which it is here separated by the Khitai (i.e. Kerait) and Naiman episodes, owing to TR's reversal of the order (see above, ¶5, n. 1). *Carpini* names the four tribes as *Sarruyur* (best reading), *Karanitae, Voyrat,* and *Kanana,* in that order. In general the section seems to correspond to the subjection of the forest tribes to the northwest of Mongolia by Jochi and other leaders in 1207, although only the Uirats and Sari-Uighurs can be identified with certainty. The direction southeast, peculiar to TR, is true only of the latter.

2. The Mongol Uirats, under their chieftain Kutuku, submitted voluntarily to Jochi in 1207 (Grousset, 1941, p. 199; *Secret History,* ¶239). They dwelt between the headstreams of the Yenisei, west of Lake Baikal, northwest of Mongolia.

3. The Sari-Uighurs or Yellow Uighurs lived near the Tangut country by Lake Koko-Nor, and were conquered by Subetei in 1226 (Bretschneider, Vol. 1, p. 263; d'Avezac, pp. 539–40; Beazley, *Texts,* p. 277; Martin, pp. 285, 290) during Chingis Khan's final war against the Tanguts, to whom they were allied. But the entry in *Carpini*-TR—unless it is due merely to mistaken assimilation with the Uighurs proper—may well refer to an attack on the Sari-Uighurs, unmentioned elsewhere, during Chingis Khan's campaign in 1207 against the Tanguts, who used Sari-Uighur cavalry in their army (Martin, pp. 54, 116).

4. The *Karanitae* are a mystery, for which the following four solutions seem equally feasible, though only the first two fit the context. They may be a corruption of: (a) the Kirghiz, subdued by Jochi in 1207, under their alternative name of Keregut (Grousset, 1941, pp. 199–200, 486); or (b) the Tumat or Khori-Tumat, who dwelt west of the Uirats and north of the Kirghiz, and were likewise conquered in 1207 (Grousset, 1941, pp. 200–01); they are mentioned by Carpini, ch. VII, ¶9, in the list of conquered peoples, but not by TR (see below, Excursus B, p. 105); or (c) the Karanuts (d'Ohsson, Vol. 1, p. 426), a subtribe of the Kongirats, a Mongol tribe east of the Tatars, to whom Chingis Khan's first wife Borte belonged; they had joined Jamuka's opposition in 1201, and submitted partly in 1203 and finally after the Mount Namogo battle in 1205 (Grousset, 1941, pp. 52, 65, 108, 135, 168; *Secret History,* ¶196); or (d) a doublet of the Keraits, to whose name the reading *keranitas* in TR is palaeographically very close.

frater Benedictus equitare attemptabat sed a Tartaris non est permissus ne equum perderet et personam. Residui autem in ipsa acie excercitus accesserunt et sic commissum est proelium magnum valde nimis ex omni parte Naymanorum in quo maior pars eorum interempta est et residua Cingis dominio se subiecit. Tunc *interfectis tribus filiis regis cum ampliori excercitu* Cingis ad propria est reversus.

[V, ¶7]

¶8. Deinde progrediens ad bellum *inter meridianam plagam et orientalem* cepit quatuor terras videlicet Voyrat,[(a)] Sarihuiur,[(b)] Karanitas[(c)] et *Cosmir.* Et sic iterum ad propria remeavit.

[V, ¶8]

¶9. Verum *quia cupiditas eum dominandi non sinebat* quiescere aggregata omni qua poterat *robustorum* fortitudine *iterato* processit adversus imperatorem Kitaorum. Tandem post diuturnum bellum *fugato exercitu imperatoris* ipsum imperatorem in metropoli civitate fortissima obsedit quo adusque obsidentes pro nimia penuria excepto Cingis decani cum suis decimum hominem inter se manducarent. Obsessi vero cum iam sagittarum ac lapidum ictus paterentur iactare argentum ceperunt contra hostes et precipue liquefactum. Erat enim hec civitas abundans divitiis huiusmodi. Ad ultimum autem obsidentes fecerunt viam subterraneam usque ad medium civitatis per quam in nocte irruentes in civitate imperatore cum potentibus interfecto universa que in ea fuerant possiderent. Cingis[(a)] ergo parte terre quam ceperat ordinata cum gaudio ad

[V, ¶9]

¶8. (*a*) MS *Woyrac.*   (*b*) MS *Sariphur.*   (*c*) MS *keranitas.*
¶9. (*a*) MS *Cingit.*

---

5. Cosmir is a still deeper mystery. The name should mean Kashmir, which Chingis Khan may well have touched on his journey along the upper Indus in 1221, but which was not otherwise attacked until 1253, in the reign of Mongke Khan, when a detachment under Sali Noyan was sent there from Hulagu's army in Iran and returned with great booty (Bretschneider, Vol. 1, pp. 138, 305). *Cosmir* is mentioned by *Carpini,* ch. VII, ¶9, in the list of Mongol conquests, but not by TR, ¶34. It is perhaps more significant that a tribe called *Keshimir* is named in the *Secret History,* ¶262, ¶270, along with the Kangli, Kipchaks, Russians, Bashkirs, Alans, Saksins, Circassians, Bulgars, and Hungarians, in the list of Subetei's conquests in the West. The name here has never been explained, but the context makes Kashmir impossible. It seems possible that *Keshimir* may be a misnomer in the Mongol manner (like *Keler* for *Kerel,* meaning the Hungarians, or *Keluren* for the Kerulen River) for the Cheremiss, a Finno-Ugrian tribe dwelling northward of the Mordvins and Bulgars between the Volga, Kama, and Viatka rivers (cf. d'Ohsson, Vol. 2, p. 118; Vernadsky, p. 209, and map 5, p. 318), who were conquered during Batu's western campaign *ca.* 1238. If so, the Cheremisses may be tentatively equated with *Carpini*-TR's *Cosmir.*

¶9. 1. The Kin war of 1211–15 is here telescoped, but it is true that it began with the successive routing of the main Kin armies and ended with the sacking of Peking. The incidents of the siege in *Carpini*-TR relate mostly not to Peking, which was captured by blockade, but to various other sieges in this war and, more frequently, in Ogedei's Kin of war 1231–34. See below, nn. 2–5.

2. Cannibalism is reported of the besieged Kin at Peking (Martin, p. 177) and on other occasions (Martin, p. 160; Howorth, Vol. 1, pp. 122, 124, 125; d'Ohsson, Vol. 1, p. 369, Vol. 2, pp. 42, 52–54), but not of the Mongols, who had abundant food supplies from pillaging, except on a single occasion, during a long march by Tolui's army in 1230 (d'Ohsson, Vol. 2, p. 30).

3. Apparently an allusion to the casting of arrowheads from money in the siege of Lo-yang in 1231 (Howorth, Vol. 1, p. 121), perhaps also to the various forms of bombshell, rockets, and incendiaries used by the Kin (cf. Howorth, Vol. 1, p. 122; d'Ohsson, Vol. 2, pp. 36–37).

4. Mine-tunnels under city and fortress walls were frequently made by the Mongols instructed by their captured Kin engineers (cf. d'Ohsson, Vol. 2, pp. 25–26, 37; Howorth, Vol. 1, p. 119), but not at Peking.

5. Untrue, but Juvaini (Vol. 1, p. 39) makes the same error. The commanding general at Peking, Fu-hsing, committed suicide, but the emperor Hsuan-tsung escaped beyond the Hoang-ho to Kai-feng. Probably there is a confusion with the capture of Ju-nan in 1234, when the last Kin emperor, Ai-tsung, hanged himself (d'Ohsson, Vol. 2, pp. 54–55).

order (for there is a part of this country on the seacoast which to this day the Tartars are unable to win[6]) and returned home rejoicing. Henceforth Chingis ordained that he should be called Khan, meaning Emperor.[7]

¶10. The aforesaid Kitai, although they are heathens, have an Old and New Testament, together with their own way of writing, many lives of the Fathers, hermits, and buildings [2ᵛ] like churches in which they say prayers at the appointed time. They allege also that they have certain special saints of their own. They worship one God,[1] and believe in Our Lord Jesus Christ[2] and in life eternal. They give generous alms and respect Christians, though without practicing baptism. They have no beards, are not broad in face like the Mongols, and speak a language of their own.

¶11. *After Chingis had taken the title of Khan* and had remained quiet *for a year* without making war, he prepared *three* armies, *one for each of the three quarters of the globe, intending them to conquer all men who dwell on earth.*[1] He sent one with his son Jochi, whom like himself they called Khan,[2] *to the west* against the Comans, *who dwell above the Az,*[3] and another with another son[4] against Greater India *to the northeast.*[5]

¶12. He himself[1] marched with the third against the Caspian Mountains.[2] After crossing the

---

6. This presumably refers to Southern China under the Sung dynasty, attacked by Ogedei in 1236 but not finally conquered till 1279 in the reign of Kubilai. Cf. TR, ¶32.

7. In fact, Temujin was proclaimed Chingis Khan at the kuriltai of 1206, after the defeat of the Naimans and five years before the Kin war. The friars were unaware of his birth-name Temujin, meaning "blacksmith" (Grousset, 1941, p. 51). Chingis, meaning Oceanic or Universal (from *tengis* = sea) was of course not a personal name, but part of his title. Cf. Kuyuk's title Dalai Khan (from *dalai* = ocean, as in Dalai Lama) in the seal of his letter to Innocent IV (Pelliot, 1922–23, pp. 24–25).

¶10. 1. "The Old Testament I take to be the 'Five Classics' (Wu Ching), the New Testament the 'Four Books' (*Ssu Shu*). The lives of the Fathers are probably the Confucian Analects and the works of Mencius; and Confucius, Mencius and Lao-Tzu are in all likelihood the saints referred to. The one God they worship is either *T'ien*, 'Heaven', or *T'ien Chu*, 'the Lord of Heaven'" (Rockhill, p. 155).

2. Owing to the successful persecutions in the ninth century, the Nestorian Church had "ceased to exist after 1000 A.D. in China proper" (Pelliot, 1914, p. 626). By the thirteenth century, however, Nestorianism had revived, though apparently among Ongut and other Turkish immigrants rather than among the Chinese proper, in Northern China (ibid., p. 630). However, the Buddhists had monks, churches, and alms-giving, and the friars may have mistaken Buddha for Christ (cf. Risch, pp. 119–20, nn. 13, 15).

¶11. 1. Here, where historical fact would require an account of the Khorasmian War of 1219–23, *Carpini*-TR tell a strange story of three expeditions, of which only Jochi's is partly historical. Those of Chingis Khan and Tolui form a kind of Chingis Romance compounded, with a vestigial modicum of historical basis, of elements drawn from Mongol and Turkish (Uighur) folklore, Nestorian sources, and the Alexander Romance. For a general discussion see above, pp. 47–51. The year's interval perhaps represents the period between Chingis Khan's departure from China in 1216 and his mobilization on the Irtish for the Khorasmian campaign in the spring of 1219. *Carpini*, ch. V, ¶11, says merely *"aliquantulum"*, "for a little while".

2. *Tossuc* represents *Toshi*, the Turkish form for Jochi, the *c* being no doubt parasitic from the *c* in *Tossu Can*. See Pelliot, *Horde d'Or*, pp. 18–19. All four sons of Chingis Khan were, of course, Khans of their own appanages.

3. *Az*, probably a little corrupt, is possibly the Sea of Azov, but the allusion may rather be to the Ases or Alans (cf. *"Alani qui dicunt se Azzos,"* TR, ¶34), the Comans' neighbors to the south between the Black Sea and the Caspian. For further discussion of this expedition see below, ¶20, nn.

4. Tolui, who for reasons explained below (¶23, nn. 4, 11) is never named by *Carpini*-TR.

5. The friars probably did not realize that Greater India (i.e. the main peninsula of India between the Indus and the Ganges) was southwest rather than southeast of Mongolia; but they can hardly have supposed it lay northward. "Northeast" must be a mere slip, not an error. Cf. below, ¶18, n. 1.

¶12. 1. Here again TR curiously reverses the order of *Carpini*. *Carpini* gives the three expeditions in the order Jochi-

propria est reversus. Est enim quedam pars terre maritima quam etiam usque ad hodiernam diem Tartari non prevalent obtinere. Ex tunc Cingis praecepit se can, id est imperatorem appellari.

¶10. Predicti autem Kitai quamvis pagani sint habent tamen novum et vetus testamentum et litteras speciales vitas patrum multas et heremitas et domos [2ᵛ] quasi ecclesias in quibus orant statuto tempore. Dicunt preterea se habere sanctos speciales quosdam. Hii unum deum colunt et credunt in dominum Jesum Christum, credunt etiam vitam eternam. Elemosinas dant largas et reverentur christianos, licet minime baptizentur. Barbam non habent nec in facie lati sunt ut Mongali et habent idioma speciale.　　　　　　　　　　　　　　　　　　　　　　　　　[V, ¶10]

¶11. Igitur *cum Cingis can esset*[(a)] *appellatus* et quievisset *per unum annum* sine bellis ordinavit eo tempore *tres* exercitus *ad tres mundi partes ut subiugarent cunctos homines qui habitant super terram*. Unum direxit cum filio suo Tossuc[(b)] quem etiam can nominabant contra Comanos *qui siti super Az ad plagam occidentalem,*[(c)] alterum vero cum alio filio contra Maiorem Indiam *ad orientem hyemalem*.　　　　　　　　　　　　　　　　　　　　　　　　　　　[V, ¶11]

[V, ¶12]

¶12. Ipse autem cum tertio processit contra montes Caspeos et cum transisset[(a)] terram que *Solangia*[(b)] dicitur tunc temporis eam sibi non subiciens assidue ibat *tribus mensibus homines non inveniens per desertum*. Cumque venisset prope montes Caspeos *ubi dicuntur esse inclusi ab Alexandro Iudaei quos ipsi appellabant Gog et Magog*, ecce[(c)] subito omnia ferramenta, sagitte *de pharetris, cultelli*[(d)] *et gladii de vaginis, strepe de sellis, habene de frenis, ferramenta*　　[V, ¶15]

¶11. (*a*) MS *Cingiz iam esse.*　　(*b*) MS *Cossut.*　　(*c*) MS *accidentalem.*
¶12. (*a*) MS *transset.*　　(*b*) MS *salangia.*　　(*c*) MS *Moagog. Et ecce.*　　(*d*) MS *cuttelli.*

Tolui–Chingis Khan, whereas TR has Chingis Khan–Tolui–Jochi.

2. Ordinarily "the Caspian Mountains" was an alternative name for the Caucasus, e.g. in Ptolemy's maps, in Rubruck (Rockhill, p. 119), and in Odoric (Yule, *Cathay,* Vol. 2, pp. 240, 242). At the Iron Gates of Derbend, in the narrow gap between the Caucasus and the Caspian, Alexander the Great was supposed to have shut off the lost Ten Tribes of the Jews, called Gog and Magog. Subetei and Jebe passed this point in 1221 during their great raid. Nevertheless, although TR does not mention Chingis Khan's direction at the outset—*Carpini,* ch. V, ¶15, does, however, as "east"—it is abundantly clear from the direction northeast which he takes after leaving the Caspian Mountains (¶13), and his eventual arrival in the country of sunrise, that the whole journey is conceived as lying northeast from Mongolia. The attempts of d'Avezac (pp. 565–66), Beazley (*Texts,* p. 281) and Risch (pp. 130–31) to explain *Carpini's* story in terms of Subetei's journey through the Caucasus in 1221, and to interpret *Carpini's Kergis* (see n. 3, below) as meaning not the Kirghiz of Central Asia but the Circassians of the Caucasus, therefore fall to the ground. Apart from its close connection with the Alexander Romance, the story seems vaguely connected with a tale told by the Armenian prince Hetoum in his *Flos historiarum,* Book 3, ¶6–¶8, written *ca.* 1305: that Chingis was ordered in a vision to cross Mount Belgian [*sic*], whereupon the sea miraculously receded to make a passage nine feet wide, and he passed through to conquer many lands. Hetoum's story, in turn, seems to derive partly from Chingis' retreat to the Baljuna in 1203, and partly from a Mongol legend that their people, many centuries before, had broken loose from a mountain barrier called Ergene-kun by melting a way through an iron mine with fire and bellows (d'Ohsson, Vol. 1, pp. 21–22). The story in *Carpini*-TR is unique in relating a repulse of Chingis Khan by the enclosed tribes and in saying that the mountains were magnetic. A still earlier version was told by an embassy of the Ishmaelite Assassins, seeking aid against Chormaghan from the kings of France and England in 1238: according to this, the Mongols themselves were the tribes of Gog and Magog, and had broken loose from the Caspian Mountains near the Arctic Ocean (Matthew Paris, Vol. 3, pp. 487–89; Rockhill, pp. xiv–xvii). The ungeographical transference of the Caspian Mountains from the Caucasus to the far northeast of Asia was necessitated in either version by the real position of Mongolia itself; but it may well have been aided by the idea current in the early Middle Ages, and represented e.g. in the Beatus, Ebstorf, and Hereford world maps, that the Caspian Sea was a gulf of the northern Ocean, with the Caspian Mountains and Gog-Magog in a peninsula on its eastern shore, situated in northeast Asia far eastward of its true position.

country called *Solangia*,[3] which he refrained from conquering at that time, he traveled persistently onward *for three months*[4] *through an uninhabited desert.* When he drew near the Caspian Mountains, *where the Jews called Gog and Magog by their fellow-countrymen are said to have been shut in by Alexander,* lo and behold, everything made of iron, arrows *from quivers, knives and swords from sheaths, stirrups from saddles, bits from bridles, horseshoes from horses' hooves, breastplates from bodies and helmets from heads,* flew *violently and with a tremendous clatter* toward the mountain; *and as the Tartars jestingly informed our Friar Benedict when they told this story, the heavier iron objects such as breastplates and helmets scurried along the ground to the mountain, raising a great cloud of dust and clanking, so that they were seized with blind horror.* These mountains are believed to be magnetic.[5]

¶13. Chingis *fled in terror* with his army, *and leaving the mountains on the right*[1] marched *north east.*[2] At last after toiling continuously on his journey for *three more months*[3] through the desert, *he ordered them, as food was running short, to eat one man in every ten.* After these *three* months he came *to great mountains in a country called Narayrgen, that is, Men of the Sun, for Nara is Tartar for sun, and Irgen means men.*[4] Finding trodden trackways but no [3ʳ] inhabitants, he and his men began to marvel exceedingly. Soon after he found a single native with his wife, and proceeded to ask him *through numerous interpreters* where the men of the country were. He learned that they dwelt in underground homes beneath the mountains, and sent the captured man, keeping the woman still prisoner, to ask if they were willing to come out *and fight.* While the man was on his way back day broke, and the Tartars *threw themselves face downward on the ground* at the noise of the rising sun, and many of them died on the spot.[5] The natives of the country saw the enemy and made *a night* attack on them, killing a number of the Tartars, and seeing this Chingis Khan fled with the survivors, but took the captive wife with him nevertheless.

3. The Solangs, a Tungusic tribe subject to the Kin of North China, dwelt in Manchuria from the confines of the Tatars and Kongirats to Northern Korea. The latter country is intended by Carpini in his journey-narrative, when he states that the kuriltai of 1246 was attended by "princes of the Kitai and Solangi" (ch. IX, ¶31, ¶33, ch. IV, ¶5); but Manchuria is meant here in TR, and in *Carpini,* ch. I, ¶3, where the Solangs and Kitai are given as the eastern neighbors of the Mongols. The Solangs of Manchuria submitted to Chingis Khan's brother Jochi Khasar in the winter of 1214-15 (Martin, p. 205), this expedition being the furthest northeast penetration of the Mongols recorded in history. *Carpini* here has *Kergis* instead of *Solangia,* meaning the Kirghiz, who submitted to Chingis Khan's son Jochi in 1207—an error possibly deriving from confusion of the two Jochis, and from the fact that the Kirghiz bordered on the Selenga River.

4. *Carpini* (ch. V, ¶15) says "more than a month".

5. The story of a magnetic mountain is widespread in Eastern lore, though it does not seem to be combined elsewhere with the tale of Gog-Magog and the Caspian Mountains, and is usually an island in the sea. In the *Arabian Nights* both the Third Kalandar and Sinbad the Sailor were wrecked on it, and Mandeville records it twice in the Indian Ocean, once near Ormuz (Vol. 1, p. 118) and again further east on the way to Prester John's country (ibid., p. 188). A closer parallel is the story in *Merveilles de l'Inde* (¶XLVI) of a river in China with magnetic mountains on its banks, so that ships sailing by must contain no iron, and horsemen riding over the mountains must have wooden stirrups, saddles, and bridles. The common element of noise frightening an army occurs, with reversal of roles, in Ricoldus de Monte Crucis (p. 119), when the Mongols break loose from the Caspian Mountains (this being itself a conflation of the Ergene-kun and Baljuna legends), after being deterred by the din of horses, warriors, and trumpets created "by artifice of wind", and in the Alexander Romance, when Alexander stations wind-operated trumpets to guard the enclosed tribes (Anderson, pp. 83-85). It is noteworthy that De Bridia quotes Benedict himself as authority, that Benedict had the tale from the Mongols themselves, and that they told it with due appreciation of its comic qualities.

de equorum pedibus, lorice de corporibus, galee de capitibus, versus montem *cum impetu ac maximo strepitu* processerunt *et sicut ipsi fratri nostro Benedicto commemorantes hec in quadam referebant leticia quod graviora ferramenta ut pote lorice et galee super terram ad montes properanda cum impetu magnum nimis pulverem et strepitum excitabant. Unde ipsos cecitas et horror nimius invadebant.* Creduntur autem hii montes esse adamantini.

¶13. *Territus* ergo Cingis can *fugit* cum exercitu *dimittensque montes ad dextrum*[(a)] processit [V, ¶16] *inter aquilonem* et orientem. Tandem[(b)] cum per *tres alios* menses continue in itinere per deserta laborasset *precepit deficientibus alimoniis ut decimi decimum inter se devorarent hominem.* Post hos *tres* menses venit *ad montes magnos terre quae appellatur*[(c)] *Narayrgen, id est homines solis, Nara enim tartarice sol dicitur latine Irgen homines.* Cumque invenisset itinera trita et nullos [3ʳ] homines mirari cepit cum suis vehementer. Postmodum inde invento unico viro cum uxore cepit *per multos interpretes* querere de terre hominibus ubi essent et percepto quod in domibus subterraneis sub montibus habitarent misit virum quem ceperat muliere retenta interrogans si vellent egredi *ad bellandum* sed illo redeunte Tartari[(d)] facto mane in ortu solis *prostrati sunt super terram* propter strepitum solis ascendentis et plures ibidem mortui sunt ex eis. Incole autem terre perceptis hostibus irruerunt *in nocte* super illos et plures de Tartaris occiderunt, quod cernens Cingis can aufugit[(e)] cum residuis uxorem captivam nichilominus secum deducens.

¶13. (*a*) MS *dextris.*   (*b*) MS *Tamdem.*   (*c*) MS *appellantur.*   (*d*) MS *tatari.*   (*e*) MS *affugit.*

¶13. 1. "On the right", if it will bear stressing, is remarkable. If the Caspian Mountains and Gog-Magog had been regarded here as situated in their usual peninsula on the Arctic coast or in furthest northeastern Asia, then Chingis Khan would have passed them to the left. But his passing them to the right suggests that in TR they are situated somewhere in Northern China, in a position where they were often connected with the Great Wall of China (see Yule, *Polo,* Vol. 1, pp. 292–95; Anderson, pp. 99, 103).

2. Carpini, ch. V, ¶16, has "east".

3. *Carpini* (ibid.) again (cf. ¶12, n. 4, above) says "more than a month".

4. The name *Narayrgen* is peculiar to TR, and the derivation is correct: *nara(n)* = sun; *irgen* = people (see Lessing, pp. 565, 414).

5. Similar sun legends are widespread, but are told usually of the setting sun. Tacitus (*Germania,* ch. 45) writes, so far truly, of the midnight sun over the frozen sea north of Sweden, so bright that it extinguishes the stars, and adds that the natives say it makes a loud noise when setting. Professor F. W. Cleaves (*HJAS,* Vol. 22, December 1959, pp. 28–29) quotes a Chinese story of Sha-pi-ch'a, the land where the sun sets, which no one has ever visited except Alexander the Great: "In the evening, when the sun sets, the sound is like thunder. The king of the country each evening gathers a thousand persons on the city-wall to blow horns, sound gongs, and beat drums to adulterate the sound of the sun. Otherwise the little children would die of fright". Although this tale is apparently not found in other versions of the Alexander Romance, it seems clear, from this Chinese source and from the closely related adaptation in this Alexander-laden context of *Carpini*-TR, that a version of the Alexander Romance containing such an incident was available to both the Chinese and the Mongols. Professor Cleaves' conjecture that the Chinese tale may have had a Mongol source is strongly confirmed by the story in TR. Risch (p. 135) is delightfully literal-minded in objecting that beating drums would only make the sun's noise worse (as Professor Cleaves points out, the purpose was to disguise the dreaded sound of thunder, and TR significantly mentions lightning below); but he provides (ibid., pp. 134–35) other useful parallels from eastern sources, including a story that the three Magi came from a country so far east that the people were born deaf from the noise of sunrise. The theme of the sun's noise is evidently related to the Mongol practice recorded by Rubruck (Rockhill, p. 240) of "sounding drums and instruments, and making a great noise and clamour" during an eclipse of the sun, a custom also found in China and Tibet. In the Alexander Romance (Budge, 1896, p. 226) the natives of the land of sunrise take refuge, like the people of Narayrgen, in underground homes beneath the mountains at sunrise, or lie with their faces to the ground as do Chingis Khan's men—as a protection, however, from the heat, not the noise.

¶14. *As the Tartars themselves told the friars,* she stayed with them for a long time after,[1] *and asserted without a shadow of doubt that the aforesaid country is situated at the very end of the world, and beyond it no land is found, but only the ocean sea.*[2] Wherefore, owing to the excessive proximity of the sun when it rises *over the sea at the point of summer sunrise,* a crashing and roaring of such a nature and magnitude is heard there, *due to the opposition of the sun and firmament,* that no one dares to live in the open air on the surface *until the sun proceeds through its zodiac to the south, for fear of dying instantly or being wounded as if struck by lightning.* For this reason the natives beat huge drums and other instruments *in their mountain caves,* in order to shut out the noise of the sun with the sound of their drumming. *This country is flat and fertile after the mountains are crossed, but not large.*

¶15. While Chingis Khan was hurrying home from this country with his men after his defeat, *he saw the Caspian mountains on the way, but did not go near them owing to his previous alarm. He noticed, however, that men had come out from the mountains owing to the noise made previously when the Tartars' iron-ware hurtled against them,*[1] and wished to try his strength against them. As the two sides drew near to one another, lo and behold, a cloud came between them and divided them one from the other, *like the Egyptians and the children of Israel long ago.*[2] *This makes it credible enough that these people were the Jews whom the Lord protected and warned by signs given to their fathers.* Whenever the Tartars advanced toward the cloud they were struck blind, *and some were even smitten dead, though they could see one another more or less through the cloud. However, finding it impossible after two days' journey*[3] *to cross to either side of the cloud without having it still in their way,* they began to proceed on their journey.

¶16. Traveling [3ᵛ] on foot and succumbing to starvation, they found in a state of semi-putrefaction the belly or entire entrails of an animal, *which as the Tartars believe they had left behind after eating there on their outward journey.* These entrails were brought to Chingis Khan, *who ordered them to be cooked, after merely pressing out the gross excrement by hand without any rupture or injury to the guts. This was done,* and Chingis Khan and the rest of his men ate them, now nearly dying of hunger. Chingis Khan announced that in future nothing must be thrown away from entrails excepting the gross inner part of the excrement contained in them;

¶14. 1. Cf. Benedict's statement (TR, ¶18) that he saw one of the women of the Land of Dogs with the Mongols.

    2. The compiler of the Vinland Map makes a curious but typical perversion of this statement (see p. 245 below), which does not necessarily imply actual geographical knowledge of furthest northeast Asia on the part of the Mongols, since it follows naturally from the sun's rising out of the sea at the end of the earth. However, taken with the mention of the seacoast of China (TR, ¶9), it does show that the friars were told of the oceanic limits of Asia, and were well aware that at Karakorum they were still a long way from the eastern ocean.

¶15. 1. It would be overcritical to tax this charming tale with absurdity in saying that Chingis Khan, after a journey of six months to and from Narayrgen, found the tribes of Gog-Magog had only just emerged to investigate the clatter of the magnetized equipment. But *Carpini* (ch. V, ¶16) has a different and more natural version (which follows immediately upon the material corresponding to TR ¶12, whereas in TR the story of the magic cloud is transferred to ¶15, after the visit to Narayrgen): that the tribes heard the noise and began to break through the mountain; and the Mongols returned ten years later (presumably on a different expedition), found the mountain broken, but were thwarted by the cloud when they tried to attack the enemy. *Carpini's* story of the break through the mountain recalls, with reversal of roles, the legend of the Mongols' escape from Ergene-kun (see above, ¶12, n. 5), and (as he cannot therefore have invented it) must be a more correct version of the story received from the friars' informants.

    2. Exodus 14:19, 20. The story of the cloud is somehow related to the tale told by Prince Hetoum (lib. 1, ch. 10) of a

¶14. Que postmodum *sicut ipsi Tartari referebant fratribus* cum ipsis mansit longo tempore *affirmans absque dubio quod dicta terra in extremis mundi partibus sit posita nec ulterius terra nisi solummodo mare oceanum invenitur.* Unde nimia vicinitate solis ascendentis *in mare e regione estivali tempore* tantus ac talis fragor et sonitus *ex contrarietate solis et firmamenti* auditur in ea quod nullus hominum audet sub divo habitare super terram *quo adusque sol ad meridiem per suum zodiacum progrediatur quin statim moriatur tamquam per tonitruum aut ledatur.* Inde est etiam quod eo tempore tympana maxima et alia instrumenta percutiunt *in cavernis montium* ut sono tympanorum solis strepitum intercludant. *Hec terra post transitum montium plana est et fertilis, sed non est magna.*

¶15. Dum autem de hac terra Cingis can devictus ad propria cum suis redire festinaret et *dum in reditu montes Caspeos conspexisset ad eos propter timorem pristinum*[(a)] *non accessit. Videns tamen homines iam de montibus processisse propter strepitum ante factum quod ad montes properabant ferramenta* cum eis certare cupiebat. Cumque utrique sibi appropinquare cepissent et ecce nubes divisit eos stans in medio *sicut quondam Egyptios et filios Israel. Unde satis credibile est eos esse Iudeos quos Dominus munivit et monuit signis patrum.* Et quandocunque Tartari ad nubem ascendebant cecitate percutiebantur *et quidam etiam plaga mortis. Poterant tamen se videre per nubem ad invicem quoquomodo. Postquam autem ad utramque partem nubis per duas dietas transire non possent quin super nubem haberent oppositam* ceperunt cepto itinere proficisci.

[V, ¶17]

[V, ¶15]

¶16. Igitur iter [3ᵛ] facientes Tartari pedestre[(a)] et fame deficientes invenerunt alvum seu viscera integra unius animalis satis fetentia *que ut ipsi credunt prius eis ibidem manducantibus fuerant derelicta* et cum ad Cingis can essent delata *precepit ut tantummodo grosso fimo manibus expresso absque ulla ruptione vel lesione viscerum coquerentur quod et factum est* et sic Cingis can cum ceteris iam quasi fame moriens manducavit et exinde statuit Cingis[(b)] can ut nichil de visceribus[(c)] reicerentur preter fimi grossiciem interiorem, *de quo plenius dicetur cum de tradicionibus dicetur Tartarorum.* Hiis gestis reversus est in terram suam et a tonitruo divino iudicio est percussus.

[V, ¶17]

[V, ¶18, 19]

¶15. (*a*) MS *prestinum.*
¶16. (*a*) MS *pedester.*   (*b*) MS *zingiz.*   (*c*) MS *pectoribus.*

---

district in Georgia three days' journey in circumference, where, once upon a time, a cruel emperor pursuing Christians was imprisoned by a miraculous darkness, in which he and his army still remain until the world ends. The natives say they can hear men's voices, cock-crows and neighing within, but dare not enter lest they should lose their way. Another ingredient is the tale of the Land of Darkness, based ultimately on rumors of the Arctic night, in the Alexander Romance (cf. pseudo-Callisthenes, lib. 2, ch. 39; Yule, *Polo,* Vol. 2, pp. 484–85; Budge, 1896, pp. 242–77, 372, 396). The Land of Darkness is mentioned, again in close proximity to a sun-legend, in the fragment of a Mongol Alexander Romance edited by Professor F. W. Cleaves (see above, ¶13, n. 5), in which Alexander journeys to the Land of Darkness by "setting with Mother Sun" (*Naran Eke*). We have now seen that *Carpini*-TR present a narrative about Chingis Khan in which are embodied various components of the Alexander Romance —the Caspian Mountains, the enclosed tribes, a legend of the rising sun and a people of troglodytes, the Land of Darkness; and another drawn from Alexander's battle with Porus, king of India, follows (see below, ¶17, n. 4). These are combined with other elements from the story of the Turkish hero Oghuz Khan (¶18, n. 3) and from Nestorian Christian lore. For a general discussion of these facts, suggesting that the friars were told a Chingis Romance probably derived from Nestorian Uighurs and adopted by the Mongols, see above, pp. 47–51.

3. Cf. Prince Hetoum's statement that the Land of Darkness was three days' journey in circumference (see n. 2, above).

but more will be said on this subject when I discuss the hereditary customs of the Tartars.[1] After this he returned home and by God's judgment was struck by lightning.[2]

¶17. The second army which had been sent with the second son of Chingis Khan against the Indians conquered Lesser India or Ethiopia, the inhabitants of which are black-skinned and heathen. When they reached Greater India,[1] *which the Apostle Thomas converted,*[2] the king of the country, who is always called Prester John,[3] *although he was not well prepared,* immediately sent an army against them which used a new and unheard-of device against the Tartars. They organized a special force of *three thousand* warriors carrying on the front of their saddles statues of iron or bronze containing live fire in their hollow interior, and before the Tartars' arrows could reach them they began to shoot fire against them, by blowing it with bellows *which they carried on either side of the saddle under both thighs.*[4] After the fire they began to shoot arrows, and in this way the Tartar army was put in disorder. Some burned, others wounded, they took to flight, and the pursuing Indians felled many and ejected the others from their country, so that the Tartars never returned to India. *All this the Tartars told our friars, saying that the Indians as they attacked lifted themselves on their stirrups above their horses' bodies in a regular line; "and as we wondered what this might be," they said, "they suddenly sat down on their saddles again, and instantly fire shot forth against us, followed by their arrows as well, and so our army was routed." Recently, when the Tartars had returned to their own country and the*

¶16. 1. Neither this story nor the tabu imposed by Chingis seem to occur elsewhere than in *Carpini*-TR (but cf. ¶41, n. 2, below). However, Alexander likewise on returning from the Land of Darkness saved his army from starvation by feeding them with a miraculously inexhaustible bunch of grapes (Budge, 1896, p. 262).

2. *Carpini*-TR are alone in saying that Chingis Khan was struck by lightning. In fact he died during his last war against the Tanguts on 18 August 1227, after a week's illness perhaps associated with a fall from his horse when hunting in the previous year (d'Ohsson, Vol. 1, pp. 378–84; Grousset, 1941, pp. 269, 273, 277–84; Martin, pp. 301–06). But the manner and place of his death were variously told, and the subject may have lain under a tabu. The Mongols were greatly afraid of lightning, which many of their strangest customs were designed to avert (cf. below, ¶42, nn. 1, 4; ¶48, n. 2; Rockhill, pp. 75–76), believing it to come from Tengri, the sky god. On the other hand, they thought a person struck by lightning a kind of saint (Rockhill, p. 76, n. 1); and Chingis Khan was in the habit of speaking directly to Tengri at times of crisis, and was thought to have "ascended to heaven" after his death (*Secret History,* ¶268). So the friars may well have heard a story that he was struck by lightning, as a kind of apotheosis. However, being struck by lightning was also regarded as a divine punishment for sin (Roux, Pt. III, p. 50), and the tale may equally well be one of the many elements in this Chingis Romance which show hostility to Chingis.

¶17. 1. Lesser India was the region west of the Indus, Greater India the present Indian subcontinent between the Indus and Ganges. The Horn of Africa was believed to extend eastward to the longitude of India (partly in order to allow a common source in Paradise for the Nile, Ganges, Tigris, and Euphrates, partly in accordance with the idea of a circular world), as indeed it does in the Vinland Map; so the natives of Lesser India could be described as Ethiopians, as they are, e.g., in Vesconte's early fourteenth-century world maps (*"India parva seu Ethiopia"*— Nordenskiöld, *Periplus,* figs. 20, 6). Innocent IV issued letters of recommendation on 21 and 25 March 1245 addressed to authorities in Middle Eastern countries including the Ethiopians and Nubians (Sbaralea, pp. 360–64), meaning, as the context shows and as Golubovich (Vol. 2, pp. 316–17) suggests, the natives of Lesser India between Persia and the Indus. In this light TR ¶34 is correct in naming Ethiopia and Nubia among the peoples conquered by the Mongols. Neither Tolui, who is meant here, nor Chingis Khan himself crossed into "Greater India" after the Battle of the Indus, but a detachment was sent under Torbei Tokshin in pursuit of Jelal-ed-din, which retired after ravaging Multan and Lahore (Juvaini, Vol. 1, pp. 141–42, Vol. 2, p. 413).

2. The Nestorian Christians of Syria established toward the seventh century an outpost in southern India which flourished until modern times (see G. M. Rae, *The Syrian Church in India,* 1892). Legend ascribed this foundation to St. Thomas the Apostle, who was thought to have been buried at Madras (see Yule, *Polo,* Vol. 2, pp. 353–59).

3. For Prester John see above, pp. 48–49; d'Avezac, pp. 547–64; Yule, *Polo,* Vol. 1, pp. 231–37; Beazley, *Texts,*

¶17. Secundus vero exercitus qui cum secundo filio Cingis can missus fuerat contra Indos devi- [V, ¶12]
cit Minorem Indiam id est Ethiopiam in qua sunt homines nigerrimi et pagani. Cumque per-
venissent ad Maiorem *quam Thomas apostolus convertit* statim rex terre qui *semper* appellatur Presbiter[(a)] Johannes *quamvis non bene praemunitus* misit exercitum contra eos. Fecerunt quandam novam et inauditam artem contra Tartaros, ordinaverunt enim specialiter *tria
milia pugnatorum* in quorum sellis in anteriori parte posuerunt quasdam ferreas sive ereas
imagines ignem vivum habentes in sua concavitate et ante quam sagitte Tartarorum ad ipsos
attingere possent ceperunt contra ignem emittere sufflando cum follibus *quos habebant ex
utraque parte selle sub utroque femore.* Post ignem vero sagittas iacere ceperunt et sic turbatus
est exercitus Tartarorum. Alii quidem exusti alii vero vulnerati fugam inierunt quos persequentes Indi multos straverunt et reliquos de suis finibus eiecerunt nec ultra ad Indos Tartari
sunt reversi. *Hec eadem ipsi Tartari fratribus nostris referebant dicentes quod Indi in congressu
ordinata acie super equos se in strepis elevarerunt. Cumque miraremur quid hoc esset resederunt
subito super sellas et ignis mox prosiliit adversum nos quem etiam sagitte eorum sunt secute et
sic noster exercitus est fugatus. Cumque Indi Tartarorum postquam ad se rediissent*[(b)] *infra xviii
annos aut paulo plus nichil vidissent miserunt nuper ad eos nuncios sic dicentes: vos in terram
nostram intraveratis sicut fures et non milites*[(c)] [4ʳ] *bellicosi sed nunc scitote quoniam ad-*

¶17. (a) MS *prespiter.*   (b) MS *Tartarorum ad se rederint.*   (c) MS *milites milites.*

---

pp. 278–80. The idea that successive kings were "always called Prester John" was necessitated by the long persistence
of the legend. The Prester's realm was transferred from its first site in the Karakhitayan empire to India as early
as 1177, when Pope Alexander III wrote to him as "King of the Indians, holiest of priests". His realm appears in the
furthest east as "India Superior" or as "India Inferior" [*sic*] in the Vesconte world maps (Nordenskiöld, *Periplus,*
figs. 20, 6). Simon of Saint-Quentin tells of Chingis Khan's defeat of the Nestorian Wang Khan of the Keraits in
1203 (giving the date almost correctly as 1202) as a defeat of "David son of Prester John, once Emperor of India"
(Vincent, *Speculum Historiale,* Book 30, ch. 69). The Chingis Romance of *Carpini*-TR seems unique in claiming
the victory for Prester John. This Nestorian legend is here combined with Tolui's campaign in Khorassan against
Merv, Nishapor and Herat in the spring of 1221, and with Chingis Khan's pursuit of Jelal-ed-din through Afghanistan, culminating in the victory on the Indus, 24 November 1221. But the battle here referred to, in which Tolui
[*sic*] is heavily defeated, is clearly the defeat of Shigi-Kutuku by Jelal-ed-din at Perwan north of Kabul in a two-
day battle in the late spring of 1221 (d'Ohsson, Vol. 1, pp. 301–03; Grousset, 1941, pp. 241–42; Juvaini, Vol. 2, pp.
406–07; above, p. 30).
4. The strange story of Prester John's stratagem, peculiar to *Carpini*-TR, is derived in part (with reversal of roles)
from a device used by Shigi-Kutuku in the Battle of Perwan in accordance with a Mongol custom (mentioned by
Carpini, ch. VI, ¶14, and also employed in Hungary—d'Ohsson, Vol. 2, pp. 141–42). He ordered each Mongol
horseman to tie a dummy figure on his spare mount, in order to double their apparent numbers (Juvaini, Vol. 1,
p. 406). The stratagem was unsuccessful, and this defeat, although compensated by the arrival of Chingis Khan
with the main army, was one of the most serious ever suffered by the Mongols in the time of Chingis. The story
that the puppets emitted fire derives partly from the methods of chemical warfare used against Chingis and Ogedei
by the Kin, which included the shooting of inflammable powder from a tube. The Byzantine Greeks used a similar
device known as Greek fire, employing sulphur, naphtha, and other ingredients, from the seventh century onward,
and *Carpini* (ch. V, ¶12—not in TR) intelligently says that Prester John's weapon was "Greek fire". In the Khorasmian war both the Mongols and their opponents used naphtha and other incendiaries (Juvaini, Vol. 1, pp. 92, 106,
121, 127, 176). But the basic source is Alexander's battle near the Indus with Porus King of India, when Alexander
was fabled to have routed Porus' elephants with a panzer squadron of red-hot bronze statues filled with burning
embers on iron wagons, on which the elephants scorched their trunks and fled (cf. Risch, pp. 126–27). It is noteworthy that the story in *Carpini*-TR follows an early source in describing the statues as human in shape (cf.
pseudo-Callisthenes, lib. 3, ¶3), whereas in later versions they are models of elephants (cf. Budge, 1889, p. 90;
Budge, 1896, pp. 120–21, 369–70).

Indians had seen nothing of them for eighteen years or rather longer,[5] *they sent messengers to the Tartars, saying: "You invaded our country like thieves, not like fighting soldiers;* [4ʳ] *but now take warning that we are daily preparing our own invasion. Therefore, although you will not come to us, you may expect us soon to come to you."*

¶18. The Tartars, however, *not daring to return to their own land before the appointed time, lest Chingis Khan should condemn them to death, proceeded to the southeast,*[1] and marching *for more than a month* through the desert reached the Land *of Dogs, which in Tartar is called Nochoy Kadzar; for nochoy means dog in Tartar, and kadzar means land.*[2] They found only women there without men, *and taking two of these prisoner they waited by the river which flows through the middle of the country.* They asked the women where *and of what kind* the men were, and they replied that they were dogs by nature, *and had crossed over the river on hearing of the enemy's approach. On the third day* all the dogs in the country were seen to be gathering; and *when the Tartars made mock of them, they crossed the river and* rolled themselves in the sand, which owing to the coldness of the weather then froze. *For a second and third time* they did the same, and *as the dogs were shaggy* the mixture of ice and sand froze *a hand's-breadth thick.* This done, they charged upon the Tartars, who *laughed and* began to shoot them with their arrows, but *succeeded in killing very few, as it was impossible to wound them except in the mouth or eyes.* But the dogs ran swiftly up, *throwing a horse to the ground with one bite and throttling it with the next.* The Tartars, seeing that neither arrow *nor sword* could hurt the dogs, took to flight; *and the dogs pursued them for three days,* killed very many, dismissed them from their country, *and so had peace from them ever after.*[3] *One of the Tartars*

5. I.e. *ca.* 1240. A message of defiance to Ogedei from Il-Tutmish, the Sultan of Delhi, who had made uneasy terms with Jelal-ed-din in 1222, would be feasible but does not seem to be otherwise recorded. A doubtful report of the King of the Christians [*sic*] in India submitting and promising alliance against the Saracens in 1247, the year of Kuyuk's kuriltai, is given in the letter of Sempad, Constable of Armenia (Yule, *Cathay*, Vol. 1, p. 263)—but this is probably only another Prester John story. Prester John in Marco Polo (i.e. the Wang Khan) says in contempt of Chingis Khan's army that "they are not soldiers" (Yule, *Polo*, Vol. 1, p. 240). There may well be some relation with the defiant letters sent by Porus to Alexander in the Alexander Romance (e.g. Budge, 1896, pp. 112–16).

¶18. 1. Clearly a slip (cf. above, ¶11, n. 5) for northeast, in view of the icy climate of the Land of Dogs.

2. Correct as usual. *Nochoy* = dog, *ghajar* = country (Lessing, pp. 592, 355). The Mongol name is peculiar to TR, and of the highest importance, as showing that a genuine Mongol legend is here reported. But its transmission was indirect, for *Carpini* (ch. V, ¶13) says that the story was told to the friars in Kuyuk's court "by Russian priests and others who dwelt long with the Mongols". It is perhaps only a coincidence that Chingis Khan's father Yesugei was reputed to have said that the boy was "afraid of dogs" (*Secret History*, ¶66).

3. The story of dogs with human wives is told by King Hetoum I of a country "beyond Cathay", and by Chinese sources of a land called Kou-kuo in the far northeast (d'Avezac, pp. 544–45; Rockhill, p. 36). As in *Carpini*-TR both stress the shagginess of the dogs, and Hetoum states that the women gave birth to human females and canine males. The legend has evident origins in totemism and wolf packs, possibly even in fur-clad northerners. The Mongol royal line claimed its origin in a wolf (*Secret History*, ¶1), and that of the Turks in a child brought up (like Romulus and Remus, or Mowgli) by a wolf (Howorth, Vol. 1, p. 33). A still more closely related story is told by Rashid-ed-din of Oghuz Khan, the legendary ancestor of the Turks and Mongols, when he came to "the land of Kil Berak on the frontiers of the Land of Darkness", during a journey to the northeast in which, having already subdued—like Chingis Khan—Bokhara, Urgendj, and Hindustan, he furthered his intention of conquering the whole world. The natives prepared two warriors for a duel by the similar but still more uncomfortable method of bathing them in two vats of glue, one white and one black, and rolling alternately in white and black sand, repeating the process three times. The champions thus made invulnerable were victorious. Oghuz then launched a general attack, was routed, and took refuge between two rivers. Meanwhile a fugitive from his army made himself welcome to the womenfolk and their queen, who told Oghuz how to defeat the males by strewing caltrops

ventum nostrum coctidie prestolamur. Quare etsi ad nos venire nolueritis nostrum ad vos adventum citius expectetis.

¶18. Tartari autem *redire non presumentes ad propria ante statutum tempus a Cingis can ne* [V, ¶13] *subirent sentenciam capitalem processerunt inter orientalem plagam et meridianam.* Ambulantes *plus quam mensem* per desertum pervenerunt ad terram *canum que appellatur tartarice Nochoy Kadzar. Nochoy*[(a)] *enim tartarice canis dicitur latine, ḳadzar vero tartarice terra dicitur latine.* Invenerunt tantummodo mulieres preter viros, *quibus captis remanserunt duobus iuxta flumen quod medium terre transit,* cumque interrogassent[(b)] de viris *quales et* ubi essent responderunt quod canes naturales *et audita fama hostium flumen transivisse. Tertia autem die* canes omnes qui in terra fuerant coadunari apparuerunt *sed Tartaris iocum de eis facientibus transito flumine* involverunt se sabulo quod propter temporis frigiditatem congelatum est. Sicque *secundo et tertio* fecerunt et *quia canes pilosi erant* glacies cum sabulo congelata est *ad spissitudinem unius palme.* Quo facto super Tartaros irruerunt. Qui *risum facientes* sagittis eos impetere ceperunt. Sed *quia nisi per os et oculos ledi non poterant paucissimos peremerunt.* Canes vero accurrentes citius *uno morsu equum deiciebant altero catarum strangulabant.* Tartari ergo cernentes quod canibus nec sagitte *nec gladii* nocere poterant fugam inierunt *quos canes*

¶18. (*a*) MS *nothoy cadzar. Nothoi.*   (*b*) MS *intrassent.*   (*c*) MS *cuidam.*   (*d*) MS *propterea.*

---

and by shooting "a rain of arrows on those of the enemy who were naked and not covered with glue" (Erdmann, pp. 471–72, 475–78; Risch, pp. 127–28). A more correct form, It-berak, is given elsewhere by Rashid-ed-din (Erdmann, pp. 499–500). Rashid-ed-din's description of the natives—the men are "dark brown and of mongrel visage" and covered with hair, the women "catlike in shape and doglike in manners"—suggests that he may be toning down an original in which either or both are in fact dogs. *It* is the ordinary Turkish word for dog, while *berak,* or rather *baraq,* is a fabulous dog, very hairy and fast-running, hatched from the egg of an aged vulture (letters from Sir Gerard Clausen and Dr. J. A. Boyle, citing the eleventh-century Turkish-Arabic dictionary of Kashgari, Vol. I, p. 377). Erdmann is certainly right in suggesting that this Oghuz-legend is derived from the tale of Alexander and the Queen of the Amazons, for it contains vestiges, which are still visible in *Carpini*-TR, of relations with the Queen and her women, and of the river beyond which the Amazon's mates dwell. Cf. Mandeville's story, borrowed from Vincent, that the Amazons keep their female children and slay the males, and that in the neighboring country of Albania there are fierce dogs (Mandeville, Vol. I, pp. 111–12, 102–03; Hamelius, Vol. 2, pp. 93–94, 88). A further element in the Oghuz story—an old man who, unable to keep up with the army, is hidden by his son and gives advice at crucial moments, notably a stratagem for exploring the Land of Darkness, a journey of three days, by taking mares bereft of their foals as guides for the return journey (Erdmann, pp. 478–79)—is likewise borrowed from the Alexander Romance (pseudo-Callisthenes, lib. 2, ¶39; Budge, 1896, pp. 372, 396). Perhaps the most remarkable and the earliest parallel to the TR story of Chingis Khan and his sons is found in a recently discovered manuscript recording the expedition of five Uighur envoys in the eighth century, who were sent to explore the territories in northern Asia surrounding the Uighur empire. The envoys reported the existence to the northwest of Mongolia of a tribe of dogs with human wives, sprung from the union of a princess with a dog descended from heaven. This country, the envoys were told, was first discovered by two soldiers from the army of the conquering Zama Khagan, who followed camel-tracks across the desert (Bacot, pp. 147–48). This last element, like the similar one in the Oghuz story, derives ultimately from the journey into the Land of Darkness in the Alexander Romance; and we may further compare the desert, the three days' journey, and the camel tracks with Chingis Khan's journey of three *months* across the desert to Narayrgen, and the "trodden ways" he found there (TR, ¶13). Not far from the land of dogs, the Uighur envoys further reported, was a race of ox-footed men, whom Sir G. Clausen has explained as a rumor of arctic tribes wearing snowshoes (Clausen, p. 17). These ox-footed men of the Uighur story are evidently the same as the *Ucor-colon* of TR, ¶21 (q.v.); and their juxtaposition with the dog-men further suggests that the dogs of Nochoy Kadzar in TR, ¶18 and the dog-headed *Nochoy terim* of TR, ¶21 are doublets of one and the same legend. For further discussion of the origins of the TR Chingis romance in Uighur legend, the Alexander Romance, and other sources, see above, ¶11, n. 1; ¶12, nn. 2, 5; ¶13, n. 5; ¶15, n. 2; ¶17, nn. 3, 4; pp. 47–51.

even told Friar Benedict that his father was killed by the dogs at that time; and Friar Benedict believes beyond doubt that he saw one of the dog's women with the Tartars, and says she had even borne male children from them, but the boys were monsters. The aforesaid dogs are exceptionally shaggy,[4] *and understand every word the women say, while the women understand the dogs' sign language.* If a woman bears a female child, it has a human form like the mother, while if the child is a male it takes the shape of a dog like the father.

¶19. On their way home from this country the Tartars conquered the country known as Burithebet. *Burith means wolf,*[1] *and this name suits the natives well, since* it is their custom when their father dies to collect the whole family [4ᵛ] and eat his body,[2] *like ravening wolves.* They have no hairs in their beard, but if hairs grow they pull them out with iron tweezers made for this purpose.[3] Furthermore, they are exceedingly ugly.

¶20. The third army, however, which marched west with Chingis Khan's son Jochi Khan, conquered *first*[1] *the country called Terkemen,*[2] *secondly the Bisermins,*[3] *next the Kangits,*[4] *and lastly* invaded the country of *Cuspcas*[5] or Comania. *The Comanians, however, joined forces with the whole nation of the Russians and fought the Tartars near two small rivers, one called Kalka and the other called Coniuzzu (that is, Sheep's Water, for coni means sheep in Tartar and uzzu means water), and were beaten by the Tartars.*[6] *Blood ran on both sides up to the horses' bridles, according to those who took part in this war.* After this victory the Tartars began the return journey to their own country, and *on the way* conquered several countries to the north,[7] for example the Bashkirs, or Greater Hungary,[8] *which borders on the Arctic Ocean.*

4. Evidently one of the earliest occurrences of a shaggy dog story.

¶19. 1. *Buri* means wolf in Turkish. The name occurs also in Rashid-ed-din (d'Ohsson, Vol. 1, p. 82) and in a Chinese source (Boli-tufan = tubot—Bretschneider, Vol. 2, p. 25), as the country to which the Wang Khan's son Senggum Ilka fled in 1203, where it apparently means the district of northern Tibet bordering on Tangut. A statement by the seventeenth-century Sanang Setsen (p. 89) that Chingis Khan made a campaign against Tibet in 1206 is a mere confusion with the submission of the Uighurs in 1207, and in any case is too late to explain *Carpini*-TR. A possible source is the fact that in his expedition against Jelal-ed-din, which seems the main historical basis for Tolui's journey in TR, Chingis had thought of returning through Tibet (d'Ohsson, Vol. 1, p. 318). Tibet was perhaps attacked by Ogedei (Juvaini, Vol. 1, pp. 190, 196), and certainly by Mongke in 1251 and by Kubilai in 1254, 1257, 1268 (Bretschneider, Vol. 2, pp. 23–24), but was never definitively conquered.

2. Also reported by Rubruck, but untrue, except that the Tibetans had the custom of treasuring their ancestors' skulls (Rockhill, pp. 152–53).

3. Cf. Risch, p. 129, n. 7.

¶20. 1. For the following four tribes cf. the countries recorded in reverse order on the outward journey by *Carpini* (ch. IX, ¶21–23)—*Comani, Kangitae, Bisermini*—and by Benedict (Wyngaert, p. 138)—*Comani, Kangitae, Turkya.*

2. I.e. the Turcomans, nomadic Turkish tribes between Lake Balkash and the Aral Sea. The form *Terkemen* is very close to the correct indigenous form *Turkmen,* meaning "pure-blooded Turks" (cf. Grousset, 1939, p. 203).

3. The MS form *Berezemitae* is evidently a scribal corruption of *Bisermini,* for which TR, ¶34 has *Bizerunhte,* where manuscripts of *Carpini* (ch. VII, ¶9) give the similarly corrupt forms *Besereminy* and *Bissermiti* (Wyngaert, p. 89, n. f). Bisermin or Bussurman is the Slav form of Mussulman or Moslem, applying in general to the whole Khorasmian empire, but here only to Turkestan, its northern fringe (Rockhill, pp. 13–14).

4. The nomadic Kangits or Kangli were apparently Pechenegs, closely related to the Comans, and lived in the country between the Aral Sea and the northwest Caspian (Bretschneider, Vol. 1, pp. 301–04; Rockhill, p. 119; Beazley, *Texts,* p. 291).

5. Both *Cuspcas* and *Kusscar,* which is likewise given as an alternative for the Comans in TR ¶34, are presumably corruptions of some form of the name Kipchak or Kapchat, by which the Comans were also known (Bretschneider, Vol. 2, pp. 68–73; Rockhill, pp. 92–93). Rubruck similarly says: "Comani qui dicuntur Capchat" (Wyngaert, p. 194).

6. Jochi's expedition is here combined, for reasons discussed above (pp. 45–46), with Subetei and Jebe's south Russian

persequentes per triduum interfectis plurimis a suis eos finibus eiecerunt. *Et sic pacem ab eis de cetero habuerunt. Narravit etiam quidam*[c] *fratri B. Tartarus patrem suum a canibus tunc temporis interemptum. Frater praeterea*[d] *B. credit pro certo inter Tartaros unam de canum mulieribus se vidisse quam etiam dicit peperisse a Tartaris sed pueros monstruosos. Dicti autem canes sunt magis pilosi, intelligentes omnia verba mulierum et mulieres nutus canum.* Si mulier parit feminam humanam formam matris habet si masculum canis efficitur sicut pater.

¶19. De hac terra Tartari ad propria revertentes ceperunt terram que appellatur Burithebet.[a]   [V, ¶14]
Burith dicitur lupus et bene congruit incolis terre qui tamquam lupi sevientes patrem mortuum parentela [4ᵛ] congregata commedere consueverunt. Isti pilos in barba non habent sed si pili nascuntur extrahunt eos ferreo tenaculo ad hoc facto. Multum preterea sunt deformes.

¶20. Tertius autem exercitus qui ad occidentem ivit cum Tossuc can filio[a] Cingis can subi-   [V, ¶11]
ugavit *primo terram que dicitur Terķemen secundum Biserminos* [b] *postea Kangitas* [c] *ad ultimum* intraverunt *terram Cuspcas id est Comaniam.*[d] *Comani autem coadunati cum Ruthe-nis omnibus pugnaverunt cum Tartaris iuxta duos rivulos nomen unius Calc alterius vero Coniuzzu*[e] *id est ovium aqua, coni enim tartarice*[f] *oves dicuntur latine, uzzu*[g] *vero aqua,*

¶19. (*a*) MS *burithebeht.*
¶20. (*a*) MS *Cossut can cum filio.*   (*b*) MS *Berezemitas.*   (*c*) MS *ķangitās.*   (*d*) MS *comoniam.*   (*e*) MS *talc ... coniaxzu.*   (*f*) MS *cani enim grece tartarice.*   (*g*) MS *uzzum.*

---

campaign and the Battle of the Kalka River on 31 May 1222, in a unique and highly important narrative. The *Calc* is evidently the Kalka. The *Coniuzzu* is unrecorded elsewhere, but the derivation is correct (*coni* = *qoni* = sheep; *uzzu* = *usu* = water—see Lessing, pp. 963, 887). The Kalka has generally been identified with the Kal'mius, a small stream flowing into the Sea of Azov near Mariupol, the modern Zhdanov (Grousset, 1941, p. 260). However, modern large-scale maps show two small rivers here, the Kal'chik and the Kal'mius, which unite a mile or so from their mouth (see O. A. Beloghazova, *Atlas SSSR,* Moscow, 1954, fig. 39). In the light of TR we may identify the Kalka with the Kal'chik (evidently a diminutive of Kalka) and the Kal'mius with the *Coniuzzu,* though any apparent resemblance (*Coni* = Kal'mi; *uzzu* = us?) is perhaps coincidental.

7. During their return Subetei and Jebe fought only the Bulgars, by whom they were defeated (Pelliot, *Horde d'Or,* p. 170, correcting earlier authorities, e.g. d'Ohsson, Vol. 1, pp. 346, 446, and Grousset, 1941, p. 260, who say they were victorious). Nor is it likely that Jochi, during the four brief years of his khanate, and with the intervening Bulgars still unconquered, was able to make a foray to the north. *Carpini,* ch. V, ¶29–31, is probably right as against TR in situating this expedition in the period of Batu's western campaign of 1237–42. But it is less certain that *Carpini* is correct in placing it after Batu's return from Poland and Hungary, for in *Carpini* it is wrongly preceded by the campaigns against the Mordvins and Bulgars, in that order, which in fact took place in reverse order in 1237. As it happens either the earlier or the later date is rendered possible by the existence of two northward expeditions during the period, the first in 1238 under Siban, Bujek, and Buri to the Cheremisses on the Middle Volga north of the Kama River (Howorth, Vol. 2, p. 140; de Mailla, Vol. 9, p. 222; d'Ohsson, Vol. 2, p. 118; Wolff, p. 148), and the second *ca.* 1242–43 under Batu's brother and deputy Sinkur, when the rebellious Bulgars and Bashkirs were driven past the upper Kama (Howorth, Vol. 2, p. 155; Wolff, p. 383). On one or the other of these, according to a Chinese source, the Mongols penetrated so far north that there was hardly any night, and subdued a people with fair hair and blue eyes, possibly a Scandinavian colony (Gaubil, p. 104; Wolff, p. 148).

8. The Bashkirs, who still exist as natives of the Bashkir Autonomous Soviet Socialist Republic, were remnants of the Magyars who migrated to Hungary at the end of the ninth century, dwelling north of the Kangli and east of the Bulgars (Bretschneider, Vol. 1, pp. 326–28; art. Bashkir in *Encyclopaedia of Islam*). They were conquered at the same time as the Bulgars in 1237, when a Dominican mission under Friar Julian, sent to investigate rumors of the Mongol intention to invade Europe, traveled to near the borders of their country and found them already subdued (Rockhill, p. 131; Albericus Trium Fontium in *MGH,* Vol. 23, p. 942; Erben, Vol. 1, pp. 474–76; Dudik, Vol. 2, pp. 326–40; Fejér, tom. 4, Vol. 1, pp. 50–59; Bendefy; Wolff, pp. 263–74; below, p. 104).

¶21. After leaving this country they came to the Parossits, *who are tall in stature but thin and frail*, with a tiny *round* belly *like a little cup*. These people eat nothing at all but live on steam, for *instead of a mouth they have a minute orifice*, and obtain nourishment by inhaling the steam of meat stewed in a pot *through a small opening; and as they have no regard for the flesh they throw it to their dogs.*[1] *The Tartars took no heed of these people, as they thoroughly despise all monstrous things.* Next they came to the people called Samoyeds, *but took no notice of them either, because they are poverty-stricken men who dwell in forests* and sustain life only from hunting.[2] Lastly they came to the people called *Ucorcolon, that is, Ox-feet, because ucor is Tartar for ox and colon for foot, or otherwise Nochoyterim, that is Dog-heads, nochoy being Tartar for dog and terim for head.* They have feet like oxen from the ankles down, and a human head *from the back of the head to the ears,* but with a face in every respect like a dog's; *and for that reason they take their name from the part of them which is monstrous in form.* They speak two words and bark the third, *and so can be called dogs for this reason also.* [5ʳ] *They, too, live in forests and are nimble enough when they run, and the Tartars despised them like the others.*[3] Accordingly they returned home, where they found Chingis Khan had been struck by lightning.

¶22. *The Tartars also told our friars that they had been in the country of men with only one* foot and one hand, *but could do them no harm owing to their swiftness and their strength in shooting;* for one holds the bow and another shoots the arrow *more powerfully than any other nation, while they are said to excel in swiftness not only the men of other lands, but all four-footed animals in the world. Before the arrival of our friars among the Tartars two* of the aforesaid men, *a father and son,* came to the court of the Tartar Emperor and said as follows: *"For what reason have you tried to trouble us with wars? Do we not excel you in shooting of arrows and speed of running?" A horse of exceptional swiftness was appointed to race against them, and the Tartars released the horse at full speed. The two men began to revolve swiftly like a wheel in an extraordinary manner, and suddenly set out in pursuit of the horse. Finally they turned their*

¶21. 1. The Parossits are the Permiaks, whom the Arab geographer Idrisi calls Borassits, a Finnish tribe north of the Bashkirs in the present district of Perm on the Urals. They fled from the Mongols at an unascertained time during the reign of King Haakon II (1217–63) to Norway (Torfaeus, *Historia rerum Norvegicarum*, 1711, vol. 4, p. 303; d'Ohsson, Vol. 2, p. 186; d'Avezac, p. 492; Beazley, *Texts*, p. 285). According to Pullé, p. 181, they offered the steam of cooked meat to the souls of the dead, hence the story that they lived on steam; but a similar legend is found of an Indian tribe living on the scent of apples in Pliny (Book 7, ¶2), and repeated by Mandeville (Vol. 1, pp. 143, 208).

2. The Samoyeds, a Ural-Altaic tribe of the tundra on the lower Obi and Yenisei and the Arctic coast, still exist (Beazley, *Texts*, p. 285). The Parossits and Samoyeds are marked on the Obi River in Mercator's map of Europe of 1595 (Nordenskiöld, *Periplus*, p. 93, fig. 38), where they are no doubt derived from the abridgment of *Carpini* in Vincent's *Speculum Historiale*, Book XXXII, ch. 15.

3. Once again, the correct Mongol derivations peculiar to TR show that the story genuinely came from Mongol informants. *Uķor* = ox; *ķol* = foot; *nochoy* = dog (cf. *Nochoy Kadzar*, ¶18 above); *teriun* = head; see Lessing, pp. 1003, 483, 592, 805. *Terim* is paleographically so close to *teriun* that the latter may well have been the original reading of TR. For the Ox-foots see above, ¶18, n. 3. As for the Dog-heads, except for the somewhat similar tale of Nochoy Kadzar (see above, ¶18, nn. 2, 3), parallels have been adduced only from fables of dogheaded men in the islands of the Indian Ocean told by Friars Jordanus and Odoric, Marco Polo, and others (Yule, *Polo*, Vol. 2, pp. 309–12; *Cathay*, Vol. 2, pp. 168–69, Vol. 4, pp. 93–94; Cordier, *Odoric*, pp. 209–15; Risch, p. 127). D'Avezac,

et devicti sunt a Tartaris. *Effusus est sanguis ex utraque parte usque ad frenos equorum sicut qui bello interfuerant referebant.* Victis ergo istis Tartari redire ceperunt ad terras proprias *et in reditu* ceperunt ab aquilone quasdam terras videlicet Bastarchos id est maiorem Hungariam *que est contigua mari oceano ab aquilone.* [V, ¶29]

¶21. Ab hac terra venerunt ad Paroscitas qui *longe sunt stature sed graciles sunt et debiles* habentes ventrem parvulum *et rotundum ad modum ciphi modici.* Hii nichil manducant penitus sed vapore vivunt. Habent enim *foramen parvum loco oris* et dum carnes in olla obsoletas decocunt vapore suscepto *per aperturam modicam* sustentantur. *Carnes vero non curantes proiciunt ante canes. Hos itaque non curaverunt quia multum res abhominantur monstrosas.* Post hec venerunt ad quosdam qui Zamogedi appellantur. *Sed neque istos curaverunt eo quod sint homines pauperes silvestresque* et de venacione tantummodo vitam sustentantes. Postremo venerunt ad eos *qui vocantur Ucorcolon.*[a] *Ucor tartarice latine dicitur bos colon pedes quasi boves pedis vel dicuntur Nochoyterim Nochoy canis terim caput dicitur,*[b] *id est canis caput, Latine vero dicuntur canina capita.* Habent bovinos[c] pedes a talis deorsum caput hominis *ab occipite usque ad aures* faciem autem per omnia sicut canis *et ideo a parte denominantur degeneri.*[d] Isti duo verba locuntur et tercium latrant *et idcirco etiam canes possunt* [5ʳ] *nominari. Sunt etiam silvestres et in cursu agiles competenter et hos similiter contempserunt. Revertentes* itaque ad terram suam Cingis can percussum[e] a tonitruo invenerunt. [V, ¶30] [V, ¶31]

¶22. *Retulerunt preterea Tartari fratribus nostris* quod fuissent in terra quorundam hominum qui unum pedem habent tantummodo et unam manum, *quibus nichil potuerunt nocere propter eorum velocitatem et fortitudinem sagittarum.* Nam unus tenet arcum, alter vero dirigit sagittam *fortius omni gente. Velocitate etiam sua excedere dicuntur non solum homines terrarum aliarum verum etiam cuncta quadrupedia super terram.* Unde *ante adventum fratrum nostrorum ad Tartaros duo* ex iam dictis hominibus *pater et filius* ad curiam imperatoris Tartarorum venientes sic[a] dixerunt: *ob quam causam nos bellis inquietare attemptastis; nonne in sagittarum iaculis et cursus velocitate nos excedimus? Cumque equus velocissimus statutus fuisset cum eis publice ad predicandum ad currendum miserunt equum quidem cursu veloci procedere. Ipsi vero modo mirabili se velut rotam velocius ceperunt*[b] *volvere et equum sunt subito insecuti. Tandem equo et Tartaris terga vertentes ad terram propriam cucurrerunt, quod cernentes Tartari eos amplius invadere noluerunt.*[c] Isti autem *unipedes* vocantur. [V, ¶33]

¶21. (a) MS *urcolon.*   (b) MS *Notoyterim Nothoy canis terim dicitur.*   (c) MS *caninos.*   (d) MS *diginori.*
(e) MS *percusso.*
¶22. (a) MS *sicut.*   (b) MS *se ceperunt.*   (c) MS *voluerunt.*

---

p. 493, suggests that the Mongols may have heard rumors of the Tchouds, the aboriginals of the Arctic tundra. It may be a mere coincidence that the renegade Gascon priest Ivo of Narbonne, who wrote in March 1242 from Vienna to Giraldus, Bishop of Bordeaux, concerning Batu's ravaging of Hungary, states that the Mongol princes were accompanied by warriors with dog's heads (Matthew Paris, Vol. 4, p. 27, reading *cynocephalis*). *Carpini*, ch. IX, ¶20, names the Mordvins, Bulgars, Bashkirs, Parossits, Samoyeds, and Dogheads in a list of tribes north of Comania, as does Benedict (Wyngaert, p. 138), but with omission of the Samoyeds and with the Dogheads preceding the Parossits. Dog-headed people ("*cinocephales*") are shown on the Arctic coast of Russia in the Hereford Map.

backs on both horse and Tartars and ran to their own country, seeing which the Tartars decided not to invade them again. These people are called *Unipeds.*[1]

¶23. At this juncture Chingis was succeeded by his son Ogedei through the election of the rest.[1] For Chingis Khan had left four sons,[2] namely Ogedei, *who succeeded him,* Jochi,[3] Chaghatai, and a fourth whose name *I could not gather either from the friars or from the rest of the party.*[4] There are three sons of Ogedei, namely Kuyuk, who recently became Khan (or Emperor), Koten, and Siremun.[5] The sons of Chingis' second son Jochi Khan are Batu[6] (who is next most powerful after the Khan) and Ordu (who is senior and by far the highest in honor among the generals[7]). Jochi had two other sons *from another wife,* namely Siban[8] and Tangut.[9] The sons of Chingis' third son Chaghatai are Kadan and Buri.[10] The sons of the fourth son, whose name I could not gather,[11] are Mongke (*the elder,* whose mother Sorghoktani is next in precedence among the Tartars to the Emperor's mother, and who is himself next in power to Batu[12]), and Bujek, and others whose names I did not understand.[13] The following are the names of the generals: Ordu, who marched through Poland into Hungary; Batu, Buri, *Kadan,* Siban, and

---

¶22. 1. *Carpini,* ch. V, ¶33, tells this tale of Chormaghan's expedition (1229–41), on his way to attack the Armenians (1239), saying that the embassy of the One-foots arrived in the reign of Ogedei, and citing the authority of the Russian priests at Kuyuk's court, from whom the friars obtained some of their tallest stories. Risch (p. 156) adduces distant parallels from Pliny (lib. 7, ch. 2—men with one eye and one leg on which they hop nimbly) and Plato (*Symposium,* ch. 14—the men-women in Aristophanes' jesting tale, who roll like a wheel on their four hands and four feet). *Carpini's* citation of *Cyclopodes* in Isidore of Seville (*Etymologiae,* Book 11, ch. 35, ¶24), which is an after-thought occurring only in the manuscripts of his second version, has always been assumed to be correct, and has absurdly been taken as evidence that the whole story is Carpini's own invention (Pullé, pp. 162, 171; Wyngaert, p. 11; Risch, pp. 153, 156). In fact it shows only his desire to reinforce an improbable story with a respectable authority. The context in Isidore proves the very contrary, that Isidore was not the source; for *Cyclopodes* in *Carpini* is merely a portmanteau word due to an error of memory, compounded from the names of two separate tribes of monsters in Isidore: the *Cyclopes,* who are one-eyed giants found in India, and the *Sciopodes,* i.e. "shade-feet", a one-legged tribe in Ethiopia who hop "with marvellous celerity" on their single leg, and use their huge foot as a parasol to shield them from the heat of the sun (cf. Pliny, loc. cit.).

¶23. 1. On 13 September 1229. "The spelling Okodei occurs in the *Secret History* of the Mongols, and may indicate an actual variant pronunciation" (letter from Dr. J. A. Boyle).

2. The following account of the Mongol princes and generals, in which TR and *Carpini* (ch. V, ¶20–21) differ little, is by far the fullest and most accurate in any contemporary Western source. For genealogical tables of the Chingisids by Dr. J. A. Boyle, see Juvaini, Vol. 2, pp. 726–29; also Hambis, 1945.

3. In fact, of course, Jochi was Chingis Khan's eldest son, followed by Ogedei, Chaghatai, and Tolui. For *Carpini*-TR's spelling Tossuc for Jochi see above, ¶11, n. 2.

4. This is one of the rare personal comments by De Bridia. *Carpini* (ch. V, ¶20) says simply "we do not know the name of the fourth son" (cf. n. 11, below, and ¶11, n. 4). This inability of the friars to discover Tolui's name is highly interesting; for in fact his name, which means "mirror", was made tabu after his death, when he was called Ulugh-noyan or Yeke-noyan (i.e. Great Chieftain), and even mirrors could only be mentioned by the Turkish synonym *közgu.* Similarly, although these other tabus did not hinder the friars, Jochi after death was called "Ulus-Idi" ("lord of the appanage"), Ogedei "Qa'an" ("Emperor"), and Tolui's widow Sorghoktani "Beki" ("princess"). *Carpini* (ch. III, ¶12) says "no one dares to use the personal name of a dead prince until the third generation". See Juvaini, Vol. 1, p. 40, n. 5; J. A. Boyle (1956); d'Ohsson, Vol. 2, p. 60.

5. *Carpini's* Cocten and TR's Gozen suggest that the original reading was the perfectly correct Coten. Siremun, i.e. Solomon, was in fact Ogedei's grandson, being the son of his son Kochu. Another son of Ogedei, Kadan, is named below in the list of generals in TR, where *Carpini* (ch. V, ¶21) names yet another, Karachar (cf. d'Ohsson, Vol. 2, p. 99).

6. *Carpini*-TR's Bati represents the Slavonic pronunciation of Batu (cf. Pelliot, *Horde d'Or,* p. 28).

7. True, for Ordu was the eldest son of Jochi, eldest son of Chingis Khan.

¶23. Hiis gestis Occoday filius eius imperio ei successit per electionem aliorum. Reliquerat [V, ¶25]
enim Cingis can quattuor filios scilicet Occoday *qui et successit ei,* Tossuc,[a] Schahaday, quarti [V, ¶20]
nomen *nec a fratribus nec ab aliis intellexi.* Filii Occoday sunt tres scilicet Cuiuc[b] qui modo est
can id est imperator et Cocten[c] et Cyrenen.[d] Filii secundi scilicet Tossuc[e] can filii Bati (iste
est potentior post can), Ordu.[f] Iste senior est inter duces et honorabilior valde. Alios duos filios
habuit *de alia uxore* scilicet Syban et Chauth. Tertii scilicet Schahaday[g] sunt filii Cadan[h] et
Buri, quarti cuius nomen non intellexi filii sunt Mengu[i] (*hic fuit senior,* cuius mater Serectam
quae post matrem imperatoris est inter Tartaros nominata, et est potentior praeter quam Bati),
alter Bechac.[j] Aliorum filiorum nomina non intellexi. Hec sunt autem nomina ducum: Ordu [V, ¶21]
(iste transivit per Poloniam in Hungariam), Bati, Buri,[k] *Kadan,* Syban, Bugiec[l] (isti fuerunt
[5ᵛ] in Hungaria), Cyrbodan (iste adhuc contra Soldanum *Damasci* proeliatur); sed in terra
Tartarorum remanserat Mengu,[m] Cocten,[n] Syrenen et alii quamplures quos nominare non
oportet.

¶23. (*a*) MS *eis Cosut.*   (*b*) MS *Cuiur.*   (*c*) MS *Gozen*   (*d*) MS *Cyreuen.*   (*e*) MS *Cossu.*   (*f*) MS
Ozdu.   (*g*) MS *schaday.*   (*h*) MS *can.*   (*i*) MS *aingoy.*   (*j*) MS *betaht.*   (*k*) MS *burin.*   (*l*) MS *bu-*
giet.   (*m*) MS *Mango.*   (*n*) MS *Orten.*

---

8. Siban or Shiban is a Turkish form of Stephen, which, like Siremun = Solomon (n. 5, above), is a Nestorian
Christian name (Pelliot, *Horde d'Or,* pp. 46–47). Batu's mother was probably named Oki, and Ordu's mother was
Sarkan. Jochi's chief wife was Bek-tutmish, but her children and the mothers of his other sons are unknown (Pelliot,
ibid., pp. 28–31).

9. TR's *Chauth* is apparently a mishearing of Tangut as Ta'ut. *Carpini* here names two other sons of Jochi, "Bora"
(i.e. Bura) and "Berca" (i.e. Berke), and in the list of generals adds two more, "Sinocur" (i.e. Sinkur) and "Thuate-
mur" (i.e. Togha-Temur).

10. *Carpini* adds here: "we don't know the names of his other sons". The sons of Chaghatai were in fact Mochi
(named by *Carpini* below in the list of generals), Metiken, Yesu-Mongke, and Baidar. Buri was Chaghatai's grandson, being a son of Metiken, while Kadan was a son of Ogedei (see n. 5, above).

11. I.e. Tolui (cf. n. 4, above).

12. *Carpini*'s best form, *Mengu,* is the Turkish form of the Mongol *Mongke* (Juvaini, Vol. 1, p. 4, n. 1). These remarkable comments on the hierarchy of power show the friars' intimate acquaintance with the inner politics of
the Mongol court, the discovery of which was indeed one of the chief purposes of their mission. Batu, "the Maker
of Khans", although he had no desire to become Khan himself, was truly "most powerful after the Khan". Batu's
policy was directed to ensuring undisturbed possession of his own appanage, which in fact was destined to be the
most stable and durable of the Mongol sub-empires. He hated Kuyuk, having inherited the family feud with the
branches of Ogedei and Chaghatai which began with Jochi's quarrel with his brothers at the siege of Urgendj in
1221; but he was on the best of terms with Mongke, the eldest son of Tolui, who had loyally secured his rear in
the Russian campaign by conquering the Alans in 1239–40, and had fought by his side at Kiev in December 1240.
Mongke's mother and Tolui's widow, the Nestorian Christian Sorghoktani, was wealthy, powerful, just, and uni-
versally respected. In the series of state trials and investigations into the transactions of Turakina's regency which
followed Kuyuk's accession, though Kuyuk overthrew many of his own mother's favorites and ministers, he was
forced to acquit Sorghoktani of any misdoing (Juvaini, Vol. 2, pp. 549–53). After Kuyuk's death, with Batu's support, Sorghoktani secured Mongke's election in 1251 by a kuriltai composed solely of representatives of the houses
of Jochi and Tolui, and this *coup d'état* was followed by the liquidation of the Ogedeid and Chaghataid dissidents.
TR's form *Serectam,* together with the *Carpini* variants *Sorocan* and *Seroctan,* seems to point to the more accurate
form *Soroctan* (Pelliot, 1932, pp. 44–45). The "Emperor's mother" was Ogedei's widow Turakina, regent in 1242–46
between Ogedei's death and Kuyuk's accession, who, unknown to the friars, had died soon after their departure
from Karakorum. For Bujek, see Juvaini, Vol. 1, p. 269, n. 3.

13. Tolui's other sons were Kubilai, the future Khan (named below in the list of generals by *Carpini,* but not by
TR), Hulagu, Arig-Boke, Moge, Sogedu, and Subetei (to be distinguished from his namesake the great general
Subetei).

Bujek, who were [5ʳ] in Hungary; Chormaghan, who is still fighting the Sultan of *Damascus;*[14] while Mongke,[15] *Koten,* Siremun,[16] and many others whose names need not be given remained in the country of the Tartars.[17]

¶24. Ogedei, however, being very strong in numbers, organized *three of his father's armies.*[1] He placed *his brother's son* Batu in command of the first *and sent him to the west against God's Church and all the provinces of the west.*[2] Batu on his journey conquered the country of the Altisultan[3] and the land of the Bisermins,[4] who are Saracens and speak the Comanian language.[5] He also captured in the same country a very strong city called Barchin, although only after a lengthy war.[6] Another city called Iankint surrendered voluntarily, and accordingly he did not destroy it, but took booty and put *the nobility* to death, as is the Tartar custom, and then leased the city to other men after having the inhabitants transported.[7] Then he proceeded against Ornas,[8] a very large city full of Christians, that is Gazars and Alans, and others who are Saracens from various countries, situated on a river which *enclosed a large part of* the sea and ran through the city. The Tartars blocked the upper course of the river and then let the water flow violently down, drowning the city and everything in it.

¶25. At the same time Batu conquered *the countries of Terkomen, the Kangits,*[1] *Great Comania,*[2] *and* Russia, and captured Kiev, the metropolis of Russia, a very large and famous city,

14. For the form *Cyrpodan* = Chormaghan, cf. Juvaini, Vol. 1, p. 190, n. 31. In fact Chormaghan had died or retired in 1241, five years before the friars' arrival at Kuyuk's court, and the Sultan of Damascus was not attacked until 1260 (cf. below, ¶31, nn. 4, 5). Significantly, only the first version of *Carpini* follows TR here in naming the Sultan of Damascus, whereas the second version reads, more correctly: *"contra Soldanos quosdam terre Sarracenorum, et alios qui sunt ultra mare"*—"against certain Sultans of the land of the Saracens and others who are in the Middle East".

15. In fact Mongke had fought in Batu's western campaign (see above, n. 12), but returned to Mongolia before the death of Ogedei to watch his own interests and Batu's.

16. All the generals listed here by TR have appeared above among the Chingisids except Chormaghan, who was not of royal birth. *Carpini* omits Kadan and Koten.

17. In view of the much fuller list given by *Carpini,* this remark is probably another sign of De Bridia's unintelligent editorial intervention. *Carpini* names ten others in the list of generals who stayed in Mongolia, two of whom (Bura and Berke) he had already mentioned above (cf. n. 9). The remainder (best readings given) are: *Hubilai* (i.e. Kubilai); *Sinocur* (i.e. Sinkur, son of Jochi, though in fact he fought in the west); *Seremum* (i.e. Saraman, son of Chaghatai); *Tuatemur* (i.e. Togha-Temur, son of Jochi); *Karanchay* (i.e. Karachar, son of Ogedei); *Sibedei,* "the old man whom they call soldier (*miles*)", (i.e. the great Subetei *bahadur,* Subetei the Warrior, though he, of all people, did not "stay at home"); *Mauci* and *Corenza* (i.e. Mochi, son of Chaghatai, and Khurumsi, son of Ordu, both of whom the friars had encountered on their outward way to Batu—see p. 36, above).

¶24. 1. The arrangement in a simultaneous triad of the campaigns ordered by Ogedei in Russia (1236–42), Persia (1230 and onward) and China (1231 and onward) resembles the similar presentation of the semimythical campaigns of Chingis Khan, but is more justifiable. Ogedei himself seems to have ordained them, or to have been reputed to have done so, at the beginning of his reign—cf. Juvaini, Vol. 1, p. 190, who says that Ogedei immediately after his accession "dispatched armies to all the climes of the world", and ibid., pp. 198–99.

2. As we have seen, TR has already (¶20, above) given an apparently unique and authentic account of the conquests of Jochi in Turkestan and western Asia, in the order: Turcomans, Bisermins, Kangits, and Comania. Now the same narrative is told, giving much greater detail to the campaign of 1219–21 in northern Khorasmia when Jochi captured Barghalikent, Yanghikent, and Urgendj, by *Carpini* for the first time, and by TR, unwittingly, for the second time, but substituting Batu for Jochi and regarding the whole as forming part of Batu's western campaign of 1236–42. It seems likely that the friars recorded in Batu's territory the whole series of Jochi's and Batu's campaigns in chronological order, but without ascertaining the point at which Jochi's ended and Batu's began. Their respective errors—*Carpini's* omission of Jochi (except for the mention of Comania, ch. V, ¶11) and TR's duplica-

¶24. Occoday^(a) vero cum esset fortis multitudine *tres ex patris* exercitus ordinavit. Primo pre-   [V, ¶25]
fecit Bati *filium fratris* et misit *ad occidentem contra ecclesiam dei et omnes provincias occi-*
dentis. Qui veniendo subiugavit terram alti soldani et terram Biserminorum.^(b) Hii Sarraceni
erant Comanicum loquentes. Cepit ibidem etiam fortissimam civitatem nomine Barchin licet
cum bello diuturno. Alia vero civitas sponte se reddidit nomine Iankint^(c) qua de re civitatem non   [V, ¶26]
destruxit sed acceptis spoliis et interfectis ut moris eorum est *nobilioribus* aliis hominibus civitatem locans incolas transferri fecit et processit adversus Ornas^(d) civitatem maximam repletam
christianis scilicet Gazaris et Alanis necnon et aliis Sarracenis partium diversarum. Est autem
sita super fluvium *magnam habentem partem* maris et qui transibat civitatem. Tartari obstru-
entes *in superiori parte fluvium demiserunt*^(e) *aquam cum impetu* et submerserunt civitatem
cum omnibus que in se civitas continebat.

¶25. Preterea Bati^(a) tunc temporis subiugavit *terram Terkomen et terram Kangitarum*^(b)   [V, ¶27]
atque *Magnam Comaniam*^(c) nec non et Rusiam^(d) et capta Kyovia^(e) metropoli Rusie civitate
maxima et nominatissima per stragem multam populorum *et bella plurima que ad praesens*
transeo quia scriptorem exigit specialem.

¶24. (*a*) MS *octoday.*   (*b*) MS *bisermenorum.*   (*c*) MS *Iakint.*   (*d*) MS *ornaz.*   (*e*) MS *diuiserunt.*
¶25. (*a*) MS *Bat.*   (*b*) MS *gaugitarum.*   (*c*) MS *camoniam.*   (*d*) MS *ursiam.*   (*e*) MS *kyonia.*

---

tion—arise perhaps from the coincidence that the list contained, correctly, two adjacent campaigns against Comania,
the first at the end of Jochi's career and the second at the beginning of Batu's.

3. The precise explanation of *Carpini*-TR's epithet *alti* for the Sultan of Khorasmia remains uncertain. It surely
cannot represent the Latin *altus,* meaning high or supreme, though the friars may have wrongly thought so (cf. *Car-*
pini, ch. IX, ¶23; Rockhill, p. 15). It may well be a corruption of Shah Mohammed's first name, Ala-ed-din, or, still
more probably, of the Mongol name *Jalaldin Soltan* for his son Jelal-ed-din, whereas they called Mohammed himself
Khan Melik (*Secret History,* ¶257). In either case there is perhaps a confusion with the title *Altun Khan,* i.e. Golden
Emperor (from the Turkish *altun* = the Chinese *kin,* meaning Golden), by which the emperor of the Kin dynasty of
Northern China was generally known (*Secret History,* ¶248, ¶271, ¶273; Juvaini, Vol. I, p. 39, n. 18).

4. See above, ¶20, n. 3.

5. I.e. they were Turkish-speaking Moslems, which is correct.

6. For the form *Barchin,* cf. *Parch'in* in Kirakos's narrative of the journey of Hetoum I of Armenia in 1254–55,
and the Chinese *Pa-erh-chen* (Bretschneider, Vol. I, p. 170, Vol. 2, p. 95; Juvaini, Vol. I, p. 83, nn. 5, 7). In fact
Barghalikent surrendered to Jochi early in 1220 with little resistance and was spared (Juvaini, Vol. I, p. 87). The
only lengthy siege in this period of the war was the five-months' siege of Otrar by Ogedei and Chaghatai (*ca.*
September 1219–February 1220), hence perhaps *Carpini*-TR's confusion.

7. Yanghikent was captured by a detachment (Juvaini, Vol. I, p. 90). No details of the fate of the inhabitants are
given in eastern sources (cf. Bretschneider, Vol. I, pp. 278, 285, 291), but *Carpini*-TR may well have obtained a
correct account from informants in Batu's territory. It is true that during the Khorasmian war the Mongols generally massacred the garrison and chief citizens of towns which resisted, sent the craftsmen to Mongolia, and incorporated the adult males in their armies (cf. for Benaket, d'Ohsson, Vol. I, p. 224; for Samarkand, ibid., p. 239;
for Urgendj, ibid., p. 269; for Merv, ibid., pp. 285–86; for Nishapor, ibid., pp. 290–91). Cf. TR, ¶41.

8. See Excursus A: The Identification of "Ornas" (pp. 102–04, below).

¶25. 1. Up to the conquest of the Turcomans and Kangits the narrative relates historically to Jochi (cf. ¶20, above); Great
Comania applies both to Jochi (or rather to Subetei and Jebe considered as acting under his command) and to Batu;
subsequent events belong to Batu.

2. Here both *Carpini* and TR confuse the order of events. TR (¶27, below) transposes the campaigns against the
Bulgars and Mordvins in 1237, which ought to come here, to between the capture of Kiev (6 December 1240) and
the invasion of Poland and Hungary (spring of 1241), while *Carpini* (ch. V, ¶29) places them after the conquest
of Poland and Hungary, and follows them (ibid., ¶30, ¶31) with the expedition against the Parossits, Samoyeds
and Dog-heads, which TR has told above (¶21) of Jochi.

with great slaughter of the inhabitants *and many campaigns which I pass over for the present, because the subject demands a special author.*[3]

¶26. *And when Ogedeï's son, Batu's cousin, who is now Khan,*[1] *returned after learning secretly of his father's death,*[2] *on the way he conquered the countries of the Gazars and Alans, then the land of the Cathi, and lastly the country of the Circassians. These are countries inhabited by Christians,*[3] *but speaking different languages, and they are situated in the south near the sea.*[4] *After these conquests he returned home.*

¶27. Batu, however, made a campaign *in Russia* against the Bilers, that is, Great Bulgaria, and the Mordvins, *whom he took prisoner and enrolled in his own army.*[1] After this he proceeded against Poland and Hungary,[2] *and dividing his army on the frontier of these countries sent ten thousand soldiers under his brother Ordu against Poland. Many of these* [6ᵛ] *were routed and fell in battle on the border at the hands of the Poles of the duchies of Cracow and Sandomir.*[3] *However, envy being the greatest of all instigators to vices, instead of cherishing with mutual unity the blessing they had won, the Poles gave way to haughty pride and envied one another,*[4] *and were woefully stricken by the Tartars.*[5]

¶28. *The Tartars continued their advance into Silesia and joined battle with Henry, who at that time was the most Christian Duke of that country*[1]; *and as the Tartars told Friar Benedict, when they were themselves on the point of flight the columns of the Christians unexpectedly turned and fled.*[2] *Then the Tartars took Duke Henry prisoner, stripped him completely, and made him kneel before the body of their dead general, who had been killed at Sandomir.*[3] *Then*

3. This remark, if it is a sign of De Bridia's editorial abridgment, suggests that an account of the North Russian campaign of 1237–38 (unmentioned in *Carpini*) has been omitted here.

¶26. 1. I.e. Kuyuk.

2. This rumor is interesting, although incorrect, since Kuyuk was recalled in 1241 some months before the death of Ogedei, and according to some accounts in time to receive his father's admonishment for quarreling with Batu (d'Ohsson, Vol. 2, pp. 118–19; Grousset, 1941, p. 302; *Secret History*, ¶277; Juvaini, Vol. 1, pp. 239–40, 244). However, Ogedei suffered a slight stroke in March 1241, nine months before his death on 11 December 1241 (d'Ohsson, Vol. 2, pp. 86–87), and his wife Turakina, who was determined that her eldest son Kuyuk should succeed him, may well have warned Kuyuk "secretly" to return in view of Ogedei's ominous ill-health.

3. It is not elsewhere recorded, and is most improbable, that Kuyuk made any conquests during his hurried return. This episode clearly refers to Mongke's campaign against the Alans in the winter of 1239–40, made with the intention of securing Batu's rear. The Gazars or Khazars lay just to the north of the Alans, and it may be accepted that Mongke had to fight them also. The next two tribal names, *Th'et* and *Tartarorum*(!) are almost hopelessly corrupt. However, if we refer to *Carpini*'s list of tribes to the south of Comania (ch. IX, ¶20; cf. Benedict, ed. Wyngaert, pp. 137–38), we see that he correctly names the Circassians and the Cathi, i.e. the Kakhets or Kakhs in Georgia (d'Avezac, p. 495; Beazley, *Texts*, p. 290), and these, in reverse order, are perhaps intended here. Some such form as *Charcasi* for the Circassians (cf. Pelliot, *Horde d'Or*, p. 157, n. 5) would be very close to the TR reading. It is correct that these tribes were mainly or partly Christian.

4. I.e. south of Comania on the east coast of the Black Sea.

¶27. 1. Cf. above, ¶25, n. 2. The *Carpini*-TR form *Bileri* for the Bulgars corresponds to the Mohammedan *Beler* and the Mongol *Bolar*. Cf. *Carpini*, ch. V, ¶29, ch. VII, ¶9, ch. IX, ¶20; Benedict, ed. Wyngaert, p. 138; Rockhill, pp. 12, 121; Bretschneider, Vol. 2, pp. 81–84; *Secret History*, ¶262; Pelliot, *Horde d'Or*, pp. 135–7, 225. For the Mordvins incorporated in the Mongol armies cf. Rubruck, Rockhill, p. 99, and a letter of a Hungarian bishop to the Bishop of Paris on 10 April 1242, saying that they fought in the van "and killed all men indiscriminately" (Matthew Paris, Vol. 6, pp. 75–76).

2. The following detailed and remarkably accurate account of the campaigns in Poland and Hungary during 1241 is among the outstanding features peculiar to TR, and may be ascribed to the special interests and local knowledge of Benedict the Pole. Cf. above, p. 47.

¶26. *Cumque filius Occoday patruelis Bati qui modo est can reversus est patris occulte interitu intellecto in reditu autem cepit terram Gazarorum terram et Alanorum, postea terram † Th'et, ad ultimum terram Tartarorum † .*(a) *Iste sunt terre christianorum sed diversorum ydiomatum et posite sunt ad meridiem iuxta mare. Hiis actis ad terram propriam est reversus.*

¶27. Bati vero exivit *in Rusia* contra Bileros(a) id est Bulgariam Magnam et Morduanos *et captis eis suo eos exercitui subiugavit.* Ex tunc postea processit contra Poloniam et Hungariam, *divisoque exercitu in metis terrarum cum fratre suo Ordu misit contra Poloniam decem milia pugnatorum, ex quibus in terre principio* [6ʳ] *a Polonis Cracoviensis et Sandomericii*(b) *ducatus perturbati plurimi in prelio ceciderunt. Verum quia invidia est fomentum viciorum plurimum ideo Poloni non foventes unitate mutua bonum quod ceperant ob fastum superbie invidentes invicem a Tartaris miserabiliter sunt percussi.*

¶28. *Tartari vero ulterius procedentes in Slesiam*(a) *cum Henrico duce tunc temporis christianissimo eiusdem terre in prelio sunt congressi, et dum iam sicut ipsi fratri Benedicto referebant fugere voluissent ex insperato christianorum cunei ad fugam subito sunt conversi. Tunc ducem Henricum capientes Tartari et totaliter spoliantes coram duce mortuo qui in Sundomia*(b) *occisus fuerat flectere genua preceperunt. Sicque caput eius velut ovis*(c) *per Moraviam in Hungariam ad Bati detulerunt et inter cetera capita cadaverum postmodum proiecerunt.*

[V, ¶29]
[V, ¶28]

¶26. (a) MS corrupt. Perhaps: *Cathorum et* (or *Cachet*) *ad ultimum terram Circassorum.*
¶27. (a) MS *pilaros.*   (b) MS *apolinis o͞comin. et Sundemeric͞ii.*
¶28. (a) MS *zlesiam.*   (b) MS *sundomiam.*   (c) MS *ovi.*

3. According to the Polish chroniclers the Mongol detachments in Poland were commanded by Chaghatai's son Baidar and Ogedei's grandson Kaidu (Wolff, pp. 158; Grousset, 1939, p. 330). The provinces of Cracow and Sandomir belonged to Boleslaus IV, titular king of Poland; the remainder of Poland was divided between his relatives, Conrad Duke of Mazovia, Henry II Duke of Silesia, and Miecislav Duke of Oppeln and Ratibor (d'Ohsson, Vol. 2, p. 121). His followers seem in fact to have scored a few initial successes, notably in February 1241 after the sacking of Sandomir, when Vladimir the palatine of Cracow surprised the Mongols at Polanietz. A number of Mongols were slain in the first onset, but the rest turned and put Vladimir to flight, though their prisoners taken at Sandomir escaped in the confusion. The Mongols continued their temporary retreat into Galicia with their booty (d'Ohsson, Vol. 2, p. 122).

4. Henry and Miecislav had stayed behind to protect their own territory, instead of joining forces with their cousin Boleslaus (d'Ohsson, Vol. 2, pp. 123-24).

5. Boleslaus was routed at Chmielnik near Szydlow on 18 March 1241, and fled to a Cistercian monastery in Moravia (d'Ohsson, Vol. 2, p. 123). He survived to become Duke of Silesia, and befriended the Carpini friars on their outward journey (see above, p. 000).

¶28. 1. Henry was known by the epithet of "the Pious".

2. The Battle of Liegnitz on 9 April 1241 against Henry, Miecislav, and the Teutonic Knights began with a feigned retreat of the Mongol vanguard; the pursuers were surrounded, and the rest of the European forces were routed by panic, which they afterward attributed to supernatural causes, when trying to support them (d'Ohsson, Vol. 2, pp. 125-27).

3. Henry, accompanied by only four knights, was surrounded when trying to flee, wounded in the armpit by a Mongol lance, and beheaded. The story of a Mongol general's death in the duchy of Sandomir, and Henry's being ordered to kneel before his body, is not otherwise recorded, but may well be true. The reference is clearly to the skirmish under the palatine Vladimir near Polanietz (see above, ¶27, n. 3). The slain general, if he existed, can only have been a minor figure, since all the major chiefs survived the Western campaign. A Mongol general supposed to have been killed at Olmütz on 24 June 1241 was believed by the Polish chroniclers to be Baidar himself (d'Ohsson, Vol. 2, p. 130), though Baidar in fact appeared safe and sound at Kuyuk's installation in 1246 (Juvaini, Vol. 1, p. 249). In the effigy on his tomb at Breslau, Henry is represented as trampling on a Mongol warrior (see reproduction in Yule, *Polo*, Vol. 2, p. 493).

they took his head,[4] as if it had been the head of a sheep, through Moravia into Hungary to Batu, and then threw it among the other heads of the slain.

¶29. *While Batu himself was overrunning more than half the territory of Hungary, he was met near a certain river by a numerous army[1] under two brother kings born of the same mother, namely Bela who now reigns and Coloman of blessed memory, who at the first onslaught with his own hands hurled the chief general of the Tartars with his horse and weapons from a bridge over this river into the abyss of death.[2] And so he resisted a second and a third charge, until the Tartars turned to flight.[3] Meanwhile, however, Batu sent an army to cross the river a day or two's journey upstream to take the enemy by stealth in the rear during the battle on the bridge. They did so, and the outcome of this stratagem proved remarkably successful. The Hungarians neglected the warnings of King Coloman,[4] and the Tartars crossed the bridge. As the Tartars themselves told the story,* Batu unsheathed his sword when they were already in flight before the Hungarians and compelled them to return to battle,[5] *while the Hungarians, remaining inactive and almost heedless in their contempt for the Tartars, committed the same error at this time from presumptuous pride[6] as the Poles from envy. The Tartars charged upon them and slew a great number, and pursued Bela the king of Hungary as far as the sea.*

¶30. *While Batu was in Hungary, however, he learned of the death of Ogedei Khan,[1] who died after being poisoned by his sister[2] and was buried with the rich man in hell,[3] and immediately returned to Comania.[4] The friars saw him there on their way back from the Tartars to our Lord the Pope,* [6ʳ] *and state further that he is now returning from his own dominion to Kuyuk Khan. Moreover, there is great discord between them, and if this proceeds further the Christians may have respite from the Tartars for many years.[5]*

¶31. The second army under the command of Chormaghan[1] which had marched against the

---

4. The Mongols displayed Henry's head on the point of a lance to the garrison of the citadel at Liegnitz (d'Ohsson, Vol. 2, p. 127). His headless and naked body was recognized on the battlefield by his wife Anna from the six toes on its left foot, and buried in the Franciscan church of St. Vincent at Breslau, where it was exhumed in 1832, and again identified by the six toes (Wolff, p. 189).

¶29. 1. For the Battle of the Sayo River on 11 April 1241, and the flight of King Bela, see d'Ohsson, Vol. 2, pp. 142–60, Bretschneider, Vol. 1, pp. 324–32, and above, pp. 32–33.

2. An unnamed Mongol chieftain (*bahadur,* a title which the Chinese biography of Subetei in the *Yuan-shi* mistakes for a proper name) was in fact slain in the fight by the bridge, a mishap which Batu blamed upon Subetei for arriving late after his encircling movement (Bretschneider, Vol. 1, pp. 331–32). For the title *bahadur,* which was held among others by Chingis Khan's father Yesugei and by Subetei himself, cf. d'Ohsson, Vol. 1, p. 35; Grousset, 1941, p. 33; Martin, p. 41; Pelliot, *Horde d'Or,* p. 132, maintaining that it was sometimes used as a proper name.

3. Coloman's three brave but (despite TR) unsuccessful sorties were made not on the bridge but from the Hungarian camp after the bridge was lost (d'Ohsson, Vol. 2, pp. 143–44).

4. Coloman, as the king's brother, was effectively only a duke, but had the official title of "King of the Ruthenians and Duke of Slavonia". Bela himself calls him in an official document "Our brother Coloman, king and duke" (Fejér, tom. 4, Vol. 1, pp. 183, 203, 251).

5. According to Juvaini, Vol. 1, p. 270, Batu took a leaf from Chingis Khan's book (ibid., p. 80; Grousset, 1939, pp. 276–77) by ascending a hill (in order to commune with the sky god Tengri) and praying for a day and a night before the battle. The *Yuan-shi* says that Batu wished to retreat, dismayed by his losses on the bridge, to which Subetei replied that he would not retreat until he reached the Danube (Bretschneider, Vol. 1, pp. 331–32). But the story of Batu's rallying his men, which is given more fully by *Carpini,* ch. V, ¶28, is entirely in the spirit of Mongol epic narrative, though not recorded elsewhere, and no doubt has a Mongol source. *Carpini* says that Batu cried: "Fly not, for if you fly none will escape, and if we must die, let us all die; for what Chingis Khan said will come to pass, that we must all be slain; and if that time is now come, let us endure it."

¶29. *Ipso autem Bati intrante Hungariam ultra medium terre ipsius spacium occurrerunt ei iuxta quemdam fluvium cum multitudine copiosa duo reges fratres uterini Bela videlicet qui adhuc regnat et Colomanus felicis memorie qui manu propria de ponte ipsius fluvii princi-palem ducem Tartarorum in primo congressu cum equo et armis mortis precipitavit in abyssum. Sicque restitit eis etiam secundo et tercio, quoad usque*[(a)] *in fugam Tartari sunt conversi. Medio autem tempore Bati misit exercitum ultra flumen in superiori parte ad dietam unam sive duas qui istis in ponte pugnantibus caute super hostes irruerent*[(b)] *ex adverso. Quod et factum est. Nam rei eventus se mirabiliter hic probavit. Spernentibus enim Hungaris monita regis Colo-mani*[(c)] *pontem Tartari transiverunt et quod etiam ipsi Tartari referebant videlicet quod ipsis iam fugientibus ante Hungaros Bati evaginato gladio redire eos compulit ad bellandum et dum* [V, ¶28] *Hungari quasi securi quiescerent vilipendentes Tartaros quod Poloni*[(d)] *invidia hoc temporis presumptuosa superbia commiserunt. Nam Tartari irruentes straverunt plurimos et usque ad mare Belam regem Hungarie sunt secuti.*

¶30. *Bati vero in Hungaria existens percepta morte Occoday can qui impocionatus periit a sorore et sepultus est cum divite in inferno statim rediit in Comaniam, quem*[(a)] *etiam viderunt fratres ibidem ad dominum papam a Tartaris* [6ʳ] *redeundo. Dicunt praeterea fratres quod iam ad Cuiuc*[(b)] *can ex ipsius imperio revertatur. Insuper inter eos est discordia magna que si processum habuerit Christiani poterunt per plures annos a Tartaris*[(c)] *respirare.*

¶31. Secundus autem exercitus cui preerat Cyrpodan[(a)] qui iverat contra meridiem subiugavit [V, ¶32]

¶29. (a) MS *quo adusque*.　　(b) MS *irruerunt*.　　(c) MS *Colomoni*.　　(d) MS *polonis*.

¶30. (a) MS *quam*.　　(b) MS *cuino*.　　(c) MS *tataris*.

¶31. (a) MS *Gyrpodan*.

---

6. Apparently an echo of the words of the Emperor Frederick in a letter of 3 July 1241 to King Henry II of England, appealing for help against the Mongols and criticising Bela's negligent contempt for the Mongols ("*sprevit negligenter*") and his sloth and excessive heedlessness ("*deses et nimis securus*"). See Matthew Paris, Vol. 4, p. 113.

¶30. 1. The news of Ogedei's death on 11 December 1241 reached Batu in the early spring of 1242, soon after the sacking of Gran in a campaign west of the Danube (d'Ohsson, Vol. 2, p. 155).

2. Similarly, *Carpini,* ch. IX, ¶36, says that after his accession Kuyuk held a court of justice; "an aunt [reading *amita* for the evidently incorrect *amica* of the printed texts] of that emperor [Kuyuk] was arrested, who had killed his father [Ogedei] with poison, at the time when their army was in Hungary; and on this account their army retreated; and she was put to trial with many others, and they were executed". *Carpini*-TR's statements are a curious misunderstanding of the state trial and execution of Kuyuk's mother Turakina's favorite, Fatima, on a charge of having caused through witchcraft the death not of Ogedei but of Kuyuk's brother and rival Koten (Juvaini, Vol. 1, pp. 244–46; above, p. 38). In fact Ogedei died of drink (d'Ohsson, Vol. 2, pp. 86–87).

3. Luke 16:22: "*Mortuus est autem et dives et sepultus est in inferno*"—"the rich man died also, and was buried in hell".

4. Batu returned slowly to his seat on the Volga, arriving early in 1243, after aiding his brother Sinkur to repress a rebellion of the Comans (d'Ohsson, Vol. 2, p. 159; Bretschneider, Vol. 1, p. 333).

5. This remark, which again shows the friars' remarkable and prophetic insight into the internal politics of the Mongols (cf. above, ¶23, n. 12), suggests that a summons from Kuyuk had already reached Batu in time for them to hear of it on their arrival at his camp in May 1247 during their return journey, and that Batu's return to Mongolia to settle accounts with Kuyuk, which he began only in the spring of 1248 (Grousset, 1939, p. 338), was then already rumored. In fact Batu's plans for western conquest were halted by his quarrel with Kuyuk no less than by the death of Ogedei. He could no longer hope for the cooperation of the other Mongol princes and their armies, which was essential for a resumption of the war against Europe, and henceforth desired only to maintain the *status quo*.

¶31. 1. For Chormaghan's campaigns in the Middle East (1230–41) see above, pp. 31–32; d'Ohsson, Vol. 3, pp. 47–79; Grousset, 1939, pp. 325–27.

south conquered the country called Kirgiz.[2] The inhabitants of this land are pagans, and grow no hair on their faces, and when a man's father dies he cuts a strip of skin along his chin from one ear to the other to show his grief and sorrow for his father's death. Chormaghan also conquered Armenia, Georgia, *Nubia*,[3] *Turkey,* Baghdad[4] and the sultans of the Saracens, and many others, and is said to be still at war with the Sultan of *Damascus*.[5]

¶32. *The third army is now fighting certain eastern nations which are still not wholly subject to the rule of the Tartars.*[1]

¶33. *After the death of Ogedei Khan the Tartars were without a Khan for seven years,*[1] *and therefore made no attack in the direction of the west.* However, when our friars were present among them, they elected Ogedei's son Kuyuk as Khan *by a majority of one.*[2] As soon as he was elected, he raised a triumphal standard against the church of God and the dominion of the Christians and all the kingdoms of the west, and allocated *a third* of all his force for the conflict.[3] The Tartars are coming to fight for eighteen years in succession,[4] and will not depart until they have left neither ruler nor emperor nor kings, although they know they must be slain meanwhile by the Christians, *but do not know the day or the country in which God has ordained this, to the end that the God of vengeance may unexpectedly avenge the blood of the unavenged.*[5]

¶34. The names of the countries conquered by the Tartars are as follows: Kitai, Solangi, Ethiopia, Uirat, Keranite, Buritebet, Uighur, Kirgiz, Sariuighur, Merkit, Mecrit, Nayman, Karaki-

2. Probably untrue. The Kirghiz here have been generally supposed to mean the Cherkesses or Circassians northwest of the Caucasus (d'Avezac, pp. 568–70; Risch, pp. 130–31, 154–55). But these dwelt north of the Georgians, and would therefore be out of topographical order here, while the ethnographical remarks of *Carpini*-TR apply to the Kirghiz of the upper Yenisei in Central Asia, and are quite untrue of the Circassians, who were bearded Christians. However, Chormaghan arrived in Persia to attack Jelal-ed-din with the utmost speed, and it is most unlikely that he lingered on the way to fight the Kirghiz, who lay well to the north of his route, and do not seem to have rebelled after their submission to Jochi in 1207. It is equally unlikely that Chormaghan pursued his campaigns in Georgia in 1236–39 (d'Ohsson, Vol. 3, pp. 75–76) as far as the Circassians, who belonged to Batu's territory, and were conquered under his command by Kadan at this very time, in 1238 (d'Ohsson, Vol. 2, pp. 118, 626).

3. For Nubia, as meaning not Africa but the country on the Indian Ocean between the Persian Gulf and the Indus, cf. above, ¶17, n. 1. This may well have been included in the terms of reference of Chormaghan's command, but he made no campaign there.

4. As before (¶23 above, n. 14), the friars are unaware that Chormaghan had died or retired in 1241 and been replaced by Baiju. It was Baiju who subjugated the Seljuk Turks (1242–43)—see Grousset, 1939, p. 328; d'Ohsson, Vol. 3, pp. 78–84. Chormaghan threatened Baghdad in 1238 but was repulsed by the Caliph Mustansir (d'Ohsson, Vol. 3, pp. 73–74), and Baiju attacked with the same lack of success in 1245–46 (ibid., pp. 88–89). An envoy from Baghdad attended Kuyuk's accession (Juvaini, Vol. 1, p. 250), but the city was only captured by Hulagu in 1258 (Grousset, 1939, pp. 427–30). However, the *Secret History* records (¶260)—although this may be a mere anachronism—that Chingis Khan had ordered Chormaghan to advance on Baghdad in 1221, after the capture of Urgendj, but apparently without outcome; and again (¶270), that Ogedei sent Chormaghan "against the Sultan Chalibai [i.e. the Caliph] of the Baghdad-folk whom his father [Chingis Khan] had failed to conquer"; and (¶274) that Chormaghan "overthrew the people of Baghdad", implying that he exacted annual tribute, as is also stated by *Carpini*, ch. V, ¶34. The friars seem therefore to have obtained their information on Baghdad from an authentic though exaggerative Mongol source.

5. The Mongols under Baiju exacted tribute from Aleppo in 1243 and from Damascus in 1245 (d'Ohsson, Vol. 3, pp. 84, 88), though these cities were not captured until 1260, when the Mongols were immediately expelled by the Mamelukes of Egypt (Grousset, 1939, pp. 436–39). The Sultan of Aleppo sent his brother to Kuyuk's election (Juvaini, Vol. 1, p. 250). Only the manuscripts of the first version of *Carpini* read "Damascus" with TR; those of the second version read *Alapie* = Aleppo (Wyngaert, p. 75, n. s). Cf. above, ¶23, n. 14.

¶32. 1. The war against the Sung dynasty of southern China, begun by Ogedei in 1236 and still in progress (cf.

terram que appellatur Kirgiz. Homines terre huius pagani sunt nec habent pilos in barba, et cuiusque pater moritur ab una aure usque ad aliam per mentum incidit corrigiam de morte patris ostendens gemitum et dolorem. Item subiugavit Armeniam, item Georgianiam, *item* [V, ¶33] *Nubiam, item Turchiam,* item Baldac et Sarracenorum soldanos, alios quamplures. Iste adhuc [V, ¶34] soldanum *Damasci* dicitur impugnare.

¶32. *Tercius autem exercitus pugnat contra quosdam orientales qui adhuc non subiacent per omnia dominio Tartarorum.*

¶33. *Mortuo igitur Occoday can Tartari caruerunt can vii annis et ideo ad plagam occidentalem minime pugnaverunt.* Presentibus autem fratribus nostris Cuiuc[(a)] filium eius in can *per unius* [VIII, ¶2] *arbitrium* elegerunt. Qui mox ut electus est erexit vexillum triumphale contra dei ecclesiam et Christianorum imperium et regna omnia occidentis et de omni sua fortitudine destinavit [VIII, ¶4] partem *tertiam* ad bellandum. Veniunt autem xviii annis continue pugnaturi nec aperciantur quin nec potentem nec imperatorem[(b)] neque reges relinquant[(c)] et quamvis sciant quod de- [VIII, ¶3] beant interfici medio tempore a[(d)] christianis *nec tamen diem neque terram in qua hoc deus* [V, ¶19] *disposuerit fieri ut ex insperato sanguinem inultorum ulciscatur deus ultionum.*

¶34. Nomina autem terrarum quas subiugaverunt Tartari sunt hec: Kytai, Solangi, Ethiopia, [VII, ¶9] Voyrath, Keranite, Buritebet,[(a)] Uihur, Kirgiz, Saruihur, Merkit, Mecrit,[(b)] Nayman, Karaki-tai,[(c)] Turkia, *Nubia,* Baldac, *Urumsoldan,* Bisermini,[(d)] Cangite, Armenia,[(e)] Georgiania, Alani qui dicunt se Azzos, Circasi, Gazari, Comani qui dicunt se Kusscar, Mordui, Bascart, id est magna Hungaria, Billeri,[(f)] Corola, *Cassidi,* Parossiti,[(g)] *Canina,* Zamogedi, Nestoriani, *Nusia,* Persarum Soldani (omnes isti Sarraceni per se vocantur).

¶33. (*a*) MS *cuiūt.*　(*b*) MS *impatorem.*　(*c*) MS omits (e.g.) *relinquant.*　(*d*) MS omits *a.*
¶34. (*a*) MS *Huritebet.*　(*b*) MS *Vihur kyrgiz Sarumhur Merkyte Metrum.*　(*c*) MS *Kyrakytarum.*　(*d*) MS *Bizerunhte.*　(*e*) MS *Armienia.*　(*f*) MS *Bylee.*　(*g*) MS *Parozici.*

---

above, ¶9, n. 6, and pp. oo). *Carpini*-TR do not mention separately Ogedei's previous conquest of the province of Ho-nan, the last remnant of the Kin empire, in 1231–34, which they have confused with the Kin war of Chingis Khan (cf. above, ¶9, nn. 1–5).

¶33. 1. In fact the interregnum lasted only four years and eight months, from 11 December 1241 to 24 August 1246.

2. The election of Kuyuk was, of course, unanimous, but the friars no doubt heard of the alternative candidatures of Siremun and Koten (see Juvaini, Vol. 1, p. 251).

3. This event is recorded in *Carpini, ch. IX,* ¶38, also ch. VIII, ¶3, where it is said that Kuyuk ordered the friars "to return to Turakina's residence the day before, because he wished to raise his standard against the whole terri- tory of the west, as we were firmly told by people who knew, for he did not wish us to be aware of it". The standard was the famous white banner with nine yak-tails, the original tribal standard of Chingis Khan, the *tugh,* which was erected before the emperor's tent as a formal declaration of war (Grousset, 1941, pp. 159, 180, 477). In fact Kuyuk renewed the declaration of war on Southern China and the Middle East, assigning for the latter alone two men in every ten (Juvaini, Vol. 1, p. 256), but not against Europe, which he could not attack before dealing with Batu. However, Kuyuk's letter to Innocent shows his sinister interest in the West, and *Carpini,* ch. VIII, ¶5, says, no doubt truly: "He declared with his own mouth that he intended to send an army into Livonia and Prussia".

4. *Carpini,* ch. V, ¶19, says that the Mongols have fought for forty-two years and will fight for eighteen more. Risch (p. 136, n. 7) suggests that this period of sixty years was regarded as a complete cycle by the Mongols and Chinese, which corroborates the authenticity of this superstition, though it does not seem to be recorded in other than western sources. Another version is given in Bishop Peter's communication to the Council of Lyons in 1245, stating that the Mongols "say they have been commanded by God to exterminate the whole world for thirty-nine years" (Matthew Paris, Vol. 4, p. 387).

5. Perhaps an echo (cf. above, ¶2, n. 1) of Innocent's letter to Kuyuk of 13 March 1245, in which he threatens divine vengeance in somewhat similar words—"*Omnipotens Deus . . . gravius ulciscatur*" (Wadding, Vol. 3, p. 135).

tai, Turkia, *Nubia*, Baghdad, *Urumsoldan,* Bisermins, Kangits, Armenia, Georgia, the Alans who call themselves Azzi, the Circassians, Gazars, the Comans who call themselves Kusscar, Mordvins, Bascart otherwise Great Hungary, Billeri, Corola, *Cassidi,* Parossits, *Dog-heads,* Samoyeds, Nestorians, *Nusia,* the sultans of the Persians, all of whom call themselves Saracens.[1]

¶35. *Having described the wars of the Tartars and their origin*[1] *I must now explain the position of their country.* Part of it is very mountainous and part very flat. It is infertile because the soil is sandy, and the climate is very intemperate, perhaps owing to the alternation of mountains and plainland. Violent winds are frequent, and they also have lightning, thunder, and storms [7ʳ] out of season. *They told our friars that in the last few years their climate had undergone a remarkable change, for frequently clouds seem to contend with clouds near the surface of the ground, and they added that a little before the arrival of the friars fire descended from heaven and consumed many thousand horses and cattle with all but a few of their herdsmen.* While the friars were present at the election of the Khan or Emperor hail fell in such quantities that more than a hundred and sixty men were drowned by its sudden melting and their property and huts were swept far away, *but did no damage whatever to the friars' dwelling which was nearby.*[2] While the friars were watching and suffering the same calamity with the others, a violent wind sprang up and raised such a cloud of dust that no one could ride or even stand.

¶36. These Tartars are generally of low stature and rather thin, *owing to their diet of mare's milk, which makes a man slim, and their strenuous life.* They are broad of face with prominent cheekbones, and have a tonsure on their head like our clerics from which they shave a strip three fingers wide from ear to ear. On the forehead, however, they wear their hair *in a crescent-shaped* fringe reaching to the eyebrows, but gather up the remaining hair, and arrange and braid it *like the Saracens.*[1]

¶37. As to their clothing, one needs to know that men and women wear the same kind of garments *and are therefore not easy to tell apart; and as these matters seem more curious than useful I have not troubled to write further about their clothing and adornment.*[1]

¶38. Their houses are called stations and are of round shape, made of withies and stakes. At the top they have a round window to let out the smoke and let in the daylight. The roof and door are of felt. They differ in size and are movable insofar as the size permits them to be carried. The "stations" of the Khan and princes are called hordes. They have no towns but are organized in stations in various places. They have one city called Karakorum, from which our friars were a half a day's journey when they were at the Emperor's Sira Ordu or superior court.[1] Owing to shortage of wood neither nobles nor commoners have any fuel but cattle dung and horse dung.[2] *According to the tradition of some, Chingis Khan was the founder of the Tartars, but the friars, although they stayed with them a long time, were unable to discover more about their origin.*[3]

¶34. 1. See Excursus B: The *Carpini*-TR lists of peoples conquered by the Mongols (pp. 104–06, below).

¶35. 1. The remainder of TR, comprising an account of the homeland, daily life and customs of the Mongols (¶35–55), followed by a discussion of their methods of warfare (¶56–61), contains comparatively little material that is not found in much greater detail in *Carpini*. The order perhaps represents that of the hypothetical original draft from which both *Carpini* and TR were diversely elaborated. The former section is transposed in *Carpini*, ch. I, ¶4–ch. IV, ¶11, to before the account of Mongol history forming ch. V, which it immediately follows in TR.

2. The hailstorm of 15 August 1246, which was considered an unfavourable omen and caused the postponement of

¶35. *Descriptis igitur bellis*[a] *Tartarorum et unde ortum habuerint ubi etiam eorum terra sit nunc sciendum est.* Terra[b] eadem est in parte aliqua montuosa multum in aliqua plana valde. [I, ¶4]
Infertuosa quia arenosa est in aere nimis distemperata *et hoc forte ratione moncium et plani-* [I, ¶5]
tiei.[c] Ventis fortissimis abundat: sunt etiam ibi fulmina tonitrua et tempe- [7ʳ] states et
extra tempus. *Dicebant enim fratribus quod a paucis annis incepissent mirabiliter aput eos*
tempora immutari. Nam sepe nubes contra nubes iuxta terram quasi pugnare videntur. Dice-
bant enim preterea quod parum ante adventum fratrum ad eos ignis de celo descendit et con-
sumpsit equorum multa milia et pecorum cum servis omnibus pascentibus preter paucos.
Fratribus autem presentibus in electione can id est imperatoris tanta grando cecidit quod ex sui [I, ¶5]
resolutione subita plus clx homines submersit et res cum habitaculis procul duxit, *fratrum vero*
habitaculum quod prope erat penitus non offendit. Fratribus insuper videntibus et cum aliis
hoc idem pacientibus maximus ventus exurgens tantum pulverem excitavit quod nemo equitare
poterat neque stare.

¶36. Isti Tartari sunt stature mediocris generaliter et satis graciles *ratione lactis iumentini*[a] [II, ¶2]
quod subtilem facit hominem et laboris. In facie vero sunt lati genas prominentes habentes,
coronam preterea sicut nostri clerici habent in capite a qua radere solent[b] versus utramque
aurem spacium trium digitorum. In fronte vero habent crines usque ad supercilia *in modum*
lunule, deprehendentes reliquos autem crines componunt et nectunt[c] *sicut Sarraceni.*

¶37. De vestibus eorum sciendum est quod uniformes vestes habent viri cum feminis *et ideo* [II, ¶4]
non subito disnoscuntur, et quia hec magis curiosa quam utilia videntur, idcirco de vestibus
cetera et ornatu eorum scribere non curavi.

¶38. Domus eorum stationes vocantur et sunt rotunde facte de virgis et de sudibus. Superius [II, ¶6]
rotundam habent fenestram propter fumum et lucem. Tectum et ostium sunt de filco. Differunt
tamen in quantitate et duci possunt secundum quod quantitas exigit ad portandum. Stationes [I, ¶5]
can et principum ordea Tartarice appellantur. Villas non habent sed in diversis locis per sta- [I, ¶4]
tiones ordinantur. Civitatem unam habent que Caracaron[a] dicitur iuxta quam fratres nostri
fuerunt ad dietam dimidiam quando erant apud Syram ordea imperatoris scilicet curiam meliorem. Habent fomentum ignis non nobiles et simplices propter lignorum paucitatem nisi de

---

¶35. (*a*) MS *sellis.* (*b*) MS *est quod terra.* (*c*) MS *placiei.*
¶36. (*a*) MS *iumentum.* (*b*) MS omits *solent.* (*c*) MS *mit'u't.*
¶38. (*a*) MS *Cratura.*

Kuyuk's election until 24 August (cf. *Carpini,* ch. IX, ¶32). For the horrors of Mongolian weather cf. Risch, p. 53, nn. 6-8.

¶36. 1. Cf. Risch, pp. 54-56, nn. Rubruck gives a similar account of Mongol hairdressing (Rockhill, p. 72).

¶37. 1. *Carpini,* ch. II, ¶5, gives a meticulous description of Mongol women's dress, and TR would no doubt have repeated it, had not C. de Bridia thought the subject slightly improper.

¶38. 1. The Mongol word is *ordu,* meaning a royal encampment (Lessing, p. 617). The friars perhaps heard the Coman form *orda* (cf. Pelliot, *Horde d'Or,* p. 30). Cf. Rockhill, p. 57, and Rubruck's account of Mongol tents (ibid., pp. 53-57). *Sira* in fact means "yellow" (Lessing, p. 714).

2. Rubruck on entering Mongke Khan's palace found "a fire of briars and wormwood roots and cattle-dung in a grate in the centre of the dwelling" (Rockhill, p. 173, cf. ibid., p. 133).

3. "First ancestor" was, in fact, one of the posthumous titles of Chingis Khan (Rockhill, pp. 80, 82). The Mongols, however, had a good knowledge of their history for several generations before Chingis Khan, and legends reaching back to remote antiquity (d'Ohsson, Vol. 1, pp. 21-36; *Secret History,* ¶1-67).

¶39. They believe in one God, creator of things visible and invisible and giver in this world of good and evil alike.[1] But for all that they do not worship Him as is right, for they have various idols. [7ʳ] They have certain images of men made of felt which they place on either side of the door of their station above udders of felt likewise, and they assert that these are the guardians of their herds, and offer them milk and meat. But their chiefs give greater honor to certain silken idols which they keep on the wagon, or on the roof or door of their station, and if anyone steals anything therein he is immediately slain. But the captains of thousands and hundreds keep a goatskin *stuffed with hay or straw* in the middle of their station[2] and offer it milk of all kinds. When they begin to eat or drink, they offer to the idol on the wagon the heart of the animal on a platter, and take it away and eat it next morning. They place before the station of every Khan an idol which they first made in the image of Chingis Khan,[3] and offer it gifts. The horses which are offered to it are never ridden again. They offer first to it the animals which they slaughter for food, and they do not break their bones. They bow southward to the same idol as to a god and compel many of their captives to the same act, especially noblemen.

¶40. Hence it happened recently that when Michael, one of the grand dukes of Russia, submitted to their rule but refused to bow down to the aforesaid idol, saying that this was forbidden to Christians, and persisted in his constancy to the faith of Christ, he was ordered to be kicked with the heel of the foot to the right of the heart; and when his attendant knight urged him to endure even to martyrdom, his *throat* was cut with a knife and the knight who exhorted him was beheaded.[1] They make offerings also to the sun, the moon, water, and earth, usually in the morning.

¶41. They keep certain traditional laws made by Chingis Khan,[1] who laid down (as has been stated above) that the filth contained in an animal's belly must not be extracted by opening up the entrails, but be squeezed out by hand, and the bowels be prepared for eating after cleansing

¶39. 1. Tengri, the sky-god. Kuyuk's letter to Innocent IV begins with the formula: "In the power of the eternal Tengri" (Pelliot, 1922–23, p. 24). Mongke Khan told Rubruck: "We Moal believe that there is only one God, by whom we live and by whom we die" (Rockhill, p. 235). Cf. Risch, pp. 63–65, nn. 2, 3; Roux, passim.

2. In this passage Carpini and Benedict seem to have variously misunderstood their own or each other's notes. *Carpini,* ch. III, ¶2, obviously correctly, states that the theft of any object from *"the wagon of the idol"* is punished by death, but then, obviously wrongly, that the captains have a *goat (hircum)* in the middle of their huts. The TR text, explicitly describing a stuffed goatskin, refutes Wyngaert's (p. 37, n. 2) absurd emendation of *Carpini's hircum* into *hercium,* which he explains as *"Iovis nomen"*—apparently taking it for the Homeric and Classical Greek Ζεὺς ἑρκεῖος, Zeus god of the household, from ἕρκος, meaning "front court", in which his statue stood. The idols made of felt, the stuffed goatskin, and the tabu on touching the idol-waggon are all mentioned by Rubruck (Rockhill, pp. 58–59, 149).

3. *Carpini,* ch. III, ¶3, mentions the golden image of Chingis Khan in front of Kuyuk's tent, and Benedict (Wyngaert, p. 137; Rockhill, p. 35) records the same of Batu's tent, saying that the friars refused to bow down before it, and were let off with a mere nod of the head.

¶40. 1. Duke Michael of Chernigov and his faithful knight Feodor were thus martyred by Batu on 20 September 1246, during the friars' absence at Kuyuk's court, and were made saints by the Russian Orthodox Church (Spuler, p. 27; Vernadsky, pp. 143–45). The friars must have received an eyewitness account of the tragedy on their return to Batu's camp in May 1247. The kicking of Duke Michael was an honor according to protocol, and the cutting of his throat an extra punishment for his contumacy. The Mongols scrupulously avoided shedding the blood of royalty, since the soul was thought to reside in the blood. Thus Jamuka was executed "without shedding of blood" (*Secret History,* ¶201), the Russian princes captured at the Battle of the Kalka were crushed beneath a platform of boards (*Novgorod Chronicle,* p. 64), and the Dowager Empress Oghul Ghaimish and Siremun were drowned

boum stercoribus et equorum. *Tradicione quorundam Tartarorum Cingis can inventor extitit sed plurimum auctores fratres inter eos longo existentes tempore minime invenerunt.*

¶39. Credunt tamen unum deum creatorem rerum visibilium et invisibilium et datorem bono- [III, ¶2]
rum in hoc seculo pariter et malorum. Nec tamen ideo eum venerantur sicut decet, habent
enim idola [7ᵛ] diversa. Quasdam imagines hominum de filco habent quas ponunt ex utraque
parte hostii stacionis super ubera de filco similiter, et has affirmant esse custodes pecorum et eis
offerunt lac et carnes. Sed quedam idola sericea⁽ᵃ⁾ plus honorant potentes super currum, tectum,
aut hostium stacionis, et si quis in eo quid furatus fuerit mox necatur. Millenarii autem et
centenarii pellem hircinam⁽ᵇ⁾ *repletam feno vel stramine* habent in medio stacionis, offerunt- [III, ¶3]
que ei lac omnis generis. Idolo vero quod est in curru commedere sive bibere incipientes offerunt
cor animalis in scutella quod mane auferunt et manducant. Fecerunt preterea primo Cingis
can idolum quod ante stacionem cuiuslibet can ponunt offerentes ei munera. Equi autem qui
ei offeruntur ulterius non equitantur. Animalia etiam quae occidunt ad manducandum ei
prius offerunt, os animalis non confringunt. Eidem idolo inclinant ad meridiem quasi deo et
ad idem multos compellunt precipue nobiles subiugatos.

¶40. Unde nuper accidit quod dominus Michael de maioribus Rusie ducibus dum se eorum [III, ¶4]
dominio subiaceret et nollet dicto idolo inclinare dicens hoc illicitum esse Christianis et dum
constans in fide Christi persisteret iussus est calce pedis ad precordia percuti ad dextrum.
Exhortante autem eum milite suo ad constanciam martyrii *guttur* ei cultello precisum est et
caput amputatum militi exhortanti. Libant etiam munera soli lune aque terre et hoc precipue [III, ¶5]
mane facere consueverunt.

¶41. Habent preterea quasdam tradiciones a Cingis can quas observant, qui statuit ut interior [V, ¶17]
grossicies ventris animalis sicut dictum est superius per apercionem viscerum non purgetur sed
exprimatur manibus et venter sic purgatus ad comedendum preparetur. Item si quis per super- [V, ¶18]
biam auctoritate propria can esse voluerit mox necetur. Ideo ante electionem Cuiuc⁽ᵃ⁾ can
nepos Cingis can occisus fuit quia ad imperium aspiravit. Item statuit ut omnes terras mundi
subiugarent et cum nullis pacem facerent nisi simpliciter se eis redderent sine pacto, *et tunc
precepit quod omnes nobiliores interficiantur rusticis reservatis.* Prophetatum est etiam eis [V, ¶19]
quod ad ultimum debent omnes interfici *in terra christianorum,* pauci tamen residui tenebunt
legem terre in qua patres [8ʳ] eorum diversis mortibus occidentur. Item statuit esse in exercitum decanos centenarios millenarios⁽ᵇ⁾ et decamillenarios id est decem milia sub uno *quod*⁽ᶜ⁾
Ruteni solent tumbas appellare.

¶39. (*a*) MS *cericea.*   (*b*) MS *ircynam.*
¶41. 1. Chingis Khan commenced his law code, the Yasa, after his inauguration in 1206, and completed it in 1225

---

at Mongke's order (Grousset, 1941, pp. 310–11). Even princes, however, were beheaded in cases of particular out-
rage (cf. *Secret History,* ¶136, ¶156).
¶41. (*a*) MS *cygniz.*   (*b*) MS *esse temerarios decanos in exercitum millenarios.*   (*c*) MS *quia.*
after his return from the Khorasmian war. The Yasa was written on rolls in Uighur script, and kept in the treas-
uries of the chief Mongol princes (Juvaini, Vol. 1, p. 25). The surviving fragments are discussed by Riasanovsky,
pp. 57–69, Vernadsky, pp. 99–110, d'Ohsson, Vol. 1, pp. 404–16. In *Carpini,* ch. V, ¶18, ¶19, this brief account of
the Yasa occurs in the historical section, between the story of the entrails during Chingis Khan's return from
Narayrgen and his death.

in this manner.[2] Again, should any man attempt out of pride to become Khan by his own personal influence, he must instantly be slain. Accordingly before the election of Kuyuk Khan, a nephew of Chingis Khan was killed because he aspired to be emperor.[3] He also ordained that the Tartars should conquer every country in the world and make peace with none unless they surrendered unconditionally and without treaty, *and even then he ordered that all of nobler rank should be slain and only plebeians be spared.*[4] It has been prophesied to them that in the end they must all be killed *in the land of the Christians,* except that the few survivors will adopt the law of the country in which their fathers [8ʳ] are destined to be slain by various deaths.[5] He ordered, moreover, that the army should be commanded by leaders of ten, a hundred, a thousand, and ten thousand—that is, one man to command ten thousand, *which the Russians call tumbas.*[6]

¶42. Moreover, owing to dread handed down from their ancestors, they assert that certain things are great sins. One of these is to poke a fire or touch it in any way with a knife, or to take meat from a pot with a knife, or to chop wood with an axe near a fire, because they affirm that this causes the fire to be beheaded, or to lean on the whips with which they lash their horses (for they do not use spurs), or to touch arrows with a whip, or take young birds *from a nest,* or to strike a horse with a bridle, or to urinate in a hut. If this last is done intentionally, the culprit is slain; if unintentionally, he must pay a sorcerer who performs a rite of purification by making them carry their huts and property between two fires, and until this is done no one dares to touch anything in the hut.[1] If anyone spits out a morsel of food (*or a mouthful, which comes to the same thing*) once it is put in his mouth, being unable to swallow it, a hole is dug under his hut through which he is dragged out and instantly put to death.[2] If anyone treads on the threshold of a chief's hut, he is slain without mercy, and our friars were therefore instructed not to do so.[3] They also consider it a sin to pour mare's milk on the ground intentionally,[4] and *when the friars told them it was a sin* to shed human blood, *or to get drunk,*[5] or to steal the property of others, *they laughed at this and paid no attention whatever.* They do not believe in the eternal life of the blessed or in perpetual damnation, but only that they live again after death and increase their herds and eat. They practice drug-potions and spells, but believe the demon's

2. Cf. above, ¶16. Possibly a misunderstanding of the Yasa article on the slaughter of animals: "When an animal is to be eaten its feet must be tied, its stomach must be ripped and its heart pressed with the hand until the animal dies; then its meat must be eaten" (Riasanovsky, p. 57).

3. In fact the conspirator was Chingis Khan's youngest brother, Otegin, who in 1242, shortly after the death of Ogedei, had made an abortive attempt to usurp the Khanate; and his trial and execution took place immediately after, not before, Kuyuk's accession. Juvaini remarks, in exact conformity with *Carpini*-TR, that Otegin was put to death "in accordance with the Yasa" (Juvaini, Vol. 1, pp. 244, 255; d'Ohsson, Vol. 2, pp. 194–95, 203).

4. Cf. above, ¶24, n. 7.

5. Cf. above, ¶29, n. 5; ¶33, n. 4.

6. *Carpini* says twice (ch. V, ¶19; ch. VI, ¶2) that the Mongols call a division of ten thousand "darkness" (*tenebrae*), and the corrupt "*tumbas*" in the TR manuscript should probably be emended to *tenebras*. The similarity in sound between the Turkish words *tuman* = ten thousand and *thuman* or *duman* = darkness is coincidental and without philological connection, since the former is of purely Altaic stock, while the latter is a loan word of Indo-European origin, found in various forms in many languages, including the Sanskrit *tama*, the Latin *tenebrae*, and the Russian *t'ma*, but apparently introduced into Turkish via the Iranian *dunman*. Owing to the similarity of sound to the Turkish *tuman*, which they learned from early contact with the Comans or other Turkish tribes, the medieval Russians adopted the alternative meaning "ten thousand" for their own words of Indo-European origin, *tuman* =

¶42. Ex terrore preterea[(a)] patrum suorum peccata quedam asserunt esse magna. Unum est [III, ¶7]
figere ignem vel quoquomodo tangere in cultello. Item carnes de caldario extrahere cum cultello.
Item iuxta ignem ligna scindere cum securi. Post hoc enim caput[(b)] ignis asserunt amputari.
Item appodiari ad flagella equorum quia calcaribus non utuntur vel flagello sagittas tangere
vel iuvenes aviculas *de nido* accipere. Item cum freno equum percutere. Item in stacione urinare
quod si facit voluntarie tunc necatur, si non[(c)] oportet ut det pecuniam cantatori qui purificet
inter duos ignes per ipsos staciones cum rebus faciens pertransire, et priusquam fiat hoc nullus
audet res stacionis attrectare. Item si quis morsellum, *siue bolum quod idem est,* sibi impositum
de ore eicit deglutire non prevalens suffoditur statio eius et per illud foramen extrahitur et mox
necatur.[(d)] Item si quis calcat limen stacionis ducis absque misericordia vita caret. Ideo fratres [IX, ¶11, ¶33]
nostri super limen docti fuerant non calcare. Item peccatum reputant in terra sua sponte lac [III, ¶7]
effundere iumentinum[(e)] et *quando fratres dicebant eis peccatum esse* humanum sanguinem [III, ¶8]
fundere, *inebriari,* aliena rapere *et huius ridebant et penitus non curabant.* Non enim credunt
esse sanctorum vitam eternam nec dampnacionem perpetuam, sed tantummodo quod post [III, ¶9]
mortem vivant iterum et greges multiplicent et manducent. Attendunt etiam veneficia et in- [III, ¶10]
cantationes. Responsa vero demonis credunt dei quem deum appellant *Iuga* sed Comani *Codar.*
Nec cogunt quempiam fidem suam relinquere *dum modo per omnia eis obediat in preceptis.* [III, ¶5]
Alioquin[(f)] *cogunt violenter aut occidunt.* Unde fratrem iuniorem ducis Andree in Rusia quem [III, ¶6]
falso iudicio interfecerunt coegerunt fratris relictam accipere etiam eos[(g)] in uno lecto coram
aliis publice componentes.

¶43. Item in principio lunacionis vel in plenilunio solent incipere quodque opus. Item dicunt [III, ¶10]
lunam magnum esse imperatorem et genibus flexis adorant eam. Solem vero dicunt esse matrem

---

¶42. (*a*) MS *preterita.*   (*b*) MS *capit.*   (*c*) MS *nam.*   (*d*) MS *extraitur et non calcatur. Carpini* has: *extra-*
hitur . . . et sine ulla miseratione occiditur.   (*e*) MS *iumentum.*   (*f*) MS *alioquim.*   (*g*) MS *in eos.*

---

fog, and *t'ma* = darkness, which has survived into modern Russian. Cf. M. Vasmer, *Russisches etymologisches*
Wörterbuch, Heidelberg, 1958, Vol. 3, pp. 152, 162; F. Miklosich, *Lexicon palaeoslovenico-graeco-latinum,* Vienna,
1862–65, p. 1021; d'Avezac, pp. 578–79. The remark in TR is of great interest, as giving one of the earliest dated
attestations of this borrowing. The Mongol word for ten thousand, which *Carpini* (loc. cit.) is mistaken in interpreting as meaning also "darkness", is *tumen* (Lessing, p. 853), as is mentioned by Rubruck (Rockhill, p. 201).
For Chingis Khan's decimal reorganization of his army in 1206 cf. Riasanovsky, pp. 59–61; Martin, p. 22; Grousset,
1939, p. 282; Juvaini, Vol. 1, pp. 31–32.

¶42. 1. Because the spilling of liquid would attract lightning—cf. n. 4 below, and the Yasa article: "Whoever urinates
into water or ashes is put to death" (Riasanovsky, p. 57).

2. A slight misunderstanding of the severe tabu against rejecting food put into one's mouth by a guest of honor
(cf. Risch, p. 74, n. 6). This and the next prohibition, against treading on the threshold of a prince's tent, occur
together in Riasanovsky (p. 60), and perhaps retain the original sequence of the Yasa.

3. The friars were so warned at the camp of Khurumsi (*Carpini,* ch. IX, ¶11), at Batu's (ibid., ¶16), and at Kuyuk's
court (ibid., ¶33). So too was Rubruck at the camp of Batu's son Sartak (Rockhill, p. 104) and at Mongke's palace,
where his companion Friar Bartholomew clumsily trod on the threshold and was arrested but pardoned on plea
of ignorance (ibid., pp. 188–89, 192). Friar Julian records the same prohibition (Dudik, Vol. 1, p. 332).

4. Cf. the statement of Rashid-ed-din (d'Ohsson, Vol. 2, p. 618): "They say that if anyone spills wine, kumiss, milk
or whey on the ground, lightning strikes their herds and especially the horses".

5. The Yasa itself deprecated drunkenness, but was here honored more in the breach than in the observance. "If
a man must drink," said Chingis Khan, "he should try to get drunk only thrice in a month; twice or once would
be better still, and never at all would be best of all—but where shall such a man be found?" (d'Ohsson, Vol. 2,
p. 412).

replies come from a god whom they call *Iuga* and the Comanians call *Codar*.[6] They do not force anyone to abandon his faith *provided he obeys their orders in every way;*[7] *otherwise they compel him by force or kill him,* as they compelled the younger brother of Duke Andrew in Russia, whom they wrongfully condemned and slew, to take his brother's widow to wife, and even laid them publicly together in the same bed in the sight of the rest.[8]

¶43. They are accustomed to begin any undertaking at the new moon or full moon. They say the moon is a great emperor, and worship it on bended knees, and that the sun is the moon's mother, because the moon takes its light from thence *and because of its fiery nature, which they revere above all things,* for they believe everything is purified by fire. For this reason all messengers and the gifts they bring must be brought to their masters between two fires, [8ᵛ] so that any poison or spell they have brought may be purged. Accordingly, even our friars passed between fires.[1]

¶44. When one of them is gravely ill, a spear nine cubits long bound in black felt is erected near his dwelling, and henceforth no one outside his family dares to enter the bounds of that hut.[1] When his death-agony begins, it is unusual for anyone to stay by him, because no one who was present at his death could enter the horde of any chief or of the emperor until the ninth moon began.[2]

¶45. When a rich man dies, he is buried secretly in the open country, sitting in his dwelling with a basket full of meat and a jar of mare's milk, and with him is buried a mare and foal, a horse with bridle and saddle, *and a bow with quiver and arrows.* His friends eat the flesh of a horse and its hide is stuffed with hay and raised on a wooden scaffold. They believe he needs all these things in the future life, the mare for milking, the horse for riding, and so on, *and gold and silver is in like manner laid with him.*[1]

¶46. Certain more important persons are buried as follows. They make a secret pit in open country *with a small square opening* but widened both ways inside, *and another near his hut openly and publicly in which they pretend to bury the dead man;* and they put the slave who was his favorite in life under the dead man's body in the still open grave. If the slave survives after lying in torment for three days beneath the corpse, he is freed and is honored and powerful in the whole family of the deceased. After this they cover up the grave *and drive mares or cattle over the place*[1] *all night, so that when it is flattened out the treasure buried with him may not be discovered by strangers,* and sometimes they even replace the turf taken from the site.

6. A description of the shaman prophesying in an autohypnotic trance (cf. Rubruck, Rockhill, p. 246). *Carpini*, ch. III, ¶10, gives the better reading *Itoga*. Etugen or Itugen was the Mongol earth goddess (see Lot-Falck, passim), the "Natigay, god of the earth" of Marco Polo (Yule, *Polo*, Vol. 1, pp. 257-59). The friars and Polo are not quite mistaken in calling her a god, as she was often given male epithets (Lot-Falck, pp. 194-96). *Carpini*, ch. III, ¶10, says incorrectly that the Coman equivalent is *Kam*, which in fact is the Turkish for a shaman—an error perhaps arising from confusion with the Mongol *idughan*, meaning a female shaman (Lot-Falck, pp. 191-92). In TR "*Codar* could stand for *Codai* or the like, i.e. the Persian Khudā(i) "God". Cf. the *kudai* of the Kirghiz and the Altai Tatars. See Harva, *Die religiösen Vorstellungen der altaischen Völker*, p. 142" (letter from Dr. J. A. Boyle). Less probably, it might represent the form *Iediiar* = Itugen, attested for the Western Turks (Lot-Falck, p. 181).

7. Cf. the Yasa article: "He (Chingis Khan) orders that all religions shall be respected, and that no preference shall be shown to any of them" (Riasanovsky, p. 58).

8. *Carpini*, ch. III, ¶6, states that the victim was accused, "though the charge was unproven", of selling Mongol horses outside Mongol territory, and that the incident "occurred while we were still in the land (of the Mongols)"— i.e., presumably, before their return to Batu's camp. The story has been doubted, on the grounds that no Duke

lune eo quod ab eo lumen recipiat *et quia ignee nature est, quam ipsi pre omnibus reverentur,* credunt enim per ignem omnia purificari. Unde nuncios qualescumque et munera que portant inter duos ignes ad dominos eorum [8ᵛ] transire opportet ut venenum si quid portaverint aut maleficium expurgetur. Qua de re ad ignes transiverunt etiam fratres nostri. [IX, ¶14]

¶44. Cum aliquis inter eos infirmatur graviter hasta novem cubitorum circumdata filco nigro [III, ¶11] erigitur circa stacionem eius et extunc nullus alienus audet intrare terminos illarum stacionum. Cum autem agonizare ceperit raro aliquis aput eum remanet quia nullus posset qui morti interesset[a] ordan ducis alicuius aut imperatoris introire nisi prius nona lunacio inchoaretur.

¶45. Quod si dives moritur occulte in campo sepelitur cum stacione sua sedendo in ea et cum [III, ¶12] alveolo pleno carnibus et cipho lactis iumentini. Sepelitur etiam cum eo iumentum cum pullo, equus cum freno et sella, *arcus cum pharetra[a] et sagittis.* Unum autem equum commedunt amici et coreum eius repleto feno elevatum super ligna. Credunt quod hiis omnibus indigeat in futuro iumento scilicet ad lactandum equo ad equitandum et sic de aliis. Simili modo ponitur aurum et argentum.

¶46. Quosdam etiam maiores sic sepeliunt. Unam occultam foveam in campo faciunt *cuius* [III, ¶13] *orismum est quadrum et satis parvum,* interius autem ad utramque partem dilatatur *et aliam faciunt prope staciones publice et aperte in quam se mortuum simulant sepelire.* Servum[a] vero quem pre ceteris dilexit in vita ponunt subtus corpus mortui sepulcro aperto remanente, qui si tertio sub eo agonizando surrexerit liber erit et in tota parentela illa honorabilis atque potens. Post hoc sepulcrum operientes *iumenta seu pecora agunt[b] per noctem desuper locum ut planato loco non possit ab extraneis thesaurus cum eo positus inveniri.* Quandoque etiam prius reposita gramina supponunt.

¶47. Duo praeterea[a] cimiteria habent in terra propria *unum simplicium* aliud imperatorum [III, ¶14] ducum et nobilium et si quomodo fieri potest de omnibus terris in quibus occiduntur ad istud mortui nobiles redducuntur *sicut de hiis factum fuit* qui in Hungaria fuerunt interfecti. Si quis

---

¶44. (*a*) MS *interesse.*

¶45. (*a*) MS *cum probaretur.*

¶46. (*a*) MS *sercium.* (*b*) MS *etiam.*

¶47. (*a*) MS *propterea.*

Andreas of Chernigov is known between the Duke of that name who was slain at the Battle of the Kalka in 1222 and another who succeeded to the dukedom in 1261 (Risch, p. 71, n. 20). However, the Andreas named by the friars may well have reigned for only a few months after the martyrdom of his predecessor Duke Michael (see above, ¶40, n. 1), and have remained otherwise unknown. *Carpini* (loc. cit.) states that the younger brother of Andreas visited Batu with the dead man's widow to plead to be allowed to inherit the dukedom. For this purpose, according to Mongol law, it was necessary for him to marry his brother's widow (cf. below, ¶49, n. 2), a union which in Christian eyes was within the forbidden degrees and therefore incestuous.

¶43. 1. At Batu's camp on the outward journey (*Carpini,* ch. IX, ¶14; Benedict, ed. Wyngaert, pp. 136–37). Rubruck was excused this ceremony at Mongke's court, as he had brought no gifts (Rockhill, p. 240).

¶44. 1. Cf. Rubruck (Rockhill, pp. 82–83).

2. Cf. Rubruck (Rockhill, p. 80). Rubruck says "for a year". The reading in *Carpini,* ch. III, ¶11, is *ad novam lunationem,* i.e. "till the new moon", where *novam* should evidently be emended to *nonam* as in TR.

¶45. 1. Cf. Risch, pp. 81–83, nn. 5–9.

¶46. 1. Cf. Risch, pp. 84–85, nn. 12–15. This detail, not found in *Carpini,* is quoted from a Chinese source in Yule, *Polo,* Vol. 1, p. 248.

¶47. They have two cemeteries in their own land,[1] *one for ordinary people* and one for emperors, chiefs, and noblemen, and if at all possible dead noblemen are brought back there from every land where they are slain, *as was done with those* who were killed in Hungary. If anyone but the guardians[2] enters this cemetery, he is ill-treated in many ways. Our friars who entered it unknowingly would have given grave offense if they had not been messengers *of the great Pope, whom the Tartars call Yul* [9ʳ] *Boba,* which means Great Pope.[3]

¶48. When anyone dies, everything appertaining to his dwelling has to be purified. Two fires are accordingly prepared, near which two spears are set upright and bound together at the top with a thong to which shreds of buckram are tied. Under this thong between the spears and fires must pass all the men, the animals, and the hut itself, and two witches stand on either side throwing on water and reciting spells. If a wagon is touched by the spears when passing or anything falls from it, it becomes the lawful perquisite of the witches.[1] Similarly if anyone dies from being struck by lightning, all his possessions are shunned by everyone until purified in the aforesaid manner.[2]

¶49. They have as many wives as they can afford, and generally buy them, *so that except for women of noble birth they are mere chattels.*[1] They marry anyone they please, except their mother, daughter, and sister from the same mother. When their father dies, they marry their stepmother, and a younger brother or cousin marries his brother's widow.[2] The wives do all the work, and make shoes, leather garments, and so on, while the men make nothing but arrows, and practice shooting with bows.[3] They compel even boys three or four years old to the same exercise, and even some of the women, especially the maidens, practice archery and ride as a rule like men.[4] If people are taken in adultery and fornication, man and woman alike are slain.[5]

¶50. They are more obedient to their lords than other nations, more even than priests are to bishops, the more so as no mercy is shown to transgressors, and the emperor therefore holds them in his power in every way; for whether they are sent to their death or to live they must do their task with all speed. The emperor can take to himself the daughters, wives, or sisters of anyone he wishes, and after he has enjoyed them, if he does not want to keep them for himself, he gives them to whomsoever he pleases.[1]

¶51. Envoys sent by him or to him are given their keep free of charge together with post-horses, but foreign envoys are given only meager keep, for two *or three* could eat what is doled out to *five* men.[1] *I shudder therefore to describe or enumerate the hardships undergone by our friars, since they themselves who endured them marvel how the grace of Jesus Christ sustained them in opposition to human nature.* [9ᵛ] *Oh, how often they rode more than thirty Bohemian*

¶47. 1. *Carpini,* ch. III, ¶14, no doubt rightly, distinguishes the two cemeteries as one for the Khans, princes, and nobility, the other for those slain in Hungary. Risch (p. 86, n. 18) is certainly wrong in suggesting that the latter cemetery was actually in Hungary, for (a) the friars did not travel through Hungary; (b) the Mongols would never have buried their great dead in a country which they did not occupy permanently; (c) *Carpini* (loc. cit.) says both cemeteries were *"in terra eorum"*, i.e. in Mongolia; (d) the new evidence of TR states explicitly that the dead were brought back from Hungary to Mongolia.

2. For the cemetery guards cf. Rubruck, ed. Rockhill, pp. 80–81.

3. *Yul boba* in fact represents the Turkish *Ulugh baba*, Great Pope, not the Mongol *baba yek̲*. TR perhaps alludes specifically to Kuyuk's letter to Innocent IV, in which the surviving original Persian text has *papai-kalan,* with the same meaning, "Great Pope". Cf. Pelliot, 1922–23, p. 18.

ad hoc cimiterium accesserit exceptis custodibus male multimodis pertractatur. Unde et fratres nostros qui ignoranter intraverant offendissent graviter quin fuissent nuncii *magni pape quem vocant Tartari yul* [9^r] *boba id est magnus papa.*

¶48. Mortuo^(a) autem aliquo oportet purificari omnia que ad eius pertinent stacionem.^(b) Preparantur itaque duo ignes iuxta quos eriguntur^(c) due haste in directum in cacumine colligate zona habente in se quasdam scissuras de bukerano alligatas. Sub hac zona inter hastas et ignes opportet transire homines bestias et stacionem. Due autem incantatrices stant hinc atque inde aquam proicientes et carmina recitantes. Quod si currus transeundo tangitur seu res^(d) alique ceciderint mox eas incantatrices accipiunt ipso iure. Similiter si quis a tonitruo percussus moritur omnia que habuit contempnuntur ab hominibus quousque dicto modo fuerint expurgata.   [III, ¶15]

¶49. Quotquot possunt in expensis tenere uxores tot habent, emunt autem eas generaliter omnes, *ideo sunt quasi proprie preter nobiliores,* et ducunt indifferenter excepta matre et filia et sorore ex eadem matre. Novercam mortuo patre ducunt et relictam fratris iunior frater vel cognatus. Uxores faciunt omnia opera scilicet calceos pellicea et huiusmodi cetera, viri^(a) sagittas tantummodo et exercent cum arcubus sagittando. Compellunt etiam pueros trium aut quatuor annorum hoc similiter excercere. Mulieres preterea quedam et precipue virgines utuntur sagittis et equitant generaliter sicut viri. Si qui in adulterio et stupro deprehensi fuerint vir et mulier pariter occiduntur.   [II, ¶3] [IV, ¶11] [IV, ¶10] [IV, ¶11] [IV, ¶9]

¶50. Obediunt praeterea^(a) dominis suis plusquam cetere naciones aut etiam religiosi prelatis suis et eo potius quod^(b) aput eos transgressoribus locus misericordiae^(c) non prestatur et ideo imperator eorum habet eos ad omnimodam potestatem. Nam sive ad mortem sive ad vitam mittuntur celerius explere hoc oportet. Potest etiam imperator tollere sibi quando vult filias aut uxores quorum vult^(d) aut sorores, postquam autem eas habuit et pro se retinere noluerit tribuit ei cui placet.   [IV, ¶2] [V, ¶22]

¶51. Nunciis quos mittit vel qui mittuntur ad ipsum dantur gratis expense et equi subducticii, extraneis tamen nunciis dantur expense tenues. Nam duo vel *tres* comederent quod *quinque* hominibus ministratur. *Ideo quae quot et qualia mala fratres nostri passi fuerunt perhorresco scribere cum et ipsi qui hoc toleraverunt fratres mirentur qualiter ipsos contra naturam humanam substentaverit* [9^v] *gratia Jesu Christi. O quam sepe plusquam xxx boemica miliaria*   [V, ¶23]

¶48. (*a*) MS *coortuo.*   (*b*) MS *stacioni.*   (*c*) MS *eriguntur in directum.*   (*d*) MS *frangitur seu tres.*
¶49. (*a*) MS *et huius cateri vero.*
¶50. (*a*) MS *propterea.*   (*b*) MS *pacius quo.*   (*c*) MS *misericordi.*   (*d*) MS *vult filias.*

¶48. 1. Cf. Rubruck, ed. Rockhill, p. 240. The "witches" are, of course, female shamans.
   2. Cf. Juvaini, Vol. 1, p. 205.
¶49. 1. Cf. Risch, pp. 56–57, nn. 5–8.
   2. Cf. above, ¶42, n. 8; Rubruck, ed. Rockhill, pp. 77–78.
   3. Cf. Rubruck, ed. Rockhill, pp. 75–76.
   4. Cf. Risch, pp. 105–06, nn. 9, 10; Rubruck, ed. Rockhill, p. 74.
   5. Cf. the Yasa article: "An adulterer is put to death, whether he is married or not" (Riasanovsky, p. 57).
¶50. 1. Cf. the Yasa article: "He (Chingis Khan) orders them to present all their daughters . . . at the beginning of each year so that he may pick out some of them for himself and his children" (Riasanovsky, p. 59).
¶51. 1. *Carpini,* ch. V, ¶23, says: "so little is given to ten men that scarcely two can live on it". Perhaps "ten" is named merely as a round figure—but it may well be the actual number of the friars and their bodyguard.

miles in a single day on the Tartar's post-horses,[2] *tasting neither bread nor water, but obtaining with difficulty at noon or in the night only a little thin broth of boiled millet!*[3] *That they rode so far is not surprising, for as soon as their horses grew weary, even before they could begin to rest, the Tartars brought up fresh strong mounts.*

¶52. All homesteads are subject to the Khan in their settlings *and movements,* for he fixes the stations of the chiefs, who in turn assign their posts to the leaders of a thousand, these to the leaders of a hundred, and these to the leaders of ten. All are exceedingly covetous, both nobles and poor, and unrivalled in the extortion of gifts. *If they do not receive immediate gifts, they torment envoys with starvation and pettifogging, in order that those who have neglected to give of their own free will may be compelled to do so later against their will.* For this reason our friars spent for the most part on gifts the alms of good men which they had received on the way (with the exception of the spiritual envoy of the Apostolic See), for otherwise they would have been greatly hindered and indeed despised in the business of the Universal Church.[1]

¶53. Of all men they are the most given to despising other nations. Hence Tartar *interpreters,* even when of lowly station, take precedence in walking and sitting over the envoys entrusted to their care, *whether* these are envoys or legates of the Apostolic See or of kings.[1] Moreover, they are devoid of honesty in their dealings with foreigners; for it is their inhuman way to promise many good things at the beginning, but to practice endless cruelties at the end. Their promise is like a scorpion, which *although it pretends to flatter with its face,* strikes suddenly *with the poisonous sting in its tail.*

¶54. They are more given to drunkenness than any other nation on earth, and however much excessive drink they unload from their bellies, they at once begin again to drink on the spot, *and it is their habit to do so several times in the same day.* They also are accustomed to drink every kind of milk. They eat immoderately all forms of unclean food, wolves, foxes, dogs, *carrion,* afterbirths of animals, mice, and, when necessary, human flesh. *Similarly, they reject no species of bird, but eat clean and unclean alike.*[1] They do not use napkins or tablecloths [10ʳ] at dinner and so eat in excessive filth. They wash their platters rarely and very badly, and the same applies to their spoons.[2]

¶55. Among themselves, however, they are peaceable, fornication and adultery are very rare, and their women excel those of other nations in chastity, except that they often use shameless

---

2. An impossible exaggeration. The Bohemian mile—a measurement appropriate to both Benedict and his audience—measured about seven kilometers or four and three-eighths modern English miles, being the average distance covered by a pedestrian in two hours; so thirty Bohemian miles would be over 130 modern miles! Roman numerals were easily corrupted, the later scribes of TR were probably not familiar with the Bohemian mile, and we should perhaps read "*xv*" or "*xx*" instead of "*xxx*". However, it need not be doubted that the friars often traveled uncomfortably far in a day, since their daily average from Batu's camp to Kuyuk's court, not allowing for detours, delays, and rest days, was nearly thirty miles (cf. p. 37, above). Rockhill (p. 85) assesses a stage on the postroads of Central Asia as up to thirty miles, depending on the distance between water supplies. But Rubruck claims to have averaged "about the distance between Paris and Orleans"—i.e. about sixty miles—through the Kangit country, and says he "sometimes changed horses two or three times a day" (Rockhill, p. 131). *Carpini* (ch. IX, ¶12, ¶21, ¶28) repeatedly affirms the same, showing that the friars frequently traveled two or more stages in a day. This killing pace was enjoined by Batu (*Carpini*, ch. IX, ¶28), in order to ensure their arriving in time for the great kuriltai.

3. This starvation diet applied only to Lent, 22 February to 8 April 1246, when the friars were traveling from Khurumsi's camp to Batu's, and presumably to Fridays and other fast days subsequently, as is shown by *Carpini,* ch. IX, ¶19. Rubruck was given millet gruel, a staple diet of the Mongols to this day, for breakfast, and stewed

una die equitabant super equos subductitios[(a)] *Tartarorum non gustantes panem neque aquam sed tantummodo in meridie aut in nocte parumper de tenuissimo brodio cocti milii vix habebant. Nec mirum si tantum equitabant, deficientibus enim equis etiam priusquam pausare poterant alios fortes et recentes Tartari adducebant.*

¶52. Ad imperium etiam can omnes manent stationes *et moventur,* ipse namque assignat loca ducibus qui millenariis qui centenariis qui decanis. Omnes insuper nobiles et pauperes avarissimi sunt et maximi munerum extorsores. *Statim etiam si*[(a)] *munera non recipiunt multa fame ac cause protellatione nuncios affligunt ita ut qui sponte dare neglexerint cogantur offerre munera postmodum sine sponte.* Hinc est quod fratres nostri elemosinam bonorum hominum quam peragendo excepto nuncio sedis apostolice spirituali acceperant pro magna parte in muneribus expenderunt, alioquin multum fuissent in negocio universalis ecclesie impediti pariter et contempti.   [V, ¶22] [IV, ¶6] [IX, ¶3]

¶53. Inter homines aliarum nacionum[(a)] sunt latissimi contemptores. Unde etiam *interpretes tartarici licet contemptibiles precedunt tamen nuncios sibi commendatos*[(b)] in ambulando et sedendo *sive sint nuncii vel legati sedis apostolice sive regum.* Item[(c)] nullam veritatem servant alienis. Sunt enim multa bona in principio promittentes sed ad ultimum infinitas crudelitates inhumaniter exercentes. Eorum namque promissio est ut scorpio qui *licet facie blandiri videatur* percutit tamen *subito caude aculeo venenoso.*   [IV, ¶4] [IV, ¶5] [IV, ¶6]

¶54. Item[(a)] inebriantur super omnes naciones huius mundi. Quantumcumque enim de nimia potacione per ventrem se evacuant bibere statim in eodem loco incipiunt iterato *et hoc in die una sepius facere*[(b)] consueverunt. Solent praeterea[(c)] lactis bibere omne genus. Item[(d)] omnia immunda commedunt absque modo lupos vulpes canes *morticina* adluviones[(e)] mures et in necessitate carnes humanas. *Similiter et inter volatilia nulla reiciunt sed commedunt munda pariter cum immundis.*[(f)] Pannis et men- [10ʳ] salibus ad prandia non utuntur et ideo immunde commedunt super modum. Scutellas raro et pessime lavant simili modo fiunt cocleariis.   [IV, ¶8] [IV, ¶7] [IV, ¶8]

¶51. (*a*) MS *subductios.*
¶52. (*a*) MS *si si.*
¶53. (*a*) MS *Inter hominum aliarum naciones.*   (*b*) MS *commendati.*   (*c*) MS *Inter.*
¶54. (*a*) MS *Inter.*   (*b*) MS *iacere.*   (*c*) MS *propterea.*   (*d*) MS *inter.*   (*e*) MS *adluuones.*   (*f*) MS *mundis.*

mutton with broth, which he found "a most delicious drink and very nourishing", for dinner. Being less scrupulous in this respect than Carpini and his companions, Rubruck ate this evening meat, "though it distressed me sorely", even on Friday fast days (Rockhill, p. 132). *Carpini,* ch. IV, ¶8, gives the same account as Rubruck of Mongol staple diet—millet gruel in the morning and stewed meat with broth in the evening—and this was doubtless the friars' normal fare.

¶52. 1. The friars were compelled to spend part of the alms given for their support during the journey on buying beaver pelts at Cracow as gifts for the Mongols (*Carpini,* ch. IX, ¶2, ¶3; above, p. 36).

¶53. 1. *Carpini,* ch. IV, ¶5 gives as examples among the envoys to Kuyuk's kuriltai the Russian Grand Duke Yaroslav, Prince David of Georgia, "many and great Sultans", and a prince of Korea, whose interpreters took precedence of them at Kuyuk's court (cf. Juvaini, Vol. 1, p. 250, n. 7; *Carpini,* ch. VII, ¶4, ¶7; Risch, pp. 188–90, nn. 3–6).

¶54. 1. The usual meats of the Mongols were, of course, beef, mutton, and horseflesh from their abundant herds; but *Carpini*-TR list only those which seem to them strange and unclean. Similarly, Juvaini (Vol. 1, p. 21) mentions "dogs, mice and other dead things", Rubruck, mice and rats (Rockhill, p. 69), and Marco Polo, dogs and Pharaoh's rats (Yule, *Polo,* Vol. 1, p. 252).

2. Cf. Rockhill, pp. 63–64, 76; Risch, p. 100, nn. 13–15.

words when jesting.[1] Theft is unusual among them, and therefore their dwellings and all their property are not put under lock and key. If horses or oxen or other animal stock are found straying, they are either allowed to go free or are led back to their own masters.[2] They are richer in horses and mares, oxen, cows and sheep than any other men on earth. They are kind enough among themselves, and share their property willingly by reciprocal concession. They are very hardy, for even when they fast for a day or two they sing and jest as if they had eaten excellently well. They willingly help one another to positions of honor. Rebellion is rarely raised among them, *and it is no wonder if such is their way, for, as I have said above, transgressors are punished without mercy.*[3]

¶56. Now I must briefly discuss their warfare and the methods by which they can be opposed.[1] *Whenever the Tartars plan to attack any countries, the army directed to conquer them marches speedily but with great caution in wagons and on horseback, taking with it whole families, including wives, boy children, and servant-maids, with their tents and all their chattels, herds, and sheep, and a vast stock of arms, bows, quivers, and arrows.* When the Tartars begin to draw near, they send ahead their swiftest skirmishers to spread terror unexpectedly and kill, *and to prevent an army from being quickly mobilized against them. If they meet with no obstacle, however, they continue to advance, and the multitude follows with all their families without concealment.*

¶57. If they see their opponents are too numerous to defeat, they immediately withdraw to the main body and draw up their forces in the following manner. *They dispose the main strength of the army in abundant numbers round the triumphal standard in the middle,* and on the wings place two smaller forces, one on each side, at a small distance but projecting a long way forward. They leave a few to [10ᵛ] guard the women, sick, boys, and the chattels brought with them.

¶58. When they are on the point of joining battle with the enemy, *a number of them, each supplied with several quivers complete with arrows, begin to shoot before their opponents' arrows can reach them, sometimes even ahead of time when they are not in range. As soon as their arrows can reach the mark unhindered they are said owing to the density of their fire to rain arrows rather than to shoot them.*[1] If they find their enemies unprepared, they surround them suddenly in a ring leaving only a single way of escape, and attack them fiercely with a hail of javelins, so that anyone who does not resist in the middle perishes in flight. *I consider therefore that it is better to die bravely fighting than to take refuge in cowardly flight.*

¶59. *It must be further noticed that if they meet with success, they press ever onward and leave in their rear stations of a thousand or a hundred men, according to their resources in men and livestock, the nearer ones being the stronger and larger.*

¶60. *If any cities or fortified places remain in the countries they have conquered, these cities can hold out very well against them, where the position is such that arrows can be aimed or*

¶55. 1. "They have not changed since then", remarks the experienced Rockhill (p. 79, n. 2).

2. Cf. Risch, p. 90, n. 5; Yule, *Polo*, Vol. 1, pp. 403, 407, n. 4.

3. Cf. above, ¶50.

¶56. 1. TR's discussion of Mongol warfare is perfunctory and unintelligent as compared with *Carpini*, chs. VI–VIII—so much so that perhaps Benedict as well as De Bridia must be blamed. However, the vivid account of a Mongol army on the march in TR ¶56, ¶59 is peculiar to TR, and can have been omitted from *Carpini* only by an oversight. For Mongol strategy and tactics cf. Martin, pp. 26–41; Vernadsky, pp. 110–20.

¶55. Sed tamen inter se pacifici, fornicatio et adulterium inter eos parciter valde raro. Mulieres   [IV, ¶2]
eorum castitate excedunt feminas aliarum nacionum excepto quod in trufa sepe proferunt verba   [IV, ¶3]
impudica. Furtum inter eos esse non consuevit, ideo staciones et omnes res earum non serantur.   [IV, ¶2]
Si qui autem equi aut boves aut aliqua huiusmodi inventa fuerint aut libere ire permittuntur
aut ad proprios dominos reducuntur. Abundant enim equis et iumentis bobus vaccis et ovibus   [II, ¶7]
magis quam aliqui homines super terram. Satis etiam humani sunt inter se et res suas libenter   [IV, ¶2]
communicant ad invicem concedendo. Patientes praeterea[(a)] sunt multum. Sepe namque licet
per diem aut per duos nichil commedant tamen cantant et iocantur tamquam peroptime manduc-
cassent. Libenter namque etiam unus alium promovet ad honorem. Raro autem seditiones inter   [IV, ¶3]
eos excitantur *nec mirum si servant talia quia ut dixi superius transgressores inter eos absque*
misericordia puniuntur.

¶56. Nunc de preliis eorum et qualiter eisdem occurri possit breviter est notandum. *Quando-*   [VI, ¶1; VIII, ¶1]
cumque Tartari terras aliquas proponunt impugnare exercitus qui ad eas dirigitur expugnandas
cum omni familia uxoribus videlicet pueris et ancillis tentoriis et omni superlectili cum armentis
et ovibus in curribus et in equis properat valde caute ducens secum in maxima multitudine arma
arcus pharetras et sagittas. Cumque Tartari propinquare ceperint premittunt velocissimos cur-   [VI, ¶11]
sores qui terreant ex insperato homines et occidant *et ne possit contra eos exercitus subito con-*
gregari. Quod si obstaculum non habuerint procedunt semper et multitudo sequitur cum suis
omnibus satis plane.

¶57. Si autem viderint turbam insuperabilem confestim ad suos resiliunt[(a)] et exercitus ordi-   [VI, ¶13]
nant tali modo. *Robur exercitus disponunt circa vexillum triumphale in medio cum multitudine*
copiosa in cuius lateribus duas minores ponunt utrimque unam[(b)] parum distantes et eminentes   [VI, ¶14]
ante magnum. Paucos autem relinquunt in [10ᵛ] custodia mulierum debilium puerorum et
eorum que duxerunt.

¶58. Cum itaque congredi debent cum hostibus *plures ex ipsis se pluribus muniunt pharetris*
et sagittis et antequam adversariorum eos possint sagitte attingere suas dirigunt quandoque
etiam ante tempus ad plenum iacere non valentes. Quando vero sine obstaculo sagittis possint
attingere compluere pocius dicuntur quam iacere cum sagittis et hoc propter sagittarum nimiam
densitatem. Quod si hostes incautos reperierint circundant eos in modum corone subito dimit-   [VI, ¶14]
tentes eis unicam viam ad fugiendum. Eos impetunt iaculis valde absque modo ita ut si quis
in medio exorsus non fuerit pereat fugiendo *qua de re melius arbitror pugnando bene mori*
quam conspicere malam fugam.

¶59. *Notandum praeterea*[(a)] *si eis prosperatum fuerit quod semper procedendo ordinant post*
tergum[(b)] *staciones per millenarios centenarios secundum quod eis expedit cum hominibus et*
iumentis, ordinant tamen viciniores sibi fortiores et maiores stationes.

¶60. *Et si que civitates sive castra in terris quas expugnaverunt manserunt et bene possunt*   [VIII, ¶12]
subsistere ante eos ubi sagittarum impetus potest dirigi et iactus machinarum[(a)] *et ubi expense*

¶55. (*a*) MS *propterea.*
¶57. (*a*) MS *resilirent.*   (*b*) MS *unum.*
¶59. (*a*) MS *propterea.*   (*b*) MS has *se* deleted before *tergum.*
¶60. (*a*) MS *manithearum.*   (*b*) MS *audacia apl'orum situm in terra antiquorum saxatini.*

¶58. 1. Almost the same remark is made by the Dominican Friar Julian: "In the first onset, as it is said, they seem to
rain arrows rather than to shoot them" (Dudik, Vol. 1, p. 332).

missiles from war engines be shot against them; and where supplies of food, drink, or wood give out, the courage or daring of the opposing forces can compensate for the deficiencies of the position. So it happened in the country of the Old Saxons,[1] who *made repeated sorties in small numbers from their city and killed many of the Tartars,* and while *the women* extinguished the fires in the burning town the men defended the walls against the Tartars; and when the Tartars emerged through an underground passage in the middle of the town, they slew many and put the rest to flight. *It is impossible for men to hide away from them in any forests which are accessible in summer and winter, since they lie in wait for men as they would for wild animals. However, safety from them can be had on the sea or in the places mentioned above.*[2]

¶61. The proper method of resisting the Tartars *can be understood easily enough from the various accounts of the Maccabee kings, where the tactics of sending out archers ahead of the main army and laying different kinds of ambushes against the enemy are described.*[1] *In my opinion, however, peace between our rulers is absolutely necessary,*[2] *with a view to their massing together and drawing up three or more armies against the enemy* [11^r] *as demanded by the quality of their soldiers, not omitting to post ambushes on the wings fitted with the best horses. Crossbow-men must be posted in front of the armies in three ranks at least, and these must shoot their arrows even before they can reach the Tartars' front line, in the right manner and in good time, to prevent our own front rank from being put to flight or disordered. But if the enemy take to flight, the crossbow-men with the archers and the ambushers must pursue them, and the army must follow a little way behind. If, however, there are no crossbow-men to spare, then cavalry with armored horses must be placed in the van, and these must take cover behind a wall of strong shields on the horses' heads and immediately baffle the Tartars' arrows. I leave other details concerning warfare to those who are instructed in its practice more by experience than by book-learning.*

¶62. *I beseech your fatherly authority therefore to attribute any disorder in the matters I have set down in writing to my ignorance rather than to my intention.*[1] *Completed on 30th July in the year 1247*[2] *after the Incarnation of Our Lord. So ends the Life and History of the Tartars.*

¶60. 1. The Saksins or Sakassins, probably a Turkish tribe of Mohammedan religion, dwelt on the lower reaches of the Volga, south of the Bulgars and northeast of the Gazars. Their capital city was an important merchant town on an island or peninsular in the Volga delta, and must presumably be the same as Summerkent (i.e. reed-town) visited by Rubruck, who says the Mongols "were round it for eight years before they captured it" (Rockhill, p. 258). Its exact site has not been identified, though Pelliot, most tantalizingly, would evidently have propounded a solution if he had lived to complete his discussion of the matter. See d'Avezac, pp. 576–77; d'Ohsson, Vol. 1, p. 346; Bretschneider, Vol. 1, p. 296; Risch, pp. 312–24; Juvaini, Vol. 1, pp. 42, 190, 249, Vol. 2, p. 557; Pelliot, *Horde d'Or,* pp. 165–74; Bartold, *Four Studies,* Vol. 3, 1962, pp. 126–27. The emendation *Saxorum* in TR, although the form is incorrect, is confirmed by *Carpini,* ch. VII, ¶10 ("*Saxi . . . civitatem Saxorum*"), while Benedict himself gives *Saxi* as the first tribe southward on their journey through Comania, followed correctly by the Alans and Khazars (Wyngaert, p. 137). Benedict states incorrectly that they were Christians, and says "we believe them to be Goths", evidently misconstruing their name as indicating a kinship with the Saxons of Germany, and further supposing them to be related to the actual enclave of Goths in the Crimea. These were a remnant of the Ostrogoths, who had

cibi et potus defuerint aut ligna potest tamen situm loci supplere fortitudo aut audacia adversariorum. Sic in terra antiquorum Saxorum[b] fuit factum qui *sepius pauci egressi de civitate*   [VII, ¶10]
plures ex Tartaris occidebant et *mulieribus* extinguentibus succensam civitatem a Tartaris viri
menia defendebant necnon egressos Tartaros in medio civitatis per viam subterraneam peremerunt et reliquos fugaverunt. *In nullis autem silvis abscondi possunt homines ubi estate et*
hyeme accedi potest, morantur homines tamquam feras. In mari tamen securitas est et in locis
superius pretaxatis.

¶61. Qualiter autem Tartaris sit occurrendum *satis*[a] *intelligi potest ex diversis regum Macha-*   [VIII, ¶1]
beorum historiis ubi et precedentes sagittarii exercitum et insidie hostibus diversimode posite de-
scribuntur. Summe tamen necessariam arbitror pacem principum[b] *ob hoc factam ut in unum*
congregati ex adverso hostium tres aut plures exercitus ordi- [11ʳ] *nent prout pugnancium qua-*
litas hoc exposcit ex latere nichilominus in insidiis in equis optimis adaptatis. Ballistarii vero ad
minus tribus ordinibus ante exercitus disponantur qui iacere sagittas debent prius etiam quam
possint Tartarorum aciem attingere bono modo ut sit tempestive, ne[c] *nostrorum acies aut fugiat*
aut turbetur. Quod si hostes fugam ceperint ballistarii eos cum sagittariis arcuum necnon et hiis
qui sunt in insidiis persequantur paulatim exercitu subsequente. Si autem alii ballistarii non
fuerint tunc faleratis equis utentes ponantur anterius qui se inclinantes sub fortissimis clipeis
iunctis in equorum frontibus sagittas confundant subito Tartarorum. Cetera de bellis supplenda
relinquo hiis qui in huiusmodi sunt exercitio edocti experimento plusquam scripto.

¶62. *Vestre igitur paternitati supplico quatenus si qua minus ordinate in scripto posui non volun-*
tati sed ignorancie mee potius imputetis. Actum ab incarnacione domini m°.cc°.xl°.vii° iii° kalen-
dis augusti. Explicit vita et historia Tartarorum.

¶61. (*a*) MS deletes *intelligendum est* after *satis.*   (*b*) MS *principium.*   (*c*) MS omits *ne,* or may be otherwise corrupt.

---

stayed at home when their fellows invaded Europe in the third century A.D. They are mentioned by Rubruck, and a vocabulary of their language, still recognizably Teutonic, was collected by the traveler Busbeck in the sixteenth century (Rockhill, p. 51; d'Avezac, pp. 498–99). TR therefore calls them the "Old Saxons", just as for the same reason Benedict calls the Bashkirs the "Old Hungarians" (Wyngaert, p. 138). However, the TR manuscript reading *saxatini,* though corrupt, seems to retain a trace of the true name of the Saksins or Sakassins, and perhaps represents an original (e.g.) *Sacassinorum.*

2. An allusion to the Hungarian campaign, in which the refugees were ruthlessly hunted down in the summer and winter of 1241 (d'Ohsson, Vol. 2, pp. 160–64), while King Bela escaped to an island in the Adriatic off Trau (ibid., pp. 158–60).

¶61. 1. Cf. Maccabees 1.9.11: "the horsemen were divided into two troops, and the slingers and archers went before the army" (". . . *sagittarii praecedebant exercitum*"). The result was not promising, however, for Judas Maccabeus was slain and his army routed. Ambushes are described in Maccabees 1.9.38–40, 1.10.79–82. However, the two books of Maccabees, stirring as they are, cannot be recommended as manuals of military tactics.

2. An allusion to the conflict between the Emperor Frederick II and the Papacy, which continued unabated despite the menace of the Mongols. Cf. d'Ohsson, Vol. 2, pp. 166–74. For European tactics against the Mongols cf. Oman, Vol. 2, pp. 315–35.

¶62. 1. A prayer to be echoed by all editors.

2. Cf. above, pp. 21, 40.

EXCURSUS A: THE IDENTIFICATION OF "ORNAS" (TR, ¶24).

Controversy has raged concerning the identity of "Ornas", and the view of d'Avezac and Risch (see below), that the port of Tana at the mouth of the Don is intended, seems at present to hold the field. Bretschneider's suggestion of Otrar (Vol. 2, p. 56) and Rockhill's of Otrar or Eshnars (p. 15) may be dismissed as having no recommendation except a vague resemblance in sound and a situation on the Syr-daria River. The arguments of d'Avezac and Risch in favor of Tana are demonstrably incorrect. The text of *Carpini,* now reinforced by the new evidence of TR and of other contemporary western documents to be quoted below, points beyond reasonable doubt to Urgendj. It may be admitted, however, though not for the reasons adduced by d'Avezac and Risch, that the friars have contaminated Urgendj in certain details with some maritime town or towns in South Russia, perhaps Matrica and Soldaia, but probably not Tana. The following phonetic, historical, contextual, and topographical arguments seem decisive for Urgendj. (1) Ornas tallies well enough in sound with Urgendj, which is *Urganch* in Juvaini (Vol. 1, p. 123), and *Urunggechi* in Mongol (*Secret History,* ¶258, ¶260, ¶263). The variant readings *Oznac, Osna* (*Carpini,* ch. V, ¶26), *Orpar* (*Carpini,* ch. IX, ¶23), and *Ornam* or *Ornarum* (Benedict, ed. Wyngaert, p. 137) seem to be paleographically easy corruptions, rather than alternative forms. The similar forms Tornax, Ornacia, Ernac, Ornachi, and Ornach are found, in contexts which clearly apply to Urgendj, in the three contemporary western documents cited below. (2) The account of the flooding of Ornas is historically true of Urgendj, where the Mongols destroyed the city after its capture by breaking the dams of the Amu-daria (d'Ohsson, Vol. 1, p. 270; Barthold, 1928, pp. 436–37), but is recorded of no other town captured by the Mongols. (3) The context, as further clarified by the new evidence of TR, of a town besieged by Jochi (though here confused with Batu) in the Khorasmian war after the capture of Barghalikent and Yanghikent, fits no town but Urgendj. (4) *Carpini* in his journey-narrative (ch. IX, ¶23) states that after passing through the country of the Kangits the friars entered that of the Bisermins, "in which is a great river on which are towns called Iankint, Barchin and Ornas". Although in fact the first two are on the Syr-daria whereas Urgendj is on the Amu-daria, the topographical error is small and natural, and leaves the situation of Ornas in Turkestan indubitable. The friars apparently obtained information in that very district, where *Carpini* (ibid.) says they found "innumerable ruined cities and broken fortresses and deserted towns" (i.e. those on the Syr-daria), and Benedict (Wyngaert, p. 138) states that they actually passed through Iankint (i.e. Yanghikent).

Nevertheless, though there can be no doubt that the present episode relates to Urgendj, it seems clear that the friars themselves confused the information they had received on Urgendj with entirely separate material concerning a port in South Russia. *Carpini's* location of Ornas "on a river which flows through Iankint and the country of the Bisermins" (ch. V, ¶26) is a rectification, found only in his second version, of the statement in his first version that it is situated on the Don (Wyngaert, p. 71, nn. b, c). Similarly, Benedict in his journey-narrative places it between the Alans and Gazars and the Circassians (Wyngaert, pp. 137–38)—that is, somewhere toward the northeastern quarter of the Black Sea. It may well be that the friars had heard of the sacking of Soldaia—the only capture of a South Russian seaport by the Mongols known in history—by Subetei and Jebe in 1222. But the situation of "Ornas" on a river "enclosing a large part of the sea", which is peculiar to TR, applies exactly and exclusively to Matrica, the great merchant-city on the eastern side of the straits of Kerch, where the Sea of Azov meets the Black Sea. As Rubruck explains (Rockhill, p. 45), the straits were regarded as the true mouth of the Don, and the Sea of Azov was considered to be part of the river, which may therefore well be said to enclose a large part of the sea. *Carpini*-TR's statement that "Ornas" is inhabited by Christians, including Gazars and Alans (*Carpini* adds "and Russians") applies equally to both Matrica and Soldaia but is of course entirely inappropriate to Urgendj.

It follows that the arguments of d'Avezac (pp. 509–11) and Risch (pp. 296–304) for the total identification of Ornas with Tana must be rejected in favor of Urgendj, though a partial confusion with a South Russian port should be admitted. With a single exception, no positive evidence in favor of Tana remains. Indeed, it seems probable from the absence of any mention of a medieval Tana before the early fourteenth century, and from the silence of Rubruck, who describes Soldaia, Matrica, and the remainder of the region without mentioning Tana, that this city did not yet exist at the time of the friars' journey (cf. Rockhill, pp. 13, 15; Hallberg, pp. 503–04). However, it remains to examine a passage in the *Chronica* of Albericus Trium Fontium from which d'Avezac (loc. cit.) alleged a phonetic equivalence of Ornas with Tana. Under the year 1221 Albericus tells of the conquest by the Mongols under their "King David, called Prester John" of "a certain kingdom in the East next to Persia"; then "king David, or as some say his son, came into Comania and slew many thousands of Russians; and it is further said that they destroyed the great city of Tornax, that is, Ornacia, to which merchants from distant countries resorted"—"*quod magna civitas Tornax (v.l. Tenex), id est Ornacia, ab eis destructa est, ad quam mercatores de longinquis partibus ibant*" (*MGH,* Vol. 23, p. 911). Here we have, in terms of the prevalent Nestorian identification of Chingis Khan with Prester John, a correctly dated mention of the conquest of the Khorasmian Empire, an independent confirmation of the friars' belief that the expedition of Subetei and Jebe was under the command of his son Jochi, and a report of the destruction, not of Tana, but of Urgendj. Although the last episode follows the mention of the Mongols' victory in Russia, it does not follow, as d'Avezac supposes, that Albericus means to imply that "Tornax" is in Russia. Still less is *Tornax* or *Tenex,* as d'Avezac maintains, a corruption of Tana. Both forms can be paleographically explained as products of the sequence *Ornas* > *Ornax* > *Cornax* > *Tornax* > *Tenex,* or, better still, *Tornax* or *Cornax* may represent *Gurgandj,* the indigenous form for Urgendj, just as *Ornacia* may represent the Mongol form *Urunggechi.* Two other contemporary documents confirm, though confirmation is hardly necessary, the equation Ornas = Urgendj. A certain Bishop Peter from Russia, in a report made to the Council of Lyons in 1245, describes how Chingis Khan and his sons "issued forth with innumerable armies and besieged a certain very great city called *Ernac,* which they captured together with its governor whom they immediately slew, and pursued his nephew Curzensam through many provinces, ravaging those which had given him refuge" (Matthew Paris, Vol. 4, pp. 386–90). Here again we have the destruction of Urgendj, followed by the pursuit of Mohammed (whose title Khorasm-Shah produces the name *Curzensam*) and his son Jelal-ed-din. Curiously enough, Bishop Peter repeats the capture of Urgendj as of Batu, independently sharing the friars' confusion between Jochi and his son; for he further states that the three [*sic*] sons of Chingis Khan after their father's death divided their armies, and that "Bathatarcan", presumably Batu Khan, "marched against *Ornachi,* and sent his chieftains against Russia, Poland and many other kingdoms". Finally, there exists the unduly neglected narrative of the

Dominican Friar Julian, who in 1237 traveled to the Bashkirs in Old Hungary east of the Volga at the request of King Bela of European Hungary (the same who was crushed by Batu in 1241), to investigate rumors that the Mongols intended to invade Comania and Hungary in Europe (Dudik, Vol. 2, pp. 326–40; Fejér, tom. 4, Vol. 1, pp. 50–59; for critical edition see Bendefy; cf. Albericus Trium Fontium, in *MGH*, Vol. 23, p. 942). Julian sailed with three other friars from Constantinople to Matrica, which he found inhabited by Christians (like Ornas in *Carpini*-TR), with priests of the Greek Church using Greek service-books. Two of his companions returned, the third, Friar Bernard, died of hardship; but Julian traveled to Bulgar in the service of a Saracen merchant, and found the Old Hungarians near the Volga. They still spoke intelligible Hungarian, and he converted several to Christianity. They had already submitted to the Mongols, who were preparing a winter campaign (that of 1237–38) against Russia. A Russian priest told him that the Mongols were the Midianites who fled from Gideon (a variant of the Gog-Magog story) and that they lived by a river called Thartar (cf. TR, ¶3, n. 3). Julian tells a curious story of their leader Gurgachan (Jochi Khan, the name perhaps confused with Kuchluk, Gurkhan of the Karakhitayans) conquering the Sultan of *Ornach* (i.e. Urgendj), and afterward Persia and Comania (the campaign of Subetei and Jebe again attributed to Jochi). Gurgachan is now dead, but his son Chaym (Batu, who was also called Sain Khan, i.e. the Good Khan—Grousset, 1939, p. 317) had succeeded him and resided at Ornach (untrue, for Batu's base camp was now on the Volga; but Urgendj, which Jochi had so regretted the necessity of destroying, had revived and was still the capital city of Khorasmia and the chief city of Batu's appanage).

EXCURSUS B: THE *CARPINI*-TR LISTS OF PEOPLES CONQUERED BY THE MONGOLS (TR, ¶34).

Of the thirty-six names of peoples conquered by the Mongols listed in TR, ¶34, thirty-one have already been mentioned, some with variant forms, in the text of TR, and are discussed in the notes (q.v.) in the following order: ¶3, *Merkit, Mecrit;* ¶5, *Uihur;* ¶7, *Naiman, Karakitai;* ¶8, *Uirat, Saruihur, Keranitae;* ¶9, *Kitai;* ¶12, *Solangi;* ¶17, *Ethiopia;* ¶19, *Buritebet;* ¶20, *Bisermini, Kangitae, Comania, Bastarci;* ¶21, *Parossiti, Zamogedi, Canina capita;* ¶26, *Gazari, Alani; Circassi* (?) ¶27, *Billeri, Mordui;* ¶31, *Kirgiz, Armenia, Georgiania, Nubia, Turkia, Baldac, Soldani.* Nine other names are mentioned in the text (see notes) but not in the present list: ¶3, *Zumoal;* ¶6, *Esurscakita;* ¶8, *Cosmir;* ¶20, *Terkemen;* ¶25, *Rusia;* ¶26, *Th'et* (i.e. *Cachet* ?); ¶27, *Polonia, Hungaria.* The following five names occur in the TR list but are not mentioned in the text: *Urumsoldan, Corola, Cassidi, Nestoriani, Nusia. Urumsoldan* is the Seljuk Sultan of Rum, comprising the greater part of Asia Minor, who was conquered by Baiju in 1242–43 (see above, ¶31, n. 4). He is mentioned by Carpini, ch. V, ¶34, under the similar form *Soldanus de Urum.* The name is a doublet of *Turkia* in the TR list and text (¶31), although in his journey narrative Benedict uses *Turkia* for Turkestan east of the Aral Sea (Wyngaert, p. 138). However, the use of *Turkia* for the Sultanate of Rum is attested, e.g., by Rubruck (Rockhill, pp. 41, 272). *Corola* occurs in the *Carpini* list as *Korola,* where in view of the new evidence of TR the variants *Karola, Corota, Catora,* and *Colona* can be rejected. The name has not previously been explained. It cannot represent the homonym *Qorola,* one of the many subtribes of the Mongols in their homeland (Grousset, 1941, pp. 23, 410; *Secret History*, ¶120, ¶141), since, of course, none of these were counted among the Mongol conquests. It may well represent the Mongol word *Kerel* (*Secret History*, ¶262, 270; *Keler* in Juvaini, Vol. 1, pp. 199, 270–71), derived from the Hungarian word *király* = king, and meaning the Hungarians (Pelliot, *Horde d'Or*, pp. 115–23). The *Cassidi* are perhaps the *Kesdi(yin)*, mentioned in the *Secret History*, ¶239, among the forest tribes of the upper Yenisei subdued along with the Kirghiz and Uirats by Jochi in 1207. Probably the *Cassidi* are the same as the *Cassi* in the *Carpini* list, in which case the TR form should be preferred. If *Cassi* is correct, however, then it may represent *Cashi,* or *Qasin,* the former name of Tangut, which was given to a son of Ogedei born when Chingis Khan conquered that country, but became tabu when Cashi died of drink in early youth (d'Ohsson, Vol. 1, p. 95; *Secret History*, ¶150 and n., p. 155; Boyle, 1956, p. 154)—rather than the Saksin of the lower Volga (as Pullé, p. 197), or the Kakhets of the Caucasus (as d'Avezac, p. 574). As for *Nestoriani,* the Nestorians are treated as a tribe in both the TR and the *Carpini* lists, although in fact this Christian sect was spread over the greater part of Asia. The *Carpini* list, in first-version manuscripts only, also mentions another oriental Christian sect, the Jacobites. Both are described as nations by Prince Hetoum and other eastern sources (Risch, p. 194, n. 10), being concentrated in Syria, Iraq, and Persia, and this region in Chormaghan's and Baiju's territory is perhaps intended here (cf. d'Avezac, pp. 572–74). Finally, *Nusia* is in all probability a mere corruption of *Rusia,* i.e. Russia.

The *Carpini* list (ch. VII, ¶9), which differs considerably in order and somewhat in names from the TR list, is as follows, the best readings being given: (1) *Kitai* (2) *Naymani* (3) *Solangi* (4) *Karakitai* (5) *Comana* (6) *Tumat* (7) *Voyrat* (8) *Karaniti* (9) *Huyur* (10) *Sumoal* (11) *Merkyti* (12) *Mecriti* (13) *Sarihuiur* (14) *Bascart* (15) *Kergis* (16) *Cosmir* (17) *Sarraceni* (18) *Bisermini* (19) *Turcomani* (20) *Bileri* (21) *Korola* (22) *Tomiti* (23) *Buritabet* (24) *Parossiti* (25) *Cassi* [(25a, in first-version MSS only) *Jacobitae*] (26) *Alani* (27) *Georgiani* (28) *Nestoriani* (29) *Armeni* (30) *Kangit* (31) *Comani* (32) *Brutachi* (33) *Mordui* (34) *Torci* (35) *Gazari* (36) *Samogedi* (37) *Perses* (38) *Tarci* (39) *Ethiopia* (40) *Circassi* (41) *Rutheni* (42) *Baldach* (43) *Sarti.* The TR list has six names not in the *Carpini* list: *Turkia, Nubia, Urumsoldan, Cassidi, Nusia,* for which see above, and *Canina,* i.e. *Canina capita,* the Dog-heads or *Nochoyterim.* The *Carpini* list has thirteen names not in the TR list: *Sumoal, Cassi, Jacobitae,* for which see above, *Cosmir* (see TR, ¶8, n. 5), *Turcomani* (see TR ¶20, n. 2), *Rutheni* (i.e. the Russians, cf. *Nusia* above), and *Comana, Tumat, Tomiti, Brutachi, Torci, Tarci,* and *Sarti.* *Comana* is perhaps the same as *Kanana,* mentioned in *Carpini,* ch. V, ¶8 with variant readings including *Coluna* and *Comana,* in the conquests of Chingis Khan following the Uighurs (cf. TR, ¶8, n. 1). This is perhaps the district called Cuman to which the Wang Khan's son Senggum Ilka fled in 1203 via Tangut and Buritebet, on the border of Kashgar (d'Ohsson, Vol. 1, p. 82; d'Avezac, p. 541). For *Tumat,* see TR, ¶8, n. 4. The readings for *Tomiti* (v.l. *Comity, Thorati*) are perhaps too dubious for valid identification, but the emendation *Comuci,* indicating the Qumuqs of Daghestan, remains a possibility (d'Avezac, p. 575; Risch, p. 193, n. 8; Pelliot, *Horde d'Or*, p. 157). The *Brutachi* are mentioned in *Carpini,* ch. IX, ¶20, as a Jewish tribe in the Caucasus (cf. Risch, p. 231, n. 5). *Torci* should perhaps be *Turci,* i.e. Turks, and *Tarci* probably represents *Tarsi,* a name for the Uighurs used by Prince Hetoum (Mandeville, Vol. 1, p. 176), and the Bianco and Catalan world maps (see Yule, *Cathay*, Vol. 1, p. 205, n. 1; Pelliot, 1914, p. 636; Hallberg, pp. 515–17). The *Sarti,* Mongol *Sarta'ul,* were the sedentary and mercantile Mohammedan inhabitants of Turkestan and Transoxiana, possibly derived from Iaxartes, the classical name of the Syr-daria River (d'Avezac, p. 571; Bretschneider, Vol. 1, pp. 268–69; Risch, p. 197, n. 16; *Secret History,* ¶152, ¶177, ¶181–82, etc.).

In either list the order of the conquered peoples follows neither the historical nor the narrative sequence; yet there are evident traces of a purposeful grouping, especially in TR. A first group, from *Kitai* to *Sariuihur,* seems to list conquests in the time of Chingis Khan in the regions surrounding Mongolia; a second group, *Merkyte* to *Karakitai,* represents Chingis Khan's subjugation of Mongolia in the order of TR; a third group, *Turkia* to *Georgiania,* covers the campaigns against the Mohammedan world mainly in the reign of Ogedei; and the last group, from *Alani* to *Nusia* (= Russia ?), belongs to the western appanage of Jochi and Batu, though *Nestoriani* and *Persarum Soldani* have intruded from the preceding series. The whole list irresistibly recalls the similar conquest-catalogues in the *Secret History,* notably that of the forest tribes subdued by Jochi in 1207 (¶239, including the Uirat, Tumat, Kirghiz, and Kesdiyin [= Cassidi ?]), and still more that of Subetei's conquests, which corresponds strikingly to the last group above (¶262, ¶270, including the Kangits, Kipchaks or Comans, Bashkirs, Russians, Alans, Circassians, "Keshimir" [= *Carpini's Cosmir* = the Cheremisses ?], Bulgars, and "Kerel" [= *Corola ?* = the Hungarians]). For a similar circular list see Clausen, p. 19. The arrangement in TR has obvious affinities with the Mongol fan-shaped division of their armies and empire—as if the whole world were one vast battlefield covered by one unified army—into left wing (the East), center, and right wing (the West)—cf. Grousset, 1939, pp. 282–83. The two lists, in view of their order and the substantial number of peoples not previously mentioned in the narrative, cannot have been compiled by the friars themselves from the materials already available to them. It seems likely that they had access, presumably through an interpreter, to an actual Mongol document, possibly an inscription—or rather perhaps to two different documents, since the *Carpini* list diverges so considerably in content and in order from the TR list (cf. p. 47 above). The reconstruction of the original document or documents, and the explanation of the divergence of the *Carpini*-TR lists therefrom and from one another, constitutes one of the most important and fascinating problems in *Carpini*-TR, and calls for further investigation.

THE VINLAND MAP

R. A. Skelton

CONTENTS

I. DESCRIPTION OF THE MAP

1. PHYSICAL DESCRIPTION OF THE VINLAND MAP

AND ITS RELATIONSHIP TO THE MANUSCRIPT[1]

The map is drawn on a single sheet of vellum measuring 27.8 × 41 cm. (about 11 x 16 inches), folded down the center and trimmed to a rectangle corresponding in size to that of the other sheets in the codex, of which it forms a preliminary unsigned quire. The vellum appears to be identical in texture, color, and thickness with a conjugate pair of vellum leaves (l_1, l_{16}) used in the text. The physical association of the map with the manuscript is demonstrated beyond question by three pairs of wormholes which penetrate its two leaves and are in precise register with those in the opening text leaves of the *Speculum*. The brown stain round one pair of wormholes is repeated in a few leaves of the text. A fourth pair of holes in the map-leaves (very small in the second leaf) does not recur in the text-leaves. Two other small flaws in the vellum, not matching in the two leaves of the map, are perhaps (as Mr. Witten has suggested) "the result of an accidental slip of the knife in the manufacture of the vellum". Along the central fold the vellum has cracked and fractured; this has been repaired by a strip of later vellum pasted along the back. Similarly, a square patch of vellum has been pasted on the back of the sheet underlying each of the ten small holes. As Mr. Witten reasonably surmises, these repairs "were doubtless carried out at the time of the binding repair and separation of the map and Tartar relation from the Vincent of Beauvais". An irregularly shaped piece, measuring (at its greatest) about 5 cm. wide and 1.2 cm. high, has been cut away from the foot of the vellum, in the center. The vellum sheet, which has plainly been kept flat under pressure for a very considerable time, has not much "cockle".

On the blank recto of the first leaf of the map, that is, on the first page of the quire, are written the words: *Delineatio 1ᵉ ꝑs: 2ᵉ ꝑs. 3ᵉ ꝑs. specl'i*—"Delineation of the first, second, third part of the *Speculum*". The handwriting and ink appear to be similar to, if not identical with, those of the legends on the face of the map.

The outlines, names, and legends of the map are executed in a somewhat diluted brownish ink flecked with black. As Dr. Marston shows, the handwriting is similar in character to that of the manuscript and shows the same idiosyncracies in individual letters.[2] The map was therefore prepared by the scribe who copied the texts of the *Speculum* and the Tartar Relation. The writing on the map is in two sizes, a larger for the nomenclature (about 3 lines = 1 cm.) and a smaller for the longer legends (about 4 lines = 1 cm.). The letter-formation is regular, and the use of rules for the legends (though not for the names) is apparent.

That the map and the manuscript were juxtaposed within their binding from a very early date cannot be doubted. The physical analysis given above, together with the endorsement of the map, points with a high degree of probability to the further conclusions that the map was drawn immediately after the copying of the texts was completed, and in the same workshop or scriptorium, and that it was designed to illustrate the texts which it accompanied. These texts may have included, in addition to the surviving books (XXI–XXIV) of the *Speculum* and the

---

1. This section was written from examination of the manuscripts at Yale in February–March 1961, supplemented by Mr. Laurence Witten's careful description of them (October 1958).

2. See above, pp. 6–8.

Tartar Relation, other books of the *Speculum* conjectured to have formed the missing quires a–d and a lost final volume of the original codex.[3]

The association of the map with the texts is reinforced by palaeographical examination, which has enabled the hands of the map, of its endorsement, and of the texts to be confidently attributed to one and the same scribe. Further evidence on their relationship and on its character must be sought in the content of the map.

2. FORM AND CONTENT

The map depicts, in outline, the three parts of the medieval world—Europe, Africa, and Asia—surrounded by ocean, with islands and island-groups in the east and west. Those to the east are named *Insule Sub aquilone zamoyedorum* and *Postreme Insule;* in the west are the Atlantic archipelagos—*Desiderate insule, Beate Ysule fortune, Magnæ Insulæ Beati Brandani Branziliæ dictæ*—and (to the north and northwest) *isolanda Ibernica, Grŏnelāda, Vinlanda Insula.*[4] The map is drawn with north to the top, that is, with names and legends written in horizontal east–west alignment. Whether the northerly orientation is deliberate or represents the most convenient method of arranging the elements of the map within the rectangular space at the cartographer's disposal cannot be positively determined.[5]

In the design of the Old World the map belongs to the class of circular or elliptical world maps in which, during the 14th and 15th centuries, new data were introduced into the traditional mappamundi of Christian cosmology. The derivation of the map, in this respect, from a circular or oval prototype is betrayed by the general form of Europe, Africa, and Asia, which is rounded off (or beveled) at the four oblique cardinal points, although the artist had a rectangle to fill with his design.[6]

Within the coastal outlines hydrographic features (rivers and inland seas) are represented; orographic features are absent, and the five cities named[7] are not marked by symbols. The whole design is drawn in a coarse inked line, with evident generalization in some parts and considerable elaboration in others. In certain regions, such as East Asia, the precision of detail is doubtless illusory; in others, notably the Mediterranean coasts, Western Europe, and the British Isles, it is as plainly derived from experience, if at several removes.

Written on the face of the map are sixty-two geographical names and seven longer legends, in Latin. The features named are seas and gulfs, islands and archipelagos, rivers, kingdoms, regions, peoples, and cities. The nomenclature is densest in Asia, where (as will be seen) it is

3. See above, pp. 23–27.

4. The nomenclature and legends of the map are analyzed below, pp. 127–43.

5. But see below, pp. 115, 118. The influence exercised by the space to be filled upon the medieval cartographer's choice of shape and orientation for his map is a factor which must often be taken into account, particularly in respect of maps in codices or on skins of vellum. It is relevant, for instance, to consideration of the shape of Ranulf Higden's world maps (see Konrad Miller, *Mappaemundi*, Heft 3, p. 109) and to that of world maps which retain traces of prototypes of a different shape (see below, n. 6). Cf. also R. Uhden, "Die Weltkarte des Isidorus von Sevilla", *Mnemosyne*, Ser. III, Vol. 3 (1936), pp. 3–4.

6. The Catalan Atlas of 1375, drawn on six panels forming a rectangle, also appears to have been based on a circular or oval model. In the northeast (that is, at the top righthand corner, the map being oriented to the north), the coast of Asia is rounded off; and it has been conjectured that the southern half of the map, which would restore the proportions and framework of an ovoid, may have been lost or never executed.

7. Rome, Jerusalem, Mecca, Cairo, Alexandria.

largely borrowed from the Tartar Relation or a similar text. The sources of the names and legends are examined in detail below.[8] Although they are carefully written, some fragmentary forms and corruptions point to errors by the copyist or to his failure to read or understand what he transcribed.[9] That his original was a map containing (in the manner of medieval cartography) drawings of monarchs with pavilions, cities, or standards is suggested by the frequent indication of kingdoms as *Rex* ... or *Imperium* ...[10]

3. THE MAP AND ITS PRECURSORS

Before proceeding to analyze the geographical delineations of the map in detail, we may briefly survey the antecedent materials, cartographic and textual, to which comparative study of it must refer. It is, of course, not to be supposed that its anonymous maker had direct access to all surviving earlier works with which his shows any affinity in substance or design; but identification of common elements will help us to reconstruct the source or sources upon which he drew. Moreover, in the light thrown on the cartographer's work-methods and professional personality by his treatment of sources which are to some extent known, we may visualize his mode of compilation or construction from materials which have not come down to us. We may even catch a glimpse of these materials, as they are reflected in the map before us, and of the channels by which they could have reached a workshop in Southern Europe.[11]

As noted above, the representation of Europe, Africa, and Asia in the map plainly derives from a circular or oval prototype. Even when the world maps of the later Middle Ages, drawn for the most part in the scriptoria of monasteries, attempted a faithful delineation of known geographical facts (outlines of coasts, courses of rivers, location of places), they still respected the conventional pattern which Christian cosmography had in part inherited from the Romans and in part created. Until the second half of the fifteenth century, the habitable world continued to be represented as a circular disc surrounded by the ocean sea, with Jerusalem at the center and east (with the Earthly Paradise) to the top; and the symmetrical pattern of the T–O (or "wheel") diagrams was still reflected in the more elaborate mappaemundi. Underlying their wealth of geographical detail and (in some cases) legendary lore, this was the model for the world maps of Hereford and Ebstorf (thirteenth century), of Fra Paolino Minorita and of Petrus Vesconte (*ca.* 1320), of Ranulf Higden (*ca.* 1350), of Andrea Bianco (1436), of Giovanni Leardo (1442–52/3).[12]

Variations of this basic pattern were introduced to admit new geographical information or ideas or new cartographic concepts. Some of these changes are shown in summary form in the

8. See below, pp. 127–43.

9. E.g. in Europe, *Apusia, aben;* in Africa, *Bela . . . rex, Rex Marr;* in Asia, names relating to Carpini's mission. See below, pp. 141–42.

10. Such drawings were a regular feature of mappaemundi and of the Catalan charts of the fourteenth and fifteenth centuries. The use of the word *Rex* . . . plainly implies an iconographic representation of a monarch.

11. This assumes that the ascription of the manuscript to a scriptorium of the Upper Rhineland is valid (see above, p. 16).

12. For these maps, see in general K. Miller, *Mappaemundi* (1895–98); C. R. Beazley, *The Dawn of Modern Geography,* Vol. 3 (1906); M. C. Andrews, "The study and classification of mediaeval mappae mundi", *Archaeologia,* Vol. 75 (1926); R. Uhden, "Zur Herkunft und Systematik der mittelalterlichen Weltkarten", *Geographische Zeitschrift,* Vol. 37 (1931); G. H. T. Kimble, *Geography in the Middle Ages* (1938); and separately published facsimiles of, and memoirs on, individual maps. See also the Bibliographical Postscript, p. 240, and Fig. 2 (p. 156).

table opposite. From the early fourteenth century the representation of Asia and the Far East is amplified by information from the missions to the Tartars or (exceptionally) the travels of Marco Polo, and from the middle of the fifteenth century by the reports of Nicolò de' Conti. The delineation of Africa and the Atlantic islands, in the fifteenth century, is progressively extended and improved by the Portuguese voyages of discovery and by the information of merchants and other travelers in the Sudan and Near East. The maps in the Byzantine manuscripts of Ptolemy, brought to Italy at the beginning of the century, introduced a radically different world picture, especially in regard to the Indian Ocean.

The circular form of the medieval world map, in the hands of some fourteenth- and fifteenth-century cartographers, is superseded by an oval or ovoid; and even in the fourteenth century rectangular world maps begin to appear, mainly under the influence of nautical cartography. The traditional orientation, with east to the top, came to be abandoned by more progressive cartographers, who drew their maps with north to the top (following the fashion of the chart-makers) or south to the top (perhaps under the influence of Arab maps).

Most of these variations in the form and design of world maps were adapted from the practice of nautical charts and, in the fifteenth century, of the Ptolemaic maps.

Like the maps of Ptolemy, the portolan charts—or compass charts—were drawn with north to the top; and they were as a rule rectangular in shape.[13] These were not documents of the study, but practical works whose design betrays their function, as aids to navigation by compass or wind-direction. Hence their orientation; hence, too, the network of rhumbs or bearing lines radiating from centers or windroses arranged on the circumference of a circle. The drawing of the coasts is characterized by geometrical forms (arcs for bays, pointed headlands, rectangular or crescent shapes for islands) and by the writing of names at right angles to the coastline. The "normal" portolan charts of the fourteenth and early fifteenth centuries embraced the shores of the Mediterranean, of the Black Sea, and of western Europe. Those of Italian authorship, with few exceptions, represented only features on or adjoining the coasts, with the more important rivers which carried trade inland; but charts drawn in the workshops of Catalonia and Majorca attempted a more detailed delineation of the interior. The world maps executed by chart-makers—Petrus Vesconte, Abraham Cresques, Andrea Bianco—tended to reproduce features of design customary in nautical cartography, particularly the network of rhumb-lines.

If the Vinland Map was drawn in the second quarter of the fifteenth century, and perhaps early in the last decade of that quarter, it would take its place, in the table of world maps opposite, after that of Andrea Bianco and would be contemporary with the output of Leardo, whose three maps are dated 1442, 1448, and 145- (1452 or 1453). While the work of Leardo is considerably more sophisticated in compilation and more "learned" in its incorporation of varied geographical materials than that of Bianco, the world maps of both these Venetian cartographers plainly depend for their general design on models of the fourteenth century.

Whether and to what extent the author of the Vinland Map made use of textual information for certain parts of his map, and what its character may have been, will emerge from the de-

13. On the orientation and general design of the portolan charts, see Theobald Fischer, *Sammlung mittelalterlicher Welt- und Seekarten italienischen Ursprungs* (1886); A. E. Nordenskiöld, *Periplus* (1897); K. Kretschmer, *Die italienischen Portolane des Mittelalters* (1909).

PRINCIPAL WORLD MAPS OF THE FOURTEENTH AND FIFTEENTH CENTURIES

(Shape: C, circular; O, oval; Od, ovoid; R, rectangular. Orientation: E(ast), N(orth), S(outh) to top.)

Author or Description	Date	Place of Origin	Shape	Orientation	New information on:	Remarks
Giovanni da Carignano	ca. 1310	Genoa (Italy)	R	N	The Baltic and Africa	A land map of the Western World drawn in portolan style, with much detail on the interior of Africa.
Fra Paolino Minorita	ca. 1320	Avignon (France)	C	E	Asia and the Far East	Including some geographical data from Rubruck. (See R. Almagià, *Monumenta Cartographica Vaticana*, Vol. 1, pp. 3–8 and pl. I.)
Petrus Vesconte	ca. 1321	Genoa (Italy)	C	E	Asia and the Far East	Ten world maps either signed by him, or of his authorship and included in Marino Sanuto's *Liber Secretorum Fidelium Crucis*. Apparently based on the map of Fra Paolino.
Ranulf Higden	ca. 1350	Chester (England)	O, Od	E	—	—
World map in Laurentian ('Medici') sea atlas	1351	Italy	R (after a prototype C)	S	The Baltic, the Atlantic islands, Africa, Asia	Perhaps the earliest map to show the Azores. The southward extension of Africa is a later addition.
Marco and Francesco Pizzigano	1367 1375	Venice (Italy)	R	N	Africa	A land map and atlas of the Western World, drawn in portolan style.
Abraham Cresques, Catalan atlas	1375	Majorca	R (after a prototype C or O?)	N	Asia and Far East, Africa	The first map to incorporate the discoveries of Marco Polo in detail. Drawn in portolan style.
Borgia world map	15th cent. (first half)	S. Germany?	C	S	—	Archaic in character.
Pirrus de Noha	1415(?)	Italy	R	N	—	Ptolemaic in form.
Albertinus de Virga	ca. 1411–15	Venice (Italy)	C	N	—	Probably derived from the Laurentian sea atlas.
Andrea Bianco	1436	Venice (Italy)	C	E	The Baltic, the Atlantic islands, coast of W. Africa	See below, pp. 124–27.
Giovanni Leardo	1442–52/3	Venice (Italy)	C	E	Asia and the Far East	Eclectic works, including data from Nicolò de' Conti and from Catalan maps.
Andreas Walsperger	1448	Constance (Switzerland)	C	S	—	—
Catalan-Este world map at Modena	ca. 1450–60	Majorca?	C	N	Africa	Similar in content and representation to the Catalan Atlas of 1375. Sometimes ascribed to the fourteenth century.
'Genoese' world map	1457	Genoa (Italy)	Od	N	—	An eclectic work, similar in content to the Leardo maps.
Fra Mauro	1459	Venice (Italy)	C	S	Many regions	A conspectus of fifteenth-century geographical knowledge, cast in medieval form.

tailed analysis in the following chapters. The textual sources on which the mapmaker could have drawn in this period may be roughly grouped:

(a) Geographical treatises of classical authors (Strabo, Pliny, Ptolemy, Pomponius Mela) and of medieval writers (Vincent of Beauvais, John Sacrobosco, Pierre d'Ailly, the fourteenth-century *Libro del Conoscimiento*).

(b) Travelers' reports (e.g. for Asia, Marco Polo and missionaries or merchants before and after him, Nicolò de' Conti; for Africa, the Portuguese voyages along the west coast, the journeys of merchants into the Sahara or up the Nile).

(c) The texts contained in the manuscripts which accompany, or formerly accompanied, the Vinland Map, namely the surviving books (XXI–XXIV) of Vincent's *Speculum Historiale*, the conjecturally missing sections of the *Speculum*, the Tartar Relation of C. de Bridia describing Carpini's mission, and perhaps other texts which contributed to delineations or legends on the map.[14]

Of these three groups, the last was plainly that most accessible to the cartographer. The degree to which he limited his compilation processes to this group of materials (so far as we can reconstruct them), or extended his search for geographical data beyond it, will help to determine the character of his map, as a representation of the known world, and the purpose for which it was drawn.

4. THE TRIPARTITE WORLD IN THE MAP

The outlines of the three continents form an ellipse or oval, the proportions between the longer horizontal axis and the vertical axis[15] being about 2 : 1. Since the map is oriented with north to the top, the longer axis lies east–west, and the two greater arcs at top and bottom are formed by the north coasts of Europe and Asia and by the coasts of Africa respectively. The elliptical outline is interrupted, in its western quadrant, by the Atlantic Ocean and by the gulfs or seas of western Europe, and in its eastern by a great gulf named *Magnum mare Tartarorum;* the curvilinear outline is however continued southeastward from Northern Asia by the coasts of the large islands at the outer edge of this gulf. The only parts of the design which fall outside the elliptical framework are the representations of Iceland, Greenland, and Vinland, in the west, and (less certainly) the outermost Atlantic islands and the northwest-pointing peninsular extension of Scandinavia.

It is not necessary to assume that the prototype followed by the cartographer was also oval in form. In fact his map has striking affinities of outline and nomenclature with the circular world map in Andrea Bianco's atlas of 1436, preserved in the Biblioteca Nazionale Marciana, Venice.[16] The features common to both maps, and in some cases peculiar to them, are sufficiently numerous and marked (as their detailed analysis will demonstrate) to place it beyond reasonable doubt that the author of the Vinland Map had under his eyes, if not Bianco's world map, one which was very similar to it or which served as a common original for both maps. If this original was circular, the anonymous cartographer's elongation of the outline to form an ellipse may be

14. See above, pp. 25–27.
15. As measured between the extremities of the inked design.
16. See below, pp. 125–26; also Pl. VI and Fig. 2.

a pattern into which elements not in the original, notably his de-
d Vinland and his elaboration of the geography of Asia, could be
ps also, or alternatively, by the need to fill the rectangular space
f a codex. These two explanations, taken together, may account for
obably made by the cartographer to his prototype. The northerly
uld perhaps be attributed to expediency rather than to the adoption
model, for it enabled the names and legends to be written and read
ts which followed the map in the codex.[17]

nland Map corresponded generally in form and content to Andrea
the variations introduced by its author are not less significant than
Apart from the change in orientation and the north–south compres-
associated with the adoption of the elliptical shape, they include the
land, and Vinland; a different delineation (not certainly deliberate)
the Atlantic extremity of Scandinavia; a variation in the drawing of
sion of the design of East Asia within the framework of the original
of the iconography—pictures of cities, pavilions, and monarchs—
ver Bianco's map, was presumably also in the prototype and (as noted
the nomenclature of the Vinland Map.

graphical outlines of the Vinland Map with those of Bianco suggests
erally following his model, was inclined to exaggerate prominent fea-
tures, such as capes or peninsulas, and to elaborate, by fanciful "squiggles", the drawing of a
stretch of featureless coast. His personal style of drawing, save perhaps in the outlines of certain large islands, shows no sign of the idiosyncracies of the draftsmen of the portolan charts,
although these have left a clear mark on the execution of Bianco's world map. Some apparent
differences in the rendering of particular regions in the Vinland Map, which may be due to the
use of a different cartographic prototype or simply to negligence by the copyist, are discussed
in the detailed analysis which follows.

EUROPE

With the reservations made in the preceding paragraph, the cartographer's representation of the
regions embraced by the "normal" portolan chart of the fifteenth century—the Mediterranean
and Black Seas, Western Europe, and the Baltic—closely resembles that of Bianco in his world
map, which reflects his own practice in chartmaking. The orientation and outline of the
Mediterranean agree exactly in the two maps, although in the Vinland Map it has a considerably greater extension in longitude, in proportion to the overall width of Eurasia. The distinctive shapes in which Bianco draws the Adriatic, Aegean, and Black Seas reappear in the
Vinland Map. The Peloponnese and the peninsula in the southwest of Asia Minor are treated
with the anonymous cartographer's customary exaggeration. The outline of Spain is depicted
with slight variation from Bianco's, the Atlantic coast trending NNW (instead of northerly)
and the north coast being a little more arched. The remaining continental coasts of Western

17. See R. Uhden, loc. cit. above, n. 5; and on oval or elliptical maps of the classical and medieval periods generally,
T. Fischer, *Sammlung*, pp. 157–58.

Europe are drawn precisely as by Bianco. This correspondence is particularly marked in the north-trending line from Flanders to the Skagerrak; in the flat-headed outline of Denmark (peculiar to Bianco and to the Catalan world maps);[18] and in the orientation and shape of the Baltic, typical of the portolan charts and of world maps derived from them.[19]

Scandinavia, as in all maps before the second quarter of the sixteenth century, lies east–west in both maps; but there is a conspicuous divergence in their treatment of its western end, which both cartographers extend into roughly the longitude of Ireland. Bianco shows Scandinavia as terminating in an indented coast projecting westward with a large unnamed island offshore, divided from it by a strait; but the author of the Vinland Map has altered the island to a peninsula and the strait into a deep gulf by drawing an isthmus across the south end of the strait. This seems a more probable explanation of the feature than to suppose that it represents the gulf of the northern ocean supposed by medieval geographers to cut into the Scandinavian coast and drawn in various forms by cartographers of the fourteenth and fifteenth centuries, from Vesconte to Fra Mauro.[20] If the delineation by Bianco and that in the Vinland Map rest on authentic information and not on the draftsman's adherence to a cartographic model, it must be admitted that the source for it is unknown. A legend on Fra Mauro's map indeed refers to the shipwreck of the Venetian Pietro Querini on the Norwegian coast in 1431, and it has been suggested[21] that Fra Mauro obtained oral information on Scandinavia from Querini, who spent some time in Norway and Sweden and wrote an account of these countries.[22] If Querini's evidence could have been used by Fra Mauro, it was doubtless no less available to Andrea Bianco (also a native of Venice), who is recorded to have assisted in the preparation of Fra Mauro's world map and who included in his atlas of 1436 a special map of Scandinavia and the Baltic, showing knowledge of the Norwegian fisheries and an enriched nomenclature.[23]

In its delineation of the British Isles, the Vinland Map again diverges from that in Bianco's world map. In both, Ireland has the same shape and coastal features, derived from the representation in contemporary Italian charts; and Bianco's version of Great Britain also is that of the portolan chartmakers, with the English coasts deeply indented by the Severn and Thames estuaries and the Wash, with a channel or strait separating England and Scotland, and with Scotland drawn as a rough square with little indentation.[24] The design of Great Britain in the Vinland Map is markedly at variance with Bianco's: the southwest peninsula is considerably extended, the Isle of Wight is laid down off the southeast coast (not, as by Bianco, in its correct position), the Thames estuary has almost disappeared, the channel between England and Scotland is not shown, and Scotland has a distinctly different outline, with a much more indented

18. See N. E. Nørlund, *Danmarks Kortlægning* (1944).

19. H. Winter, "The changing face of Scandinavia and the Baltic in cartography up to 1532", *Imago Mundi,* Vol. 12 (1955), pp. 45–54; A. Spekke, *The Baltic Sea in Ancient Maps* (1961).

20. F. Nansen, *In Northern Mists* (1911), Vol. 2, pp. 222–23, 258–59; see also below, pp. 163–64.

21. By T. Fischer (*Sammlung*, p. 47).

22. See Nansen, Vol. 2, p. 286. Querini's report was first printed by Ramusio, *Navigationi et Viaggi*, Vol. 2 (1559); see also C. Bullo, *Il viaggio di M. Piero Querini* (1881).

23. It is unnecessary, and probably unsafe, to postulate the influence of Claudius Clavus (see below, pp. 176–77) on Bianco's representation of the North, although this is chronologically possible.

24. M. C. Andrews, "The British Isles in the nautical charts of the 14th and 15th centuries", *Geographical Journal,* Vol. 68 (1926), pp. 474–80; "Scotland in the portolan charts", *Scottish Geographical Magazine,* Vol. 42 (1926).

east coast and the north coast trending WSW–ENE (instead of W–E as in Bianco) to end in a conspicuous cape.

These differences seem too great to fall within the limits of the licence in copying which the author of the Vinland Map evidently allowed himself in those parts of his design which agree basically with Bianco's rendering and may derive from a common prototype. In view of the novel elements in the northwest part of the map, we must reckon with the possibility—but no more—that its author found this version of the British Isles in a map of the North Atlantic which may have served him as a model for this part of his work and from which may stem not only his representations of Iceland, Greenland, and Vinland, but also his revisions of Scandinavia and Great Britain and of the islands between.[25]

The Atlantic islands lying off Europe and Africa will be considered in a later section of this chapter.

In the Vinland Map, Europe is devoid of rivers, save for a very muddled representation of the hydrography of Eastern Europe. The lower course of the Danube is correctly drawn as falling into the Black Sea; but the copyist or compiler appears to have erroneously identified it with the Don (which debouches on the Sea of Azov), for the name *Tanais* is boldly written just above the river, with a legend about the Russians. The "Danube" is shown as rising just south of the Baltic and turning eastward in about the position of Poland; at this point it forks, and a branch flows in a general southeasterly direction to fall into the Aegean. On the source of this farrago, which is in marked contrast with the relatively correct river pattern drawn in Central Europe by Bianco and the chartmakers, it is perhaps idle to speculate; it seems to involve a confusion of the Oder, the lower Danube, and the Struma.

The twelve names on the mainland of Europe are, with two exceptions, those of countries or states. The only European city named in the Vinland Map is Rome, while Bianco's world map marks only Paris.

AFRICA

The general shape and proportions of Africa, extending across the lower half of the Vinland Map, correspond to a type followed, with variations, in most circular world maps of the fourteenth and fifteenth centuries, and deriving ultimately from much earlier medieval and classical models.[26] The great arc of the southern coast, extending from Morocco to East Africa and

25. The representation of Great Britain in the Vinland Map is paralleled in a considerably later map, that included in a MS recension of C. Buondelmonte's *Insularium,* drawn and illuminated by Henricus Martellus Germanus, *ca.* 1490, and preserved in the Biblioteca Laurenziana, Florence (Pl. 29, 25); the map of Great Britain in this codex is reproduced by A. E. Nordenskiöld, *Bidrag til Nordens äldsta kartografi* (1892), pl. II, and in his *Periplus* (1897), pl. XXXII. Here we see the same features which distinguish the delineation in the Vinland Map from that in the portolan charts or in the Ptolemy maps: the SW and NE prolongation of the island, the outline and orientation of the Scottish coasts, and the position of the Isle of Wight. In the Martellus map these characteristics may, in part at least, be ascribed to the fact that the map appears to be an extract, or copy of a detail, from a map of a larger area on a trapezoid projection, in which Great Britain lay well to the west of the central meridian, with consequent NE–SW inclination of its meridian lines.

26. The ultimate source is the world picture of Isidore of Seville (seventh century), subsequently adjusted to the model established by Idrisi and other Arab cartographers, perhaps under the influence of Ptolemy. The sources drawn on by Fra Paolino and Petrus Vesconte (early fourteenth century), with whose world maps Bianco's map of 1436 has a close affinity, are analyzed by R. Almagià, *Monumenta Cartographica Vaticana,* Vol. 1 (1941), pp. 3–8.

bounded by the encircling ocean, is common to Fra Paolino (*ca.* 1320) and to Petrus Vesconte, to the Catalan-Este map, to Andrea Bianco (1436), to Leardo, and to Walsperger (1448). That this representation shows an open seaway from the Atlantic to the Indian Ocean does not necessarily imply that the authors of these maps had any knowledge or conviction of the existence of such a passage or that they explicitly repudiated (if they knew) Ptolemy's concept of a landlocked Indian Ocean.[27] Bianco's atlas of 1436 indeed presents both versions, for his circular mappamundi is followed by a world map on the Ptolemaic model. In the Vinland Map, as in the other circular maps mentioned, the form of Africa is dictated by the traditional cosmographical pattern of land environed by ocean and by the medieval trend toward symmetry and analogy in design. "Thus geographers of that time could speak of a double Gades or a double Strait of Gibraltar, of the Pillars of Hercules in the west and the Pillars of Alexander in the east."[28]

Alike in the general form of Africa (with one major variation) and in the detailed outlines of the continent, the Vinland Map agrees with Bianco's circular map of 1436 (which itself has, in this part, close affinities with the design of Petrus Vesconte). The northwest coast was by this date known as far as Cape Bojador, and this section is traced with precision in both maps. Beyond it the coast line, conventionally drawn, trends southeastward with two estuaries or bays, similarly shown by both cartographers, although the anonymous map has a slight difference in the river pattern. This coastline forms the first section of the great southerly arc, which is continued by Bianco in an unbroken, conventionally drawn curve to the eastern horn of the continent; within this line, and in the center of the arc, he has described a reverse chord, and the resulting indentation, named *nidus ahimalion*[29] and decorated by two heraldic dragons, is painted in the color (green) of the surrounding ocean. The cartographer of the Vinland Map has, however, flattened the great curve, the central part of which (amounting to about one half of its total length) is drawn as a roughly horizontal line, with the words *Sinus Ethiopicus* below it. This modification in the outline of a model which was certainly circular or oval admits of only one explanation: compression due to lack of space at the draftsman's disposal. Since the vellum sheet on which the Vinland Map is drawn allows ample room, at the foot, for the tracing of the full curve called for by the design, it may be inferred that the modification had already been made in the immediate prototype from which the copyist worked. We have here a suggestion (however slight) either that the Vinland Map as we have it is a servile copy of an original with the same content, or that its compiler or author took little trouble to "edit" or correct his originals, at any rate in parts of the map in which his interest may have been less lively than in others.

If the linear outline can thus be accounted for in cartographic terms, its identification in those of historical geography is no less patent. The *Sinus Ethiopicus* is adumbrated, in the same position but without name, in two of the world maps drawn by Petrus Vesconte; in the Borgia map, which is probably to be dated a little earlier than Bianco's, it is conspicuously marked,

---

27. See (for example) T. Fischer, *Sammlung*, pp. 162–63.

28. O. Peschel, *Der Atlas des Andrea Bianco vom Jahre 1436* (1869), Vorwort, p. 13.

29. Misread by all previous commentators as *nidus abimalion*. Interpreted by V. Formaleoni (*Saggio sulla nautica antica dei Veneziani*, 1783) as "nest of winged dragons", referring to the legendary dragons who guarded the Fruits of the Hesperides. More probably (as Mr. Painter suggests) a scribal corruption of *sinus ethiopicus*.

with the name *Mare Ethiopie;* and in the Catalan-Este and Leardo maps it is transferred further west, appearing as a deep gulf which perhaps reflects vague information, going back to the fourteenth century, about the Gulf of Guinea.[30] The author of the Vinland Map, who does not in fact draw the gulf, gives it a name, classical in form, which is different from Bianco's somewhat cryptic name but may have stood in a common original, is identical with Fra Mauro's, and, although not to be found in Ptolemy, might be deduced from his text.[31] Apart from this, the Vinland Map, like that of Bianco, shows no other trace of the two deep indentations, penetrating southwest and southeast Africa, seen in the Catalan-Este world map and (in somewhat different form) in the maps of Leardo. In its delineation of East Africa, the Red Sea, the Arabian peninsula, and the Persian Gulf, its agreement with Bianco is complete.

The hydrographic pattern of the African rivers in the Vinland Map is a somewhat simplified version of that drawn by Bianco, with the Nile (unnamed) flowing northward from sources in southern Africa to its mouth on the Mediterranean and forking, a little below its springs, to flow westward to two mouths on the Atlantic; the western branch is named *magnus [fl]uuius.*[32] (Here again, Bianco's representation closely follows that of Petrus Vesconte.)

The African nomenclature of the Vinland Map—some fourteen names—is conventional, over half the forms corresponding to those of Bianco. Errors made by the anonymous cartographer in common with Bianco, or derived from their common prototype, are the transference of *Sinicus mons* (Mount Sinai) to the African side of the Red Sea and the location of *Imperiũ Basora* (Basra) in the eastern horn of Africa.[33] The single African legend in the Vinland Map relates to Prester John.[34]

ASIA

If we are justified in supposing the cartographer's prototype to have been circular, he—or the author of the immediate original copied by him—has adapted the shape of Asia, as of Africa, to the oval framework by vertical compression rather than lateral extension. Thus, in place of the steeply arched northern coast of Eurasia shown by Bianco, we have a flattened curve which abridges the north-south width of the land mass.

It is in the outline of East Asia that the maker of the Vinland Map introduces his most radical change in the representation of the tripartite world which we find in other surviving mappaemundi and particularly (in view of the affinities noted elsewhere) in that of Andrea Bianco. The prototype is, in this region, not wholly set aside—for traces of it remain—but rather adapted to admit a new geographical concept which, significantly enough, can be considered a gloss on the Tartar Relation. This concept is the *Magnum mare Tartarorum* with, lying be-

---

30. See G. R. Crone, ed., *The Voyages of Cadamosto* (1937), p. xviii.

31. Ptolemy, IV.8. Also perhaps from Pomponius Mela; the 'Genoese' world map of 1457 here has a barely decipherable legend, which has been read as "Preter tolemei tradicionem hic est guffus sed pomponius eum tradit cum eius insula", translated by Kimble (*Geography in the Middle Ages*, p. 197) as "Contrary to the opinion of Ptolemy, this is a gulf, but Pomponius speaks of it with its islands".

32. See G. H. T. Kimble, ed., *Esmeraldo de Situ Orbis* (1937), pp. 173–75.

33. Bianco also incorrectly places the Old Man of the Mountain (*el ueio dala montagna;* not in the Vinland Map) in Africa instead of Asia.

34. See below, pp. 131, 142.

yond it and within the encircling ocean, three large islands which appear to derive from the cartographer's interpretation of passages in C. de Bridia's text.[35]

This version of East Asian geography is found in no other extant map, and its relationship to the prototype followed for the rest of the Old World is best seen by comparison with Bianco's delineation, which itself descends from an ancient tradition.[36] In the sector of his world map lying, by his orientation, between NE (*G* = *greco*) and ESE (below *L* = *levante*), Bianco draws the coastal outline as a curve interrupted by a semicircular bay[37] with a large island (*tenplon chatai*) and trending SE to a prominent cape (*gog magog*) followed by a deep gulf and another cape (with the *paradixo terrestro*), after which the coast runs SW to join that of the island-studded sea which in maps of this type represents the Indian Ocean. In the Vinland Map, allowing for the flattening of the curve forming the northern edge of Eurasia, we find some evident correspondence with Bianco's design. The outer coasts of the three large islands (*Insule Sub aquilone* and *Postreme Insule*) plainly repeat the outline and orientation of sections of Bianco's coast; the channel dividing the mainland from the first, or most northerly, of these islands is laid down in the position of the semicircular bay in Bianco;[38] and the strait between the second and third islands coincides with the deep gulf in the east of Bianco's map. The inner or western coasts of the three islands and the eastern coast of the mainland, fringing the Sea of the Tartars, have no counterpart in any known cartographic document, but are drawn with elaborate detail of capes and bays. Considering that this sea represents (so far as we know) the cartographer's interpretation of a textual source, it may be suspected that the outline of its shores was seen by him in his mind's eye and not in any map.[39]

Whatever view we may have formed of our mapmaker's independence of judgment in the parts of his work so far analyzed, it is a striking fact—and one which perhaps does credit to his realism—that, in order to admit into his drawing of the Far East a representation derived from a new source under his hand, he has gone so far as to jettison the Earthly Paradise from the design.[40]

The remaining islands of Asia are drawn in the Vinland Map very much as by Bianco, with some simplification and generalization, and may be taken to have been in the prototype. The three small islands in the Persian Gulf appear in both, though Bianco's crescent outline for them (of portolan type) is not reproduced by the anonymous cartographer; the large archipelago depicted by Bianco (again in portolan style) in the Indian Ocean is reduced to four islands, and the two bigger oblong islands to the east of them are in both maps.[41] So too is the large island lying still further east in the ocean, roughly rectangular in shape, with its longer axis

35. See below, pp. 152–53.

36. See above, n. 26.

37. The concept of the Caspian Sea (Hyrcanum mare) as one of the four gulfs of the outer ocean was inherited by medieval cartography from Strabo and Isidore of Seville. Rubruck was the first traveler to refute it: "It is not true what Isidore reporteth, namely that this sea is a bay or gulf coming forth of the ocean: for . . . it is environed on all sides with land". See below, p. 151.

38. I.e. the traditional Caspian Sea (see the preceding note).

39. This interpretation is doubtless to be ascribed to the compiler rather than to the copyist of the Vinland Map as we have it; see below, p. 151.

40. This innovation would be even more remarkable if the cartographer was a religious.

41. Unnamed by Bianco.

N–S, and named by Bianco *ixola perlina;* comparison with earlier maps of this type identifies the island as Taprobana, that is, Ceylon.[42]

The representation of the interior of Asia in the Vinland Map is considerably curtailed by its author's modifications of his prototype (assuming this to have been a circular mappamundi similar to Bianco's): in the north, by vertical compression to fit the elliptical outline adopted; in the west, by the drawing of Europe on a larger scale; and in the east by the interpolation of the Sea of the Tartars. Instead of Bianco's representation of the Arctic zones of Eurasia (with two zonal chords, delineations of skin-clad inhabitants and coniferous trees, and a descriptive legend), the Vinland Map has only the two names *frigida pars* and *Thule ultima.* The elimination of East Asia by the western shoreline of the sea of the Tartars has affected the distribution of place names in the Vinland Map and its delineation of the hydrography. The four streams issuing from Eden, shown by Bianco as the headwaters of two rivers flowing west and falling into the Caspian Sea from the northeast and south, have disappeared from the Vinland Map, in which we see only the two truncated rivers entering the Caspian from the east and south respectively. A third Asian river (representing the Volga and the Kama) is drawn in Bianco's map with a T-shaped course, rising from two headstreams and flowing south to a delta on the northwest Caspian. In the Vinland Map the double headstreams are absent, and the river is traced from the Caspian to the ocean in northeast Asia, where it is given the name *Tatartata fluuius;* this delineation is not paralleled in any surviving map and doubtless springs from the cartographer's misreading of the Tartar Relation.[43] The general form of the Caspian Sea, as a rough oval, is similar in the two maps.[44] The Aral Sea is not represented in either.

Within the restricted space allowed by his revision of the river-pattern and of the coastal outlines, the author of the Vinland Map has grouped the majority of his names in two belts from north to south, on either side of the river which runs from the Caspian to the ocean. The nomenclature for Asia, with twenty-three names, is richer than that for the other two continents; some names come from the common stock found in other mappaemundi, but the greater number are associated with the information on the Tartars and Central Asia brought back by the Carpini mission. The location and arrangement of the names cannot, in general, be connected with Carpini's itinerary (or any other itinerary order), nor with any systematic conception of Central Asian geography. They appear, rather, to be dictated by the cartographer's need to lay down names where the design of the map allowed room for them. The four longer legends written in Asia or off its coasts are all related, by wording or substance, with the Tartar Relation.

ATLANTIC ISLANDS

Both the "normal" portolan charts and the mappaemundi of the fourteenth and fifteenth centuries included the islands and archipelagos of the eastern North Atlantic, so far as they were known;[45] and it is evident that they were in the prototype followed in the main by the author

42. The name Taprobana, given by classical geographers to Ceylon, was in the Middle Ages variously applied to this island and to Sumatra.

43. See above, pp. 56–57.

44. Thus in these, as in other medieval maps, two Caspian Seas are drawn; see above, n. 37, and below, p. 151.

45. The literature on this is extensive; see C. R. Beazley, *The Dawn of Modern Geography,* Vol. 3 (1906), ch. iv; also A. Cortesão, *The Nautical Chart of 1424* (1954), chs. ii–v, with a full bibliography.

of the Vinland Map for his representation of the tripartite world. His delineation of them, indeed, closely resembles that in Bianco's world map, which is in turn a generalization, with nomenclature omitted, from the fourth and fifth charts (or fifth and sixth leaves) in his atlas of 1436. The affinity between the two world maps, in this respect, is so marked as to distinguish them from all other surviving fifteenth-century maps and to confirm the hypothesis that one has been copied from the other or that both go back to a common model for their drawing of the Atlantic islands.

It is convenient (leaving Iceland, Greenland, and Vinland for separate consideration) to examine first the islands shown in the eastern Atlantic, from north to south.

To the north of the British Isles, the Vinland Map marks two islands, presumably representing either the Orkneys and Shetlands or these two groups and the Faeroes. The two islands appear, in exactly the same relative positions, in Bianco's world map, although they are absent from the charts of his atlas.[46]

To the west of Ireland the Vinland Map has an isolated island, also in Bianco; and to the southwest of England another, drawn by Bianco as a crescent. In Bianco's fifth chart they are named, respectively, *y*ᵃ. *de berzil* (i.e. Brasil) and *y*ᵃ. *de uentura*.[47]

Further out, and extending north–south from about the latitude of Brittany to about that of Cape Juby, Bianco's world map shows a chain of about a dozen small islands, drawn in conventional portolan style. These islands—the Azores of fifteenth-century cartography and the Madeira group[48]—are represented in the Vinland Map, in more generalized form and without Bianco's characteristic geometrical outlines, by seven islands, having the same orientation and relative position as in Bianco's map, and with the name *Desiderate insule*. In the fourth chart of Bianco's atlas, which depicts the chain of islands as in the world map, the names given to the "Azores" (north to south) are *corbo marino, coruos, y*ᵃ. *de sanzorzi, y*ᵃ. *de bentusta, y*ᵃ. *di colonbi, y*ᵃ. *de brasil, chapusa* and *lobo;* and those of the Madeira group are *porto santo, y*ᵃ. *de madera, y*ᵃ. *dexerta*.[49]

Further south, the Vinland Map lays down the Canaries as seven islands lying off Cape Bojador, with the name *Beate īsule fortune*.[50] The grouping differs slightly from that of Bianco, who arranges the seven islands—as in all charts which show them before the date of his atlas—in a line lying roughly ENE–WSW. It seems unlikely that the anonymous cartographer's redisposition of the islands, any more than the difference in their outlines from the chart-designs of Bianco, has any special significance. In the fourth chart of Bianco's atlas, the islands are named (from east to west) *y*ᵃ. *del fero, y*ᵃ. *de le palme, y*ᵃ. *de gomera, y*ᵃ. *de inferno, y*ᵃ. *de chanaria, p*ᵒ. *santo, forte uentura, paruego*(?), *p*ᵒ. *sable, gracioxa, y*ᵃ. *de lancilotto, rocho*.[51]

In the ocean to the west of the *Desiderate insule*, the Vinland Map has two large islands, irregularly rectangular in shape with the longer axis north–south; the name *Magnæ Insulæ Beati*

---

46. See below, p. 129.
47. See below, p. 137.
48. On the cartographic representation of the Azores in the fourteenth and fifteenth centuries, see Cortesão, passim, and fig. 5; also below, Part II, ch. 5.
49. Cortesão (table II) gives a comparative table of nomenclature for the islands.
50. See below, pp. 137–38.
51. For the nomenclature in other maps, see Cortesão, table II.

Brandani Branziliæ dictæ is written between them. Their agreement in outline with the two large islands laid down in exactly the same positions at the western edge of Bianco's world map is striking: in particular, the indentation of the east coast of the more northerly island and the peninsular form of its southern end, the squarish northern end of the other (and larger island) and its forked southern end, are common to both maps. These islands (unnamed in the two world maps) are Satanaxes and Antillia, which make their first appearance in a map of 1424 and have been the subject of extensive discussion by historians of cartography. In point of date, Bianco's atlas of 1436 is the third known work to show the Antillia group, and the fourth chart of the atlas names the two major islands *y*ª. *de la man satanaxio* and *y*ª *de antillia*.[52] Since the outline given to these two islands both in the world map and in the fourth chart of Bianco's atlas is easily distinguishable from that in any fifteenth-century representation of them,[53] the concordance with the Vinland Map in this respect is significant. Here again we have plain testimony to the derivation of the Vinland Map from a cartographic prototype, and to the character of this prototype. It does not appear necessary to trace back the history of the delineations of Atlantic islands which the mapmaker found in his model and which have been the subject of a copious literature.[54]

5. ICELAND, GREENLAND, VINLAND

In the extreme northwest and west of the map are laid down three great islands, named respectively *isolanda Ibernica, Gronelãda,* and *Vinlanda Insula a Byarno re p̄a et leipho socijs,* with a long legend on Bishop Eirik Gnupsson's Vinland voyage above the last two. That they lie outside the oval framework of the map suggests that they were not in the model—apparently a circular or elliptical mappamundi—which (as we have seen) the cartographer followed in his representation of Europe, Africa, and Asia.

The three islands are drawn in outline, in the same style as the coasts in the rest of the map; and there can be no doubt that the whole map, including this part of it, was drawn at the same time and by a single hand. For this part of the map there are no earlier or contemporary prototypes of kindred character for comparison, and indeed (except in respect of Iceland) no representations with much apparent analogy can be cited before the late sixteenth century.[55] Any attempt to divine the cartographer's sources of information and their character can only proceed from analysis of his delineation, in the light of impressions formed about his working methods and style; from examination of the knowledge of lands in the northwest Atlantic available in Europe in the early fifteenth century, and of the channels by which it may have been transmitted; and from the scrutiny of later maps or texts for data that might have survived from the period in which the Vinland Map was made. Here we have at once the most arresting feature and the most exacting problem presented by this singular map. The questions of sources

52. The Antillia question is fully studied, with bibliographical references, by Cortesão, who discusses the probable origins of these names. The two earlier works to show Antillia are the Pizzigano chart of 1424 (now in the James Ford Bell Collection, University of Minnesota) and the chart of Battista Beccario, 1435 (Biblioteca Nazionale, Parma). See below, Part II, ch. 5.
53. Cf. Cortesão, fig. 4; and below, Fig. 3 (p. 158).
54. Listed by Cortesão, pp. 113–16.
55. See below, Part II, chs. 7, 8.

and parallels will be considered in later chapters;[56] the present section is confined to a brief description of what is visible in the map.

Iceland lies to the west and a little north of Scandinavia, and NNW of the British Isles. It is drawn as a rough rectangle, with a prominent west-pointing peninsula in the northwest, the E–W axis being considerably longer than the N–S axis. Greenland, somewhat larger than Iceland, is doglegged in shape, with its greatest extension from north to south. Its outline, on the east side, is deeply indented and in the form of a bow, the northeast coast trending generally NW–SE to the most easterly point, and the southeast coast trending NNE–SSW to a conspicuous southernmost promontory, in about the latitude of north Denmark; from this point the west coast runs due north, again with many bays, to an angle (opposite the easternmost point) after which it turns NW and is drawn in a smooth unaccidented line to its furthest north, turning east to form a short section lying W–E. The approximation of the east coast and of the southern section of the west coast to the outline in modern maps leaps to the eye.

Between Greenland and Vinland lies a channel slightly wider than that between Iceland and Greenland. The northernmost point of Vinland is shown in about the same latitude as the south coast of Iceland and somewhat lower than the north coast of Greenland; and its southernmost point in about the latitude of Brittany. Between these points Vinland is drawn as an elongated island, the greatest width being roughly a third of the overall length; the somewhat wavy details of the outline, if compared with this cartographer's technique in other parts of his map, seem to be conventional rather than realistic. The island is divided into three great peninsulas by deep inlets penetrating the east coast and extending almost to the west coast. The more northerly inlet is a narrow channel trending ENE–SSW and terminating in a large lake; the more southerly and wider inlet lies roughly parallel to it. The name *Vinlanda Insula . . .* is written to the right of the northernmost peninsula.

No off-shore islands are shown round the coasts of Iceland, Greenland, or Vinland.[57]

NOTE A. ANDREA BIANCO AND HIS ATLAS OF 1436

Since a comparative study of the Vinland Map has involved frequent reference to the manuscript atlas of 1436 by Andrea Bianco, a brief account of this cartographer and his work is here given.[58]

Bianco was an experienced ship master and navigator of Venetian merchant galleys. The Archives of the Republic record his certification, at various dates between 1437 and 1451, as

56. Part II, chs. 6–9.

57. The circle visible off the SE coast of Greenland is in fact a hole in the vellum, easily identified (like the other holes) by the square outline of the patch at the back of the vellum, showing through to the face.

58. On Bianco and his maps, see V. Formaleoni, *Saggio sulla nautica antica dei Veneziani, con una illustrazione di alcune carte idrografiche antiche della Biblioteca di S. Marco* (1783); Santarem, *Essai,* Vol. 3 (1852), pp. 366–98; O. Peschel, *Der Atlas des Andrea Bianco von 1436* (1869); T. Fischer, *Sammlung* (1886), pp. 207–10; G. Uzielli and P. Amat di S. Filippo, *Studi biografici e bibliografici sulla storia della geografia in Italia,* Vol. 2 (2d ed. 1886), pp. 67–68; A. E. Nordenskiöld, *Periplus* (1897), pp. 61–62; K. Kretschmer, *Die italienischen Portolane des Mittelalters* (1909), pp. 130–32; T. Gasparrini Leporace, *Mostra dei navigatori veneti del quattrocento e del cinquecento: catalogo* (1957), pp. 80–81 (archival references) and 92–93. The entire atlas of 1436 was reproduced in the *Raccolta* of F. Ongania (no. IX, 1871), and four of its charts by Nordenskiöld (*Periplus,* pls. XX, XXI); the world map has often been reproduced; the chart of 1448 was reproduced by Ongania (no. XI, 1881). See Pl. VI, IX, X herewith. Bianco has also been the subject of a romantic novel by F. G. Slaughter, *The Mapmaker* (1957).

ammiraglio and *uomo di consiglio* in ships plying the trade routes to Tana (Black Sea), Flanders, Beirut and Alexandria, Rumania, and Barbary. He signs his chart of 1448 from London as *comito de galia*.

Two cartographic works from Bianco's hand have survived. These are the atlas of ten leaves, with nine charts or maps, dated 1436 and preserved in the Biblioteca Nazionale Marciana, Venice (MS It., Fondo antico Z. 76), and the nautical chart of 1448, preserved in the Biblioteca Ambrosiana, Milan (F. 260 Inf.). The latter is the primary cartographic authority (since no Portuguese charts of this period are extant) for the Portuguese exploration of the Atlantic and of the African coast up to the year 1445, extending southward to Cape Verde. This chart, which has been frequently reproduced, has been the subject of much discussion in regard to its representation of the Azores and of islands shown at the southern edge of the chart—two off Cape Verde (conjecturally identified as the Cape Verde Islands) and *ixola otenticha,* to which further reference will be made in this study.[59] The chart is signed *Andrea biancho. venician. comito di galia me fexe a londra. m. cccc.xxxx.viij;* it is thus the earliest surviving nautical chart prepared in England, and testifies to the manner in which intelligence of new discoveries could reach England in the fifteenth century.[60] Bianco is also recorded to have assisted Fra Mauro in the preparation of his world map at Murano in 1459.[61]

The atlas of 1436, with which we are principally concerned, comprises ten leaves of vellum, measuring 29 × 38 cm., in an eighteenth-century binding. Until 1813, when it came to the Biblioteca Marciana, it was in the possession of the Venetian family of Contarini, and there is no evidence that it ever left Venice, where Bianco seems to have executed and signed it.

The designs on the leaves are as follows:

> I. Description of the Rule of Marteloio (*la raxon de marteloio*) for resolving the course, with the "circle and square", two tables and two other diagrams;[62] to the right a windrose. Above is the signature: *Andreas. biancho. de ueneciis me fecit. m.cccc. xxxvj.*
>
> II. FIRST CHART: coasts of the Black Sea.
>
> III. SECOND CHART: coasts of the Eastern Mediterranean.
>
> IV. THIRD CHART: coasts of the Central Mediterranean.
>
> V. FOURTH CHART: coasts of Spain and Portugal, NW Africa, and Atlantic islands (Azores, Madeira, Cape Verde Islands, *Antillia, Satanaxio*).
>
> VI. FIFTH CHART: coasts of North Spain, France and Flanders, the British Isles.
>
> VII. SIXTH CHART: coasts of the Baltic, Denmark and Scandinavia (Pl. IX).

59. See below, p. 159.

60. On geographical culture in England in the fifteenth century, see E. G. R. Taylor, *Tudor Geography 1485–1583* (1930), ch. i; R. A. Skelton, "English knowledge of the Portuguese discoveries in the 15th century: a new document", *Congresso Internacional de História dos Descobrimientos, Actas,* Vol. 2 (1961), pp. 365–74; J. A. Williamson, *The Cabot Voyages and English Discovery under Henry VII* (1962), p. 18. Nordenskiöld remarks that Bianco's chart of 1448 is the only portolan chart before the sixteenth century known to have been executed outside the Mediterranean area.

61. Placido Zurla, *Il Mappamondo di Fra Mauro Camaldolese* (1806), p. 85.

62. On the *raxon de marteloio,* see E. G. R. Taylor, *The Haven-finding Art* (1956), pp. 117–21.

VIII. SEVENTH CHART, on a smaller scale (Pl. X): all the coasts of Europe and NW Africa comprised in the previous six charts.

IX. Circular world map, 25 cm. in circumference (Pl. VII).[63]

X. Ptolemaic world map on Ptolemy's first (conic) projection, with graduation.

The first five charts are drawn and colored in the usual portolan style, with strongly accented coastlines; they are on a common scale, and oriented with south to the top (as indicated by the writing of names and legends not on the coasts). The sixth chart is drawn in somewhat different style, with the coastlines traced in smooth broad curves, suggesting less detailed knowledge or information from hearsay. The seventh chart embraces the "normal portolan" area, with some extension to the north (from the sixth chart) and to the south and west (from the fourth chart). The geographical delineations in this and in the circular world map agree on the whole with those in the six special charts and seem to be generalizations from them.[64] The world map has iconographic representations of kings, natives, and so on.

The affinities noted between the Vinland Map and Bianco's circular world map do not extend to the charts of the atlas; for where these differ from the circular map, it is the latter version which the delineation in the Vinland Map reflects. It is clear indeed that, however much Bianco drew on his charts for the *outlines* of his circular map, he followed quite distinct models for the construction and form of one and the other.

The incongruous appearance of a circular mappamundi of archaic design and a Ptolemaic world map in this company has prompted the suspicion that one or both may have been added to the atlas at a later date.[65] The similarity of the handwriting in these two maps and in the rest of the atlas, however, leaves little doubt that they were executed at the same time as the other charts, or else (as Peschel surmised) little later and certainly at the same time as one another.

In its general character the circular world map faithfully reproduces the pattern introduced by Fra Paolino and Petrus Vesconte over a century earlier, augmented only by the representation of northwest Africa and the Atlantic islands borrowed from Bianco's charts. Neither in design nor in content does its author seem to have sought novelty; there is no attempt at originality of design as in Pirrus de Noha's world map, or at conscientious scrutiny of sources, as in the maps of Leardo and Fra Mauro. Rather than dismiss Bianco as "a casual and untutored cartographer",[66] it is tempting to speculate (no more than speculation is justified) that in adding the two world maps to his atlas he was deliberately presenting side by side the old world picture and the new, the geographical lore of the Christian Middle Ages and the lately discovered geography of Ptolemy[67]—just as sixteenth-century editors of the *Geographia* printed a modern world map, based on experience, alongside the traditional maps of the Ptolemaic atlas. This is perhaps

63. As noted by Kretschmer (p. 131), the map is in fact slightly elliptical, the N–S diameter being 26 cm., and the E–W diameter 25 cm.

64. The only substantial difference is in Northwest Europe and Scandinavia, as represented in the seventh chart and the world map.

65. Cf. Peschel, pp. 14–15, and Kretschmer, p. 131.

66. T. Fischer, *Sammlung*, p. 77.

67. The first Latin translation of Ptolemy's Greek text was completed by the Florentine Jacopo d'Angiolo in 1406, and the maps were turned into Latin soon after. Bianco's copy of the Ptolemaic world map, made in Venice in 1436, testifies to the diffusion of the Latin manuscripts of the *Geographia* and has a possible relevance to the Ptolemaic echoes in the nomenclature of the Vinland Map, few and faint though they are; see below, pp. 141–42.

fanciful; but it is nonetheless remarkable that the author of the Vinland Map, with so much new material, not yet seen in maps, at his disposal, chose so elderly a stock on which to graft it.

6. NAMES AND LEGENDS IN THE VINLAND MAP

The nomenclature and longer legends in the map, like its geographical outlines, are in part paralleled in surviving maps or texts, in part drawn from sources not now known. The comparative notes which follow do not attempt a complete, or even a fairly full, record of other maps or texts in which any one name or legend (in the same or a similar form) occurs. Parallels are cited from what may be called proximate sources—in particular, among maps, Bianco's world map of 1436, and, among texts, the Tartar Relation of C. de Bridia and other accounts of the missions of Carpini and Rubruck.[68] Other cartographic and textual documents are cited where their use of a name, in a particular form or position, throws light on its appearance in the Vinland Map or on the background of knowledge or belief against which this map was compiled. Some general inferences on the toponymy of the map and on the cartographer's sources for it are drawn after the list.

The following abbreviations are used:

MAPS

FP	Fra Paolino, *ca.* 1320.
Ves	Petrus Vesconte, *ca.* 1321.
Laur	Laurentian ('Medici') atlas, 1351.
CA	Catalan atlas, 1375.
Borgia	Borgia world map, 15th century.
Bi	Andrea Bianco, world map, 1436.
Bi¹, Bi²...	First, second, etc., charts in Bianco's atlas of 1436.
(icon.)	Iconographic representation in Bianco's world map.
Wal	Andreas Walsperger, 1448.
Le	Giovanni Leardo, 1442–52/3.
CE	Catalan-Este world map, *ca.* 1450–60.
Gen	'Genoese' world map, 1457.
FM	Fra Mauro, 1459.

TEXTS

TR	The "Tartar Relation" of C. de Bridia, reproduced and translated herewith.
Ca	The "Historia Tartarorum" of Carpini, ed. M. A. P. d'Avezac, in *Relation des Mongoles ou Tartares* (1858); ed. C. R. Beazley, *Texts and Versions* (1903); ed. A. van den Wyngaert, in *Sinica Franciscana,* Vol. 1 (1929).
Ru	The "Itinerary" of Rubruck, ed. d'Avezac (1858); trans. and ed. W. W. Rockhill, *The Journey of William of Rubruck* (1900); ed. Beazley (1903); ed. Wyngaert (1929).

68. Collation of C. de Bridia's text with the other accounts of the mission exposes their relationship and the dependence of the author of the map upon C. de Bridia, as shown by Mr. Painter in his contributions to this volume. Where TR is cited in the following list, reference should be made to Mr. Painter's annotated text.

LITERATURE

Beazley, *Dawn*. C. R. Beazley, *The Dawn of Modern Geography* (1897–1906).

Beazley, *Texts*. C. R. Beazley, ed., *The Texts and Translations of John de Plano Carpini and William de Rubruquis* (1903).

Björnbo and Petersen. A. A. Björnbo and C. S. Petersen, *Der Däne Claudius Clausson Swart* (1909).

Bretschneider. E. Bretschneider, *Mediaeval Researches from Eastern Asiatic Sources* (1888).

Cortesão. A. Cortesão, *The Nautical Chart of 1424* (1954).

T. Fischer. Theobald Fischer, *Sammlung mittelalterlicher Welt- und Seekarten italienischen Ursprungs* (1886).

Hallberg. I. Hallberg, *L'Extrême Orient dans la littérature et la cartographie de l'Occident des XIIIᵉ et XIVᵉ siècles* (1907).

Hennig. R. Hennig, *Terrae Incognitae* (2d ed. 1945–56).

Hermannsson, *Cartography*. H. Hermannsson, *The Cartography of Iceland* (1931).

Hermannsson, *Wineland*. H. Hermannsson, *The Problem of Wineland* (1936).

Kretschmer. K. Kretschmer, *Die italienischen Portolane des Mittelalters* (1909).

Miller. K. Miller, *Mappaemundi* (1895–98).

Nansen. F. Nansen, *In Northern Mists* (1911).

Pauly-Wissowa. *Enzyklopädie der klassischen Altertumswissenschaft* (1894–).

Yule, *Cathay*. Sir H. Yule, *Cathay and the Way Thither* (1913–16).

Yule-Cordier. Sir Henry Yule, ed., *The Book of Ser Marco Polo,* 3d ed., rev. H. Cordier (1903).

Names and legends are transcribed *ad litteram,* with indication of line divisions; contractions are not extended. Translations of the legends only are given. To facilitate location of the names and legends on the original map, numbers have been added, keying them to the reproduction on Pl. VII.

EUROPE

(a) The British Isles and other islands of NW Europe

1 Anglia/terra/insula: Bi *engeltera;* = *England.*
[Isle of Wight, unnamed: also unnamed in Bi; Bi⁵ *huic.*]
[Ushant, unnamed; also unnamed in Bi; Bi⁷ *vsenty.*]

2 Ibernia: Bi *irlanda;* = *Ireland.*

3 Ierlanda insula: perhaps a variant of *Irlanda,* as a doublet of *Ibernia* (cf. Bi⁵ and Bi⁷ *Ibernia Yrllanda;* Laur *Irllanda uel iberni*); but more probably, in view of the position of the name, a corruption of one of the names current in 14th and 15th century cartography for islands or island groups north of Scotland (see below, pp. 164–66). These are shown in Catalan maps as a large elliptical island (CA *stillanda;* CE *stillant;* Laur *Sillant;* Bi⁷, *stilanda*), with two smaller islands aligned NW of it (CA *orchansa, chatenes;* CE *arcana, coronas;* Laur *Orbenas, State*); in Bi the elliptical island disappears. Closer in form is the name *Herlant* (= Shetland) in maps of the North deriving from Claudius Clavus, later in date (*post* 1466) but going back to earlier models; see Björnbo and Petersen, pp. 28–29, and below, pp. 176–77.

[Two islands, unnamed, north of the British Isles: also unnamed in Bi; unrepresented in Bi[5] and Bi[7]. Residual from the representation described under the previous name, the large elliptical island being suppressed. Presumably intended for the Orkneys and Shetlands, or one of these groups and the Faeroes; see above, p. 122.]

(b) Northern Europe

4 Dacia: Bi *dacia;* = Denmark. The form (for *Dania*) common in mediaeval cartography, and found in many charts and world maps; see Björnbo and Petersen, p. 107.

[An island, unnamed, in the mouth of the Baltic: also unnamed in Bi; Bi[8] *y*[a]. *lasant;* = Sjælland.]

[An island, unnamed, at the head of the Baltic: also unnamed in Bi and Bi[7]; = Gotland.]

5 Rex/Noruicorum: Bi *noruega;* = Norway.

6 Rex Suedorum: Bi *sueda;* = Sweden. Bi and VM both place this name south of the Baltic.

7 frigida pars: Bi *in [h]ac parte est maximum frigus* ... Mediaeval world maps, such as Bianco's, commonly show a pair of such legends, indicating the regions, outside the *oikoumene,* too cold or too hot for human habitation.

(c) Central and Eastern Europe

8 Apusia: not in Bi; TR (¶2) *aprusia;* Prussia. The insertion of the *r* above the line by the corrector of TR shows that the original reading was *apusia.*

9 Buyslaua: not in Bi; = Breslau (*Bratislava*), where Carpini's party stopped on the outward journey and was joined by Friar Benedict.

10 Rusij: Bi *rosia, inperiō rosie magna* (icon.); = Russia.

11 Rusij habent imperiũ contiguum ex parte oriētis mogaloχ tartaroχ / m. ḳan ex parte boreali habent mare frigidum et magnum flumen / quod medium montiũ insularum q' transit inter glacies borealis occeani / progrediens ("The Russians have their empire adjoining on the east that of the Mongols and Tartars of the Great Khan, to the north they have the frozen sea and a great river which passes through the midst of the mountains and islands, debouching amongst the ice of the northern ocean"). This legend is based in general on the text of TR, ¶¶2, 3. The account of the "great river", which has no exact textual counterpart in TR, recalls that of the Tanais (Don) by Rubruck (ed. Rockhill, pp. 97–98), as "the eastern boundary of Russia, and takes its rise in the Maeotide fens, which extend to the ocean in the north. The river flows southward forming a great sea ... before it reaches the Sea of Pontus." While the members of the Carpini mission, unaware of the existence of the Caspian (in its true position), supposed the Volga to flow into the Black Sea, Rubruck's description of the course of the Don seems to contain the elements of the representation of the great river (*Tatartata fluvius*) in VM, extending from the Caspian to the northern ocean; see below, p. 151. No direct debt of VM to Rubruck need however be inferred.

12 Tanais: Bi *tanai;* = river Don. To the Venetians, and to Bianco, engaged in the trade with Russia through their principal factory at Tana in the Crimea, the geography of this region was well known; and Bianco correctly shows the Don, with its marked sweep to the east, flowing into the Sea of Azov (see T. Fischer, pp. 114–15). The author of VM has omitted the river (see above, p. 117) and seems to have mistaken its name for that of a region or kingdom. Cf. the narrative of Friar Benedict: ". . . the great river Ethil, which the Russians call Volga, and which is believed to be the Tanais" (Rockhill, p. 34); and the note above on the legend *Rusii habent* . . .

(d) Mediterranean countries

13 Rex/francorū: Bi *rex frācoron* (icon.); = France.

14 Hispanorū rex: Bi *rex ispanea e castilie* (icon.); = Spain.

15 aben: plainly a corrupt and probably truncated form, which cannot be assimilated to any name on the south coast of Spain in Kretschmer's list or in other charts and maps of the 14th and 15th centuries not collated by him. Bi⁷, however, has, on the SE coast, *malien* (Bi⁴ *molinij* = Torremolinos), the *i* being undotted, so that the word could easily be misread *maben;* this is of course a long shot, which would imply knowledge of the charts in Bianco's atlas (at any rate the general chart of Europe and the Mediterranean) by the author of the Vinland Map or of its prototype.

16 vrbs/Roma: not in Bi; = Rome.

17 Imperium/romanorum; Bi *inperion romanie, inperiū romanorō* (icon.). Written in SE Europe, denoting the Eastern Empire.

(e) The Mediterranean

[The islands of Majorca and Minorca, Corsica and Sardinia, Sicily, Corfu, Cephalonia, Crete, Cyprus, and the Aegean Archipelago are drawn but unnamed: so too in Bi.]

AFRICA

(a) West of the Nile

18 Rex/Marr: Bi *rex de maroco* (icon.); = Morocco. Although the second word is truncated, no trace of further letters can be seen in ultraviolet light.

19 Bela . . . /rex: Bi *rex belmarin* (icon.). The Beni Marin dynasty which ruled in Fez and Morocco in the 13th century and in Tlemcen until 1407 (Santarem, *Essai,* Vol. 3, p. 368).

20 Tunesis/rex: Bi *tunis.*

21 Maori: not in Bi; = *Mauri?* The name is, however, placed too far inland and too far east for Mauretania, and this may be a corruption of another name in the prototype, e.g. the second element of *Syrtis maioris* (Ves *Syrtes maiores*).

22 Phazania: not in Bi; = Fezzan. The Roman name, first used by Pliny (v.33); also in Ptolemy (IV.7.10), but not in his maps. This name does not seem to occur in any other medieval map.

23 *magnus* ⎫
 magnus ⎭ [*fl*]*uuius:* not named in Bi; Bi⁵ *flm̄ main.* The concept of the Western Nile, or "Nile of the Negroes", represented in mediaeval cartography arose from the identification of the Niger, by some classical writers, as a western branch of the Nile and from subsequent confusion of the Niger, the Senegal, and the Rio do Ouro (south of C. Bojador). The name *Magnus fluvius* is not in any other map, but is implied in some texts, e.g. the *Libro del Conoscimiento* (*ca.* 1350): "The river [Nilus] forms two courses, the greater, flowing to the westward, called the Rio del Oro"; and Alvise Cadamosto (*ca.* 1468): "This river is said to

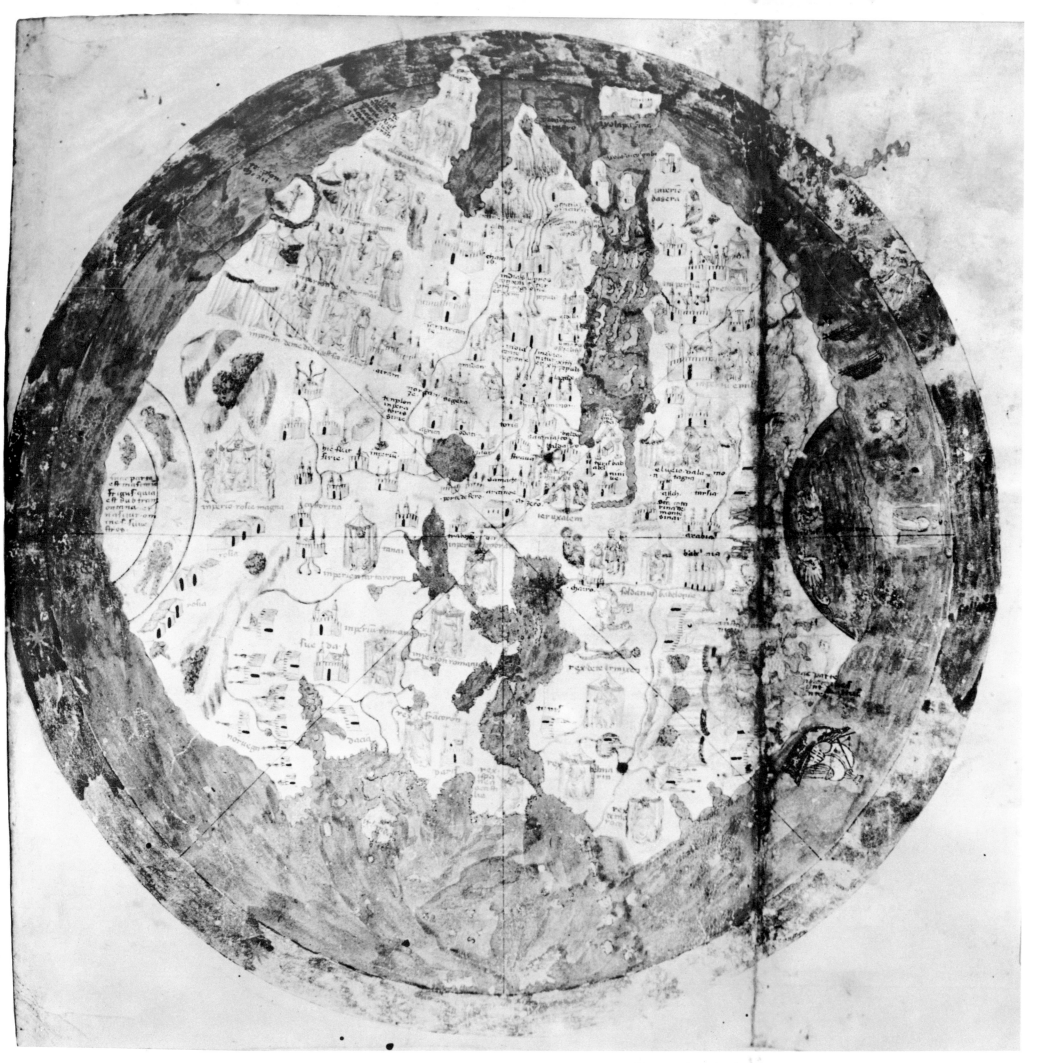

VI. World Map in the Atlas of Andrea Bianco, 1436. Biblioteca Nazionale Marciana, Venice.

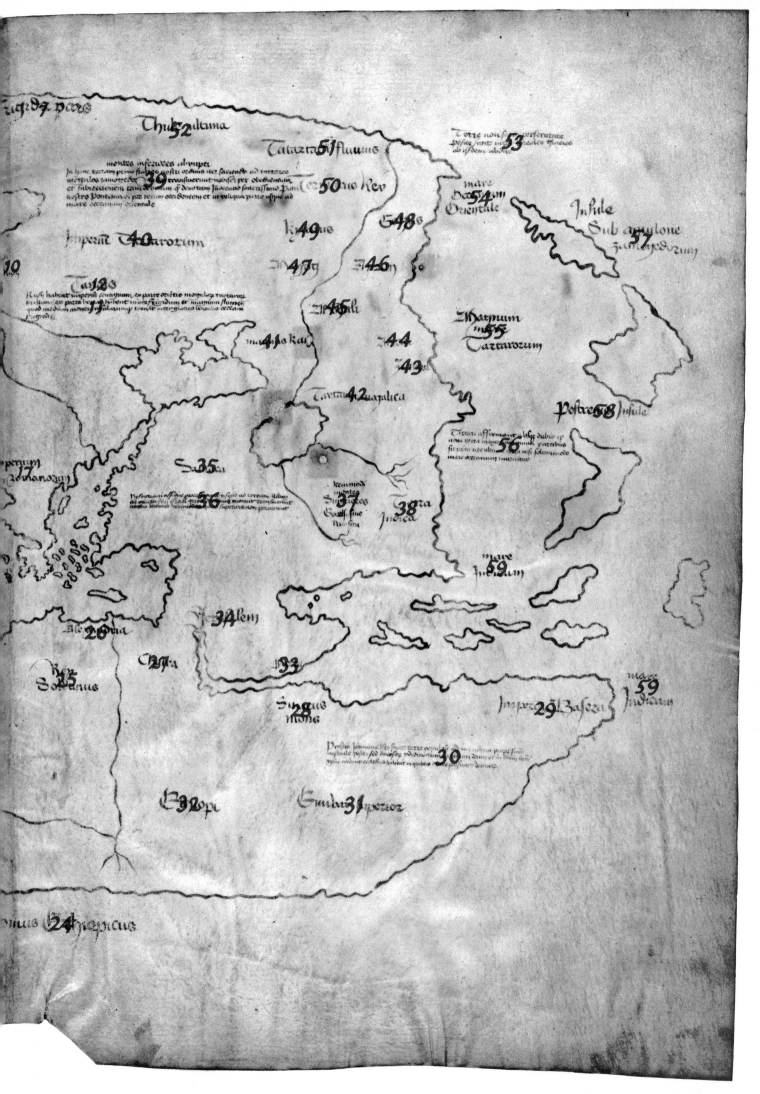

VII. Names and Legends of the Vinland Map, Keyed by Numbers to the Annotated List, pp. 128–41.

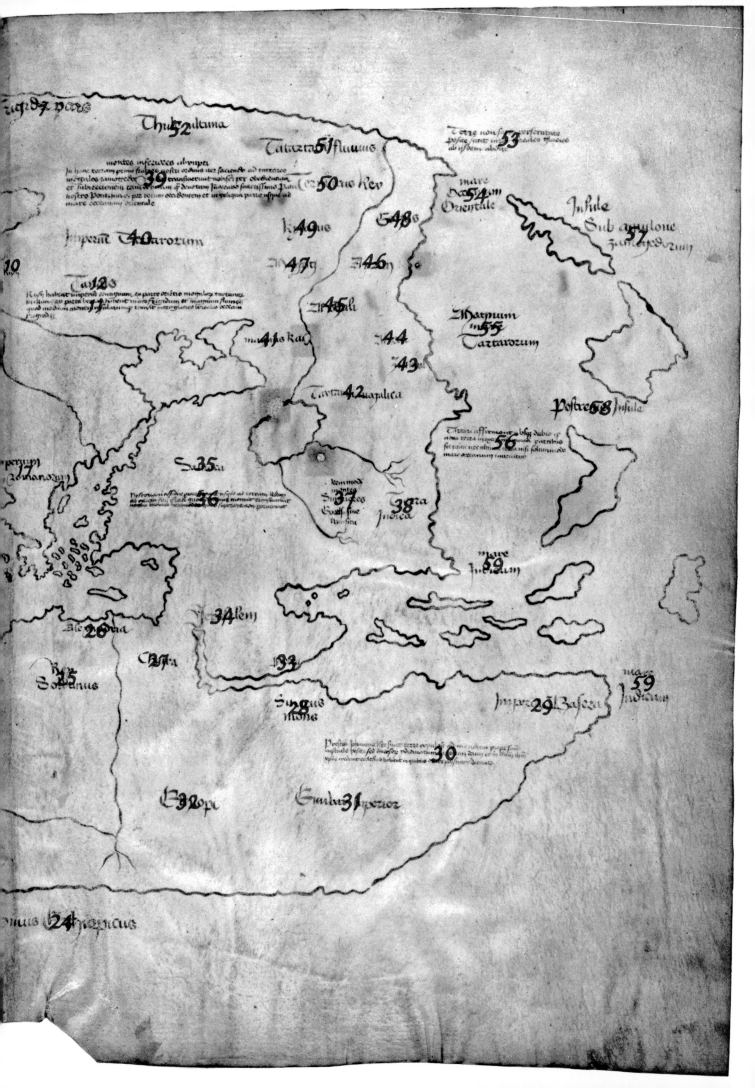

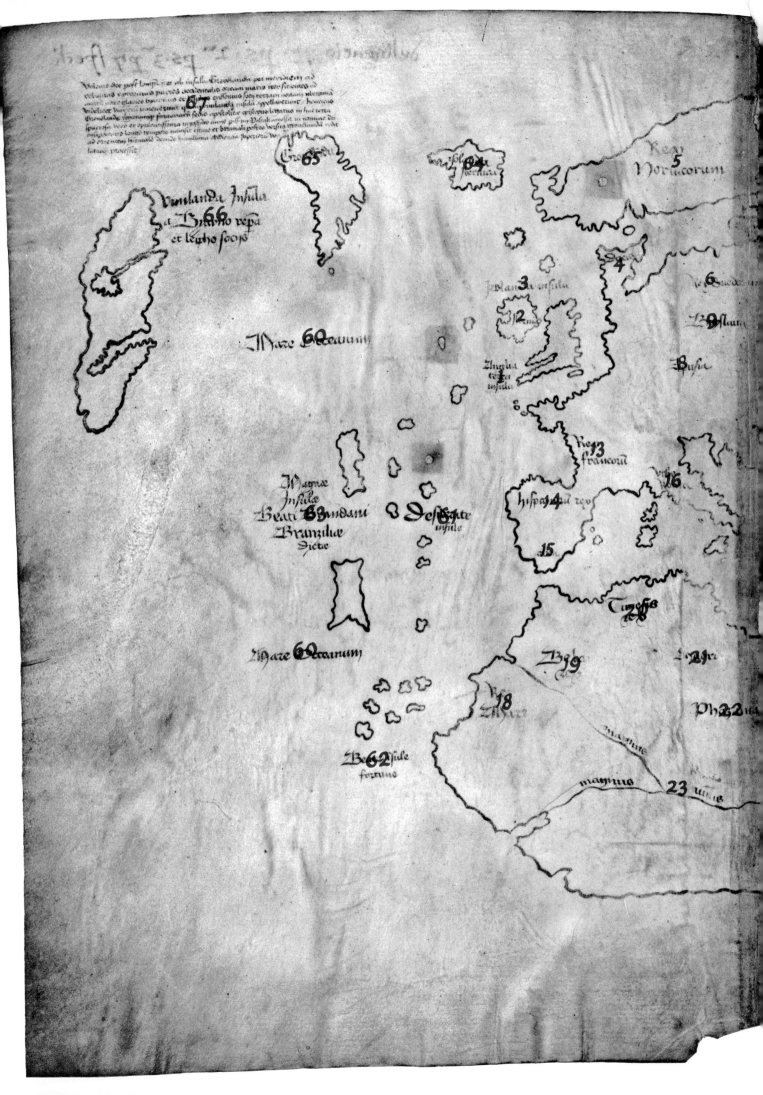

Volens deo post longissime ab insula Groenlanda per meridiem ad
occiduas extremasq́ partes occidentalis oceani maris reversionem ad
iunior inter glacies hyperius et ☩ ryssimus soci certam noviñ plenissima
videlicet hanc viñ invenerunt q́ Frislandia insula appellaretur: henricus
Groenlande revorumq́ ſinuarum sede apostolice episcopus lotharius in hac terra
spaciosa vero et opulentissima imposito anno post n̄i Pascali accessit in nomine dei
omnipotento longo tempore mansisse et iam et britanno postea westia Groenlanda redit
ad extremum hyemale deinde humillima oblonaia superiora W ...
litatis processit

Regñ
Norwcorum 5

Croenea 65

Vinlanda Insula
a Bralio repa
et leutho focys 66

mar sol ...
hercina 64

4

le Sueda 6

Iselandia insula 3
12 mar

L Dstani 9

Bassia

Islanda
terra
insula

Mare 60 ceanum

Magne
Insule
Beati 63 andani
Brazilie
dicte

Desesgte 61
insule

Regñ 13
francorum

vru 16

hispalia 14 al regñ

15

Mare 60 ceanum

Tunesis 17

B 19

L 21 n

18
Zilia

Ph 22 n...

Be 62 sile
fortune

magnus

23 uus

be a branch of the river Nile . . . This river has many other very large branches, besides that of Senega, and they are great rivers on this coast of Ethiopia".

24 *Sinus Ethiopicus:* Bi *nidus ahimalion* (apparently a scribal corruption of *sinus ethiopicus*); Borgia *Mare Ethiopie;* FM *Sinus Ethiopicus.* See above, p. 119.

25 *Rex/Soldanus:* Bi *soldanus babelonie* (icon.); = Egypt (*Babilonia* being the medieval name for Cairo).

26 *Alexandria:* not in Bi; Bi⁷ *alesandria.*

(b) East of the Nile

27 *Chaira:* Bi *chairo* (written on the west bank of the Nile, whereas VM has the name somewhat to the east of the river).

28 *Sinicus/mons:* Bi *sta catarina de monte sinai;* = Mount Sinai. Bi and VM both place this on the African side of the southern end of the Red Sea.

29 *Imperiū Basora:* Bi *inperio basera* (icon.); = Basra. Bi and VM both place this at the eastern tip of Africa.

30 *Prestīs̄ Johannis Iste sunt terre populose ad meridiem prope sinum / australē posite sed diuersoᵖ ydiomatum in unum deum et in dn̄m ihm / xp̄m credunt ecclesias habent in quibus orare possunt dicunt[ur]* ("These are the populous lands of the Prester John situated in the south near the southern gulf. Although of diverse languages it is said that they believe in one God and in our Lord Jesus Christ and have churches in which they can pray"): Bi *inperiū prete ianis* (icon.). Like all Europeans in the 13th century, C. de Bridia (TR, ¶17), here closely following Carpini (ed. d'Avezac, p. 655), locates Prester John in Asia. See Yule-Cordier, Vol. 2, pp. 231–37, and Rubruck, ed. Rockhill, pp. 150, 162; also F. Zarncke, *Der Priester Johannes* (1879–83). As Yule observes, "when the Mongol conquests threw Asia open to Frank travellers in the middle of the 13th century, their minds were full of Prester John". In spite of the confident identification of Prester John as "Unc Can" by Marco Polo, reports on the Christian kingdom of Ethiopia reaching Europe in the early 14th century suggested that Prester John was to be located in Africa. The first writers to identify him as the ruler of Ethiopia were the Genoese cartographer Giovanni da Carignano in 1306 (though his work is now lost) and Friar Jordanus in 1321 (ed. d'Avezac, p. 56), and the earliest mapmaker to record a Christian kingdom in Ethiopia was Angelino Dulcert in 1339; see R. A. Skelton, "An Ethiopian Embassy to Western Europe in 1306", in *Ethiopian Itineraries,* ed. O. G. S. Crawford (1958), pp. 212–15. By the beginning of the 15th century the location of Prester John in NE Africa was generally accepted by writers and cartographers; Bianco and the author of VM therefore reflect the current opinion of their day. (See Fischer, pp. 197–99; Beazley, *Texts,* pp. 278–80; Hallberg, pp. 281–85; E. D. Ross, "Prester John and the Empire of Ethiopia", in *Travel and Travellers of the Middle Ages,* ed. A. P. Newton, 1926, pp. 174–94.) Maps which place Prester John in Asia are FP, Ves, Wal, Gen (also in Africa!); those which place him in Africa are CA, CE, Borgia, Bi, Le, Gen (also in Asia!), FM. The other details given in the legend in VM are borrowed from the text of TR: ¶26, referring to the countries conquered by Batu, *Iste sunt terre christianorum sed diversorum ydiomatum et posite sunt ad meridiem iuxta mare;* and ¶10,

Kitai . . . habent . . . domos quasi ecclesias in quibus orant . . . Hii unum deum colunt et credunt in dominum Iesum Christum. In both passages TR agrees with Carpini's account.

31 *Emibar superior:* Bi *inperiũ emibar* (icon.); = Zanzibar. The forms of the name in Bi and VM (perhaps deriving from a debased form in a common source) are corruptions of the medieval name for the coastal region of East Africa known to the Arabs as Zanzibar: FP, Ves *zinc vel ziziber,* FM *xengibar.*

32 *Ethiopi:* not in Bi.

ASIA

(a) South of the Black and Caspian Seas.

33 *Mecca:* Bi *la mecha.*

34 *Ierusalem:* Bi *ieruxalem* (icon.).

35 *Samaca:* Bi *samachi* (icon.); Ru *Samag;* = Shamaka, in the eastern Caucasus, NW of Baku. See Rockhill, p. 264; Hallberg, p. 445.

36 *Nestoriani assidue processerunt usque ad terram Kitay / itē reliqui filij israel quos dominus monuit transiuerunt / uersus montes hemmodos quos superare non potuerunt* ("The Nestorians pressed on assiduously to the land of Cathay. The remaining children of Israel also, admonished by God, crossed toward the mountains of Hemmodi, which they could not surmount"). This legend has no textual counterpart in TR, nor in the other narratives of Carpini's mission. The first part of it seems to be distilled from references, in TR (¶7) and in Friar Simon's account, to the defeat of "Nestorians" by Genghis Khan and their diffusion in Asia; there is an echo in Rubruck (ed. Rockhill, p. 157): "Living mixed among [the Mongols] . . . are Nestorians and Saracens all the way to Cathay [*usque in Cathaiam*]". The second part of the legend relates to the medieval belief that the ten tribes of Israel which forsook the law of Moses and followed the Golden Calf were shut up by Alexander the Great in the Caspian mountains and were unable to cross his rampart. This story is found in many authors, including Vincent of Beauvais, the Alexander Romances, and Mandeville (ed. Letts, p. 184). TR, ¶12, seems to have a faint echo of it. Carpini (ed. d'Avezac, p. 659) refers to the "homines inter Caspios montes conclusi". The "shut-up nations" were also identified with Gog and Magog and with the Tartars, who were held to be descended from the Ten Tribes. Among the maps with legends relating to this, usually placed in the Far East in association with Gog and Magog, are Ves, CA, CE, Bi, Le, Wal, Gen, FM. See below, under *Magog, Gogus;* also Yule-Cordier, Vol. 1, pp. 56–7; Rockhill, pp. xvi–xvii, xxxi, 114; Hallberg, pp. 260–65; Hennig, Vol. 2, p. 169; A. R. Anderson, *Alexander's Gate, Gog and Magog, and the Inclosed Nations* (1932). For "Hemmodi", see the note on the next name.

37 *Kemmodi/montes/Superiores/Excels. siue/Nimsini:* not in Bi; Gen *Ymaus mons;* FM *Mons Imaus;* = the Himalayas. The name *Hemmodi,* of which *Kemmodi* in the legend is an obvious corruption, is not in the text of TR, nor in any other account of the Carpini mission, and it is not used by Rubruck; nor have I found it in any other medieval map. It corresponds to the *Emodus* or *Emodorum montes* of Ptolemy (vi.15, 16), dividing Scythia intra Imaum from Scythia extra Imaum, and to *Imaus mons promontorium Emodorum* in Pliny

(vi.64); and Pauly-Wissowa (*s.v.* Emodon) notes that the form given by Pomponius Mela 1.81), *Hammodes* or *Haemodes,* comes nearest to preserving the Sanskrit aspirate. See also T. Fischer, pp. 189–90; Hallberg, pp. 197, 259–60. *Nimsini* doubtless represents the Naiman, a tribe of Turkish origin conquered by Chingis Khan; they are mentioned by Carpini and Rubruck, and also in TR (¶¶7, 34), following Carpini. The location of this tribe indicated by Carpini—in the Altai, west of the Land of the Tartars—may have suggested the position of the name in VM, coupled with *Kemmodi montes* and adjacent to *Terra Indica.* See Hallberg, pp. 366–67; and below, p. 142.

38 *Terra/Indica.* This name is placed in the approximate position of *India media* of Bi, who (like most medieval geographers) distinguished three Indias—*minor, media,* and *superior.* For the threefold division, see Yule-Cordier, Vol. 1, pp. 425–26; Beazley, *Texts,* p. 278.

(b) North of the Black and Caspian Seas

39 *montes inferiores abrupti / In hanc terram primi fratres nostri ordinis iter faciendo ad tartaros / mōgalos samogedos [et] indos transiuerunt nobiscꝫ per obedientiam / et subieccionem tam debitam q̄' deuotam Iñocentio sanctissimo Patri / nostro Pont. max. per totum occidentem et in reliqua parte usque ad mare occeanum orientale* ("Steep mountains, not very high. The first to cross into this land were brothers of our order, when journeying to the Tartars, Mongols, Samoyedes, and Indians, along with us, in obedience and submission to our most holy father Pope Innocent, given both in duty and in devotion, and through all the west and in the remaining part [of the land] as far as the eastern ocean sea"). The first three words are taken from TR, ¶7 (*montes inferiores . . . per ipsa abrupta montium*). The formula *per obedientiam . . . quam deuotam* is used by C. de Bridia (addressing his superior) in the first sentence of TR; and the expression *iter faciendo* (in a temporal sense, as commonly in medieval Latin) recurs frequently in TR. Association of the *Montes abrupti* with the *Riphaei montes* of classical geographers and medieval mapmakers (Ves, Wal, Le, FM; not Bi), suggested by the similarity of position and of form, is unjustified. The legend which follows, summarizing the journey of the Carpini mission, appears to be abstracted from TR, in which the names of the four peoples mentioned all occur, although the text does not contain any reference to Pope Innocent by name. If (as seems probable) C. de Bridia did not accompany the mission into Asia, the interpolation of the word *nobiscum* by the 15th-century cartographer is the more curious; if a rhetorical device for linking the map to the Tartar Relation, and so emphasizing the authority of the map, it would provide further support for the hypothesis that the map was drawn to illustrate the text or texts accompanying it (see above, p. 114). As Mr. Painter suggests, however, the word could perhaps imply that the author of the map and legend was of the same order as the *fratres nostri ordinis,* sharing a common obedience. The claim that Carpini's mission traveled "as far as the eastern ocean sea" is unsupported even by the text of TR; but see the note below (p. 136) on *Magnum mare Tartarorum.*

40 *Imperiũ Tartarorum:* Bi *inperion tartaroron* (written on the River Don).

41 *magnus ka[n].* The form *Magnus Canis* is found in many world maps (Ves, CA, Gen; not in Bi), usually following Marco Polo; it is not used by Carpini or Rubruck, or in TR (¶15 and elsewhere, *can*). The position of the name in VM, between the Sea of Azov and the

Volga, is curious, since Carpini only reached the camp of Kuyuk Khan *after* entering "the country of the Mongols, whom we call Tartars" (ed. Rockhill, pp. 18, 37), i.e. in Mongolia, far to the east. The cartographer has perhaps confused the Great Khan (Kuyuk) with Batu, Khan of Kipchak, whom the Carpini mission encountered on the Volga.

42 *Tartaria mogalica.* Presumably Carpini's "country of the Mongols, whom we call Tartars" (see previous note), i.e. Mongolia. On the origin and history of the names Mongol and Tartar, see Rockhill, pp. 112–13; Beazley, *Texts*, pp. 322–23.

43 *Zumoal:* TR (¶¶3, 4) *zumoal.* According to Carpini (ed. d'Avezac, p. 645), one of the nations of the Mongols: ". . . *Su-Mongal,* or Water-Mongols, though they called themselves Tartars from a certain river which flows through their country and which is called Tatar (or Tartar)". The passage in TR follows Carpini closely, adding "zu enim Tartarice aqua dicitur latine moal terra". Also described by Rubruck (ed. Rockhill, p. 196): ". . . people called *Su-Moal,* which is 'Moal of the waters'." Dr. J. A. Boyle comments: "It is interesting that TR has this Turkish form (Sumoal), whereas Carpini, whom one would expect it to follow, has Su-Mongol. The Sumongol or Water Mongols are specifically identified by Carpini with the Tartars, i.e. the Tatar, but the Shui Ta-ta (of the Chinese), with whom they are more obviously identical, were apparently a different tribe with which the Mongols did not come into contact until after their invasion of China: Carpini presumably confused them with the Tatar proper, who, as a separate entity, had been obliterated by Chingiz-Khan many years before". See above, pp. 56–57; Beazley, *Texts*, p. 274; Hallberg, p. 493.

44 *Moal:* TR (¶¶3, 4) *moal;* Ru *Moal.* Dr. Boyle writes: "Rubruck's Moal represents the Turkish *Moghal* or *Moghol,* the native Mongolian word being *Mongghol.*" See also Beazley, *Texts*, pp. 322–23; Rockhill, p. 112.

45 *Mōgali:* TR (¶6) *Mongali.*

46 *Ayran:* Bi *airam* (NE of the Caspian); not identified with any name in TR, Ca, or Ru. Perhaps Sairam in Turkestan, described by Bretschneider (Vol. 2, pp. 94, 250) as a station on the old highway, east of Chimkent and N.E. of Tashkent.

47 *Magog* }
48 *Gogus* } TR (¶12) *Moagog;* Bi *gog magog.* As early as the 13th century (e.g. in the Ebstorf mappamundi) the cannibal nations of Gog and Magog, enclosed within the mountain rampart built by Alexander, were placed by Europeans in northern Asia. Hence their identification with the Tartars and their location by Marco Polo (Bk. I, ch. lix) in Tenduc, with a probable reference to the Great Wall of China (Yule-Cordier, Vol. 1, pp. 293–94). "The theory that the Tartars were Gog and Magog led to the Rampart of Alexander being confounded with the Wall of China or being relegated to the extreme N.E. of Asia, as we find it in the Carta Catalana" (Yule-Cordier, Vol. 1, p. 57); Gog and Magog are thus represented, usually behind Alexander's wall, in NE Asia by most cartographers of the 14th and 15th centuries, including Ves, CA, CE, Bi, Le, Wal, Gen, and FM. (See also Rubruck, p. xxxi; Yule-Cordier, Vol. 1, pp. 56–57, 292–93; Hallberg, pp. 225–30; and the note above, p. 132, on the legend *Nestoriani assidue . . .*) In VM, the intrusion of the *Magnum mare Tartarorum* has shifted the names westward. Gog and Magog are not mentioned in the other accounts of Carpini's mission, or by Rubruck. The corrupt form in TR recalls the etymology suggested

in the Itinerary of Friar Ricold of Monte Croce: "Mogoli, quasi corrupto vocabulo Magog-oli" (cited by Beazley, *Dawn,* Vol. 3, p. 194).

49 *Kytanis:* TR (¶6) *Kitai,* Ca *Kitai, Kythai;* Bi *inperion catai, chataio;* = Cathay. The Khitai, who ruled in China for three centuries before the Mongol conquests under Ogedei and Kublai, "originated the name of *Khitai, Khata* or *Cathay,* by which for nearly 1000 years China has been known to the nations of Inner Asia" (Yule-Cordier, Vol. 1, p. 12). See also Yule, *Cathay,* Vol. 1, pp. 146–48; Hallberg, pp. 303–04; P. Pelliot, *Notes on Marco Polo,* Vol. 1 (1959), pp. 216–29. The name in VM is misplaced to NW (instead of SE) of the land of Mongols.

50 *Termacus Rex:* Bi *inperion de termaxo* (icon.); FM *Termes;* = Sarmatia, shown by FM as a town near Bokhara, on the Amu Darya. Not in TR, Ca or Ru.

51 *Tartartata fluuius:* TR (¶3): *a fluvio . . . qui . . . dicitur Tatar.* The form *Tatartata,* which occurs in no other map or text, is plainly a misreading of TR by the author of VM (see above, pp. 56–57). Carpini's statement that "they called themselves Tartars from a certain river which flowed through their country" (see above, under *Zumoal*) reflects the opinion of other 13th-century writers, of whom Rockhill (p. xvii) cites Matthew Paris; for the history and etymology of the name Tartar, see Rockhill, pp. 113–14, and above, pp. 56–57. The course of the river of the Tartars, as depicted in VM, recalls Rubruck's statement (ed. Rockhill, p. 118) that the Etilia (i.e. Volga) flowed from Bulgaria Major, on the Middle Volga, southward, "emptying into a certain lake or sea . . . called Sea of Sirsan [? = the Mare Hyrcanum of 14th- and 15th-century world maps, i.e. the Caspian]". See also Beazley, *Texts,* p. 274; and above, p. 121.

52 *Thule ultima:* not in Bi; not mentioned in TR, by Ca or by Ru. In medieval cartography generally (as by Bi) Thule is represented as an island north or NW of Great Britain; some writers identified it as Iceland (see Nansen, *In Northern Mists,* Vol. 1, passim). VM's location of the name, in the extreme north of Eurasia, places Thule (as Ptolemy and other classical authors did) under the Arctic Circle.

(c) Inland seas

[The Black Sea and Sea of Azov are drawn but not named, as in Bi.]

[The Caspian Sea is drawn but not named, as in Bi. Carpini and his companions seem to have confused the Black, Caspian, and Aral Seas, the last of which was probably not visited by Rubruck and remained unknown to Marco Polo and to the mapmakers who followed him. VM, like Bi, correctly distinguishes the Black and Caspian seas. Following an older model, they also represent the Caspian as a gulf of NE Asia; see Beazley, *Texts,* pp. 318, 324, and above, p. 120, n. 37.]

(d) Ocean and islands

53 *Terre non satis perscrutate / posite sunt inter boreales glacies / ab iisdem abdite* ("Lands not sufficiently explored. They are placed among the northern ice and concealed by it"). No textual parallel in TR, from which the substance could however be inferred, e.g. from the account of northern peoples subjugated by Batu (¶21; here closely following Carpini's text).

54 mare Occeanum Orientale. This phrase does not occur in the text of TR, only the northern ocean (*mare oceanum aquilonis*) being named. Cf. the note above, p. 133, on the legend *Montes inferiores abrupti . . .*

55 Magnum mare Tartarorum. Neither named nor implied anywhere in the text of TR. The name and delineation probably embody the mapmaker's interpretation of what he had read or been told of the Caspian Sea. The name *Magnum Mare* was applied by Carpini and Friar Benedict to the Black Sea (Rockhill, pp. 8–9), while Rubruck called it *Mare maius.* Members of the Carpini party were somewhat confused about the courses of the rivers flowing into the two seas, supposing the Volga to enter the Black Sea. On their supposed discovery of the Caspian (for which see below, p. 151), Friar Benedict reported: "Post Turkyam intraverunt terram que vocatur Karakytai . . . in qua invenerunt mare a sinistris quod credimus esse Caspium mare. Post hanc terram intraverunt terram Naymanorum . . . Post hanc intraverunt terram Thartarorum" (Wyngaert, pp. 138–39; not in d'Avezac and Rockhill). Reading this passage in the light of the belief—presumably shared by the Carpini mission— that the Caspian was a gulf of the ocean sea (see below, p. 151), we can perceive the basis both for the cartographer's representation of the Great Sea of the Tartars and for his claim (in the legend *Montes inferiores abrupti . . .*) that the mission reached the eastern ocean sea. Benedict's narrative was dictated to an ecclesiastic in Cologne after his return; and the use of the first person and present tense (*quod credimus . . .*) in this and other passages suggests glosses or interpretations by the scribe who wrote down his words, and not perhaps by Benedict himself. One more possibility may be mentioned: that the name *Mare Tartarorum* is a corruption or mishearing of *Mare Gazarorum,* or Sea of the Khazars, another name applied to the Caspian (see Rockhill, p. 36).

56 Tartari affirmant absq' dubio q' / noua terra in extremis mundi partibus / sit posita nec ultima terra nisi solummodo / mare occeanum inuenitur ("The Tartars affirm beyond doubt that a new land is situated in the outermost parts of the world, and beyond it no land is found but only the ocean sea"). This legend closely follows a passage in TR (¶14), which refers to the woman of the country of *Narayrgen* taken by the Tartars: *Que postmodum sicut ipsi Tartari referebant fratribus cum ipsis mansit longo tempore affirmans absque dubio quod dicta terra in extremis mundi partibus sit posita nec ulterius terra nisi solummodo mare oceanum invenitur.* C. de Bridia's account of this episode generally agrees with that of Carpini; but, of the texts derived from the Carpini mission, only TR has this passage and gives the name *Narayrgen,* which represents Mongolian *nara[n]* = "sun" and *yrgen* = "people". (See above, pp. 64–65.) The sole change of sense introduced by the cartographer lies in the substitution of *noua terra* for *dicta terra,* bringing in the idea (unsupported by the original text in TR) that the land in question remained to be discovered. How far this perversion of his source is sufficient to account for the concept and form of the islands laid down by the mapmaker in the eastern ocean, or whether they reflect information about real lands (Korea or Japan?) transmitted by Mongols or Chinese, will be considered later (below, pp. 152–53). It is certainly irrelevant to cite in this connection possible Chinese knowledge of American lands; see Beazley, *Dawn,* Vol. 1, pp. 492–503. The last phrase of the legend is inconsistent with the geographical ideas of the Mongols, contrasting with those of the Franks, as reported by Rubruck: "as to the ocean sea they [the Tartars] were quite unable to understand that it was endless, without bounds" (ed. Rockhill, p. 133).

57 *Insule Sub aquilone zamogedorum.* These islands are not mentioned in TR, which does however (¶21, here following Carpini) refer to the land of the Samoyedes as adjacent to the people who dwelt on the shores of the northern ocean. These islands, and the *Postreme Insule,* are associated with the cartographic concepts in the two preceding legends (see notes on *Magnum mare Tartarorum* and on *Tartari affirmant . . .*).

58 *Postreme Insule.* Not in TR; see the preceding note, and p. 152 below.

59 *mare Indicum:* not named in Bi.
   [Three small islands, unnamed, in the Persian Gulf; also, unnamed, in Bi.]
   [Six large islands, unnamed, in the Indian Ocean: Bi *ixole di colonbi,* with many more islands; = the Maldives and other archipelagos of the western Indian Ocean.]
   [A larger oblong island, unnamed, to the east of the six islands: Bi *ixola perlina;* Le *Taprobana* (and so in other maps); = Ceylon.]

THE ATLANTIC AND ITS ISLANDS

60 *Mare Occeanum.* Twice written.
   [An island, unnamed, west of Ireland: also unnamed in Bi; Bi^5 *y^a. de berzil;* = Island of Brasil. Thus, with characteristically circular shape, in many charts of the 14th and 15th centuries. See Cortesão, table II; T. J. Westropp, "Brasil and the legendary islands of the North Atlantic", *Proceedings of the Royal Irish Academy* (1912); W. H. Babcock, *Legendary Islands of the Atlantic* (1922).]
   [An island, unnamed, SW of England: also unnamed in Bi; Bi^5 *y^a. de uentura.* The usual name for this crescent-shaped island, in 14th- and 15th-century charts, is *I. de Man* (or *Mam*), sometimes *Mayda.* See the references cited above.]

61 *Desiderate/insule.* This is written in the center (between the fourth and fifth, counting from the north) of the chain of seven unnamed islands extending in a line N–S from the latitude of Brittany to that of C. Juby, and represented in Bianco's world map by about a dozen unnamed islands (see above, p. 122, where their names in Bianco's charts are listed). These are the Azores, laid down in charts with this position and orientation from the middle of the 14th century to the end of the 15th (see Cortesão, chap. III, also table II and fig. 5), and the Madeira group. In many 15th-century charts the chain has (usually written in larger lettering to the north of Madeira) the general name *Insule Fortunate Sancti Brandani,* or variants. The classical Insulae Fortunatae were the Canaries, the only group known in antiquity, and the association with St. Brendan arose in the Middle Ages (T. Fischer, pp. 15–16; Cortesão, chap. II); thus in the Hereford mappamundi (*ca.* 1290), *Fortunate insulee sex sunt insulae sct brandani,* and in the Pizzigani map (1367), *Isolae dictae fortunatae sive isole ponentur (?) sancti Brandany.* The general name *Desiderate insule* given in VM to these islands is not found in any other map; the only explanation we can hazard is that it may allude to the Portuguese attempts at discovery and colonization of the Azores from, probably, 1427 onward (Cortesão, p. 55).

62 *Beate ƚsule/fortune.* The Canaries, represented as seven unnamed islands. Also unnamed in

Bianco's world map; for his delineation and for their nomenclature in his charts, see above, p. 122. As noted above, many late medieval maps and charts combine, in a single name for the Azores-Madeira group referred to above, elements of the classical Insulae fortunatae (= Canaries) and of St. Brendan's Islands; instances near in date to VM are Battista Beccario's two charts of 1426 and 1435 (*Insulle fortunate sancti brandany*) and Bianco's chart of 1448 (*y^a. fortunat de s^a. beati brandan,* for one of the Azores). These provide a parallel for the association of words in VM's name, but the cartographer has (correctly) moved the name to the south so that it refers only to the Canaries, unlike the other charts cited, in which the name is attached to the Azores-Madeira chain. See also below, pp. 155–58.

63 *Magnæ/Insulæ/Beati Brandani/Branziliæ/dictæ.* The name is placed westward of, and between, two large unnamed islands, to which it plainly refers. They are unnamed also in Bi and correspond to his Satanaxio and Antillia, named in Bi⁴ (see above, p. 123). As the examples already cited show, the name *Insulæ Sancti Brandani* (in variant forms) is commonly ascribed by chartmakers to the Azores-Madeira chain. VM is the earliest known map to move the name further out into the ocean and apply it to the Antillia group, the word *magnæ* being added to justify the attribution and make a clear distinction from the smaller islands to the east. The alternative form *Branziliæ* (or *Branzilia*), suggesting an association with the name of the legendary island of Brasil, is not found in any other surviving map. The name Brasil, in many variants, was generally applied by cartographers of the 14th and 15th centuries (a) to a circular island off the coast of Ireland (see above, p. 137), and (b) to one of the Azores, perhaps Terceira; the variant forms of the name include Brasil, Bersil, Brazir, Bracir, Brazilli. Its etymology has never been satisfactorily determined, and none of the scholars who have discussed it has postulated a connection with, or derivation from, St. Brendan. The most likely etymological affinity seems to be with the Irish *breas-ail* (= blessed), suggesting association with the Fortunate Isles; but Brasil is not mentioned in medieval Irish literature, nor is it among the islands which St. Brendan is supposed to have visited. (See Hennig, Vol. 4, pp. 325–32; G. Ashe, *Land to the West,* 1962, pp. 294–95.) Mr. Laurence Witten has shrewdly pointed out that this legend in VM supplies a key to a possible onomastic evolution (by normal processes of contraction and copying): *Brandani insulæ > Branziliæ > Brāziliæ > Braziliæ > Brasil.* Whether this sequence represents the historical development of the name Brasil, up to the point of its emergence in maps, or merely an etymological and *ex post facto* interpretation by the author of VM or of its original, must be held an open question in the present state of our knowledge. Since the name makes its first cartographic appearance about a century before VM was drawn (in the chart of Angellino de Dalorto 1325), further—and preferably earlier—evidence is needed before the first hypothesis can be confidently accepted and the second eliminated.

ICELAND, GREENLAND, VINLAND

64 *isolanda Ibernica.* In no other map or text is the form *Isolanda* found, or the epithet *Ibernica* annexed to the name for Iceland. Medieval mapmakers, from the 10th century (Cottonian map) onward called the island *Island* or *Ysland* (v.l. *Hislant*), *Islandia* or *Yslandia*. (See Björnbo and Petersen, p. 127; Hermannsson, *Cartography,* ch. i.) The form *Isolanda* ap-

pears to stem, by elision, from *Iso[la Is]landa.* (If this hypothesis be accepted, we may suppose, from the form *isola,* an Italian original to have furnished the name.) FM in fact has the name *Isola Islandia* (for the island of Sjælland, which in his map represents Denmark). Derivation of *Isolanda* from Old Norse *Isaland* (= island of ices) is improbable; the Norse name for the island was always Island. The epithet *Ibernica* also admits of possible explanation on cartographic grounds. The anonymous Franciscan author of the *Libro del Conoscimiento* (*ca.* 1350), who probably had a Catalan map before him as he wrote, uses the name *Ibernia* when, from the context, Iceland seems to be meant; and in the Catalan chart of Mecia de Viladestes, *ca.* 1413, one of the islands to the north of Scotland is named *Ibernia,* the cartographer having apparently "misunderstood the legend about Hibernia generally found in this place on the earlier maps, and therefore added an island of Ibernia, north of Stilanda (he has Irlanda in its proper place) . . ." (Hermannsson, *Cartography,* p. 8; see also above, p. 128). Ibernia was so placed by some medieval geographers, e.g. Adam of Bremen. Alternative explanations deserving consideration (though without dogmatism) are that the author of VM had access to Norse or Irish sources from which he learnt of the Irish missionaries who preceded the Norsemen in Iceland, or that he had heard of the part taken by Irish in the settlement of Iceland during its colonial period. It is again, possible —although perhaps less likely—that the cartographer associated Iceland with the reputed voyages of St. Brendan in the 6th century.

65 *Gronelāda.* The Icelandic name *Groenland,* in variant forms (including the latinization *Terra viridis*), is used in all early textual sources. The name was introduced into cartography by Claudius Clavus (1427) as *Gronlandia;* a Catalan chart of the 15th century, in the Biblioteca Nazionale, Florence, has *mar de Gronlandia;* and another, in the Biblioteca Ambrosiana, Milan, has *Illa verde.* See Björnbo and Petersen, pp. 129–30, 188–89; Björnbo, *Cartographia Groenlandica* (1910), passim; and below, pp. 177–78, 182.

66 *Vinlanda Insula a Byarno re p̄a et leipho socijs* ("Island of Vinland, discovered by Bjarni and Leif in company"). If the large island to which this name is applied represents the three lands —Helluland, Markland, and Vinland—discovered by Leif Eiriksson from north to south and divided in VM by the two deep inlets, either the name *Vinlanda* is here used collectively for all three, or it has been erroneously placed against the northernmost instead of the southernmost land. In the earliest written record of Vinland, that of Adam of Bremen (*ca.* A.D. 1070), it is referred to as an island; in the 12th-century Icelandic Geography, Helluland and Markland are said to be islands, and it is suggested that Vinland is "connected with Africa"; none of the other Norse sources referring to Vinland, from the earliest in the *Íslendinga bók* of Ari Frode (*ca.* 1122–24), contains any indication that Vinland was thought to be an island. The Icelandic name was Vínland, variants of which are used in all the medieval texts. Apart from instances in which this or a similar name evidently relates to Wendland or Finland (see Nansen, Vol. 1, pp. 382–83; Vol. 2, pp. 31–33), the earliest known map— other than VM—to show the name in its correct reference is that of Sigurdur Stefánsson, *ca.* 1590. (The geography of Vinland and its delineation in VM and in other maps are discussed in a later section of this study, Pt. II, ch. 8.

The American landfall of Bjarni Herjolfsson in A.D. 985 or 986 and his sale of a ship to

Leif Eiriksson in (probably) A.D. 1001 rest on the sole authority of the "Tale of the Green-landers" in the 14th-century Flatey Book; for this reason, these events have been rejected as unhistorical by some writers (e.g. G. Storm, J. Fischer, H. Hermannsson). None of the Icelandic accounts of Leif's voyage of discovery states that Bjarni accompanied him. The legend in VM, if it faithfully reproduces a genuine record, accordingly authenticates Bjarni's association with the discovery of Vinland and adds the significant information that he sailed with Leif. We must however admit the possibility that the cartographer, or the au-thor of his source for this matter, has confused the two voyages, that of Bjarni in 985 or 986 and that of Leif in 1002, or—since no patronymic is assigned to Bjarni in the legends of VM—that there has been a confusion between Bjarni Herjolfsson, to whom the earlier discov-ery is ascribed in the Flatey Book, and Bjarni Grimolfsson, who accompanied the Icelander Karlsefni to Vinland *ca.* A.D. 1020. The latter hypothesis has been advanced, to account for the already known record of Bjarni's voyage, by adverse critics of the Flatey Book, e.g. J. Fischer (*Norsemen,* p. 14; contested by Gathorne-Hardy, *Norse Discoverers,* pp. 105–06) and Hermannsson (*Wineland,* pp. 34–36). (This question is considered in more detail be-low, Pt. II, chs. 9, 10; see also the note on the next legend.)

67 *Volente deo post longū iter ab insula Gronelanda per meridiem ad / reliquas extremas partes occidentalis occeani maris iter facientes ad / austrū inter glacies byarnus et leiphus erissonius socij terram nouam uberrimā / videlicet viniferā inuenerunt quam Vinilandā [?or Vim-landā] insulā appellauerunt. Henricus / Gronelande regionumq finitimarū sedis apostolicae episcopus legatus in hac terra / spaciosa vero et opulentissima in postmo anno p. ss. nrj. [= pontificis or patris sanctissimi nostri] Pascali accessit in nomine dei / omnipotētis longo tempore mansit estiuo et brumali postea versus Gronelandā redit / ad orientem hiemalē deinde humillima obediencia superiori vo– / lūtati processit* ("By God's will, after a long voyage from the island of Greenland to the south toward the most distant remaining parts of the western ocean sea, sailing southward amidst the ice, the companions Bjarni and Leif Eiriksson discovered a new land, extremely fertile and even having vines, the which island they named Vinland. Eric [*Henricus*], legate of the Apostolic See and bishop of Greenland and the neighboring regions, arrived in this truly vast and very rich land, in the name of Almighty God, in the last year of our most blessed father Pascal, remained a long time in both summer and winter, and later returned northeastward toward Greenland and then proceeded [i.e. home to Europe?] in most humble obedience to the will of his superiors.") Two historical events are here described: first, a voyage of discovery by Bjarni [no patro-nymic] and Leif Eiriksson "southward" from Greenland to Vinland; and second, a visit to Vinland by Bishop Eirik [Gnupsson] in a specified year, viz. A.D. 1117, his stay in the coun-try, and his return.

The voyage of Bjarni and Leif is also referred to in the legend *Vinlanda Insula . . .* ; the additional information in the longer legend relates to the course ("southward amidst the ice"), to the character of the land discovered ("extremely fertile and even having vines"), and to the bestowal of the name Vinland by the discoverers. These data will be examined and collated with other records of the Norse voyages in a later section (Pt. II, chs. 9, 10).

Bishop Eirik Gnupsson's visit, ascribed in the Icelandic Annals to the year 1121, is the latest recorded historical event relating to Vinland. Either the bishop made two voyages to Vinland, or the legend in VM corrects the date of the visit as given in the Annals, expressing it in an ecclesiastical form which carries conviction of its authenticity. The legend also adds to the meager allusion in the Annals details about the duration of the bishop's stay in Vinland and about the circumstances of his return. *Humillima . . . voluntati,* while no doubt a stock phrase, seems to echo TR, ¶1. Bishop Eirik's status and the chronology and purpose of his visit to Vinland will be discussed later (pp. 223–26), with a comparison of the evidence in VM with that of other records.

Analysis of the nomenclature and of its affinities with other maps or texts suggests some general remarks about the Vinland Map and about its mode of compilation. In respect of toponymy, as of outline and design, the correspondences between this map and Bianco's world map of 1436 are almost certainly too extensive to be explained by coincidence. It seems to be an inescapable inference that the author of the Vinland Map (or of its immediate original) employed no eclectic method of selection and compilation from a variety of sources, but was content to draw on a single map—which must have been very like Bianco's—for the majority of the names, as well as the outlines, in Europe, Africa, and part of Asia. For convenience of reference, this Bianco-type original, which has not survived, will be cited as O1. The fact that, in regard to a few names or delineations, the Vinland Map seems to show affinities with charts in Bianco's atlas of 1436, rather than with his world map, may suggest that O1 was of Bianco's—or at any rate of Venetian—authorship.

In those parts of the map in which (as noted above) the influence of O1 predominates, there are very few names which cannot be traced to it or to the common stock of toponymy found in contemporary cartography (and therefore perhaps in O1). Some of these anomalies (*Apusia, aben, Maori*) are plainly the product of truncation or corruption in transcription, and indicate that the draftsman lacked the knowledge to correct his own errors in copying. In two other cases (*Rex Marr, Bela . . . rex*), it seems probable that names were never completed, perhaps because the draftsman could not read his model, or because he omitted a line containing the second half of a divided word. These instances suggest that the draftsman of the Vinland Map, as we have it, may not have been its compiler, but that the map may have been copied from an immediate original or preliminary draft (having the same content) by a clerk or scribe who was no geographer and did not have access to the compilation materials. This hypothetical preliminary draft will be referred to as O2 (see diagram on p. 142).

On this assumption, some other names (if they were not in O1) and all the legends (which can hardly have been in O1) must be attributed to the compiler of the map, i.e. the author of O2. Thus, in Europe, *Ierlanda insula* may perhaps arise from his misinterpretation of O1 or of some other map in which the names for Ireland and for the islands north of Scotland misled him; and *Buyslava* may come from the reports of the Carpini mission. In Africa, *Phazania* must have been taken by the author of O1 or O2 from Pliny or Ptolemy; and *magnus fluuius* (if not a coinage of the cartographer) perhaps from a geographical text of the 14th or early 15th century. *Sinus Ethiopicus* could have been deduced from Ptolemy's text; Andrea Bianco's connection with Fra Mauro, in whose map this very name is found, and his conjectural association with O1 lend substance to the possibility that this name stood in O1, although corrupted in Bianco's own world map. The transfer of Prester John from Asia to Africa was already made by Bianco and presumably in O1; but the compiler, or author of O2, has enriched the plain name, found in Bianco, with details copied from the Tartar Relation, in which Prester John is recorded as an Asian king.

In this case the geography of the Tartar Relation has been corrected from that of O1. In Asia however, while a number of names and the basic geographical design derive from O1, the authority of the Tartar Relation—or of other Carpini information—generally prevails in the toponymy. The degradation of names from this source points again to carelessness or ignorance in the copyist, although in one instance—*Gogus, Magog*—he, or the compiler of O2, has emended the debased form (*moagog*) in the Tartar Relation by reference to O1.[69] The only name which cannot be traced to either O1 or the Tartar Relation is *Hemmodi* (v.l. *Kemmodi*) *montes,* where a borrowing from a classical text (such as Pomponius Mela), in which the rendering of the initial aspirate was retained, may be suspected; the form in the Vinland Map could hardly have been derived from Ptolemy's. While the coupling of this name, in the Vinland Map, with one from the Tartar Relation (*Nimsini*) may however mean that *Hemmodi* too came from a Carpini source, it is more likely that the cartographer was here trying to integrate his two sources.

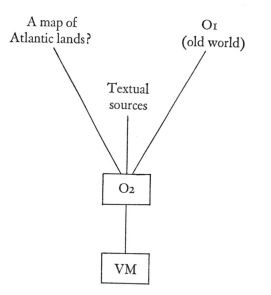

Whether the novelties in the nomenclature of the Atlantic island groups were in O1 or were introduced by the compiler of O2 cannot be determined; the affinities between their delineation in the Vinland Map and in surviving charts suggest that the names also may have been found by the compiler in maps which have not survived. The names for Iceland and Greenland may point to literary sources, perhaps of Norse origin.[70] So, with more certainty, do the name and legends relating to Vinland.

At each stage of derivation—from O1 to O2, and (less probably) from O2 to the Vinland Map

69. Unless we assume that the compiler of O2 was working from an earlier and more correct text of the Tartar Relation and that, if the same scribe copied the Tartar Relation and the Map, he failed to notice the discrepancy between the two.

70. These names, however, may have been in cartographic sources used by the compiler.

in its present form—there must have been a process of selection or thinning out of names. For Europe and Africa, Bianco's world map has considerably more names than the Vinland Map; in Asia the balance is redressed by the introduction of names from the Tartar Relation. In the absence of the prototype O1, we cannot say whether its author or the compiler of the Vinland Map was responsible for introducing the few names in the Old World which must have come from classical or medieval literary sources and the nomenclature for the Atlantic islands. The names for Iceland, Greenland, and Vinland, with the legend on Vinland, must—like their delineations—be held not to have been in O1 (see above, p. 123).

II. THE GEOGRAPHY OF THE VINLAND MAP
IN RELATION TO ITS SOURCES

1. CHARACTER AND PURPOSE OF THE MAP

To the question "what kind of map is this?" the answer must be: a very simple map—simple both in intention and in execution. The links between the map and the surviving texts which accompany it strongly suggest (as we have seen) that it was designed to illustrate C. de Bridia's account of the Carpini mission (the Tartar Relation). They also prompt the suspicion that missing sections of the original codex may have been illustrated by the other novel part of the map, namely its representation of the lands of Norse discovery and settlement in the north and west of the Atlantic.[1] It might be said that the dominant interest of the compiler or cartographer lay in the periphery of geographical knowledge, to which indeed the accompanying texts relate; and such a polarization of interest is exemplified in the themes of the seven legends on the map.

In finding cartographic expression for the geography of his texts, the maker of the map has practised considerable economy of means. The design is reduced to its barest elements of coastal outlines and nomenclature. There is hardly a superfluous line in the drawing; any decorative detail which the compiler may have found in his map sources has been suppressed; no representation of topographical facts, such as relief, is attempted; and from the stock of names commonly found in world maps of the fourteenth and fifteenth centuries—even in small ones like that of Andrea Bianco—only a meager selection has been made. In a map of this form, drawn—like the circular mappaemundi—on no systematic projection, we do not of course expect to find graduation for latitude and longitude, even if the quantitative cartography of Ptolemy had been known to its author.[2] The only mark of modernization in design is the orientation of the map to the north.

Examination of the nomenclature has suggested that the Vinland map, in the form in which it has survived, is the product of a stage of compilation (the work of the author or cartographer) and a subsequent stage of copying or transcription (the work of a scribe who was perhaps not a cartographer). There is a decided incongruity between—on the one hand—the care and finish which characterize the writing of the names and legends, with their generally correct Latinity,[3] and—on the other hand—the occurrence of onomastic errors which knowledge of current maps and geographical texts or reference to the prototype used by the compiler would have corrected. What other undetected changes or corruptions the copyist may have introduced into the final draft we cannot tell, since his original—the compiler's preliminary draft—is lost. If Bianco's world map be assumed to have resembled, in form and content, the model followed by the compiler for the tripartite world, we can however assess the performance of the final copyist by comparison of his work with Bianco's map, so far as it takes us. He emerges from this test on the whole creditably, for the outlines of the two maps are (as we have seen) in general agreement. The chart-forms characteristic of Bianco's style of drawing are not reproduced in the

---

1. This suggestion, with that made in the following sentence, was first made by Mr. Witten in 1958.
2. Cf. Bianco's inclusion of a medieval mappamundi and a Ptolemaic world map in his atlas of 1436 (above, p. 126).
3. See above, p. 8.

Vinland Map; at what stage these disappeared we do not know, and they were not necessarily in the original model followed by the compiler. All the major divergences, in the geographical elements of the Vinland Map, from the representation in Bianco can be traced to its compiler's reading of the Tartar Relation or to changes forced upon him by the design adopted.

The process of simplification described above was presumably carried out in the compilation stage. If we are justified in supposing the scribe who made the surviving transcript of the map to have been ignorant or naïve in matters of geography, the draft which he had before him for copying must have been the product of selection and combination already exercised by the compiler.

These considerations must govern our judgment of the date and place of origin to be ascribed to the map. The evidence, internal and external, which indicates that the manuscripts were produced in the Upper Rhineland in the second quarter of the fifteenth century can only apply to the map included in the codex.[4] If, as we suggest, this is a more or less faithful copy from an earlier draft, any inferences on the date, place, and possible authorship of the preliminary draft—that is, of the compilation of the map—must be drawn from study of its content and of the source materials which went into it. This will furnish a *terminus post quem* for the making of the map and some evidence of the character and resources of the cartographer.

2. SOURCES

For the purpose of analysis the map divides itself into two distinct parts. In its representation of Europe, Africa, and Asia it can be referred to, and collated with, not only extant cartographic works of similar character and design, but also a text which is bound in the same volume and to which its content is clearly related. For its delineation of lands in the north and west Atlantic, the cartographic prototypes (if it had any) either have not survived or have been so transformed as to be difficult to identify; and if the codex once included a text relating to these lands, this too has now disappeared.

The representation of the Atlantic, with Iceland, Greenland, and Vinland, was (as we have seen) almost certainly not in the prototype used for the tripartite world, but was added to it by the cartographer from another source or other sources. The lucky accident that his sources for the Old World can be easily identified or reconstructed allows us to hazard some inferences about his treatment of his sources for the Atlantic part of his map. His apparent preference for the simple solution or the single source admits the possibility that the western part of his map also derives, in the main, from one prototype rather than that it combines features from several; it may have been modified by interpolation or correction from another source (as is the representation of Asia from the Tartar Relation), and this too must be taken into account. That the prototype—like that for the Old World—was a map also deserves consideration. This hypothesis indeed, while it must be tested by collation of other extant maps from which the prototype may be reconstructed, has (*prima facie*) some support both from the analogy of the cartographer's treatment of the tripartite world and also from the uniformity of style which characterizes all parts of the drawing, alike in the east and in the west—in those parts where we know, and in those where we suspect, a cartographic model to have been followed. The historical

---

4. See above, pp. 141–43.

statements about Vinland contained in the map, on the other hand, doubtless come from a textual source, as those in Asia and Africa can be shown to do.

The materials from which the cartographer derived the geographical representations and the
historical lore synthesized in the Vinland Map are studied in detail in the chapters which follow.
Most of these materials (as will appear) are considerably older than the extant copy of the map.
They will enable us to compose the world picture which the compiler distilled into his map and
to assess the value of the map as a historical document.

3. THE MODEL FOR THE TRIPARTITE WORLD

The world picture of the fourteenth century, which was taken over into the mappaemundi of
the next century, including the prototype used in the Vinland Map, owed its general form and
plan to geographical concepts of classical origin, confirmed and modified by the authority of
the Christian Fathers. Patristic geography, as formulated in the *Etymologiae* of Isidore of Seville
(seventh century), envisaged the habitable world as a disc—the *orbis terrarum* of the Romans—
encircled by the Ocean and divided into three unequal parts, Europe and Africa occupying one
half and Asia the other half of the *orbis,* with the Earthly Paradise in the east. This theoretical
and schematic construction did not necessarily imply belief in a "flat earth", although it is uncertain whether Isidore himself admitted the sphericity of the earth.[5] The T–O map was simply
a diagram designed to bring home to the reader certain basic geographical ideas in an easily
apprehended form, and serving as a vehicle for biblical and legendary iconography. In the later
Middle Ages the framework of the tripartite world was modified by elements from Arab cartography; thus the eastward horn of Africa, as a survival of the coast by which Ptolemy closed the
Indian Ocean on the south, passed from Idrisi into European maps.

On this pattern were to be grafted geographical facts derived from experience and unknown
to the creators of the model. New lands reported beyond the bounds of the known world were
laid down as islands in the encircling ocean; rivers were moved about the map to accord with
the progress of discovery; and a feature might be represented twice on a map—in the form
handed down by tradition and in that recorded by a traveler.[6] The accommodation of new
knowledge from land journeys in Africa and Asia during the thirteenth and fourteenth centuries
and from oceanic discovery in the Atlantic during the fourteenth and fifteenth centuries confronted the mapmakers with "the task of pouring the new wine into the old skins". That they
were not daunted by this task is illustrated by the mappaemundi from Fra Paolino to Fra Mauro;
and the Vinland Map, or its prototype, exemplifies this harmonizing process in a peculiarly
interesting way.

In Europe, Bianco's world map of 1436 shows little difference from those drawn by Fra Paolino and by Petrus Vesconte over a century earlier, except in its general proportions and some
regional details.[7] Here the author of the Vinland Map is following a well-established model,

5. See Uhden, "Die Weltkarte des Isidorus von Sevilla", pp. 4–8.
6. Such as the Caspian Sea in the maps of Fra Paolino, Petrus Vesconte and later cartographers; see above, p. 120,
and below, p. 151.
7. See below, pp. 149, 228.

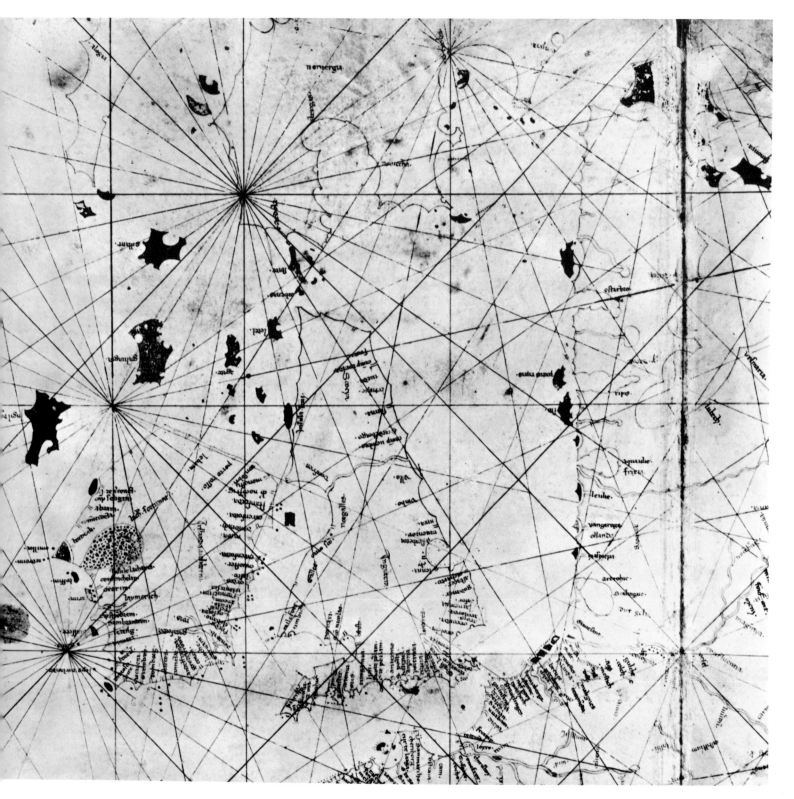

VIII. Northwest Europe in the Laurentian Atlas, 1351.

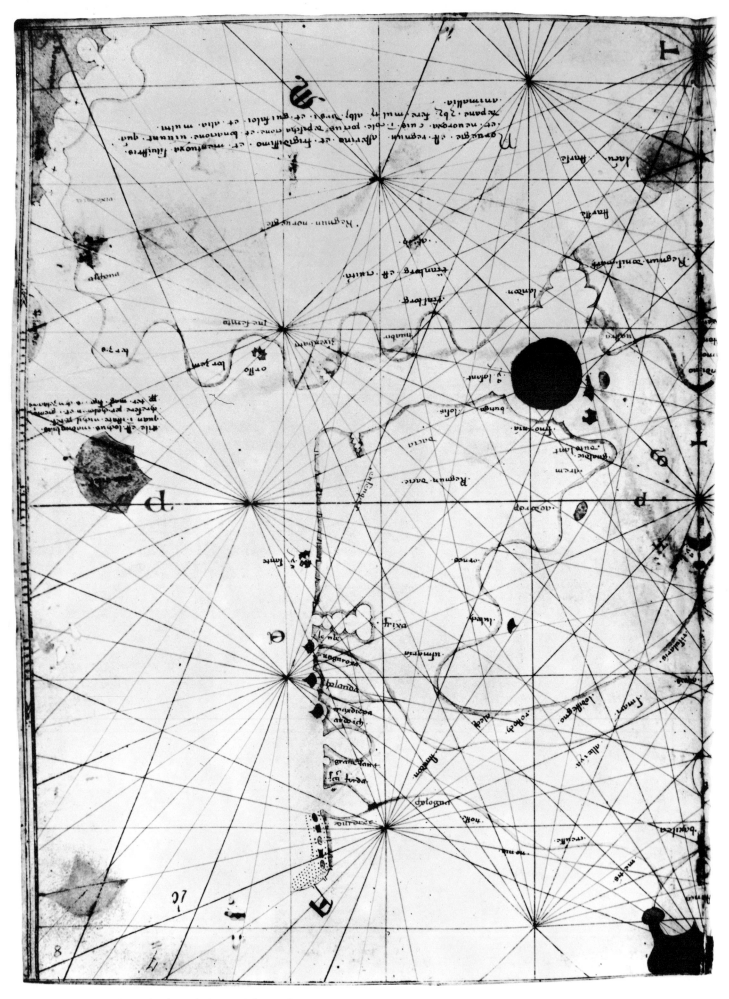

IX. Scandinavia in the Sixth Chart of Bianco's Atlas, 1436.

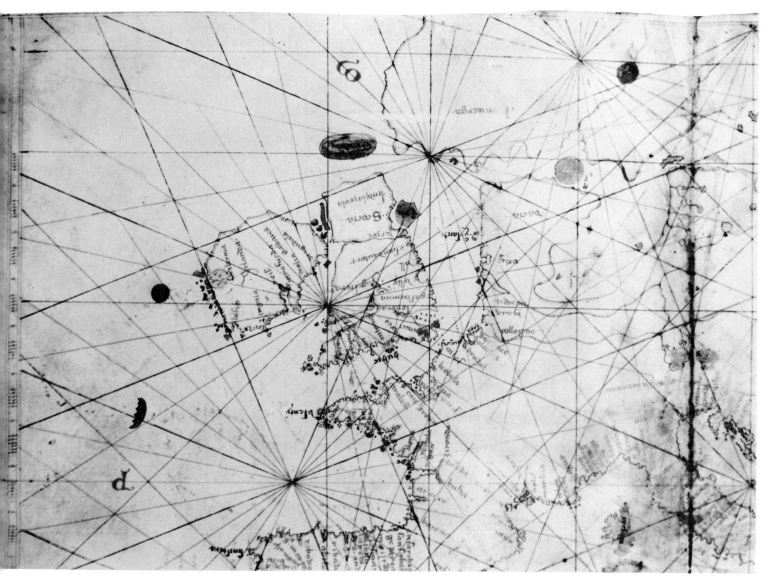

X. Northwest Europe in the Seventh Chart of Bianco's Atlas, 1436.

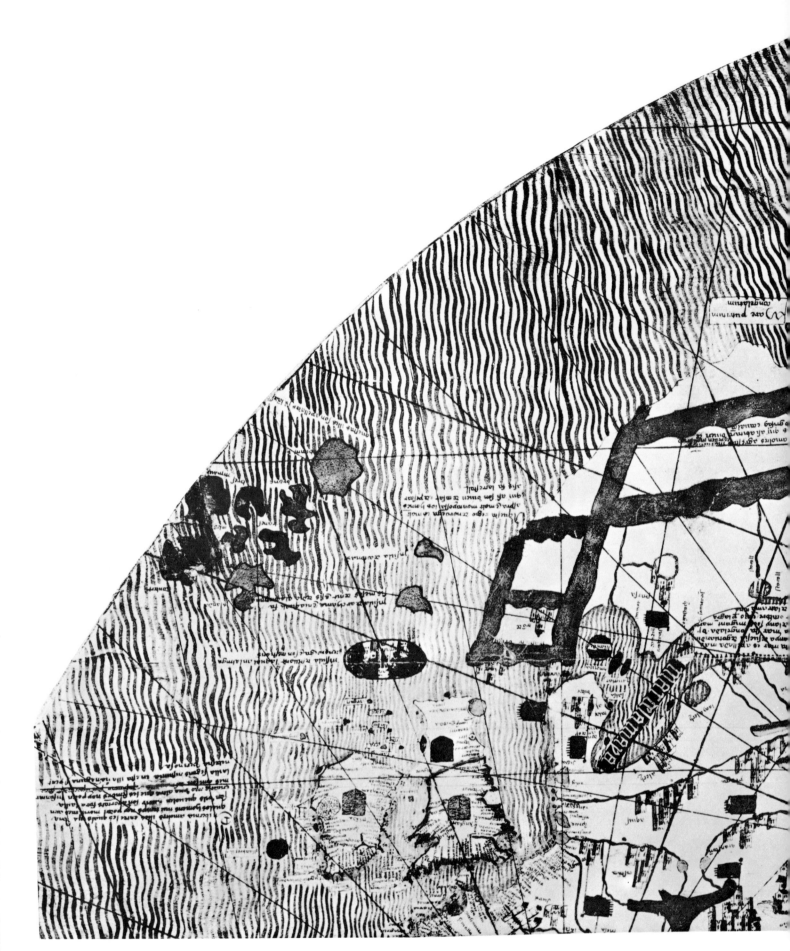

XI. Northwest Europe and Iceland in the Catalan-Este Map, *ca.* 1450–60. Biblioteca Estense, Modena, C.G.A.1.

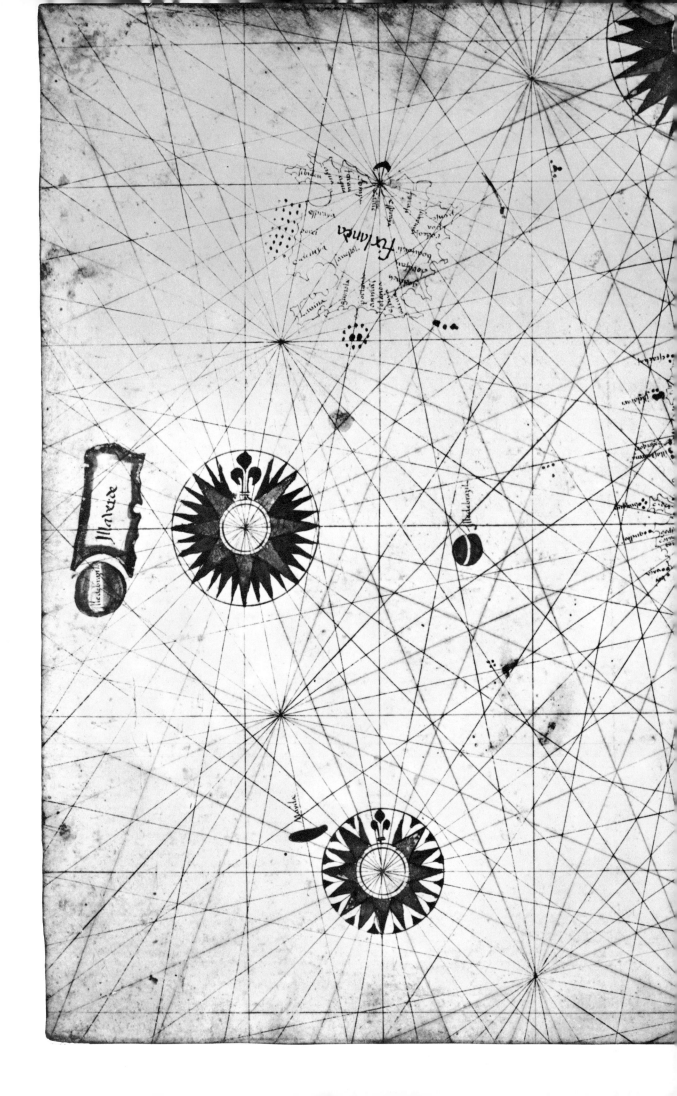

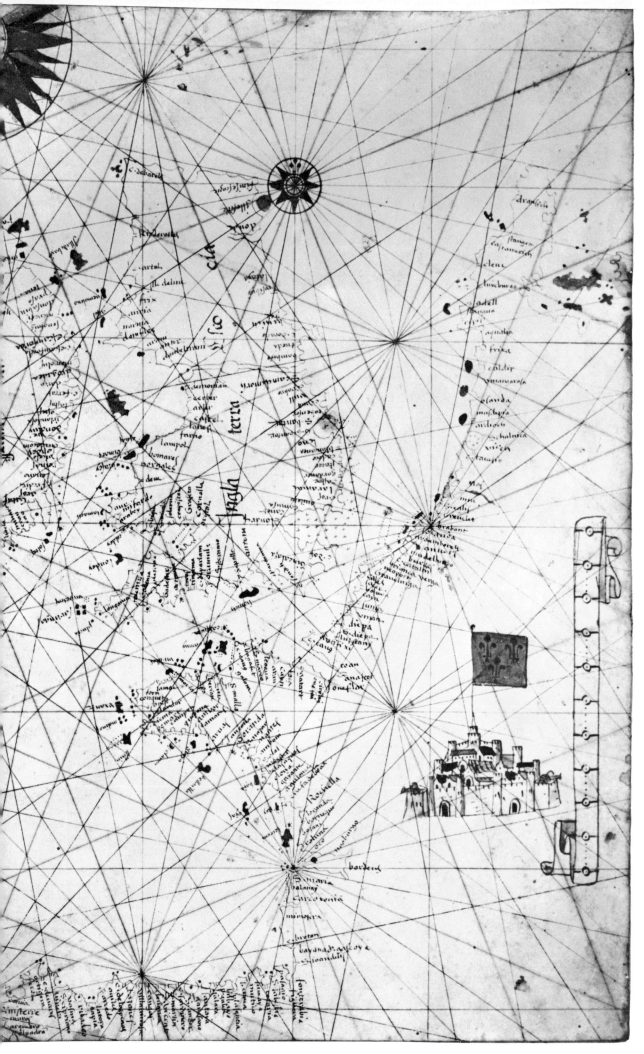

XII. Northwest Europe and Iceland in a Catalan Map, *ca.* 1480? Biblioteca Ambrosiana, Milan, S.P. II.5.

XIII. The Arctic in the Globe of Martin Behaim, 1492.

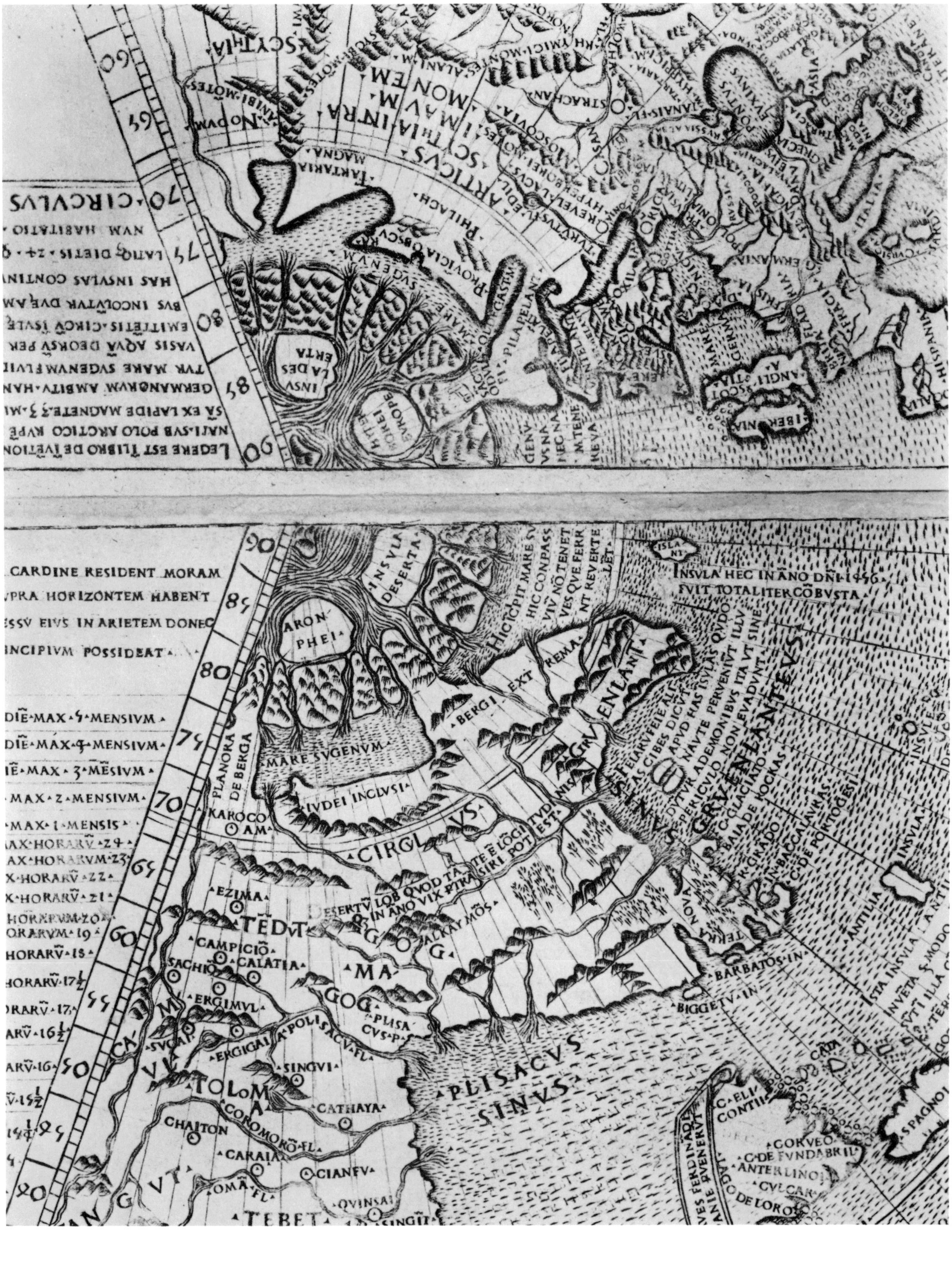

XIV. The Arctic in the World Map of Johan Ruysch, 1508.

XV. The Arctic in Mercator's World Map of 1569 (inset).

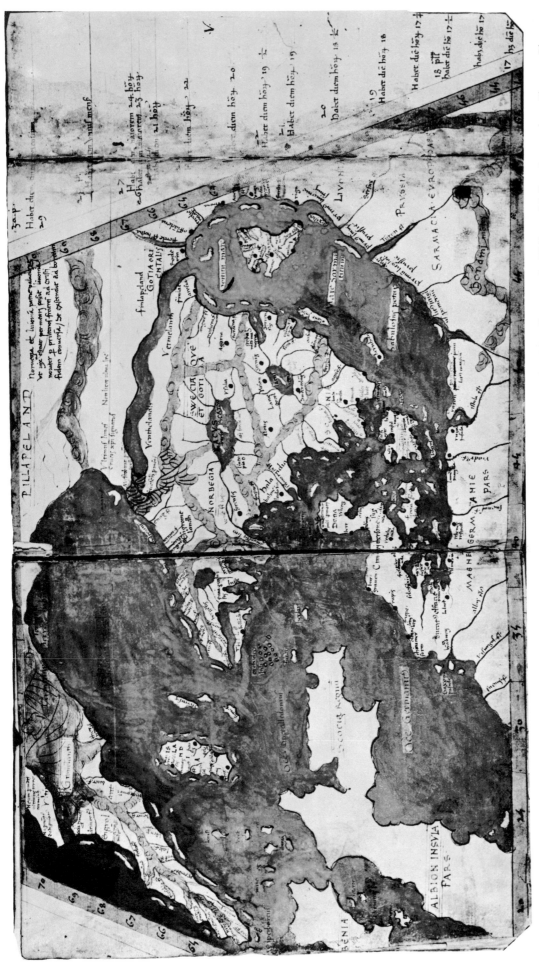

XVI. Map of the North by Henricus Martellus, *ca.* 1480. Biblioteca Mediceo-Laurenziana, Florence, Pl. 29.25.

Characterum in hac mappa
occurrentium, explicatio
ipsius Auctoris.

A Hi sunt ad quos Angli per
venerunt, ab ariditate nomen
habent, tanquam, vel solis vel
frigoris adustione torridi et
exsiccati

B His proxime est Vinlandia
quam propter terræ fæcun-
tatem et utilium rerum ube
rem proventum, Bonam
dixere. Hanc a meridie
oceanum finire voluere nostri, sed ego ex recentiorum
historiis colligo, aut fretu
aut sinum hanc ab America
distinguere.

C Regionem Gigantum vocant
quod ibi Gigantes cornuti sint
quos Skrickfinna dixere.

D Orientaliores sunt, quos klo
fina ab unguibus appella
runt.

E Jotunheimar idem est
ac regio Gigantum mon-
strosorum, hic Regiam
Geruthi et Gudmundi fu-
isse existimare licet.

F Sinum hic ingentem intelligimus in Russiam excurrentem.
G Regio petrosa, hujus in historia sæpe fit mentio.
H Hæc quæ sit insula nescio nisi ea forte quam Venetus ille invenit Frislandiamq Germani vocant.

Autor hujus tabellæ Geographicæ perhibetur esse Sigurdus Stephanius Islandus vir eruditus, Scholæ
Schalholtinæ quondam Rector dignissimus, qui etiam alia nonnulla ingenii et eruditionis specimina edidit
videlicet Descriptionem Islandiæ, quam apud Sereniss.ᵉ Regiæ Maj.ᵗˢ Antiquarium Thormodu Torfæum vidisse me
memini, nec non opusculum de Spectris quod præterita æstate ab amico quodam in Patria mecum
comunicatum, penes me asservatur. Delineationem autem hanc suam, ex antiquitatibus Islandiæ
maxima sui parte desumpsisse videtur. De Hellulandia Marclandia et Skralingialandia, videri
poterit Arngrimus Ionas, qui ad calcem opusculi de Gronlandia, Gronlandorum aliquot navigationes
ad has terras annotavit, in terrarum etiam hyperborearum ultra Gronlandiam delineatione, ubi
Risaland et Iothunheima collocat, antiquitates quoq Islandicas secutum esse Autorem, sat scio, sed
an authenticæ illæ sint dubito. Cum priore Gronlandiæ mappa Dñi Gudbrandi, parum consentire
hanc satis constat. Islandia hic justo majorem habet latitudinem, Promontorium etiam Biriolfsnes, in-
gentis continentis potius quam isthmi vel promontorii speciem præ se fert, ut cætera omittam, quocum-
ca curiositatis potius quam necessitatis ergo hanc mappam annotavi.

XVII. Sigurdur Stefánsson, Map of the North, *ca.* 1590. Royal Library, Copenhagen, G.K.S. 2881, 4°.

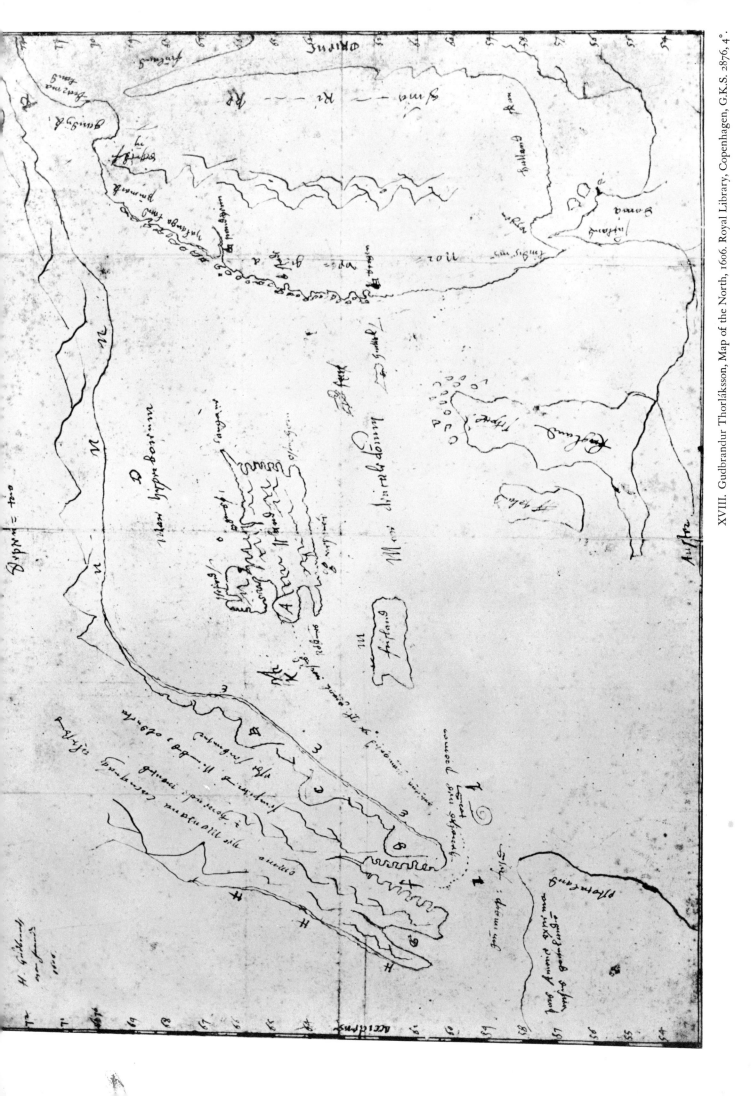

XVIII. Gudbrandur Thorláksson, Map of the North, 1606. Royal Library, Copenhagen, G.K.S. 2876, 4°.

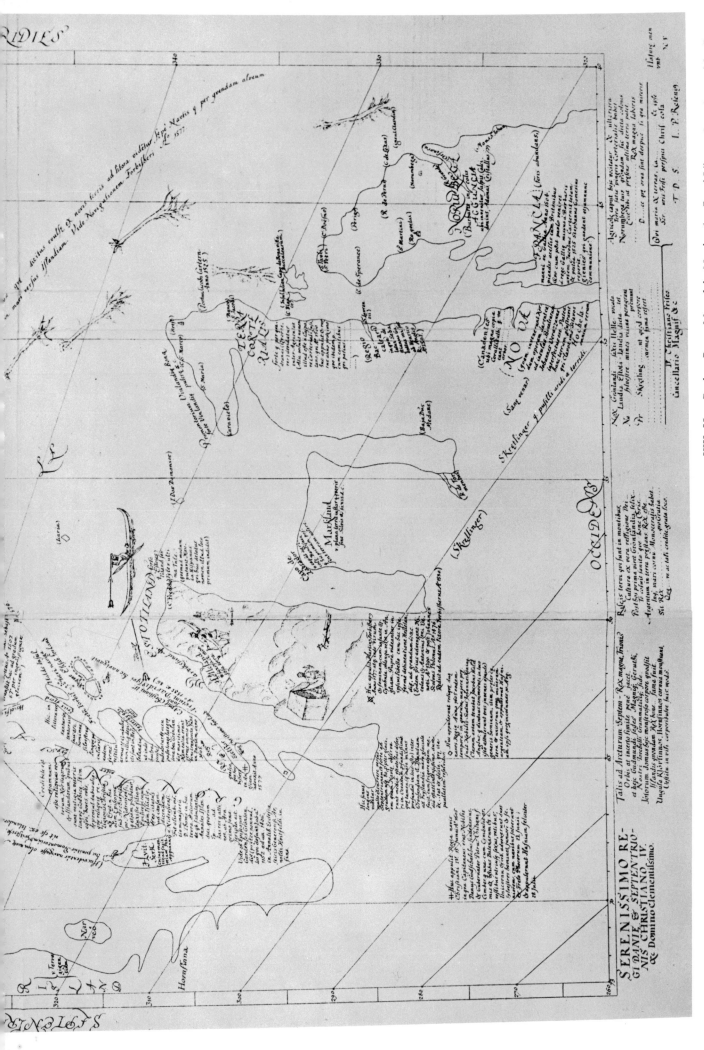

XIX. Hans Poulson Resen, Map of the North, 1665. Royal Library, Copenhagen, Map Room.

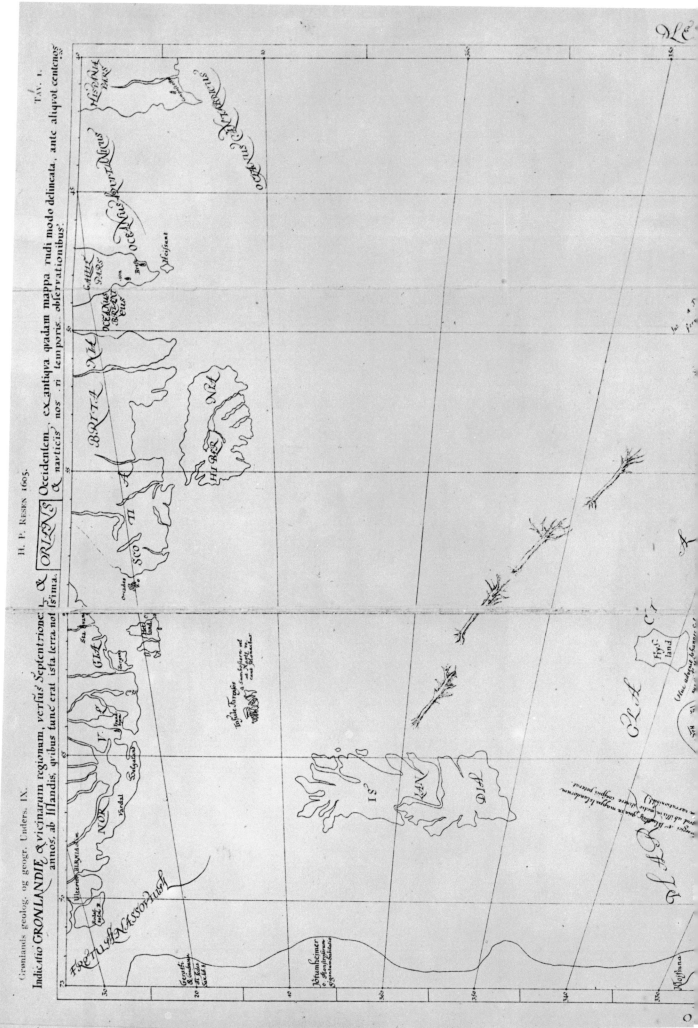

Grønlands geolog. og geogr. Unders. IX.

H. P. RESEN 1605.

TAV. 1.

Indicatio GRONLANDIE & vicinarum regionum, versus Septentrionem & ORIENS Occidentem, ex antiqva qvadam mappa rudi modo delineata, ante aliqvot centenas annos, ab Islandis, qvibus tunc erat ista terra notissima, & navticis nostri temporis observationibus.

from which he diverges only in his representation of Great Britain, of Scandinavia, and of the European rivers.[8]

Africa is the continent in which we have noted some striking links between the Vinland Map and Bianco's world map of 1436. It also seems, although no doubt deceptively, to provide the latest *terminus post quem* for dating both. They have in common the precise tracing of the northwest coast as far south as Cape Bojador,[9] and if they shared a common prototype, this (it might be supposed) could not have been executed before the voyage of Gil Eannes in 1434. Yet this section of coast had been laid down in very similar form on earlier maps; as Kimble puts it, "Cape Non ceased to be 'Caput finis Africa' about the middle of the fourteenth century", and "the ocean coast as far as Cape Bojador (more correctly, as far as the cove on its southern side) was known and mapped from the time of the Pizzigani portolan chart (1367)".[10] No documentary record of any voyage south of Cape Bojador before 1434 survives; but the fact that it is marked and even named in earlier maps (as in the Catalan Atlas of 1375,[11] *buyetder*) forbids us to assume that Bianco's representation and that of the prototype followed in this part of the Vinland Map must postdate 1434.[12]

The great advance in the knowledge which, from the second half of the thirteenth century, reached southern Europe about the interior of West Africa and the Sudan was reflected in many maps, from the information collected by merchants on the Saharan trade routes and in the markets of Northwest Africa.[13] The wealth of detail for this region recorded by Carignano, the Pizzigani, and the Catalan cartographers is wholly absent from Bianco's world map and from the Vinland Map. The latter repeats Bianco's anachronistic reference to the Beni-Marin and his erroneous location of two names;[14] but these aberrations, which appear to be peculiar to Bianco, do not help in dating. Nor was the transference of the Prester John to Africa a novelty in the middle of the fifteenth century.[15] The other names in Africa all come from older stock, and the marked similarity of outline between the Vinland Map and Bianco's may go back to an earlier prototype now lost.

For Asia the compiler of the Vinland Map shows the same conservatism in his use of sources as for Africa; and, apart from the modifications introduced from his reading of the Tartar Relation, this part of the map could very well have been drawn over a century earlier. The cartographer's neglect to use any information from Marco Polo or from the travelers in his footsteps, notably Odoric of Pordenone, is common to all maps before the Catalan Atlas of 1375 (in which

8. The first two of these distinctive delineations are discussed elsewhere in this study (Part I, ch. 4; Part II, chs. 5, 6).

9. *Cabo de* ... (name illegible) in the fourth chart of Bianco's atlas of 1436.

10. Kimble, p. 114. See also R. Mauny, *Les Navigations médiévales sur les côtes sahariennes antérieures à la découverte portugaise (1434)* (1960).

11. In association with the legend and picture relating to Jacme Ferrer's voyage for the River of Gold in 1346.

12. It is true that by 1448, when he drew his later chart, Bianco had obtained (no doubt when calling at Lagos or Lisbon on the Flanders voyage) intelligence of the Portuguese traverse of the African coast as far as Cape Verde, i.e. up to 1445; but the time lag between discovery and mapping was usually much greater.

13. See C. de La Roncière, *La Découverte de l'Afrique au Moyen-Age* (1925-27); Kimble, ch. V; E. W. Bovill, *The Golden Trade of the Moors* (1958), ch. 11.

14. See above, p. 131.

15. See above, p. 131.

East Asia is drawn entirely from Marco Polo) and to most maps of the first half of the fifteenth century.[16] The Asian geography of Fra Paolino and of Petrus Vesconte in the early fourteenth century, while it owes nothing to Marco Polo, betrays the influence of Rubruck in its nomenclature and in the corrected delineation of the Caspian Sea (although it retains the classical version of that sea, in duplicate).[17] Nothing is added to this stock of information either by Bianco or—apart from the data furnished by the Tartar Relation—by the author of the Vinland Map.

The latter, however, deserves credit for originality in his removal of the Earthly Paradise—"an almost constant component of the mappamundi"—from his map; for (as Kimble observes) "the vitality of the tradition was so great that this 'Garden of Delights', with its four westward flowing rivers, was still being located in the Far East long after the travels of Odoric and the Polos had demonstrated the impossibility of any such hydrographical anomaly, and the moral difficulties in the way of the identification of Cathay with Paradise".[18]

The geography of the Carpini mission of 1245–47, as illustrated in the Vinland Map, is discussed in the next chapter. Here we may note only that the cartographer's delineation of the *nova terra* in the east as islands in the ocean conforms to the convention of the Latin mappaemundi and to their authors' usage in incorporating fresh matter of this kind into their design.[19]

Lastly, it is evident that the geographical outlines of the map owe no direct debt to Ptolemy and that the few and faint traces of Ptolemaic nomenclature to be found in its toponymy are so ambiguous[20] as to arouse the strongest doubt whether its author knew or used the *Geographia*.

4. GEOGRAPHY OF THE CARPINI MISSION

Friar John of Plano Carpini styled his Book of the Tartars a *libellus historicus,* that is, a work descriptive of the Mongols, their lands, manners, and way of life. The narrative of his journeys across Asia, out and home, concludes this general report (ch. IX of his original text; bk. XXXII, chs. XIX–XXV and XXXIII, in the *Speculum Historiale* by Vincent of Beauvais). Brief though the account of his own traverse of Asia is, Carpini is scrupulous in stating dates and length of stages, and in giving indications of orientation. Thus it is possible to recover from his text both his itinerary and the geographical ideas which he formed from observation and report.[21]

Although Carpini nowhere mentions a map of any kind, we may assume that the mental image of the geography of Asia with which he set out was that of the thirteenth-century mappaemundi.[22] If so, the length of his journey to Mongolia must have surprised him. From none of the Europeans who preceded him had any information on Central Asia reached the map-

16. See Yule-Cordier, Introductory notices, secs. XII, XIII; Kimble, pp. 144–46.

17. Cf. above, p. 121. Almagià (*Mon. Cart. Vat.,* I, p. 8) thought it "far from improbable" that Fra Paolino had information direct from Rubruck, who was also a Franciscan. It was certainly the maps of Paolino and (following him) Vesconte that introduced geographical data from Rubruck into the stock of fourteenth-century cartography.

18. Kimble, p. 185, citing Bianco's world map of 1436 as an example of such archaism.

19. See above, p. 146.

20. See above, pp. 141–42.

21. In this chapter the geography of the Vinland Map is confronted mainly with that of the accounts by Carpini and Benedict; the geographical system to be derived from the Tartar Relation is essentially identical, though it contains no itinerary.

22. Such as those of Ebstorf and Hereford and the Psalter Map in the British Museum. Preconceived ideas of the geography of Asia are hinted at in only a few passages in the original texts of the Carpini mission; among these are Carpini's allusions to peoples and monsters of medieval legend, to Prester John, to the river systems of Asia and

makers,[23] whose design, conforming to a traditional pattern, ascribed roughly the same longitudinal extension to Asia (from the Holy Land to the Far East) as to the Mediterranean.[24] Yet from Kaniev, on the Dnieper, where he and Friar Benedict arrived on 4 February 1246, it took them sixty days to reach the camp of Batu, on the middle Volga; and, although "passing through Comania we rode most earnestly", Carpini drily comments, as they traversed the steppes eastward, "thus far had we traveled from the beginning of Lent until eight days after Easter". They left Batu's camp on Easter Monday (8 April), were crossing the steppeland east of the Ural river on Ascension Day (17 May), and a month later were in the land of the Karakhitai, east of the Aral Sea; passing by the south of Lake Balkhash,[25] along the northern Tien Shan, they entered the country of the Naiman, in the western uplands of the Altai, on 28 June, and eventually, riding "without intermission" eastward over the mountain passes, they came to Kuyuk's camp near Karakorum, south of Lake Baikal, on 22 July.[26] The return journey is described by Carpini more summarily; leaving Kuyuk's camp on 13 November 1246 and traveling "all winter long", they arrived at that of Batu, on the Volga, on 9 May 1247. For the extraordinary speed of the outward journey (some 3,000 miles in 106 days), credit is no doubt due to the post system of the Mongols; yet, as Kimble remarks, the Franciscans' achievement is "remarkable by any criterion; not least by mileage".[27]

Carpini was thus the first traveler to demonstrate, from experience, that Eurasia extended much further to the east than European geographers and mapmakers supposed; and this process of education was continued by Rubruck, Marco Polo, and Odoric. How far the continent stretched beyond the limits of his information remained a matter of surmise to Carpini, who reports (for instance) that Mongolia is "on the north side . . . environed with the Ocean Sea".

---

to the ocean sea, and Benedict's reference to the Caspian Sea (above, p. 136). We may also cite C. de Bridia's phrase *habitabilis mundi huius machina* (TR, ¶2). Rubruck contrasted the Latin world picture with that of the Mongols (see pp. 136–37).

23. On the Christians found by Rubruck in 1254 in the camp of Mongke Khan, at Karakorum, see L. Olschki, *Marco Polo's Precursors* (1943), pp. 52–53; and his *Guillaume Boucher: A French Artist at the Court of the Khans* (1946). Carpini too had oral information from "a certain Ruthenian called Cosmas, a goldsmith, and a great favourite of the emperor" (ed. Rockhill, p. 26). Olschki diagnoses the "profound and persistent ignorance of Central and Eastern Asia" which prevailed in Europe up to the time of the missions *ad Tartaros:* "No actual experience of warriors, travellers and traders contributed to the clarification of geographical and ethnological details concerning those regions known only by persistent erudite and literary traditions" (*Marco Polo's Precursors,* p. 1). See also the same author's *Marco Polo's Asia* (1960), ch. ii.

24. These proportions are found even in the world maps of Fra Paolino and of Petrus Vesconte (*ca.* 1320). During the fourteenth century however, as the Mediterranean sea-chart was (in Professor E. G. R. Taylor's words) "incorporated into the Mappa Mundi", its more correct estimation of the length of the Mediterranean, which it reduced to about 50 degrees, improved the design of the world map. In Bianco's of 1436, for instance, the longitudinal extent of Asia is about twice that of the Mediterranean.

25. And apparently within sight of it. Although the lake or "small sea" which they rode along in June 1246, in the Karakitai country, is usually identified (as by Rockhill, pp. 16–17, 159–60) with the Ala Kul, about 100 miles east of Lake Balkhash, the topographical indications in the texts, including the statement that they traversed it "for the space of many days", support the identification with Lake Balkhash. See above, p. 136; below, n. 36; and Fig. 1.

26. On the location and site of Karakorum, see Yule-Cordier, Vol. 1, pp. 227–30; P. Pelliot, *Notes on Marco Polo,* Vol. 1 (1959), pp. 165–69.

27. Kimble, *Geography in the Middle Ages,* p. 135. For the rapidity of Carpini's journey the "nomad peace" and the post system introduced by Ogodei Khan in 1236 were not perhaps so much responsible as was the elaborate organization for Kuyuk Khan's enthronement, attended by Carpini in August 1246. On this see Juvaini, *The History of the World-Conqueror,* trans. and ed. J. A. Boyle (1958), pp. 248–51; and above, p. 36.

From the observations made on his journey Carpini was also able to describe the character of the interior and to distinguish its geographical regions: the "plain ground" of the steppelands, the Turanian desert, the complex mountain systems of the Tien Shan and the Altai, and the stark homeland of the Mongols—"in some part full of mountains, and in other places plain and smooth ground, but everywhere sandy and barren". The principal Mongol peoples are named (not, however, without some misapprehensions) and located, as are the peoples against whom they made war; and it would be easy to lay them down on a map from Carpini's account.[28] To knowledge of the hydrography of Asia he made a less significant contribution than Rubruck; for, although he differentiated, and gave their Slav names to, the four great rivers Dnieper, Don, Volga, and Ural, he supposed them all to fall into the Black Sea. There is no evidence that he was aware of the existence of the Caspian, although the compiler of the Vinland Map seems to have derived an adventurous piece of geography from a speculation by Friar Benedict or his scribe;[29] and the inland Caspian Sea which begins to appear in the world maps from the early fourteenth century was derived from Rubruck's report.[30]

Whether through the mapmakers' conservatism or through their lack of curiosity and diligence in research, Carpini's report left no mark on fourteenth-century cartography; and it is only in a figurative sense that we can agree with Beazley's dictum that "Carpini really begins the reliable western map of Further Asia".[31] This is an odd accident of cartographic history, since it was Carpini's account of the Mongols, and not Rubruck's, which Vincent brought into currency by publication in the *Speculum Historiale,* and it was on Carpini's work (as abridged by Vincent) that Mandeville drew for the passages on the Tartars in his widely read book.[32]

The Vinland Map is therefore exceptional in rendering information from Carpini's mission in cartographic form. (The only element from Rubruck, namely the inland Caspian, was doubtless taken by the author of the map from his Bianco-type original.) Carpini's geography has suffered a good deal of change and indeed degradation on its way to the map. It seems to have been known to the cartographer through the medium of the Tartar Relation of C. de Bridia, and not from Carpini's own account or Vincent's abridgement of it. As Mr. Painter shows,[33] the geographical matter in the Tartar Relation is already at one remove from the observer; and it is from the cartographer's further interpretation of it, perhaps nearly two hundred years later, that its delineation in the Vinland Map is derived.

It is not surprising that in its rendering of Carpini's geography the map is not only decidedly meager but also more than a little confused. By drawing Europe and the Mediterranean on a larger scale (in proportion to the rest of the Old World) than in his original, and by the representation of the Sea of the Tartars, abridging Eastern Asia, the cartographer has ludicrously restricted the longitudinal extension of Asia and the length of Carpini's journey to Mongolia.

28. Cf. the maps in C. d'Ohsson, *Histoire des Mongols* (2d. ed. 1834–35), Vol. 1; Rockhill, *Rubruck;* R. Grousset, *L'Empire des steppes* (1939), esp. nos. 20–22; and Fig. 1 herewith.

29. See above, p. 136, and below, p. 151.

30. Initially by Fra Paolino and Petrus Vesconte; see R. Almagià, *Monumenta Cartographica Vaticana,* Vol. 1, p. 8. Bianco doubtless derived this feature in his world map from a cartographic tradition, not directly from Rubruck's report or any other text.

31. C. R. Beazley, *Prince Henry the Navigator* (1895), p. 91.

32. See *Mandeville's Travels,* ed. M. Letts (1953), Vol. 1, pp. xxxii–iii.

33. See above, p. 42.

The location of the Mongol country is roughly indicated by the name *Tartaria mogalica* north-east of the Caspian, and that of two of its peoples by the names *Moal* and *Zumoal* to the east. Further north we have *Mōgali* and *Tatartata fluius,* illustrating Carpini's belief that here Mongolia was "environed with the ocean sea". *Kytanis,* wildly misplaced in this area, represents the Khitai (Cathay) southeast of the Mongol country; this error was not made by Carpini. Here, too, we find, interspersed with the "Carpini" nomenclature, names from the map prototype—*Termacus rex, Gogus, Magog.* The *Imperiū Tartarorum,* between the Baltic and the Black Sea, presumably relates to the Kipchak Tartars, Batu's khanship of the Russian steppes, or perhaps refers generally to Mongol expansion westward through Asia and Europe; and the name *Magnus kan* east of the Black Sea probably alludes to Batu. Carpini's list of the peoples against whom the Mongols campaigned is copied by C. de Bridia, but only two of their names are reproduced in the map: the Khitai and the Naiman (*Nimsini*)—the former wrongly and the latter correctly located. The linking of the Naiman, who lived in the Altai uplands west of the Mongol country, with a classical name (*Hemmodi*) which undoubtedly referred to the Himalaya betrays however ignorance of the mountain systems of Central Asia—an ignorance which the travels of missionaries and merchants had by the middle of the fourteenth century already done much to dispel. The compiler of the map may be inferred to have had no knowledge, since he made no use, of the reports of Rubruck, Marco Polo, Odoric, and Montecorvino, or of such merchants' handbooks as that of Pegolotti.[34]

The *Magnum mare Tartarorum* is a feature of the Vinland Map which (so far as we know) had no cartographic precedent and found no imitator; and we take it to be a deduction by the compiler of the map from his textual sources of information. Carpini's description of the geography of Asia, followed by the Tartar Relation, contains several vague indications that the land of the Mongols, "lying in that part of the world which is thought to be most northeasterly", was bounded to east and north by the ocean sea. It was in this quarter that, in the tradition of the later Greek geographers, Isidore and the mapmakers who followed him placed the Caspian or Hyrcanian Sea, as a gulf of the outer ocean; and it was doubtless with this image in his mind's eye that Friar Benedict, or the scribe who wrote down his account, conjecturally identified the "sea" (in the Karakhitai country), along the southern shore of which he and Carpini rode in June 1246, as the Caspian.[35] This identification is not made by Carpini in the corresponding passage of his own account (in the text which has survived), and it is not paralleled in the Tartar Relation of C. de Bridia. But if Friar Benedict or his reporter could make it, so too could the compiler of the Vinland Map, who, by a similar process of thought, plainly arrived at the conclusion that the mission had reached the shore of the eastern ocean. In his map this conclusion is expressed graphically by the delineation of the Great Sea of the Tartars, textually by the name *Mare Occeanum Orientale* and in the legend *montes inferiores abrupti . . . fratres . . . transiuerunt usque ad mare occeanum orientale.* Thus, to the two representations of the Caspian Sea found in Bianco (and no doubt in the prototype of the Vinland Map), the cartographer has added yet a third.

34. On these, see Beazley, *Dawn,* Vol. 3, ch. ii passim.

35. This was probably Lake Balkhash (see above, n. 25); they had it, Benedict wrote, on their left, and he presumably supposed them to be traversing the west or south side of the gulf. If the conjectural identification were indeed his, their further journey must surely have disillusioned him. See above, p. 149.

To account for the form in which the three large islands, east of the Sea of Tartars, are drawn is perhaps less simple. The medieval cartographer found it natural to depict new lands, of which he heard, as islands in or adjacent to the environing ocean; and the outer coasts of the *Insule Sub aquilone* and *Postreme insule* plainly repeat the outlines of eastern Asia in Bianco's world map, or in the common prototype, which therefore dictated the spacing of the three islands. But what are we to make of their inner or western coasts, which are drawn with particularity of detail and boldly marked features? We have the choice between supposing them a figment of the cartographer's mind or admitting the possibility that he drew them from more precise information about islands to the east—perhaps Korea, perhaps the larger Japanese islands, whose outline indeed the delineation in the Vinland Map strongly recalls.

That Chinese or Korean information about Japan was available to the Mongols in the first half of the thirteenth century must be credited, even if it is apparently undocumented. Between 1211 and 1241 they had conquered Korea and campaigned in China; Chinese prisoners or envoys who visited the Great Khan's camp could have talked of islands in the ocean; so too could the Chinese artisans whom Rubruck noticed in the "street of the Cathayans" at Karakorum. It is difficult to determine, from the sparse hints picked up by European travelers, how precise were the geographical ideas formulated by the Mongols at this early period about countries which they had not yet seen. They appear to have led Rubruck to suppose Korea an island;[36] but this error (which was not made in Chinese or Korean maps) may have arisen from misunderstanding of what was said to him. Rubruck has, however, left an indication of the world-picture visualized by the Mongols, who (he writes) "were quite unable to understand that [the ocean sea] was endless, without bounds".[37] This calls to mind a group of world maps preserved in later Korean copies but traced by Professor H. Nakamura to an otherwise lost Chinese model not later than the eleventh century.[38] In maps of this type the ocean, which (as normally in Chinese cartography) runs round the world-continent, is itself surrounded by a ring of land, within which lie many conventionally drawn islands, including those of Japan.

It is not incredible that the Mongols should have known or even possessed Chinese world maps, nor that Carpini might have seen them at Karakorum, although (if so) it might be thought that he or Benedict would have mentioned them. Even if we admit this, and if we add the further, and more unlikely, assumption that the map or maps seen by them depicted Japan with the detail ascribed to the outer islands in the Vinland Map, we face considerable difficulties when we try to envisage the process by which the representation was conveyed from Carpini or Benedict to the compiler of the Vinland Map, whether through C. de Bridia or another intermediary.

We can at once dismiss the hypothesis that so detailed and precise a design, if founded on reality, could have been communicated orally or by any other medium than a map or sketch. If it derives from Carpini or Benedict, we must presume that he obtained or copied a Chinese map, some version of which eventually came into the hands of the author of the Vinland Map.

36. He heard of "certain people called Caule [Koreans] and Manse, who live on islands, the sea around which freezes in winter, so that at that time the Tartars can make raids thither" (ed. Rockhill, pp. 200–01). The frozen sea is perhaps the Yalu River, on the Manchuria–Korea border, which freezes from November to March.

37. Ed. Rockhill, p. 133. Cf. above, pp. 136–37.

38. H. Nakamura, "Old Chinese world maps preserved by the Koreans", *Imago Mundi*, Vol. 4 (1947), pp. 3–22; also J. Needham, *Science and Civilisation in China*, Vol. 3 (1959), pp. 565–68.

There is no evidence that, for his illustration of Carpini's geography, the cartographer used any other source than the Tartar Relation of C. de Bridia. If this text was ever accompanied by a map, perhaps (let us conjecture) one found by C. de Bridia in Carpini's papers or sketched for him in the course of conversation by Friar Benedict, we still have to postulate a chain of transmission over an interval of a century or more to its incorporation in the Vinland Map.

Not one of the assumptions which form the links in this hypothetical argument is impossible, although each is (in our opinion) weak. By making one link depend on the other, we do not increase the strength of the chain but reduce it. The difficulties presented by the argument as a whole seem to us far greater than those involved in the supposition that the three islands depicted in the Vinland Map owe their design to the cartographer's fancy, rather than to any graphic representation transmitted to him from (ultimately) a member of the Carpini mission.

It is in East Asia, as we have seen, that the author of the Vinland Map introduces his most substantial and significant modification of an original design; and since we can here reconstruct his prototype, it is possible to analyze, hypothetically, his modes of thought and interpretation. Though essentially conservative, with a tendency to cling to his original, he has sought to extract from his textual sources (primarily the Tartar Relation), and to incorporate into his map, geographical matter which struck him as new. This included names from the Carpini stock, the geographical or historical concepts alluded to in the legends of the map, the river of the Tartars, and the *Magnum mare Tartarorum*. His two principal sources for Asia were his map-prototype and the text (or texts) on the Carpini mission. Where these were in conflict, he has in one conspicuous instance—the location of Prester John—preferred the authority of the map; or perhaps, in the middle of the fifteenth century, he considered the concept of Prester John as an Asian monarch to be too anachronistic. Elsewhere in the map we find indications that its compiler has made attempts to reconcile his authorities; but they are rather perfunctory. He had apparently read Pomponius Mela, from whom the name Hemmodi must surely be derived, but the bracketing of the Naiman with the Himalaya is not very happy. This must be the only medieval map to separate Gog and Magog—a severance apparently dictated by the space available for writing in the names. The interpolation of the Sea of the Tartars into the design of the map-prototype is an ingenious graphic construction, but the retention of Rubruck's inland Caspian Sea from the original is a startling dittography, in a geographical sense. The significance which the cartographer attached to this new delineation is betrayed by his willingness to abandon a basic feature of the traditional mappamundi, the Earthly Paradise, and by his perversion (accidental or wilful?) of the passage in the Tartar Relation transcribed in his legend. Yet while snatching at geographical concepts suggested by the Carpini materials, he is apparently unaware of the great body of information on Asia brought back by later travelers; this neglect is, it is true, common to most mapmakers up to the middle of the fifteenth century, and (as we have seen) the Vinland Map is primarily an attempt to illustrate the accompanying texts. In general, we can envisage the compiler of the map as one whose imagination was easily kindled by novelties in his sources but uncontrolled by a broad geographical culture or a strict critical sense.

5. CARTOGRAPHY OF THE ATLANTIC

The global geography of the Greeks, following the pattern developed by Crates of Millos (*ca.* 150 B.C.), envisaged the habitable world as one of four land masses, divided by seas which extended along the equatorial zone and between the poles. In the northern hemisphere were the *oikoumene*, or habitable world, and the lands of the *perioikoi;* south of the equator lay the continents of the *antoikoi* and the *antipodes*. This world view held its own among the Roman geographers alongside their formulation of a circular or disc-shaped model, the *orbis terrarum,* for the *oikoumene* alone. During the Middle Ages, however, the concept of Crates can be traced only residually in maps or diagrams (such as those in manuscripts of Macrobius) illustrating the theory of climatic zones and in a few late derivatives from Roman cartography.[39] The classical vision of an "opposite continent" beyond the western ocean had faded from European consciousness.

Thus, to the patristic geography of the early Middle Ages, the Atlantic—the "Sea of Darkness" of the Arabs—was simply that part of the outer ocean which marked the western boundary of Europe and Africa. In Isidore's words, "the philosophers say that beyond the ocean there is not any land". Ptolemy's longitudes were reckoned only eastward from the Canaries, and medieval cartographers—as late as the fourteenth and fifteenth centuries—took in, at the western edge of their world maps and charts, no more of the ocean than was needed to accommodate the islands and archipelagos known or supposed to exist there. Such were the islands of fable— St. Brendan's Isles, Brasil, Mayda or Man, Antillia, and Satanaxes—and the islands revealed by discovery or by trade and settlement—Madeira, the Canaries, the Azores, Iceland. The American landfalls of the Norsemen before and after A.D. 1000 did not pass into the general stock of European ideas and failed to create a common image of the Atlantic. Yet it is conceivable that even the "mythical" islands laid down by cartographers in the Atlantic embodied folk memories and traditional—if distorted—rumors of westerly voyages, perhaps earlier than those of the Norsemen. A recent writer has persuasively detected a factual basis in the *Navigatio Sancti Brandani,* inferring that "there were Irishmen in the tenth century who knew that America was there"; and he may well be justified in suggesting that "in the mediaeval maps . . . the notions of Atlantic islands spread by Irish literature are chiefly preserved".[40] Certainly, from the thirteenth century onward, geographers in Europe came to visualize the ocean increasingly as a way of access to lands lying within or beyond it.[41]

Eastward from his prime meridian Ptolemy's *oikoumene* embraced only 180 degrees of longitude. Very soon after the manuscripts of his *Geographia* reached Western Europe, his concept of the distribution of land and water was being challenged, as by Pierre d'Ailly (*ca.* 1410), who, in a passage later to be noted by Columbus, cited other classical authority for the view that "the sea is little between the farthest bound of Spain from the east and the nearest of India from the west" and that "this sea is navigable in a few days if the wind is favorable".[42] The maps (or charts), depicting the intervening ocean, which Toscanelli sent from Florence to the King of Portugal in 1474 and to Columbus before 1481 are now lost, but can be reconstructed from

---

39. Notably in the world map of the Carthaginian Martianus Capella (fourth century), preserved in MSS (twelfth and thirteenth century) of the *Liber floridus* of Lambert of St. Omer. See R. Uhden, "Die Weltkarte des Martianus Capella", *Mnemosyne,* Ser. III, Vol. 3 (1936), pp. 97-124.

40. G. Ashe, *Land to the West* (1962), pp. 291, 293.

41. On this, see generally Beazley, *Dawn,* Vol. 3, ch. iv; also J. A. Williamson, *The Voyages of the Cabots* (1929), Part II, ch. i.

42. P. d'Ailly, *Imago Mundi,* cap. 19. These arguments go back to Roger Bacon's *Opus Majus.*

the text of his letter and from two surviving cartographic works embodying his ideas.[43] These are the world map of Henricus Martellus Germanus (*ca.* 1490), now at Yale, and the Nuremberg globe of Martin Behaim (1492)—the only two extant non-Ptolemaic world maps of the fifteenth century to be graduated in latitude and longitude and so to convey a precise estimate of the width of the ocean between westernmost Europe and easternmost Asia.[44]

To Toscanelli the goal was Marco Polo's Cathay, and within the intervening ocean he was aware of no considerable land other than the two large islands of Antillia and Cipangu.[45] The discovery of America at the end of the fifteenth century was also a discovery, or rediscovery, of the Atlantic, as an ocean with bounds defined by continental seaboard lands to east and west. Thus, so long as the Norse (or any previous) discovery remained unknown to cartographers, or at any rate unrecorded in a form which they could use, no true Atlantic chart could be made before the discoveries of Cabot and Columbus came to the notice of the mapmakers; and none has in fact survived.

The western part of the Vinland Map, taken as a whole, has therefore no extant antecedent and may be cited as the oldest map of the North Atlantic Ocean in existence. This representation however may be said (with slightly less confidence)[46] to have found no imitators and to have established no cartographic tradition. Whether it was derived by its author from a single map or chart embracing the whole area, from the coasts of Europe and Africa westward, or was pieced together by him from disjunct materials is a question on which opinions may well differ. Examination of the separate elements in the composition, but leaving Greenland and Vinland aside for study in later chapters, may help in forming a judgment.

Throughout the fourteenth and fifteenth centuries there is abundant evidence, both in records of voyages and in maps, that the Atlantic, "as a field of discovery", excited the strongest curiosity among the seamen and cartographers of Southern Europe. As Dr. Williamson observes, "there was yet no thought of voyaging to India or . . . Cathay"—still less of picking up the landfalls of the Norsemen in the west: "the common mind ran upon islands, not continents".[47] The Canaries had been rediscovered in 1336 and first laid down on a chart only three years later. The Madeira group, perhaps also sighted in 1336, was delineated in the Laurentian sea-atlas

43. The authenticity of Toscanelli's letter and lost maps, formerly challenged by H. Vignaud, appears now to be established beyond dispute.

44. In its general geographical design the Behaim globe derives from a map of Martellus type, if not by him. The Yale map by Martellus does not show the western ocean, being bounded in the east by Cipangu and in the west by the Canaries; but its graduation in longitude admits an interval of 90 degrees between the Canaries and Cipangu. Toscanelli allowed 85 degrees; and the corresponding figure in Behaim's globe is 110 degrees.

45. Cipangu only is in the Martellus map at Yale; both islands are shown on Behaim's globe. Alternative opinions on the western ocean were expressed by a French writer *ca.* 1452, i.e. nearly contemporary with the scribe of the Vinland Map: "Oultre ce pays d'Illande [Ireland] ne trouveres terres ne ysles aultres devers le couchant. Et disent aucuns que se une nef tiroit tout droit a la longue qu'elle se trouveroit en la terre de prestre Jehan [i.e. Asia]. Et les aultres disent que c'est le bout des terres du coste d'occidant" (*Le Livre de la Description des Pays de Gilles Le Bouvier dit Berry*, ed. E. T. Hamy, 1908, p. 123). Mr G. R. Crone is doubtless right in suggesting "that the belief that the east could be reached by the west was being reconsidered in geographical circles before the second half of the 15th century, possibly in the 14th"; see below, pp. 157–59 and n. 57.

46. In making any such generalization, caution is dictated by the very great wastage and loss known to have occurred among maps before (roughly) the middle of the sixteenth century.

47. Williamson, *Voyages of the Cabots*, p. 123.

Fig. 2. Outline of Five World Maps of the 14th and 15th Centuries:

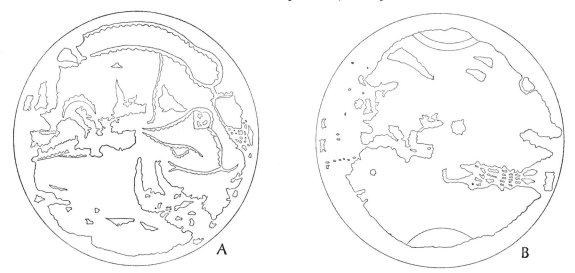

A. Petrus Vesconte, *ca.* 1321

B. Andrea Bianco, 1436

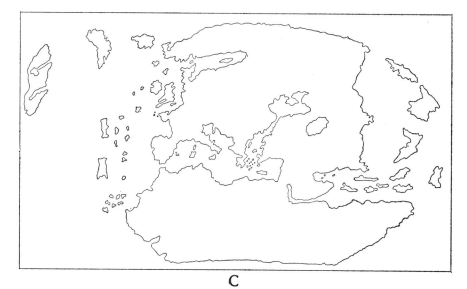

C. The Vinland Map, *ca.* 1440

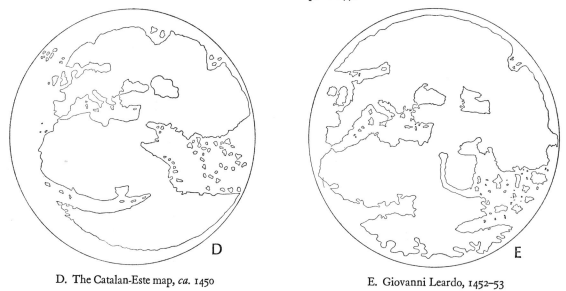

D. The Catalan-Este map, *ca.* 1450

E. Giovanni Leardo, 1452–53

The maps are reduced to a common scale, based on the N–S diameter. The originals of A, B, and E were drawn with East to the top; they are here reoriented with North to the top, for convenience of comparison.

(1351) and in all subsequent maps; Portuguese settlement there began in 1418. The evidence for a fourteenth-century discovery of the Azores is the representation of a chain of eight or nine islands, extending north–south, in the Laurentian atlas (1351) and in most later charts. Beazley's assertion[48] that in the atlas of 1351 "the whole group is mapped with remarkable precision", even "with the fullness and accuracy of a pilot-chart", has not gone unchallenged by later historians;[49] but it is indisputable that, from the time when Portuguese colonization began in 1427, the real Azores were identified by cartographers with the "supposed" Azores laid down in maps from the middle of the preceding century.

Thus the delineation of these archipelagos in the Vinland Map represented, at the date when the existing copy of the map was made, fact verified by experience; but the form in which they are depicted (doubtless with some simplification or generalization) is considerably older, although it remained in currency until nearly the end of the fifteenth century. Only the nomenclature is original and (apparently) peculiar to this map. As we have seen, the representation of these groups is common to the Vinland Map and to Bianco's world map of 1436. So, too, is that of the two imaginary islands west of the British Isles; their characteristic shape (though lost in the Vinland Map) and location, with the names *Brasil* and *Mayda* or *Man* (*berzil* and *uentura* in the fifth chart of Bianco's atlas), had become standardized in cartography before the end of the fourteenth century, as in the Catalan Atlas of 1375.

The two large oblong islands west of the Azores, named in the map *Magnæ Insulæ Beati Brandani,* drawn precisely as in Bianco's world map and in the fourth chart of his atlas, and named in the latter *Satanaxio* and *Antillia,* constitute one of the unsolved enigmas of cartographic history. Scholars have been unable to agree on the derivation of the name Antillia or on the significance to be attached to the delineation of this island group in maps from 1424 onward throughout the fifteenth century. On the one hand, *Antillia* is considered to be derived, by corruption, from *Getulia* (the classical name for northwest Libya), and its representation to be a *romanticismo insulare* created by the mapmakers and subsequently associated with the Portuguese discovery of the Azores.[50] On the other hand, it is contended that the name is made up of the Portuguese words *ante* (or *anti*) and *ilha,* indicating an island lying off a continent and pointing to a pre-Columbian discovery of the Antilles and perhaps the American mainland.[51] We need not go into these issues here, but will merely note, first, that the Antillia concept originates in the work of Venetian cartographers, probably drawing on Portuguese sources of information; second, that the version in the Vinland Map most closely resembles that of Bianco, whose atlas was prepared twelve years after, and in the same city as, the earliest chart to lay down Antillia; and third, that the concept takes its place among other testimony to a general

48. Beazley, *Dawn*, Vol. 3, pp. 422, 524; see also Cortesão, *The Nautical Chart of 1424,* p. 47.

49. E.g. S. E. Morison, *Portuguese Voyages to America in the 15th Century* (1940), pp. 15–18.

50. G. R. Crone, "The 'mythical' islands of the Atlantic Ocean", *Comptes rendus du Congrès International de Géographie, Amsterdam 1938* (1938), Vol. 2, pp. 164–71; "The origin of the name Antillia", *Geogr. Journal,* Vol. 91 (1938), pp. 260–62. Cf. also Morison, *Portuguese Voyages,* pp. 16–17. To Crone "the oblong shape of the 'island' strongly suggests that the outline may have been derived from a border around an inscription". This is not the only case in which fifteenth-century cartographers attributed this, or a very similar, shape to islands of which they knew (or thought they knew) the name and approximate location or direction but little or nothing more. We may compare the *Illa verde* in some charts (see below, p. 182), the *Giava major* (= Japan) of Fra Mauro's world map, and the *Cipangu* of Henricus Martellus; perhaps also the *ixola otenticha* in Bianco's chart of 1448 (see below, p. 159).

51. Cortesão, *The Nautical Chart of 1424,* passim.

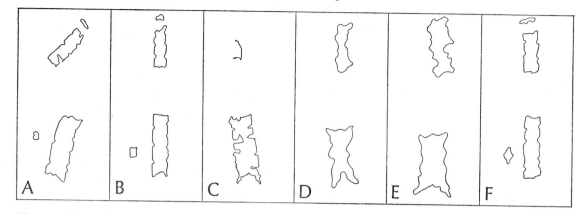

Fig. 3. Antillia and Satanaxes in Six Maps of the 15th Century: A. Pizzigano, 1424; B. Beccario, 1435; C. Bianco, 1436 (regional chart); D. Bianco, 1436 (world map); E. The Vinland Map, *ca.* 1440; F. Benincasa, 1463. All reduced to the scale of E, which is approximately original size. A, B, and F after Armando Cortesão, *The Nautical Chart of 1424.*

(if ill-defined) belief, in the early fifteenth century, that out in the ocean there was land waiting to be discovered.[52]

The Portuguese seamen learned the practice of oceanic navigation from their regular traffic with the Azores and also from the African voyages.[53] Returning home from the coast of Africa beyond Cape Bojador, they had to face adverse winds (the northeasterly trades) and currents, and they solved their problem by reaching northwest into the ocean until they were out of the trade-wind belt, in the latitude of the Azores, before laying course for Portugal. The further south they went on the outward voyage, the wider was the westward sweep made on the homeward: the *volta do mar largo* brought them back from Gambia, the *volta da Mina* or *volta do Sargaço* from Guinea. Bianco's atlas of 1436 indeed is often cited as evidence that by this early date the Portuguese had already navigated to the west of the Azores; the fourth chart has, in the extreme west, the legend *questo xe mar di baga* (here is the sea of weed). Since *baga* is a Portuguese word, this information must have come from a Portuguese source, and it suggests that the Sargasso Sea had been reached and recorded.[54]

Whether any Portuguese ship went further and made an American landfall before the men of Bristol or Columbus or John Cabot need not be considered here, for the Vinland Map provides no testimony for or against.[55] Out in the islands, evidence of land to the west could be picked up

52. Such rumor seems to have been prevalent in Bianco's native city of Venice (see below, p. 159). The earliest charts to depict Antillia were the work of Venetian or of Italian cartographers in touch with Venice—Pizzigano, 1424 (Venice); Beccario, 1435 (Genoa); Bianco, 1436 (Venice); Pareto, 1455 (Genoa). Grazioso Benincasa, in several of whose works Antillia appears, did not add it to his representation of the Atlantic until after his move to Venice in 1463. See Fig. 3 herewith.

53. See A. Teixeira da Mota, *A Arte de navegar no Mediterrâneo nos séculos XII–XVI e a criação da navegação astronómica no Atlântico e Índico* (1957), pp. 8–9.

54. See (for instance) Jaime Cortesão, *Os Descobrimentos Portugueses,* Vol. 1 (1959), pp. 259–69; and (for the skeptical view) Morison, *Portuguese Voyages,* pp. 15–33. A possible allusion to the Sargasso Sea in the *Navigatio Sancti Brandani* is noted by Ashe, *Land to the West,* pp. 101–03. In Bianco's chart of 1448, which does not show Antillia, the name *yⁿ fortunat' de sⁿ beati blandan* is attached to an island group (the Azores) lying further out in the ocean than the "supposed" Azores.

55. On conjectural western discoveries by the Portuguese, see V. Magalhães Godinho, *Documentos sobre a expansão portuguesa,* Vol. 3 (1956), ch. vii; also the above-cited works by S. E. Morison and A. Cortesão, passim.

on beaches after any gale. In Dr. Williamson's words, "all the time the unknown world was sending out signals of its existence . . . Year by year the tale mounted until Antillia and St Brandan's and Brasil became obsessions with every mariner whose business took him west of Cape Clear and Finisterre".[56] To the same climate of opinion and surmise belong references in two other documents of the second quarter of the fifteenth century, both from Venice. In his *Liber de omnibus rebus naturalis* (*ca.* 1450), the Venetian physician Giovanni da Fontana wrote, of the Atlantic Ocean: "Et ab eius occasu finitur pro parte etiam terra incognita" (And in the west it is bounded in part by unknown land).[57] And Bianco's chart of 1448 has, at the bottom edge of the parchment and southwest of Cape Verde, the outlines of two islands or a continental coast with the obscure and much-debated legend *ixola otenticha xe longa a ponente 1500/ mia,* i.e. "authentic island lying (*or* extending) 1,500 miles to the west". This has variously been interpreted as a representation of Brazil, or of some more northerly part of America, or of one of the Cape Verde Islands (usually Santiago), or of the Bissagos Islands south of Cape Verde.[58] The discovery of the Vinland Map encourages us to launch yet another explanation, perhaps little more far-fetched than the earlier ones. That the Vinland Map and Bianco's world map of 1436 are somehow connected can hardly be doubted, although we do not know in what relationship; nor can we suppose that Bianco ever saw the Vinland Map or the prototype for its delineation of the Atlantic, which is not reproduced in his work or in any other extant map. May he not, however, have obtained indirect or hearsay information about such a map and its representation of America, to which his vague indication of an *ixola otenticha* in 1448 perhaps refers?[59] And if so, could not Fontana, writing at Venice then or thenabouts, have picked up some similar rumor of a map which showed transatlantic land?[60]

However this may be, we are perhaps justified in conjecturing a Venetian original, perhaps

---

56. J. A. Williamson, *The Voyages of the Cabots*, p. 127.

57. Venice edition (1544), fol. 94; cited by A. Cortesão, *The Nautical Chart of 1424*, pp. 99–100, from Lynn Thorndike, *A History of Magic and Science*, Vol. 4 (1934), p. 159. That this concept was of greater antiquity, however, is shown by a quotation by Thorndike (p. 160) from Bernard of Verdun, *ca.* 1300: "Capitulum tertium de quantitate terre inhabitate earum insularum que habitantur alchalidat appellatis in oceano occidentali et sunt 6 numero . . . " The Arabic influence on belief in Atlantic lands, exemplified in this passage, is discussed by many authors; and G. R. Crone ("The 'mythical' islands of the Atlantic Ocean", p. 166) has pointed to a "connection between the mythical islands of the West and the body of oriental 'marvels' associated with islands". Belief in the "mythical" islands was fostered by new discoveries, as their representation by mapmakers shows. Thus the "supposed" Azores of fourteenth century cartography are assimilated to the discovered and settled Azores in the next century; in Battista Beccario's chart of 1435 the Antillia group has the legend *Insulle de nouo r'pte* (newly discovered islands); and in several of Benincasa's later charts it is similarly described, e.g. in that of 1482: "Fortunarum Insule que multa nomine reperiuntur ut dicit Isidorus 1° xv e a beato Brandano insule fortunate . . . etiam insule st' uocate . . . " This legend neatly illustrates all the hypothetical stages through which Crone (p. 171) supposes the delineation of legendary islands to have passed: "representation of the classical islands; identification of St Brandon's islands with these; insertion of further islands owing to the popularity of islands in accounts of the East; appearance of Antillia through a mistake; impetus to belief in these islands given by actual discoveries". See also above, n. 45.

58. See Morison, *Portuguese Voyages*, pp. 119–25, and the literature cited by him; also Duarte Leite, "Uma ilha enigmática", in *História dos Descobrimentos*, Vol. 1 (1958), pp. 339–45.

59. "The inscription indeed strongly suggests that the island was 'reported but not seen' " (Morison, *Portuguese Voyages*, p. 124). We may see a possible analogy, respecting both shape and conjectural location, in the mapmakers' representation of *Illa verde;* see above, n. 50, and below, p. 182.

60. See above, n. 57. According to Thorndike, Fontana's *Liber* may have been begun before 1450 and was completed not later than 1454.

of the first half of the fifteenth century, to have served for this part of the Vinland Map, which lies within the field of Mediterranean geographical ideas, and indeed within the coverage of the maps and charts produced by Italian craftsmen, including Bianco, in this period.

The more northerly lands of the Atlantic lay largely beyond the range of Mediterranean commerce, observation, and precise geographical knowledge in the early fifteenth century. Here the Vinland Map grafts on the Italian world picture alien cartographic elements which must be traced to other sources. The old and the new overlap to some extent. Ireland is in a common portolan form; but Great Britain is taken from a different model, and the representation of islands north of it is revised. The Baltic and Scandinavia are drawn after a pattern established in the fourteenth century by Mediterranean cartographers. Iceland is given an outline which, although known and reproduced in Majorca and Italy during the fifteenth century, was not generally adopted into southern cartography until the sixteenth. While the rendering of Greenland invites comparison with a representation given currency during the fifteenth century by maps drawn by the Dane Claudius Clavus between 1424 and 1430, it is in fact irreconcilable with the maps and concepts of Clavus and with those of all other geographers of this period. The delineation of Vinland has no counterpart in any other map or geographical text of the fourteenth and fifteenth centuries from either northern or southern Europe.

Whether the new or non-Mediterranean elements in this part of the Vinland Map were found by its author in a single map or drawn together by a process of compilation is a question to which no positive answer can be given. If they derive from a variety of sources, we must allow for an eclecticism of method not exemplified elsewhere in the map. If one map source only is involved, this was of a type which very probably antedates the middle of the fourteenth century. In the following chapters some attempt will be made to define the source, or sources, by analysis of the representations of the British Isles, Scandinavia, and Iceland; of Greenland; and of Vinland.

6. GEOGRAPHY OF THE NORTH

The associations of the Vinland Map so far examined are with southern Europe and the Mediterranean cultural area. When we attempt to trace to their origin its delineations of regions or lands beyond the vision of southern geographers and mapmakers, or only dimly perceived by them, we have also to consider what knowledge or opinion of these regions prevailed in the North, in what form it was recorded, and whether—and by what channels—it could have come to the notice of a cartographer working in southern Europe. By a long road we may arrive at a point where we can visualize the materials which lay before him as he drew these parts of his map. We must further try to determine the extent to which his own modes of interpretation and representation have transformed these materials, and to account for the odd circumstance that the Vinland Map is the only document of its period to preserve this complex of information on the north and west, some of which is not even remotely paralleled in text or map for at least a century and a half earlier, and a century and a half later, than its presumed date.

NORTHERN EUROPE AND ICELAND

By the beginning of the fourteenth century, when the earliest surviving portolan charts were made, Italian seaborne trade with Flanders and England was well established. The northern terminals of the regular sea routes plied by the Italian seamen were Antwerp and London, with the ports on the south and west coasts of the British Isles. To the markets of Flanders, where Genoa and Venice had factories, goods from the Baltic and Scandinavia were conveyed in shipping of the northern countries; and this trade was the jealously guarded preserve of the Hanse merchants and shipowners. An Italian seaman who might, like Bianco, also be a cartographer had no opportunity for hydrographic observation and recording of the coasts and waters of the North Sea, the Baltic, and the Norwegian Sea; nor had he any occasion to use charts in waters which he rarely, and never regularly or voluntarily, navigated. The precise, detailed, and generally correct coastal mapping in portolan charts of the fourteenth and fifteenth centuries ends at the estuaries of the Scheldt and Thames, for this was the limit of the observation and experience available to their makers.[61]

This is not to say either that no Italians traveled in the northern countries or that there were no maps of these countries derived from direct experience. We have, on the first point, not only documentary but also cartographic evidence that information came into the hands of Mediterranean mapmakers; and, on the second point, such arguments as that of Dr. A. W. Lang that "while the southern Europeans, with few exceptions, continued to cling to their cartographic beliefs which matured about 1350 . . . seamen in Northern Europe . . . created the foundations for a new cartographic picture of the continental North Sea coast".[62]

Two recorded visits by Italians to the North exemplify the character of the information brought back and the use made of it by cartographers. In 1313 Marino Sanuto sailed to Flanders in a Venetian trading galley and made his way overland into northern Germany, visiting the Hanseatic ports of Hamburg and Lubeck and going as far east as Stettin on the Baltic. The later maps of Petrus Vesconte, which accompany manuscripts of Sanuto's *Liber Secretorum Fidelium Crucis* (1318–21), and the world map of Fra Paolino Minorita have a developed representation of the Baltic and Scandinavia, with correctly placed names of countries; and it is reasonable to suppose that this was based on Sanuto's report.[63] In the next century Pietro Querini, traveling overland after his shipwreck on the north coast of Norway in 1431, encountered other Italians established in Sweden, and the relation of his experiences and observations written down after his return to Venice was known to Fra Mauro (who cites it explicitly) and perhaps also to Andrea Bianco;[64] this provided southern geographers with their earliest firsthand information on the coasts north of Trondhjem and on the Lofotens.

The delineations deduced by cartographers from such hearsay and verbal information betray the nature of their sources, and justify animadversions like that of E. T. Hamy on Carignano's world map, in which "la Scandinavie, prise à quelque source nautique, allonge dans le haut de

61. A good summary of the matters discussed in this paragraph is given by T. Fischer, *Sammlung,* pp. 33–55. See also Nansen, ch. xiii; H. Winter, "The changing face of Scandinavia and the Baltic in cartography up to 1532", *Imago Mundi,* Vol. 12 (1955), pp. 45–54.

62. A. W. Lang, "Traces of lost North European sea charts of the 15th century", *Imago Mundi,* Vol. 12 (1955), pp. 31–44; Dr. Lang, however, does not claim that there were any native charts of northern waters before the second half of the fifteenth century.

63. E. T. Hamy, "Les origines de la cartographie de l'Europe septentrionale", in *Études historiques et géographiques* (1896), p. 22; Nansen, Vol. 2, pp. 222–25; T. Fischer, p. 36; Winter, pp. 45–46.

64. See above, p. 116.

la carte d'excentriques digitations".[65] Even in a special chart of the Baltic coasts, such as the sixth chart of Bianco's atlas of 1436, or in the much more mature representation by Fra Mauro, coastal outlines are formal and generalized, names are transposed or misplaced, and there are considerable errors in the orientation, relative position, and latitude of hydrographic features. Such defects are common in cartographic representations derived from textual or oral information; and even if this included, for the delineation of the North, sailing directions of northern origin or merchants' guidebooks such as the Bruges Itinerary, which might perhaps be picked up in the markets of Flanders, these could add no further or more exact data than distances and perhaps bearings between places.[66] Whether there was any indigenous cartography of northern waters is a question which will be considered later, as will be the contribution made by Claudius Clavus, in the second quarter of the fifteenth century, to the image and map of the North.[67]

We will begin with the British Isles, taking as a basis for comparative study the analysis of M. C. Andrews.[68] The outline of Ireland in Bianco's atlas (in the separate charts as in the world map), with greater extension E–W than N–S, is extremely defective, and most nearly resembles that in the earlier work of Petrus Vesconte (Andrews, type Ia), although nearly contemporary charts by Perrinus Vesconte (type Ib), with a better outline and richer nomenclature, indicate that "Irish seaports and harbours were well-known at this period [the early fourteenth century] to navigators of the Mediterranean".[69] Bianco's model for Ireland is followed in the Vinland Map, in which (as in Bianco's world map, but not in his detailed charts) it lies within the same latitudes as Scotland; this error plainly springs from the reduction in N–S length which England and Scotland have suffered (in Bianco's representation) when transferred from a chart on a larger scale to a map on a smaller.[70]

The representation of England and Scotland in the Vinland Map has little affinity with Bianco's or indeed with any of the types identified by Andrews in the portolan charts, and can be paralleled, from southern sources, only in a later map of quite different character and construction.[71] The erroneous representation of the west coasts of Wales, England, and Scotland, which, to the north of the Bristol Channel, were unfrequented by Italian shipping even in the mid-fifteenth century, is not unusual (cf. Andrews, types I–III); but we should not expect to find the Thames estuary, which was well-known to the Italian seamen, so inconspicuously drawn, nor the east coasts of England and Scotland, of which they had only a vague knowledge,

65. Hamy, p. 25.

66. On sailing directions, see below, pp. 168–70. The Bruges Itinerary has been published by Lelewel, *Géographie du moyen-âge*, Épilogue (1852), pp. 285–308; and by Hamy, in *Le Livre de la Description des Pays de Gilles Le Bouvier* (1908), pp. 157–216. Lelewel ascribed it to *ca.* 1380, Hamy merely to the fifteenth century; the use of it by Claudius Clavus, demonstrated by Storm and by Björnbo and Petersen (p. 162), suggests that it, or its content, must have been in existence before 1424.

67. See below, pp. 176–77.

68. "The British Isles in the nautical charts of the 14th and 15th centuries", *Geogr. Journal*, Vol. 68 (1926), pp. 474–80. Mr. Andrews's collection of photocopies illustrating the evolution of the map of the British Isles is in the possession of the Royal Geographical Society, London.

69. Andrews, p. 476. See also T. J. Westropp, "Early Italian maps of Ireland from 1300 to 1600, with notes on foreign settlers and trade", *Proc. Royal Irish Academy*, Vol. 30 (1912), pp. 361–428.

70. See below, p. 164.

71. See above, p. 117.

delineated in so much detail.[72] These considerations, together with our estimate of the cartographer's methods, dictate caution in ascribing the design of Great Britain in the Vinland Map to a different—and perhaps northern—prototype, rather than to haphazard copying or adaptation by its compiler. The misplacing of the Isle of Wight and the conventional drawing of the coasts on the other side of the North Sea point in the same direction. Common also to the design in Bianco's world map (but not his other charts) and to that in the Vinland Map is the gross underestimate of the length (north–south) of Great Britain, the northernmost point of which is laid down in the latitude of southern Denmark, instead of that of southern Norway.

In the delineation of the west coasts of Flanders, Holland, and Denmark, from the Scheldt to Cape Skagen, and in that of the Baltic coasts, the author of the Vinland Map (as we have seen) closely follows the pattern of Bianco's world map, although he has drawn the Baltic, like the Mediterranean and the rest of Europe, with a much greater west–east extension than is justified by the proportions of his map. Bianco, both in his world map and in the special charts of his atlas, here adopted a model established over a century earlier in the charts of Dalorto (1325) and Dulcert (1339). In these, and in later charts of the fourteenth century, we find all the principal features of Bianco's design: the sacklike shape of the sea, oriented east–west and narrowing in the center, with no trace of the Gulfs of Bothnia, Riga, and Finland; two large islands (Sjælland and Gotland) at the mouth and the head of the sea; a marked indentation (Lubeck Bay) on the south, and another on the north, into which flows a river, with a lake (*lacus starse* in Bianco's sixth chart) in its middle course, the river being identifiable as the Gota Älv from the name *scarsa* or variants (= Skara) placed here by the fourteenth-century cartographers.[73] All these features, with the exception of the river and lake, reappear in the Vinland Map.

For Scandinavia—or rather southern Scandinavia, since no more is represented in detail— the model followed in Bianco's world map and in the Vinland Map is no less traditional, although a curious variant is introduced in each.[74] The great peninsula reaching westward into the longitude of the west coast of Great Britain, common to both cartographers (cf. Pls. VI, X, XI), first appears in the fourteenth-century charts of Carignano, Dalorto, and Dulcert; in the sixth and seventh charts of Bianco's atlas it does not extend quite so far to the west. Its curved (or retroussé) outline on the north coast, in Bianco's world map, may be residual from a feature which is more marked in some earlier maps, such as those of Petrus Vesconte, and probably derived from the thirteenth-century concept of a gulf of the northern ocean cutting into the Scandinavian coast and forming "a little piece of continent, which looks out upon the sea washing it on both sides".[75] The outline in the Vinland Map suggests this image more vividly than does that in Bianco's world map; but (as we shall see) another origin for it is more probable.

---

72. Cf. Andrews, pp. 476–79.

73. This route, by Lake Vänern, carried an important inland trade. See Nansen, Vol. 2, pp. 226–36; Björnbo and Petersen, p. 123; Winter, pp. 45–46. Nordenskiöld (*Facsimile Atlas,* pp. 54–55), while pointing to a "common prototype" for the representation of the Baltic in the early charts, instances details, like the sketch of a reindeer in the Catalan chart at Florence, which have "the appearance of having been drawn by a Scandinavian, or by a foreigner who had visited the Scandinavian countries"; see above, pp. 161–62.

74. The only elements traceable to experience or firsthand information in Bianco's chart of the Baltic are a legend descriptive of Norway, some names in Norway and Sweden, and the word *stocfis* in the approximate position of the Lofotens (T. Fischer, *Sammlung,* pp. 52–53); all this may have come from Querini (see above, p. 161).

75. Saxo Grammaticus, cited by Nansen, Vol. 2, p. 223.

In each of the maps in Bianco's atlas which take in Scandinavia, namely the world map, the sixth chart (of the Baltic) and the seventh chart (of Europe), the southwestern coast of the peninsula is drawn in the same form, with a series of bays or indentations from the Skagerrak to the northwest promontory; but all three maps differ in their representation of the Norwegian Sea and the islands to west and south. In the seventh chart (Pl. X), Scotland extends north to the latitude of southern Norway; in a bay of its west coast is a large circular island (the *Tile* of fourteenth-century cartography; Andrews, type III), and to the north there is another large island elliptical in shape, bearing the name *Stilanda* and corresponding to the island laid down with the same outline and position (v.l. *Stillanda, Estilanda*) in Catalan charts of the fourteenth and fifteenth centuries.[76] The sixth chart (Pl. IX) includes none of the British coasts, but has Tile in the same shape and position as in the seventh chart and with the legend *tile est lochus inabitabilis* . . . ; facing the western coast of Scandinavia are two sections of coastline of which the remainder is cut off by the border, the lower one being the eastern tip of Stilanda (and so named), the upper one—facing *nidroxia* (= Trondhjem)—with the names y^a *Rouercha* and *stocfis*. In the general map (which names none of the islands), Tile is in its place off Scotland, Stilanda has disappeared, and the two fragments of land shown to the west of Scandinavia in the sixth chart are run together to form the east coast of a large island, unnamed and irregularly oblong in shape, with its longer axis N–S.

This feature, which occurs in no earlier map and does not seem to have caught the eye of any commentator,[77] is of some interest, not the less as the three maps by Bianco give alternative, if not progressive, renderings of the geography of this section. In the first place, the large island introduced in Bianco's world map (and partially in his seventh chart) accounts for the delineation in the Vinland Map, whose author (whether deliberately or inadvertently, we cannot say) seems to have transformed the island of his Bianco-type model into a peninsula, by drawing an isthmus to close the south end of the strait; in all other respects the outlines are practically identical. Secondly, we have to consider whence Bianco derived this representation and what he supposed it to indicate. Is he interpreting in cartographic terms a geographical text such as that cited above from Saxo? and if so, has the compiler of the Vinland Map corrected Bianco by reference to the original authority? Or has Bianco borrowed the outline of the island from some other map, in which it was perhaps drawn in a different place, at the same time suppressing "Stilanda" (found in his separate charts, after a regular convention, but not in his world map, nor in the Vinland Map) as a duplication? Does it in fact represent his concept of Ptolemy's Thule or Iceland?

From the time of the union with Norway, in 1263, the Icelandic trade had been largely restricted to Bergen, but during the fourteenth and fifteenth centuries it came to be increasingly drawn into the orbit of European commerce, as communications with Norway declined. The

---

76. Cf., for instance, the Catalan Atlas of 1375 and the Catalan charts in the Biblioteca Estense, Modena (Pl. XI), the Biblioteca Nazionale, Florence (reproduced by Nansen, Vol. 2, pp. 232–33) and the Biblioteca Nazionale, Naples (reproduced by Björnbo and Petersen, *Anecdota Cartographica Septentrionalia* [1908], pl. I). See also above, p. 128, and Pls. IX–XII.

77. It is not mentioned by Peschel, T. Fischer, Nordenskiöld, Björnbo, Kretschmer, Nansen, or other writers who refer to Bianco's atlas of 1436. Nordenskiöld does, however, take the names y^a *Rouercha, stocfis* and *Stilanda* in the sixth chart to be evidence "that Greenland and Iceland were vaguely known to the mariners from whose reports the map was compiled" (*Facsimile Atlas*, p. 53).

first two decades of the fifteenth century produce evidence of voyages from the east coast ports of England; Bristol entered the trade a little later (*ca.* 1425) and was to become the principal English vent for Icelandic goods.[78] The *Libelle of Englyshe Polycye,* written about 1436 and first printed by Richard Hakluyt, describes the traffic:

> Of Island to write is little nede,
> Save of stock-fish: Yet forsooth in deed
> Out of Bristowe, and costes many one,
> Men have practised by nedle and by stone
> Thider wardes within a litle while,
> Within twelve yere, and without perill
> Gon and come, as men were wont of old
> Of Scarborough unto the costes cold.

At about this time the Hanse merchants also began to deal in Icelandic goods, and Gilles Le Bouvier (writing about 1450) refers to the Icelanders' trade with Flanders, especially in "stocphis", mutton, wool, and salmon.[79] The Bruges Itinerary, compiled for the use of merchants at an uncertain date but doubtless earlier than this, gives the stages Bergen–Iceland and Iceland–Greenland.[80]

Thus, even if there was no direct traffic between Mediterranean seaports and Iceland,[81] southern geographers did not lack opportunities for gleaning information about Iceland in the fifteenth century, and perhaps even earlier. That this was little but hearsay or rumor is indicated by the uncertainty and variety of the delineations found in the maps, principally those of Catalan authorship, and by the conflicting views regarding its location. In the Middle Ages it was identified with the classical Thule (as by Adam of Bremen, eleventh century: *Thyle nunc Island*), and this misled academic geographers into placing it too far north, under the Arctic Circle.[82] The island of Stilanda, laid down (as noted above) to the north of Scotland by Catalan mapmakers from the second quarter of the fourteenth century, doubtless originally represented the Shetlands, since the legend accompanying it in the earliest charts refers to the Norwegian speech and Christianity of the inhabitants.[83] It is nonetheless apparent that, as the existence of Iceland became vaguely known to the mapmakers, they tended to confuse it with Stilanda (Shetland), partly no doubt because of the similarity of nomenclature.[84] Thus Bianco's omis-

---

78. See E. M. Carus-Wilson, "The Iceland trade", in *English Merchant Venturers* (1954), ch. ii; G. J. Marcus, "The first English voyages to Iceland", *The Mariner's Mirror,* Vol. 42 (1956), pp. 313–18.

79. *Le Livre ... de Gilles Le Bouvier,* ed. Hamy (1908), p. 104.

80. See above, n. 66; and below, p. 171. It must be observed that the length of these stages, as given in the Itinerary, is erroneous.

81. If (as now seems probable) we are to accept Columbus' story that he visited Iceland in 1477, he doubtless did so in a Bristol ship: "to this island ... come English with their merchandise, especially they of Bristol". See H. Hermannsson, *The Cartography of Iceland* (1931), p. 16; S. E. Morison, *Admiral of the Ocean Sea* (1942), pp. 24–25.

82. Cf. below, p. 172.

83. Björnbo and Petersen, *Anecdota,* table on p. 16.

84. Cf. the variant forms in the table cited in the preceding note. The onomastic muddle prevailed all through fifteenth-century cartography: Fra Mauro has *Isola Islandia* (= Sjælland), *Ixilanda* (NW of Great Britain), *Isola di giaza* (NW of Norway), and a chart of 1497 by Conte Freducci has *Isola di Issilanda*. See Hermannsson, *Cartography,* ch. i. Perhaps there was also an association with Ptolemy's Thule (Tile—Stilanda) shown in his maps to the north

sion of the elliptical Stilanda from the world map, in which he has inserted the large island off Scandinavia, would have some significance if he equated Stilanda with Thule or Iceland.

Two different cartographic renderings of Iceland emerged. In a couple of Catalan maps, probably of the first half of the fifteenth century, both of which have the elliptical Stilanda, a group of islands is conventionally drawn to the northwest, near the edge of the vellum, with names which include *islanda* and *islandes*. This representation must rest on some traveler's report, such as that of Gilles Le Bouvier: "Puis y est l'isle de Yslande qui vaut autant à dire en alemant comme pais d'ysles".[85] It also perhaps throws a little light on the mind of the scribe who wrote down *Isolanda* as the name for Iceland in the Vinland Map; and the name suggests that this scribe was Italian of speech, if he was not copying or compiling from an Italian original.[86]

In the other interpretation of Iceland by the mapmakers we find for the first time some indication of firsthand experience. First faintly adumbrated in the shape given to *Sillant* in a chart of the Laurentian Atlas (1351),[87] it appears in mature form in one Catalan chart (that of the Biblioteca Ambrosiana, Milan) and in one Genoese chart (in the Bibliothèque Nationale, Paris), both undated but of the fifteenth century.[88] The Milan chart (Pl. XII) gives Iceland a markedly particularized outline, as a rough rectangle, with the longer axis east–west, much indented, and with the west coast divided into three peninsulas by deep bays; it has the general name *Fixlanda* and twenty-five local names along the coasts. In the Paris chart, Iceland is drawn with the same shape and the legend "Hec insula pprio uocabulo dicitur islanda latine nūcupatur thile"; to the south of this, another island with the name *Frixlanda,* drawn much smaller but with similar outlines, apparently duplicates the representation of Iceland.

The affinity between this design for Iceland and that in the Vinland Map is unmistakable; the latter only diverges in the outline of the west coast, where but one (the northernmost) of the three peninsulas is shown, and in the location of the island, which is placed in correct relationship with the British Isles and southern Norway, whereas in the Milan map it lies west of Ireland. That the *Sillant* of the Laurentian Atlas and the large island off Norway in Bianco's world map belong to the same type or family is not out of the question, for there is a general similarity of outline (though not of orientation).

While this model for Iceland was to have a long life in the next century, in manuscript charts of the Majorcan school and also (through the Zeno map) in printed cartography, its antiquity and sources are unknown. In Hermannsson's view, "the contours [of the Milan chart] . . . leave no doubt that this type owes its origin to some person or persons who were fairly well acquainted with Iceland from personal experience, and we doubtless owe it to some traders or fishermen, but of what nationality it is not possible to determine"; and he draws attention to the English

---

of Scotland; in the maps of Claudius Clavus (1424–30), Thule was in fact incorporated into southwestern Norway (Nansen, Vol. 2, 257–58), although by a process and in a form which preclude the possibility of borrowing by Bianco from Clavus.

85. *Le Livre . . . de Gilles Le Bouvier,* p. 104. The two charts here referred to are those in the Biblioteca Nazionale, Florence, and in the Biblioteca Estense, Modena; see Nansen, Vol. 2, pp. 231–33, and above, n. 76.

86. See above, pp. 138–39.

87. Also, in generalized form, in the world map of the Atlas.

88. The first is reproduced by Nansen, Vol. 2, p. 280; the second by Nordenskiöld, *Bidrag,* pl. 6, and by C. de la Roncière, *La Carte de Christophe Colomb* (1924).

aspect of the names *Fixlanda* and *Porlanda*.[89] Nansen, declaring the outline of Iceland on this chart to be "incomparably better than on all previous maps", goes further in suggesting that, "as the place-names point to an English source, it is possible that the cartographer may have received information from Bristol, which city was engaged in the Iceland trade and fisheries".[90] The precise detail of the drawing in the Milan chart strongly suggests that the "information" which had come into the cartographer's hands was a map, not a text or verbal report. If an Italian seaman and chartmaker could find his way to Iceland in 1477,[91] could not another have done so, by a like route, earlier in the century?

The excellence of the southern prototype thus established for Iceland, and followed in the Vinland Map, is in notable contrast with the poverty of the "minimal" contribution made to Icelandic cartography, in the fifteenth century, by academic geographers of the north, such as Claudius Clavus, whose earlier map (1424–27) "indicates hardly any knowledge about Iceland" and whose later map (*ca.* 1430) merely reproduces the *Sillant* of the Laurentian Atlas, adding however—perhaps as a scholastic joke!—twenty-two fictitious names derived from those of the runic characters.[92] The model used in the Vinland Map and in the two other fifteenth-century charts which reproduce it may now be held to have originated before about 1440, and perhaps (if we admit the rather slender evidence of Bianco's world map and the Laurentian Atlas) before the middle of the previous century.

NORSE NAVIGATIONS AND THE VINLAND MAP

For the representation of the North in the Vinland Map, or rather for those parts of it so far examined, we have been able without much difficulty to find analogues in southern cartography. These may—indeed, insofar as they are founded on experience, must—have been derived from reports or descriptions or drawings originating in the north, although whether furnished by natives of the southern countries or by Scandinavians we do not know. Among the materials for the cartography of the north and northwest which Nordenskiöld supposed to have existed in Italy at the end of the fourteenth and beginning of the fifteenth century, besides the portolan charts and the maps of Ptolemy and Claudius Clavus, he postulates "a [lost] map of the Scandinavian peninsula, Iceland, and Greenland, composed ere the northern mariners became acquainted with the use of the compass, perhaps in the beginning of the thirteenth century".[93] That such a map, of Scandinavian origin, may have existed is not at all improbable, even if the premisses of Nordenskiöld's hypothesis have been discountenanced by later research.[94] The discovery of the Vinland Map forces us to take this possibility seriously into account, more especially as the map, besides showing Greenland in a form not paralleled in fifteenth-century

89. Hermannsson, *Cartography,* p. 12, suggesting equivalence with "Fishland" and "Portland".

90. Nansen, Vol. 2, p. 279, pointing out that the author of the Milan chart also apparently had information on Greenland.

91. As Columbus may have done (see above, n. 81). The Milan chart is usually dated fairly late in the century, as by Björnbo who ascribes it to *ca.* 1480–1500 (*Cartographia Groenlandica,* pp. 124–25).

92. See Hermannsson, *Cartography,* pp. 19–21. The epithet "minimal" is Hermannsson's.

93. *Facsimile Atlas,* p. 58.

94. That of Björnbo and Petersen, principally their discovery of the Vienna MS of Clavus' later description of the North, and their analysis of the representations derived by Donnus Nicolaus and Henricus Martellus from Clavus' work.

cartography, also takes in Vinland, on which all records from southern Europe are silent after the first quarter of the twelfth century. It is therefore relevant to consider briefly what knowledge was possessed, and what beliefs prevailed, in Northern Europe at the beginning of the fifteenth century about the north and northwest parts of the world.[95] A distinction must be made between observations founded on experience and the geographical concepts formulated by scholars.

The oceanic navigation of the Norsemen in the Viking period ranged from the White Sea to Southwest Europe and from the Baltic to the coasts of North America. Before the end of the ninth century they were in Iceland (whither Irish monks had preceded them by about a hundred years), and Óttarr had sailed north and east into the White Sea; Greenland was settled soon after A.D. 980, and the American coast probably sighted a few years later; the first three decades of the eleventh century saw the voyages for the discovery (and perhaps settlement) of Helluland, Markland, and Vinland; in 1194 Spitzbergen was perhaps discovered. Although no passage to Vinland is certainly recorded after the first quarter of the twelfth century and none to Markland after 1347, the traffic to Iceland was uninterrupted from the first colonization, and that to Greenland, although in decline during the fourteenth century, was still intermittently maintained in the fifteenth. "The *regularity* of this oceanic navigation was one of its most impressive aspects",[96] and it is the more remarkable in that these great ocean passages were made and remade by the Norse seamen without quadrant or astrolabe, without magnetic compass, and without sea-charts.

The rutters of the westerly voyages, embodied in the Icelandic sagas and annals, and the sailing directions which were written down from the thirteenth century onward illustrate both the navigation methods of the Norsemen and their views on the geographical relationship between the lands they visited. From point of departure to point of arrival the distance is stated in days' sailing,[97] and the course as a bearing given, as one of the eight "airts" or divisions of the horizon. Since most of the sea routes lay due east or due west, course could be kept by "running down the parallel".[98] This implies ability to determine latitude by observation of the meridian sun; and although the precise method remains uncertain, a great number of such observations by the Norsemen during the Middle Ages are recorded.[99] As Dr. Marcus notes, these "covered a wide range of latitudes, e.g. somewhere south of lat. 40° N. in Vinland (North America) about A.D. 1000; Flatey Island, off the north coast of Iceland (lat. 66° 10′ N.) in *c.* 1140; on the banks

95. On this, see generally Björnbo and Petersen, pp. 183–94; Nansen, ch. xiii.

96. G. J. Marcus, "The navigation of the Norsemen", *The Mariner's Mirror*, Vol. 39 (1953), pp. 112–31. The summary here is mainly based on Dr. Marcus' excellent study, which gives full bibliographical references. See also E. G. R. Taylor, *The Haven-Finding Art* (1956), ch. 4.

97. A *dægr-sigling* "sometimes covered twelve and sometimes twenty-four hours" (Marcus, p. 119). W. Hovgaard (*The Voyages of the Norsemen to America* [1914], p. 63) reckons "a day's sail as about 75 miles for a *dægr* of twelve hours, and 150 miles for a *dægr* of twenty-four hours". G. M. Gathorne-Hardy (*The Norse Discoverers of America* [1921], p. 196–99) reaches the same result by a different argument.

98. Marcus, pp. 124–25; also, "The early Norse traffic to Iceland", *The Mariner's Mirror*, Vol. 46 (1960), pp. 179–80.

99. These presuppose not merely knowledge (which the Norsemen certainly had) of the length of the day in different latitudes, but also their use (which is less securely established) of some instrument such as a "swimming gnomon" or a "sunboard". On the former, see H. Winter, "Die Erkenntnis der magnetischen Missweisung", *Comptes rendus du Congr. Int. de Géographie* (1938), p. 63, and Marcus, "The navigation of the Norsemen", p. 126; on the latter, Marcus, p. 124.

of the Jordan (lat. 32° N.) in 1150; in Baffin's Bay (lat. 74° N.) in 1267."[100] Here is a historical fact not irrelevant (for instance) to the problem of accounting for the correctness of outline with which Greenland is drawn in the Vinland Map.

In this navigation neither compass nor chart was needed, nor in fact used.[101] As late as the fifteenth century, it was believed in southern Europe that these regular tools of Mediterranean seamen were unknown to those of the North, whether in oceanic or enclosed waters. Thus Prince Henry of Portugal, in 1434, referred to "the opinion of four sailors who, coming from the Flanders voyage or from some other ports . . . are unacquainted with the needle or the sea-chart";[102] and Fra Mauro's map of 1457 has, written in the Baltic, the legend "per questo mar non se navega cum carta ni bossola, ma cum scandaio" (in this sea they do not navigate with chart or compass, but only with the lead). Yet before 1400 there is documentary evidence of compass-making in Germany and the Netherlands; by the middle of the fifteenth century compasses were included in inventories of Hanse ships; and, as the *Libelle* of 1436 shows, they were by this date in use on the English navigation to Iceland.[103] But the Norse seaman on the longer Atlantic passages, who was unaware of magnetic variation, could not have obtained as good determinations of position by the compass (even if he had had it) as he did by other methods. As Dr. Marcus points out, the thirteenth-century sailing directions correctly placed Bergen and Hvarf (in southern Greenland) in about the same latitude, and "the relative position of these two places, separated by a distance of so many hundreds of miles, must have been determined, not magnetically, but by astronomical observation".[104] It must be added that these "latitudes" were only relative, probably recorded empirically on the shadow-instrument used, and not expressed in quantitative terms, by conversion into degrees.[105]

For northern waters sailing directions were not to be supplemented by indigenous charts before the end of the fifteenth century. That they are of much greater antiquity is shown by Óttarr's rutter of his White Sea voyage about 880 and by the fragmentary rutter from northwest Germany to Acre written down by Adam of Bremen in the eleventh century or by one of his scholiasts. The Norse sailing directions, which supplied the want of charts, were compiled from dead reckoning and observations of relative latitude; and they furnished precise data on the relative position of, and distance between, the lands or islands of the Norwegian Sea and North Atlantic. The course for Iceland was seven days' sail due west from Cape Stad, the westernmost point of Norway, to Cape Horn, the southeastern point of Iceland; the actual distance is about 560 miles. From Langenes, in the north of Iceland, to Svalbardi (Spitzbergen or Jan Mayen?), four days' sail northward (in fact about 290 miles); from Reykjanes, in the south of Iceland, five days' sail to "Jolduhlaup" in Ireland (perhaps Olderfleet near Larne, i.e.

---

100. Marcus, p. 122.

101. On this, the argument *ex silentio* is agreed by most students to have force.

102. Zurara, *Crónica de Guiné*, cap. ix.

103. W. Vogel, "Die Einführung des Kompasses in der nordwest-europäischen Nautik", *Hänsische Geschichtsblätter* (1911), pp. 1–32; A. W. Lang, "Traces of lost North European sea charts", pp. 35–36; G. J. Marcus, "The mariner's compass in Northern Europe", *The Mariner's Mirror*, Vol. 41 (1955), p. 69. For the *Libelle*, see above, p. 165.

104. Marcus, "The navigation of the Norsemen", p. 124. Dr. Marcus rightly comments that "if one were to steer due west (magnetic) from Hernum to Hvarf to-day, one would certainly never arrive at Hvarf".

105. Marcus, p. 126.

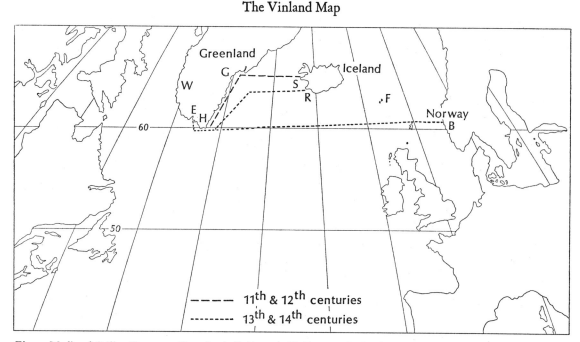

Fig. 4. Medieval Sailing-Routes to Greenland: B. Bergen; F. Faeroes; R. Reykjarnes; S. Snæfellsnes; G. Gunnbjörn's Skerries; H. Hvarf; E. East Settlement; W. West Settlement.

about 750 miles); from Sjæfellsnes, in the west of Iceland, to the nearest point of Greenland, four days' sail westward (in fact 330 miles). These data are given in a thirteenth-century re-cension of the Icelandic *Landnámabók,* the writer of which was "evidently trying to fix the position of Iceland by reference to well-known points on all sides of it".[106] He here describes the old course from Iceland to Greenland; by the fourteenth century the southward encroach-ment of ice had imposed a new course, laid down by Ivar Bardsson (*ca.* 1342) as a day and a night due west, then slightly southwest to avoid the ice, and a day and a night northwest to Hvarf, just north of Cape Farewell in South Greenland. By the end of the thirteenth century, there were already sailing directions for the direct course from Norway to Greenland; this ran from Hernum (near Bergen) in Norway due west to Hvarf in Greenland, passing north of Shetland and south of the Faeroes, but with both in sight above the horizon.[107]

For the location of the lands to the west and southwest of Greenland there are only the frag-mentary and sometimes conflicting indications of bearing and distance sailed given in the sagas; these will be considered in more detail in a later chapter. Here it will be enough to say that they point to Helluland lying some five days' sail west or southwest of southern Greenland, with Markland and Vinland further south; whether the three lands were thought to be connected or disjunct is uncertain.

106. Gathorne-Hardy, p. 201. See also Björnbo and Petersen, pp. 184–85; Hovgaard, pp. 61–64.

107. On the deterioration of climate and ice conditions which dictated the change in the sailing routes, see O. Pet-tersson, "Climatic variations in historic and prehistoric time", *Svenska Hydrografisk Biologiska Kommissionens Skrifter,* Vol. 5 (1914), pp. 7–15; also L. Koch, "The East Greenland Ice", *Med. om Grönl.,* Vol. 130 (1945). See also below, pp. 185–86, and Fig. 4.

If, to these data on the relative location of the lands visited or frequented by the Norsemen, we add their observations of the trend and features of the coastline on their traverses of Iceland, of the southern half of Greenland and east coast of Davis Strait, and of Helluland, Markland, and Vinland,[108] we have the materials for a recognizable map of the North Atlantic. That such a map could have been made is of course not to say that it *was* made or that it reached southern Europe; as we shall see, the materials for it were apparently unknown to Claudius Clavus.[109]

That the delineation in the northwest part of the Vinland Map does not, as a whole, correspond to the general picture of the North Atlantic evoked by the Norse sailing directions may well be due to the defects in the cartographer's delineation of northwestern Europe, the point of departure for the westward voyages; there may also be contributory influences in the academic geography of the North and in the pattern of the map and the space at the draftsman's disposal. In spite of this, the relative disposition of lands in the Vinland Map strongly suggests a series of courses by latitude sailing, in agreement with those described in the sailing directions. Although Iceland is laid down a little too far north, its southernmost point lies on an east–west rhumb from the westernmost point of Norway. Greenland is placed a little too far south; if it be moved slightly north, its most easterly point would be in about the same latitude as the westernmost point of Iceland, and Cape Farewell would lie due west from a point (Bergen?) in southwestern Norway. Even without this adjustment, the map indicates a due westerly course laid between the two islands (presumably the Shetlands and Faeroes) northwest of Great Britain and so across to Cape Farewell.

"Vinlanda" extends further north than the bearings and courses recorded in the sagas seem to justify; but we have to remember that, unlike the passages to Iceland and Greenland which had been in continuous use for hundreds of years and were still being made in the fifteenth century, there had been no regular voyages to Vinland since about 1030, and that, instead of codified sailing directions derived from cumulated knowledge, the route was recorded only in the intermittent data logged in the saga accounts of a few voyages. Moreover, in a geographical tradition of northern Europe, Vinland came to be located among the mist and ice of the Northern Ocean, in Arctic latitudes.

It is not easy to detect much agreement between the longitudinal intervals between lands, as shown in the Vinland Map, and the distance in days' sailing prescribed in the Norse sailing directions. Recalling that, in the map, the terminal peninsula of Scandinavia is probably a fictitious feature, we may note that, if it were omitted, the east-west distances from Norway to Iceland and from Iceland to Greenland would be about equal; this accords with the equal stages of the Bruges Itinerary, which gives 280 Flemish miles (= about 750 statute miles) for both Bergen–Iceland and Iceland–Greenland.[110] Generally, the longitudinal intervals between lands, as shown in the Vinland Map, seem to increase with latitude, as they would in a plane chart which took no account of the convergence of meridians; but we cannot attach any significance to this. The position in which Vinland is laid down by the cartographer, in relation to the Norse settlements in southwest Greenland, is not precisely consonant with the courses attributed, in the long legend

108. See below, chs. 7, 8.
109. See below, pp. 176–77.
110. See above, pp. 162, 165.

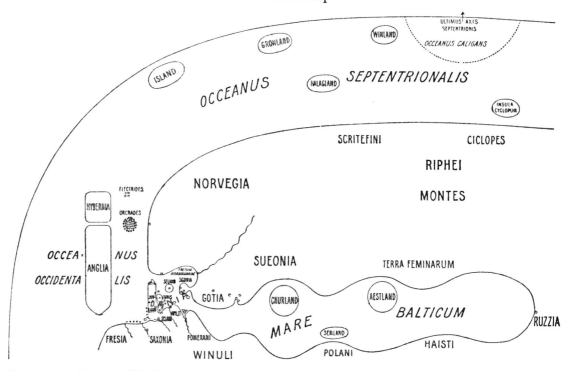

Fig. 5. Adam of Bremen's World Map Reconstructed. After A. A. Björnbo, *Cartographia Groenlandica.*

of the Vinland Map, to the voyages of Leif and Bjarni (who sailed "south" to Vinland) and of Bishop Eirik (who returned "northeast" from Vinland).

THE ATLANTIC LANDS AND THE MAPPAMUNDI

As geographers of the Scandinavian countries and northern Europe heard of the Norse discoveries in the north and west Atlantic, they assimilated them into the framework of the Latin world picture which they shared with the schoolmen of the south.[111] The facts observed and reported by the navigators were interpreted in the light of concepts derived from authority, tradition, and legendary lore. About 1070 Adam of Bremen wrote down the substance of what he had been told about Vinland by King Svein Estridsson of Denmark; and this earliest textual reference to Vinland is already colored by the cosmography of the schools. Within his pattern of the habitable world, as a circular disc surrounded by the outer ocean, Adam could not but conceive the new lands reported to him by Scandinavians, and recorded in his *Descriptio insularum aquilonis,* as islands in the ocean;[112] and he supposed Iceland to lie to the north of Norway, Greenland (facing the northern coasts of Sweden and Russia) further east, and Vinland still more to the east, under the North Pole.[113] This concept was (as we shall see) to linger on in

111. On this, see generally Björnbo and Petersen, pp. 187–91; Björnbo, *Cartographia Groenlandica,* chs. i, ii; Nansen, chs. v, xiii.

112. Cf. above, p. 152.

113. This is well illustrated in the map constructed by Björnbo from Adam's description of the North (*Cartographia Groenlandica,* p. 70; reproduced herewith, Fig. 5). Nansen (Vol. 1, pp. 201–02) thought that Björnbo had placed Vinland and the other islands too far north and had continued the north coast of Scandinavia too far west.

the geographical views held in southern Europe as late as the fifteenth century; incorporated in the tract entitled *Inventio Fortunata,* which described the northern voyage of an English Franciscan in 1360, it was adopted into Renaissance world maps; and so it passed, in the 16th century, into the main stream of European cartography.[114]

Adam's erroneous image of the Atlantic lands was not shared by Norse writers, in whose geographical literature Iceland, Greenland, and Vinland are invariably located in the western ocean.[115] They, too, sought to reconcile the new discoveries with preconceived ideas, whether those of northern tradition or those which formed the Latin mappamundi; and in this process they radically changed Isidore's world picture. The lands—or "islands"—discovered by the navigators were considered to lie within the outer ocean of medieval cosmography, and in Norse writings of the twelfth and thirteenth centuries they came to be associated with the land divisions of the tripartite world. Thus the author of the remarkable geographical work *Konungs skuggsjá* ("King's Mirror"), writing about 1250, thought Greenland to be "mainland, and connected with other mainland"; he supposed that there was no land "outside the circle of the world, beyond Greenland, only the great ocean which runs round the world; and it is said ... that the strait through which the empty ocean flows comes in by Greenland, and into the gap between the lands, and thereafter with fjords and gulfs it divides all countries, where it runs into the circle of the world". If "the lands" here represent (as is usually agreed) the American discoveries of the Norsemen, the text suggests that they lay to the south of Greenland, following the curve of the outer ocean. This concept is found more explicitly in the Icelandic Geography (composed perhaps in the middle of the twelfth century)[116] and it is repeated in other works by northern writers: "South of Greenland is Helluland, next to it is Markland, and then it is not far to Vinland the Good, which some think to be connected with Africa; and if this be so, then the outer ocean must fall in between Vinland and Markland".

The cartographic image evoked by these passages[117] is that of Vinland as a western horn of Africa, and Greenland as a similar horn of northern Eurasia arching to the west over a great gulf, with the islands of Helluland and Markland between, and divided by channels of the outer ocean. These channels (or "indrawing seas", as they are styled in the *Inventio Fortunata*) were identified by the Norsemen as Ginnungagap, the great abyss which in their mythology formed the bounds of the ocean and the world; and in seventeenth-century geographies and maps composed in Iceland, Ginnungagap was in fact located between Greenland and Vinland.[118]

The hypothesis that Greenland was a peninsula of Eurasia, connected to Bjarmeland (northern Russia), found support in observation of its animals, which "must have come from other places on the mainland"; in the discovery of land (perhaps Spitzbergen), to the north of Iceland at the end of the twelfth century; in knowledge of the Arctic pack-ice and in stories about

---

114. See below, pp. 179–82.

115. See the references above, n. 111; also J. Fischer, *The Discoveries of the Norsemen in America* (1903), ch. v.

116. It is not certain that the passage quoted was in the original text. Hermannsson (*The Problem of Wineland,* pp. 2–3) thought it "probably an interpolation of the fourteenth century"; cf. also Nansen, Vol. 2, p. 1.

117. See the reconstruction by Björnbo, *Cartographia Groenlandica,* p. 82, reproduced herewith, Fig. 6 (p. 174).

118. On Ginnungagap, see Nansen, Vol. 2, pp. 239–41, and references there cited. On the Arctic geography of the *Inventio Fortunata,* see below, pp. 179–82.

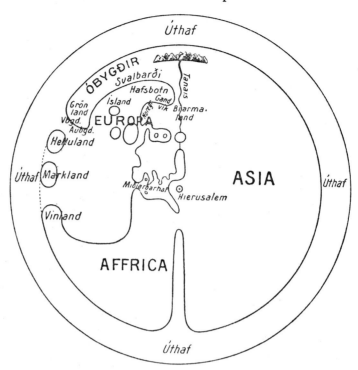

Fig. 6. The Norse World Map of the 12th–14th Centuries Reconstructed. After A. A. Björnbo, *Cartographia Groenlandica.*

travelers supposed to have gone on foot from Greenland to Norway.[119] In addition, the fact that Greenland was found to be partly inhabited, although its polar climate and ice cap suggested to the Norse geographers that it must lie in extreme northern latitudes, made a breach in the medieval belief in the uninhabitability of the cold zone of the earth; thus it could be held that the land bridge between Greenland and Eurasia was the habitat of a race akin to the native Skraelings (Eskimo) of Greenland. These people were styled Karelians[120] by northern geographers, and so in the Bruges Itinerary the stages Bergen–Iceland and Iceland–Greenland are followed by a statement that half a year's journey beyond Greenland are to be found the *Kareli.*[121]

Although this construction of the northwest parts of the world was to be introduced into southern cartography by a Danish geographer in the early fifteenth century, it is illustrated in no surviving map drawn in the Scandinavian countries before the turn of the sixteenth and seventeenth centuries, when the attempt to locate the lost Norse colonies in Greenland inspired a search of the Icelandic archives and the compilation of maps by Icelanders embodying the traditional Norse geography of the lands in the north and west Atlantic discovered, centuries

119. J. Fischer, pp. 56–57.

120. The name was transferred from the Karelians of Finland (Björnbo and Petersen, pp. 192–93).

121. "Groenland. Deinde usque Kareli". The author of the Itinerary (see above, p. 171) probably believed Iceland and Greenland to lie north of Scandinavia, toward the Pole. The note which he appends on the mountain *Iueghelberch* in the Karelian country points to a Scandinavian source for his information.

earlier, by their forebears. Only in these maps can we seek analogous representations, of northern origin and perhaps derived from much older prototypes, to those in the Vinland Map.[122]

TRANSMISSION TO SOUTHERN EUROPE

The available evidence both of texts and of maps suggests that in the Mediterranean cultural zone, where the Latin world picture originated, the northern geography exemplified in the views of Adam of Bremen not only held its own until the very end of the Middle Ages but even took on fresh vitality from the authority of the Renaissance mapmakers who derived their representation of the Arctic from the *Inventio Fortunata*.[123] As early as the twelfth century Adam's views were echoed by Ordericus Vitalis (1141): "Orcades insulae et Finlanda [Vinland], Islanda quoque et Grenlanda, ultra quam ad septentrionem terra non reperitur, aliaeque plures usque in Gollandam [Gotland] regi Noricorum subiciuntur". Three centuries later the references by ecclesiastical writers point the same way. Cardinal Fillastre, commenting in Rome about 1425 on "illas regiones que sunt ab Germania ad septentrionem versus orientem", enumerated the "sinum codanum [the Baltic] diuidens Germaniam a Nouergia et Suessia" and "alium sinum ultra ad septentrionem", and added: "Et ultra illum sinum est grolandia, que est versus insulam tyle magis ad orientem". A brief of Pope Nicholas V on the state of Greenland, addressed in 1448 to the Bishops in Iceland, speaks of the "insule Grenolandie, que in ultimis finibus oceani ad septentrionalem plagam Regni Norwegie . . . dicitur situata". That the concept was not unknown to the mapmakers is suggested by the Catalan chart at Florence (late fourteenth or early fifteenth century), in which the name *gronlandia* is by a *lapsus calami* written for *gotlandia* in the Baltic, and by the world map in Bianco's atlas of 1436, with its representation of Arctic lands in the north of Eurasia (*in* [*h*]*ac parte est masimū frigus . . .*) and delineation of skin-clad inhabitants living in forests.[124] It has been suggested, with somewhat less plausibility, that two names—*stocfis* and *y*ᵃ. *Rouercha*—in the map of Scandinavia in Bianco's atlas (sixth chart) point to knowledge of Iceland and Greenland.[125] At the very end of the century the Laon globe shows *Grôlandia* as an island to the north of Scandinavia; and Martin Behaim's globe of 1492 gives cartographic expression to the old Norse concept of islands under the Pole which he found in the *Inventio Fortunata*. This narrative of the Arctic voyage of an anonymous English Franciscan in 1360 was widely read in the later Middle Ages and Renaissance; so far as we can determine from the abstract made by Mercator in 1577 (the original being lost), it influenced geographical thought in central and southern Europe; and the known references to it are accordingly assembled in a note following this chapter.[126]

That information about the western lands discovered and partly settled by the Norsemen must have reached southern Europe is hardly to be doubted. There was regular communication between Rome and the episcopal sees of Iceland and Greenland: Scandinavian churchmen came to Rome and attended the ecumenical councils, and Papal legates went to Scandinavia; pilgrims

---

122. See Hermannsson. *Two Cartographers,* pp. 31–38; and below, pp. 199–208.

123. See generally J. Fischer, *Discoveries,* pp. 56–57; Björnbo and Petersen, pp. 191–92; Björnbo, *Cartographia Groenlandica,* ch. ii.

124. Björnbo, *Cartographia Groenlandica,* p. 124.

125. Nordenskiöld, *Facsimile Atlas,* p. 53; and see above, p. 164.

126. See below, pp. 179–82.

from the north visited Italy on their way to or from the Holy Land.[127] To such sources are no doubt to be ascribed the scraps of observation, such as references to polar bears, white falcons, reindeer, whaling, and fishing, which are found here and there in legends of the Italian and Catalan maps.[128] But the information obtained by the cartographers by such channels, so far as we can judge from their surviving work, did not bring to their notice the more correct Atlantic geography of the Icelanders, nor furnish them with materials for a map laying down Greenland in its true relationship to Iceland and northwest Europe, still less a map in which any land yet further west was shown. No such work by a southern mapmaker has been preserved.

Thus it was with the shock of novelty that Italians became aware, in the third decade of the fifteenth century, of the image of the Atlantic lands conceived by the Scandinavian geographers, who knew well that the Norse discoveries lay in the western, and not the northern, ocean. The intermediary was the Dane Claudius Clavus, who between 1424 (when he appears in Rome) and about 1430 compiled in Italy two descriptions of the North.[129] From the first, a map was drawn for inclusion in Cardinal Fillastre's manuscript copy of Ptolemy's *Geographia* (preserved at Nancy); the second account (preserved at Vienna) is accompanied by no map, but it—or its lost map—exercised (in Nansen's words) "a decisive influence on the representation of Scandinavia and to some extent of Greenland". It introduced into southern cartography the delineation of Greenland lying to the west of Ireland and forming a peninsula connected on the north to lands round the Pole.[130]

Clavus has the distinction of being the first to add a "modern" map to the Ptolemaic atlas and to apply the methods of quantitative map construction to contemporary geography; it is supposed that he learned these methods in Italy. It is, however, no longer possible, since Nansen's devastating criticism, to refer to Clavus' "marvelously correct delineation of Greenland",[131] nor to consider him a very competent representative of Scandinavian culture. His northern sources were extremely limited, and where they failed him he did not hesitate to invent. Above all, it is evident that he had with him in Italy no map of the North, and that (so far as we can judge) his knowledge of mapmaking was acquired after his arrival in Rome.

Whether Clavus himself drew the Nancy map and his lost later map (as reproduced in its derivatives), or whether they were drawn at his direction or from his description by an Italian cartographer, we do not know. It is certain that (as Nansen demonstrated) a considerably older

127. J. Fischer, pp. 101–04, gives details of this traffic. Most of the travelers whom he enumerates were ecclesiastics or pilgrims.

128. Cf. above, n. 73.

129. On Claudius Clavus, see J. Fischer, *Discoveries,* ch. v; Björnbo and Petersen, passim; Björnbo, *Cartographia Groenlandica,* ch. iii. Nansen (ch. xiii) successfully challenged the conclusions reached by these writers regarding the scope of Clavus' personal observations, the extent and character of the geographical sources used by him, his originality, and his status as a cartographer. It appears that Björnbo and Petersen "in all essentials" came round to Nansen's view (Nansen, Vol. 2, p. 255; cf. also the preface, written after Björnbo's death, to his *Cartographia Groenlandica,* p. xi); but they never recanted their earlier judgment in print. In my discussion of Clavus I have followed Nansen.

130. Clavus' description in the Vienna text reads: "Grolandie insule chersonesus dependet a terra inaccessibili a parte septentrionis uel ignota propter glaciem" (Björnbo and Petersen, p. 144). We may translate the first three words as "the peninsula, or [so-called] island of Greenland".

131. J. Fischer, p. 69.

Italian model, namely the representation of Scandinavia as drawn in the Laurentian Atlas of 1351, was adapted to serve as a cartographic illustration of Clavus' descriptive text on the northern regions. In both the world map and the chart of Europe in the Atlas, the extremity of Scandinavia is extended further westward than in other portolan charts; the westernmost peninsula of Norway (*aloga*), in the approximate longitude of the west coast of Ireland, is drawn with an outline, orientation, and features corresponding closely to those of Clavus' Greenland; and there are many other points of agreement both in design and in location.[132]

Thus, some years before the compilation of Bianco's atlas in Venice and of the Vinland Map (or its original draft) perhaps somewhere in southern Europe, Italian geographers had the materials for a map in which the lands of Norse discovery were to be found to the west—not to the north—of Scandinavia. These materials were, it is true, textual and not graphic, and Clavus in turn had derived them from textual sources: geographical descriptions, itineraries, perhaps sailing directions.[133] For "the first native cartographer of the North"[134] evidently brought no maps with him to Italy; nor is there any evidence that before his arrival in Rome in 1423–24 he had ever drawn a map, or seen a map drawn in northern Europe or by any other Scandinavian. Clavus' own maps were constructed on a recognizable projection and with graduation in latitude and longitude, after the new Ptolemaic manner, and they embodied geographical views which had been current in the Scandinavian countries since the twelfth or thirteenth century, but which had not previously found expression in the Mediterranean area. Yet the cartographic form into which Clavus or his draftsman cast this material was borrowed, as to geographical design and outline, from an Italian model at least three-quarters of a century older.[135]

In considering the antecedents of the Vinland Map, we therefore have good reason to leave out of account Clavus' maps and descriptions of the North. His maps show Greenland as a peninsula, not an island; its outline in them is that ascribed by the author of the Laurentian Atlas to the western peninsula of Norway, and no map in this atlas (which may be taken to represent Clavus' prototype) includes Greenland; Vinland was unknown to Clavus; finally, no elements from Clavus can be traced in Bianco's world map, in which the representation of the tripartite world is drawn after the same model as that in the Vinland Map. With the representation of the North derived from Clavus by later geographers—in the manuscript maps of Donnus Nicolaus (from 1466) and Henricus Martellus (*ca.* 1480–95), in printed cartography beginning with the Ulm Ptolemy of 1482 and overlapping the rediscovery of the North Atlantic by English and Portuguese—we are not concerned, for it is unmarked by any vestige of the representation of lands in the west of the Atlantic found in the Vinland Map.[136]

Here the Vinland Map stands in isolation outside the main stream of cartographic evolution. The still unidentified source whence its anonymous author drew his delineation of Greenland

---

132. See Nansen, Vol. 2, pp. 257–65, 272–75.

133. The more generous estimate of Clavus' sources made by Björnbo and Petersen, ch. viii, is cut down to measure by Nansen, Vol. 2, pp. 255–56, 265–76. Some of these sources were certainly northern; others (as Nansen points out) could have been consulted by Clavus in Rome.

134. The phrase is that of Björnbo and Petersen, *Anecdota*, p. 3.

135. Unless we suppose that in the prototype the westernmost peninsula in fact (as in Clavus) represented Greenland and that the author of the Laurentian Atlas erroneously identified it with the most westerly peninsula of Norway.

136. On these, see J. Fischer, ch. v; Björnbo and Petersen, ch. ii–v; Björnbo, *Cartographia Groenlandica*, ch. v; Nansen, ch. xiii. For a possible qualification of this judgment, see below, p. 199.

and Vinland was, at least until the end of the sixteenth century, tapped by no other mapmakers whose works have survived. Any attempt to trace it to its origin is the more speculative since we have, as point of departure, only one document—the map itself.

To limit the field of search, however, a few generalizations from the discussion in this chapter may be hazarded. The data from which Greenland and Vinland were drawn in the map were, at the time of its execution, unknown in southern Europe, and they remained unknown. From this curious fact we are entitled to make some inferences about the source of the map and about its subsequent history. The information on lands in the west can only have originated in the northern countries, most probably (as we shall see) in Iceland. By what intermediary did it find its way into the Vinland Map? In balancing the possible answers to this question, we must recall that only the surviving, or final, draft of the map is associated with the accompanying manuscript texts and to be ascribed therefore to the same date and place of execution. When, where, and by whom the presumed lost preliminary drafts were made, we cannot say. In regard to Greenland and Vinland, various alternative conjectures are open to us. The cartographer, if a southerner, may have received a document (text or map) from a Scandinavian source; if so, neither this document nor any analogous to it has yet come to light in the archives of northern or southern Europe. Or the cartographer received verbal information from a visiting Scandinavian, although the precision of the drawing in this part of the map seems to point to a graphic prototype. Or the cartographer who prepared or supplied the preliminary draft for the western part of the map was himself a native of northern Europe, seized of the authentic data on the Norse discoveries which reposed in Icelandic written records or orally conveyed tradition. The crossing of this representation, Scandinavian in origin, with a mappamundi of Italian character must surely have taken place at some meeting point of northern and southern culture. The period to which paleographical examination ascribes the execution (in their surviving form) of the Vinland Map and its associated texts is nearly spanned by the life of the Council of Basle (1431–49). The delegates who attended this Council came from northern and eastern, as well as southern, Europe; and they included churchmen from Italy, Low Germany, England, Denmark and Sweden (but not, apparently, from Norway or Iceland). In such a gathering, and among the large staff of secretaries employed by it, it is not difficult to envisage circumstances in which maps of Scandinavian and of Venetian origin or authorship may have come together under the eyes of a single scribe or into the possession—perhaps only temporary—of a single scriptorium.[137]

The weight to be given to alternative hypotheses on the source of the Atlantic section of the Vinland Map must be largely determined by our interpretation of the map itself. To the question why this representation remained without an imitator and in obscurity until its discovery

137. Lists of the delegates to the Council of Basle are printed by P. Lazarus, *Das Basler Konzil* (1912). On the impulse given by the Council to paper production and to the employment of scribes, see Paul Lehmann, "Konstanz und Basel als Büchermärkte während der grossen Kirchensammlungen", in *Erforschung des Mittelalters,* Vol. I (1941), pp. 270–80. Lehmann (pp. 270–71) refers to "das Vielschreiben und Viellesen, das Bücherbedürfnis, der Bücherhunger, die Sammellust" that prevailed at Basle during the Council; and he emphasizes the activity of Italians in searching out manuscripts, in dealing with "non-Italian connoisseurs from northern collections", and in acquiring "many an important codex in original or in copy". There is no difficulty in supposing that, perhaps by this channel, circular world maps of Italian origin (such as a version of Bianco 1436) could have reached Germanic lands. Such a map was in fact available in Austria, as shown by D. B. Durand, *The Vienna-Klosterneuburg Map Corpus* (1952), ch. xiii; and Durand (p. 69) notes that the astronomer and mathematician Johannes Keck, of the Benedictine house at Tegernsee, Bavaria, was present at the Council of Basle.

in the twentieth century, a less ambiguous answer may be ventured. Parallel cases can indeed be cited. The earlier map and description by Claudius Clavus were taken back to France by Cardinal Fillastre soon after the completion, in 1427, of the Ptolemy codex with which it was bound; they remained at Nancy until brought to light in 1835, and accordingly—unlike Clavus' second recension—they exercised no influence at all on cartography of the fifteenth century or later. Again, the *Inventio Fortunata,* one copy of which was in the fifteenth century in English ownership, has disappeared from sight since the third quarter of the sixteenth century, in spite of its extensive influence and the significance attached to it in that and the previous century. The Vinland Map, of which doubtless fewer copies existed than of the *Inventio,* might easily have suffered the same fate.

NOTE B. The *Inventio Fortunata*

The relationship of the northern land masses and the distribution of land and water in high latitudes were problems which engaged medieval geographers and which became of vital interest to those of the sixteenth century in connection with the search for northern passages to Cathay. This gives the lost tract *Inventio Fortunata*[138] its particular significance, since, although written by an Englishman, it was the principal vehicle by which the medieval Scandinavian view of the North was incorporated into European geographical ideas and cartography of the Renaissance.

Although the influence of the *Inventio* during the fifteenth century, e.g. in Clavus' descriptive texts and in the papal letter of 1448, was deduced by Nansen (who did not know the only extant summary of its contents), the earliest reference to it is made by the English merchant John Day, who in 1497 promised to send a copy of it to a correspondent in Spain, whom he addressed as "Almirante Mayor" and who may have been Christopher Columbus. It is next cited explicitly by Johan Ruysch as his authority for the representation of the Arctic in his world map printed at Rome in 1507. That the same delineation appears in the globe completed at Nuremberg in 1492 by or for Martin Behaim indicates (as Nansen inferred) that Behaim too had read the *Inventio.* It was known to Columbus' son Fernando, who cited it in his biography of his father (*Historie,* ch. ix; completed before his death in 1539); and the reference was repeated by Las Casas (*Historia de las Indias* [Bk. I, ch. xiii; written *ca.* 1527-61]). A copy of the *Inventio* came, as a loan, into the hands of an Antwerp friend of Mercator (perhaps Ortelius), but when "after many yeares" (probably in 1577) Mercator "required it again of my

138. The title is given in the earliest references as *Inventio Fortunatae* (John Day, Mercator, Dee), or *De Inventione Fortunatae* (Ruysch), *Invencio Fortunata* (Fernando Colón), *Inventio Fortunae* (Mercator, Dee), or *Inventio Fortunata* (Las Casas). Syntax seems to demand one of the last two forms, and we have (perhaps arbitrarily) here adopted the last. Mercator's letter of 20 April 1577 to Dr. John Dee, containing the only extant summary of the *Inventio,* has been printed several times with his correspondence. The best edition, accompanied by a study of the geography of the work and its later influence, is that of Professor E. G. R. Taylor, "A letter dated 1577 from Mercator to John Dee", *Imago Mundi,* Vol. 13 (1956), pp. 56-68; see also T. J. Oleson, "Inventio Fortunata", *Annual of the Icelandic National League,* Vol. 44 (Winnipeg, 1963), pp. 64-76. There are frequent references to it in Nansen, passim. Richard Hakluyt, in the *Principall Navigations* (1589), printed a translation only of the relevant legend in Mercator's map of 1569. For John Day's letter of 1497, see L. A. Vigneras, "New light on the 1497 Cabot voyage to America", *Hispanic American Historical Review,* Vol. 36 (1956), pp. 503-09; idem, "The Cape Breton landfall: 1494 or 1497", *Canadian Historical Review,* Vol. 38 (1957), pp. 219-28; R. Almagià, "Sulle navigazioni di Giovanni Caboto", *Rivista Geografica Italiana,* Vol. 67 (1960), pp. 1-12; J. A. Williamson, *The Cabot Voyages and Bristol Discovery under Henry VII* (1962).

friend . . . he had forgotten of whom he had borrowed it". Meanwhile, in 1569, Mercator had used it as the basis for the inset of the North Polar regions in his world map, giving a note on his source material in a legend; and eight years later, when John Dee wrote to ask him about the "Authority whereupon he fasshioned unto us that strange plat of the Septentrionall Ilands", Mercator prepared from his notes and sent to Dee an abstract of the text of the *Inventio* which he had made. This abstract is preserved (although damaged by fire) among Dee's manuscripts in the British Museum (Cotton MS Vitellius C. vii, fols. 264v–269v), and it was printed in full, with an English translation and commentary, by Professor E. G. R. Taylor in 1956.

Mercator's abstract (which is mainly in Flemish) is therefore the only surviving record of the contents of the *Inventio*. The version which he had seen was apparently contained in an account of the northern regions by a native of the Low Countries, Jacob Cnoyen of 's-Hertogenbosch, about whom nothing more is known. Cnoyen, after describing the islands of the Polar Sea, in terms derived from the *Gesta Arthuri* (a work which is also lost), goes on to say that in A.D. 1364 eight people returned to the Norwegian coast from a voyage to the "northern islands". One of these was a priest with an astrolabe, who told the King that in A.D. 1360 "an English Minorite from Oxford . . . a good astronomer" had visited the northern islands and had "journeyed further through the whole of the North, etc.", and that on his return he had written a description of the North, from 54° N to the Pole, in a book called *Inventio Fortunata,* which he gave to the King of England (Edward III). Cnoyen, as recalled by Mercator, concludes with a summary of the English friar's book; and he adds that the friar had "since journeyed to and fro [i.e. between England and Norway] five times for the King of England on business".

Dee identified the friar with the Oxford mathematician Nicholas of Lynn, and this identification has been accepted by modern writers. But Professor Taylor has pointed out that Nicholas was a Carmelite, and (reviving a conjecture in a contemporary gloss on Mercator's letter to Dee) she puts forward a rival candidate in Hugh of Ireland, a Minorite who, according to John Bale, quoting in 1557 from an older catalogue of authors, "travelled widely about the world . . . wrote a certain journey in one volume . . . [and] is said to have flourished in A.D. 1360 in the reign of King Edward III". On the other hand (as Professor D. B. Quinn points out in a private communication) "English" and "Irish" are terms as distinct as "Minorite" and "Carmelite", and perhaps less liable to confusion by a writer of the fourteenth—or the sixteenth—century.

Cnoyen's report seems (as Professor Taylor suggests) to indicate that he had himself, in Bergen in 1364, gathered his information from the priest with the astrolabe and perhaps also from the Oxford friar. Be that as it may, his geography of the north, like that of the *Inventio* which he quotes, is in close accord with that of the old Scandinavian geographical treatises of the thirteenth century, notably the *Historia Norvegiae* (*ca.* 1200) and the "King's Mirror" (*ca.* 1250). It was surely in Norway that the author of the *Inventio,* and Cnoyen also, picked up their concept of islands in the north (including "Grocland") divided by channels, or "indrawing seas", which poured into the polar ocean. These plainly correspond to the "fjords and gulfs" which, according to the "King's Mirror", divide all countries as they flow "into the circle of the world" from the outer ocean (see above, p. 173). Again, the whirlpool, "into which empty the four indrawing seas which divide the North" (according to the *Inventio*), while mentioned by many medieval Latin writers, strongly recalls the Ginnungagap of Norse lore, which is in fact drawn as a maelstrom in the Icelandic maps of the early seventeenth century, evidently after ancient tradition (see below, Note D, pp. 201–02). The isthmus supposed by the Scandinavians to connect the uninhabited northeast parts of Greenland with northern Eurasia is also described in the *Inventio,* with the pygmies, or Eskimos, whom the author claimed to have seen there.

If Professor Taylor's searching study of the *Inventio* does not perhaps bring out boldly enough the debt which its author and Jacob Cnoyen owed to Norwegian theoretical geography of the polar regions, she effectively points to the significance of some elements in their narratives which seem to lead back to experience or observation—whether that of the authors or of their informants we cannot be sure. There are details which seem to relate to Greenland—the Eskimos, whose height is precisely given as four feet, the hewn timbers of abandoned habitations, driftwood including "planks of ships and tree trunks", the mountain walls of the fjords, the contrast between frozen sea in the east and open water (in the same latitude) in the west.

The chronology of these references is not without interest. Jacob Cnoyen's text, from which Mercator claims to have copied his extracts "ad verbum exactum", permits the following reconstruction of the sequence of events described. In or before 1360 the English Minorite from Oxford, who had an astrolabe with him, went to the Eastern Settlement of Greenland, perhaps (as Professor Taylor suggests) in the royal *knarr* or supply ship from Bergen; in the course of his travels about the country, he gave a local priest his astrolabe in exchange for a testament; he may have visited the deserted Western Settlement, and perhaps even the American mainland. Four years later, in 1364, a year in which the *knarr* is known to have returned from Greenland, the priest who had acquired the astrolabe came to Bergen with (as seems to Professor Taylor "almost certain") "a band of the Norse settlers in Greenland, or even, since they excited so much interest, from Markland (Labrador)". Here the priest was interviewed by Jacob Cnoyen, who also got from him—or possibly from the Oxford friar making one of his later visits to Norway—a copy of the *Inventio Fortunata.*

Even if Greenland is accepted as the furthest west reached by the Minorite, we have a fact of some relevance for the next section of our study. For the story shows that at least one traveler to Greenland in the fourteenth century was equipped with the most accurate practical instrument of the day for measuring the angular elevation of sun and stars, and that it was left behind in the country for four years after his own return thence. The Oxford mathematicians of this century were familiar with the use of the astrolabe in determining latitude; and the *Inventio* supplies the only known testimony to the presence, and perhaps employment, of such an instrument in the western Atlantic before the end of the fifteenth century. If the Greenland priest, who was evidently a man of intellectual curiosity, had learned from the English friar how to use it, he could have made a contribution to the mapping of Greenland much in advance of the simple methods of finding their northing employed by the Scandinavian seamen. It is at any rate clear that the author of the *Inventio* thought in terms of a graduated map, for he begins his description "at latitude 54°" and records the extension of the pygmies' country as "more than 6 degrees broad" and "10 degrees long", although he also translates these distances into the equivalent number of days' journey. Mercator indeed, quoting Jacob Cnoyen in the polar legend of his map of 1569, seems to imply that the *Inventio* contained a list of latitudes, from the Englishman's observations, which he took over into his map: ". . . in the yeere 1360, a certaine English Frier . . . came into those Islands [Greenland?], who leaving them, & passing further [to Markland?] . . . described all those places that he sawe, & took the height of them with his astrolabe, according to the forme that I have set down in my map, and as I have taken it out of the aforesaid Jacob Cnoyen" (Hakluyt's translation). It is nevertheless difficult to detect, in the design of Mercator's map in high latitudes (Pl. XV), any evidence that he corrected his other sources from the "English Frier's" data; and Professor Oleson was perhaps justified in approving the skeptical comment by the Tudor mathematician Thomas Blundevill (*A briefe Description of Universall Mappes and Cardes* (1589), sig. C2): "Neither doe I beleeve that the Fryer of *Oxford* . . . ever came so nigh the Pole to measure with his Astrolabe those colde parts togither with the foure floods, which *Mercator & Barnardus* [Bernard van den Putte] do describe both in the front, and also in the nether end of their Maps . . . And therfore I take them in mine opinion to be meer fables."

7. THE MAPPING OF GREENLAND

There is evidence to suggest that, in some map workshops of southern Europe untouched by the influence of Claudius Clavus, Greenland was, during the fifteenth century, conceived as an island out in the western ocean. The Catalan chart in the Biblioteca Ambrosiana, Milan, already noticed for its delineation of Iceland (*Fixlanda*),[139] shows to the west of Ireland an island drawn as a conventional rectangle lying north–south and named *Illa verde;* in a bay formed by its southern horns is the circular *Illa de brazil*. A chart inserted in a manuscript of Ptolemy in the Bibliothèque Nationale, Paris, has a like representation accompanied by the legend *Insula uiridis de qua fit mentio ĩ geographia*.[140] These maps are probably of the late fifteenth century, and their testimony is ambiguous. We can accept the equivalence of the names with Greenland, for which such forms are found in Latin texts;[141] but the close similarity of the shape with that ascribed by cartographers to Antillia and other islands of hearsay or speculation throws doubt on the authority on which the representation rests.[142] The further equation Brasil = Markland, proposed by Nordenskiöld and Joseph Fischer, may be thought too far-fetched for serious consideration.

The rendering of Greenland in these two maps and that in the maps (also of southern authorship) which descend from Clavus must alike be regarded as constructions of the mind only faintly related to geographical fact. While the Vinland Map is not the earliest, among surviving maps, to show Greenland correctly in the west, it is almost certainly the first to depict the country—or part of it—with geographical outlines apparently derived from observation or survey, and not merely embodying an academic hypothesis or a vague rumor about an island "out there". We have to consider, first, whether and in what respects these outlines correspond to reality; second, from what data they could have been drawn; and third, whence the cartographer could have procured his information. We must also note, and seek an explanation for, the fact that Greenland is represented as an island.

To identify the delineations in an early map with the real facts of topography is an agreeable and often profitable exercise—but one which may be misleading if undisciplined by judgment of historical possibility and probability. Thus the *Insule postreme* in the east of the Vinland Map

139. See above, p. 166 and Pl. XII.
140. Reproduced by Nordenskiöld, *Bidrag,* pl. V.
141. See J. Fischer, *Discoveries,* p. 94; Björnbo and Petersen, pp. 188–89.
142. Cf. the comment on the shape of Antillia in the charts, above, p. 157 and n. 50.

may seem, from inspection of their outline and orientation, to show a convincing similarity to the islands of Japan; and it is by no means impossible that Carpini could have heard of them from Mongols or Chinese at the Khan's court. That such a report could have come to him in a form precise enough to draw a recognizable map of Japan is in the highest degree improbable, and (as we have seen) examination of the cartographer's working methods and proximate sources suggests an explanation nearer at hand and considerably easier to credit. No less caution is needed in drawing conclusions from the form given to southern Africa or to western Scandinavia in the Vinland Map; both can be explained by reference to its original.

The representation of Greenland is of entirely different character and origin, justifying comparison with the modern map. Before the end of the tenth century southern Greenland had been discovered and settled by Europeans. Their sea route took the Norsemen west from Iceland and southwestward along the east coast of Greenland; from their colonies on the west coast the hunters and fishermen ranged the shores of Davis Strait as far as the ice permitted. This traffic, not casual but regular, was carried on for over 400 years by seamen who learned to locate and orient themselves by signs in the sky and the sea and by marks on the land, without the help of charts. It took them into high latitudes along the Greenland coasts—perhaps higher than we now conceive possible; and it was chronicled in Icelandic records of factual character, which furnish materials for plotting the courses taken, the landfalls made, and the coasts traversed. From these records, intermittent and ambiguous though they often are, maps were to be constructed by Icelanders at the end of the sixteenth and in the seventeenth century; but by the Norsemen who frequented these waters from the tenth to the fifteenth century no map was needed, and none is known to have been made.

The agreement, both in general and in detail, between the outline given to Greenland in the Vinland Map and that of the modern map is impressive (cf. Fig. 7). The principal axes of the country are correctly oriented, as is the general trend of the coastlines, apart from that in the northeast which lies NW–SE instead of north–south. The conspicuous formal features are clearly evoked. We recognize, for instance, the bow-shaped east coasts, with a marked bend in the center; the coast running southwest to the tapered southernmost point; the sharp angle at which the trend of the west coast changes from south–north to SE–NW. It follows that the design conveys a visual impression of correctness in shape and proportion.

Still more extraordinary is the fact that it appears possible to identify some of the details in the outline. The deep indentation in the center of the east coast vividly suggests Scoresby Sound, with the peninsular Liverpool Land and a more shallow inlet (King Oscar's Fjord?) immediately north of it, and further north still the fjords of King William Land. Southwest of "Scoresby Sound", and midway to Cape Farewell, is another deep bay or fjord extending in a northerly direction into the land. It is difficult to resist the inference that this represents Sermilik (Egede Fjord, on which Angmagssalik stands), or possibly Kangerdlugsuak.[143] The contrast between the southeast coast and the much more sharply indented fjord coasts on the northeast and southwest emerges from the delineation in the map. The peninsular character of the south-

___

143. Alternatively, if the southernmost fjord shown on the Vinland Map be taken for Sermilik, that which we have associated with Scoresby Sound might be Kangerdlugsuak, the orientation of which would agree with the delineation; and in this case Scoresby Sound (if represented) would be one of the indentations marked north of the easternmost point of Greenland in the map. See Fig. 7 (p. 184).

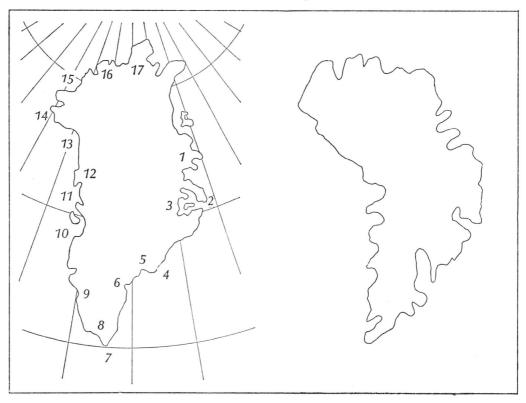

Fig. 7. Greenland in the Modern Map (*left:* polar projection) and in the Vinland Map (*right:* assumed extension 60°–80°N.lat.), on the same scale. The numbers in the modern map indicate the following places or features: 1. King William Land; 2. Liverpool Land; 3. Scoresby Sound; 4. Cape Dan; 5. Kangerdlugsuak; 6. Angmagssalik; 7. Cape Farewell; 8. Julianehaab (the East Settlement); 9. Godthaab (the West Settlement); 10. Disko Bay; 11. Umanak Fjord; 12. Upernavik; 13. Melville Bay; 14. Cape York; 15. Kane Basin; 16. Petermann Fjord; 17. Peary Land.

ern tip of Greenland, at Cape Farewell, is conveyed, with a fjord feature (Eiriksfjord or Einarsfjord?) in the position of Julianehaab, the site of the Eastern Settlement. Further north, four bays are drawn before the coastline veers northwestward; while it would be fanciful to propose, in this area, precise identifications in so generalized a drawing, we may venture the suggestion that a mapmaker could hardly overlook the Godthaab fjords where the Western Settlement lay, Disko Bay, and Umanak Fjord, nor the conspicuous headlands adjacent to them. The smoothly drawn coast to the northwest suggests a want of precise information; it may, no less, indicate the edge of pack ice extending across Melville Bay from Upernavik or Cape Svartenhuk (north of Umanak) to Cape York in the north. Lastly, while we dare not suggest that the representation of the north coasts has the same authority as the rest, it must be noted that a deep indentation might be taken for Petermann Fjord and that their general trend as far as the marked northeast angle of Peary Land is consistent with that of the modern map.

This singular degree of concordance between the Vinland Map and that of today compels the question whether the delineation derives from actual discovery, and (if so) at what point experience ends and conjecture or theory begins. The answer must be sought in correlation of the outlines and features in the map with the coasts known to have been discovered or frequented by the Norsemen.

In determining the extent of Norse navigation we shall be misled if we suppose it to have been controlled by a climatic situation identical with that of the present. It is clear that, during the Viking age, a milder climate allowed the Norse voyagers to use sailing routes, and to carry out exploration in high latitudes, that would be impossible in the ice conditions of the later Middle Ages or of today. Modern climatologists are agreed in regarding the period between about A.D. 950 and 1200 as "a climatic optimum with unmistakable evidence of being warmer than now in Iceland and Greenland, presumably implying higher ocean temperatures in the northern Atlantic, and much less extensive ice in the Arctic seas"; the subsequent climatic decline which set in during the thirteenth century, with increasing ice in the Arctic seas affecting the navigation routes, culminated in the "Little Ice Age", which began in the fifteenth century. Recent synoptic studies in paleoclimatology generally substantiate the theory of cyclic changes in climate developed by Otto Pettersson over half a century ago.[144] Pettersson, who ascribed these changes to "variations of the tide-producing force" of the sun and moon, postulated a "minimum period of the tide-generating force", accompanied by stable and uniform climate, in the sixth century A.D., and a maximum tidal effect, with harsh and even catastrophic climatic conditions, in the fifteenth century. This span of nearly a thousand years brackets the rise and decline of the oceanic navigation of the Norsemen; and in their historical records Pettersson found confirmation of his theory.

The time intervening between the climacterics falls into three phases. In the first, up to about 1100, the Arctic Ocean was almost free of polar ice; little or no ice was brought down by the Labrador and East Greenland currents, and the warm waters of the Gulf Stream—or of its effluent the Irminger current, from Iceland to Greenland—could flow further to the westward. "The ice-melting took place at higher latitudes in Baffin's Bay, in the arctic sea and even in the polar basin". Iceland and Greenland enjoyed a more temperate climate, and the east and south coasts of Greenland were ice-free. The narratives of the Greenland voyages in this period contain no mention of ice as a hazard to navigation, and Eirik the Red's route—today impracticable —was regularly followed due west from Iceland to Greenland, south along the coast, and through the sounds north of Cape Farewell. "Nor was navigation hampered by the ice in Davis Sound or in the sea between Greenland and North America; ice was first met with in the far north at the fishing places of Baffin's Bay". This is the time in which the Vikings made their pioneering voyages, embracing the settlement of Iceland and Greenland, exploration northward up Baffin Bay and perhaps Kane Basin, and their discovery of America. The second phase of the period, toward the end of the twelfth century and during the thirteenth, is marked by a deterioration of climate, with "the first signs of an ice-blockade of Iceland" and a southward

144. See H. H. Lamb and A. I. Johnson, "Climatic variation and observed changes in the general circulation", *Geografiska Annaler,* Vol. 41 (1959), pp. 94–134, and Vol. 43 (1961), pp. 363–400; I. I. Schell, "The ice off Iceland and the climates during the last 1200 years, approximately", *Geografiska Annaler,* Vol. 43 (1961), pp. 354–62; H. H. Lamb, "On the nature of certain climatic epochs which differed from the modern (1900–39) normal", *Proc. of the WMO/UNESCO Rome 1961 Symposium on Climatic Changes* (Paris, 1963), pp. 125–50, with bibliography. On Pettersson's hypothesis, see his "Climatic variations" (cited above, n. 107), esp. pp. 7–15, 21–22, 26, from which quotations in the next paragraph are taken; C. E. P. Brooks, *Climate through the Ages* (2d ed. 1949); and, for a convenient summary, Rachel Carson, *The Sea around us* (paperback ed., 1960), pp. 136–41.

movement of the Greenland Eskimos following the advancing ice edge for their sealing and fishing in Baffin Bay. While the old route from Iceland still remained in use, the *Konungs skuggsjá* reports a dense drift of ice floes along the Greenland coast lying "to the north-east [of Iceland]", and there is a first reference to icebergs; seamen are warned not to try "to make the land too soon", but to steer "southwesterly and westerly" to round the ice-drift. The final phase, in the fourteenth and fifteenth centuries, saw the destruction of the Western Settlement by the Eskimos; Ivar Bardsson's revision of the sailing directions (*ca.* 1360); the permanent freezing of the ground in southern Greenland (*ca.* 1400); and, as "the icedrift from the polar sea steadily increased towards the time of the maximum of the tide-generating force", the rupture of communications with Greenland.

If this reconstruction of the climatic changes be accepted, it must color any interpretation of the Vinland Map as a record of the medieval voyaging and exploration of the Norsemen.[145]

The first leg of the ancient course from Iceland took them from Snæfellsnes due west to "Gunnbjorn's Skerries", said to be midway to Greenland (i.e. to the settlements in the southwest); these were islands off Cape Dan in the vicinity of Angmagssalik (about 66° N). Today this is the only part of the coast facing Denmark Strait which is, in the late summer and autumn, free from the pack ice which closes the coast northward and southward of it to navigation; north of 70°, however, where the "ice river" drifting down from the Arctic is not compressed into a channel, the Greenland coast is accessible to ships, while north of 75°, facing the sea dividing it from Spitzbergen, it is again blocked by the pack ice. In eastern Greenland archaeology has brought to light no Norse remains north of Kangerdlugsuak (66° 30′ N), and it is commonly stated that the limit of the Norsemen's knowledge of this coast was Scoresby Sound (71° N). Of the "uninhabited region" of eastern Greenland the Icelandic records say little, apart from the tale of ships wrecked on its coasts.[146] Nansen maintained indeed "that the Norwegians and Icelanders sailed over the whole Arctic Ocean, along the edge of the ice, when hunting seals and the valuable walrus";[147] here, if they ranged along the Arctic ice from northern Greenland to Nova Zemlya, may be the origin of their medieval concept of a land connection between northern Russia and Greenland, enclosing a great gulf of the ocean (*Hafsbotn*).[148] Nansen observes that, to reach the Greenland coast north of 70°, "it is nearly always necessary to sail through ice . . . a somewhat tricky piece of sailing, which requires an intimate knowledge of the ice conditions"; but (he concedes) "it is nevertheless not entirely impossible that they should have reached the northern east coast, since it may be comparatively free from ice in late summer and autumn".[149] Bruun, on the other hand, asserts bluntly that "the old Norsemen . . . were

---

145. In the cursory survey which follows I have used, generally, Nansen, chs. vii, viii, xi, xii; W. Hovgaard, *The Voyages of the Norsemen to America* (1914), ch. ii; D. Bruun, *The Icelandic Colonisation of America* (1918); P. Nörlund, *Viking Settlers in Greenland* (1936); O. Pettersson, "Climatic variations", pp. 9–14. I have left out of account episodes which are recorded so vaguely or ambiguously as to leave their location uncertain; e.g. Adam of Bremen's stories of the Polar expeditions of the Frisian nobles in 1036 and of King Harald Hardrade in 1065, and the discovery of western land (probably East Greenland) by the Icelanders Adalbrand and Thorvald Helgesson in 1285, noted in the Icelandic Annals. Cf. Fig. 4 (p. 170).

146. The references are collected by Nansen, Vol. 1, pp. 280–85; see also Nörlund, pp. 92–94.

147. Nansen, Vol. 1, p. 287.

148. See Fig. 6 (p. 174); and Nansen, Vol. 2, pp. 171–72.

149. Nansen, Vol. 1, p. 287. Nansen had personal experience of such "tricky sailing" in July 1888, when he and

never afraid of sailing through the ice"; in common with some other historians, he identifies Svalbard, discovered in 1194, as northeast Greenland ("probably Scoresby Sound is Svalbard"), and he adds a suggestion "of the Norsemen staying here during the summer on account of the good hunting".[150] Although land north of 70° is reported to have been seen several times in the seventeenth century, mainly by Dutch whalers, it remained for explorers of the nineteenth and twentieth centuries, beginning with Captain William Scoresby, to survey and map the northern east coast of Greenland in detail. Neither their experiences along this coastline nor the summer ice conditions seem to exclude the possibility that the medieval Norsemen, on their hunting expeditions, could have reached the land, perhaps as far north as 75°, with less obstruction from ice, and obtained a general knowledge of its trend and character.[151]

The course from Iceland adopted in the fourteenth century was more southwesterly, to get round the ice which came "out of the sea bays near to Gunnbjorn's Skerries", and it brought the navigator on a northwest tack right up to Hvarf.[152] On the older course, pioneered by Eirik the Red, the coast was in full view as he ran along the ice all the way from Angmagssalik to Cape Farewell; and the oldest accounts of the voyage evoke the dominant features of the coastal topography—the glaciers of Midjokull, where Eirik made his landfall, the peak of Blaserk (Ingolf's Fjeld?), which served as a landmark, and so on.[153] Finally, Ivar Bardsson (fourteenth century) gives the names of a number of coastal features in East Greenland, which cannot be confidently identified; these (as Nansen suggests) were probably places to which "expeditions for seal-hunting were made . . . from the Eastern Settlement, and they must have lain near it, just north of Cape Farewell".[154]

In the southern section of the west coast the Norsemen planted their two settlements, or rather groups of settlements. The more southerly, the so-called Eastern Settlement, occupied the cluster of fjords from about 60° 30′ to 61° 30′ N; then, at a distance of "six days' rowing with six men in a six-oared boat", past other fjords where Norse remains have been found, the Western Settlement lay in the deep fjords about Godthaab, from about 64° to 65° N.[155] At the present day, although some ice is carried round Cape Farewell by the East Greenland current, the Greenland coast of Davis Strait is kept relatively ice-free, in July and August, as far north as Melville Bay (about 74° N), by warmer water flowing in from the North Atlantic, and the floes from the

---

Sverdrup, taking to their boat 2½ miles off shore, south of Sermilik, only got to land after a fortnight of arduous beating and drifting.

150. Bruun, pp. 22, 172. Svalbard is more generally supposed to be Spitzbergen or Jan Mayen; cf. Nansen, Vol. 2, pp. 166–72.

151. Cf. Björnbo and Petersen, pp. 177–78; V. Stefansson, *Greenland* (1943), ch. xiii; U.S. Hydrographic Office, *Ice Atlas of the Northern Hemisphere* (1946).

152. Hvarf, formerly identified (from the indication in the sailing directions) as Cape Farewell, is now thought to be the headland of Kangek on Sermersok island (60° 10′ N) or that of Cape Desolation on Nunarssuit (60° 40′ N), both on the southwest coast, one to the south and the other to the north of the Eastern Settlement; or perhaps it refers simply to the "great massive block" of mountains at the south end of Greenland, "round about the Ilna fjords and Cape Farewell" (Nörlund, p. 105).

153. Nansen's discussion (Vol. 1, pp. 286–96), illustrated by his drawings, is admirable.

154. Nansen, Vol. 1, p. 296; Bruun, pp. 172–73; Pettersson, pp. 12–13.

155. Björnbo and Petersen, p. 178; Bruun, ch. xi; Nörlund, pp. 23–25. Bruun estimates a "day's rowing" as 24–24½ miles. Nansen (Vol. 1, p. 300) put "the northern extremity of the Western Settlement . . . at Straumsfjord, about 66½° N lat." Cf. Fig. 7 (p. 184).

Arctic are driven against the western shores of the Strait by the Labrador Current and by south-easterly winds off the Greenland ice cap. How well the medieval Norsemen understood the physical geography and meteorology of Greenland is testified by the description of the country in the *Konungs skuggsjá;* and that their settlers and hunters ranged far north in Davis Strait in the summer months is demonstrated by literary and archaeological evidence. In this region lay the *Nordrsetr,* or northern stations; and whether or not (as Nansen suggests) Eirik the Red himself explored "right up to north of Davis Strait",[156] his successors certainly did so for fishing and sealing or to recover the driftwood which was brought down by the Polar Current (but which they supposed to come from Markland). Place names are mentioned in the Greenland literature: "Greipar" (probably between Holstensborg and Egedesminde, in 67° or 68° N), described as the "land's end", i.e. the end of the habitable land not covered by inland ice, and "Kroksfjardarheidi" (Kroksfjord heath), doubtless in the neighborhood of Disko Bay or Vaigat.[157] A medieval chorography of Greenland, copied and printed in the seventeenth century, contains a rutter of the west coast of Greenland which gives distances in the rowing time for six men in a six-oared boat: from the Eastern Settlement to the Western, 6 days rowing, thence to Lysufjord 6 days, thence to Karlbudir 6 days, thence to Bjarneyjar ("Bear islands") 6 days, "twelve days rowing round [an unnamed feature], Eisunes, Ædanes in the north". Although ambiguous, this passage has suggested that Bjarney was Disko Island (69°–70° N) and that the capes last named were on Nugssuak peninsula, where (in 70° 45′ N) a bear trap possibly of Norse origin has been found.[158]

The distances in this rutter are from dead reckoning, but the story collected by the priest Halldor from "men of Nordrsetr, who had gone farther north than had been heard of before" in the year 1266, describes astronomical observations which help to fix the positions reached. Their farthest north was four days' sailing and rowing from Kroksfjardarheidi, so that (in Nansen's view), "if they started from the northern end of Vaigat in 70½°, they may have been as far north as 74° N lat., or about Melville Bay"; since on St. James's day (July 25, i.e. July 20 in 1266) they noticed the sun above the horizon at midnight, "they must at any rate have been north of 71° 48′".[159] The report also records an observation of the sun at noon, when it was "only so high that, if a man lay athwartships in a six-oared boat, the shadow of the gunwale [sun-board?] nearest the sun fell upon his face". These data have been variously interpreted to mean that the party reached Lancaster Sound or Jones Sound (i.e. above 76° N), or the western shores of Baffin Bay, or Inglefield Gulf and Kane Sound on the Greenland coast (i.e. in nearly 80° N).[160] The most careful analysis of the observation points to a latitude of about 74° N, that is, in the southern part of Melville Bay, thus approximating to Nansen's conclusion.[161]

Finally, one piece of undisputed archaeological evidence comes from a high latitude on this coast. This is the runic stone discovered in 1824 (but now lost) on the island of Kingiktorsuak, in 72° 58′ N, north of Upernavik. The inscription has been read as a record left by three Norse-

156. Nansen, Vol. 1, p. 269. Nörlund (p. 18) suggests that Eirik explored the east coast also.

157. Nansen, Vol. 1, pp. 298–301, 306–07; Hovgaard, pp. 36–38; Bruun, p. 223; Nörlund, pp. 130–31.

158. Nansen, Vol. 1, pp. 301–02; Hovgaard, pp. 38–39; Bruun, pp. 223–24.

159. Nansen, Vol. 1, pp. 308–11.

160. Fischer, pp. 33–34; Björnbo and Petersen, p. 180; Nansen, loc. cit.; Hovgaard, pp. 37–38; R. Hennig, *Terrae Incognitae,* 2d ed., Vol. 3 (1953), pp. 68–78.

161. O. S. Reuter, *Germanische Himmelskunde,* pp. 595–603.

men in a year variously read as 1135 or 1333; but its authenticity and Norse origin appear to be unmistakable.[162]

Fragmentary and intermittent though they are, these scraps of evidence take us some way—perhaps quite a long way—along the road to accepting that by the fourteenth century the Icelanders and Greenlanders, enjoying easier conditions for high-latitude travel than the modern explorer, may have had as much knowledge of the Greenland coasts, at least up to 75° N, as is displayed in the Vinland Map. It would be by no means hazardous to suppose that this knowledge extended north of the 75th parallel, especially on the west coast, where William Baffin in 1616, in a ship probably no better found than those of the Norsemen, attained the latitude of nearly 78° N. If it be admitted that the Greenlanders practiced a simple method of ascertaining their northing by observation of the heavens, we are entitled to make the further inference that they could determine the approximate latitude of conspicuous coastal features. Since, like the Norwegian coasts where these men or their forebears learned their seamanship, the coasts of Greenland which they frequented lay mainly north–south, it follows that their navigation of these coasts supplied them, probably before the end of the thirteenth century, with the materials for drawing a recognizable map, had they desired to do so.

The evidence summarized in this chapter may suggest that the design of Greenland in the Vinland Map could have been—indeed must have been—derived, if perhaps at more than one remove, from information gathered by the Norse settlers who frequented these coasts. It gives us no help at all in seeking the author who first incorporated this information in a map, in determining when and for what purpose such a map was prepared, or in conjecturing how and in what form it came to the notice of the compiler of the Vinland Map. For the representation in the Vinland Map we find no analogy in any antecedent, contemporary, or subsequent cartographic work. If it had been furnished with place names, some starting-point for inquiry might have suggested itself. As it is, we can only compare it with maps of two other families, which we will call (for convenience) the Clavus group and the Icelandic group.

The delineation of Greenland by Claudius Clavus could not, in the view of Björnbo and Petersen,[163] have been constructed from written sources only; and, although they did not fail to point out its defects, such as the incorrect orientation of the east and west coasts and the fictitious names supplied by Clavus (from the words of a Danish folk song), they were so far impressed by its general resemblance to the true form, at a time when communication between Greenland and Europe had almost ceased, that they felt compelled to accept Clavus' claim to have visited the country. But Nansen established (and Björnbo apparently later admitted) the derivation of Clavus' drawing of Greenland, in the surviving Nancy map, from that of the westernmost peninsula of Norway in the Laurentian ('Medici') Atlas of 1351;[164] and it is consequently the merits or validity of the latter, as a possible representation of Greenland, that we have to consider. This need not take us long, even were we to make the improbable assumption that the cartographer is here depicting Greenland. The erroneous orientation, the formal or conventional

162. Nansen, Vol. 1, p. 297; Hovgaard, pp. 39–40; Nörlund, pp. 129–31. The date in the inscription—25 April—shows that the voyage was made far earlier in the summer than would today be possible, because of ice. Stefansson (pp. 132–38) has inferred from the evidence of archaeology and Eskimo folklore that the Norsemen may have gone as far north as 79° on the west side of Smith Sound.

163. Pp. 180–82.

164. See above, pp. 176–77; also Pl. VIII and Figs. 8, 9 (p. 190).

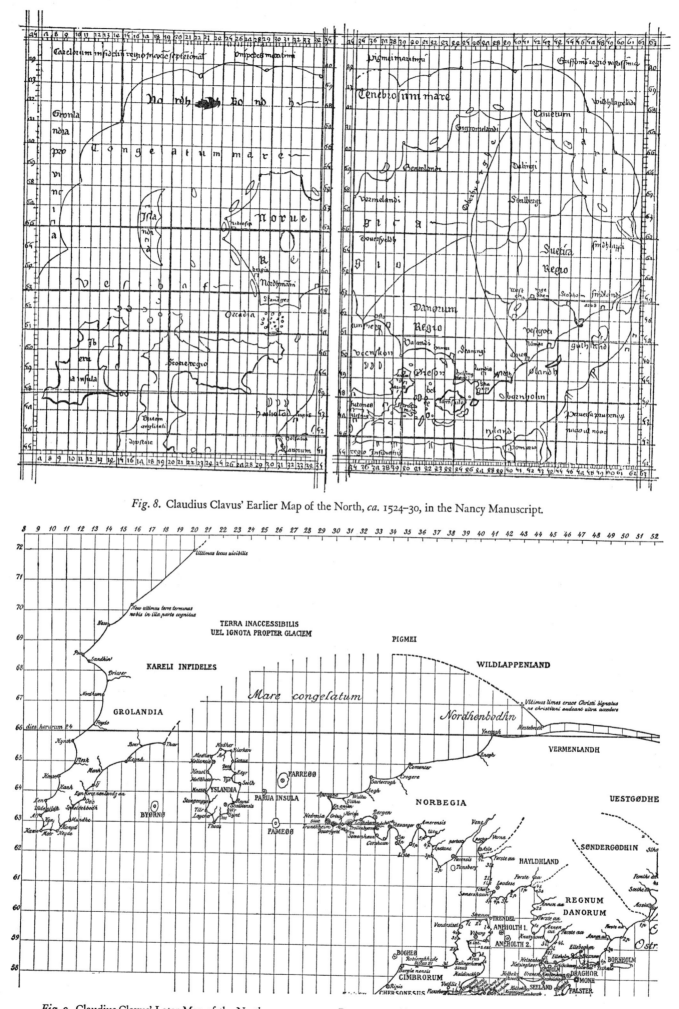

Fig. 8. Claudius Clavus' Earlier Map of the North, *ca.* 1524–30, in the Nancy Manuscript.

Fig. 9. Claudius Clavus' Later Map of the North, *ca.* 1524–30, as Reconstructed by Björnbo and Petersen from the Vienna Text.

relationship to the land to the northeast, and finally the association of the peninsula with Norway by the name *aloga* (= Halogaland)—all these characteristics combine to place any connection between the peninsula shown in the Laurentian Atlas and the Greenland of the Vinland Map out of the question.

We cannot dismiss quite so lightly the possibility that there may be a link of some kind, perhaps in a common source, between Clavus' lost second map (the counterpart of the Vienna manuscript of his descriptive text) and the Vinland Map; and although such a connection, however weak, seems to us unlikely, it deserves mention for further investigation by any student who may think the exercise profitable. Clavus' later map can be visualized from two reproductions: first, its reconstruction by Björnbo and Petersen from the data in the Vienna text,[165] and, second, the various copies of it (those of the so-called "A-type") in manuscript maps by Donnus Nicolaus Germanus (from about 1466) and Henricus Martellus Germanus (from about 1485).[166] Nansen argues that the west coast of Greenland in Clavus' second map "bears an altogether striking resemblance to the west coast of the corresponding peninsula on the Medicean mappa-mundi, so that there can be no doubt that this coast is copied from it".[167] This argument is convincing enough if (in Nansen's words) "we confine ourselves to Björnbo and Petersen's reconstruction of the coast after the text of Clavus";[168] but it does not apply with equal force to the maps of the A-type derived from Clavus' later map. While the major errors of the Nancy map, as to orientation and peninsular form, are repeated, the coastlines are drawn with much more particularity of detail, and it is possible to distinguish individual features, the forms of which seem to be deliberately differentiated. Nordenskiöld's redrawing of the oldest of these maps on a different projection[169] and Miller Christy's superimposition of the Zeno chart of 1558[170] (whose delineation of Greenland is borrowed from a map of the A-type) on the modern map show how far the outline of Greenland in these maps bears comparison with that in the modern map. Here we leave this speculative line of thought, noting only that, if Clavus or Donnus Nicolaus had access to a map of Greenland related to the prototype of the representation in the Vinland Map, this must have suffered a good deal of degradation before being incorporated into the Clavus derivatives of the A-type.

The Zeno map of the North, although late in the series of those descended from Clavus' second map, was to exercise an influence on explorers and mapmakers not surpassed by any of its predecessors. The origin and character of this curious map (Fig. 9) are described in a note at the end of the present chapter.[171] Whatever may be thought of its authenticity, its consequences

165. Björnbo and Petersen, pl. II; reproduced by Nansen, Vol. 2, p. 273.

166. See Björnbo and Petersen, ch. ii, where these derivatives are listed and described; also Fig. 9 and Pl. XVI herewith. The "B-type" is the later modification (exemplified in the Ulm Ptolemy of 1482 and many later printed maps), by which Donnus Nicolaus transferred Greenland, still as a peninsula, to the north of Scandinavia, perhaps under the influence of earlier views on the geography of the North (see above, pp. 172–73).

167. Nansen, Vol. 2, pp. 273–74. The west coast of Greenland is not included in the Nancy map.

168. It is probable that, in drawing their reconstruction of the west coast of Clavus' lost second map, Björnbo and Petersen were guided to some extent by the representation in the Laurentian or Medici Atlas.

169. *Facsimile Atlas,* p. 61 (fig. 33), where the map by Donnus Nicolaus in the Zamoiski codex (*ca.* 1466–68) at Warsaw is redrawn on the projection of that in the Brussels codex.

170. Christy, *The Silver Map of the World* (1900), pl. III and Appendix B. See also below, p. 199.

171. Note C, on pp. 197–99.

for cartographic history are clear.[172] It was carried on his first voyage for the northwest passage, in 1576, by Captain Martin Frobisher, who sighted the Greenland coast in about 60° N, that is, far to the south of its position as laid down in the Zeno map, and accordingly took it to be the island of "Frisland" shown in the map some ten degrees to the east, and a little south, of the southern point of "Engroneland". When John Davis, on his Arctic voyages of 1585–87, demonstrated the continuity of the west coast of Greenland up to 73° N, thus discrediting its identification as "Frisland", a reinterpretation of Frobisher's discoveries became necessary. The mapmakers, beginning with Emery Molyneux in his globe of 1592, reconciled the reports of Frobisher and Davis by transferring eastward all the landfalls made by Frobisher: that on Greenland into the position of "Frisland" on the Zeno map, and those on the coasts of Baffin Land to southern Greenland.[173] This reorientation of opinion, which took place between 1587 and 1592, gave rise to a spectacular geographical misconception and was to mislead mapmakers until the nineteenth century. It was also to color the representations of the Norse discoveries in the west drawn by Icelanders in the seventeenth century.

The rediscovery of Greenland credited to Frobisher and Davis reawakened interest among Scandinavians in the lost Norse colonies. Neither of these explorers recognized any traces of the settlers, nor (in all probability) had they any knowledge of the medieval Norse voyages and colonization. By 1605 King Christian IV of Denmark was making plans to rediscover the Greenland settlements and to ascertain the fate of their European inhabitants; and the three voyages which he promoted in 1605–07 were the first in the long succession of Danish expeditions which extended over two and a half centuries and only reached their successful culmination in the nineteenth century.[174]

The ancient records and literature of Iceland were the principal repository of information on medieval Greenland and (so far as they went) on Vinland. They were collected and copied by Icelandic scholars, particularly Bjorn Jónsson of Skárdsa (1574–1656); some early documents, such as the old chorography of Greenland cited above,[175] are now known only in Jónsson's transcripts.[176] Whether, among the records which they rummaged and brought to light, the Icelanders found any early maps is uncertain. No such maps have survived, and the only evidence that they may have existed is to be sought in the maps drawn at this late period in Iceland; to this evidence we may now add that of the Vinland Map.

In the Icelandic maps[177] the information derived by their authors from ancient records of the medieval voyages and discoveries was superimposed on the "base-map" of the late sixteenth century. Their immediate prototype for Greenland may have been Mercator's world chart of 1569, in which the representation of the Zeno map is followed, but modified by a strait dividing Greenland from lands in the northeast; this strait, though not in the Zeno map, is found in the Icelandic

---

172. In Nordenskiöld's words, it "exercised an influence on the mapping of the northern countries to which there are few parallels to be found in the history of cartography" (*Facsimile Atlas*, p. 26).

173. See Christy, pp. 26–36.

174. See K. J. V. Steenstrup, "Om Østerbygden", *Meddelelser om Grönland*, Vol. 9 (1889), pp. 1–51; H. Hermannsson, *Two Cartographers: Gudbrandur Thorláksson and Thórdur Thorláksson* (1926), pp. 31–38; V. Stefansson, chs. xii–xiv.

175. Above, p. 188.

176. Printed in *Grönlands historiske Mindesmærker*, Vols. 1–3 (1838–45).

177. A fuller account of these maps, with bibliography, is given in Note D, below, pp. 199–208.

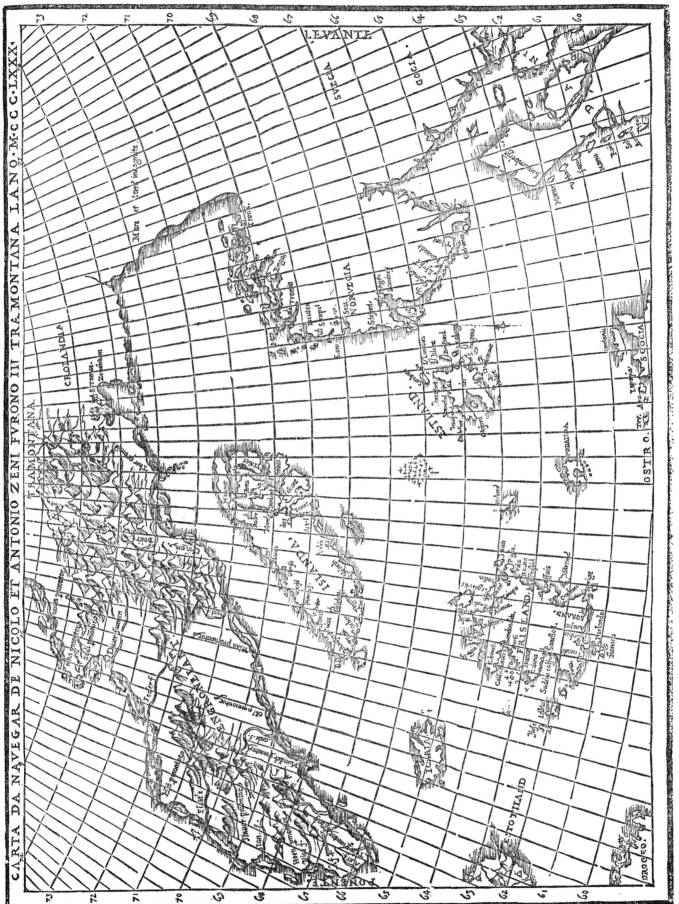

Fig. 10. The Zeno Map of the North Atlantic, 1558. From Nicolò Zeno, *Commentarii*, Venice, 1558.

maps.[178] In other respects the outline of Greenland in these maps, and its relationship to Eurasia, are decidedly of the Zeno type, with additions or alterations suggested by interpretation of the voyages of Frobisher and Davis. Unlike the compiler of the Zeno map, however, the Icelandic cartographers set out to illustrate the Norse discoveries and settlements; in their maps they depicted Helluland, Markland, and Vinland, and—perhaps partly arising from this addition to the "base-map"—they radically changed the orientation of Greenland to a general SE–NW alignment. It has been argued by Gathorne-Hardy that this reorientation arose from the cartographers' mistaken belief that the Eastern and Western Settlements lay (as their ancient names suggested) east and west of one another, instead of north and south.[179] This explanation finds support in the earliest of the Icelandic maps: in those of Sigurdur Stefánsson (*ca.* 1590; Pl. XVII) and Bishop Hans Poulson Resen (1605; Pl. XIX) the west coast of Greenland is turned anticlockwise so that it faces southwest, while in that of Bishop Gudbrandur Thorláksson (1606; Pl. XVIII), which—exceptionally—aligns Greenland SW–NE as in the Zeno map, the two settlements are represented by deep fjords in the much broadened south coast, and the east coast is declared to be uninhabited.

The geographical or historical information on Greenland and the sea routes thither, which the Icelandic cartographers added to their sixteenth-century "base-map", comprises ancient place or feature names such as Hvitserk, Herjolfsnes, and Vesterbygdsfiord, the track of the old navigation from Iceland to the Eastern Settlement (plotted as a line of dots by Thorláksson, verbally described by Resen), the location of the settlements, and copious legends (in Resen's map) on the old Norse voyages and colonies. All this matter, without exception, insofar as it relates to Greenland (for which relatively recent maps supplied the outline) and not to the lands further west (for which we know no cartographic prototype), could have been taken from the textual sources—the Icelandic historical literature, medieval geographical or chorographical works, the old Norse sailing directions and rutters—which were studied and transcribed by Icelanders in the seventeenth century. Stefánsson's map was believed by the seventeenth-century scholars who copied it to have been derived "from ancient memorials of Iceland" (*ex antiquitatibus Islandicis*).[180] In respect of its delineation of Greenland, and that in the maps of Thorláksson and Resen, it would be unnecessary to postulate the existence of any map among these "ancient memorials", were it not for two considerations. The first is, of course, the representation of the Norse discoveries on the American mainland; this will be discussed in the next chapter. Secondly, Resen twice cites an older—apparently much older—Icelandic map among his sources: in the title of his map ("Indicatio Gronlandie & vicinarum regionum . . . ex antiqua quadam mappa rudi modo delineata, ante aliquot centenos annos, ab Islandis, quibus tunc erat ista terra notissima") and in his legend on the sailing route to Greenland (". . . in mappa Islandorum hic

---

178. Though in a different association. In Mercator's map (as in the world map of Oronce Finé, 1531), the strait results from his adoption of the Polar geography of the *Inventio Fortunata* (see above, pp. 179–82). In the Icelandic maps, which do not extend so far north, the strait cuts through the land bridge between northeast Greenland and northern Russia (Biarmaland) and represents the passage (Yugorski Shar) by which the Dutch penetrated into the Kara Sea in 1594–95. Sigurdur Stefánsson calls it "sinum . . . in Russiam excurrentem", Resen names it "Fretum Nassovium" (the name given to Yugorski Shar in Dutch maps from 1596 onward).

179. G. M. Gathorne-Hardy, *The Norse Discoverers of America* (1921), pp. 295–96.

180. So in the note written by Thormod Torfaeus to accompany his engraving of Bishop Thórdur's copy of the Stefánsson map, in *Gronlandia antiqua* (1706), pl. 11. See Pl. XVII herewith.

ponitur Promontorium Hvitserck quod . . . in medio itinere conspici poterat, ut est ex Islandorum narrationibus"). To Resen's testimony may be added the argument that, in spite of their
general family likeness, the Icelandic maps show mutual differences, in their representation of
Vinland, which have suggested that they are derived from a common map-prototype rather
than copied from one another.[181] The ancient Icelandic map mentioned by Resen as an authority
was "some centuries old", and it plainly embraced the whole extent of medieval Norse voyaging
in the western Atlantic. The form in which it delineated Greenland cannot now be visualized
or reconstructed. No such map, nor even any seventeenth-century transcript of it, has turned
up in the archives and libraries of Iceland and Denmark; and the authors of the Icelandic maps
preferred a more recent cartographic model for their draft of Greenland, limiting themselves
only to a correction of its latitudes.[182]

Thus neither the later Clavus map and its derivatives nor the Icelandic maps drawn from
about 1590 onward lead us back unquestionably to an original which could have supplied the
design of Greenland found in the Vinland Map. For an evaluation of this design and its source
we must return to the map itself.

As we have seen, there is not much real difficulty in supposing the drawing of the coasts south
of about 75° N (i.e. south of King William Land, on the east, and of Melville Bay and perhaps
Cape York on the west), with their relatively correct orientation and location of main features,
to be the product of experience. The completion of the outline by the drawing of a north coast,
and the consequent insular form given to Greenland, are very much more difficult to explain,
and we will limit ourselves to stating alternative hypotheses, for none of which can a high degree
of probability be claimed. Since the northern coastline appears to be drawn with not less precision of detail than the rest of Greenland, can we suppose that for it, too, the cartographer had information of similar quality to that used for the coasts further south? It may well be thought
that the formidable difficulties of travel in this very high latitude categorically forbid any suggestion that the medieval Norsemen could have anticipated Peary in circumnavigating Greenland by the north;[183] yet Pettersson's chronology of climatic change opens the door on the possibility that, in or before the thirteenth century, they may have found this coast free of ice. Or
are we to think that the cartographer, having come to the limit of his authentic information,
perhaps in about 75° N, has speculatively completed the design by adding a theoretical north
coast? We have found such a process apparently at work elsewhere in the Vinland Map (in the
design of the Great Sea of the Tartars). If it also lay behind the tracing of a north coast for
Greenland, it must be assumed that the author of the map was ignorant of the peninsular type of
design exemplified (for western Norway) in the Laurentian Atlas and (for Greenland) in the
maps by Clavus and in any other source which may have contributed to the outline in the second
Clavus map or in its Italian derivatives;[184] or else that he rejected such a design under the in-

181. See Gathorne-Hardy, pp. 289–93, and Note D, below.

182. That is, if they were using the Zeno map itself, which laid down Greenland much too far north, with its
southernmost point in 65° 40′ N. Mercator in his world map of 1569, in which Greenland is drawn after the representation in the Zeno map, with Cape Farewell in about 66° N, did not make this correction; yet it was the Mercator
map, or a derivative from it, that the Icelandic cartographers followed in general. Cf. G. Storm, "Studies on the Vineland voyages", *Mémoires de la Société Royale des Antiquaires du Nord* (1888), pp. 334–35. See also below, n. 272.

183. A more sanguine view of this possibility is taken by V. Stefansson, ch. x.

184. Miller Christy's argument, from the Zeno map, that it derives from unknown fifteenth-century originals in

fluence of a geographical dogma or fixed idea that lands out in the ocean must be islands.

If the sources from which this map of Greenland could have been constructed remain in large measure obscure or conjectural, it must be admitted that the further questions, by whom and when it was drawn, and for what purpose, are still more enigmatic. That the author of the prototype was an Icelander is suggested by his access to information about the Norse navigations which was (so far as we are aware) unknown outside Iceland, and perhaps Scandinavia, until the seventeenth century. Bishop Resen's references to an old Icelandic map, which point the same way, may also be taken as evidence—slight as it may seem in the absence of any extant examples —that maps were drawn in Iceland during the Middle Ages. We are entitled to go no further than this in surmise. We may guess, however, that the original, of which the Greenland of the Vinland Map is a copy (doubtless simplified and reduced), was carried to southern Europe by a Scandinavian, perhaps a churchman.[185] Had it not then been lost or destroyed, the course of cartographic history and of geographical thought would have been even more radically altered than by the Clavus and Zeno maps.

To what extent, and in what way, communication with Greenland may have continued after the last recorded voyage thither by Icelanders, in 1406–10, is uncertain.[186] Officially, it had perhaps broken down even earlier; the last *knarr*, or royal supply ship from Bergen, sailed in 1369 but never reached its destination, and there was no resident Bishop in Greenland after 1377. Some evidence nevertheless exists to suggest, if ambiguously, that intermittent contact with the country may have been maintained during the fifteenth century. This evidence comes from archaeological finds, from documentary records, and from cartography. Excavation of the Norse graves at Herjolfsnes has yielded European clothing mainly of the fourteenth and early fifteenth centuries but including caps which must apparently be of the second half of the fifteenth century;[187] the papal briefs of 1448 and 1492 betray information, doubtless from report by way of Iceland, about the state of the Christians in Greenland;[188] and it has been claimed that Clavus' second map and the Italian maps of the same type provide "the earliest and best representation we have of the results of the ancient Scandinavian explorations of Greenland".[189]

Yet by the middle of the fifteenth century the detailed knowledge accumulated by the Norsemen about the lands in the west had passed out of European consciousness; the exploratory enterprise of the three following centuries in this direction depended largely on false premisses; and not until the second half of the nineteenth century did it again become possible to draw an outline of Greenland comparable in general accuracy with that included in the Vinland Map.

which "Greenland can only have been represented . . . as a result of the early Scandinavian intercourse with that country" can refer only to the Clavus maps of the A-type introduced by Donnus Nicolaus; and his supporting argument that "the Zenian delineation of Greenland is more detailed and more like the actual Greenland" than that given by Nicolaus and Henricus Martellus seems to us perverse. Miller Christy, pp. 62–66; see also below, p. 198.

185. See above, p. 178.

186. On this see generally Nansen, ch. xi; Nörlund, chs. iv, v, vii; V. Stefansson, chs. x, xi.

187. Nörlund, ch. v. It has been conjectured (e.g. by Stefansson, p. 151) that these articles were brought from Iceland by the expedition supposed to have been conducted by Didrik Pining and Hans Pothorst, with Johannes Scolvus, in 1472–73 or 1476; but the documentary evidence for this voyage is late and equivocal.

188. The authenticity of the letter of 1448 (see above, p. 175) has been doubted. Assuming it to be genuine, Stefansson (p. 156) suggests that details in it may have come from an Icelander "Björn, called the Rich, who was driven to Greenland in 1446 and spent the following winter there".

189. Christy, p. 66; see above, n. 184.

By its delineation of Greenland, casting a solitary shaft of light through the darkness of five centuries, the map makes its strongest claim on our curiosity; and it is this feature, perhaps even more than the delineation of Vinland, which most clearly seems to lift the map out of its period and might suggest—were the converging evidence to the contrary less strong—the work of a counterfeiter.

NOTE C. THE ZENO MAP

The Zeno map of the North (Fig. 10), a woodcut with the title "Carta da navegar de Nicolo et Antonio Zeni furono in tramontana lano M.CCC.LXXX", was published at Venice in 1558 with the *Commentarii* edited by a later Nicolò Zeno and describing the travels of members of his family in the fourteenth and fifteenth centuries. The second part of the book, that illustrated by the map, has the subtitle *Dello scoprimento dell'Isole Frislanda, Eslanda, Engroueland, Estotilanda, & Icaria, fatto per due fratelli Zeni M. Nicolò il Caualiere, & M. Antonio . . . col disegno di dette Isole.*[190]

The narrative of the voyages of the Zeni brothers in the north and west Atlantic in 1380–87 has been shown by F. W. Lucas to be largely a compilation from earlier printed works of the sixteenth century. That shipwrecked Italians could have reached Iceland and Greenland in company with Scandinavians during the fourteenth century is, of course, not impossible; but the account of their experiences printed in 1558 cannot be taken as a reliable record, and it is scarcely to be credited that they went further west still. Historical criticism has not yet explained away every statement in the work, and a modern writer can still find in it "strong suggestions that the romance of the Zeni brothers . . . had some foundation in old family papers" and argue that (for instance) "the relation of the Latin books found in the King's library in Estotiland . . . could easily arise from a story of an Italian trader's visit to Greenland—or even to Markland".[191] But the unscrupulous methods of the sixteenth-century editor place an onus on believers to find supporting evidence for such inferences from the annals of the Zeni.

While, according to Nicolò Zeno (the compiler), the text was put together from letters written by his forebear Antonio in the fourteenth century, he does not claim the same origin for his map. It was (he says) copied by him from "a navigating chart which I once found that I possessed among the ancient things in our house, although all rotten and many years old". The map in fact owes its delineation and nomenclature of Scandinavia, Iceland, and Greenland to an Italian derivative of Clavus' second map (of the A-type, as in Pl. XVI), with Iceland modified after the map of the North by Olaus Magnus (1539). Although no manuscript map of the Clavus

---

190. The bibliography is considerable. The principal modern works are R. H. Major, ed., *The Voyages of the Venetian Brothers Antonio and Nicolò Zeno to the Northern Seas in the XIVth Century* (1873); F. W. Lucas, *The Annals of the Voyages of the Brothers Nicolò and Antonio Zeno* (1898), with full bibliography; M. Christy, *The Silver Map of the World . . . Including . . . Remarks on the Zeno Narrative and Chart of 1558* (1900); R. Hennig, *Terrae Incognitae*, Vol. 3 (2d ed. 1953), pp. 393–405. A recent attempt (W. H. Hobbs, "Zeno and the cartography of Greenland", *Imago Mundi*, Vol. 6, 1949, pp. 15–19) to re-establish, in Major's footsteps, the authority of the Zeno map leads its author into some positions which are difficult to defend, e.g. that Olaus Magnus' map, published 19 years before the Zeno map, was copied from it and that the mariner's compass was in general use in the North Atlantic in the fourteenth century.

191. E. G. R. Taylor, "A letter dated 1577 from Mercator to John Dee" (as above, n. 138), p. 66; idem, "A fourteenth-century riddle—and its solution", *Geogr. Review*, Vol. 54 (1964), pp. 573–76. The possibility that the compiler of the Zeni narrative had access to the *Inventio Fortunata* is not to be excluded.

A-type now survives in any Venetian library, the "navigating chart" copied by Nicolò Zeno was plainly of this character.[192] To it he added representations to illustrate the geography of the Zeni narrative—the islands of Estland, Frisland, Icaria, and others, and the western lands of Estotiland and Drogeo. Their outlines were borrowed or adapted, and their names transposed or altered, from earlier maps.[193] For only two names (Estotiland and Drogeo) could Lucas find no carto-graphic parallel; the first of these is doubtless a corruption of Stilanda.[194] Miller Christy's argument that the Zeno map represents "a survival of ancient geographical knowledge long since almost lost and forgotten" rests on an unfounded belief that it is more detailed and more accurate, in its delineation of Greenland, than the Clavus-type maps from which it descends.[195] Apart from the intrusion of the Zenian geography, the compiler of the map has made only one substantial modification of his principal source; while Donnus Nicolaus and Henricus Ger-manus, following Clavus, laid down the southern point of Greenland in about 63° N (already over three degrees north of the correct latitude) the Zeno map moves it even further north, to 65° 40′.[196]

The authority of the Zeno map was established by its inclusion in the Venice Ptolemy of 1561 and by its incorporation into Mercator's world map of 1569 (Pl. XV) and into the editions of Ortelius' atlas from 1570. Mercator was the first cartographer to identify Estotiland as part of the American continent, placing the name in the position of Baffin Land. While he modified the Zeno representation of Greenland by drawing a strait to divide it, in the northeast, from one of the four large polar islands deduced by him from the *Inventio,* he followed the latitudes of the Zeno map. The first correction of them, made in consequence of the voyages of Frobisher (1576–78), is found in Michael Lok's world map of 1582, in which, by drawing Frisland without a north coast and about ten degrees west of its position in the Zeno map, he provides an alternative position for Greenland, with its southern point in 59° N; and this delineation reappears in the map by "F.G." included in Hakluyt's edition of Peter Martyr, 1587. The voyages of John Davis (1585–87) and consequent reinterpretation of Frobisher's discoveries led (as we have seen) to the second revision of the Zeno version of Greenland.

While adopting the Zeno outline for Greenland, as modified by Mercator, and accepting his identification of Estotiland, the Icelandic mapmakers introduced a correction in the latitudes of Greenland (Pls. XVII–XIX). Its southernmost point is placed by Sigurdur Stefánsson in

192. See Björnbo and Petersen, pp. 79–83, 181. In his later work *Cartographia Groenlandica* (1912, ch. xi), however, Björnbo maintained that the Zeno map and Mercator's of 1569 derived their representation of Greenland, Iceland, Frisland, etc., independently from an anonymous MS Portuguese chart (the "Carte du Dépôt, 1.0.4") in the Biblio-thèque Nationale. This strange inversion of the order of descent finds no support from chronology. The Portuguese chart is now ascribed to Sebastião Lopes and to *ca.* 1583 (A. Cortesão and A. Teixeira da Mota, *Portugaliae Monu-menta Cartographica,* Vol. 4, 1960, pp. 17–21, and pl. 408); and the appearance of the Zenian geography of the north in it and in the contemporary maps of Bartolomeu Lasso merely testifies to the extensive influence of the Zeno map after its publication. Cf. Fig. 10 (Zeno) and Pl. XV (Mercator) herewith.

193. Lucas, ch. viii and app. iv.

194. On the source of the name Estotiland, Bishop Resen added a gloss to his map: "forse Esto(es) Tiland seu Tyle v. ultima Tule". Cf. also, in the chart drawn by Albino de Canepa at Genoa in 1482, the form used for Stilland: *insulla destitilant.*

195. Christy, pp. 61–66.

196. Clavus' latitudes are generally too high; the southern point of Greenland is placed in 63° 15′ in his first text, in 62° 40′ in his second (Figs. 8, 9). It is really in 59° 46′ N. Nansen (Vol. 2, p. 261) suggests that he "may have obtained the latitudes of some places" from the *Inventio Fortunata.*

61° and by Gudbrandur Thorláksson in 60½°; Resen, however, puts it back to 63°. Although the authority for Greenland followed by these cartographers doubtless seemed to them the latest and best available, it represented in fact a model which (as we have shown) originated in the fifteenth century. It still remains for consideration whether this prototype incorporated any authentic information on Greenland which may have come into Clavus' hands or into those of the mapmakers in Italy whose work reflects his later views on northern geography.

An answer to this question can perhaps be sought in comparison of the outline of Greenland in the Vinland Map with that in maps of the Clavus A-type (Fig. 9, Pl. XVI), making allowance for differences in the projection and character of drawing (which in the maps of Nicolaus and Henricus Martellus is influenced by the style of nautical charts). The two delineations have in common some markedly similar features, not all of which can be traced to the older prototype represented by the Laurentian Atlas. These include the general north–south orientation of southern Greenland, tapering to its southernmost point; the indentation of the east coast, with its SW–NE trend; and the conspicuous northwesterly sweep of the upper part of the drawing of the west coast, ending in a promontory described, in Clavus' Vienna text and in the A-type maps, as "the extreme limit of known land" and laid down by him in 70° 10′ N, with "the last land visible" about a degree to the north.

Against these apparent affinities we have to balance (on the one hand) the features of the Vinland Map not paralleled in the maps after Clavus—e.g. the more precise drawing of fjords and capes, the continuation of the coasts further northward, the insular form—and (on the other hand) the limitations of the information revealed in the Clavus maps. These limitations are the more difficult to explain if the maps were drawn from firsthand knowledge of Greenland; for instance, Clavus' names for coastal features are of his own invention, and (as Nansen points out) if his claim to have visited the country were justified, he must have been unlucky in meeting no Greenlander from whom he could have learned the names in local use.[197]

We are inclined, therefore, to ascribe the apparent points of similarity between the Vinland Map and the maps after Clavus to "one of those accidental coincidences that sometimes occur, and that warn us to be careful not to draw too many conclusions from evidence of this nature."[198] Whether the representation of Greenland in the Vinland Map rests on direct experience or not, it seems fairly certain that that of Clavus and that of the Zeno map, which ultimately derives from Clavus, have no such basis.

NOTE D. THE ICELANDIC MAPS

The maps drawn in Iceland and Denmark from the close of the sixteenth century and during the seventeenth were the first to incorporate geographical information from the ancient Icelandic records. They have accordingly been cited in connection with the mapping of Greenland, and further mention of them will be made in discussing the cartographic representation of Vinland. For convenience of reference, a brief list and summary of their character and contents is given here. For bibliographical details of the manuscript maps, the following works have been used: K. J. V. Steenstrup, "Om Østerbygden", *Med. om Grönl.* (1889); H. Hermannsson, *Jón Gudmundsson and his Natural History of Iceland* (1924); and H. Hermannsson, *Two Cartog-*

197. Nansen, Vol. 2, p. 273.
198. Ibid., p. 274.

raphers: Gudbrandur Thorláksson and Thórdur Thorláksson (1926). Manuscripts of the Royal Library, Copenhagen, are cited by their class-mark (Gl. kgl. Saml.). The list of reproductions is selective only.[199]

I. Sigurdur Stefánsson (Sigurdus Stephanius), "1570" [*ca.* 1590].[200]

    a.   Original, lost.

    b.   Copy by Bjorn Jónsson of Skárdsa, lost.

    c.   Copies by T. Thorláksson, 1669 (Gl. kgl. Saml. 2881, 4°; and 997, fol.). 14½ × 12½ cm. and 15½ × 13 cm., respectively.

    d.   Engraving of I*c* in T. Torfaeus, *Gronlandia antiqua* (1706), pl. II.

    Repr. Steenstrup, p. 7 (I*c*); Lucas, p. 142 (I*d*); Storm, *Studies on the Vinland Voyages,* p. 333 (I*c*); Nansen, Vol. 2, p. 7 (I*d*); Gathorne-Hardy, p. 290 (I*c,* redrawn); herewith Pl. XVII (I*c*).

II. Hans Poulson Resen, 1605.

    a.   Original (Royal Library, Copenhagen: Map Room), 76½ × 56½ cm.

    Repr. Steenstrup, pl. 1 (redrawn); Gathorne-Hardy, p. 290 (redrawn); herewith Pl. XIX.

III. Gudbrandur Thorláksson, 1606.[201]

    a.   Original (Gl. kgl. Saml. 2876, 4°), 44½ × 32 cm. Endorsed by H. P. Resen: "H. Gudbrands egen Haand 1606".

    b.   Copy of III*a* by H. P. Resen (Gl. kgl. Saml. 2880, 4°).

    c.   Other 17th-century copies (Gl. kgl. Saml. 2880, 4°).

    d.   Copies of III*b* by T. Thorláksson (Gl. kgl. Saml. 2881, 4°, and 997, fol.).

    e.   Engraving of III*d* in Torfaeus, pl. I.

    Repr. Hermannsson 1926, facing p. 32 (III*a*); herewith Pl. XVIII (III*a*).

IV. Jón Gudmundsson, *ca.* 1640.

    a.   Original, lost.

    b.   Copies of IV*a* by T. Thorláksson (Gl. kgl. Saml. 2881, 4°, and 997, fol.). 16 × 14½ cm. and 17 × 15½ cm., respectively.

    c.   Another copy of IV*a* (Gl. kgl. Saml. 2877, 4°).

    d.   Engraving of IV*b* in Torfaeus, pl. III.

    Repr. Nansen, Vol. 2, p. 34 (IV*d*); Hermannsson 1924, pl. I (IV*c*).

V. Thórdur Thorláksson, 1668.

    a.   Original (Gl. kgl. Saml. 2881, 4°), 21 × 12½ cm.

    b.   Engraving in Torfaeus, pl. IV.

    Repr. Hermannsson 1926, facing p. 35 (V*a*).

VI. Thórdur Thorláksson, 1669.

    a.   Original (Gl. kgl. Saml. 997, fol.), 23½ × 14½ cm.

199. Fuller references to reproductions are given in the works cited above. See also *Sixteenth-Century Maps of Canada* (1956), pp. 1–4.

200. The date 1570 on the oldest copies of the map is plainly erroneous, because of the reference to an English voyage, presumably one of Frobisher's (1576–78). Since its author died in 1594 at the age of 25, it is supposed that the digit "9" in the original map may have been miscopied as "7". Sometimes cited as the "Skálholt map".

201. This date is that of Resen's note on the map; if it indicates the date when he received it, Thorláksson may have drawn it a year or two earlier. Sometimes cited as the "Hólar map".

VII. Thórdur Thorláksson, *ca.* 1670.

 a.   Original (Sökortarkivet), 66 × 37 cm.

 Repr. Steenstrup, pl. 7; Hermannsson 1926, facing p. 37.

The engravings in Torfaeus' *Gronlandia antiqua* are accompanied by notes on the maps by their authors and by Bishop Thórdur Thorláksson, whose versions of them (in Gl. kgl. Saml. 2881, 4°) served as copy for the Danish engraver. All the manuscript originals and copies listed were drawn in Iceland, with the exception of that by Bishop H. P. Resen, which was prepared in Copenhagen.

In respect of their geographical content, the maps of Stefánsson, Resen, and Gudbrandur Thorláksson form a more or less homogeneous group. That of Stefánsson (in its oldest surviving copy) is on a smaller scale and more sparsely annotated than the other two. Its outlines and place names correspond closely to those in Resen's map, which is, however, much richer in nomenclature and explanatory legends. The map by Thorláksson embraces a smaller area than the other two, taking in only Greenland in the west and a small corner of the American mainland in the southwest; unlike the other two maps, it does not draw or name Helluland, Markland, and Vinland, and it is also distinguished from them by retaining the NE–SW orientation given to Greenland by Mercator and other cartographers. All three maps are graduated in the margins, but they differ considerably in the latitudes assigned to the western lands.

With these divergences, the maps of this group have so much general affinity with one another as to point, if not to mutual influence or copying, at least to use of common sources. Storm and Steenstrup, followed by later writers, have in fact supposed Resen's map to be derived from that of Stefánsson, although this is contested by Gathorne-Hardy, who held them to be derived independently from a common earlier prototype. This question will be discussed below.

For their representation of the Atlantic, these three cartographers depended in the first instance on the type introduced by Mercator's world map of 1569 (Pl. XV), namely that of the Zeno map, modified by the introduction of a strait in the northeast dividing northern Russia from the eastward extension of Greenland. Here the Icelandic mapmakers insert names from the old Norse geography—Biarmaland, Jotunheim, Riseland. Frisland appears in all three maps, though differently located in each. In Thorláksson's (Pl. XVIII), the old course from Iceland to Greenland ("antiqua navigatio ex isl. grönl. versus") is laid down by a dotted line running southwest until it turns north into Eiriksfjord. Hermannsson has inferred that this cartographer correctly conceived the Norse settlements, which he draws as fjords penetrating a broadened southern coast, to be on the west coast of Greenland; but this seems uncertain, since his note about the "third mountain" on the southward run along the east coast instructs the navigator to "keep it to the north when entering Grönlandsfjord [i.e. Eiriksfjord]".[202]

South of Greenland, Thorláksson's map has a broad strait, with the name *Ginnungagap* and a representation of a whirlpool (*vorago*), for which he cites the ancient belief that it caused the tides. The opposite shore of the strait bears the names *Estoteland* (as in Mercator's map) and *pars Americae versus gronlandā;* and Thorláksson's note on this (in Torfaeus' rendering) reads: "Fretum inter Gronlandiae oram extremam, austrum versus & aliam Continentem, quam recentiores Americam vocant, per quod fretum olim Gronlandi excurrentes Vinlandiam invenerunt quam Estotilandiam Pagini [G. A. Magini] forte quis recte existimaverit, ipsum hoc

202. Cited from Torfaeus' Latin version.

fretum, veteribus Ginnungagap, quasi amplas fauces dixeris. Existimamus autem ex Estoti-
landia, si haec Winlandia est, versus aquilonem in Gronlandiam recta perveniri".

Here Bishop Gudbrandur's map comes to an end. His solicitude to reconcile the geography of
the old Norse world, which he had studied in the ancient records of his country, with that of
more recent European explorers and mapmakers, characterizes the work of the other Icelandic
cartographers also. They were studious men who had collated the geographical literature and
maps of their day, and who were careful to mention the authorities for their delineation or those
from whom they dissented. In their maps, and glosses on them, they cite—besides medieval
geographers like Saxo Grammaticus and indigenous sources in the Icelandic annals and sagas—
Gemma Frisius, Peter Apian, the Zeni narrative, Mercator, G. A. Magini. The voyages or reputed voyages to which explicit reference is made in their maps, particularly that of Resen, include those of the Zeni (1380), Johannes Scolvus (1476), the Cabots and the Corte Reals, Verraz-
zano (1524) and Estevão Gomes (1525), Cartier, Frobisher (1576–78) and Davis (1585–87), and
the first Danish expedition to Greenland (1605). The Icelandic maps therefore represent a
serious attempt to relate the old Norse discoveries and settlements to the geography of the
Western Atlantic as known about 1600 and to assign locations to them in terms of the "modern"
map.

Two critical questions present themselves in connection with this early group of Icelandic
maps. First, did they number among their sources any old cartographic document such as the
Icelandic map "made some centuries ago" which Bishop Resen claims to have used? Second,
with what real coasts and localities did their authors identify those visited by the Norsemen five
centuries earlier? These are related questions. For if any medieval map prototype for the Norse
discoveries in America existed, and was still extant in 1600, it would take us back considerably
nearer to the events recorded in it; it might therefore, like the delineation of Greenland in the
Vinland Map, have been, at least in part, derived from observation and experience; and had the
later Icelandic mapmakers disposed of a cartographic source containing elements recognizably
related to the actual geography, they could have come near the mark when they collated the
earliest recorded American landfalls with those of explorers in the fifteenth and sixteenth centuries. The answers to these questions must be sought in scrutiny of the maps themselves.[203]

In Gudbrandur Thorláksson's map, the broad sea-passage (Ginnungagap) south of Greenland plainly represents Davis Strait, and the land fragment south of it the peninsular feature
which in Mercator's map of 1569 is named Estotiland and corresponds to Baffin Land. The Icelandic cartographer however, presumably after reading the old sailing directions and the
saga narratives of the Norse voyages, had misgivings about Mercator's delineation, which are
expressed in his transfer of it five degrees to the south and by his suggestion (in the gloss quoted
above) that, if Estotiland be Vinland, it must lie southwest of Greenland, so that the course
thence to Greenland would be northeasterly.

The outlines in the maps by Stefánsson (Pl. XVII) and Resen (Pl. XIX), which extend further
to the south than Thorláksson's, might have been drawn in answer to this criticism. By turning
the main axis of Greenland through almost a right angle, so that it lies SE–NW instead of
SW–NE, they bring its southernmost point into a position roughly northeast of Markland and
Vinland. In these two maps, as in Mercator's, Davis Strait appears as a closed gulf, trending ap-

203. Unless they are to be found in the unpublished manuscript writings of the cartographers, particularly Resen.

proximately northwest; south of it is the peninsula of Estotiland (named *Helleland* by both cartographers), which is separated by another gulf to the south of it from the peninsula of *Markland*. South of this is a third gulf, after which comes a deep narrow bay running southward into the land, with (on the east side of it) the conspicuous north-pointing *Promontorium Vinlandiae* and, inland, the regional name *Terra Corte Rialis*. Here Stefánsson's outline ends; south of the Vinland promontory Resen shows a broad estuary leading westward into the land and, below it, the peninsula of Norumbega. In both maps the mainland to the west of Vinland is indicated as the habitat of the *Skraelinge* (i.e. Eskimos), who in earlier maps, following Clavus and including Mercator, were located northeast of Greenland.

It is quite evident that the geographical representations in the maps of Stefánsson and Resen are identical. If we compare the outlines of Greenland and America, which appear in these maps as part of a continuous land mass extending in a great arc from north of Scandinavia to the coast of Maine, we find that in both maps Greenland has the same orientation and the same number of inlets on the two coasts; in both maps the mainland southward to the Vinland promontory is interrupted by three westward-trending gulfs forming two broad peninsulas; and the distinctive feature formed by the *Promontorium Vinlandiae* and the deep bay on its west side is common to, and drawn in exactly the same form in, the two maps.

The relationship between the maps, which closely concerns our study of the Vinland Map, has been somewhat perfunctorily treated by historians. On balance of the arguments deployed, the view, sustained by Storm and Steenstrup, that Resen copied his design from Stefánsson's map has the upper hand in the debate. Gathorne-Hardy supports his contrary contention that the two maps are derived independently from a common original by pointing to details in the later map which are not in the earlier; but this argument will not hold water, for all these additions (unless normal copyist's variants) could have been got by Resen from Icelandic textual sources, either directly or through his correspondents in Iceland. Gathorne-Hardy's thesis hangs, in fact, on the one slender thread of Resen's explicit claim to have copied a medieval Icelandic map, "rudi modo delineata".

The further conclusion reached by Storm, that the geographical outlines of Stefánsson's map (and so, in Storm's view, of Resen's also) were constructed from a reading of the sagas, and not after an older map, demands critical scrutiny, for the possible alternative hypotheses have not yet been seriously expounded. Gathorne-Hardy sees in the cartographers' delineation of Helluland, Markland, and Vinland "a striking resemblance to the actual form of Baffin Land and northern Labrador"; believing it to be "quite clear . . . that both Stefánsson and Resen considered that their maps represented Baffin Land and Labrador", he ascribes to them "a better knowledge of the appearance of these localities" than other contemporary cartographers succeeded in formulating; and he suggests accordingly "that these maps are evidence of voyages to America subsequent to those of which we have any record". His argument is vulnerable. Even if the "striking resemblance" to the actual outlines is not one of those "accidental coincidences" misleading to the historian, this visual impression provides a narrow foundation for so heavy a structure of theory. The assertion "that both Stefánsson and Resen considered that their maps [*scil.* the section from Greenland to Vinland] represented Baffin Land and Labrador", so far from being "quite clear", is demonstrably false and betrays a superficial acquaintance with Resen's map.

Only one detail appears to justify this suggestion, namely the indication of Skraelings inland from the Vinland promontory, accompanied—in Stefánsson's map—by a reference to English discovery ("A—Hi sunt ad quos Angli pervenerunt"), which must relate to Frobisher's expeditions to Baffin Land. The juxtaposition of these data no doubt arises from Frobisher's reports on the Eskimos he encountered and from the cartographer's association of them with the natives of Vinland, whom the Icelandic historians supposed to be of the same race as the Skraelings of Greenland.[204] The fact that they are located in the same place in Resen's map must surely indicate that he knew Stefánsson's, or some other map which also presented this feature.

That the two cartographers, however, conceived the lands represented by these outlines to extend far south of Baffin Land and Labrador is apparent from the latitudes assigned to them and from Resen's descriptive notes on the character of the country. The mouth of Frobisher Bay, in the south of Baffin Land, lies in 62°–63° N; we may compare this with the north latitudes in the following tables:

TABLE 1

	Stefánsson's latitude	Resen's latitude
C. Farewell (southern Greenland)	62½°	63½°
Helluland	63°–60½°	62°–59°
Markland	59½°–57½°	58½°–54°
Promontorium Vinlandiae	56°	53½°

TABLE 2

(latitudes in the two maps adjusted to the true latitude, 59° 46′ N, of C. Farewell)

	Stefánsson	Resen
C. Farewell	[59¾°]	[59¾°]
Helluland	60¼°–57½°	58¼°–55¼°
Markland	56¾°–54¾°	54¾°–50¼°
Promontorium Vinlandiae	53¾°	49¾°

Bearing in mind the fact that the latitude of his discoveries, as determined by Frobisher, was correctly laid down in the maps drawn immediately after his expedition,[205] and that Resen explicitly locates them on the coast of *Helleland* in his map,[206] the two cartographers cannot be supposed to have identified any other part of their representation as Baffin Land. This is confirmed by Resen's characterization of the lands delineated (Helluland stony and mountainous, Markland flat and wooded), which is derived from the saga accounts, and by his association of the Norse landfalls with those of explorers nearer to his own time, as depicted in the sixteenth-century maps.

204. Thus Ari Frode, in the *Íslendingabók*, refers to the Eskimos of Greenland as "the same kind of people who have settled in Vinland, and whom the Greenlanders call skraelings".

205. E.g. in Lok's map of 1582, and in that by "F.G." in Hakluyt's edition of Peter Martyr, 1587.

206. By marking *Warvikssund* (a Frobisher name) on the northeast coast of his Helleland-Estotiland, and by a legend on the Eskimos described by Frobisher "in ipsius libello". Resen adds drawings of Eskimo life copied from woodcuts in the French and German editions (published respectively at Geneva 1578 and Nuremberg 1580) of Dionysius Settle's account of Frobisher's second voyage.

Resen's nomenclature plainly follows that of Mercator's map of 1569, or of a printed map of the same type, e.g. in Ortelius' *Theatrum*. From Davis Strait southward, he has twenty-three names of coastal features (capes, islands, rivers, places), of which all but four are from Mercator's stock,[207] although (as we shall see) some are rearranged; and of Resen's nine regional names only the three taken from the Norse voyages are not in Mercator.[208] While the outline is not that of Mercator, the location of names in Resen's map indicates that he took Helluland to be Baffin Land, and the bay to the south Hudson Strait; Markland to be Labrador (with *Capo de Labrador* = C. Chidley), and the bay to the south Belleisle Strait; and the *Promontorium Vinlandiae*, with the mainland west of it (*Terra Corte Rialis* and *Regio Baccalearū*), to be Newfoundland.[209] South of this are the St. Lawrence estuary, New France, and Norumbega, as in Mercator and generally in maps of the late sixteenth century.

The recent cartography and travel literature, which supplied the names and legends for the maps of Stefánsson and (notably) Resen, did not furnish their geographical outlines. The delineation by Mercator evidently did not satisfy the Icelandic cartographers, who, in rejecting or altering it, substituted one of their own which is difficult to parallel in maps of the period. Only in the post-Frobisher and pre-Davis cartography, particularly in Michael Lok's map of 1582, do we find anything similar. Lok shows, in the region concerned, four western openings —Davis Strait (not yet so named, of course), Frobisher's "strait" (in 62°–63° N), *Gamma baya* (in 56°–58° N) and *Grand bay* (in 47°–52° N)—the last two of which may be taken as Hamilton Inlet and the St. Lawrence. Allowing for the difference that Lok distinguishes Davis Strait and Frobisher's "strait" and shows them both as open passages to the west, we can see a marked affinity between his representation and that of the four inlets or gulfs in Resen's map.[210] Whether this is due to chance or design we will not venture to pronounce.

It may be noted also that Lok's peninsular *Corte real,* as a generalized delineation derived from the *Terra Corterealis* which in Mercator's 1569 map represents Labrador and Newfoundland combined, has a north-pointing extremity which recalls that of Resen's *Promontorium Vinlandiae.* The coastal place names in Resen's map here offer a possible clue to his line of thought. Along the outer coast of the *Promontorium,* he has three names (south to north: *C. S. Marco, S. Maria* and—at the tip—*Caravielo*) evidently derived from Mercator's map, in which they are applied to features along the Labrador section of the *Terra Corterealis,* with the *Ilha do Marco* and *Y. de carauielo* as (respectively) the southernmost and northernmost in a chain of three long narrow islands lying parallel to the main coast, in 57°–59° N.[211] To have transmuted this chain of islands into a promontory, and the strait between them and the mainland into a

---

207. The four exceptions are *Warvikssund* (see previous note), *Capo de Labrador* (C. Chidley), *Portus Jacobi Carterii* (Cabot Strait) and *Sang venar* (Saguenay). The last three are from the common stock of late sixteenth-century cartography.

208. *Helleland, Markland,* and *Promontorium Vinlandiae Bonae.*

209. Stefánsson, in his gloss on the deep inlet between the *Promontorium* and the mainland, suggests a doubt about the interpretation of his conflicting authorities: "Hanc à meridie oceanum finire voluere nostri [i.e. the Scandinavian geographers?]. Sed ex recentiorum historiis colligo, aut fretum aut sinum hanc ab America distinguere". This presumably refers to Belleisle Strait, leading into the St. Lawrence estuary.

210. Of these, the three more northerly are of course also in Stefánsson's map.

211. In Ortelius' map of America, in the *Theatrum* (1570), the three islands are named *Carauielo, fortuna,* and *S. Ioan,* while *S. Maria* and *C. Marco* are capes on the mainland facing.

deep narrow bay, is by no means beyond the limits of the licence which contemporary cartographers allowed themselves under the control of alternative geographical concepts or information; and we cannot exclude the possibility that Stefánsson's and Resen's representation of the Vinland promontory was adapted in this way by them, or by the author of a common prototype, from a detail of Mercator's map, or of a map (perhaps by Ortelius) belonging to the same family and amended in accordance with Frobisher's discoveries. If such an original is to be postulated, supplying the Icelandic cartographers with a model for the main coastal features from Davis Strait to the St. Lawrence, it was certainly later than 1569 and probably later than 1577 or 1578.

It is, of course, permissible to think the *Promontorium Vinlandiae,* as drawn by Stefánsson and Resen, too strongly marked and idiosyncratic a feature of the design to have been thus adapted, and to suppose it to come from an independent source. Its form is, in fact, not precisely paralleled in any other map of the period, except in the shape given to the Zenian island of Drogeo, shown by Lok (following Mercator and the Zeno map) out in the ocean west of Nova Scotia, and with a north coast tapering to a sharp point like a wedge; we may note, too, that in maps from the Molyneux globe of 1592 onward Drogeo came to be identified with Labrador and the name placed on the mainland in the same area as Mercator's *Caravielo* group of names (which were, as we have shown, associated by Resen with Vinland). This may seem oversubtle; but it is the only other analogy from sixteenth-century cartography which can be cited for this delineation.

If all such parallelisms are rejected, it is still possible to discredit Resen's claim to have made use of a medieval Icelandic map by supposing (as Storm did) his outline of Vinland to be a mental projection of the geographical features—a deep bay, a north-pointing ness—which he found described in the saga narratives of the Norse voyages.

In trying to recapture the processes of thought and synthesis which went into the construction of these maps, we have to distinguish the several materials which the cartographers sought to combine and to reconcile. In the Icelandic records and the old geographical texts of Scandinavian authorship, they found placenames, descriptions of countries and native peoples, sailing courses; much of this verbal information came down from personal experience gathered before the day of instrumental navigation, or indeed of written record, and was therefore not very precisely located—unless in Resen's "ancient map". The body of knowledge about North America accumulated by the date of Mercator's world map embraced a considerable number of placenames bestowed by explorers and associated with outlines pieced together from the discontinuous coastal traverses of various expeditions. To these geographical delineations and the nomenclature attached to them the map gave an illusory aspect of certainty, defining their positions, relatively and absolutely, by the coordinates of latitude and longitude. How fallible such determinations must be, and how speculative their assembly into the coherent framework of the map, had been demonstrated, in the lifetime of the Icelandic cartographers, by the changes imposed on Mercator's representation by the English discoveries in the northwest. Geographical features and names had to be shifted to east or west, or north or south; bays were revisualized as straits, islands as capes; and consequent adjustments had to be made to combine the parts into a continuous coastline.

The maps of Stefánsson and Resen are doubtless, in large part, end products of such a process.

They, or the author of their common original, selected details from the printed cartography of their time and adjusted them to the geography of the Norse voyages deduced from the Icelandic texts—by changes in form, orientation, or latitude, and by adding the toponymy of the sagas. In the course of all this Resen fortunately leaves clues for us to follow, in the place names retained from his prototype and moved into a different position along with the outline to which they were attached.[212] If such a process of adaptation of elements from recent cartography, combined with geographical interpretation of the Icelandic texts, be thought sufficient to account for the whole delineation of America in the maps of Stefánsson and Resen, then there is no need to postulate the use of a medieval Icelandic map, and we must suppose that, if it existed, it has left no mark on the work of these cartographers. We must then, with Hermannsson, deem their maps to be "of no importance, because the old tradition had been interrupted, and they merely represent the ideas of the cartographers themselves".[213]

Even if Storm made little attempt to trace to their recent sources the American outlines in Stefánsson's map (still less in Resen's), there is consequently good reason to admit, with him, that they were "constructed after the Saga of Erik the Red on arbitrary parallels, and, though well worth examining as illustrative of the idea an Icelander about the year 1590 had formed as to the early discoveries of his countrymen, will not help us to determine them geographically".[214] To shake this hypothesis it would be necessary to demonstrate *either* that visual inspection and comparison of the outlines left a residuum not accountable to derivation from sixteenth-century cartography, *or* that a medieval Icelandic map of American lands existed and could have been consulted by the mapmakers of *ca.* 1590–1605. The first alternative is perhaps (as we have seen) not very easy to sustain without invoking the second, which will be considered in the next chapter.

The later Icelandic maps, and copies from the earlier ones, made in the seventeenth century do not concern us, for they are no more than graphic systematizations of the records of the Norse voyages, as interpreted by their authors, and they contain no hint of any medieval map among their sources. They have been well described by Hermannsson,[215] and a very brief summary is sufficient here.

Even if the Danish expeditions of 1605–07 expected to find the lost colonies on the east coast of Greenland, they were prevented by ice from landing there, and they failed to discover the relics of the colonists on the west coast. A version of Ivar Bardsson's description of Greenland, which came into currency in Holland and England, provided Dutch cartographers with the place names of the Norse settlements and hunting grounds; and the Dutch maps, beginning with those of 1626 and 1634 by Joris Carolus of Enkhuizen,[216] set down many of these names on the east coast of Greenland. In this they were followed by the Icelandic mapmakers—Jón Gudmundsson, Bishop Thórdur Thorláksson, and Torfaeus; and thus, in Hermannsson's words, "the fateful error was committed which was the cause of so many futile and disastrous

212. For instance (as noted), the three coastal names along the Vinland promontory; also the names *R. de Tormentus* and *Baja Dus Mejans,* in the gulf south of *Markland* (Labrador), which correspond to names placed by Mercator in the large bay named *Golfam de Merostris* and lying (in his map) *north* of Labrador.

213. Hermannsson, *The Problem of Wineland* (1936), p. 77.

214. Storm, "Studies", p. 335.

215. Hermannsson, *Jón Gudmundsson,* pp. xxvii–viii; and *Two Cartographers,* pp. 33–38.

216. Björnbo and Petersen, *Anecdota,* pl. xi; see also Hermannsson, *Cartography of Iceland,* pp. 36–37.

efforts to reach that coast, upon which it was taken for granted that the Eastern Settlement was situated".

So the map of Jón Gudmundsson (*ca.* 1640), with many names from the "mythical-heroic sagas", lays down the Eastern Settlement on the east coast with, north of it, *Kroksfiord* and *Greiper;* to the south the American coastline is sketched in as a great projection of land, with only one name (*Helleland*) relating to the Norse discoveries.[217] Bishop Thórdur's maps are mere elaborations of that by Bishop Gudbrandur, revised in the light of his own reading of the old texts and in accordance with more recent Dutch cartography. In none of these maps are Markland and Vinland delineated.

8. THE MAPPING OF VINLAND

The surviving copy of the Vinland Map was made less than forty years after the last authenticated voyage between Norway and Greenland. Intermittent communication with Greenland (as we have seen) may have continued into the very period when the copy, or even perhaps the original draft, of the map was made. If, however, its compiler derived this part of his map from an antecedent cartographic model, his prototype must have been a good deal older than this; and its detailed delineation of the west coasts of Greenland may be supposed to antedate the abandonment of the Western Settlement in the first half of the fourteenth century. It may indeed go back even further in time, perhaps to the early thirteenth century, when the description in the *Konungs skuggsjá* attests an intimate and realistic knowledge of Greenland.[218]

It is curious that the *Konungs skuggsjá,* compiled about the year 1250, makes no mention of Vinland and the other western discoveries of the Viking Age. While this omission in itself may have no special significance (the work being apparently unfinished), it illustrates aptly enough an essential difference, arising from chronology, between the sources available to the author of the Vinland Map for his delineations respectively of Greenland and of the lands to the west, considered as geographical records. For the series of Norse voyages to Helluland, Markland and Vinland had taken place over four centuries before the extant copy of the map was drawn; they were over by about A.D. 1030 (at the latest), and resulted in no permanent settlement such as that of Greenland; only three possible later American landfalls are recorded, but so equivocally (in regard to two of them) as to fall far short of proof.[219] Any basis of experience from which a map of Vinland could have been constructed in the early fifteenth century was therefore remote in time, and the four hundred years' interval was bridged only by Icelandic records in which the events of the tenth and eleventh centuries were preserved. Although the surviving recensions of the two sagas which form the principal sources for the Norse discovery of America are no older than the fourteenth century, their narratives doubtless stem ultimately from an oral tradition unbroken from the Viking period. While it is true that (in Gathorne-Hardy's words)[220] "the compilers of those versions which we now possess must have worked in the main . . . from earlier written sagas", it must also be remembered that none of the Icelandic

217. Bishop Thórdur, copying Jón Gudmundsson's map, thought it a fanciful work: "hanc mappam curiositatis potius quam exempli ratione adjeci".
218. See Nansen, Vol. 2, pp. 246–48.
219. See below, pp. 222–27.
220. Gathorne-Hardy, p. 99.

tales was committed to writing until the beginning of the twelfth century, when Ari Thorgilsson (born 1067) inaugurated the age of documentary history. Gathorne-Hardy, emphasizing the reliability of oral tradition, suggests—no doubt rightly—that "the exploits of those who fought, litigated or explored in the tenth and eleventh centuries were carried with truth, impartiality and accuracy over the brief interval which separated them from the age of written history, which dawned with Ari the Learned".[221] Yet we must attribute to this gap of about one hundred years, or three generations, a somewhat greater significance in the *cartographic* history of North American discovery.

The technique of Norse navigation occasioned neither the use nor the making of charts, to which none of the medieval records makes any reference in this connection; and it appears the more unlikely that any map of the American discoveries was drawn before "the age of written history".[222] The narratives or logs of the expeditions, handed down with remarkable particularity in the stories of the saga tellers, conveyed the geographical circumstances of these voyages with sufficient precision to satisfy their audience and to make a map even more supererogatory, and indeed inconsistent with this mode of transmission, than a written transcript. We have also to remember that the Norse voyages to America, unlike those to Greenland and along its coasts, were isolated episodes, covering only a brief span of time, and that (so far as we know) they were not followed up by any regular navigation.

But a map, like other graphic records, cannot be substantially communicated by word of mouth. Even an observer, if he draws from visual memory, and without the aid of sketches made *ad vivum,* a map of the coasts which he has traversed, must generalize and formalize his outlines; and this process necessarily plays a much greater part in the construction of a map by someone who does not carry in his mind's eye an image of these coasts from direct visual experience. If (as we think probable) no map illustrating the American landfalls of the Norsemen was drawn before the twelfth century at earliest—that is, long after the death of the adventurers who made them—its chain of transmission must have been verbal, not graphic. In these circumstances we could expect from such a map no more than a general indication of the coasts in question and of their most conspicuous features, with the data of direction from known lands, of location, of trend, orientation, and form stated with no greater precision than a verbal relation, whether spoken or written, could offer. This hypothesis will be tested by scrutiny of the outline in the Vinland Map.

WRITTEN RECORDS

Before returning to the map we may conveniently make a cursory survey of the surviving textual records of the Vinland voyages;[223] of the chronology of the voyages to be reconstructed from these accounts; and of the geographical data on the lands visited which may be extracted from the texts.

221. Ibid., p. 93.

222. See above, p. 183. We do not overlook that some races to whom the art of writing was unknown have been found to practice that of mapmaking; but their cartographic works are generally so specialized in function and form as to place them in a different category from the geographical map as conceived by Europeans. Nor do we suggest that the Viking seamen lacked the data of observation from which to draw a chart; see above, p. 189, and below, p. 214.

223. These are described by A. M. Reeves, *The Finding of Wineland* (1890); by H. Hermannsson, *The Problem of Wineland* (1936), pp. 1–48; and in Hermannsson's edition, *The Wineland Sagas* (1944).

The first reference to Vinland comes from Denmark, where Adam of Bremen picked it up and wrote it down in his "Descriptio insularum aquilonis" (*ca.* 1070); this shows that at so early a date the name of the country and information on its character had reached Europe, although Adam gives no details of the voyages or of the discoverers. The earliest Icelandic mention occurs in the *Íslendingabók* (*ca.* 1124) of Ari Thorgilsson, who makes a glancing allusion to Vinland as the home of the same race as the earlier inhabitants of Greenland.[224] The Icelandic geographical text prefixed to an itinerary to the Holy Land compiled by Abbot Nicolaus Bergsson of Thvera (died 1159) enumerates the lands in the western ocean—Helluland, Markland, and Vinland—and refers to the discovery of Vinland by Leif Eiriksson and to the expedition of Thorfinn Karlsefni; but this passage may be a later interpolation.[225] The sections on Leif's voyages in the Saga of King Olaf Tryggvason (thirteenth century) are perhaps derived from the Saga of Eric the Red "in an oral form"; but the original recension of the *Landnámabók,* dated by Hermannsson to "the latter part of the twelfth century, or somewhat later", probably made no reference to the discovery of Vinland by Leif.[226] The relative barrenness of information about Vinland in these early Icelandic historical writings, or the offhand way in which it is introduced, is held by some scholars (e.g. Gathorne-Hardy and Hermannsson) to show that "the story about Vinland was well-known" to their readers; a not less likely explanation may be the remoteness of the events associated with the discovery. Nevertheless, the references (as Hovgaard remarks) "testify to a firmly established and generally known tradition, which reaches back to the time of Ari Frode [Thorgilsson] and the first settlement of Greenland".[227] They certainly will not sustain Nansen's thesis that, though the Norse discovery of America be historical, the details of it in the two fuller narratives were invented, or elaborated from classical and Irish folklore, by the Icelandic saga writers.

These narratives are, it is true, preserved in manuscripts of later date than those so far cited, and their accounts of the voyages, which are difficult to reconcile, have been the subject of vigorous and unresolved debate by historians. The Saga of Eirik the Red (or Saga of Thorfinn Karlsefni) has come down to us in two variant texts, the *Hauksbók* written by or for Hauk Erlendsson in the early fourteenth century and a manuscript collection of sagas written in the fifteenth century.[228] The Flatey Book, a codex from the last two decades of the fourteenth century, is a compilation from various sagas which incorporates, in that of Olaf Tryggvason,

224. Ari Thorgilsson is also believed to be the authority for the report in the *Landnámabók* (in Hauk Erlendsson's *Hauksbók*) about the landfall made by Ari Mársson, apparently about 983, on Hvítramannaland, i.e. White Men's Land, "which some call Great Ireland". The name of this country was again picked up from Eskimos of Markland by Karlsefni on his return voyage, according to the Saga of Eirik the Red; but Hermannsson (*Wineland,* p. 25) thinks it "obvious that this passage is a later addition . . . and that the land is a fabulous one as Storm, Nansen and others have shown". The data however can be shown to fit Greenland, as Mr G. Ashe has argued (*Land to the West,* ch. v). In any case, the Vinland Map makes no reference to Hvítramannaland, and this disputed issue lies outside the scope of our present study. Cf. below, n. 269.

225. Hermannsson, *Problem of Wineland,* pp. 2–3.

226. Ibid., pp. 4–6.

227. Hovgaard, p. 127.

228. Royal Library, Copenhagen, AM 544, 4°, and AM 557, 4°, respectively. Gathorne-Hardy cites them independently as Hauk's Book and the Saga of Eirik the Red; but since both texts derive from a common original, we follow Hermannsson's convenient practice of referring to this version, without discrimination of MS, as the Saga of Eirik the Red, or briefly the Saga.

two sections relating to Vinland and its discoveries and entitled respectively the Tale of Eirik the Red (in three chapters) and the Tale of the Greenlanders (in seven).[229]

The two principal sources, namely the Saga of Eirik the Red and the Tale of the Greenlanders, appear to represent (respectively) Icelandic and Greenlandic versions of the Norse discovery of America. Their divergences in recording the sequence of events are profound and various. The Saga records two voyages which reached Vinland and one which failed; the Tale recounts five voyages which made or sighted the country and one which failed. The majority of modern students, drawing attention to discrepancies, absurdities and mythical or supernatural elements in the Tale, have tended to discredit it and, following Storm, to hold that its testimony, where it differs from the Saga, must be rejected and, where unsupported by the Saga, must be considered doubtful; Hermannsson goes even further in his assertion "that, in trying to find a solution to the problem of Wineland, we need pay very little, if any, attention to the Tale".[230] Some historians, on the other hand, consider that the discrepancies and errors in the Tale are not sufficient wholly to invalidate its authority as a factual report and that the numerous and circumstantial details found in it (but not in the Saga) can be accounted for only as a record of experience. Adding the a priori argument that (in Gathorne-Hardy's words) "the normal course of tradition is rather to blend many voyages into one than to expand one voyage, in one and the same story, into many", such critics have considered themselves justified in constructing from the Saga and the Tale a consecutive narrative of events. This procedure, adopted by Hovgaard and Gathorne-Hardy, although condemned by Hermannsson as "against accepted principles of textual and historical criticism", plainly goes further to explain the geographical and navigational details of the various accounts—and consequently to establish the authenticity of those in the Tale—than a hypothesis which rests on more general considerations of inherent probability, leaving a large residuum of factual reporting unaccounted for except as fiction. The wealth of nautical detail, for instance, in the report of Bjarni Herjolfsson's chance discovery, which (being in the Tale but not in the Saga) is discarded by Storm, surely justifies Gathorne-Hardy in claiming that "whatever criticisms have been passed upon Bjarni's voyage by those who are unable to fit it into their theories . . . if all the rest of our material had been destroyed, this voyage would be regarded as in itself sufficient to substantiate the fact of Norse discovery".[231] We may add that the two legends in the Vinland Map, by associating Bjarni with the discovery of America, provide a further justification for accepting the historical and geographical evidence of the Tale; the sources of these legends and their implications for the chronology of the voyages will be examined in the next chapter.

With the detailed arguments respecting the degree of authority to be ascribed to the two accounts we need not concern ourselves here. As a working assumption, we shall (with Hovgaard and Gathorne-Hardy) take it that both narratives contain authentic elements. The resultant chronology of the voyages, as developed by Gathorne-Hardy from this premise, is shown in column A of the table below; column B gives the chronology deduced by Storm from the Tale of the Greenlanders alone; and column C that which he extracted from the Saga of Eirik the Red.

229. Royal Library, Copenhagen, Gl. kgl. Saml. 1005, fol. Cited by Gathorne-Hardy as Flatey Book; here, following Hermannsson, as the Tale of the Greenlanders, or briefly the Tale.

230. Hermannsson, *Problem of Wineland*, p. 47.

231. Gathorne-Hardy, p. 245.

	A Tale + Saga (GATHORNE-HARDY)	B Tale (STORM)	C Saga (STORM)
Bjarni's voyage from Iceland to Greenland, and chance discovery of America	986	985	—
Bjarni's voyage to Norway and return to Greenland	1000–1001	1001–1002	—
Leif's voyage from Norway to Greenland, and chance discovery of Vinland	—	—	1000
Leif's expedition to Vinland	1002–1003	1003–1004	—
Thorvald's expedition to Vinland	1004–1007	1005–1006	—
Thorstein's abortive voyage and death	1008	1007	1001
Karlsefni's arrival in Greenland	*ca.* 1019	1008	1002
Karlsefni's expedition to Vinland	*ca.* 1020–*ca.* 1023	1009–1011	1003–1006
Freydís's expedition to Vinland	*ca.* 1024	1012–1013	—

The outstanding differences between the two versions may be briefly summarized. The Tale alone records Bjarni Herjolfsson's voyage and accidental discovery, and represents Leif Eiriksson's voyage as deliberately undertaken, in consequence of Bjarni's, with the object of exploration and settlement; the Saga makes Leif's discovery an accident of his return voyage from Norway. Thorvald Eiriksson's voyage and death in Vinland are reported in the Tale, while the Saga makes him merely a member of Karlsefni's expedition on which he met his death. Freydís' voyage is unmentioned in the Saga.

GEOGRAPHY OF THE VOYAGES

Admitting the chronological sequence of voyages as enumerated in the first column of the table, and consequently the authenticity of the texts on which it is based, we may extract the geographical information which they furnish on the discoveries.

In A.D. 986 Bjarni Herjolfsson, sailing from Iceland for Greenland, is driven to the south of his course by "the persistent northerly and easterly winds which often prevail in the North Atlantic during the early summer months".[232] He sights land, wooded and not mountainous, and, knowing himself to be south of his latitude, turns northward, leaving it to port; after two days' sailing he comes to another land, flat and wooded; sailing out to sea for three days before a southwesterly wind, he comes to a third land, mountainous and with ice upon it, which he takes to be an island; and the same wind, strengthened in force, brings him in four days sail to Cape Herjolfsnes in the south of Greenland.

Fourteen years later Bjarni goes to Norway, where he tells his story. On his return to Greenland in A.D. 1001, he sells a ship to Leif Eiriksson for a voyage to the lands discovered in the west. Leif, sailing by Bjarni's homeward track, comes to the country which Bjarni found last, a flat

232. Hovgaard, pp. 123–24.

rocky coast with glaciers behind, which Leif names Helluland; and then to Bjarni's second land, low and wooded with wide expanses of white sand, which he calls Markland. Sailing out to sea for two days, he discovers another mainland, with an island north of it, and, entering "the sound which lay between the island and the cape which ran north from the mainland", he runs west past the cape; after running aground, the Norsemen take their ship up a river and into a lake, where they erect houses. Here "day and night were more equally divided than in Greenland or Iceland", as they note from observation of azimuths of the midwinter sun in the forenoon and afternoon. If these bearings refer precisely to sunrise and sunset, they indicate a northern limit of roughly 50° latitude for the position.[233] The country has no frost in winter and bears vines, so that it is given the name Vinland. After wintering there, Leif returns "with a fair wind" to Greenland in the next spring.

In the following year (1004) Thorvald Eiriksson, Leif's brother, takes a ship to Vinland and winters in Leif's old camp. In the next summer the country to the west is explored by boat and found to be wooded, with white sands and many islands. The summer after, Thorvald sails east "and along the more northerly part of the country", to a cape which he names Kjalarnes (Keelness) and eastward to fjords and a headland, where Thorvald is killed in an affray with natives and buried, so that the headland is called Krossanes (Crossness). After the winter his crew return to Greenland.

A year later (1008) Thorstein Eiriksson sets out for Vinland in his brother Thorvald's ship, but is carried by weather far out into the Atlantic and eventually reaches the Western Settlement, where he dies.

About the year 1019 the Icelander Thorfinn Karlsefni comes to Greenland, where in the next year he marries Thorstein's widow and sets out an expedition with two ships to make a settlement in Vinland. They sail north to the Western Settlement and the Bjarneyar (Bear Isles), and after two days at sea with a north wind they come to land with many flat stones and with arctic foxes; to this they give the name Helluland. Sailing thence for two days, still with a north wind, and changing course "from south to southeast", they reach a wooded land, which they call Markland, with an island offshore. Coasting southward for two days, they come to Keelness, naming the long sandy beaches Furdustrands; and while they lie at anchor in one of the bays, grapes and self-sown wheat are found. Sailing on, they come to a fjord with an island and strong currents, which they name Straumsfjord; here they winter. In the spring Thorhall takes one of the ships north past Keelness in search of Leif's Vinland, and Karlsefni with his companions in the other ship coasts southward "a long time" until they come to a river flowing through a lake and across a gravel bar to the sea; on this estuary, which they call Hóp, they find vines and self-sown wheat. After wintering there, they return to Straumsfjord, where they pass the third winter before returning with a south wind to Markland and Greenland.

Next year (*ca.* 1024) Freydís, Leif's sister, goes with two ships to his camp in Vinland.

Such, in barest outline, are the geographical data which the narratives of the Vinland voyages yield and which have been the subject of widely differing interpretations and identifications. They can be roughly classified in five groups:

233. The interpretation of the *eyktarstad* and *dagmálastad* observation recorded in the Tale is much disputed; the latitudes computed by various students range from 49° to 36° N.

(1) Details of navigation (particularly for the voyages of Bjarni and Karlsefni) such as might be extracted from a seaman's log, recording course and distance made good, winds, shoals, bearings and appearance of landmarks, and the like. From these a conception of the relationship of the various landfalls can be formed, but in general only and subject to fairly wide "spread" in view of the uncertain length of a day's sail and the practice of stating courses in terms of wind direction. Only the nearest cardinal points were used; "in at least two cases the Icelanders placed their north in the direction of our north–east";[234] the wind need not be kept astern, for the Norse ships could sail "with the wind somewhat forward of the beam";[235] and there must have been considerable leeway or drift with ocean currents. Thus, when Bjarni sailed on a southwesterly wind from his second landfall to his third and thence to Greenland, this does not necessarily imply a northeast course but one which may lie between north and east; and Karlsefni's course from the west coast of Greenland, two days before a north wind, may well have had some westing in it.

(2) The discovery of three distinct land masses or sections of continental coast. Hovgaard prudently observes that "different names may have been given to the same land, and the same name may have been applied to different lands by different explorers. Thus . . . the Markland of one expedition may have been the Vineland of another, and the Helluland of one expedition may not have been the Helluland of another".[236] The only equations which are explicitly stated in or justified by the textual evidence are: Bjarni's 3rd land = Leif's Helluland = Karlsefni's Helluland; and the Vinland of Leif, Thorvald and Freydís (since both the later expeditions went to Leif's camp, which Karlsefni apparently never found). If, as the legends of the Vinland Map suggest, Leif was accompanied by Bjarni, his identification of Bjarni's discoveries, recorded in the Tale, carries more weight. There is no mention in the narratives of any coasting voyages by Leif and Thorvald before they reach Vinland, nor by Karlsefni before he reaches the Straumsfjord area. Thorvald's exploration of the coast north of Vinland may be linked to that of Karlsefni, approaching Straumsfjord from the north, by the common feature of Keelness. The texts contain no indication whether these explorers considered the three lands of their discovery to be part of a single mainland or to be separated by sea passages.

(3) The conditions of climate and vegetation ascribed to the three lands. While by no means consistent, these indicate certain limits of latitude. Thus the wild vines found by Leif in Vinland and by Karlsefni at Hóp would today locate these regions south of Nova Scotia, as would the reference to winters free of frost; but evidence of this kind must be interpreted in the light of climatic changes, and allow for the milder climate which (as meteorologists agree) prevailed in the eleventh century.

(4) The solar observations made on the shortest day in Vinland. Because of the uncertainty whether this is to be taken as a precise statement of the length of the day or simply as a general statement that the day was much longer here than in the homelands of the Norsemen, it is

234. Hovgaard, pp. 64–65.
235. Ibid., p. 61.
236. Ibid., p. 221. Edward Reman (*The Norse Discoveries and Explorations in America,* 1949) took the Saga as the sole source for Karlsefni's voyage; suggested that the agreement of the descriptive names given by the Norsemen did not imply identity of the lands to which they were applied; and held that "Leif's Markland was not Karlsefni's", nor Thorvald's Kjalarnes that of Karlsefni.

probably unwise to take this as an accurate record of the latitudes, or of the northern limit of the latitudes, in which Vinland lay.[237]

(5) Description of the lands discovered and of their prominent features. Helluland is stony, with glaciers; Markland low and wooded, with beaches; Furdustrands has long sandy beaches; Keelness is a north-pointing cape, with a sound or bay on the west; Straumsfjord has strong currents; Hóp is a landlocked tidal estuary. It is the difficulty of reconciling these physical attributes with the other circumstances of the Norse discoveries that has occasioned the strongest conflict of opinion regarding the identification of the lands named in the narratives. The possibility that, in the process of transmission, details may have been transferred from one voyage to another, or even introduced into the saga narratives from some extraneous source, cannot be disregarded; and this gives a certain air of unreality to much of the debate.[238]

THE REPRESENTATION IN THE VINLAND MAP

It must be admitted that the Vinland Map reproduces very little of the geographical detail noted in the narratives of the Norse voyages. We find only the outline of a single land mass, divided into three by two deep inlets and the prominent capes, pointing northward or northwestward, on the south of their entrances. Before examining these features more closely, we have to consider the location and extent of the land represented in relation to the other parts of the map and to the data in the textual records.

The description of Vinland as an island and the apparent application of this name to the whole land mass have already been commented on. The threefold division is plainly deliberate, and it accords with the accounts of the various discoveries; but the narratives furnish no authority for the combination of the three lands discovered into a single great island, nor for the tracing of a continuous east coast, still less of a west coast. Are we to suppose these to be cartographic constructions evolved by the author of the map to justify his theoretical concept of "Vinland" (that is, the complex of lands discovered by the Norsemen) as an island?

To the exaggerated longitudinal interval between Greenland and Vinland—somewhat wider than that between Greenland and Iceland, and nearly as great as that between Greenland and Europe—no special significance need be attached, in view of the general unreliability of east-west distances in medieval world maps. We should not be justified in drawing from this alone an inference that the representation of Greenland and Vinland might have been derived from a single map prototype on a different scale from that used for the Old World. It is nonetheless permissible to presume that the delineation of Vinland reflects the cartographer's views (whatever their source) on the geographical relationship of the Norse discoveries in the west to Greenland.

We must first consider the latitudinal position and extension ascribed to Vinland in the map. Its northernmost point is laid down in about the same latitude as the section of the west coast of Greenland north of Disko Bay or Umanak Fjord (as we have conjectured),[239] as the south coast of Iceland, and as the westernmost point of Norway; its south coast on the parallel of

237. See Gathorne-Hardy, pp. 211–20; Reman, pp. 83–85.

238. In Mark Twain's words, "the researches of many commentators have already thrown much darkness on this subject, and it is probable that, if they continue, we shall soon know nothing at all about it".

239. Above, p. 184.

Brittany. While it would be unsafe to assume Vinland and Europe to be drawn to a uniform scale, and so to attempt a correlation of latitudes on opposite shores of the Atlantic, we may remark that this would seem to place Vinland (that is, the whole western land so named in the map) between the limits of about 60° N and 48° N, with the more northerly of the two inlets in about 58° N and the more southerly in about 56° N.

We have already observed that Iceland is laid down a little north, and Greenland a little south, of the true positions. If these necessary corrections are made, it is not difficult to reconcile the relative positions of Atlantic lands in the map with the navigational data of the Norse voyages. We can see, in the first place, how Bjarni, sailing from Iceland and driven south of his course for Greenland by northeasterly winds, inevitably made a landfall on the American coast, perhaps as far south as Nova Scotia, perhaps on Newfoundland or Labrador; his second and third landfalls lie northward of his first, and thence a southwesterly wind brings him, doubtless on a course more east than north, to Cape Herjolfsnes. Leif's course to Helluland and Markland follows that of Bjarni in reverse; and, after crossing a sound and passing a north–pointing cape to the east of it, he comes to the land which he named Vinland. This topographical description is plainly reflected in the delineation of the more southerly inlet and cape in the Vinland Map. This cape perhaps also corresponds, in the cartographer's mind, to the Kjalarnes of Thorvald's and Karlsefni's voyages. Karlsefni adopts a different outward course; and if the "Bjarneyar" of his narrative correspond to the similarly named islands of the old chorography of Greenland already cited,[240] he may have gone as far north as Disko Island (69°–70° N) before turning his ship's head westward. Hovgaard's suggestion that the open coastal channel had to be followed "at least as far as the Western Settlement" before Karlsefni could find a passage through the East Pack neglects the probability that at this date Davis Strait was free of ice.[241] With a northerly wind, and thus (we may suppose) on a southwest or westerly course, Karlsefni crosses Davis Strait and picks up land in two days. If we discount the map's longitudinal error, these courses agree reasonably enough with the delineation of Greenland and the most northerly section (Helluland) of "Vinlanda Insula". Karlsefni's subsequent landfalls all lay to the southward, and he returns from Straumfjord to Markland and then Greenland with a south wind, doubtless on a general northeasterly course.

Thus, if we were able to take the delineation in the map "at its face value", by supposing its scale to be equivalent to that of the European coasts, correlation of the American lands depicted in it with the geographical conditions prescribed by the written sources would justify the identification of the two large inlets as Hudson Strait or Ungava Bay and as the Gulf of St. Lawrence, and of the three land sections respectively as Baffin Land, Labrador (perhaps with Newfoundland), and the Maritime Provinces of Canada. The lake into which the more northerly inlet broadens at its head might be thought to represent Hudson's Bay; but there is no authority for this feature in the texts, and since medieval mapmakers commonly draw a lake at the head or source of a river we may not, without further supporting evidence, think this anything but a cartographic convention. There may nevertheless have been in the cartographer's mind some thought of the river flowing out of a lake where Leif set up his Vinland camp, although if this were so the feature has been transposed to the north of Markland. The delineation of the more

240. See above, p. 188.
241. Hovgaard, pp. 228–29.

southerly inlet clearly evokes a landlocked tidal estuary corresponding to the description of Hóp.

The matter of identification is however not so simple, as the dissident conclusions of the commentators show; and we shall return to it.[242]

The delineation of "Vinlanda Insula" in the map does not, in our view, derive from a carto-graphic model drawn from experience. The general appearance and conventional style of the outlines, the elements evidently born of theory or conjecture, and plainly contrasting with a few features which are clearly and boldly depicted as they are described in the narratives; the want of particularity elsewhere and the omission of numerous other geographical details mentioned in the texts—all these aspects of the design persuade us that it owes its ultimate, if not immediate, origin to a graphic reconstruction of the geography of the voyages, compiled from the saga accounts or from hearsay, and generalized in transmission. This is indeed a conclusion which the a priori considerations enunciated at the beginning of this chapter might lead us to expect.

That the author of the Vinland Map made use of a map prototype compiled in this way is of course very probable. The prototype, whose maker must have enjoyed access to the texts of the saga narratives, was—with little less probability—drawn in Iceland; and this naturally prompts a comparison with the Icelandic maps of the Norse discoveries drawn at the turn of the sixteenth and seventeenth centuries, particularly those of Sigurdur Stefánsson (*ca.* 1590) and Bishop Hans Poulson Resen (1605).

The later maps are, as we have seen, ex post facto attempts to locate the medieval discoveries on the "modern" map of America resulting from the exploratory voyages of the fifteenth and sixteenth centuries as interpreted by European cartographers. Stefánsson and Resen were aware, as the author of the delineation in the Vinland Map could not have been, of the continental character of North America; and it is not surprising that they should have shown Helluland, Markland, and Vinland as sections of a mainland coast, nor that they should have correlated these lands with those of more recent discovery in a way which is not inconsistent with the representation in the Vinland Map.

Between the outlines also in the later maps and in the Vinland Map there are some obvious similarities, more marked perhaps in the case of Resen's map. Leaving aside his peninsular representation of Greenland, we find, both in this map and in the Vinland Map, the three land divisions of Helluland, Markland, and Vinland separated by deep inlets, the more southerly of which has a prominent cape at the southern point of its entrance. Resen's *Promontorium Vin-landiae* however is drawn with more particularity than the cape in the Vinland Map, which —unlike Resen—does not indicate the sound described in the narrative as lying to the west of the cape.

In the absence of extant originals, and if uncontrolled by comparison of toponymy, the iden-tification of common elements of design in maps by different compilers may be perilous;[243] and it must be asked whether the similar features in Resen's map and in the Vinland Map could have come into existence independently, without postulating a common original. This is a ques-

242. See Note E, pp. 218–22.

243. We might, for instance, point to the striking similarity between the representation of Greenland and "Terra Nova" in Ruysch's world map of 1507 and that of Greenland and Vinland by Stefánsson, *ca.* 1590; or to the hardly less remarkable affinity of outline shared by "Vinlanda Insula" of the Vinland Map and by the delineation of Labrador and Newfoundland (from the Corte Real voyages) in the world maps of Mercator (1538) and Caspar Vopell (1545).

tion to which individual judgment may dictate differing answers. To our mind the two delineations are sufficiently generalized in character, and yet divergent where they particularize, to make the presumption of a common derivation unnecessary. If Resen (as he claims) had indeed at his disposal a medieval Icelandic map, we need not suppose this to have been of the same authorship as the prototype of the Vinland Map. Both originals could, in our view, have been compiled independently from the geographical data in the texts of the narratives and have owed any resemblance we may detect to the use of the same written sources. So far as Vinland is concerned, the matter could have been wholly furnished by the narratives in the Flatey Book. Beyond this point in speculation we cannot go; but the representation of Vinland, as of Greenland, in a map of the early fifteenth century lends some support to the suggestion that the medieval records of Iceland once contained maps of indigenous authorship which are now lost.

NOTE E. IDENTIFICATION OF THE NORSE DISCOVERIES

Although the Vinland Map is of only limited value as an aid to geographical identification of the lands mentioned in the narratives, we summarize in this Note, for convenience of reference, some of the opinions propounded on this controversial issue. They are, of course, derived from interpretation of the textual sources colored by their authors' judgment on the reliability of these sources. We need not refer here to the supposed Norse remains discovered in North America—the Dighton Rock, the Kensington Stone, the Newport Tower—nor to the hypotheses founded on them regarding the extent of the Norsemen's travels. It is within possibility that archeological investigation may uncover better authenticated relics of Norse exploration or settlement and so help to define the regions of discovery more confidently and precisely than is at present permissible.[244]

We take first the theories of historians who deny the authority of the Tale and so have only to elucidate the geography of the voyages by Leif (from Norway) and Karlsefni (from Greenland), as described in the Saga.

A. Gustav Storm[245] took *Helluland* to be Labrador; *Markland* (reached by Karlsefni after changing course to southeast) to be Newfoundland; and all the other places mentioned in the Saga to be on Cape Breton Island or in Nova Scotia. These identifications have been criticized on the grounds that the last two do not fit the geographical conditions found by Leif and Karlsefni, and that "far more space" is needed to accommodate Karlsefni's explorations.

B. W. H. Babcock,[246] following Storm, interpreted *Helluland* as Labrador and *Markland* as Newfoundland; and he identified Cape Breton Island as *Kjalarnes,* the Nova Scotia coast as *Furdustrands,* Passamaquoddy Bay (New Brunswick) as *Straumsfjord,* with its strong tidal currents. Reviving an older theory, he supposed Karlsefni's southward exploration to have taken him across the Gulf of Maine and round Cape Cod to *Hóp* in Mount Hope Bay, adjoining Narragansett Bay.

C. H. P. Steensby,[247] considering the whole navigation to have been coasting, placed *Helluland* on the east coast of Labrador and *Markland* on its south coast, where he located *Furdu-*

---

244. See below, pp. 220–21.
245. "Studies on the Vinland voyages" (1888).
246. *Early Norse Visits to North America* (1913).
247. *The Norsemen's Route from Greenland to Wineland* (1918).

strands and *Kjalarnes;* taking the voyages through Belleisle Strait into the St. Lawrence estuary (*Straumsfjord*), he found *Hóp* upstream at St. Thomas.

D. Hálldor Hermannsson[248] supposed Leif, blown south of his course from Norway to Greenland, to have made his landfall near Cape Cod (*Vinland*) and to have sailed north along the coast of New England and Nova Scotia to Cape Breton Island, thence across the Gulf of St. Lawrence (out of sight of land) to Labrador, out through Belleisle Strait, up the east coast of Labrador and across Davis Strait to Greenland. This hypothesis of course disregards the evidence of the Tale for Bjarni's previous voyage and for Leif's identification of Bjarni's landfalls. Hermannsson traced the route of Karlsefni's expedition from the Western Settlement across Davis Strait and along the northeast coast of Labrador (*Helluland*) to Hamilton Inlet, which he thought the explorers took for a strait;[249] along the southeast coast of Labrador (*Markland*) and its south coast (*Furdustrands*); across the St. Lawrence estuary, rounding the east point of Anticosti Island (*Kjalarnes*), and into Chaleur Bay (*Straumsfjord*). The location of *Hóp* Hermannsson supposed to be "impossible to determine", but he thought it was probably "somewhere south of Cape Cod, in Barnstable, Buzzard Bay, or thereabout". He also inferred from the text of the Saga "that sometimes the term Wineland was used loosely so as to cover Straumsfjord as well as Hóp".

Unlike these historians, those who have admitted the evidence of the Tale in addition to that of the Saga have been able to make use of data furnished by Bjarni's voyage, by the outward voyage of Leif from his point of departure in Greenland, and by Thorvald's independent expedition. They have generally placed the northern limit of the Norse discoveries in a higher latitude than the writers whose theories are cited above.

E. William Hovgaard[250] identified Bjarni's three landfalls as northeast Newfoundland, east Labrador near Hamilton Inlet, and Resolution Island off the southeast coast of Baffin Land. Hovgaard accepted the Saga's account of Leif's chance landfall, probably near Cape Cod, on his return voyage from Norway and interpreted Leif's discoveries on his later expedition from Greenland as Baffin Land (*Helluland*), Nova Scotia (*Markland*), and the Cape Cod peninsula or Nantucket Sound (*Vinland*), with Cape Cod as Thorvald's *Kjalarnes*. The localities visited by Karlsefni were placed much further north: his *Helluland* as northern Labrador, his *Markland* as the Labrador coast near Nain, *Straumsfjord* as Sandwich Bay,[251] *Furdustrands* as the southern part of the east Labrador coast, and *Kjalarnes* as Cape Bauld (the northernmost point of Newfoundland). Supposing the story of vines and wild corn to be an interpolation from Leif's narrative, Hovgaard conjectured that Karlsefni's *Hóp* was Sop's Arm, an inlet of White Bay, on the east coast of Newfoundland south of Cape Bauld, and consequently that Karlsefni never reached Vinland. Hovgaard's hypothesis, resting on his views of geographical probability, involved him in some arbitrary manipulation of the saga texts.

F. G. M. Gathorne-Hardy,[252] from a closely reasoned analysis of the nautical and geographical data, held Bjarni's three landfalls to have been the Barnstable peninsula (in Massachusetts), Nova Scotia, and Newfoundland; and Leif's *Helluland* to be in Labrador or Newfoundland,

---

248. *The Problem of Wineland* (1936).
249. It may be remarked that Hamilton Inlet, like that in the map, broadens at its head.
250. *The Voyages of the Norsemen to America* (1918).
251. Sandwich Bay also widens at its head.
252. *The Norse Discoveries of America* (1921).

Markland probably Nova Scotia, and *Vinland* the coast west of Cape Cod (Thorvald's *Kjalarnes*). Gathorne-Hardy identified Karlsefni's *Helluland* as Labrador or Newfoundland (which he supposed the explorers to have believed one country); *Markland* (ignoring Karlsefni's southeast course, which Gathorne-Hardy discredited) as Nova Scotia; *Furdustrands* as the Cape Cod peninsula; *Straumsfjord* as Long Island Sound, and *Hóp* as the estuary of the Hudson River. Some of Gathorne-Hardy's arguments from courses (which he too generally assumed to be in exactly the reverse sense of the winds named) lack conviction by being over-rigid; but it must be said that, given his textual premises, his geographical conclusions are coherent.

G. Some later writers (Matthias Thordarson,[253] Wilfred Bovey[254]) supposed, like Storm, that the explorations of Leif and Karlsefni did not extend south of the Gulf of St. Lawrence and Nova Scotia; Bovey indeed thought *Kjalarnes* to be Cape Gaspe, *Straumsfjord* to be Perce, and *Hóp* to be Port Daniel, on the north shore of Chaleur Bay.

H. Edward Reman,[255] taking the Tale alone as authority for the voyages of Bjarni, Leif, Thorvald, and Freydís, supposed the last three of these expeditions to have followed the same course, by way of *Helluland* (Resolution Island, off southern Baffin Land) and *Markland* (Newfoundland) to *Vinland,* on the Maine coast, facing Grand Manan Island at the mouth of the Bay of Fundy. To Karlsefni's expedition, for which Reman chose to use only the Saga, he assigned more northerly routes, on the assumption that Karlsefni sought, not Leif's settlement, but "the much larger landmass to which the name *Vinland* had come to be extended in consequence of Thorvald's explorations", i.e. toward Markland. Reman accordingly traced Karlsefni from Baffin Land and Resolution Island (*Helluland*), south to Ungava Bay (*Markland*), through Hudson Strait, and across Hudson Bay to Chesterfield Inlet (*Straumsfjord*) and Port Nelson (*Hóp*).

The speculative nature of these and other attempts to elucidate the geography of the Vinland voyages is betrayed by the range or spread of the divergent identifications which result from them, and by the fact that their authors are, without exception, compelled to discredit or explain away some part of the evidence for the sake of consistency. The question "To what parts of America did the Norsemen go?" cannot be answered in more generally accepted terms until new and less equivocal evidence turns up.

In 1960 in fact, the Norwegian explorer Helge Ingstad identified as Norse a habitation site on the north coast of Newfoundland, in about 51° 36′ N and 55° 32′ W, some five miles west southwest of Cape Bauld.[256] The site, near the hamlet of L'Anse-aux-Meadows, is on an old beach terrace, 100 yards from the sea in Épaves Bay, on the east side of Sacred Bay, and the excavations carried out by Dr. Ingstad in 1961, 1962, and 1963 have uncovered the foundations of seven turf buildings, with indications of smith's workings. The largest structure measures 60 ×

---

253. *The Vinland Voyages* (1930).
254. "The Vinland voyages", *Trans. Royal Society of Canada* (1936).
255. *The Norse Discoveries and Explorations in America* (1949).
256. This paragraph (written in January 1963) is based on reports in two periodicals (*New York Herald Tribune,* 18 October 1962, p. 10; *News of Norway,* issued by the Norwegian Information Service, Washington, 15 November 1962); on a lecture by Professor Ian R. Whitaker, "Vinland Discovered" (*Daily News,* St. John's Newfoundland, 26 October 1962, p. 5); on Dr. Ingstad's paper, "Discovery of Vinland" (*The Arctic Circular,* published by the Arctic Circle, Ottawa, Vol. 15, no. 1, January 1963); and on information courteously given me in conversation by Dr. William Taylor, of the National Museum, Ottawa, in December 1962. (See Bibliographical Postscript, p. 240.)

45 feet (thus much bigger than any Eskimo building), and one of its five rooms is a large hall with an open stone hearth. Carbon 14 tests of charcoal samples are reported to yield dates from the seventh to the eleventh centuries, with a cluster about A.D. 900, and there are signs that the site was subsequently visited and stripped by Eskimos. It is understood that, at the time of my writing (February 1963), Dr. Ingstad is preparing his report for publication. Canadian archaeologists seem to accept that the settlement cannot be Eskimo, but "to reserve judgment on whether it is indeed Vinland",[257] as claimed by Dr. Ingstad.

Such caution is certainly justified. On the one hand, it appears possible that Norse sites have hitherto gone unrecognized or unrecorded, whether along the American mainland to the south and west, or on the coasts of Labrador, Ungava Bay, and Baffin Land to the north. On the other hand, the saga accounts mention several wintering-places of the Norsemen, and it is hardly to be expected that, even if the Viking origin of the settlement at L'Anse-aux-Meadows can be established, it will yield any evidence to determine which expedition established itself there, and when. The location of the site, on the west side of Cape Bauld and at the entrance of Belleisle Strait, together with the configuration of the adjacent coasts, does indeed call to mind the north-pointing cape, lying as a wedge between the ocean on the east and a sound on the west, where Leif built his winter quarters in "Vinland". It recalls, no less, the Kjalarnes of Thorvald and of Karlsefni, and may suggest that the settlement at L'Anse-aux-Meadows was the work of the Karlsefni expedition (thus supporting Hovgaard's conjectural geography for this voyage). The wedge-shaped north-pointing cape reappears in the *Promontorium Vinlandiae* of the Icelandic maps drawn at the end of the sixteenth century, and it is worth noting that (as we have shown) their authors identified this feature with northern Newfoundland—that is, in the vicinity of Cape Bauld. Until Dr. Ingstad has published his discovery, it would be rash to carry surmise further.

Confronted with the Vinland Map, we may still ask whether the geographical hypotheses of the commentators can be tested against its delineation of America, if not against archaeological evidence. It cannot be too strongly emphasized that, in studying an early map, it is hazardous and may be extremely deceptive to construct a latitude scale for lands represented in the west of the Atlantic from that of lands in the east; the risk of error is greater when, as here, two different prototypes seem to have been used. We may nonetheless allow ourselves the purely hypothetical exercise of identifying the principal features of "Vinlanda Insula" on the assumption that the parallels of latitude are continued right across the map and that its European latitudes are correct. Some obvious correspondences emerge. In the modern map Cape Chidley, on the south of the entrance to Hudson Strait, lies on approximately the same parallel as Cape Farewell, in southern Greenland, and Bergen, in Norway. Recalling that, in the Vinland Map, Greenland is drawn somewhat south of its correct position, we can accordingly identify the northernmost section of "Vinlanda Insula" as Baffin Land, separated by Hudson Strait and Ungava Bay from Labrador, the central section; the eye of fancy might even see a delineation of Hudson's Bay in the large lake into which the inlet representing Hudson Strait broadens at its head. Southward on the modern map, the Labrador-Newfoundland coast is interrupted by a number of more or less prominent openings: Nain Bay (in about the latitude of northern Denmark), Hamilton Inlet and Sandwich Bay (in that of Friesland), Belleisle Strait (in that of the Scheldt

257. These comments were collected by the Ottawa correspondent of the *New York Herald Tribune*.

estuary), White Bay (in that of Land's End), with Cabot Strait roughly in the latitude of Brittany. This might suggest, for the more southerly inlet and conspicuous cape of "Vinlanda Insula", identification with Hamilton Inlet and Cape Porcupine, on the Labrador coast. If, however, the great size of this feature in the Vinland Map and its marked southward bend prompt us to look for an alternative, we must assume a northerly error of some three degrees in the map and pitch on Belleisle Strait and Cape Bauld; or a northerly error of seven or eight degrees, taking us to Cabot Strait and the St. Lawrence, with Cape Breton. The last solution only could be reconciled with the "eyktarstad" observation of the length of the shortest day, if strictly interpreted to determine the latitude of Leif's Vinland. It does not rule out the possibility that in the Vinland Map the more southerly cape may correspond to the *Promontorium Vinlandiae* of the Icelandic maps and therefore to Cape Bauld.

It is nevertheless to be hoped that, until we know more about the map and its sources, this speculative analysis will not be adduced to support one or other of the geographical theories extracted from the saga narratives.

9. THE NORSE DISCOVERY OF AMERICA AND ITS AFTERMATH

The initial discovery of America is credited in one of the principal sources to Bjarni Herjolfsson, in the other to Leif Eiriksson, both being said to have made it by chance. There is no other written testimony to confirm the account of Bjarni's voyage contained in a chapter of the Flatey Book, nor indeed is there any other mention of him in Icelandic literature, although his father Herjolf is recorded elsewhere as an original Greenland settler. Bjarni's claim has been roughly handled by critics of the school of Storm and Hermannsson, and even the temperate Reeves discusses it with a measure of skepticism.[258] Bjarni Herjolfsson is said to be "a totally unknown character", perhaps a projection of Bjarni Grimolfsson who accompanied Karlsefni on his expedition; such events as the story recounts, it is affirmed, "only happen in fairy tales and lying sagas", and they are perhaps "a faint, garbled reminiscence of Leif's voyage";[259] finally the unexplained gap of sixteen years before Bjarni's alleged discovery was followed up defies historical logic.

This destructive criticism, much of which seems captious, has been effectively answered by Gathorne-Hardy. The barrenness of Bjarni's discovery of western land, "whatever may be its historical interest to persons of a post-Columbian age", is inconsistent with an attempt to build up a rival hero to Leif; "such inaccuracy as characterizes tradition has . . . the effect of merging the exploits of the less well-known with those of the more popular hero", and "the creation of a fictitious hero in addition to the real one is . . . the reverse of the normal process".[260] The accidental American landfalls ascribed by the Flatey Book to Bjarni and by the Saga of Eirik the Red to Leif, each being blown off course on a westerly voyage to Greenland, have indeed elements of similarity; but this is uncertain ground for refusing credit to the report of Bjarni's voyage, which is far richer in details of seamanship and navigation than that of Leif's,

258. A. M. Reeves, *The Finding of Wineland the Good* (1890), pp. 55–56.
259. Hermannsson, *Problem of Wineland*, p. 36.
260. Gathorne-Hardy, p. 116.

and which Gathorne-Hardy is surely justified in claiming as "a very clear and correct account of the way in which America was discovered, whether by Bjarni or by another".[261]

The first chapter of the Tale of the Greenlanders, later in the Flatey Book, introduces its account of Leif's expedition to Vinland by narrating how Bjarni Herjolfsson, after the death of King Olaf Tryggvason in September 1000, went from Greenland to Norway, where he told the story of his American voyage; how he returned in the following summer to Greenland, where "there was now much talk of exploration"; and how he sold a ship to Leif Eiriksson for the latter's expedition. No more is heard of Bjarni Herjolfsson in the Tale, or in any other Icelandic history.

The Vinland Map contains two statements that Bjarni (whose patronymic is not given) and Leif Eiriksson—who are named in this order twice over—discovered Vinland in company. If this be fact, it is unrecorded in any surviving textual source for the voyage and must derive from an oral or written tradition otherwise lost. The legends of the map, if we may suppose them to have a historical foundation, consequently supplement the known narratives of the discovery of Vinland, in the first place, by establishing the association of a certain Bjarni, whose parentage is not stated, with that discovery, and, secondly, by reporting that he sailed with Leif. The Tale of the Greenlanders, while it does not again refer to Bjarni Herjolfsson after telling of the sale of his ship to Leif, contains no word to preclude the supposition that he could have gone with the expedition to Vinland.

It is to be noted, however, that the statements in the Vinland Map contain no allusion to the lone discovery made, according to the earlier chapter of the Flatey Book, by Bjarni Herjolfsson in his own ship. For this reason we cannot dismiss the possibility that, either in the mind of the cartographer or in that of the author of his immediate or remoter source, the voyages of Bjarni and of Leif, recorded in the Flatey Book as distinct, may have been confused and merged into one. Such a conflation of two events would in fact reflect a common process in the evolution of tradition, as Gathorne-Hardy has noted.[262] There is no reason to think that the Bjarni of the legends in the map relates to Bjarni Grimolfsson.

The longer legend in the Vinland Map contains information about the voyage of Bjarni and Leif "southward amidst the ice", about their discovery of a land "extremely fertile and even bearing vines", and on their bestowal of the name Vinland. All this seems to be culled from a narrative similar to that in the Tale, which mentions the glaciers of Helluland, the vines of Vinland, and the naming of the country.

The Vinland Map makes no verbal allusion to any of the other Norse voyages to America described in the two saga narratives. Its longer legend does, however, give some account of an event which is the subject of the latest reference to Vinland (though not to America) in the medieval Icelandic Annals, namely the voyage thitherward of Bishop Eirik Gnupsson early in the twelfth century.[263] This episode has been interpreted by some modern historians as evidence of the survival of a Norse colony in America into this period.

Several compilations of Icelandic Annals contain, under the year 1121 and with slight vari-

---

261. Ibid., p. 244. See also above, p. 211.

262. See above, p. 223.

263. On this, see Reeves, pp. 79–82; Gathorne-Hardy, pp. 18, 283; Hermannsson, pp. 76–77; R. Hennig, *Terrae Incognitae*, Vol. 2 (2d ed. 1950), pp. 384–95.

ations in wording, the same statement about Bishop Eirik's voyage.[264] The Annales Reseniani, probably the oldest collection, perhaps compiled before 1319, have the entry: "Bishop Eirik sought Vinland". The Lawman's Annals, also of the fourteenth century, give the name as "Bishop Eirik Uppsi"; other collections give it in the form "Eirik, Bishop of Greenland" or "Eirik, the Greenlanders' Bishop". The entry in the Annals included in the Flatey Book reads: "Eirik, Bishop of Greenland, went in search of Vinland". This Bishop Eirik Uppsi has been confidently identified with the Icelander Eirik Gnupsson, mentioned as "the Greenlanders' bishop" in the *Landnámabók* (Uppsi, i.e. "pollock", being a nickname).

An earlier voyage by Bishop Eirik, presumably from Norway or Iceland to Greenland, is recorded in the Lawman's Annals under the year 1112, and in those of the Flatey Book under 1113. His name appears at the head of a list of the bishops at Gardar (the episcopal seat in Greenland), included in the twelfth-century Icelandic work *Rimbegla*. Whether he occupied the see of Gardar is (as will be seen) very doubtful. The Icelandic Tale of Einar Sokkason describes the petition sent by the Greenlanders to Norway in 1123, requesting the creation of a diocese; the Norwegian Arnald was ordained as Bishop of Gardar in 1124 and arrived in Greenland in 1126.

No original record of Bishop Eirik's ordination is known; but his entry in the list of bishops of Gardar compiled by Luka Jelič and based in part on that of Gams[265] may rest on a papal document seen by one of these authors, although not cited or published by them:

1. *Erich* (Eirikr); a. 1112–1113 consecratur in episcopum regionarium Groelandiae regionumque finitimarum; a. 1211 [*scil.* 1121] pergit Vinlandiam ubi moritur (a. 1122?).

A. 1123 Groelandenses petunt erectionem sedis episcopalis in Groelandia.

2. *Arnoldus,* a. 1124 consecratus; a. 1126 sedem figit Gardari . . .

The statements in this list as to Eirik's consecration, as to his title, and as to his death in Vinland, conjecturally in 1122, are unconfirmed by medieval Icelandic sources, or indeed by any other known documentary record; and no explicit authority is given for them. The date 1112–13 for the ordination may be derived from the report, in two Annals, of the voyage by Bishop Eirik made in one of those years; the wording of the title, which seems to bear the mark of authenticity, is of some significance, although no source for it can now be traced; for the statement about the bishop's death in Vinland we do not know the authority, and were this voyage identical with that recorded in the Vinland Map, the statement would conflict with the account of his American mission preserved in the map.

To various details of this chronology the longer legend in the map brings confirmation, correction or amplification. The formula for Eirik's episcopal style (". . . Gronlande regionumque finitimarum sedis apostolicae episcopus legatus") closely parallels that quoted by Gams and Jelič. If he made a Vinland voyage (as the legend states) in the last year of Pope Paschal II, it must have been in 1117, since this Pope died in January 1118 and the voyage was presumably made in the preceding summer. The point of departure, not named, was doubtless Greenland;

---

264. This paragraph and that which follows it are based on Reeves, pp. 79–82.

265. P. B. Gams, *Series episcopum Ecclesiae Catholicae* (1873), p. 334; L. Jelič, "L'évangélisation de l'Amérique avant Christophe Colomb", *Le Missioni francescane*, Vol. 8 (Rome, 1897), pp. 556–60. Gams cites only modern authorities, going back no further than Torfaeus, who compiled the first printed list of the Gardar bishops. For Bishop Eirik, Jelič seems to have found no source unknown to Gams. The text of the list cited here is that of Jelič, p. 557.

and, according to the legend in the map, Bishop Eirik remained in Vinland for at least a year ("longo tempore mansit estiuo et brumali") before returning to Greenland and thence—if we construe the text correctly—on to Europe under orders from his superiors,[266] perhaps (since he was a papal legate) in consequence of the Pope's death. The sequence of events here detailed and the account given in the Icelandic Annals and by Gams and Jelič are not irreconcilable; there may have been two voyages, a first in 1117–18 and a second, on which the bishop died, in 1121. We may, alternatively, suppose that there was only one voyage, that it was entered under the wrong year in the Annals, and so copied by Gams or his source, and that Bishop Eirik's death was inferred by Gams from the absence of further information about him and from the appointment of a Greenland bishop in 1124. The version in the legend of the Vinland Map carries conviction because of its circumstantial character and the ecclesiastical expression of the date, in a form less liable to error in copying than a year number.

The purpose of the Bishop's voyage recorded in the Annals under the year 1121 has been the subject of much historical debate. Was it made (as Nansen suggests) in search of a land whose very existence was doubtful, or (as supposed by Storm and Hermannsson) in search of one which was known to exist but the route to which, unfrequented for nearly a century, had been forgotten? Or did the bishop (as held by Hennig and others) sail by a familiar navigation route to a land where Norse settlers still maintained themselves and needed the ministrations of the Church?

The discussion of this question has turned mainly on two issues: the precise sense of the Icelandic words *leitadi* and *fór at leita* (here translated as "sought" and "went in search of"), and Bishop Eirik's standing and duties. The best philological opinion, supported by the Icelandic scholarship of Storm, Reeves, and Hermannsson, holds that "the verb *leita* can, in this connection, only have the meaning 'to search for something which is undetermined, or lost' ".[267] If this be admitted, it follows that there could hardly have been a Norse colony surviving in Vinland and that the motive for the bishop's visit must have been evangelization of the heathen. Hermannsson draws the compelling conclusion that, since Eirik "could not have been ordained bishop of Greenland so long as there was no see established there, he probably was bishop *in partibus infidelium* and his voyage to Wineland would thus have been a missionary expedition to the Skraelings who had been found there by Leif Eriksson or Thorfinn Karlsefni. And Ari's reference to those aborigines[268] may be given for similar reasons, indicating that there was, perhaps, within the domain of the Icelandic church a field for missionary work".[269] To this view the legend in the Vinland Map lends unmistakable support, for the formula used to indicate Bishop Eirik's rank, office, and territorial responsibility carries the clear implication that he was charged with the spread of the Christian faith beyond Greenland. The fact, unrecorded elsewhere, that he was also a papal legate, and therefore appointed by the Pope as his representative

---

266. Mr G. D. Painter suggested this interpretation of the passage to me.

267. Hermannsson, p. 76; see also Reeves, p. 80.

268. In the *Íslendingabók,* written about 1124, i.e. very near the date of these events. See above, p. 210.

269. Hermannsson, *The Book of the Icelanders* (1930), p. 83; also his *Problem of Wineland*, pp. 76–77. Hermannsson, discussing Hennig's view that Bishop Eirik's mission was not to "establish" but to "strengthen" Christianity in Vinland, which was part of his diocese, supposes the German scholar's interpretation to be "put forward in support of his stubborn, though futile, efforts to show that Hvítramannaland was not a legendary, but a real, country somewhere in the west, inhabited by Irish, or Norse, Christians". Cf. above, n. 224.

for specific duties, points the same way, besides making it probable that (unlike the see of Gardar, established in 1124 as suffragan of the archbishopric of Hamburg-Bremen) Bishop Eirik's sphere of authority lay outside the formal ecclesiastical organization.[270]

Previous writers have accepted the probability that Eirik did not return from his voyage of 1121; and Storm suggested that he never even found Vinland.[271] If the evidence of the legend in the map be credited, the bishop not only reached Vinland but also stayed there at least a year and returned safely with geographical information about the country, which he may have brought to Europe and from which the details given in the map legend were perhaps extracted. Here, then, we seem to have the latest information on Vinland which, so far as our knowledge goes, could have been derived from observation; if so, it was transmitted to Iceland within the age of written records, and perhaps to Europe. The bearing of these circumstances upon the compilation and preservation of the Vinland Map is evident, although (in the absence of collateral evidence) not precisely definable.

Whence the compiler of the map had his intelligence on Bishop Eirik Gnupsson we do not know. It is a fair guess (if no more) that its ultimate source, like that for the information on Bjarni, was Icelandic.[272] However this may be, the map here, by supplementing and glossing a bald sentence in the Icelandic Annals, reinforces the conclusion that the voyages made to America in the early eleventh century had been without sequel. Barely a hundred years after these voyages, no Europeans were established in the westernmost lands of Norse discovery, and the sailing directions for navigation to these lands had been forgotten.

That intermittent later voyages, of chance or design, were made to the American coasts is suggested by two further entries in the Icelandic Annals. In 1285 they record, in variant forms, the discovery of "new land" to the west of Iceland by the brothers Adalbrand and Thorvald Helgesson; whether this was the Greenland coast or some land further west remains uncertain. In 1347 a Greenland ship fetched the west coast of Iceland, having been driven off course on her return voyage from Markland, whither (as Nansen conjectures) her crew had gone to collect "timber or wood for fashioning implements, which was valuable in treeless Greenland".[273] The Greenland Annals compiled from older materials in the seventeenth century in fact record that the people living on the west coast of Greenland "take up trees and all the drift that comes from the bays of Markland". Though we cannot determine with what part of America the Markland of these references is to be identified, they testify at least that the name was still known

---

270. Torfaeus, in his *Gronlandia antiqua* (1706), pp. 239–40, writing of Bishop Eirik, "quem fidem Christianam in Vinlandia plantasse . . . tradit", seems to have suspected this: "Nam Eiricus, qui primus Gronlandorum Episcopus habetur, iis annumerandus videtur, qui nullam certam sedem aut reditus obtinuerint, sed . . . circumeuntes regiones ecclesias aedificabant . . . qui postea Vinlandiam exquisivit".

271. "Studies", p. 332.

272. A possible channel of transmission has been conjectured in the doubtfully documented Norwegian expedition of Paul Knutsson which, commissioned by King Magnus Eiriksson in 1354 to go to Greenland to sustain the Christian colonies there, may not have returned until 1363 or 1364. Nothing is known of the proceedings of this expedition; and no evidence exists to support the suggestion that it visited Markland and Vinland and that some member of it made the Icelandic map "several centuries old" which Bishop H. P. Resen cited among the sources for his map of 1605 (see above, pp. 194–95). It is nonetheless worth noting that the year 1364, in which according to Storm the Greenland expedition may have returned, is also that in which Jacob Cnoyen had his information, from a priest (perhaps a Greenlander) whom he encountered at the Norwegian court, about the English friar who had traveled through the northern islands and taken the "height", i.e. latitude, of places with his astrolabe (see above, pp. 181–82).

273. Nansen, Vol. 2, pp. 36–37.

and used in the later medieval period, and that the Greenlanders' voyage thither in 1347, which came by accident to the notice of an Icelandic chronicler, was almost certainly not the only one of its kind.

To our knowledge of such occasional communication with America the Vinland Map adds nothing. The map nonetheless reflects the strong probability that in medieval Iceland the historical recollection of the Norse discovery of America was sustained by graphic as well as written memorials which have not survived.

III. THE VINLAND MAP AS A HISTORICAL DOCUMENT

1. THE DATE OF THE MAP

The nature of the Vinland Map limits its virtue as a historical document. The surviving copy of it is undated and furnishes neither the name of its author or transcriber nor that of its place of origin. The content of the map, as a whole, cannot be assigned confidently to a single phase or horizon of geographical knowledge. Its outlines are in part transcribed from a map prototype or prototypes not precisely identifiable with any extant work; in part they illustrate texts, not all of which have come down to us. The information taken by the author of the map from these sources (graphic and textual) relates to events and concepts of various periods; most of it is older by at least a century, and some of it by much more, than the presumed date at which the existing copy of the map and of its accompanying manuscript texts was made. The delineations in the map before us are separated by long intervals of time not only from the original experience which they reflect, but also from the direct records of it. For the mapmaker was working always at one remove, sometimes (we cannot doubt) at two or more removes, from firsthand records; and it is evident that, to a degree and in senses which it is difficult for us to divine, he exercised his judgment in selection from and in adaptation of his sources, which are themselves partly unknown to us.

All this is very unsatisfactory if we are to study the Vinland Map as a historical document and to extract its testimony on the course of events or the state of thought at a specific point in time. The more peremptory, for these reasons, is the need to assign a date, and particularly a lower limit of date, to the chronological levels of knowledge and geographical consciousness represented in the various parts of the map.

The delineation of the Old World (as we have seen) closely parallels that in a Venetian world map drawn in 1436. Andrea Bianco was not (we may say) a conspicuously original cartographer;[1] and in his delineation of Europe, Asia, and Africa he undoubtedly followed, in the main, an older model in which he made few, if any, modifications. If we compare his design for the tripartite world with that of Fra Paolino or Petrus Vesconte about 1320, we note only five major revisions: the reduction in the longitudinal extent of the Mediterranean in proportion to that of Eurasia as a whole, better delineations of the Black Sea and the Baltic, the transference of Prester John from Asia to Africa, and a fuller representation of the Atlantic coasts and islands. Most of these improvements had already been made by mapmakers of the fourteenth century; they are found (to take a dated example) in the Catalan Atlas of 1375. Common also to the world maps of the early fourteenth century and to that of Bianco, as indeed to nearly all the intervening maps which survive, is their neglect of the recent Asian travellers, with the exception of Rubruck, for the geography of the East.[2] None of these cartographers drew on Carpini's report; none but the Catalans made any use of Marco Polo.

Although we cannot escape the conclusion that the design of the Old World in the Vinland

1. The first five charts in his atlas of 1436 closely resemble, not only in outline and nomenclature but also in scale and sheet-division, those in four atlases by Giacomo Giroldis, also drawn at Venice, three dated 1426, 1443, 1446, and one undated. If Bianco was not copying Giroldis, both cartographers must be supposed to have followed a common model, in existence before 1426. See T. Fischer, *Sammlung*, pp. 153–54.

2. See above, p. 150.

Map and that in Bianco's world map are intimately related, it does not follow that the connection was a direct one. The prototype for this part of the Vinland Map, as for Bianco's, could have been drawn in the second half of the previous century, or at any time after Cape Bojador (marked and named in the Catalan Atlas of 1375) became known to the mapmakers.[3] Convincing as the affinities between the Vinland Map and that of Bianco may seem, the high degree of wastage of early maps forbids us to exclude the possibility that the two cartographers drew on a common source which may have been considerably earlier than 1436. This possibility looms larger if we consider how much that was known to the compiler of the Vinland Map was seemingly unknown to Bianco.

Although it is therefore unsafe to take the date of Bianco's atlas as a *terminus post quem* for the compilation (as distinct from the copying) of the Vinland Map,[4] we must note that the islands of Antillia and Satanaxes, which are drawn in so closely parallel a form in the two works, make their first appearance in the Pizzigano chart of 1424. We cannot assume that earlier and now lost maps did not contain this representation; a conjectural date-bracket for its origin is suggested by the fact that Antillia is absent from the Pizzigani world map of 1367 and atlas of 1373, both by members of (presumably) the same family of Venetian cartographers as the author of the 1424 chart.[5] It is permissible to surmise, with all the reservations due to the imperfect state of our knowledge, that this representation may have entered cartography in the first quarter of the fifteenth century, or not much earlier; and that it may have been introduced by a Venetian mapmaker, perhaps from Portuguese information.[6]

Outside his map prototype, the only significant source used by the author of the Vinland Map for the geography of the Old World was the Tartar Relation of C. de Bridia. The surviving copy of this text seems to justify the inference that it is in substantially the form in which it was written down soon after Carpini's return to Europe in 1247. We do not know whether the manuscript from which the text was transcribed was accompanied by a map, nor (if so) what this map looked like. It is in any case clear that the Carpini information of C. de Bridia is considerably older than the "base map" from which the compiler of the Vinland Map copied his representation of the tripartite world, and that it must have been in his hands when he did so. The author of the "base map", of Bianco-type, did not possess the Carpini information; or at least he made no use of it.

The lands, or islands, drawn by the cartographer in the northwest and west Atlantic provide little help in dating the composition of the map. Iceland is depicted with a maturity and a correctness of outline and orientation which might be supposed not to antedate the regular trade with England and Flanders initiated in the first half of the fifteenth century;[7] but if a model of Scandinavian, and specifically of Icelandic, origin was available for the representation of Iceland, as it almost certainly was for that of Greenland and Vinland, this might well have been appreciably earlier. In attempting to date the delineation of Greenland we have no firm ground

3. See above, p. 147.

4. We must also concede that the very high degree of probability that Bianco's world map is contemporaneous with, and from the same hand as, the rest of the atlas does not amount to absolute certainty. The signature and date are only on the first leaf of the atlas; the world map is unsigned and undated. See above, p. 125.

5. See Cortesão, pp. 20, 59–60; Gasparrini-Leporace, pp. 93–94, and references there cited.

6. See above, pp. 157–58.

7. See above, pp. 166–67.

to stand on. We may see a possible *terminus ad quem* in the extinction of the Western Settlement during the first half of the fourteenth century. Alternatively, the return of Ivar Bardsson to Norway, by 1364, or the uncertainly documented Norwegian expedition of Paul Knutsson in 1354, together with the (perhaps related) geographical observations of the Oxford friar and the Greenland priest picked up in Norway in 1364 by Jacob Cnoyen, may be thought to suggest a *terminus post quem*. While none of this amounts to more than guesswork, unsupported by concrete evidence of association with the design of Greenland in the Vinland Map, we see least difficulty in the supposition that the materials for the design were assembled and brought back to Iceland or Norway before the Greenland settlers had ceased to frequent Baffin Bay and before their communications with Iceland and Europe had been broken. This would indicate an earlier date, perhaps even in the thirteenth century, rather than a later one, for the map of Greenland.

If the outline of Vinland and the legends relating to it are derived (as we suppose) from a common textual source, this cannot have been committed to writing before the first quarter of the twelfth century, when the "age of written history" dawned in Iceland—that is, at about the same time as Bishop Eirik Gnupsson made his Vinland voyage or voyages. This lower limit of date may be conjecturally raised if we bring the source, and the map outline derived from it, forward into the early fourteenth century, in which the first Icelandic annals were composed and the oldest surviving texts of the Vinland sagas were written down. For the upper limit of date at which the delineation of Vinland may have been drawn, we have no testimony other than the general considerations adduced for that of Greenland.

That the representation of Atlantic lands in the Vinland Map shows a general concordance with the old Norse sailing directions, which were written down in the thirteenth century, may also point to an Icelandic model not older than this. The question how and when this model was transmitted to southern Europe cannot be positively answered unless and until we learn more about the history and authorship of the group of manuscripts in which the surviving copy of the Vinland Map has come to light.

So far as the evidence goes, and (for the rest) on a balance of probabilities, we reach the provisional conclusion that the map is constructed from two prototypes, neither of which is now known to exist. That for the Old World presumably dated from the last decades of the fourteenth century or the beginning of the fifteenth; that for the Atlantic and the lands to the northwest and west was probably somewhat older, and may have come into existence in the thirteenth or early fourteenth century. In the collocation of these prototypes, the author of the Vinland Map (as we now see it) has fused two geographical traditions. Various considerations suggest that he may have found occasion to do so in the ambience of the Council of Basle, during the second quarter of the fifteenth century.[8]

2. TRADITION AND EXPERIENCE

In the images traced by the early cartographer on paper or vellum and transmitted in his map we can detect a tendency toward inertia. He preferred old bottles into which to pour new wine; traditional patterns were adapted to accommodate new information or concepts. These profes-

8. See above, pp. 105 (palaeography and paper), 178 (map).

sional characteristics are plainly illustrated in work which, like the Vinland Map, is the product of a relatively naïve cartographer making use of a limited range of models and source materials. Such maps, even if all their delineations are not in equal measure witnesses of truth, have particular value for the light which they throw on the processes of thought and expression involved in their compilation. Like other historical documents, they provide not only "evidence of what did actually occur historically" but also "evidence of what men thought was occurring, and of what they thought about what they thought was occurring".[9] In taking the testimony of an early map, it is the historian's business to sift representations which record experience from those dictated by tradition or interpretation; yet the intermingling of such diverse elements, of varying degrees of authority, is itself a historical fact which deserves study and explanation.

The author of the Vinland Map, like Bianco, was content to copy his outlines of the Old World from a model which was already well-worn, although no other example of it has come down to us. On it he superimposed, apparently about the turn of the fourteenth and fifteenth centuries, information from two other sources, which were not available to Bianco. The consequent revisions are applied to the "base map" in quite distinct ways, exemplifying the fusion of old and new matter in different combinations.

The Vinland Map is the earliest known map to illustrate the geography of Carpini's expedition, or (more properly) to incorporate data from Carpini's journey in its representation of Asia, yet within the framework of the circular "base map". In doing so, the cartographer has overlooked or failed to apprehend the most striking geographical result of Carpini's journey, namely his discovery that continental Asia extended much further to the east than had been accepted. So far from increasing the longitudinal extension of the continent in accordance with Carpini's itinerary, the design in the Vinland Map actually reduces it, and so makes nonsense of the source. This curious and retrograde error exemplifies some behavior patterns typical of early cartographers. In admitting new data into the world picture their critical judgment was frequently at fault, whether by dependence on an imperfect authority or by failure to take into account and to collate a sufficient variety of available evidence. In the Tartar Relation the author of the Vinland Map, who apparently disposed of no other source for Carpini's journey, found none of the precise details of direction and duration of travel recorded by Carpini himself; and he did not supply them from the reports of later travelers to the Far East. Characteristically, he confined himself to a graphic modification which admitted, without going outside the basic pattern of the map prototype, his interpretation of the geographical matter deduced from a somewhat incoherent text. The resultant design conveys only a faint, and much distorted, reflection of Carpini's experience.

The cartographer's handling of the lands in the northwest and west is so markedly different as to justify us in supposing his source to have been here not only different in kind but also superior in definition and more closely related to experience. By no amount of ingenious manipulation could these lands be brought within the framework of the tripartite world map. That they are located in approximately correct relationship to the eastern seaboard of the Atlantic and to one another suggests that their representation derives ultimately from knowledge of the ocean passages to them. This could have been extracted from the Norse sailing directions; but the precision with which the coasts of Iceland and Greenland are traced points insistently to a graphic

9. Durand Echevarria, in *The John Carter Brown Library Conference: a report* (1961), p. 46.

source, in a map or maps, for this part of the design. The delineation of Vinland, unlike that of Iceland and Greenland, can hardly have been made directly from observation or surveys; but even if (as we suppose) a construction from oral or written report, this too must be attributed to the same origin as the drawing of Iceland and Greenland. Although these representations are therefore of differing types, in part derived from visual experience, in part from textual inference, there can be little doubt that they had already been formulated graphically when they came to the notice of the compiler of the Vinland Map. That it was a Scandinavian, and very probably an Icelander, who first reduced these materials to cartographic shape seems to us indisputable. If this conclusion be justified, the Vinland Map has preserved the only surviving example of a medieval Norse map, and in a form which (to judge from the faithfulness with which the author of the Vinland Map elsewhere followed his map model) closely mirrors that of the original. As such, it is entitled to a respectable and indeed significant place among the documentary testimony to the Norsemen's navigation of the North Atlantic and its coastal lands and to their discoveries in the west. The credit to be attached to the cartographic delineation, or at least to its northern origin, is enhanced by the legends relating to Vinland, the authenticity of which appears to stand up to the test of historical criticism.

3. THE OLDEST SURVIVING MAP OF AMERICAN LANDS

If the delineation of land to the west of the Atlantic found in the Vinland Map had ever come under the eyes of Andrea Bianco, it is impossible to think that he would not have reproduced it. Allowance must be made for the possibility that other works from his hand have been lost; yet his chart of 1448, which is precisely a representation of the Atlantic and its islands, is later than the date probably to be assigned even to the extant copy of the Vinland Map.[10] Considering the very close correspondence, in regard to the Old World, between the Bianco world map of 1436 and the Vinland Map, we may affirm with some confidence that any common original from which both stemmed cannot have included the representation of Iceland, Greenland, and Vinland, and that this representation had to be taken by the compiler of the Vinland Map from another source, which (as we suggest) was probably a map.

To what extent the "mythical" islands of the Atlantic laid down by late-medieval cartographers reflect real discoveries, or a belief in them, remains a matter of speculation. Greek lore of an "opposite continent", exemplified in Plato's Atlantis or in the world pattern constructed by Crates from his reading of Homer, had been in the main lost, although echoes of it, conveyed through later Latin writings and Irish scholarship, have been detected in the tenth-century *Navigatio Sancti Brendani*.[11] The extensive diffusion of the tale of the Irish saint's voyages is sufficient to account for the Islands of St. Brendan and Brasil which, as "relics of Irish geographical learning with a potential value for explorers", made their appearance in maps from the

---

10. The fact that the 1448 chart does not show Antillia may suggest that in it Bianco made only selective use of his materials on the Atlantic. It is, however, possible, and even likely, that in this chart the Antillia of the 1436 atlas has evolved into the large *y^a fortunat' s^a beati blandan* (of similarly conventional shape) in the island group drawn to the west of the "supposed" Azores, by a fusion of Bianco's earlier Antillia concept with his knowledge of Portuguese navigation to the true Azores. The *ixola otenticha* of the 1448 chart may also (as we have seen) point to a rumor of western land. See above, pp. 157, 159.

11. G. Ashe, *Land to the West,* chs. iii, iv.

thirteenth century onward.[12] It is just within possibility that these delineations dimly reflect a memory of actual landfalls, seen through a haze of folklore or literary tradition; it is also arguable that the later representation of Antillia, to be associated by cartographers with the legendary Island of the Seven Cities, may embody hearsay or rumour of land sighted out in the ocean. It is not less evident that none of these or other conventionally depicted islands owed its formal design in the maps to observation or visual recording, and that none of them was associated in the mapmakers' minds with the Norse landfalls in the west. Greenland was unknown to, or unnoticed by, cartographers of southern Europe until the visit of Claudius Clavus to Italy. Vinland seems to be mentioned by only two non-Scandinavian writers before the fifteenth century— Adam of Bremen (*ca.* 1070) and Ordericus Vitalis (*ca.* 1140); and it is neither depicted nor named in any medieval map so far known.[13] There could hardly be clearer testimony to the lack of precise communication of geographical knowledge between the Scandinavian and the Latin worlds.

In the Vinland Map, therefore, we see the only known cartographic delineation of American lands before the discoveries of Columbus and Cabot. This was drawn solely from records of the Norse voyages, and it illustrates no other American landfall. The different parts of the design exemplify the character and reliability of the information on these lands available to the mapmaker or to his original. If Iceland and Greenland are depicted from experience, the outline of Vinland must have been constructed from written or oral report. The map nevertheless records in graphic form the only documented pre-Columbian discovery of America. So far as the evidence goes, this unique record remained unnoticed by geographical writers, by projectors and explorers, and by cartographers.[14] We may still ask whether, more positively than all the hints of western land accumulated in fifteenth-century maps and texts, it served in some way to bridge "the gap between two epochs of Atlantic discovery".[15]

4. THE VINLAND MAP AND THE DISCOVERY OF AMERICA

The western part of the Vinland Map presents a chart of the Atlantic which (as we have seen) appears to be put together from two distinct sources. In central latitudes the cartographer has drawn the island groups of the Canaries, Madeira, and the "supposed" Azores; this chain is extended northward by Mayda and Brasil, lying off the southwest coasts of (respectively) England and Ireland, and westward of it are the larger islands of Antillia and Satanaxes, with the name *Magnæ Insulæ Beati Brandani*. All this matter was common to Italian nautical cartography from the early fifteenth century. In higher latitudes the three great islands of Iceland,

---

12. Ashe, p. 295.

13. Adam of Bremen's work, as suggested by its manuscript diffusion, was not widely read or well known in southern Europe. Ordericus Vitalis (*Historia Ecclesiastica,* bk. X, cap. 5) merely includes "Vinlandia" in a list of islands under the King of Norway; while this allusion may be derived from Adam, Nansen suggests that Ordericus (1075–1143), an English monk who spent most of his life in Normandy, "may well have had communication with Irishmen". See Nansen, Vol. 2, p. 31; Beazley, *Dawn,* Vol. 2, p. 547. Nansen (Vol. 2, pp. 31–32) is doubtless right in supposing the "Wyntlandia" in Ranulph Hygden's world map (*ca.* 1350) to represent Wendland, not Vinland. Cf. also Miller, *Mappaemundi,* Heft 3, p. 106.

14. It is perhaps just possible that the map and its representation of land out in the ocean had been, if not seen, at least heard of and talked about. Cf. above, p. 159.

15. Ashe, p. 296.

Greenland, and Vinland form a vast arc curving out and westward from Norway across the ocean and southward approximately to the parallel (not drawn) which would cut the northern end of Satanaxes and the western point of Brittany. This representation was unknown to the mapmakers of southern Europe and must have come from a Scandinavian, and probably Icelandic, source by a chain of transmission which remains obscure.

If the two parts of the Atlantic chart, thus clearly distinguished both by origin and by design, be considered in relation to the prevalent wind systems, they can be seen to indicate alternative westward ocean passages on which the navigator might hope to pick up land. Taking his departure from a port of the Iberian Peninsula and sailing down into the zone of the northeasterly trade winds, he could then lay a course west or southwest on which he would find Antillia lying across his bows. These were in fact the courses set by Columbus in the late summer of 1492, and Antillia was the first land which he expected to sight on his westward passage from the Canaries.[16] A mapmaker who thought in terms of a globe could locate Antillia somewhat further west than might be suggested by an ungraduated mappamundi or portolan chart in which it was drawn at the lefthand edge of the parchment. Toscanelli (as he told Columbus) supposed Antillia to lie 35 degrees west of his prime meridian through the Canaries; and it is in just this longitude, a little north of the equator, that Martin Behaim lays down, in his globe of 1492, the Island of St. Brendan, with an outline very like that of Antillia in the fifteenth-century charts and in the Vinland Map.[17] This concept is not, in substance, different from that expressed in the relevant part of the Vinland Map and there copied from a model similar to Bianco's world map of 1436, in which the design is compressed within the limits of the available space at the extreme left of the vellum sheet.

Two northern sea routes, by parallel sailing, are suggested by the disposition of lands in the Vinland Map. One is that of the Norse navigation due west from Norway to Iceland and Greenland, or direct from Norway to the south point of Greenland.[18] The other, using the northeasterly winds of early summer and of autumn in this zone, makes a course westward from southern England or Ireland, with perhaps a sight of Brasil or Mayda on the way, to a landfall in Vinland. It was by this route that, from 1480 or earlier, the Bristol merchants set forth regular voyages in search of "the Island of Brasylle on the west part of Ireland", or "to thentent to search & fynde a certain Isle called the Isle of Brasile", and that at some date before 1494 their search was crowned by the discovery of a mainland which they called Brasil.[19] In Dr. Williamson's words, "it was these unknown men who first worked out the course from the British Isles to the north-east corner of America";[20] and Bristol was the base selected by John Cabot for his western voyages to find (as he supposed) Cathay. This port offered him at once the best point of departure for a transatlantic crossing and also crews who were already familiar

16. As we may assume from Toscanelli's reference, in his letter to Columbus, to "the island of Antillia which is known to you", in the latitude of Cipangu.

17. Behaim gives it the name *Insula de sant brandan*. This apparent association of Antillia and St. Brendan in Behaim's mind echoes that in the Vinland Map. We must note, however, that the globe also shows *Antilia*, as a triangular island lying on the Tropic of Cancer (thus nearly due west of the Canaries) and about 10 degrees east of St. Brendan's Island.

18. See above, Fig. 4 (p. 170).

19. See D. B. Quinn, "The argument for the English discovery of America between 1480 and 1494", *Geogr. Journal*, Vol. 127 (1961), pp. 277–85.

20. J. A. Williamson, *The Cabot Voyages and Bristol Discovery under Henry VII* (1962), p. 62.

with the navigation. In May–June 1497 Cabot's course, which was doubtless that of the preceding expeditions of the Bristol men, took him along the south coast of Ireland, north for "some days", and then west for thirty-five days on an ENE wind to his landfall. The land which he discovered was "assumed and believed to be the mainland that the men from Bristol found" some years earlier. On his return voyage in July, with favorable west winds, Cabot made a passage of fifteen days from (probably) Cape Race in Newfoundland to a landfall in Brittany.[21]

The course of the pioneering voyages to the west which resulted in landfalls authenticated by documents is therefore consonant with the geography of the Atlantic portrayed in the Vinland Map. This is very far from proof that the map or its content was known to the promoters and leaders of these enterprises. Voyages made in the fifteenth century by a number of Portuguese venturers in search of land in the western Atlantic are also attested, more or less loosely, in documents of various kinds. Most of them set out from the Azores, Madeira, or the Cape Verde Islands; and there is no serious evidence, until near the end of the century, that they sought or found any objective more substantial than the imaginary islands—Antillia, the Seven Cities, St. Brendan—displayed in contemporary charts and granted by royal letters-patent to the expectant discoverers.[22] Some of these stories were collected by Columbus in support of his project; and some no doubt were transmitted to Bristol, the principal English terminus of the trade with Portugal and Madeira, by seamen's gossip. It can even be argued that such "an exchange of ideas between men with a common interest in the farther Atlantic" justifies us in seeing the Portuguese voyages out into the ocean as an impulse behind the Bristol interest in the search for distant islands, which is attested from 1480 onward.[23]

That there was a two-way traffic of ideas is conceivable and even likely. This enables us to visualize a possible route by which geographical information available in Iceland, where the Atlantic representation in the Vinland Map doubtless originated, could have been conveyed at least to Portugal, if not to other countries of southern Europe. The Bristol trade with Iceland initiated about 1424 had by the second half of the fifteenth century become substantial and regular, and the Icelandic grounds were frequented by Bristol fishermen.[24] Iceland was the repository of the knowledge about Greenland and lands further west preserved both in folk memory or orally and in the written literature of the sagas and annals; and among the documentary records we may now count a map or maps, no longer extant except in a derivative represented by the western part of the Vinland Map. That the Bristol merchants and fishermen had any access to Icelandic documents is of course exceedingly unlikely; but, in Dr Williamson's words, "the

21. The details of the courses out and home are given in the letter of John Day, discovered by Dr. L. A. Vigneras in the Simancas archives in 1956. See L. A. Vigneras, "New light on the 1497 Cabot voyage to America", *Hisp. Amer. Hist. Review*, Vol. 36 (1956), pp. 503–09; idem, "The Cape Breton landfall: 1494 or 1497", *Canadian Hist. Review*, Vol. 38 (1957), pp. 219–28; R. Almagià, "Sulle navigazioni di Giovanni Caboto", *Rivista geogr. italiana*, Vol. 67 (1960), pp. 1–12; Quinn, loc. cit.; Williamson, introduction, chs. ii–v, and doc. 25. The Spanish text of the letter is printed by Vigneras (1956) and Almagià; English translations are given by Vigneras (1957) and Williamson.

22. The evidence for these expeditions is surveyed by S. E. Morison, *Portuguese Voyages to America in the Fifteenth Century* (1940), ch. i, "The northern voyages". Two of them have been claimed to have reached Newfoundland or the Grand Banks. As Admiral Morison shows, the course of Diogo de Teive and Pedro de Velasco in 1452, as described by Las Casas, could not have brought them to the Banks; and the late testimony to an American landfall by João Vaz Corte Real in 1472 seems far too slight to carry any burden of proof.

23. This suggestion is made by Williamson, pp. 14–17.

24. See the extracts from the Bristol customs records printed by Williamson, pp. 175–77; and his introduction, chs. i, ii.

story of lands to the west and south, and their traditional names, must have been current in vague form among the illiterate people of the ports and coast with whom the English inevitably had dealings. We do not know if the Bristol men had any intellectual contact with the few who knew the history recorded in the sagas, but it seems very probable that they heard of Markland and Wineland and perhaps of western fisheries which the Icelanders themselves had no need to exploit".[25] Such a hypothesis not only goes far to explain (as Professor D. B. Quinn suggests) both the interest of the Bristol merchants in Brasil as "a territorial key to a fishery" and "the lack of publicity about the discovery of new and extremely rich grounds".[26] It also illustrates the means by which, despite this "policy of secrecy", some of the Icelandic talk about western lands might have been transmitted from Bristol to Lisbon or Seville by a similar chain of gossip and hearsay on the quayside and in the counting-house. Professor Quinn has demonstrated that a "leakage" of this kind would have been enough to attract John Cabot, in 1494 or 1495, from Spain or Portugal to England, where "he could propose to use the Isle of Brasil as a half-way house to a more northerly part of the Asiatic coast, with a still shorter sea passage than that followed by Columbus, so as to tap the commerce of Cathay and the Spice Islands".[27]

A phrase in John Day's letter describing the Cabot voyage of 1497, which must have been written at the end of 1497 or beginning of 1498, indicates that its recipient already had knowledge of the earlier Bristol discovery of "mainland" in the North Atlantic. The letter is addressed to the "Almirante Mayor", whom (as Dr. L. A. Vigneras has shown) there are grounds for identifying with Christopher Columbus, Admiral of the Ocean Sea.[28] Acceptance of this identification admits the possibility that news of the English discovery may have been in Columbus' possession before he sailed in 1492 and have contributed to his "conviction that there was land to be found within the range of distances which he anticipated".[29] It may be added that, if Columbus in fact visited Iceland in 1477, it was very probably in a Bristol vessel that he made the trip, and, if so, that he could have shared the Icelandic information picked up by Bristol seamen.[30]

That such a "leakage" from Iceland to Bristol and from Bristol to Lisbon or Seville embraced anything more than oral report, and that it extended to documents, let alone a map, may be considered out of the question. But if we make the reasonable assumption that the geographical information of the Vinland Map, or of its Icelandic original, corresponded in its main features to that orally transmitted by the channels suggested above, we have to consider how it fits into the ideological background of the enterprises of Columbus and Cabot. In other words, had either of these imaginative men become aware of the information contained in the Vinland Map, to what use would he have turned it in planning and promoting his enterprise?

Columbus made copious notes on all reports of land or islands in the west that came to his notice, and these were gathered together in the biography by his son Fernando.[31] From the fact

25. Williamson, p. 14.

26. Quinn, p. 282; cf. Williamson, p. 43.

27. Quinn, p. 284.

28. Vigneras, "The Cape Breton landfall", p. 226.

29. Quinn, p. 284.

30. We do not go so far in skepticism as Admiral Morison, who writes: "The Vinland story was not likely to come [Columbus's] way, unless he had learned Icelandic and attended saga-telling parties ashore" (S. E. Morison, *Admiral of the Ocean Sea* (1942), Vol. I, p. 35).

31. *Historie,* ch. x.

that they include no mention of Vinland, Admiral Morison has concluded "that Columbus never heard of it" and that, "if we accept Ferdinand's positive evidence of the Iceland voyage, we must also accept his negative evidence that Columbus found no useful evidence there".[32] Whether the first of these inferences is justified or not, the second is indisputable, if we suppose the information available to Columbus from Iceland to have corresponded to that in the Vinland Map. All the evidence which he could collect indicated that both his objective and the best route thither lay in tropical latitudes. Like Toscanelli, he took Antillia to lie on or near the Tropic of Cancer; and if (as we suppose) the world maps he consulted included one like that by Henricus Martellus now at Yale, which reflects Toscanelli's views, he could see that a course along the same parallel would bring him to Cipangu and to Mangi, the "cape of Asia". Any Portuguese expeditions which may have attempted a passage from Madeira or the Azores to land in the northwest were doubtless beaten back by the westerly winds of the North Atlantic; and his experience in the Portuguese navigation to Africa had taught Columbus how to use the wind systems of the central Atlantic. Thus he inevitably thought of a voyage with the northeast trade winds.[33] The southern point of Vinland, as drawn in the Vinland Map, is in the latitude of the English Channel, 25 degrees north of Columbus' point of departure in the Canaries. Not only was the knowledge reflected in this map (if he had it) not "useful" to his enterprise; it was simply irrelevant.

Had therefore the two men met after John Cabot's 1497 voyage to his American landfall in about 45° N, Columbus might have told him (in the words of Captain Luke Foxe): "You are out of the way to Japon, for this is not it".[34] But Cabot's adoption of the northern route proceeded from geographical premises quite distinct from those of Columbus; they appear, ironically enough, to have included Cabot's disbelief in Columbus' own claim to have reached Asia in 1492–93.

Unlike Columbus, John Cabot has left no explicit statement either of his objectives and of the means by which he proposed to attain them, or of the experience and reasoning by which his project was formulated. On all these matters no writing from his hand or of his composition survives. We can only visualize them from the statements which he is reported by contemporaries to have made and by deduction from his recorded actions. The evidence, as surveyed most recently by Dr. Williamson and Professor Quinn,[35] points to certain conclusions which are logically related to one another and to the Atlantic ventures of the Bristol men and of Columbus; and they are here summarized, with the reservations dictated by the possibility that new evidence may alter the perspective.

Cabot, like Columbus, sought a westward passage to Cathay by the shortest sea route. He was probably present in Valencia to witness Columbus' triumphant return in 1493; but he could not credit Columbus' identification of his discoveries with the Asian mainland. Study of the globe would show him that, because of the convergence of the meridians, a passage in higher latitudes would be shorter than that made, almost within the tropic, by Columbus. If and when news of the Bristol discovery of land in the northwest reached him, he must have realized, first, that here

32. Morison, *Admiral of the Ocean Sea,* Vol. I, p. 35.
33. Ibid., pp. 207–08.
34. *North-West Fox* (1635), p. 223. Foxe made this facetious remark to Captain Thomas James, when he encountered him in the south of Hudson's Bay in the summer of 1631.
35. Williamson, introduction, chs. iii–vi; Quinn, pp. 281–84. The documents are printed by Williamson.

were men who had mastered the winds and navigation for a westward passage in these latitudes; and, second, that the "Brasil" found by the Bristol venturers might turn out to be at worst an island which would serve as "a half-way house to a more northerly part of the Asiatic coast",[36] at best "the north-east corner of Asia, projecting more towards Europe than the tropical region", which could be coasted south-west "to Cipango and the rich tropical part of the Great Khan's empire. These would be in Columbus's latitudes, but they would be far beyond Columbus in longitude".[37] That Cabot probably adopted the more sanguine of these two interpretations is suggested by his confident report, after his return in 1497, that he had "discovered mainland 700 leagues away, which is the country of the Great Khan".[38] The geographical picture which he had in mind before he sailed would then correspond to that illustrated in the later world maps of Contarini-Rosselli (1506), Ruysch (1507–08), and Vesconte Maggiolo (*ca.* 1510 and 1511).[39] These cartographers show the recently discovered coasts of Labrador and Newfoundland, in the longitude of the eastern Antilles, as the Atlantic seaboard of a great promontory jutting eastward from northeast Asia, with its southern coast trending first west and then south to the point of Mangi, in Cathay. In this representation the Spanish discoveries in the Caribbean are separated by a broad sea passage both from the English and Portuguese landfalls in the northwest and from the mainland of Asia.

This was the pattern of land and water which probably ruled Cabot's thought before he sailed from Bristol in 1497, and certainly did so after his return and in the planning of his next voyage. How would he have reconciled it with the delineation in the Vinland Map, if this map or the information in it had, through a Bristol intermediary, come to his knowledge? To simplify the argument, let us make the improbable assumption that Cabot had seen some version of the map itself. Comparison of its representation of the North Atlantic with the courses and distances logged by the Bristol pilots would undoubtedly have led him to identify the lately discovered "Brasil" with the southern part of Vinland as shown on the map. This would provide him with mutual confirmation of the reliability of his two sources. He would see that Vinland extended, on the map, little south of the latitude of Bristol and that, if it were an island (as it is depicted) and not mainland, it would not bar an onward voyage to Cathay on a course changed slightly south of west. On the other hand, he might well note that the western coast of Vinland appears to be drawn from conjecture and not from discovery, and conclude that the question whether the Vinland of the map represented an island or the eastern face of a continental coast remained open for investigation. Any of these hypothetical interpretations of the map was consistent with his plan, and the plan could be modified to accord with what he found. That in June–July 1497 he coasted 300 leagues of land in a month, from west to east, must have convinced him that the "continental" interpretation was correct and that "Brasil" and "Vinland" were sections of the mainland of Asia.

It is to be understood that the reconstruction of Cabot's line of thought in the preceding paragraph is wholly speculative and depends on assumptions which, even if true, will probably never

36. Quinn, p. 283.

37. Williamson, p. 47.

38. Recorded by Lorenzo Pasqualigo, 23 August 1497 (Williamson, p. 208).

39. On these maps, see R. A. Skelton, "The cartography of the voyages", in Williamson, pp. 300–06. La Cosa's map dated 1500 presents, in substance, a similar delineation.

be verified. It does nevertheless demonstrate that the Icelandic information exemplified in the Vinland Map, had it come to John Cabot's notice, would have seemed to him compatible with his own preconceptions, with the discoveries in the North Atlantic known to him, and with his plan for further exploration.

The Vinland Map is the only surviving graphic record of the western voyages of the Norsemen to contain any element of experience. As such, it must have exercised a potent influence on the mind of any seaman under whose eyes it came. We cannot yet point to any direct link between it and the rediscoverers of North America at the end of the fifteenth century. Yet it is conceivable that they had heard of the Viking voyages, even if in a form much less precise than the carto-graphic record of them in the Vinland Map, and that the example of the Norse seamen served as an incentive for their own ventures. As Nansen wrote of the Norse voyages: "For the first time explorers had set out with conscious purpose from the known world, over the surrounding seas, and had found land on the other side. By their voyages they taught the sailors of Europe the possibility of traversing the ocean".[40] Of this initiative the Vinland Map is a memorial.

40. Nansen, Vol. 2, p. 38.

BIBLIOGRAPHICAL POSTSCRIPT

(November 1964)

This study of the Vinland Map was written without access to the important works on the Icelandic voyages and settlements by Jón Dúason (*Landkönnun og Landnám Íslendinga i Vesturheim,* Reykjavik, 1941–48), the late Professor T. J. Oleson (*Early Voyages and Northern Approaches,* Toronto, 1963), and Professor Gwyn Jones (*The Norse Atlantic Saga,* London, 1964). The first of these works was, at the time of writing, not yet in the British Museum Library; the second and third were published after the paper had been delivered for printing (February 1963). Insofar as these scholars, drawing on archaeological and anthropological evidence, are concerned with the range and extent of the Greenlanders' navigation, with the evidential value of the sagas, and with the character of the American voyages, their conclusions are consistent with the hypothetical opinions advanced here. Although Professor Oleson was reluctant to admit the strong evidence for climatic deterioration between the ninth and fifteenth centuries, this factor (so far from weakening) would have strengthened his thesis that racial and cultural intermingling took place, from an early date, between the Icelandic settlers of Greenland and of the Canadian Arctic and the aboriginal inhabitants of these regions (Skraelings). Professor Jones, on the other hand, accepts the chronology of climatic change constructed by recent students, but rejects Dúason's hypothesis of "absorption".

The fluctuation of opinion on the historicity of the Icelandic sagas, from the seventeenth to the twentieth century, has recently been surveyed by Dr. Theodore M. Andersson, *The Problem of Icelandic Saga Origins* (Yale University Press, 1964). In the present study it has been assumed that the saga accounts of the Viking voyages to America rest upon an oral tradition with a firm basis in fact, even if subjected to some later deformation or interpretation.

Dr. Helge Ingstad's investigation of a site in northern Newfoundland, claimed to be Norse, has been the subject of many further articles in newspapers and periodicals. To the English-language references given above, page 220, note 256, may be added: *Evening Telegram* (St. John's), 24 August 1962, 5 February 1964, 10 March 1964; *Providence Journal,* 9 and 20 November 1963; *New York Times,* 6 and 23 November 1963; and an article by Dr. Ingstad in the *National Geographic Magazine,* November 1964. None of these adds much to the material published up to January 1963, and Dr. Ingstad's scientific report is still awaited.

To the works on medieval mappaemundi enumerated on p. 111, n. 12, may now be added a full inventory: *Mappemondes, A.D. 1200–1500. Catalogue préparé par la Commission des Cartes Anciennes de l'Union Géographique Internationale, rédacteur-en-chef Marcel Destombes,* Amsterdam, 1964 (Monumenta Cartographica Vetustioris Aevi, Vol. I).

THE TARTAR RELATION

AND THE VINLAND MAP

An Interpretation

George D. Painter

As we have seen, the compiler of the Vinland Map used the Tartar Relation as one of his chief sources for the captions which he included in his map. Conversely, it seems that one of his intentions in compiling the Vinland Map was to construct a cartographic illustration of the geography of the Tartar Relation in terms of the world map which he used as his model. In our appraisal of the value of the Vinland Map as documentary evidence it is of primary importance to assess the compiler's attitude toward his sources and the use he has made of them. We must endeavor to distinguish the features in map and captions which are due to his intervention from those features which were already present in his cartographic or textual sources. The compiler's own conceptions or misconceptions can then be set aside, as being merely arbitrary figments of his mind; but the residue will represent the pre-existing cartographic or historical traditions which constitute the chief significance of the Vinland Map.

In the following study the Vinland Map is approached, as in some degree was the method of the compiler himself, from the point of view of the Tartar Relation. In the compiler's treatment of the Old World his activities can be detected with some certainty, since we are able to compare his two chief sources—the Tartar Relation and his map model as adumbrated by the surviving world maps of Andrea Bianco, Petrus Vesconte, and others—with the results of their embodiment in the Vinland Map. For the New World portions of the Vinland Map we possess neither the cartographic nor the textual sources used by the compiler, except insofar as they are revealed in the Vinland Map itself; but here the attitudes disclosed by his handling of the Old World may help us to deduce the extent of his intervention, and to assess the authenticity and significance of the remainder.

I am grateful to Mr. Vietor and to Mr. Skelton for their generous encouragement in inviting me to present the personal and sometimes hazardous views put forward in this "interpretation". In the presence of a document as unexpected, complex, and problematic as the Vinland Map, it has seemed allowable and even useful to explore certain possibilities up to the utmost limits permitted by the evidence. The reader will understand that these views, insofar as they supplement or differ from Mr. Skelton's on the same topics, are offered only as a "second opinion", as more or less tenable alternatives, and without controversial intention.

The purpose of the compiler of the Vinland Map, as his title shows, was to supply a cartographic illustration to the *Speculum Historiale* of Vincent of Beauvais, and further, as the wording of many of his captions indicates, to make special reference to the Tartar Relation, which was appended to the Vincent manuscript available to him. Nevertheless, the map seems devoid of any particular application to the text of the *Speculum Historiale*, nor is any apparent attempt made to illustrate the detailed survey of world geography in the *Speculum*, Books I and II. The compiler seems to have worked under the simple concept that a world history would be appropriately illustrated by a world map.

The compiler, of course, must not be identified with the scribe of the surviving exemplar of VM, which is itself a copy, perhaps at several removes, from the lost original. It is possible, though not at all necessary, that the compiler may have worked, perhaps several decades before, in the same scriptorium, which may well have specialized in the multiplication of manuscripts of the *Speculum Historiale* augmented with TR and VM. As we shall see, neither the cartography nor the captions of VM show any certain sign of acquaintance with the journey-narrative of Carpini as embodied in the *Speculum Historiale,* Book XXXII, or with the other Mongol material in Books XXX–XXXII. This suggests (a) that the compiler was not the person who originally appended TR to the *Speculum,* since this addition was evidently made in recognition of the relevance of TR to the closing books of the *Speculum;* and further (b) that the compiler was not the scribe who copied the *Speculum* manuscript to which VM was first appended, since the operation of copying would have supplied him with the information which is lacking in the map.

In one of his map captions the compiler refers to Carpini and his companions as "the friars of our order", quoting verbatim from TR, ¶7, and adding that they made their journey "with us"—*"nobiscum"*. Even if we assume that he intended the map to speak for the author of TR, these expressions still appear strange. Was the compiler himself a Franciscan? He has access to the all but lost TR, a Franciscan narrative edited by a Franciscan at the command of a Franciscan. His map shows special interest in missionary journeys and Christian communities in outlying parts of the world—central Asia, Greenland and Vinland, the Nestorians of China, the realm of Prester John; and the Franciscans, ever since their foundation, had engaged in missionary exploration more energetically than any other order, even the Dominicans. The lost *Inventio Fortunata* on the countries of the Far North, though it is unlikely that this treatise was used by the VM compiler, was the work of a Franciscan.[1] Possibly the expression *"fratres nostri ordinis"* implies also that the map compiler was a Franciscan. Were the Vincent and TR manuscripts copied, and VM compiled, in one and the same Franciscan monastery of Western Germany?

Several of the longer legends in VM are adapted bodily from passages in TR, and phrases from TR appear in nearly all the remainder. The compiler's attitude toward his textual source is important to our visualization of his cartographic source. Did he modify his map source to suit TR, or modify TR to suit his map source, or both?

In fact the compiler shows a strikingly unscientific disregard for TR as an objective source of information,[2] with an equally curious borrowing of the phraseology of TR as a source of verbal expression. In accordance with his Bianco-form map source, and probably with his own

1. The author of the *Inventio Fortunata* was apparently not aware of the tenth-century Norse discovery and colonization of Greenland (which he, or rather his reporter Jacob Cnoyen, attributed to King Arthur in the sixth century!), still less of the Norse discovery of America. His minimal information on Greenland and his semi-fabulous geography are in deplorable contrast with the authoritative northwestern captions and cartography of VM. Nevertheless, he provides a possibly significant example of Franciscan interest in, experience of, and writing about the northwest, within a lifetime before the compilation of VM. Incidentally, it may be noticed that the *Inventio Fortunata* account of the two expeditions allegedly sent by King Arthur to Greenland, apparently based by Cnoyen on the lost *Gesta Arthuri,* is strikingly reminiscent of the story of Eirik the Red, and was presumably fabricated therefrom. King Arthur first sends a reconnaissance expedition, which returns to report; he then sends a colonizing fleet of twelve ships, from which five are "driven on the rocks in a storm", while the remainder reach Greenland and settle there. Similarly Eirik the Red's first expedition to Greenland was a reconnaissance (A.D. 982–85), while in the second, which established the first colony (A.D. 986), "twenty-five ships set sail . . . but only fourteen arrived at their destination: some were driven back, and some were lost". Cf. Gathorne-Hardy, pp. 22–23; E. G. R. Taylor, in *Imago Mundi,* Vol. 13 (1956), pp. 56–68.

2. Moreover, he neglected to use more than the first half of TR. The last passage in TR used in his captions occurs in the Prester John caption (no. 30), and is derived from TR, ¶26. Indeed, with this exception and that of the two captions mentioning the Samoyeds (nos. 39, 57, from TR, ¶21), his material is taken only from TR, ¶1–¶16, comprising merely the first quarter of the text. It seems that he worked through TR until he felt he had filled sufficient space with his captions, and then lost interest in the remainder. References to the VM captions are given here and below by number from Mr. Skelton's "Names and Legends in the Vinland Map", pp. 127–41 above.

fifteenth-century ideas, he places Prester John in eastern Africa (no. 30), which involves an out-right contradiction of TR's location of the Prester in India (TR, ¶17). Wishing, however, to express the notorious fact that Prester John's realm was Christian, and searching for appropriate wording in TR, he adapts for this purpose statements concerning various Orthodox Christian tribes between the Black Sea and Caspian in TR, ¶26, and the Kitai in TR, ¶10! He affirms (no. 39), in defiance of TR, that the friars traveled not only to the Tartars and Mongols but also to the Samoyeds, Indians, and the ocean sea, all three of which TR mentions as reached not by the friars themselves but by various expeditions of the Mongols (TR, ¶21, ¶17, ¶14). Here his intention seems to be to authenticate his map by pretending that the friars' journey covered not only central Asia but also the furthest north, south, and east. This caption is appended, rationally enough except that it is much too far north, to the "steep mountains, not very high" in the country of the Naimans, through which, as TR states (¶7), the friars actually passed. He perverts (no. 56) the report of the woman from Narayrgen, the People of the Sun, that her country ("*dicta terra*") "is situated at the very end of the world, and beyond it no land is found, but only the ocean sea" (TR, ¶14), by substituting the words "a new land" ("*nova terra*"),[3] and attributing the statement to the Tartars themselves.

Further captions, motivated by the compiler's desire to describe areas of his map concerning which TR was inadequate or silent, seem to suggest that he had access to other, unidentified sources. The note (no. 36) that "the Nestorians pressed on assiduously to the land of Cathay" is surely extraordinary in a fifteenth-century writer, whether it refers to the arrival in Northern China of Nestorian missionaries from Syria in the seventh century A.D. or to the revival of Nestorian Christianity there in the thirteenth century before and during the Mongol occupation—although, as Mr. Skelton suggests, there may be an echo of Rubruck's remark that Nestorians are found "all the way to Cathay" (Rockhill, p. 157).[4] The placing of the caption near the Nestorians' primary center in the Middle East is perhaps significant, and possibly some unidentified map source should be suspected here. The remainder of this caption, concerning the Enclosed Tribes of the Jews, is worded in part after TR, ¶15; but the identification of the mountains which shut them in as the *Hemmodi* or Himalaya is in contradiction not only with TR's mention of the Caspian Mountains (¶12, ¶15) and the location of Gog-Magog in the far northeast in VM, but with all known tradition. Here, too, we may suspect a lost map source, or an inference therefrom, rather than a textual source, possibly the same from which the compiler drew the adjacent caption to the east (no. 37), "*kemmodi montes* . . . ".[5] The remainder of the latter caption, ". . . *Superiores Excels [issimi]. sive Nimsini*", seems to be inferred, though quite absurdly, from TR, ¶7. The "*montes inferiores abrupti*" in the country of the Naimans (no. 39) are evi-

3. The very concept of a "new land" is surely noteworthy, though not unparalleled, at this time, more than half a century before Columbus and his successors showed that undiscovered lands in fact existed. The expression is significantly repeated in the longer Vinland caption (cf. below, p. 251). The (early) fifteenth-century date here assigned to the compiler is intended as a convenient approximation, and without prejudice to Mr. Skelton's demonstration that he may conceivably have worked as early as the closing decades of the fourteenth century (see pp. 228–30 above).

4. It is not suggested, however, that the compiler actually had access to the then little-known narrative of Rubruck; if he had, he would surely have made some demonstrable use of it. This and other possible parallels to Rubruck are no doubt entirely coincidental.

5. The form "*kemmodi*" is doubtless a mere corruption of the more correct form "*hemmodi*" used in the Nestorian caption, since the basic form is "*Emodi*". The name is found in the Ptolemaic atlases, where the eastern extension of the Himalayas is marked as "*Emodii montes*".

dently meant to correspond with these "higher, very lofty mountains" (cf. *"duos montes altissimos"*, TR, ¶7) also in the territory of the Naimans (corrupted in VM to *Nimsini*); and our compiler, perhaps encouraged by the words *"longe valde ab exercitu"* which separate the two mountain features in TR, ¶7, was not to be deterred by the immense distance at which he has parted the two captions, one in the far north, the other in the far south.

It may be noted that the corrupt form *"Nimsini"* is further evidence that the surviving VM is the end product of one or more stages of copying from the lost original, since the compiler could not have misread the clearly written *"Naymani"* in TR. The corruption *"kemmodi"* (for *"hemmodi"*) and the ungrammatical *"possunt dicuntur"* in the Prester John caption (no. 30) are possibly but not necessarily due to the same cause.

Two of the Eurasian captions (nos. 11, 53) refer, in a manner which is not only without support from TR but apparently without exact parallel in earlier medieval maps, to the ice of the Arctic Ocean;[6] and to these may be added the unusual location of *Thule ultima* in northern Eurasia (no. 52). It is tempting to link these with the mention of arctic ice in the Vinland caption (no. 67), and to wonder whether the compiler had recourse for all four captions to an account of the northern regions included in his unknown textual source for the Vinland caption, or to his map source based thereupon. Equally unsupported by known cartographic or textual sources is the "great river", not marked on the map, "which passes through the midst of the mountains and islands, debouching amongst the ice of the northern ocean" in the country of the Russians (no. 11).[7]

As Mr. Skelton has shown, the main source for the cartography of VM, except for the north-western regions, was a map of Bianco form. However, it seems possible to suggest a non-Bianco element in certain features of the northeast. *Kytanis* (Cathay) is strangely located (no. 49) to the northwest of the Mongols, instead of to the east, as might be deduced not only from Bianco but from TR, ¶5; but this error is matched in Vesconte maps, where Cathay is marked northwest of the Great Khan.[8]

The river-systems flowing into the Caspian in VM diverge notably from Bianco. In VM the northward river flows into the Arctic, whereas in Bianco it is drawn correctly, although un-named, in accordance with the Volga, with two headstreams of which the western corresponds to the Volga proper, the eastern to the Kama. No doubt the VM compiler was influenced by the need to show the "Tartartata" river (TR, ¶3), for which he had left no room further east, although the actual course and outlet of this river is not stated in TR; possibly he also had in mind the great river of his Russian caption, with its Arctic mouth. But it is noteworthy that in Vesconte maps, which show two Caspians, the Volga-like river is absent. In its place we have rivers flowing northeast from each Caspian to meet near a common source in the mountain

6. The expression *"inter glacies"* seems to suggest pack ice, which would not be a familiar concept at this period to a southerner, and might be held to suggest a northern source. The severe cold of the arctic zone was, of course, an accepted idea throughout medieval times, and is expressed by such map captions as *"Regio inhabitabilis propter algorem"* in Vesconte maps, or *"In hac parte est maximum frigus"* in Bianco, etc.; but this is hardly a true parallel. The caption *"terra inaccessibilis vel ignota propter glaciem"* for the supposed land mass northeast of Greenland in the Vienna text of Claudius Clavus (Björnbo and Petersen, 1904, p. 111 and pl. II) is perhaps a little closer.

7. If this Arctic river has any geographical reality, it might suggest the Dvina, flowing through northern Russia into the White Sea, which river was known and used as a predatory and commercial highway by the medieval Norsemen (cf. Nansen, Vol. 2, pp. 135–42).

8. Cf. Nordenskiöld, *Periplus*, figs. 6, 20; *Facsimile-Atlas*, fig. 28.

peninsular where, in these maps, not the Jews but "the Tartars are enclosed" (*"Hic sunt inclusi Tartari"*); and a further river springs at the same point to debouch in the Arctic Ocean, so drawn that it is not difficult to mistake the whole system for a single stream.[9] It seems possible that in this feature the Bianco-form model of VM may have been influenced by a Vesconte-form map.

The possibility of a non-Bianco origin may likewise be inferred for the two rivers flowing southwestward from the Caspian in VM. In Bianco these are continued far eastward to rise in the Earthly Paradise, and Mr. Skelton suggests (p. 121 above) that the VM rivers are merely truncated forms of Bianco's. In Leardo's and Fra Mauro's maps, however, as also in Ptolemy, these rivers are drawn and named as the Iaxartes (Syr-daria) and Oxus (Amu-daria), which when the Aral Sea was as yet unknown were supposed to flow into the Caspian. Here again we may suspect a non-Bianco element in the model for VM; and as between VM and Bianco the error here would be in Bianco, not VM.

It seems, so far, that the VM compiler has drawn his map in conformity with his original, and that even features not found in Bianco's world map (always excepting the northwestern portions of VM) may well have existed in that original. In his captions drawn from TR he has consistently altered TR to fit the map, rather than the map to fit TR. He has used a few topographical names from TR—*Mongali, Tartaria mogalica, Moal, Zumoal, Gogus, Magog* (nos. 45, 42, 44, 43, 48, 47, respectively), etc.—not always situating them very happily. Two of these, *Nimsini* (no. 37, as an alternative name for the *hemmodi montes*) and *Tatartata fluvius* (no. 51) are exceptional as applying new names taken from TR to actual geographical features probably present in his model. With these exceptions he has avoided any sustained effort to make the map an illustration of TR. Otherwise, if he had treated TR scientifically as a source of cartographic knowledge, he could have laid down more or less in their correct positions such regions as *Merkit, Mecrit,*[10] *Esurscakita,*[11] *Nayman,*[12] and many others for which TR gives bearings in relation to the Mongol homeland.[13]

This perfunctory attitude toward his textual source helps to explain the curious fact that the compiler has made little use—or rather, in the present writer's view, none at all—of the epitome of Carpini's journey-narrative in the *Speculum Historiale,* Book XXXII, or of Carpini's complete treatise, or of Benedict's journey-narrative. We do not know that the latter two texts were available to him, and, possible as it may be otherwise, we should require conclusive evidence in VM to assume his knowledge of them. But the first was certainly in his hands, as forming part of the *Speculum Historiale* manuscript to which TR was appended. From Vincent's abridgment of

9. *Ibid.* The Tartar river is apparently first marked—entirely independently, of course, of the Vinland Map—in G. Mercator's world map, 1569 (reproduced by E. G. R. Taylor, "John Dee and the map of Northeast Asia," in *Imago Mundi,* Vol. 12, 1955, p. 104). Here the *"Tartar flu."* is shown as flowing through the country of the *"Yek Mongul"* and *"Sumongul"* into the Arctic Ocean in extreme northeast Asia. Mercator's source is evidently *Carpini,* presumably as reprinted from the *Speculum Historiale* version in Ramusio's *Navigazioni,* vol. 2, Venice, 1559, or in the separate 1537 edition.

10. TR, ¶4.

11. TR, ¶6.

12. TR, ¶7.

13. It is uncertain whether his silence with regard to Narayrgen, Nochoy Kadzar, and other fabulous lands is due to the same indifference or to well-founded skepticism. Perhaps, however, in marking Zumoal southeast of Moal (nos. 43, 44) he is attempting, in his cramped space, to follow the statement of TR that Zumoal is "adjacent to Moal on the east" (TR, ¶3).

Carpini's journey-narrative he could have marked, if ever he went to the trouble of studying it, not only the names and relative positions of tribes and places along the friars' route, but even (by deduction from the number of day's journeys between them) their approximate distances apart. The resulting map would have given a representation of the vast extent of central Asia more accurate than any in medieval maps until the rediscovery of Ptolemy, instead of the uniquely absurd truncation actually found in VM. The compiler did not do so. We can be sure that all the captions relating to the Carpini mission are taken solely from TR, not only because none includes material not found in TR, but because when the material is common to TR and other Carpini sources the wording is always that of TR, which, as we have seen, is always different from the wording of *Carpini*. In view of this it is reasonable to assume that the rather few names in VM which are common to TR and the other Carpini sources were in fact taken from TR only; and this is demonstrably the case in the three peculiar forms of *Moal, Zumoal,* and *Tatartata*.[14]

There seem to be only two possible instances of material not found in TR which could have been derived from the other Carpini sources. One of these is trivial, while the other is of major importance; but it may be argued that both can easily and more satisfactorily be explained otherwise.

The Pope who despatched the Carpini Mission is correctly named as Innocent IV in VM (no. 39); whereas in TR, *Carpini,* and Benedict's journey-narrative he is never named, but is called simply "dominus Papa"—"our Lord the Pope", and the like, as was customary when referring to the reigning Pope.[15] It is true that the compiler could have obtained the name from the *Speculum Historiale;*[16] but he would surely have been aware of it from common knowledge, or by deduction from the date 30 July 1247 at the end of TR. His insistence on providing a historical and ecclesiastical context for his caption by giving the Pope's name is interestingly paralleled by his naming of Pope Pascal in the Vinland caption (no. 67), and accounts for his going outside TR at this point; but it is unnecessary to infer that he had recourse to the *Speculum Historiale*.

A far more important claim for influence by Carpini texts other than TR may be made in respect of the three large islands in the far east (nos. 57, 58), and the vast sea, *"Magnum mare Tartarorum"* (no. 55), which divides them from the mainland. These features, indeed, and the curtailment of eastern Asia which they cause, form the most remarkable peculiarity of the entire *Vinland Map,* other than Vinland itself and Greenland. It would be unsatisfactory to explain such a bold and decisive concept as deriving from the random sprinkling of imaginary islands round the eastern shores of Asia which is found in other medieval maps, such as the Hereford Map, or Vesconte's, or Fra Mauro's; and it is equally difficult, as Mr. Skelton shows (pp. 151–53 above), to postulate real knowledge of the three main Japanese islands in the VM compiler or his sources.[17]

Mr. Skelton has argued strongly (pp. 151–53 above) that the *"Magnum mare Tartarorum"* is a product of the VM compiler's fancy, influenced by his textual sources, and without any basis in his map model. The sea would then represent his interpretation of the Caspian as a gulf of the

14. See TR, ¶2, n. 5; ¶3, nn. 2, 3, respectively.

15. E.g., TR, ¶2, ¶47, ¶52, ¶53; *Carpini,* Prologus, ¶2, ch. IX, ¶40, ¶48; Benedict, ed. Wyngaert, pp. 135, 141, 142.

16. E.g., from Book XXXI, ch. 152, Book XXXII, chs. 1, 2.

17. As a reductio ad absurdum we may notice the obviously meaningless coincidence that, if we rotate the two northern islands to the southeast, a plausible likeness of Australia and New Guinea is obtained!

northern ocean, a concept found in the Ebstorf and Hereford Maps, ostensibly shared by Benedict (Wyngaert, p. 139), and associated with the *Mare Magnum,* or Black Sea, into which Carpini, who was unaware of the existence of the true Caspian, supposed the Volga and the Ural River (*Iaec*) to flow (*Carpini,* ch. IX, ¶13); and the islands would derive from his misunderstanding of TR, ¶14, as showing that the friars reached the ocean sea, and that the Tartars knew of a "new land" beyond it. It must be admitted that this argument, if its premisses be granted, accounts for the facts; but an alternative view seems possible.

It may well be that the friars themselves believed the Caspian was a gulf of the northern ocean, for in the mid-thirteenth century no other view was available, whether from cartographic or textual sources; but such a belief is nowhere stated in the texts of *Carpini,* Benedict, or TR. The sea briefly recorded by Benedict in the country of the Karakhitai as "a sea on the left hand" was evidently Lake Balkhash, as is clear from the fuller description in *Carpini* (ch. IX, ¶25) of "a not very large sea—*mare non multum magnum*", along the southern ("lefthand") shore of which the friars traveled for "several days", noticing its many islands, and crossing the many small rivers which flowed into it.[18] The friars would be cognizant of its relatively short length by journeying along it, and of its still narrower width by seeing the mountain circuit of its northern shore. They cannot possibly have mistaken it for an ocean-gulf Caspian; and this erroneous inference was in fact made not by Benedict himself but by his Cologne audience, as is shown by the wording "which we believe to be the Caspian Sea—*quod credimus esse Caspium mare*", followed shortly after by "And the same Friar Benedict the Pole told us . . .".[19] Similarly it may be objected that Carpini's statement that the Volga and Ural flow into the Black Sea is a misconception relating not to the Caspian (of which it shows, on the contrary, the friars' unawareness) but to the Black Sea itself. The expression *"mare magnum"* applies here, as always, to the Black Sea and not the Caspian, and does not support the view that the VM compiler chose the words *"Magnum mare Tartarorum"* as being synonymous with the Caspian.

This reasoning, however, though it clarifies the true meaning of the texts of *Carpini* and Benedict, hardly proves that the VM compiler could not have misinterpreted the texts in the manner proposed by Mr. Skelton. Here one can only appeal to the foregoing analysis, which seems to show that, in other instances, the compiler did not use *Carpini* or Benedict, employed TR only to name existing features or fill existing spaces in his model, did not reason from textual sources to alter the outlines in his model, and recorded non-Bianco forms in his map only when these were already found in his model. It seems improbable, a priori, that in this one case he should have made a major alteration to his original, through a complex process of reasoning involving *Carpini* and Benedict as well as TR, and further, under the influence of a cartographical concept (the ocean-gulf Caspian) which at his time was obsolete by at least a century, is not paralleled elsewhere in VM, and of which he may well never have heard.

We must consider, therefore, whether the three islands and the sea which they enclose could

18. Rockhill's identification of this "sea" as the small lake of Ala Kul to the east of Lake Balkhash is plainly inadequate (cf. Rockhill, p. 16, n. 2), and the friars' route through the Karakhitai district has been corrected in the present map (facing p. 27 above) to show them as skirting the southern shore of Lake Balkhash. Rubruck's description of Lake Balkhash, which he says is twenty-five days' journey in circumference (Rockhill, p. 140), is closely similar to Carpini's. Rubruck traveled along the southern shore on his outward journey, as did the Carpini mission, but along the northern shore on his return.

19. Wyngaert, p. 139.

have existed in his map source. It appears not impossible that they may have. As Mr. Skelton shows, the outline and orientation of the eastern shores of the two southern islands coincide with the two east Asian peninsulas in Bianco's map, containing Gog-Magog and the Earthly Paradise respectively, and with the deep gulf between them.[20] These features are also found in non-Bianco maps, such as Vesconte, the Borgia map, and the Estense Catalan map; and in these one or the other is represented as enclosed along the base by mountain ranges or rivers, which it would not be difficult to misinterpret as straits of the sea. If we imagine a model in which this error has occurred, and an evolution in which the resulting straits have been widened, then the configuration found in VM would be fully accounted for. If indeed, as elsewhere, the compiler here drew in accordance with his model, then his tendency to caption his map through adaptation or distortion of TR would come into play. The words *"dicta terra"* were altered to *"nova terra"* to fit the islands; from *"nec ultima terra"* came the name *"Postreme Insule"*; and the northernmost island was naturally called *"Insule* (sic) *Sub aquilone zamogedorum"*, because in the caption on the friars' journey he had already used the Samoyeds from TR as an emblem of the Far North. In naming the sea enclosed by the islands TR could give no help, and *"Magnum mare Tartarorum"* is apparently the only name in all VM which the compiler has entirely invented. But he had to describe a sea adjacent to the country of the Tartars and surrounded by land; and the term *"Mare magnum"*, which was regularly used of both the Mediterranean and the Black Sea as meaning a large, land-locked sea, was ready to hand. It seems possible, therefore, that this major and surprising peculiarity of VM—the three islands, the enclosed sea, and the consequent curtailment of eastern Asia—was not a figment of the compiler, but was already present or adumbrated in his model.

It remains to examine whether the foregoing analysis of the compiler's attitude toward TR and his map source bears any significance for the Vinland and Greenland portion of VM. Here, at least, is a most extraordinary instance of his departure—a departure which, if it had not actually occurred, we should have to regard as psychologically improbable—from the cartographic model that he had apparently followed without alteration in his representation of the Old World. There is no indication which excludes the possibility that the Vinland captions were already present in his second, or Vinland, map original, though perhaps, as we shall see, in a slightly different wording. By analogy with his treatment of the Old World, however, it seems preferable to visualize a Vinland map source used in conjunction with a Vinland textual source, a method corresponding to the compiler's supplementation of his Old World map source from the textual authority of TR. If there is any truth in the suggestion made above[21]—that the northern captions of VM were taken partly from an unknown textual source relating to the northern regions, and including arctic Eurasia as well as Vinland and Greenland—the psychological difficulty of the compiler's readiness to embody further sources would be eased. We may even conjecture that this very discovery, of a source which enabled him to create new captions for northern Eurasia, led him to incorporate its much more astonishing information on the northwest.

20. See above, p. 152. This orientation is confirmed by the position of the island corresponding to *Taprobana,* in Bianco southeast of the Earthly Paradise peninsula, in VM correspondingly southeast of the southern island of the *Postreme Insule.*

21. See above, p. 246.

Analogy from the TR captions in the Old World, in which we are able to control the compiler's divergences from his textual source, would imply the possibility of equally grave distortions in the Vinland captions. We need only imagine how erroneous a reconstruction of TR would be if the original text were lost and only the VM captions survived to adumbrate it. Such, however, is our unwelcome position with regard to the unknown Vinland source. It seems, indeed, that the compiler has continued his old habit of adapting the phraseology of TR to fit an unrelated context. As in the farrago of the Prester John caption (no. 30), or as the Russian caption (no. 11) begins with words from TR but continues supposedly from the unknown source, so in the longer of the two Vinland captions (no. 67) the phrases *"ad . . . extremas partes"* (cf. TR, ¶14), *"iter facientes"* (cf. TR, ¶7), *"terra spaciosa et opulentissima"* (cf. TR, ¶5), and *"humillima obediencia superiori voluntati"* (cf. TR, ¶1), though individually they are commonplace enough, must surely be echoes from TR. It is also the compiler's habit to re-echo his own captions; and accordingly *"terram novam"* in conjunction with *"extremas partes"* chimes with the *"Tartari affirmant . . ."* caption (no. 56), and *"inter glacies"* recurs twice in the northern Eurasian captions (nos. 11, 53). Here, then, we can detect the compiler in the act of rewording his textual source.[22] Fortunately, however, we can confirm the main elements of the sense of the caption from independent primary sources, and conclude, in the French expression, that it "sweats authenticity". The novel details, such as Bishop Eirik's title, the year-date of his voyage, his wintering in Vinland, his return to Greenland, and his retirement (to Iceland, Scandinavia, or Rome?) at the order of his superior are likely enough in themselves, and do not sound like inventions of the compiler, who when he invents does so for the benefit of his map and less sensationally.[23] Perhaps, however, the unusual and probably erroneous statement that Bjarni and Leif Eiriksson were "companions" is more naturally explained as a conflation by the compiler, rather than as already present in his source.[24]

In the Vinland captions, then, the compiler is apparently more trustworthy than the habits revealed by his Old World captions would lead us to expect. A contrary habit has been found in his faithful treatment of his Old World map-source, and it is intrinsically probable that he has shown the same fidelity in his drawing of Vinland and Greenland. Here, in all likelihood, we see still the outlines and orientation he saw in his model; except that the profusion of minor squiggles in the outline of Vinland seems to reflect the same personal foible which has been noticed (p. 115 above) in his outlines of the Old World.

The compiler's probable fidelity to his model, however, does not necessarily imply that his model was itself faithful to its own, perhaps remote archetype. The outline of Greenland, in view of its extraordinary accuracy, has presumably suffered little alteration. But the portrayal of

22. The intrusion of phraseology from TR might be held to suggest that the compiler is abridging, throughout the chief Vinland caption, a considerably longer source; for otherwise he would have had no need to reword the source. If so, since his caption is already of unusual length for a map caption, this is perhaps further evidence that his source was a text rather than a mere caption from his map original.

23. See below, pp. 255–61. The phrases adapted from TR contain no suspicious features which would imply that the compiler altered the *sense* of his original. We need not doubt, in particular, that his source declared Vinland to be "extensive and most wealthy", and gave superior command as the reason for Bishop Eirik's departure from Greenland, though in different words. The former statement concords with the traditional name "Vinland the Good" (Gathorne-Hardy, pp. 75, 97) and with numerous descriptions in the sagas (e.g. Gathorne-Hardy, pp. 42, 44, 55, 57, 63), while the latter is entirely credible in its historical context (see below, p. 260).

24. See below, p. 255.

Vinland, it may well seem, has the air of being the end product of a long process of exaggeration. The two inlets could hardly be deeper or narrower, and the northern one is on the point of turning into a river, with a conventional lake at the head. If these features are indeed corruptions, it may be felt that in all the Vinland Map there is no more important challenge than the reconstruction of the original form of Vinland.

The archetype itself was doubtless a mere inference from the saga tradition, a schematic representation retaining no real link with geographical experience. The three-part island of VM still retains the essential archetypal features of the three landfalls of Helluland, Markland, and Vinland; but we should expect, on the evidence of the sagas, that the three coasts would be separated by much wider and probably much shallower gulfs. The deep narrow inlets of VM are quite inappropriate to the saga story, and we might reject them with some confidence even if no further evidence for reconstruction of the archetype were forthcoming.

If any such evidence exists, it can only be looked for in the maps of Stefánsson and Resen; for these alone have any tenable claim, with the new exception of the Vinland Map, to preserve a cartographical tradition antedating the fifteenth- and sixteenth-century rediscovery of the northeast American coast.

In the Stefánsson map (dated 1570 probably in error for 1590) and in Bishop Resen's map (dated [1605])[25] we have outlines of the three Norse landfalls in America which strikingly resemble those in the Vinland Map, and thus suggest a common source or group of sources. Resen himself twice states that he has followed an Icelandic map, which he considers to be "several centuries old"; and the differences between Stefánsson and Resen's outlines may be held to confirm independent origin. Further, the two wide but shallow gulfs which separate the landfalls in Stefánsson seem to represent the original form from which VM has diverged, while the deepening and narrowing of the gulfs in Resen is already close to the exaggerated form of VM.

In order to dispute these natural conclusions it would be necessary to hold (a) that Resen's map, despite its differences from Stefánsson's and affinities to VM, is copied from Stefánsson's, (b) that Resen's claim to have copied from an ancient map is fraudulent, (c) that Stefánsson constructed his map from textual sources, and (d) that its similarity to VM is entirely coincidental. It must be admitted that Mr. Skelton (pp. 201–07 above) has convincingly argued the possibility, at least, of these theses, and there is no point in which his destructive criticism can be disproved. However, it seems worth while to state a case, as a feasible alternative, for the separate origin of Stefánsson and Resen, and for the common origin of these and the VM version of Vinland.

Resen entitles his map "A sketch of Greenland and neighbouring regions to the north and west, from an old map crudely drawn several centuries ago by the Icelanders, and from the observations of seamen of our own time". He again cites this original for the coast of eastern Greenland: "Norwegian and Icelandic mariners seem to have sailed hither in the past, since in the Icelanders' map Cape Hvitserk is placed here". Perhaps even a bishop is not on oath when

25. The date 1605, generally accepted for the composition of Resen's map, is apparently deduced as being the latest mentioned in his map captions (where it relates to the Greenland expedition sent in that year by King Christian IV of Denmark, to whom Resen's map is dedicated), and is therefore only a *terminus post quem*. It seems uncertain whether Resen drew his own map before, at the same time as, or after receiving Bishop Gudbrandur Thorláksson's sketch map in 1606. Cf. the following n. 26.

compiling a map, and a motive for fraud is provided by Resen's evident intention to show that the new discoveries on the northeastern American coast had been anticipated long before by his own countrymen. But the very existence of VM shows that Resen could have seen such an Icelandic map, and should perhaps make us ashamed of our suspicion.

The differences between Stefánsson's and Resen's maps in the American coastline, and the closer resemblance of Resen's to VM, have been mentioned above. Divergences in the outline of imaginary coast linking northeast Greenland with Russia seem likewise easier to explain as appearing in their different source maps than as due to careless copying of Stefánsson by Resen. Less weight can be attached to different spellings of the captions (Skraelinge Land and Huidserk in Stefánsson, Sketlinger and Hvitserk in Resen), or to the naming of Vesterbygdsfjord, Eiriksfjord, and Osterbygd found only in Resen; yet these, too, may perhaps be traces of differences in their source maps.[26]

The outline of Greenland in Stefánsson and Resen is nearly enough the same, with four prominent capes on the western coast and two on the northeastern. It is not easy to regard these features as fanciful when we find, in a less exaggerated form, the same number of capes in the same positions in the Vinland Map. We may conclude that these capes (or inlets) were all present in the old Icelandic maps from which VM, Stefánsson and Resen are here considered to be independently derived. Such a view is not inconsistent with Mr. Skelton's demonstration (p. 201 above) that in their representation of Greenland Stefánsson and Resen used a map of Zeno type, perhaps Mercator's world map of 1569, if we suppose that in Greenland, as in the American coast, they attempted to superimpose the old map upon the new. The deep fjords of southeast Greenland, however, are peculiar to VM.

The captions of Stefánsson and Resen show little trace of knowledge of the saga narratives, except that Resen marks Eiriksfjord in Greenland, while both are aware that "Helleland" [sic], as the name implies, is stony. Resen is singularly far out when he explains Markland as a "flat country like a sea, without woods and rocks",[27] apparently deriving the name from the Latin *mare* or sea, and unaware that Markland means a land of forests. One would expect Stefánsson and Resen, if they knew the facts, to provide more documentation on the Norse discoveries; and

26. The version of Resen's map redrawn by Gathorne-Hardy (p. 290) is misleading as representing Osterbygd (the Eastern Settlement) in its true position on the southwest coast by Eiriksfjord. In fact Resen marks Osterbygd at the foot of a long caption written along the *east* coast, concerning the possibility of the survival there of the Norse settlers and the Christian religion, and mentioning the fabulous monastery of St. Thomas (a fabrication of the Zeno narrative) as situated there. H. R. Holand's argument (*Explorations in America before Columbus*, 1956, p. 271) supporting the antiquity of Resen's source on the grounds that he locates Osterbygd correctly on the west coast, is based on Gathorne-Hardy's error and is in this respect inadmissible. On the other hand, although Resen was thus deceived by the Zeno narrative and map (cf. Lucas, pp. 11–15, 29, pl. XI) into believing that the Monastery of St. Thomas, and with it the Osterbygd, was on the east coast, he nevertheless contradicts his own mistaken theory by marking Eiriksfjord, the very center of the Osterbygd, in its correct position on the west coast within Herjolfsnes. Bishop Gudbrandur's sketch map of 1606, which marks the whole east coast as uninhabited, follows the Zeno-type outline of Greenland, and therefore cannot as a whole have derived from an Icelandic "old map", nor indeed from Stefánsson or Resen. In the southwest coast, however, Stefánsson-Resen-Gudbrandur are alike, except that Gudbrandur marks Osterbygd in its correct position, while Stefánsson in the surviving copies names only Herjolfsnes; but in his lost original Stefánsson may well have named all four features. In fine it must be admitted that the southwest coast features in these three maps do not permit diagnosis between the alternatives of independent use of an "old" map or maps, or of copying from Stefánsson; though we may still hold that Stefánsson, at least, used an "old" map here.

27. "Markland, vel plana terra instar aequoris sine silvis et saxis &c".

it is difficult to visualize a textual source at once bare enough to account for their ignorance as displayed in their captions and rich enough to account for the plausibility of their outlines. Yet each marks the prominent northward-pointing Vinland Promontory, with Skraeling Land within the inlet to its northwest, implying knowledge of Keelness, the northern limit of Vinland proper, and of Thorvald Eiriksson's disastrous encounter with the Skraelings in the bay behind it to the northwest.[28] These last features convey perhaps the strongest impression of all that the Stefánsson and Resen maps derive from map sources rather than a textual source.

If we agree that the natural trend of the above evidence favors the copying of the American outlines in Stefánsson's and Resen's maps from members of the same hypothetical group of earlier maps to which the Vinland Map belongs, then we are at liberty to use all three in the conjectural reconstruction of the VM's prototype.

Stefánsson and Resen, indeed, in the light of their contemporary sources, have laid down the Norse landfalls as forming part of the recently rediscovered American continent. But we need not doubt that VM accords with its prototype in showing Helluland, Markland, and Vinland as an island encircled by the ocean. Stefánsson himself seems to hint at this when he remarks of Vinland that "our countrymen [i.e. the Icelanders] maintained that this country ended in the ocean on the south, but I gather from the narratives of more recent authorities that a strait or inlet divides it from America".[29] As already suggested, we may infer that the broad and shallow gulfs separating the three landfalls in Stefánsson are closest to the prototype, and that the deeper, narrower inlets marked by Resen represent a halfway stage toward the corrupt form of VM. A still more interesting inference may be made from the bold drawing of the "Vinland Promontory" in Stefánsson and Resen. In the light of their versions it is surely permissible to identify the much less marked headland of VM, which commences the southern peninsular corresponding to Vinland proper, as a vestigial form of this Vinland Promontory; and in the prototype of VM we may conjecture a larger and bolder form resembling Stefánsson's and Resen's. If this is so, then here alone in the VM outline is it possible to point to an actual geographical feature mentioned in the sagas, other than a mere coastline; for here we see the figuration of Keelness, with the bay where Thorvald's men fought the Skraelings on its northwestern coast, and the long beaches of Furdustrands extending southwest to Vinland proper on its other side.

Neither VM, however, nor its prototype so far as we can visualize it, throws any light on the actual location of the Norse discoveries. This "map of the Icelanders" is nothing more nor less than an attempt to draw, from a minimal knowledge of the saga story, the landfalls of Helluland, Markland, and Vinland, including, as it seems, Keelness; but it manifestly bears no cartographic link with real experience. In particular, we are not entitled, on the evidence of the Vinland Map, to deduce the geographical location of the Keelness of the sagas, on which the identification of Vinland itself largely depends. We cannot infer from the Vinland Map that this promontory, the northern limit of Vinland proper, is Cape Cod, as supporters of "southern" theories have maintained, nor that it is Cape Bauld, Cape Breton, or any other headland favored in "northern" theories. The Vinland Map, precisely because it represents a generalized

---

28. Gathorne-Hardy, pp. 45–48.

29. Although the idea that Vinland was an island does not appear in the saga-narratives, it is cited as early as *ca.* 1075 by Adam of Bremen (Gathorne-Hardy, p. 98). See also Mr. Skelton, p. 172 above.

and degenerate simplification of the saga narratives, can be wrested to support any possible theory, whether "northern" or "southern"; but in fact it gives evidence for none.

For genuinely new evidence on the Norse discoveries we must return to the captions of VM. The statement that Bjarni (Herjolfsson) and Leif Eiriksson sailed together may be explained as a conflation, not untypical of the VM compiler's mentality, of their separate voyages as related in the Flatey Book; or such a conflation may already have existed in his source. But the possibility suggested by Mr. Skelton (p. 223 above), that Bjarni sailed for a second time with Leif, cannot be excluded. Bjarni's sailing with Leif is not easy to reconcile with the Flatey Book version,[30] but it may conceivably have been alleged in some lost saga, or even have occurred in historical fact.

Perhaps it is no coincidence that the VM compiler or his source has chosen to conjoin, of all the known and unknown Vinland voyages, those of Leif and Bishop Eirik. Leif (though the caption does not mention it) introduced the first priest to Greenland, while Eirik was Greenland's first bishop. The compiler, with the special interest in church affairs which he has shown in certain Old World captions, may have selected the account of Bishop Eirik from other information which we cannot know; but it may well be that his textual source itself was of church rather than lay origin, as indeed the ecclesiastical phraseology of the following sentence suggests.

> *Henricus, bishop legate of the Apostolic See in Greenland and the neighbouring regions, entered this extensive and most wealthy country (Vinland) in the last year of our most Holy Father Pascal, in the name of God Almighty; he remained for a long time both in summer and in winter, and then returned north-east to Greenland, whence in most humble obedience to superior command he proceeded ...*

This sober and weighty statement, both as a whole and in detail, seems hardly open to adverse criticism. It could be dismissed as a fabrication only by an act of arbitrary incredulity, and we may take it *ex hypothesi* as authentic. When seen in its historical context it is both confirmed and illuminated.

Bishop Eirik's mission falls precisely within the period when Pope Pascal II (1099–1118) was spreading and re-organizing the papal control of Scandinavia and the Norse colonies. In 1106 Pascal had appointed John the first bishop of Holar, the northern see of Iceland, and the establishment of a Greenland bishopric was a natural next step.[31] The motives of Rome, as shown by the emphasis on the proper collection of Peter's pence in the thirteenth-century bulls relating to Greenland,[32] were in part hierarchical and financial; but the obligation to improve the pastoral ministrations of the Church among the little-tended Greenland flock was no doubt paramount. Similarly the motives of the Greenlanders in requiring a bishop must have been not only religious but also political and commercial; and here it is permissible to argue back from

---

30. If this concept had been present in the mind of the author of the Flatey Book version, he would hardly have recorded that Leif bought his ship from Bjarni (Gathorne-Hardy, p. 40) without mentioning that Bjarni accompanied him; still less would he have related Leif's taunt on landing in Helluland—"We have not failed to land like Bjarni" (ibid., p. 41) without recalling that Bjarni was actually present.

31. See Mann, Vol. 8, pp. 201–03. Eirik's departure for Greenland (and ordination?) is said to have occurred in 1112–13 (see p. 224 above).

32. See R. B. Anderson, pp. 145–54, 161–62; Heywood, pp. 1–8.

the circumstances of the installation in 1124 of Arnald, first true Bishop of Greenland, as told in the grim Saga of Einar Sokkason.[33]

The Norwegian Arnald was appointed by Sigurd Jorsalfar, King of Norway, at the request of a Greenland parliament called by Sokki of Brattahlid and his son Einar, then the most powerful men in Greenland. A few years—apparently *ca.* 1131[34]—after his arrival in 1126, when he chose his seat at Gardar, the bishop was involved in a complex and bloody quarrel with Norwegians over shipwrecked goods, in which Bishop Arnald perforce took the part of Einar and the Eastern Settlement against the Western Settlement and a party of Norwegian merchants under the Westerners' protection. At Gardar the bishop's authority, property and existence depended on the favor of the Easterners. We may conjecture that Eirik Gnupsson, likewise, was summoned and utilized by the Easterners as a measure of political and commercial centralization, in order to strengthen their hand in dealings with the Western Settlement, with Norwegian merchants, and with the Norwegian crown. It seems that Eirik, too, may have had trouble with his powerful and violent sponsors and their enemies, and have brought news of his trials to Norway on his return. For Arnald, when asked by King Sigurd to accept the appointment, protested that "he thought he would find the Greenlanders hard to deal with", to which the King unsympathetically replied that "the more sorely he was tried by his flock, the greater would be his merit". Arnald then compelled Einar Sokkason to swear an oath "to support and strengthen the bishopric, and to protect those properties which are given to God, to punish those who try to deprive the bishopric of its property, and to be protector in every respect". Eirik, then, may have been requested in furtherance of the same policies of the Eastern Settlement Greenlanders, and have met with the same difficulties, as Arnald a decade later.

Eirik's title, "bishop legate of the Apostolic See in Greenland and the neighboring regions", carries great weight for our reconstruction of his functions.[35] He was a papal legate appointed directly by the Pope; a bishop in virtue of his legateship, and not by appointment to an already existing see; and it was only after Eirik had prepared the ground for the future see of Greenland that Arnald could be installed in it. We may expect that Eirik brought priests with him and ordained others among the colonists, built or improved churches in the outlying Greenland settlements,[36] and set in order and increased existing resources for baptism, mass, confession, marriage, and burial according to the rites of the Roman Church. Above all, he would establish temporary enjoyment of episcopal tithes and property, and obtain the promise of continuance of these for the first regular bishop who would succeed him. So, indeed, Einar's oath to Arnald strongly suggests.

Still more remarkable, however, is the expression "of Greenland and the neighboring regions".

33. Text in V. Stefánsson, *Greenland*, pp. 105–16.

34. Nörlund, pp. 36, 93–94.

35. The VM version of Bishop Eirik's title is possibly corroborated by Jelič's statement that Eirik was *"episcopus regionarius Groelandiae regionumque finitimarum"*, if we believe the similarity to be too strong for coincidence; but the document (if any) on which Jelič relied has yet to be rediscovered. Cf. Mr. Skelton's discussion, above, p. 224.

36. Of the twelve parish churches recorded in the East Settlement and four in the West Settlement, nine and three respectively had been discovered by the 1930s, while the total has since risen to seventeen. The second church at Brattahlid apparently antedates Bishop Eric, while that at Hvalsey near Julianehaab and others belong to the first half of the twelfth century, and might have been erected either by Eric or by his successor Arnald. The earliest of all, the first church at Brattahlid built by Thjodhild wife of Eric the Red *ca.* 1000 (Gathorne-Hardy, p. 39) was discovered in 1961 (*The Times*, 14 July 1962, p. 9). Cf. Nörlund, pp. 32 ff.

This does not sound like a meaningless legal formula; a bishop of Iceland, for example, would certainly not be called "bishop of Iceland and the neighboring regions". The only conceivable "neighboring regions" related to Greenland were the Norse discoveries on the American continent—Vinland, that is, and possibly Markland. Pope Pascal, therefore, must have been informed that other territories were associated with Greenland, and have been persuaded to include these in Eirik's jurisdiction. It would follow that Eirik's visit to Vinland was not a voyage of exploration undertaken in dereliction of his proper function, but a tour of duty made in accordance with the terms of his appointment.

The possibility of the existence of twelfth-century Norse settlement in America is so far-reaching, not to say romantic, that it has hitherto—when the sole documentary evidence was the entry in the Icelandic annals for 1121 that "Bishop Eirik set out for Vinland"—been rightly regarded with the gravest skepticism. The suggestion has often been made, by way of obviating the need for this startling hypothesis, that Eirik went to convert the American Skraelings,[37] the native dwellers in Vinland (and Markland) who figure prominently in the saga-narratives, but thereafter, from a period at least a century before Bishop Eirik's voyage, make little further appearance in existing documentary records until the maps of Stefánsson and Resen. On examination, however, this conjecture seems to be no true alternative. A purely altruistic missionary journey to convert distant savages dwelling out of all contact with European civilization or commerce is not only inconceivable in a twelfth-century context but manifestly impracticable owing to language difficulties. If, as may willingly be granted, Eric's duties as "bishop legate of the Apostolic See in Greenland and the neighboring regions" included the conversion of American Skraelings, then his journey surely implies the contemporary existence of Norse settlers in Vinland. This alone would provide a sufficient motive for his mission, in the facilitation of peaceful relations with hostile tribes, together with adequate means of interpretation, in the availability of Skraelings who had learned to speak Norwegian, or Norsemen who had learned to speak Skraeling. Conversely, if we grant the existence of Norse settlers, then the conversion of their predatory and warlike Skraeling neighbors would become an urgent necessity, which could well have been mentioned in the Greenlanders' petition for a bishop legate, and be alluded to in the wording of his title.

The probable nature of the hypothetical Vinland settlements may be inferred from our knowledge of the parent colony in Greenland. In Vinland, too, there would be the same pattern of the chieftain's holding, with its main building consisting of hall and smaller rooms, and outhouses including cattle byres, hay barns, smithy, corn mill (for wild lyme grass or other grain), and perhaps even a church.[38] The building materials, however, would be wood and

37. Cf. Hennig, Vol. 2, p. 386; Hermannsson, 1936, p. 76; Gathorne-Hardy, p. 283.

38. Cf. Nörlund, pp. 37–40, 63–80. Of this type, it may be, was the turf-built settlement recently excavated in Newfoundland at L'Anse aux Meadows some five miles west of Cape Bauld, which included a large hall with four adjoining rooms, and eight other buildings, one of which was a smithy with anvil, bog-iron, and slag. (Cf. above, pp. 220, 240, and references.) Dr. Ingstad's hypothesis that this site represents the settlement of Leif Eiriksson himself in Vinland may be doubted. The hall with adjoining rooms would seem a transitional type between the one-roomed all-purpose hall, as built by Eirik the Red at Brattahlid, and the later twelfth-century "passage-house", and would suggest a date nearer ca. 1100. Cf. Nörlund, pp. 74–79. Perhaps L'Anse aux Meadows was a Markland timber station more or less contemporary with Bishop Eirik, who may well have put in there on his way southwest to Vinland. But it would be premature to adduce the L'Anse aux Meadows discovery as evidence in support of the present theory (which it might otherwise tend to confirm), until the site has been fully published and its Norse origin conclusively proved.

turf, rather than stone and turf as in the treeless Greenland; and in the presence of hostile natives there would be few if any of the outlying farms which in Greenland spread to the limits of habitable land. It may be doubted, however, whether the need for self-supporting farmland away from the population pressure of Greenland could alone suffice to motivate settlement in so unfriendly a country. The saga-narratives suggest stronger motives in exploitation and export of the natural resources of the country, and in fur trade with the Skraelings. The Skraelings, indeed, dangerous as they were, were not so much an obstacle as a necessary condition for commercial settlement.

The chief Vinland exports which the Norsemen could gather unaided were timber, including the famous *mösur*-wood (whatever this may have been)[39] and grapes, which would be particularly welcome in the aleless and wineless Greenland.[40] Leif, we are told, took home a cargo of both timber and grapes, thus gaining "both wealth and honor";[41] Thorvald Eiriksson's party brought grapes,[42] Karlsefni's timber and grapes,[43] and the murderess Freydis "all the good things which they could collect".[44] Karlsefni, however—despite the continual outbreaks of violence and bloodshed on both sides, which led to his departure under the conviction "that though this country had good resources yet they would live in a perpetual state of warfare and alarm on account of the aborigines"[45]—engaged assiduously in fur trading with the Skraelings during his second summer and winter in Vinland.[46] In the spring after his return to Greenland he took his cargo of furs—"it is said that no richer ship ever left Greenland"—to Norway, where he "sold his wares, and both he and his wife were honourably received by the noblest men in Norway".[47] Fur trade with the Skraelings, then, was perhaps a paramount purpose of the Vinland settlements. Timber and grapes would be a valuable import for Greenland only; whereas furs could be exchanged, along with the walrus and narwhal ivory which formed the basic Greenland export,[48] for all the goods of Europe, either through direct shipping via Greenland to Norway, as by Karlsefni, or by commerce in Greenland itself with such parties of Norwegian merchants as those who litigated *ca.* 1131 with Bishop Eirik's successor Arnald.

The saga-narratives, as we have seen, may legitimately be used by extrapolation to suggest conditions prevailing a century later, since the motives, practices, and experiences of the twelfth-century settlers would not differ greatly from those of the eleventh-century discoverers. The further possibility arises that the sagas, which evolved over the whole period, may well emphasize or select elements common to both epochs; or even that features and incidents belonging historically to the twelfth-century settlements may then have been anachronistically embodied

---

39. This mösur-wood was found by Leif (Gathorne-Hardy, p. 76) and exported by Karlsefni, who sold a *húsa-snotra* (house beam?) made from it to a Bremen merchant in Norway (ibid., p. 71). It has generally been identified as maple.

40. Cf. Nörlund, pp. 85–86. Adam of Bremen was told *ca.* 1075 by Svein Estridsson, King of Denmark, that the grapes of Vinland "produced the best wine" (Gathorne-Hardy, p. 98). For an account of "strong and heady", if not "best" wine produced from American wild grapes by seventeenth-century colonists, see ibid., pp. 254–55.

41. Gathorne-Hardy, pp. 44–45.

42. Ibid., p. 48.

43. Ibid., p. 86.

44. Ibid., p. 70.

45. Ibid., p. 63.

46. Ibid., pp. 61–62, 83–84.

47. Ibid., pp 70–71.

48. Cf. Nörlund, pp. 96–100.

in the narratives of the age of discovery. Such a possibility seems especially inviting in the accounts of Karlsefni's alternate battles and fur trading with the natives, which present a remarkably complete and varied paradigm of how, and how not, to deal with Skraelings. Among apparently "late" and *ex post facto* features we may note the Skraelings' preference for red cloth (which Karlsefni could not have foreseen) and for iron weapons as trade goods, the prohibition against bartering such weapons, Karlsefni's protection of his house with a palisade, the subsequent trading over the palisade, and the capture in Markland of native boys, whom the voyagers took home to Greenland, christened, and taught to speak Norwegian, and from whom they in turn picked up a few words of Skraeling tongue.[49] This last incident, though quite credible in itself, may be held to foreshadow the establishment of communication with the Skraelings through native interpreters, which was perhaps available to Bishop Eirik a century later.

We may conjecture, then, that the Vinland settlements were homesteads adapted from the Greenland model, made self-supporting through the cattle rearing, hunting, fishing and food gathering of which the Karlsefni narratives have so much to tell, and installed chiefly for the export of timber and for fur trade with the Skraelings. The above hypothesis and discussion of the existence and nature of these settlements is perhaps nothing more than a more or less profitable exercise in speculation. On the other hand, it may be claimed that the concept is supported by testimony of real strength and abundance, including the new evidence of the VM caption, arguments of probability from the saga-narratives, and the suggestion that the sagas themselves contain material reflecting conditions in Vinland subsequent to the generation of the first Norse discoveries. The hypothesis requires further testing by a full reassessment in this light of all existing evidence concerning the Greenland colony and the Norse discovery of America, and by search for new evidence, both documentary and archaeological. As to the number and duration of the settlements, our present evidence can imply only that they existed in the first quarter of the twelfth century, and were sufficiently important to receive a protracted visit from Bishop Eirik at the express order of Pope Pascal, half the world away.

The VM caption's date for Bishop Eirik's voyage to Vinland, "in the last year of our most Holy Father Pascal", presumably indicating the late summer of 1117,[50] is in conflict with the

---

49. Gathorne-Hardy, pp. 61–65, 83–86. Karlsefni's prohibition against parting with iron weapons would often be circumvented, either by illegal trading or in war; and this might possibly account for some of the many alleged finds of Norse weapons on the American continent, if any of these are indeed authentic. See H. R. Holand, *Explorations in America before Columbus* (1956), pp. 137–38, 195–206, and references. Such finds sometimes show a suspicious correlation with areas of nineteenth-century Scandinavian immigration, and genuine medieval ironware may well have been brought from Scandinavia and planted in modern times. The so-called "small halbards" are known to have been manufactured in the 1890s for cutting plug tobacco! Finds made in Minnesota and other districts far inland have been used to substantiate the fraudulent runic inscription on the Minnesota Stone and the fantastic theory of a fourteenth-century Norse land expedition through the heart of the continent. On the other hand, it would not be surprising if Norse ironware acquired by Indians from trading settlements on the Vinland coast should have passed from tribe to tribe far inland. The whole rather scabrous question of these alleged finds perhaps deserves more serious investigation than it has hitherto received from competent archaeologists.

50. The papal year was normally dated from a pope's accession. Pascal II was elected on 14 August 1099, and his "last year" would therefore extend from 14 August 1117 to his death on 21 January 1118 (see Mann, Vol. 8, pp. 8, 81). If the VM date is to be taken in this strict sense, Eirik would have sailed in the late summer of 1117. On the other hand, the expression may conceivably have been used loosely to mean the complete year 14 August 1117—13 August 1118, or even the calendar year 1118; in which case Eirik may have sailed a year later, in the spring or summer of 1118. Pascal's successor Gelasius II reigned briefly from 24 January 1118 to 29 January 1119, and was followed by Calixtus II on 2 February 1119.

well-known entries in the Icelandic annals, that "Bishop Eirik set out for Vinland" in 1121. The VM date is certainly preferable, not only by reason of its circumstantial form, which would hardly be liable to corruption, but because 1121 can now be seen to be improbably late, leaving too little time for Eirik's lengthy sojourn in Vinland, his return to Greenland, the termination of his mission and his reporting to Europe, the Greenlanders' petition for a permanent bishop sent in 1123 to King Sigurd Jorsalfar in Norway, and the consecration of Bishop Arnald at Lund in 1124.

The statement that Bishop Eirik sojourned in Vinland "for a long time both in summer and in winter" is unfortunately ambiguous. Its very vagueness, we may feel, possibly suggests a period of more than one year and more than one winter; but the question remains open. The emphasis on summer and winter is a distinctly "northern" feature, with numerous parallels in the saga-narratives, and no doubt supplies a direct link with Eirik's actual experience. His arrival "in this extensive and most wealthy country"[51] "in the name of God Almighty" is doubtless no idle phrase but rather a manifesto. Bishop Eirik's duties in Vinland would include, as in Greenland, the installation of priests, the consecration of churches, and the provision of the indispensable sacraments of the Roman Church. He may also have wished to supervise on the spot the col-lection of tithes in "this most wealthy country"; and we have studied the possibility that he undertook for reasons both religious and commercial the conversion of the fur-trading Skrael-ings, perhaps through native interpreters educated from childhood, like Karlsefni's Markland captives, by the settlers.

After the completion of his Vinland mission Eirik returned to Greenland, and "thence"—or perhaps "thereupon"—"proceeded in most humble obedience to superior command". He presumably received these last instructions after his return to Greenland; and his recall may well have been due to the death of Pascal II, which would have terminated his appointment as papal legate. The date 1121 was perhaps that of his arrival in Iceland on the homeward journey, and the erroneous entries in the Icelandic annals may easily be explained as a careless abridgment from a fuller source.

Two further problems posed by the annals entry are settled by the VM caption. The expres-sions *"leitadi"* or *"fór at leita"* ("sought", or "went to seek") would in fact normally indicate a search for something lost or unlocated, and have often been taken as meaning not only that the position and even existence of Vinland were then uncertain, but that Eirik never arrived, or perished there.[52] We now know that he both arrived and returned; and the doubtful words mean here, as occasionally elsewhere, simply "set out for", as Gathorne-Hardy had already maintained.[53] Secondly, it has generally been inferred that Eirik died, either in Vinland or Greenland, before the consecration of his successor Arnald in 1124. Ordinarily, indeed, the accession of a new bishop would necessarily mean that his predecessor had died, whether within or outside his diocese; but the difficulty is now solved by the evidence that Eirik was only a bishop legate, and his appointment was therefore temporary and terminable within his lifetime.

The destination of Eirik's "proceeding", and the identity of the superior whose command he

51. Although the wording of this phrase is derived from TR, we need not doubt that its equivalent in meaning occurred in the VM compiler's source (cf. above, n. 3).
52. Cf., e.g., Nansen, Vol. 2, p. 30; Hennig, Vol. 2, p. 386 and references; Hermannsson, 1936, p. 76.
53. Gathorne-Hardy, p. 152.

"most humbly obeyed", remain open to doubt. He must surely at least have reported to his archbishop at Lund,[54] and not merely have retired to his native Iceland. In accordance with his function as a papal legate, however, Eirik may well have "proceeded" to the papal court, like Carpini a century and a quarter after him, and have discussed the results of his mission at Rome with Pope Calixtus II (1119–24), who is known to have continued Pascal II's policy of interest in the Scandinavian church.[55] Perhaps it is not idle to hope that further documents on Eirik's unique and amazing legateship may remain to be discovered in Scandinavian archives or in the Vatican.

The bare words of the VM caption concerning Bishop Eirik, we may reasonably consider, are authentic and true. On the other hand, the above attempt to reconstruct their possible background, though based on abundant and weighty evidence both circumstantial and direct, is necessarily speculative, and the reader must be warned to accept none of it as ascertained fact. But the Vinland Map is a document of such vast importance as to enjoin upon us the investigation of both its minimum and its maximum implications. It admonishes us that our knowledge of one of the great events in human history was incomplete, and may be destined to be supplemented still further, if the archivists of the Old World and the archaeologists of the New should accept its urgent challenge. Meanwhile, at the very least, the Vinland Map has given us the authentic account of a papal bishop-legate's visit to Vinland in the early twelfth century, and the first known pre-Columbian representation, however schematic, of the very coast upon which he landed.

The chief considerations discussed in the foregoing study, with their varying degrees of possibility or cogency, may be summarized as follows:

(1) The appending of the Tartar Relation to a manuscript of Vincent of Beauvais' *Speculum Historiale,* the subsequent compilation of the Vinland Map for inclusion with these, and the joint transmission of all three culminating in the surviving Yale exemplar were possibly the work of Franciscans in a Franciscan monastic scriptorium.

(2) The VM compiler, often with a marked degree of arbitrariness and unobjectivity, adapted information and phraseology from the Tartar Relation to fit his cartographic source; he did not alter his cartographic source to fit the Tartar Relation.

(3) Two Asian captions (those on the Nestorians and the Himalayas) are perhaps in part influenced by captions which existed in his map model.

(4) Certain "Arctic" captions perhaps derive from an unknown source (whether textual, cartographic, or both) relating to the northern regions; it is suggested, more doubtfully, that this source may have been the same as, or conjoined to, that used in the Vinland and Greenland portions of VM.

(5) The compiler made no use of texts relating to the Carpini mission other than the Tartar Relation.

(6) Certain non-Bianco features in the Old World cartography of VM, including the

---

54. The Scandinavian church, including Iceland, was under the archbishopric of Hamburg-Bremen in the eleventh century, and was transferred to the new archbishopric of Lund in Denmark by Pascal II in 1106. In 1152 Norway received its own archbishopric of Trondhjem, which thenceforward had jurisdiction over Iceland and Greenland.

55. See Mann, Vol. 8, pp. 202–03.

Magnum mare Tartarorum, can be satisfactorily explained as having already existed in the compiler's map model, rather than as inferences from textual sources or inventions due to the compiler.

(7) In fine, the Old World portion of the Vinland Map outlines may be accepted as a substantially true rendering of the lost map model, and as presenting no significant concept due to the intervention of the compiler.

(8) In his Vinland captions the compiler has again introduced phraseology from the Tartar Relation, but apparently—in contrast with his practice in the Old World captions—without distorting the sense of his unknown textual source.

(9) His cartographic presentation of Vinland, in conformity with his treatment of the Old World, is probably a faithful rendering from the unknown map model which he used for the New World.

(10) The form of Vinland, however, has apparently diverged from the map model's archetype, which we must endeavor to reconstruct.

(11) The Vinland Map and the maps of Stefánsson and Resen may be held to derive independently from lost maps of the same family, and all three may be used for a hypothetical reconstruction of the archetype.

(12) The archetype and its descendants, however, are merely schematic inferences from the saga traditions, and preserve no direct link with geographical reality. They cannot justifiably be used as evidence for the actual locations of the Norse discoveries on the American continent.

(13) The caption concerning Bishop Eirik may be accepted as historically authentic.

(14) Bishop Eirik's visit to Vinland may be held to imply the existence of a contemporary Norse settlement in Vinland.

(15) The nature and purposes of this hypothetical settlement may be inferred from the saga-narratives; and it seems possible that the saga-narratives include anachronistic material which relates to such a settlement.

(16) Despite its necessarily speculative nature, the hypothesis of a twelfth-century Norse settlement in Vinland deserves serious consideration, and calls for further archival and archaeological research.

BIBLIOGRAPHY

ADAM OF BREMEN, *History of the Archbishops of Hamburg-Bremen*, trans. F. J. Tschan, New York, 1959.

AF. See Analecta.

AILLY, PIERRE D', *Imago Mundi*, ed. Edmond Buron, 3 vols., Paris, 1930.

ALMAGIÀ, R., *Monumenta Cartographica Vaticana* (cited as *MCV*), Vol. 1, Città del Vaticano, 1944.

———— "Sulle navigazioni di Giovanni Caboto," *Rivista Geografica Italiana*, Vol. 67 (1960), pp. 1–12.

ALTANER, B., *Die Dominikanermissionen des 13. Jahrhunderts*, Habelschugt, 1924.

Analecta Franciscanorum (cited as *AF*), Quaracchi, 1885.

ANDERSON, A. R., *Alexander's Gate, Gog and Magog, and the Inclosed Nations*, Cambridge, Mass., 1932.

ANDERSON, RASMUS B., *The Flatey Book and Recently Discovered Vatican Manuscripts*, New York, 1906.

ANDREWS, M. C., "The British Isles in the Nautical Charts of the 14th and 15th Centuries," *Geographical Journal*, Vol. 68 (1926), pp. 474–80.

———— "Scotland in the Portolan Charts," *Scottish Geographical Magazine*, Vol. 42 (1926), pp. 129–53, 193–213, 293–306.

———— "The Study and Classification of Mediaeval Mappae Mundi," *Archaeologia*, Vol. 75 (1926), pp. 61–76.

ASHE, GEOFFREY, *Land to the West*, London, 1962.

AVEZAC, M. A. P. D', "Relation des Mongols ou Tartares par le Frère Jean du Plan de Carpin," *Recueil de Voyages et de Mémoires Publié par la Société de Géographie*, Vol. 4 (Paris, 1839), pp. 397–779.

BABCOCK, W. H., *Early Norse Visits to North America*, Washington, D. C., 1913.

———— *Legendary Islands of the Atlantic*, New York, 1922.

BACOT, J., "Reconnaissance en Haute Asie Septentrionale par cinq envoyés ouigours au 8e siècle," *Journal Asiatique*, Vol. 244 (1956), pp. 137–53.

BAR HEBRAEUS, *The Chronography of Gregory Abu'l Faraj, the Hebrew Physician, Commonly Known as Bar Hebraeus*, trans. E. A. Wallis Budge, 2 vols. Oxford, London, 1932.

BARTHOLD, W., *Four Studies on the History of Central Asia*, Leiden, 1956.

———— *Turkestan down to the Mongol Invasion*, London, 1928.

BEAZLEY, C. R., *The Dawn of Modern Geography*, 3 vols. London, 1897–1906.

———— *Prince Henry the Navigator*, London, 1895.

———— *The Texts and Versions of John de Plano Carpini and William de Rubruquis*, London, 1903.

BENDEFY, L., "Fontes authentici itinera fr. Juliani illustrantes, 1235–1238," *Archivum Europae Centro-Orientalis*, Vol. 3 (1937), pp. 1–52.

BENEDICT, THE POLE, FRIAR. *See* Wyngaert; *also* Rockhill.

BIERNACKI, C., *Speculum Minorum*, Cracow, 1658.

BJÖRNBO, A. A., *Cartographia Groenlandica*, Meddelelser om Grønland, No. 48, København, 1912.

BJÖRNBO, A. A. AND PETERSEN, C. S., *Anecdota Cartographica Septentrionalia*, Havniae, 1908.

———— *Der Däne Claudius Claussøn Swart*, Innsbruck, 1909.

BLOCHET, E., *Introduction à l'Histoire des Mongols de Fadl Allah Rashid-ed-Din*, Leiden, London, 1911.

BOVEY, WILFRID, "The Vinland Voyages," *Trans. Royal Society of Canada* (1936), pp. 27–47.

BOVILL, E. W., *The Golden Trade of the Moors*, London, 1958.

BOYLE, J. A., "Iru and Maru in the Secret History of the Mongols," *HJAS*, Vol. 17 (1954), pp. 403–10.

———— "On the Titles given in Juvaini to certain Mongolian Princes," *HJAS*, Vol. 19 (1956), pp. 146–54.

BOYLE, J. A. *See also* Juvaini.

Bibliography

BRETSCHNEIDER, EMIL, *Mediaeval Researches from Eastern Asiatic Sources,* 2 vols. London, 1888.

BROOKS, C. E. P., *Climate through the Ages,* 2d ed. Cambridge, 1949.

BRUGES ITINERARY, ed. J. LELEWEL, *Géographie du Moyen-Age: Epilogue* (Paris, 1852), pp. 285–308.

—— ed. E. T. HAMY, *Le Livre de la Description des Pays de Gilles Le Bouvier* (Paris, 1908), pp. 157–216.

BRUUN, D., *The Icelandic Colonization of Greenland,* Copenhagen, 1918.

BUDGE, E. A. WALLIS, *The History of Alexander the Great, Being the Syriac Version of Pseudo-Callisthenes,* Cambridge, 1889.

—— *The Life and Exploits of Alexander the Great, Being a Series of Translations of the Ethiopic Histories of Alexander,* London, 1896.

CAHUN, L., *Introduction à l'histoire de l'Asie,* Paris, 1896.

CALLISTHENES. *See* Pseudo-Callisthenes.

CARPINI. *See* Wyngaert; *also* Avezac, Beazley, Dawson, Pullé, Risch, Rockhill.

CARRAROLI, D., *La Leggenda di Alessandro Magno,* Torino, 1892.

CARUS-WILSON, E. M., *English Merchant Venturers,* London, 1954.

CHRISTY, MILLER, *The Silver Map of the World,* London, 1900.

CLAUSEN, SIR G., "A propos du Manuscrit Pelliot Tibétain 1283," *Journal Asiatique,* Vol. 245 (1957), pp. 11–24.

CLEAVES, F. W., "An Early Mongol Version of the Alexander Romance," *HJAS,* Vol. 22 (1959), pp. 1–99.

—— "The Historicity of the Baljuna Covenant," *HJAS,* Vol. 19 (1955), pp. 357–421.

COLUMBUS, FERDINAND, *Historie del S. D. Fernando Colombo,* Venetia, 1571.

CORDIER, HENRI, *Ser Marco Polo: Notes and Addenda to Sir H. Yule's Edition,* London, 1920.

—— *Les Voyages en Asie du Frère Odoric de Pordenone,* ed. H. Cordier, Paris, 1891.

CORTESÃO, ARMANDO, *The Nautical Chart of 1424,* Lisbon, 1954.

CORTESÃO, ARMANDO, and TEIXEIRA DA MOTA, AVELINO, *Portugaliae Monumenta Cartographica,* 6 vols. Lisboa, 1960–62.

CORTESÃO, JAIME, *Os Descobrimentos Portugueses,* Lisboa, 1959– .

CRANE, F. T., "The Mountain of Nida: an Episode of the Alexander Legend," *Romanic Review,* Vol. 9 (1918), pp. 129–53.

CRONE, G. R., "The Mythical Islands of the Atlantic Ocean," *Comptes-rendus du Congrès International de Géographie, Amsterdam, 1938,* Vol. 2 (1938), pp. 164–71.

—— "The Origin of the Name Antillia," *Geographical Journal,* Vol. 91 (1938), pp. 260–62.

CURTAIN, J., *The Mongols in Russia,* London, 1908.

DAWSON, CHRISTOPHER, *The Mongol Missions,* Eng. trans. Carpini, Benedict, and Rubruck, London, 1955.

DEVIC, L. M., *Les Merveilles de l'Inde,* Paris, 1878.

DUDIK, B., *Iter Romanum,* 2 vols. Vienna, 1855.

DURAND, D. B., *The Vienna-Klosterneuburg Map Corpus,* Leiden, 1952.

Encyclopaedia of Islam, 4 vols. Leiden, 1913–36; new edition, A–D, Leiden, 1954.

ERBEN, K. J., *Regesta Bohemiae et Moraviae,* Vol. 1, Prague, 1855.

ERDMANN, F., *Temudschin der Unerschütterliche,* Leipzig, 1862.

FA. See Nordenskiöld.

FARLATI, D., *Illyricum Sacrum,* 8 vols. 1790–1819.

FEJÉR, G., *Codex Diplomaticus Hungariae,* Vol. 4, No. 1, Buda, 1829.

FISCHER, JOSEPH, *The Discoveries of the Norsemen in America,* London, 1903.

FISCHER, THEOBALD, *Sammlung mittelalterlicher Welt- und See-Karten italienischen Ursprungs,* Venedig, 1886.

FORMALEONI, VINCENZO, *Saggio sulla nautica antica dei Veneziani, con una illustrazione di alcune carte idrographiche antiche della Biblioteca di S. Marco,* Venezia, 1783.

FRIEDLAENDER, I., *Die Chadhirlegende und der Alexanderroman,* Leipzig, 1913.

GAMS, P. B., *Series Episcoporum Ecclesiae Catholicae,* Regensburg, 1873–86.

GASPARRINI LEPORACE, TULLIA, *Mostra dei navigatori veneti del quattrocento e del cinquecento: catalogo,* Venezia, 1957.

Bibliography

GATHORNE-HARDY, G. M., *The Norse Discoverers of America*, Oxford, 1921.

GAUBIL, ANTOINE, *Histoire de Gentchiscan et de toute la dinastie des Mongous*, Paris, 1739.

GIBBON, EDWARD, *The Decline and Fall of the Roman Empire*, ed. J. B. Bury, 7 vols. London, 1900.

GOLUBOVICH, G., *Biblioteca bio-bibliografica della Terra Santa e dell'Oriente Francescano*, Vols. 1, 2, Quaracchi, 1906, 1913.

GRAESSE, J. G. T., *Orbis Latinus*, Berlin, 1909.

GRØNBECH, K., *Komanisches Wörterbuch*, Copenhagen, 1942.

Grønlands Historiske Mindesmærker, 3 vols. Copenhagen, 1838–45.

GROUSSET, RENÉ, *Le Conquérant du Monde*, Paris, 1944.

——— *L'Empire des Steppes*, Paris, 1939.

——— *L'Empire Mongol*, Paris, 1941.

HALLBERG, IVAR, *L'Extrême-Orient dans la Littérature et la Cartographie de l'Occident des 13e, 14e et 15e siècles*, Göteborg, 1907.

HALLIDAY, M. A., *The Language of the Chinese Secret History of the Mongols*, Oxford, 1959.

HAMBIS, L., *Le Chapitre 107 du Yuan Che*, Leiden, 1945.

——— *La Haute-Asie*, Paris, 1953.

HAMELIUS, J. P., *Mandeville's Travels*, ed. J. P. Hamelius, 2 vols. London, 1919–23.

HAMMER–PURGSTALL, J. VON, *Geschichte der goldenen Horde*, Pest, 1890.

HAMY, E. T., "Les origines de la cartographie de l'Europe septentrionale," *Etudes historiques et géographiques* (Paris, 1896), pp. 1–94.

Harvard Journal of Asiatic Studies (cited as *HJAS*).

HAUGEN, EINAR I., *Voyages to Vinland*, New York, 1942.

HENNIG, RICHARD, *Terrae Incognitae*, 2d ed. 4 vols. Leiden, 1945–56.

HERMANNSSON, HÁLLDOR, *The Cartography of Iceland*, Ithaca, New York, 1931.

——— *The Problem of Wineland*, Ithaca, New York, 1936.

——— *Two Cartographers: Gudbrandur Thorláksson and Thórdur Thorláksson*, Ithaca, New York.

——— *The Wineland Sagas*, Ithaca, New York, 1944.

HETOUM, PRINCE, "La Flor des Estoires de la Terre d'Orient," *Recueil des Historiens des Croisades: documents arméniens*, Vol. 2 (1906), pp. 111–253.

HEYWOOD, J. C., *Documenta Selecta e Tabulario Secreto Vaticano . . . Phototypice Descripta*, Rome, 1893.

HJAS. See Harvard Journal of Asiatic Studies.

HOBBS, W. H., "Zeno and the Cartography of Greenland," *Imago Mundi*, Vol. 6 (1949), pp. 15–19.

HOVGAARD, WILLIAM, *The Voyages of the Norsemen to America*, New York, 1914.

HOWORTH, SIR H. H., *History of the Mongols*, 4 vols. London, 1876–1927.

Imago Mundi: A review of Early Cartography, Stockholm, Leiden, etc., 1935– (in progress).

INGSTAD, HELGE, "Discovery of Vinland," *The Arctic Circular*, Vol. 15 (Ottawa, 1963), pp. 2–5.

Inventio Fortunata. See Oleson, T. J.; Taylor, E. G. R., "A letter dated 1577 . . ."

Islendíngabók. See Thorgilsson.

JELIČ, LUKA, "L'Évangélisation de l'Amérique avant Christophe Colomb," *Le Missioni Francescane*, Vol. 8 (Roma, 1897), pp. 556–60.

JUVAINI, *The History of the World-Conqueror*, trans. and ed. J. A. Boyle, 2 vols. Manchester, 1958.

KIMBLE, G. H. T., *Geography in the Middle Ages*, London, 1938.

——— ed., *Esmeraldo de Situ Orbis*, London, 1937.

KOCH, LAUGE, *The East Greenland Ice*, Meddelelser om Grønland, Bd 130, Nr 3, København, 1945.

KRETSCHMER, KONRAD, *Die italienischen Portolane des Mittelalters*, Berlin, 1909.

LAMB, H. H., "On the Nature of certain Climatic Epochs which differed from the Modern (1900–39) Normal," *Proceedings of the W.M.O./U.N.E.S.C.O. Rome 1961 Symposium on Climatic Changes* (Paris, 1963), pp. 125–50.

LAMB, H. H. and JOHNSON, A. I., "Climatic Variation and Observed Changes in the General Circulation," *Geografiska Annaler*, Vol. 41 (1959), pp. 94–134; Vol. 43 (1961), pp. 363–400.

LANG, A. W. "Traces of Lost North European Sea Charts of the 15th Century," *Imago Mundi,* Vol. 12 (1955), pp. 31–44.

LA RONCIÈRE, CHARLES DE, *La Carte de Christophe Colomb,* Paris, 1924.

—— *La Découverte de l'Afrique au Moyen-Age,* 3 vols. Le Caire, 1925–27.

LE BOUVIER, GILLES, *Le Livre de la Description des Pays de Gilles Le Bouvier dit Berry,* ed. E. T. Hamy, Paris, 1908.

LEITE, DUARTE, "Uma ilha enigmática," *História dos descobrimentos,* (1958), pp. 339–45.

LELEWEL, JOACHIM, *Géographie du Moyen-Age,* 4 vols. Brussels, 1852–57.

LESSING, F. D., *Mongolian-English Dictionary,* Berkeley, 1960.

Libelle of Englyshe Polycye, ed. Sir G. Warner, Oxford, 1926.

Libro del Conoscimiento, Book of the Knowledge of All Kingdoms, trans. and ed. C. Markham, London, 1912.

LOT-FALCK, E., "A Propos d' Atugan, déesse mongole de la terre," *Revue de l'Histoire des Religions,* Vol. 149 (1956), pp. 157–96.

LUCAS, F. W., *The Annals of the Voyages of the Brothers Nicolò and Antonio Zeno in the North Atlantic,* London, 1898.

MAGALHÃES GODINHO, V., *Documentos sobre a Expansão Portuguesa,* 3 vols. Lisboa, 1943–56.

MAILLA, J. DE, *Historie Générale de la Chine,* 13 vols. Paris, 1777–85.

MAJOR, R. H., ed., *The Voyages of the Venetian Brothers Nicolò and Antonio Zeno to the Northern Seas in the 14th Century,* London, 1873.

MANDEVILLE, SIR JOHN, *Mandeville's Travels: Texts and Translations,* ed. M. Letts, 2 vols. London, 1950.

MANDEVILLE, SIR JOHN. *See also* Hamelius.

MANN, H. K., *The Lives of the Popes in the Early Middle Ages,* 17 vols. London, 1902–31.

MARCUS, G. J., "The Early Norse Traffic to Iceland," *The Mariner's Mirror,* Vol. 44 (1960), pp. 174–81.

—— "The First English Voyages to Iceland," *The Mariner's Mirror,* Vol. 42 (1956), pp. 313–18.

—— "The Mariner's Compass in Northern Europe," *The Mariner's Mirror,* Vol. 41 (1955), pp. 69–70.

—— "The Navigation of the Norsemen," *The Mariner's Mirror,* Vol. 39 (1953), pp. 112–31.

MARTIN, H. D., *The Rise of Chingis Khan and his Conquest of North China,* Baltimore, 1950.

MAUNY, RAYMOND, *Les Navigations médiévales sur les côtes sahariennes antérieures à la découverte portugaise, 1434,* Lisboa, 1960.

MCV. See Almagià.

MEYER, PAUL, *L'Histoire d'Alexandre le Grand dans la littérature française du Moyen-Age,* 2 vols. Paris, 1886.

MGH. See *Monumenta.*

MILLER, KONRAD, *Mappae Mundi: die ältesten Weltkarten,* 6 pts., Stuttgart, 1895–98.

Monumenta Germaniae Historica, Berlin, 1826– .

MORISON, S. E., *Admiral of the Ocean Sea,* 2 vols. Boston, 1942.

—— *Portuguese Voyages to America in the 15th Century,* Cambridge, Mass., 1940.

NAKAMURA, H., "Old Chinese World Maps preserved by the Koreans," *Imago Mundi,* Vol. 4 (1947), pp. 3–22.

NANSEN, FRIDTJOF, *In Northern Mists,* 2 vols. London, 1911.

Navigatio Sancti Brendani, ed. Carl Schröder, *Sanct Brandan,* Erlangen, 1871.

—— —— trans. D. O'Donoghue, *Brendaniana,* Dublin, 1893.

NEEDHAM, JOSEPH, *Science and Civilisation in China,* Vol. 3, Cambridge, 1959.

NOELDEKE, T., *Beiträge zur Geschichte des Alexanderromans,* Vienna, 1890.

NORDENSKIÖLD, A. E., *Bidrag til Nordens äldsta kartografi,* Stockholm, 1892.

—— *Facsimile-Atlas to the Early History of Cartography* (cited as *FA*), Stockholm, 1889.

—— *Periplus: An Essay on the Early History of Charts and Sailing Directions* (cited as *Per.*), Stockholm, 1897.

NÖRLUND, N. E., *Danmarks Kortlægning,* København, 1944.

—— *Islands Kortlægning,* København, 1944.

NÖRLUND, POUL, *Viking Settlers in Greenland,* London, 1936.

Bibliography

ODORIC, OF PORDENONE. *See* Cordier.

OHSSON, C. D', *Histoire des Mongols,* 2d ed. 4 vols. The Hague and Amsterdam, 1834–35.

OLESON, T. J., "Inventio Fortunata," *Annals of the Icelandic National League,* Vol. 44 (Winnipeg, 1963), pp. 64–76.

OLSCHKI, LEONARDO, *Guillaume Boucher: A French Artist at the Court of the Khans,* Baltimore, 1946.

—— *Marco Polo's Asia,* Berkeley and Los Angeles, 1960.

—— *Marco Polo's Precursors,* Baltimore, 1943.

OMAN, SIR CHARLES, *A History of the Art of War in the Middle Ages,* 2 vols. London, 1924.

ONGANIA, F., *Raccolta di Mappa Mondi e Carte Nautiche del 13 al 15 Secolo,* 17 pts. Venezia, 1881.

PARIS, MATTHEW, *Chronica Majora,* ed. H. R. Luard, 7 vols. London, 1872–83.

PAULY-WISSOWA, *Real-Enzyklopädie der Klassischen Altertumswissenschaft,* Stuttgart, 1894– .

PELLIOT, PAUL, "A propos des Comans," *Journal Asiatique,* Vol. 15 (1920), pp. 115–85.

—— "Chrétiens d'Asie Centrale et d'Extrême-Orient," *T'oung Pao,* II, Vol. 15 (1914), pp. 623–44.

—— "Les Mongols et la Papauté," *Revue de l'Orient Chrétien,* Vol. 23 (1922–23), pp. 2–30; Vol. 24 (1924), pp. 225–335; Vol. 28 (1931–32), pp. 2–84.

—— "Le Nom du Xwārizm dans les textes Chinois," *T'oung Pao,* II, Vol. 34 (1938), pp. 146–52.

—— *Notes on Marco Polo,* 2 vols. Paris, 1959–64.

—— *Notes sur l'Histoire de la Horde d'Or,* Paris, 1950.

—— "Le Vrai Nom de Seroctan," *T'oung Pao,* II, Vol. 29 (1932), pp. 43–54.

PELLIOT PAUL, and HAMBIS, L., *Histoire des campagnes de Gengis Khan, Cheng-won ts' in-tcherrg lou,* Vol. 1, Leiden, 1951.

Per. See Nordenskiöld.

PESCHEL, OSKAR, *Der Atlas des Andrea Bianco vom Jahre 1436,* Venedig, 1869.

PETTERSSON, OTTO, "Climatic Variations in Historic and Prehistoric Time," *Svenska Hydrografisk Biologiska Kommissionens Skrifter,* Vol. 5, Göteborg, 1914.

POLO, MARCO. *See* Yule.

POTTHAST, A., *Regesta Pontificum Romanorum,* 2 vols. Berlin, 1873–75.

POUCHA, P., *Die Geheime Geschichte der Mongolen als Geschichtsquelle und Literaturdenkmal,* Archiv Orientalni Supplementa, No. 4, Prague, 1956.

PREVITÉ-ORTON, C. W., *The Shorter Cambridge Medieval History* (cited as *SCMH*), 2 vols. Cambridge, 1960.

PSEUDO-CALLISTHENES, *Pseudo-Callisthenes. Nach der Leidener Handschrift herausgegeben von H. Mensel,* Leipzig, 1871.

PUBLIC ARCHIVES OF CANADA, *Sixteenth Century Maps of Canada,* Ottawa, 1956.

PULLÉ, G., *Historia Mongalorum. Viaggio di F. Giovanni da Pian del Carpine,* Firenze, 1913.

QUATREMÈRE, E., *Histoire des Mongols de la Perse,* Paris, 1836.

QUINN, D. B., "The Argument for the English Discovery of America between 1480 and 1494," *Geographical Journal,* Vol. 227 (1961), pp. 277–85.

REEVES, A. M., *The Finding of Wineland the Good,* London, 1890.

REMAN, EDWARD, *The Norse Discoveries and Explorations in America,* Berkeley, Cal., 1949.

REUTER, O. S., *Germanische Himmelskunde,* München, 1934.

RIASANOVSKY, V. A., *Customary Laws of the Mongol Tribes,* Harbin, 1929.

RICOLDUS, DE MONTE CRUCIS, *Liber Peregrinacionis,* in Laurent, J. C. M., *Peregrinatores medii aevi quatuor* (1864), pp. 101–42.

RISCH, F., *Johann de Plano Carpini: Geschichte der Mongolen,* trans. and ed. F. Risch, Leipzig, 1930.

ROCKHILL, W. W., *The Journey of William of Rubruck,* trans. and ed. W. W. Rockhill [with Carpini, ch. 9, and Benedict], London, 1900.

RONCAGLIA, M., *Les Frères Mineurs et l'Église Grecque Orthodoxe au 13e Siècle,* Cairo, 1954.

ROUX, J. P., "Tängri. Essai sur le Ciel-dieu des peuples altaïques," *Revue de l'Histoire des Religions,* Vol. 149 (1955), pp. 49–82, 197–230; Vol. 150 (1956), pp. 27–54, 173–212.

RUBRUCK, WILLIAM OF. *See* Rockhill; *also* Dawson.

SAMARAN, CHARLES, and MARICHAZ, ROBERT, *Catalogue des manuscrits en écriture latine portant des indications de date, de lieu ou de copiste,* Vol. 1, Comité International de Paléographie, Paris, 1959.

SANANG SETSEN, *Geschichte der Ost-Mongolen und ihrer Fürstenhaüser,* ed. J. J. Schmidt, St. Petersburg, 1829.

SANTAREM, VISCOUNT DE, *Essai sur l'histoire de la cosmographie et de la cartographie,* 3 vols. Paris, 1849–52.

SBARALEA, H., *Bullarium Franciscanum,* Vol. 1, Rome, 1759.

SCHELL, I. I., "The Ice off Iceland and the Climates during the last 1200 years, approximately," *Geografiska Annaler,* Vol. 43 (1961), pp. 354–62.

SCHLAGER, P., *Mongolenfahrten der Franciscaner im dreizehnten Jahrhundert,* Treves, 1911.

SCHLEGEL, G., "On the Invention and Use of Fire-Arms and Gunpowder in China, prior to the Arrival of Europeans," *T'oung-pao,* II, Vol. 3 (1902), pp. 1–11.

SCMH. See Previté-Orton.

Secret History of the Mongols, ed. E. Haenisch, *Die Geheime Geschichte der Mongolen,* 2d ed. Leipzig, 1948.

SKELTON, R. A., "The Cartography of the [Cabot] Voyages," in J. A. Williamson, *The Cabot Voyages and Bristol Discovery under Henry VII* (1962), pp. 295–325.

———— *Explorers' Maps,* London, 1958.

SPEKKE, ARNOLDS, *The Baltic Sea in Ancient Maps,* Stockholm, 1961.

SPIEGEL, F., *Die Alexandersage bei der Orientalen,* Leipzig, 1851.

SPULER, B., *Die Goldene Horde,* Leipzig, 1943.

STEENSBY, H. P., *The Norsemen's Route from Greenland to Wineland,* Copenhagen, 1918.

STEENSTRUP, K. J. V., "Om Østerbygden," *Meddelelser om Grönland,* Vol. 9 (1889), pp. 1–51.

STEFANSSON, VILHJALMUR, *Greenland,* London, 1943.

STORM, GUSTAV, *Studies on the Vineland Voyages,* Copenhagen, 1889.

TAYLOR, E. G. R., *The Haven-Finding Art,* London, 1956.

———— "A Letter Dated 1577 from Mercator to John Dee," *Imago Mundi,* Vol. 13 (1956), pp. 56–68.

———— *Tudor Geography 1485–1583,* London, 1930.

TEIXEIRA DA MOTA, AVELINO, *A Arte de Navegar no Mediterrâneo nos Séculos 12–14 e a Criação da Navegação Astronómica no Atlântico e Indico,* Lisboa, 1957.

THORDARSON, MATTHIAS, *The Vinland Voyages,* New York, 1930.

THORGILSSON, ARI, *The Book of the Icelanders, Íslendingabók,* ed. and trans. by H. Hermannsson, Ithaca, New York, 1930.

THORNDIKE, LYNN, *A History of Magic and Science,* Vol. 4, New York, 1934.

TORFAEUS, THORMODUS, *Gronlandia Antiqua,* Havniae, 1706.

U. S. HYDROGRAPHIC OFFICE, *Ice Atlas of the Northern Hemisphere,* Washington, 1946.

UHDEN, RICHARD, "Die Weltkarte des Isidorus von Sevilla," *Mnemosyne,* Ser. III, Vol. 3 (1936), pp. 1–28.

———— "Die Weltkarte des Martianus Capella," *Mnemosyne,* Ser. III, Vol. 3 (1936), pp. 97–124.

———— "Zur Herkunft und Systematik der mittelalterlichen Weltkarten," *Geographische Zeitschrift,* Vol. 37 (1931), pp. 321–40.

UZIELLI, GUSTAVO, and AMAT DI S. FILIPPO, P., *Studi Biografici e Bibligrafici sulla Storia della Geografia in Italia,* Vol. 2: Mappamondi, carte nautiche, portolani, Rome, 1882.

VERNADSKY, G., *The Mongols and Russia,* New Haven, 1953.

VIGNERAS, L. A., "The Cape Breton Landfall: 1494 or 1497," *Canadian Historical Review,* Vol. 38 (1957), pp. 219–28.

———— "New Light on the 1497 Cabot Voyage to America," *Hispanic American Historical Review,* Vol. 36 (1956), pp. 503–09.

VINCENT OF BEAUVAIS, *Speculum Historiale,* Douai, 1624.

VLADIMIRTSOV, B. Y., *The Life of Chingis-Khan,* London, 1930.

———— *Le Régime Social des Mongols,* Paris, 1948.

VOGEL, WALTER, "Die Einführung des Kompasses in der nordwest-europäischen Nautik," *Hansische Geschichtsblätter,* Vol. 1 (1911), pp. 1–32.

WADDING, L., *Annales Minorum,* Vols. 2, 3, Quaracchi, 1931.

Bibliography

WESTROPP, T. J., "Brasil and the Legendary Islands of the North Atlantic," *Proc. Royal Irish Academy*, Vol. 30 (1912), pp. 223–60.

——— "Early Italian Maps of Ireland from 1300 to 1600 with Notes on Foreign Settlers and Trade," *Proc. Royal Irish Academy*, Vol. 30 (1912), pp. 361–428.

WILLIAMSON, J. A., *The Cabot Voyages and Bristol Discovery under Henry VII*, Cambridge, 1962.

——— *The Voyages of the Cabots*, London, 1929.

WINTER, HEINRICH, "The Changing Face of Scandinavia and the Baltic in Cartography up to 1532," *Imago Mundi*, Vol. 12 (1955), pp. 45–54.

——— "Die Erkenntnis des magnetischen Missweisung," *Comptes-rendus du Congrès International de Géographie, Amsterdam 1938*, Vol. 2 (1938), pp. 55–80.

WOLFF, O., *Geschichte der Mongolen oder Tataren*, Breslau, 1872.

WRIGHT, JOHN K., *Geographical Lore in the Time of the Crusades*, New York, 1925.

——— ed., *The Leardo Map of the World*, New York, 1928.

WYNGAERT, A. VAN DEN, *Sinica Franciscana*, Vol. 1: Itinera et relationes Fratrum Minorum Saeculi 13 et 14 [including Carpini, Benedict, Rubruck, etc.], ed. A. van den Wyngaert, Quaracchi, 1929.

YOUSSOUF KAMAL, PRINCE, *Monumenta Cartographica Africae et Ægypti*, 5 vols. (15 fasc.). Cairo, 1926–50 (numbered by folios throughout; cited as *MCA*).

YULE, SIR HENRY, ed., *The Book of Ser Marco Polo*, 3d ed. rev. by H. Cordier, 2 vols. London, 1903.

——— *Cathay and the Way Thither*, 2d ed., 3 vols. London, 1913–16.

ZARNCKE, F., *Der Priester Johannes*, Leipzig, 1879–83.

ZURLA, PLACIDO, *Il Mappamondo di Fra Mauro Camaldolese*, Venezia, 1806.

INDEXES

Note: Footnote numbers are given only in reference to pp. 17–106: "The Tartar Relation," edited by George D. Painter.

I. GENERAL INDEX

INDEX II. PROPER NAMES IN THE LATIN TEXT OF THE TARTAR RELATION

INDEX III. MONGOL AND OTHER NON-LATIN WORDS IN THE TARTAR RELATION (TEXT AND COMMENTARY)

Note: *Words occurring in the text of the Tartar Relation are marked with an asterisk.*

Altun Khan, i.e. the Kin Emperor, $79n^3$

baraq, $70n^3$
* Bati, i.e. Batu Khan, $76n^6$
baba yek, $94n^3$; *see also* *yul boba
Beki, i.e. Sorghoktani, $76n^4$
Beler, i.e. Bulgar, $80(\P 27)n^1$
berak, *see* baraq
* boba, *see* *yul boba
Bolar, i.e. Bulgar, $80(\P 27)n^1$
Boli-tufan, i.e. Buritebet, $72(\P 19)n^1$
buri, $72(\P 19)n^1$; *see also* *burith
* burith, 72; *see also* buri

* can, 63
Chalibai, i.e. Caliph, $84n^4$
* Codar, 91; *see also* Etugen; Iuga
* colon, 75; *see also* kol; *ucor; *Ucorcolon
* coni, 73; *see also* *Coniuzzu; qoni
* Coniuzzu, 73; *see also* *coni; qoni; su; usu; *uzzu; *zu

dalai, $56n^5$, $62n^7$

Etugen, $92n^6$; *see also* *Codar; *Iuga

Ghajar, $70n^2$; *see also* *kadzar
Gurgandj, i.e. Urgendj, 103

idughan, $92n^6$
Iediiar, $92n^6$
* irgen, 65; *see also* *Narayrgen
it, $70n^3$
Itugen, $92n^6$; *see also* Etugen

* Iuga, 91; *see also* *Codar; Etugen

Jalaldin Sultan, i.e. Jelal-ed-din, $79n^3$

* kadzar, 71; *see also* ghajar; Nochoy kadzar
kam, $92n^6$
* kara, 59; *see also* khara
Keler, i.e. Hungarians, $61(\P 8)n^5$, 105
Keluren, i.e. Kerulen, $61(\P 8)n^5$
Kerel, i.e. Hungarians, $61(\P 8)n^5$, 106
Keshimir, i.e. Cheremisses (?), $61(\P 8)n^5$, 106
Khan Melik, i.e. Mohammed, Shah of Khorasmia, $79n^3$
khara, $60(\P 7)n^1$; *see also* *kara
Khuda(i), $92n^6$
kin, $79n^3$
kol, $74n^3$; *see also* *colon; *Ucorcolon
közgu, $76n^4$
kudai, $92n^6$

* Mengu, i.e. Mongke Khan, 77
* Moal, 57
Moghal, $56n^5$
Mongghol, $56n^5$

* nara(n), 65; *see also* *Narayrgen
Naran-Eke, $66(\P 15)n^2$
* Narayrgen, 65; *see also* *nara(n); *irgen
* nochoy, 71, 75; *see also* *Nochoy kadzar; *Nochoy terim
* Nochoy kadzar, 71; *see also* ghajar; *kadzar; *nochoy
* Nochoy terim, 75; *see also* *nochoy; teriun; *terim

Index